Rafael Carrera
and the
Emergence of the
Republic of Guatemala,
1821–1871

Rafael Carrera and the Emergence of the Republic of Guatemala, 1821–1871

Ralph Lee Woodward, Jr.

The University of Georgia Press

ATHENS & LONDON

University of Georgia Press paperback edition, 2008

© 1993 by the University of Georgia Press

Athens, Georgia 30602

www.ugapress.org

Designed by Kathi L. Dailey

Set in Mergenthaler Garamond No. 3

by Tseng Information Systems, Inc.

Printed digitally in the United States of America

The Library of Congress has cataloged the
hardcover edition of this book as follows:

Library of Congress Cataloging-in-Publication Data

Woodward, Ralph Lee.

Rafael Carrera and the emergence of the Republic of Guatemala,

1821–1871 / Ralph Lee Woodward, Jr.

xvii, 630 p. : ill., maps ; 25 cm.

Includes bibliographic references (p. 589–613) and index.

ISBN 0-8203-1448-x (alk. paper)

1. Carrera, Rafael, 1814–1865. 2. Guatemala—History—1821–1945.

3. Central America—History—1821–1951. I. Title.

F1466.45.C375 w66 1993

972.81'04—dc20   91-41812

ISBN-13: 978-0-8203-3065-5 (pbk.)

ISBN-10: 0-8203-3065-5 (pbk.)

British Library Cataloging-in-Publication Data available

For Sue and Laura

Contents

Part Three. Socioeconomic Change in Carrera's Guatemala

Illustrations

Tables

Preface

THE HISTORY OF LATIN AMERICA is endowed abundantly with great men—*caudillos*—who have led their nations to greater achievement or ruin, or simply thrived on the Latin passion for charisma and bold leadership to build powerful political machines. Guatemala, a state where one can find most of the characteristics that are generally described as "Latin American," has had more than its share of caudillos. Even before the conquistador Pedro de Alvarado established a Hispanic dictatorship on the isthmus, there were Indian *caciques* who raised the hopes and pride of Mayan nations. According to the mythology, Alvarado defeated the last of the Mayan caudillos, the Quiché Chief Tecúm Umán, in personal combat and established a regime that institutionalized the captain general as an authoritarian commander who directed the military, political, economic, and social development of what became the Kingdom of Guatemala.

A Spanish policy of rotation prevented any of Alvarado's successors from becoming too firmly entrenched in power on the isthmus, but in the nineteenth century, with Spanish and Mexican constraints removed, long-term caudillos exercising all the power once held by the captains general came to dominate Guatemala's political history. This pattern began to emerge under the United Provinces of Central America (1823–40) as Honduran General Francisco Morazán tenaciously held on to the federal presidency for a decade (1830–40), while his rivals developed military and political power in the several states that he pretended to hold together. In Guatemala, Rafael Carrera rose to power beginning in 1837, toppled Morazán in 1840, and dominated Guatemala until his death in 1865. Other caudillos followed, most notably Justo Rufino Barrios from 1871 to 1885, Manuel Estrada Cabrera from 1898 to 1920, and Jorge Ubico from 1931 to 1944, but none matched Carrera either in the length of his domination or his widespread popularity.

Biographies of uneven quality have outlined the careers of all of these men, and it is not the purpose of this book primarily to portray the life of one of Latin America's most remarkable popular leaders of the nineteenth century. It is, rather, my intent to examine more carefully than has been done before the political, social, economic, and cultural environment in which Carrera rose to power and the sort of society that evolved around him during his quarter-century dictatorship. I seek their meaning for contemporary Central America.

Much of the history of nineteenth-century Guatemala has been written by those seeking to deprecate Carrera and the conservatives who guided his state. The liberal tradition in Guatemalan historiography remains strong. The few conservatives who wrote history during the nineteenth century (notably José Milla Vidaurre and Francisco de Paula García Peláez) focused almost exclusively on the colonial period, seeking perhaps to counter the strongly anti-Hispanic tone of the liberals. Contemporary accounts were strongly polemical, epitomized by Lorenzo Montúfar's *Reseña histórica de Centro-América*, 7 vols. (1883–87), which became the basis for many subsequent liberal accounts of the period. More accurate and less passionate were the chronicles of the more moderate liberal historian of the early nineteenth century, Alejandro Marure. The liberal view of the first half century of independence was reflected strongly in the first major English-language history of the region, Hubert Howe Bancroft's *History of Central America*, which became highly influential for much of the subsequent writing on the period in that language. Antonio Batres Jáuregui, in the third volume of his *La América Central ante la historia* (1949), was the first modern Guatemalan historian to challenge the liberal historiography seriously, reflecting a more sympathetic view of the conservative years. A kinsman of Carrera, however, Manuel Cobos Batres, initiated revisionist studies defending Carrera in three little volumes published about 1935, but the most passionate defense of Carrera and the conservatives came in two rather unscientific and strongly polemical volumes by the editor of *La Hora* and former Guatemalan Vice-President Clemente Marroquín Rojas in his 1965 *Morazán y Carrera* and his 1971 *Historia de Guatemala*. About the same time, Manuel Coronado Aguilar published a sympathetic article on Carrera in the *Anales de la Sociedad de Geografía e Historia* (1965) and subsequently in his *Apuntes históricos-guatemalenses* (1975), while another study of early Guatemalan independent history sympathetic to Carrera and the conservatives appeared by Luis Beltranena Sinibaldi in 1971. Although often no more rigorous in their methodologies than the earlier liberal works, these works represented a clear revision of nineteenth-century Guatemalan history by native historians.

More recently, Marxist-trained Guatemalans—Severo Martínez Peláez, Julio Castellanos Cambranes, and Julio César Pinto Soria—have contributed more carefully researched socioeconomic studies in support of the revisionists. In the meantime, a number of foreign historians have made significant contributions. Mario Rodríguez's detailed account of the substantial role of the British Consul Frederick Chatfield from 1834 to 1852 also provided much enlightenment on the liberal-conservative struggle and on the course of Guatemalan history in the period generally. His *Cádiz Experiment* was an even greater contribution to understanding the origins of both liberal and conservative political ideology in Central America and its impact on political structures in independent Guatemala. William Griffith and his student, Robert Naylor, added considerably to our understanding of the British role in Guatemala, while other Tulane students, notably Adam Szazsdi, Shirley Lucas McAfee, Susan Strobeck, Wes Schwemmer, David Chandler, Patricia Brady Schmit, Keith Miceli, and my own work filled out details on the individuals and institutions that developed in Guatemala during the first half of the nineteenth century. Miceli's thesis was especially important in emphasizing Carrera's concern for the welfare of the peasants. Several theses done elsewhere—notably Max Moorhead's 1942 biography of Carrera based on materials at the Bancroft Library and Hazel Ingersoll's 1972 detailed examination of the War of the Mountain—contributed further to our understanding of the era. A new generation of Guatemalan historians—notably Pedro Tobar Cruz, Manuel Rubio Sánchez, and Antonio Morales Baños—added a number of new volumes on specific episodes, individuals, or institutions. More recently, the Italian historian Daniele Pompejano and Costa Rican Juan Carlos Solórzano have surveyed mid-nineteenth-century Guatemalan history.

This study builds upon this voluminous if frequently polemical literature, but it is based primarily on examination of records in public and private archives in Central America and elsewhere and on materials published during the first half century of Guatemalan independence. It reevaluates Carrera and the conservatives in terms of the evidence from their own time as well as in the light of Guatemalan experience since 1865. It identifies the issues that divided Central American leaders in their search for a political solution to the vacuum created by independence. In doing that, it examines the ideology of Guatemalan conservatism in the nineteenth century in contrast to that of the liberals. It attempts to explain how an uneducated peasant from a sparsely populated part of the country was able to rise quickly and remain as the dominant political figure on the isthmus for nearly thirty years. It also reexamines the role foreign influence played in the development of independent Guatemala. Finally, this work considers aspects of the social history of Guatemala and the changes that the first half century of independence had upon the rural masses.

This study synthesizes and refines much of the work mentioned above in a narrative of the political history of the State of Guatemala and the rise of Carrera and the conservatives. Later chapters analyze economic and social trends during the period, which lead to the conclusions presented in the final chapter.

I am indebted to many friends and colleagues who have assisted me in the preparation of this volume. The directors and staff of the Archivo General de Centroamérica in Guatemala City over the past thirty years, beginning with the late Joaquín Pardo, have been enormously helpful to me. In this regard, Rigoberto Bran Azmitia, more recently as head of the Hemeroteca Nacional, Arturo Valdés Oliva, and Hernán del Valle, deserve my special thanks. Also in Guatemala, Manuel Rubio Sánchez, Julio Castellanos Cambranes, Jorge Luján Muñoz, Ramiro Ordóñez Jonama, Víctor Perera, Fernando González-Davision, Jorge Skinner-Klée, and Julio César Pinto Soria were repeatedly helpful. At the Centro de Investigaciones Regionales de Mesoamérica, in Antigua, Chris Lutz, the late Bill Swezey, Steve Elliott, and their staff at CIRMA were all of very substantial assistance. In the United States, many people have been helpful on various occasions, beginning with my mentor and friend, William J. Griffith. Mario Rodríguez gave me valuable criticism on more than one occasion, as did Charles Stansifer, Robert Naylor, David J. McCreery, Carol A. Smith, Richard N. Adams, and Tom Schoonover. I am also most grateful for assistance given me in Tulane's Latin American Library by Tom Niehauss and Guillermo Náñez and their staff, especially Martha Robertson, Ruth Oliveira, and Cecilia Montenegro de Teague. Sue McGrady, in the Tulane Library Manuscripts Division was also very helpful, as were John Hébert and Georgette Dorn in the Hispanic Division of the Library of Congress and Laura Gutiérrez and her staff in the Nettie Lee Benson Collection at the University of Texas. I am also most grateful to many of my own students, who over the years have given me knowledge and insight, as well as providing effective sounding boards for my own ideas. Among these I am especially indebted to Charles Carreras, Rodolfo Pastor, Bill Meneray, David McCreery, Stephen A. Webre, Gene Yeager, Virginia Garrard, Regina Wagner, Richmond Brown, Jorge González, Jacquelyn Kent, Todd Little, and Oscar Peláez.

I am also most grateful for a number of research grants that contributed materially to the completion of this work, including grants from the American Philosophical Society, the Andrew Mellon Foundation, the Tulane University Senate Committee on Research, the Murphy Institute of

Political Economy at Tulane University, and for the Fulbright-Hays Advanced Research Award that enabled me to spend the 1990–91 academic year in Guatemala, during which I wrote most of this work. To all of these people and institutions I am sincerely grateful, but final responsibility for this work remains with me.

PART ONE

Liberals
and
Conservatives

CHAPTER ONE

The Colonial Burden

SPANISH RULE OF CENTRAL AMERICA, which lasted for three centuries (1524–1821), ended with a whimper. There were no bloody wars for independence as in Mexico or South America, and after a year and a half as part of Agustín de Iturbide's Mexican Empire (1822–23), on 1 July 1823 a Central American assembly meeting in Guatemala proclaimed the absolute independence of the isthmus. It then began planning boldly for a peaceful transition to a united republican federation, about which it expressed glowing expectations for prosperity and progress.

These hopes were soon dashed on the hard rock of reality, as provincial dissensions and economic and social conflicts erupted into civil war, political intrigue, and passions that led to the collapse of the United Provinces of Central America by 1840. The chaotic period that followed witnessed the emergence of brutal, ruthless, and often opportunistic caudillos whose reactionary regimes stifled and destroyed the liberal ideologies that had flourished in the 1820s. Of these caudillos, Guatemala's José Rafael Carrera stands out as the most durable and most influential. From peasant surroundings he rose on the sheer strength of charismatic leadership and brute force to dominate his state and much of the rest of Central America for nearly thirty years. In the process, he laid the foundations of the modern Republic of Guatemala.

Carrera's regime was not merely the domination by a representative of downtrodden rural masses over a cowed elite. In fact, especially after 1850, Carrera's Guatemala was run by educated gentlemen who were dedicated to the restoration and preservation of traditional Hispanic values, as well as to the maintenance of a class structure that would preserve privileges and advantages that they had gained by virtue of their birth and labors. The particular brand of conservatism that they espoused and defended, and that Rafael Carrera protected with his military genius and crude phalanxes, reflected an important phase of Latin American history. Although it may have developed more fully in Guatemala, it can be found to some extent in every Latin American nation, and Central America's experience was a microcosm of the larger experience.

Nineteenth-century conservative thought was in large measure a reaction against the liberalism of the late eighteenth and early nineteenth centuries, especially as expressed by the creoles who established the first republics. Mario Rodríguez has described the liberal development exceptionally well in his *Cádiz Experiment* (1978). Less has been said about the Central American conservative parties, which for a half-century effectively checked liberalism on the isthmus. The relatively peaceful achievement of independence in Guatemala disguises the very great changes that occurred during the "Age of Revolution" (1775–1825) in Central America. Basic changes in the economic system that had prevailed there for nearly three centuries caused severe dislocations and tension in the closing years of the eighteenth century, beginning great social pressures with which the independent government was hardly able to cope, or perhaps even to comprehend. Over more than two centuries, Guatemalan social and economic life had developed traditions and patterns that were not easily altered nor willingly abandoned by those to whom they meant security or prosperity.

At the heart and soul of Guatemalan history are the Indians, descendants of populous pre-Columbian Mayan city-states. Although the Spanish conquest and concomitant epidemics enormously reduced their numbers, they remained the most numerous ethnic element, and their labor was the most valuable commodity in the colony. Civilization developed early in the Guatemalan highlands, and although migrations to the Caribbean lowlands eventually produced more spectacular pre-Columbian cities, the numerous Maya who remained in the highlands developed a durable life style that survived the Spanish invasion. Native traders beat paths throughout the area and colorful markets were social and economic centers for the people. Unlike the Maya who had descended to the tropical lowlands and built a high civilization, only to see it wither and decline, highland Mayan civilization was still active at the time of the conquest. It produced large and abundant crops of corn, beans, and chilies, plus cacao, vanilla, and other tropical fruits and vegetables. The Maya exploited a variety of woods and fibers for construction of houses, canoes, furniture, basketry, pottery, toys, and other simple manufactures. They cultivated cotton in amounts sufficient to sustain a major textile industry, brightly coloring their woven goods with indigo, cochineal, and other natural dyes. They grew henequen from which they made roofs, rope, floor mats, and household fixtures. They produced paper and worked silver, gold, jade, and other minerals. Yet their technology was uneven, and in many respects had not matched the heights of the lowland classic Maya or of the Europeans. Anthropologists classify it generally as neolithic. Lacking domestic beasts or application of the wheel, they depended excessively on human energy, and they had a very limited concept of energy conservation and use.[1] Most of this survived the conquest and remains even today in much of rural Guatemala. Well-established customs and practices regarding use of lands surrounding their villages also survived the conquest, notwithstanding the Spanish demands for land and labor. Although they spoke a multitude of languages, their common Mayan ancestry gave them a unity they have seldom recognized. They had reached a high level of production of goods by the time of the conquest. And both a written and oral history had produced a rich mythology that reflected the Indians' identity and character. They worked hard in a land of unparalleled beauty against severe natural obstacles and frequent geologic calamity.

The Spanish conquest of the early sixteenth century had been a major shock to the Indians of Guatemala, but it was less devastating than it had been in the Caribbean or in other parts of Central America. Indian culture was destroyed in some areas and greatly diminished in others, yet Indian communities remained throughout the western highlands (Los Altos) and were important in central and eastern Guatemala as well. The conquistadors enslaved the Indians of many areas or otherwise forced them to work for them, but Indian villages of the populous highlands, where there were few Spaniards, remained remarkably intact.

While Indians survived, they were relegated to inferior status beneath the peninsular and creole master race that used military power and collaboration with Indian caciques to maintain their own superiority.[2] Indian rebellions occurred from the start, but they were systematically suppressed with a cruelty designed to terrify the Indians.[3] The Spanish imposed their own institutions and customs, so that their capital, Santiago de los Caballeros de Guatemala, became essentially an Hispanic city, provisioned and supplied by Indians, and to a lesser degree Hispanic institutions were imposed in the towns and villages as well. Labor control institutions—the encomienda and repartimiento—drawn from Spanish experience in the reconquest of the Iberian Peninsula from the Moors demanded the labor of the

Indians. The church became the principal institution for the Hispanization process, and culturally it made inroads, as village curates became not only spiritual leaders, but also the principal link between Indians and the master race.[4] A body of law evolved that not only provided for exploitation of Indian labor, but also provided a degree of segregation and protection to this class against extinction. These laws, recorded in the *Recopilación de Indias* and in evolving practice as generations passed, institutionalized dual societies of Europeans and Indians that were both interdependent and mutually exclusive.

By the seventeenth century a creole elite in Santiago de Guatemala had achieved affluence and a degree of autonomy. Historians of colonial Central America differ as to the effect, or even the existence, of the "seventeenth-century depression" in Central America. While there continued to be production for export and the presence of a fairly wealthy community of merchants in the capital, the rising risks of maritime trade and Spain's declining military and naval power at the very least arrested the growth of overseas trade. Much of Guatemala's agriculture was subsistence-oriented, and among the creole class neo-feudal institutions and practices prevailed and even expanded. Recurrent epidemics continued to decimate the native population. By the middle of the seventeenth century much of the dynamism of the sixteenth-century export economy was gone and the creoles had entrenched themselves in feudal and bureaucratic sinecures in a colony that was more isolated and less important to the empire than in earlier days. Export production was a relatively small part of the total economy, yet landholding and control of the native population thereon was the key to social advancement among the creoles. Guatemala's seventeenth-century governors were not notably competent, a factor that contributed to the rise in power of the creole elite.[5]

The eighteenth century brought significant change to this near-feudal pattern. The industrial revolution in northern Europe stimulated a notable increase in production and commerce, to which the Spanish responded belatedly with the Bourbon commercial and economic reforms. Many parts of the Spanish Empire enjoyed economic growth. Reduction of taxes on commerce, freer trade, increased incentives to production, expansion of African slavery, encouragement of new technology, improved roads and navigational facilities, more liberal credit and capital accumulation laws, easier acquisition of land for agriculture, and authorization of new commercial organizations promoted capitalist growth and a trend away from subsistence agriculture toward plantation production for export. Central America was not the most conspicuous of areas that underwent this change, but it was definitely within the pattern throughout the century. Not until the outbreak of wars arising from the French Revolution was the growth trend arrested in the Kingdom of Guatemala, leading to a serious depression during the quarter century preceding independence.[6]

Indigo accounted for the largest part of the economic expansion, responding to the demands of rising European textile production. The area around Sonsonate, in present-day El Salvador, was the center of this production, although significant amounts also came from present-day Guatemala and Nicaragua by the end of the colonial period. The increased productivity drew Guatemala more closely to the North Atlantic economic system, providing exchange for expanding imports of foreign merchandise by Central American creoles via both legal commerce and smuggling.[7]

Inevitably, this had important repercussions, and the benefits were not uniformly distributed among the population. The expansion of exports caused changes in land utilization and began a process of Ladino encroachment on traditional Indian lands. The land and labor demands of indigo and other export commodities put pressures on Indian communities in the more densely populated areas, especially in the indigo-growing regions of El Salvador and Guatemala. Moreover, the demand for capital moved the economy away from the barter that had characterized much of the domestic trade to more emphasis on cash transactions. Increased exports, legal as well as contraband, put new demands on road and port development and the Guatemalan government had to pay more attention to its inadequate transportation infrastructure. In short, although emphasis on export agriculture and mining increased production, overseas trade, and what later would be called "modernization," it also added a burden on the lower classes whose labor was exploited without commensurate compensation to extract the agricultural and mineral commodities as well as to work on roads and other public works. Together with the conversion of some land from subsistence to export use, this began a trend toward reduced food supplies at the very time when the population finally began to grow after two centuries of decline. This would eventually lead to serious malnutrition or dependence on foreign food imports, a problem that reached awesome proportions in some parts of the isthmus by the twentieth century.

One result of the Bourbon reforms and accompanying growth of capitalism was an intensification of the regionalism among the provinces of the kingdom. Regionalism had long been characteristic of Central America owing to the poor communications, relatively isolated settlement patterns of most of the provinces, and the small amount of trade either among or beyond the provinces. Larger commercial centers grew up in each province to accommodate the export trade and to provide for the greater bureaucratic administration that the Bourbons also instituted. Despite the centralizing intention of the reforms, the tendency was to increase the sense of autonomy and importance of these regional centers. This was most evident with the establishment of intendancies in El Salvador, Honduras, Nicaragua, and Chiapas in 1786. This act, reenforcing the sense of identity of the ecclesiastical dioceses in the latter three and contributing to San Salvador's demand for its own bishop, defined the geographic boundaries of the future Central American states.[8] The growth of *ayuntamientos* (municipal councils) in the late colonial period further strengthened regional identifications. After years of inactivity, several municipal corporations began to function after 1808. By 1810, not including Indian municipalities, there were active councils in the cities of Guatemala, San Salvador, San Miguel, Ciudad Real (San Cristóbal de Las Casas), Comayagua, León, Granada, Nueva Segovia and Cartago; the *villas* of Sonsonate, Tegucigalpa, San Vicente, and Rivas; and the *pueblos* of Quetzaltenango and Santa Ana. The number expanded rapidly during the Cortes of Cádiz. Thus the emergence of local political expression at the close of the colonial period augmented regionalism on the isthmus as it contributed to the separatist spirit in opposition to the domination of Guatemala City.[9]

Paradoxically, at the same time, another effect of the economic expansion of the eighteenth century was to increase economic interdependence among the provinces. Intercolonial trade had been discouraged for most of the colonial period in defense of the commercial monopolies of Seville, Mexico, and Lima. Yet the Bourbons gradually revised this policy to allow Central Americans wider trading possibilities both within and beyond the kingdom. Moreover, the rise of contraband along the Caribbean coast in the eighteenth century increased opportunities for trade among the Central Americans. Within the kingdom, there was greater movement of merchants, intellectuals, bureaucrats, and clerics than previously. Guatemala City was, of course, the metropolis for all these people, and a growing number of provincials migrated to the capital to participate in its opportunities. Conversely, there was also a migration by offspring of Guatemalan elite to the provinces to expand their economic activities. In addition, aggressive peninsular immigrants, mostly from northern Spain, came to the provinces via the capital. The provincial creoles, associating these newcomers with Guatemala, often resented the competitive Spaniards and increased their anti-Guatemalan biases. These immigrants were, nevertheless, vital to the capitalist expansion, and the latter half of the eighteenth century saw the kingdom making the transition from feudal traditions toward a capitalist, agro-export orientation, a transition directly related to the rise of industrial capitalism in Europe.[10]

The most successful of these immigrants was Juan Fermín Aycinena, who left Navarre and came to Guatemala via Mexico in the mid-eighteenth century. In Mexico he had expanded his modest wealth as owner of a string of mules, and he reinvested his profits in indigo and livestock in Guatemala and El Salvador. He also invested in Honduran silver mining, but indigo became his most lucrative investment and he established an important exporting house in the Guatemalan capital. In Guatemala, through three successive marriages he connected himself to the powerful families of Varón de Berrieza, Carrillo, Nájera, and Piñol, and soon became a leading figure in the economic, social, and political spheres. In 1780 he purchased the title of marquis, becoming the only resident holder of a noble title in the kingdom at that time. In Guatemala he sired a large family and became the leader of the local aristocracy. His descendants and their kin by marriage enlaced the principal members of the Guatemalan landholding and commercial elite by the end of the colonial period. Figure 1 indicates the close interlinking of the two prominent Spanish commercial immigrants (José Piñol and Juan Fermín Aycinena) in eighteenth- and nineteenth-century Guatemala. By the early independent period a political faction had developed that was identified by its political opponents simply as "the family."[11]

By the Carrera period, nearly all of the leading government officials and major commercial houses in Guatemala were linked to the Aycinena-Piñol family either by blood or marriage.

A pattern of economic interdependence emerged where the exporting regions and the capital depended on the other provinces for their subsistence. Nicaragua, Honduras, and Costa Rica supplied meat, grain, and tobacco to the indigo-producing regions. Cattle ranching was important to creole families in Honduras and Nicaragua and constituted their principal economic activity. While indigo, grown mostly in El Salvador, became the chief export, a growing trade in foodstuffs benefited other areas of the kingdom and drew them into the capitalist trade pattern. Nicaragua's trade for the year 1800 reflected this pattern, as nearly 70 percent of its $539,000 in exports were to points within the kingdom.[12] The accelerated efforts to improve the road and river network of the kingdom reflected the increased interprovincial commerce as well as the overseas commerce.[13] Coastal trade within the kingdom was exempted from the *avería* tax and grew rapidly after 1780.[14] A flurry of new port projects on both coasts characterized the last half century of Hispanic rule in Central America.[15]

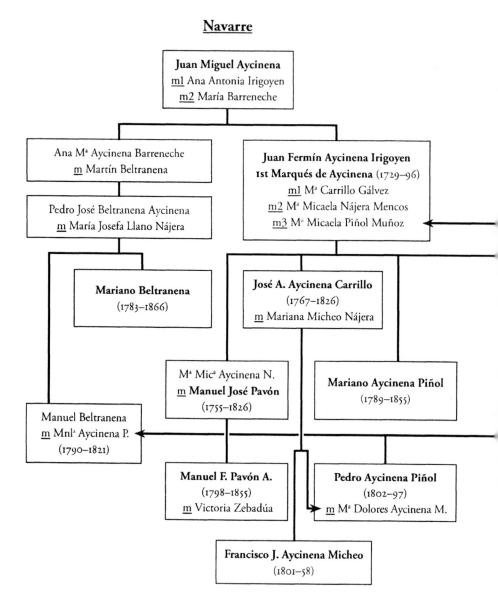

FIGURE 1. Partial Genealogy of the Piñol and Aycinena Families in Guatemala in the 18th and 19th Centuries

Navarre

Juan Miguel Aycinena
m1 Ana Antonia Irigoyen
m2 María Barreneche

Ana Mª Aycinena Barreneche
m Martín Beltranena

Juan Fermín Aycinena Irigoyen
1st Marqués de Aycinena (1729–96)
m1 Mª Carrillo Gálvez
m2 Mª Micaela Nájera Mencos
m3 Mª Micaela Piñol Muñoz

Pedro José Beltranena Aycinena
m María Josefa Llano Nájera

Mariano Beltranena
(1783–1866)

José A. Aycinena Carrillo
(1767–1826)
m Mariana Micheo Nájera

Mª Micª Aycinena N.
m Manuel José Pavón
(1755–1826)

Mariano Aycinena Piñol
(1789–1855)

Manuel Beltranena
m Mnlª Aycinena P.
(1790–1821)

Manuel F. Pavón A.
(1798–1855)
m Victoria Zebadúa

Pedro Aycinena Piñol
(1802–97)
m Mª Dolores Aycinena M.

Francisco J. Aycinena Micheo
(1801–58)

Note: Those who occupied prominent political, economic, or ecclesiastical positions are shown in bold face. Where the father had more than one wife, the mother may be easily determined by the maternal, or second, surname, which in some cases in this chart is abbreviated by the initial only (e.g., María Micaela Aycinena N. is the daughter of Juan Fermín Aycinena Irigoyen and María Micaela Nájera Mencos).

Catalonia

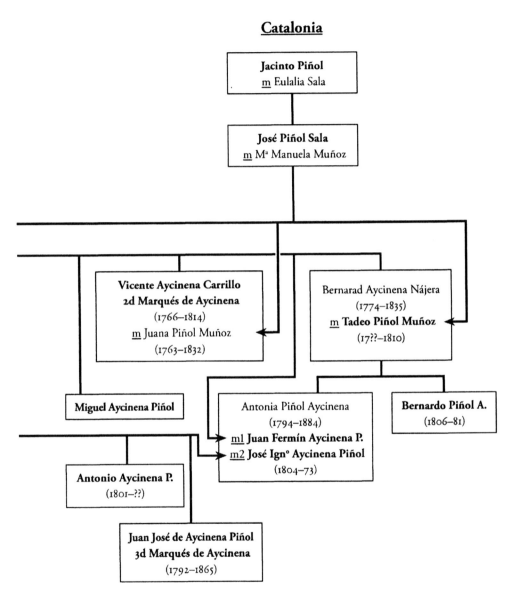

The transition to more capitalist economic structures continued into the nineteenth century, but during the last years of Hispanic rule the Kingdom of Guatemala suffered a serious economic depression. Both international and local reasons for the economic downturn made this depression especially severe and exacerbated dissensions among political factions as the region entered upon its independent course. The economic changes wrought by the Bourbon reforms inevitably caused reactions among those who did not share the gains or who were threatened by the changes. Among the elites, the emerging capitalist structure was at the root of the liberal parties that would dominate the nineteenth and early twentieth centuries in Central America. Those who doubted the methods or wisdom of the changes and who clung to traditional, neo-feudal ideas formed the core of the conservative parties. These two factions would struggle bitterly in the nineteenth century before the eventual triumph of liberalism. The growing demand for land and labor strained relationships between creoles, Ladinos, and Indians, inevitably creating doubts over the wisdom of the capitalist policies and contributing to rising tensions among the lower classes.[16]

More specifically, the growth of foreign competition began to challenge Central America's position in indigo exports. Indigo seed sent from Guatemala arrived in Venezuela in 1777, and the Caracas region quickly began to produce the blue dye in quantity. The location of its productive areas near the Caribbean gave it an advantage in access to markets over the dye produced on the Pacific slopes of Central America. In addition, other new producers, notably India and South Carolina, lowered the price of indigo in European markets.[17] Of lesser importance, but still a part of the decline was the disappearance of another dyestuff, cochineal, as a Central American export because of competition from Oaxaca.[18]

More devastating to the growth of the international trade of Central America were the wars in which Spain became embroiled from 1779 to 1821. Its vulnerable Caribbean coastal ports suffered repeated attacks during this period. Central America's role in the American Revolution rarely finds mention in United States history texts, yet Spanish forces under Captain General Matías de Gálvez repulsed a major British strike at Nicaragua and engaged the British along the Caribbean shore from Belize to Costa Rica. Although the British failed to achieve their objectives, they disrupted Spanish trade and placed a heavy defensive burden on the Central American economy. Moreover, the British activity led directly to an increase in smuggling, which would grow steadily throughout the remainder of the colonial period.[19] The French Revolution brought a more serious round of wars to Spain, which would eventually lead to the collapse of the Bourbon monarchy and the loss of most of the empire. These wars, especially after 1796, when Spain was forced to side with France against the British navy, meant disastrous losses for her overseas commerce. Central America shared these losses, as attacks on shipping and ports by British and privateer forces sent the costs of freight, insurance, and imported goods soaring. Spain, forced to rely on neutral shipping, finally abandoned the Cádiz monopoly altogether. Although British and privateer attacks were often repulsed on Central America's coasts, the cost was high and merchants and producers suffered alike. The liberalization of trade that became necessary provided some relief, but in the long run it only emphasized the collapse of Spanish commercial control. The real gainers were the foreign merchants and shippers, mostly British and North American.[20]

The Spanish expense in these wars contributed directly to the decline of the Central American economy. Spanish paper money, issued from 1779 forward, failed to relieve the scarcity of currency in an increasingly capitalist economy, and it depreciated badly after 1793.[21] The wars also required forced loans and higher taxes to finance military and defense expenditures. Beginning in 1799 these "donativos" burdened Central American commerce directly. The crown authorized an additional half of 1 percent avería tax in 1800 to help the merchants meet the $100,000 donation they had pledged to the crown.[22] Restoration of peace in 1802 brought a temporary respite, as the crown relieved the merchants of the obligation to complete the $100,000.[23] Even when war resumed, owing to the depressed state of the Central American economy, the crown did not include Guatemala in its call for a new donation of $200,000 from the merchant guilds of the empire, 70 percent of which was to come from the overseas consulados.[24]

Yet Spain became ever more desperate for funds and sought new means to secure them beyond taxation and forced loans. Among the most important of these was the Consolidation of 1804, by which the lands of "pious works" were to be sold with the proceeds going to the royal treasury, the religious organizations to receive 5 percent of the value of the properties annually, to be paid from *alcabalas* and tobacco and liquor revenues. The law exempted lands on which the members of religious orders depended for their sustenance, but a very large amount of land came under the provisions of the plan. The lands were to be sold at public auction, with minimum bids of 75 percent of their assessed value. The plan hurt many small farmers in Central America whose mortgages were held by the church. Whereas in the past they had been able to pay only the annual interest, they now were forced to pay the entire principal amount in order to hold their land. The Spanish government, which had earlier instituted the program in Spain, hoped to consolidate the wealth of the church into government control, paying the church 5 percent annual interest on the consolidated assets, which it in turn could sell for quick income. The consolidation also applied to the funds of Indian and Ladino communities, which often leased part of their land to private producers. The consolidation thus terminated mortgages that had been carried for decades, disrupting land tenure patterns and removing about 1.25 million pesos in capital from the kingdom at a time when it could ill afford it.[25] In one of its first actions following news of the overthrow of the Spanish Bourbons by Napoleon in 1808, the Guatemalan ayuntamiento terminated the consolidation processes.[26]

The defeat of the Spanish fleet at Trafalgar in 1805 left merchantmen without protection. It thus led directly to even greater commercial losses and to increased smuggling through Belize in Central America. The English used or posed as neutral (usually U.S.) shipping to trade with the Spanish Empire.[27] Once more, Spain relaxed her trading restrictions as the only means of moving her goods and exempted indigo, cacao, coffee, cotton, and sugar from payment of export taxes in an effort to stimulate production.[28]

These efforts made little difference. Carlos IV succumbed to Napoleonic pressure in 1808, turning over the empire to Joseph Bonaparte. Central American reaction to this event, consistent with the rest of Spanish America, emphatically opposed recognition of French rule. In Guatemala City, the creoles declared their allegiance to Fernando VII and the resistance junta. The merchants of the capital promptly pledged a new $100,000 "patriotic donation" on 19 September. By the end of 1809 the kingdom had sent more than a million pesos, mostly in specie and indigo, to aid the resistance to Napoleonic rule, an expression of patriotism that Guatemalan historian Ramón A. Salazar called "truly suicidal."[29] The Guatemalans also subscribed a new loan at 6 percent annual interest.[30]

To the general economic and political malaise of the Spanish Empire were added unusual local difficulties that beset Guatemala during the final half century of the colonial period. Not the least of these was a series of natural disasters among which the destruction by earthquake of the capital city in 1773 ushered in the period. The decision to move the capital to a new site was costly and diverted labor and capital from more productive enterprises. Many artisans were ruined, for their labor was required in construction work, and in the meantime the rising imports of European manufactures undermined their own craft trades, leaving them unemployed once the construction of the new city was finished.[31] The development of the new capital entailed a disruption of traditional food supplies and was a very great expense at a point when the kingdom began to face other serious economic woes. It also caused the central government to neglect the provinces, contributing to the growth of separatist sentiment on the eve of national independence.[32] In addition to the geologic catastrophe, a typhus epidemic between 1770 and 1775 caused significant demographic and economic consequences on the isthmus. The population of many areas was decimated, just as it had begun to grow. Fields were abandoned and there was notable emigration into urban centers. Many smaller agricultural enterprises failed, contributing to their resentment toward the large planters, who were better able to withstand the crisis.[33] Other major disasters near the close of the Spanish period included a series of earthquakes and violent volcanic eruptions in El Salvador in 1787, a major earthquake in Honduras in 1809, and a serious yellow fever epidemic, also in 1809, which spread death and economic loss in the Caribbean ports.[34]

But an invasion of locusts was the most devastating economic disaster to hit Central America, as these insects destroyed large parts of the indigo crops between 1799 and 1805. Earlier locust invasions had checked the growth of the industry in 1723, 1732, and again in 1772–75, but the attack at the turn of the century—combined with the declining prices, foreign competition, and other economic problems—dealt a near death-blow to the indigo industry.[35] Greatly damaged, it nevertheless survived the locust plague and grew considerably following independence, remaining the principal export of El Salvador until late in the nineteenth century.

Statistical evidence of the depression is readily available. Annual indigo production dropped from an average of more than 875,000 pounds in the 1790s to less than 460,000 pounds during the decade preceding independence.[36] David Radell and James Parsons have documented in detail the decline of the important Nicaraguan Pacific port of Realejo.[37] Textile production, which had been growing until 1780, began to suffer because of the foreign imports and went into a long period of decline.[38] Smuggling was more important for imports than for exports, so that although mineral production around Tegucigalpa was growing, most of the increased specie coined was drained off to pay for imports. Cacao continued its long decline. As the prices of foreign goods rose and exports dropped, Guatemalan standards of living declined. Public works and services lacked adequate funds to maintain them. A notable increase in mendicancy and urban crime further reflected the economic decay and brought demands for more government aid to promote new products, roads, ports, and aids to navigation.[39]

Miles Wortman, using government revenues in the kingdom as an indicator, has confirmed the seriousness of the economic depression in Central

America during the last years of Spanish rule. Providing detailed statistical tables and charts of the declining government revenues reflecting the downturn in trade and production, he shows an overall drop of 32.4 percent in government revenues for the period 1805–19 compared with the period 1790–1804.[40]

The effects of the depression were numerous. The Kingdom of Guatemala failed to produce revenues sufficient to meet the expenses of its bureaucracy, which depended on subsidies from the viceregal government in Mexico. Severo Martínez has pointed to the increase in Indian revolts, which, he says, were rebellions not against the colonial regime but against the economic system that abused them and increasingly challenged their traditional lands and exploited their labor.[41] Resentment toward a weakened Spain grew among all social classes as did tension toward each other, paving the way for independence and the bitter class struggles that followed.

The economic growth and liberalization of the Bourbon Reforms in the mid to late eighteenth century had encouraged the institutionalization of economic interest groups in the colonies. In Central America, the ayuntamiento, especially that of the capital city, had traditionally been the principal spokesman for the interests of the creole elite, and its role as defender of colonial interests increased after 1810.[42] Artisan guilds began, although not very effectively, to represent the interests of weavers and other craft people in the capital, whereas the merchants, who had traditionally depended on the ayuntamiento for representation, moved successfully to establish a *consulado de comercio* in 1793.[43] In the meantime, the indigo producers, especially the smaller Ladino farmers of El Salvador, had formed with government assistance a mutual aid fund to help them finance their crops independently of the Guatemalan merchants or the church.[44] The indigo growers' society became a fairly effective organization in defending planter interests against the merchants, especially in cooperation with the intendants of San Salvador, who encouraged the organization of the indigo growers. The indigo growers' society could not, however, overcome the devastating effects of the depression, and as its indebtedness grew its effectiveness waned.[45]

The final decade of Spanish rule in Guatemala was dominated by the authoritarian rule of Captain General José de Bustamante y Guerra, a loyal Spanish officer who worked diligently to improve the economic fortunes of the colony and to defend it from the independence movements that were sweeping Mexico and South America. Bustamante succeeded admirably in achieving these goals during his administration, but his efforts to suppress the widespread smuggling that the depression had encouraged and his Draconian political methods alienated a significant segment of the creole elite, many of whom had been engaging in smuggling or had come to enjoy the more open political process that the Spanish Constitution of 1812 provided until 1814. By the time the mild-mannered Carlos Urrutia relieved Bustamante in 1818, many of the creoles were ready to accept independence as an alternative to continued Spanish rule. The political instability that had come to characterize the peninsula, the inability of Spain to conduct a respectable foreign policy or to defend adequately the commerce of its empire, and the collapse of the Guatemalan economy all propelled major elements of the Central American society toward acceptance of independence when the opportunity came.[46] The divisions that had become exaggerated during the depression, however, left the United Provinces of Central America (established in 1823) fragmented and divisive, leading to internal strife and civil war that would go on for at least a half century more. The issues that divided the elites and increasingly alienated the rural working masses nearly all developed during the last years of the colonial period. The liberalism of the Bourbon Reforms and the Cortes of Cádiz (1810–14) has been eloquently described by Mario Rodríguez.[47] The high ideals for economic development brought forth, both in the eighteenth century and after independence, a major effort to establish a capitalist, export-led economy. Conservatives questioned the methods and effects of some parts of this policy, although rarely did they fully comprehend the full social consequences, even after the major peasant uprisings of the 1830s.

The changes in production and trade patterns during the last century of Spanish rule in Central America began a commitment to capitalist agro-export dependency that would continue to the present day on the isthmus. Disrupting the feudal haciendas and Indian subsistence agriculture that much of the kingdom had developed during the seventeenth century, the eighteenth century witnessed significant economic growth, only to be arrested at the close of the century by a combination of war, foreign competition, economic problems of the empire, and serious local misfortunes. The resulting depression during the last quarter century of the colonial era had much to do with the chaotic and unsatisfactory development of Central America during its first half century of independence, as liberal and conservative factions of the elite emerged to struggle over economic and political policies. Although the conservatives succeeded in delaying it, by the late nineteenth century Central America was well on its way to becoming a highly dependent agro-exporting region within the North Atlantic capitalist economic system, a process that by the late twentieth century would be facing serious crises because of the glaring social and economic injustices and inequities that the capitalist agrarian system engendered. In short, to understand fully the roots of the present crises in Central America, one must look to the development of the economic system over the past two centuries. Although political independence came to the region in 1821, the economic system that was launched near the close of the colonial period has grown to become the dominant force in the region.

During the first half century of national independence, however, Guatemala's course on that path was neither assured nor universally advocated. Bitter struggle both delayed the triumph of liberal agro-export economic domination and corrupted the political aspects of liberalism virtually beyond recognition. Instead of steady economic growth and political modernization through expansion of an export-led economy, Guatemala became a land of intense class struggle and caudillismo.

CHAPTER TWO

Conservatives and Liberals,
1821–1837

THE POLITICAL TURMOIL that would characterize Central America for
a half-century following independence began almost immediately after the
declaration of independence from Spain. Despite glowing promises of prosperity and progress expressed by independence proponents, unhappy times
awaited the provinces formerly comprising the Kingdom of Guatemala.
Instead of a united isthmian nation, a fragmented, feuding cluster of city
states calling themselves "republics" had emerged by 1850. In this turmoil,
conservative reaction and the caudillo Carrera came to play a formative role
in the shaping of modern Guatemala.

Central American independence has attracted less attention than separation elsewhere in Latin America, for it was not gained at the cost of a bloody
war or with serious social upheaval. Central American creoles did not
seize control of the government following Napoleon Bonaparte's invasion
of Spain, although a few tried. Peninsular rule remained in Guatemala
City until 1821, notably under the authoritarian rule of José de Bustamante (1811–18). And independence came rather suddenly, simply the act
of an assembly of notables who on 15 September accepted the fait accom-
pli of Agustín de Iturbide's Plan de Iguala. Yet, far from being politically
dormant during the first two decades of the nineteenth century, Central
America experienced severe economic stress and social dislocation during
these years. The conflicts of this period bear directly on the issues that
disrupted the Central American union during the half century following.

The period from 1810 to 1814, particularly, inaugurated political struggles that would last for decades. Creoles in El Salvador, Honduras, and Nicaragua tried to form independent juntas in 1811 and 1812, but the central government in Guatemala rather easily put them all down. Near the end of 1813, a plot by creoles in the capital itself was nipped in the bud. The strong, efficient rule of Bustamante denied success to these movements, but their real importance lies in the context of the colonial grievances and political ferment that occurred as a result of the revolutionary changes that the Cádiz government began. The Constitution of 1812 provided political definition and substance for the emerging creole liberals who had already begun to articulate economic and social grievances. It required elections, public discussion of issues, colonial representation in Spain, and provincial councils (*diputaciones provinciales*); and it encouraged free trade, threatened traditional *fueros* and monopolies, and embodied the political philosophy of the Enlightenment in providing for representative government and more democratic procedures. These new procedures allowed political dialogue in Central America that carried well beyond independence from Spain and Mexico. They laid the political foundations for the Liberal Party in Central America and for its program for the remainder of the century.[1]

Captain General Bustamante abhorred the constitution and did his best to restrain its implementation. The restoration of Fernando VII and the suppression of the Cádiz Constitution vindicated Bustamante's authoritarian dictatorship and repression of the liberals after 1814. But his successor, the mild-mannered Carlos Urrutia, relaxed the strong-armed rule. Moreover, the Spanish Revolt of 1820 restored the constitution, prompting a renewal of the dialogues of 1811–14. The constitution stimulated not only strong liberal political arguments in Central America, but also emphasized the function of local and provincial governments in making decisions for themselves and in standing up against the metropoli—Guatemala, Mexico, or Madrid.

Regional resentment was present in all of the provinces, but nowhere was it so obvious as in El Salvador. Its emergence in the late eighteenth century as the principal producer of the kingdom's exports gave San Salvador a new importance. That city grew significantly, and Salvadoran planters and creoles chafed at the monopolistic domination of society and economy by the dominant families of Guatemala City. In fact, following the destruction of Santiago de Guatemala in 1773 and its move to a new site about forty kilometers away in 1776, San Salvador probably was for a time the largest city in the kingdom. The creation of an intendancy in San Salvador in 1786 provided a degree of regional autonomy for the first time and can be seen as a first step toward Salvadoran nationality. Calls for ecclesiastical identity followed, as Salvadorans demanded their own Bishop and separation from the Diocese of Guatemala. The Cádiz reforms offered Salvadoran creoles an opportunity for self rule and justice. Thus, San Salvador became a hotbed of liberal thought and action, a position it would retain throughout much of the nineteenth century. Liberal antagonism toward the conservative families of the capital rested on the economic and social predominance that the latter exercised through their control of land and institutions such as the Consulado and the ayuntamiento. Royal appointment of José Aycinena Carrillo, a leading member of these families, as intendant in 1811 to suppress Salvadoran insurgency infuriated Salvadorans. Their resentment toward what they termed the "aristocracy" in Guatemala City was echoed in other provincial centers from Chiapas to Costa Rica.

Within the capital, the dialogue became public in the pages of two newspapers that in 1820 responded to the call for ayuntamiento elections. *El Editor Constitucional*, directed by the fiery Pedro Molina, a physician of illegitimate parentage and lacking close ties to the principal families, now challenged traditional institutions and continued Spanish rule. Answering him was *El Amigo de la Patria*, edited by José Cecilio del Valle, who had come to the capital for an education from a Honduran ranching family and stayed to become one of the colony's leading intellectuals and a prominent attorney. He had risen in position and importance during the Bustamante years as a loyal public servant. Regarded as a promoter of the Enlightenment, he enjoyed wide respect among the Guatemalan elite. His close connection to the bureaucratic establishment caused him to counsel moderation and caution regarding independence, so that by 1820, despite his ideological liberalism, he had become associated with the moderate political faction.[2]

The elections at the end of 1820 were not decisive, although Valle won election as alcalde of Guatemala City. Political lines in this election are misleading in terms of subsequent Central America politics except in the context of independence from Spain. The leading creole families, headed by the Aycinenas and fearful of the threats posed to their prestige and monopoly by the return to power of the Spanish liberals, supported Molina's rabble-rousers. Valle, on the other hand, had the support of the government and middle-sector elements in the capital. The real significance of this election was the more open political dialogue and activity which it stimulated throughout Central America.

This became evident as news of Iturbide's plan spread southward. The new emphasis on local decision making came into play as the ayuntamientos in each town took it upon themselves to decide the issue. In Chiapas, the towns of Comitán, Ciudad Real, and Tuxtla each declared separately for the Plan between 28 August and 5 September 1821. In Guatemala, Gabino Gaínza, the acting governor who had commanded the loyalist forces in the reconquest of Chile in 1814, listened privately to the proindependence arguments of Mariano Aycinena and Pedro Molina, who promised to retain him in the top position, while publicly he condemned talk of independence. On 14 September, after news had arrived from Chiapas of the Plan de Iguala, Gaínza responded affirmatively to the diputación provincial's request for a general meeting of the representatives of the corporate institutions. In a stormy session the next day, creole and peninsular leaders debated the issues while a crowd outside clamored for independence. In the end, the delegates voted 23 to 7 for independence, but changed very little else. The Spanish bureaucracy, headed by Gaínza, remained. José del Valle led the forces of moderation that in effect left the Guatemalan elite in control. Having achieved escape from the Spanish liberal regime, the Aycinenas no longer needed the alliance with Molina. They turned now to Valle, who drew up a plan of government, and thus was born the conservative party.[3]

The leadership in Guatemala City intended this act to cover the entire kingdom, but the pattern of local participation was already too popular to preclude local ratification. Accordingly, each municipality voted separately as news traveled southeastward. All echoed independence from Spain, but there were variations in their approaches to the future. In San Salvador a junta led by Father José Matías Delgado declared absolute independence and forced those who favored union with Guatemala or Mexico to leave the city. Other Salvadoran towns responded differently and trouble broke out. In Honduras, Tegucigalpa accepted Guatemalan leadership, while Comayagua insisted on independence from Guatemala as well as from Spain, but accepted annexation to Mexico. In Nicaragua, Granada promised to support the central government in Guatemala, while León declared independence from Spain and Guatemala, although it was apparently willing to unite with Mexico! By the end of September the isthmus was facing anarchy with a multitude of claimants to authority. Costa Rica, remote and generally aloof from activities in the captaincy general, seceded from Spain on 27 October, leaving its position with respect to Guatemala and Mexico ambiguous, but emphasizing its complete independence from Nicaragua. As the national period opened, Central America was politically fragmented and caught up in a wave of regional acts of separation that reflected an adolescent desire to be free of their respective immediate superiors.[4]

Annexation to Mexico became the first real issue to divide conservatives and liberals in independent Guatemala. Family names that would be the backbone of the conservative establishment during the next half century stood out in support of annexation: Aycinena, Larrave, Larrazábal, Echeverría, Piñol, Pavón, Croquer, Urruela, Irisarri, Arriaga, Beltranena, Batres, Asturias, Saravía, Arrivillaga, Arzú, Valenzuela, Barrutia, and Nájera. There were, nevertheless, individuals from the leading families who opposed annexation, most notably José Arrivillaga, José Francisco Barrundia, Antonio Larrazábal, Manuel Montúfar, and José Francisco Córdoba.[5] In general, conservatives all across Central America endorsed annexation, while liberals called for an independent republican federation. Because they controlled the apparatus of government in Guatemala and in most of the other states, the conservatives succeeded in thwarting liberal efforts to resist annexation. José del Valle kept the provisional government in Guatemala going in the weeks following the declaration of independence. His administrative ability and sound leadership checked the radicals while he consolidated the support of moderate and conservative elements. Iturbide's dispatch of a Mexican army at the end of November furthered the annexation cause. The Guatemalan government skillfully supported annexationists in the provinces against the republicans. Gaínza, who remained titular chief of state, actively persuaded many provincial leaders to support annexation. Also on the side of annexation was the powerful influence of Archbishop Ramón Casáus, who had only reluctantly accepted independence, recognizing the difficulty of Guatemala remaining a colony surrounded by independent states. Violence flared in Guatemala and Nicaragua, but only in El Salvador did the republicans gain the upper hand. On 5 January 1822 Gaínza declared that annexation was the overwhelming will of the kingdom—as expressed through the ayuntamientos—and a few days later he prohibited further opposition to the decision. The provisional junta then dissolved itself and Gaínza supervised a speedy election of delegates to the new congress in Mexico. Not surprisingly, many of the leading moderates, including Valle, won election and set out for Mexico City.[6]

Only San Salvador and Granada overtly resisted the decision, although debate continued in Costa Rica, where there was also sentiment for union with Simón Bolívar's Gran Colombia, and in Honduras, where the rivalry between Comayagua and Tegucigalpa continued. Led by Father Delgado, San Salvador turned to arms to maintain its position. Under the command of Manuel José Arce, its army first forced Santa Ana to renounce its annexation decision and then defeated Gaínza's Guatemalan army near Sonsonate, touching off a war between the two states that would continue intermittently for decades and would poison chances for a successful Central American union. A Guatemalan force under Colonel Manuel Arzú penetrated the Salvadoran capital on 3 June 1822, but then fell back before spirited resistance. This instilled confidence in the Salvadorans and had much to do with their continued resistance.

The arrival of Mexican Captain General Vicente Filísola with six hundred troops provided the imperial force to decide the issue. Filísola took office on 22 June and immediately sought a negotiated settlement. San Salvador entered into these talks apparently to buy time, for by November it was clear that the city would not submit peaceably to Mexican rule. Frantically, San Salvador sought a way out of its predicament, including a declaration of annexation to the United States. All failed, and the city capitulated to Filísola on 10 February 1823. Arce fled to the United States. In the meantime, however, Granada continued to hold out against annexation, and in April anti-Mexican forces from San José and Alajuela subdued the proimperial Cartago troops in Costa Rica.[7]

Iturbide's empire, of course, was already doomed. While Filísola had subdued the liberals in El Salvador, liberals in Mexico had pronounced at Casa Mata against the empire. After news arrived of the emperor's abdication, Filísola told the Guatemalan diputación provincial on 29 March 1823 that Mexico was in a state of anarchy. The provinces responded enthusiastically to his call for a general congress in accordance with the plan of 15 September 1821. Elections followed, and the body that began its sessions on 24 June 1823 represented all of the states except Chiapas, which had chosen to remain with Mexico.

This congress was decidedly more liberal than the previous government. Many of the conservatives were still in Mexico, and the collapse of the monarchy had discredited them anyway. Under the presidency of Delgado, on 1 July 1823 it declared Central America free and independent and adopted the name United Provinces of the Center of America (Provincias Unidas del Centro de América). The next day the congress became a National Constituent Assembly and set to work writing a constitution, incorporating reforms aimed at creating modern republican federation. Mexico recognized the United Provinces in August as Filísola and his army withdrew.[8]

The new republic began with rather naive expressions of unity and optimism for the future after nearly two years of disunion and chaos, which

TABLE I

Estimated Guatemalan Population, 1820–1870

Year	Population	Annual Growth Rate
1820	595,000	—
1830	670,000	1.2 percent
1840	751,000	1.2 percent
1850	847,000	1.2 percent
1860	951,000	1.2 percent
1870	1,080,000	1.3 percent

Sources: Ralph Lee Woodward, Jr., "Crecimiento de población en Centro América durante la primera mitad del siglo de la independencia nacional: Investigación reciente y estimados hasta la fecha," *Mesoamérica* 1, no. 1 (1980):219–29; and "Population and Development in Guatemala, 1840–1870," *Annals of the Southeastern Council on Latin American Studies* 14 (1983):5–18; Pedro Cortés y Larraz, *Descripción geográfica-moral de la Diócesis de Guatemala hecha por su arzobispo* (1958), 1:299–300, 2:301–2; José A. Barrera Túnchez, "Aspectos generales de la situación demográfica de Guatemala," in *Seminario sobre el crecimiento de la población y desarrollo* (1968), 1–9; J. D. Durand, "World Population Estimates, 1700–2000," *Proceedings of the World Population Conference, Belgrade, 30 August–10 September 1965* (1967), 2:22; Nicolás Sánchez Albornoz, *La población de América Latina desde los tiempos precolombinos al año 2,000* (1973), 108.

were now blamed on Spain, Mexico, and their "servile supporters." Despite the sudden turn of political events in favor of the liberals, serious economic and social problems and divisions stood in the way of the sort of government that the framers of the Constitution of 1824 envisioned.

Even with the loss of El Salvador and excluding Belize, Guatemala had a population at the outset of independence of nearly six hundred thousand, almost half of the entire Central American population. During the first half century of independence there were no complete censuses of the state, but, based on the survey conducted by Archbishop Pedro Cortés y Larraz in the 1770s and on Guatemalan national censuses beginning in 1880, we can estimate that the population in this period grew at a rate of about 1.2 percent per year, a rate that exceeds that generally attributed to Europe or South America during the same period, but was less rapid than in North America. Table I estimates Guatemala's population during the period.

Most of the people were illiterate peasants with little apparent voice in the future of the country. The economic depression and political turbulence of the first quarter of the nineteenth century must have had a severe effect on the social structure. Economic stress had brought hard times to the elite and they understandably looked toward expanded trade, removal of economic restrictions, and new exports, notably cochineal, as a means out of their straits. Some had already turned to contraband, principally through Belize, compounding their difficulties with the Bustamante regime. Yet they opposed economic advancement for other elements of the society, and after independence the inherent conservatism of this class became manifest. Opposing them were professional men and bureaucrats who saw in liberalism greater economic opportunity. Both factions represented only a tiny percentage of the total population, the masses of Indians and Ladinos being left out of the political debates. But the economic hard times were felt not only by the elites. Indeed, the spread of poverty among the urban poor increased social tensions at the time of independence and helped to provide soldiers for the armies of both sides in the conflicts that followed. In the absence of trained Spanish bureaucrats, who admittedly were also sometimes corrupt, public administration suffered in the hands of inexperienced newcomers who often were looking out only for their own interests. The new comptroller of customs, while assuring that "as soon as the government was settled, the receipts of the customs would be more than doubled," reported to a British diplomat that "the collection of the Customs, owing to the disorganization that had arisen from the revolution, was attended with the greatest difficulties," and "that smuggling and bribery were carried on to a serious extent." Moreover, he said, "the authorities had no power sufficient to prevent it."[9]

The issues that divided liberals from conservatives at the outset of the national period were not very different from those that divided Spaniards at the same time, and they had been delineated in the debates over the Cádiz Constitution of 1812. Conservatives felt more secure with monarchism while the successful republican example of the United States and the more open political and judicial form of the United States, France, and Great Britain enchanted the liberals. The Spanish Bourbons had not endeared themselves to either group sufficiently to allow monarchy to remain an institution long cherished by the conservatives, but even after they apparently had settled the issue of monarchy versus republic, Central American conservatives retained serious skepticism about the ability of any but the educated and propertied to govern. A more important institution than monarchy in the liberal-conservative struggle was the church. The liberals sought to disestablish and remove the church from political and economic power, while the conservatives cherished it as a defender of their privileges and a vital link to control of and support from the masses. It was, in fact, the conservatives' privileged and monopolistic control of the economy that the liberals sought to destroy, and elimination of the fueros of the conservatives—ecclesiastical, commercial, university, and so on—were all targets of the liberals. Education was an issue closely related to the church controversy, for the liberals favored secular education with mass education as a stated goal while conservatives defended the elitist educational patterns under the supervision of the clergy. Leaders in both parties, of course, recognized the need for more modern, rational approaches to the economy, as the utilitarian influence of Jeremy Bentham on both sides illustrates.[10]

The turmoil of the first two decades of independence eventually culminated in the powerful popular reaction that brought Carrera to power. Sharp disagreement among the leading landholding and merchant families and serious regional animosities were at the root of the struggle. Although political parties in the modern sense had not yet formed, factions among the elite, often following blood or matrimonial lines, had laid the foundations for the liberal and conservative parties all across Central America. Although there were exceptions on both sides, in general the conservatives represented the wealthy, established families of the late colonial period, whereas the liberals represented more especially the upper-middle sector, professional classes, and illegitimate offspring of the elite families. At the outset, there was considerable political maneuvering, but the bitter struggles that would follow removed much of the middle ground and crystallized the two parties into warring camps that would characterize Central American politics for the remainder of the century.[11]

Liberal domination of the National Constituent Assembly following the declaration of independence from Mexico (1 July 1823) meant a sharp turn away from the interests of the conservative elite. Radical liberals Pedro Molina of Guatemala and Juan Vicente Villacorta and Manuel José Arce of El Salvador made up the "Supreme Executive Power," but since Arce was still in the United States, the assembly chose another "*fiebre*," Antonio Rivera Cabezas of Guatemala, to fill his place. The assembly drafted the Constitution of 1824, establishing the basic framework for republican governments of both the federal and provincial governments. It would be the fundamental liberal document of the nineteenth century. Even before completing the constitution, the assembly challenged the class privileges that had characterized Hispanic rule. On 23 July 1823 it abolished all titles of distinction, royalty, or nobility, including even the use of *Don*, which was replaced by *Citizen*, after the French Revolution model. The same decree included anticlerical reforms, stripping bishops and archbishops of any title except *Padre*. It rejected colonial institutional terminology as well: *Audiencias* and *ayuntamientos* became, respectively, "*cortes territoriales*" and "*municipalidades.*" Later, other ceremonial forms, symbols, and aristocratic vestiges fell (21 August 1823), and "*Dios, Unión, Libertad* [God, Union, Liberty]" replaced "*Dios guarde a Ud. muchos años* [God keep you many years]" as the complimentary close on official correspondence (4 August 1823). Annulment of all acts of the imperial Mexican government and preemptory dismissal of Spanish and Mexican officials soon added to conservative resentment against the liberals.[12]

Violence flared in mid September 1823 when Captain Rafael Ariza y Torres led a revolt, ostensibly demanding back pay for his troops. It resulted in a reshuffling of the government toward more moderate interests in October, José del Valle heading the new junta, with Arce and Tomás O'Horan as the other members. Then liberal troops from El Salvador arrived in support of the former government. A major crisis passed when rival forces were kept from clashing, thereby averting civil war, but Guatemalan residents deeply resented the presence of the Salvadorans and ill feeling persisted after they left. In the meantime, the army had also been called upon to suppress a pro-Spanish revolt in September.[13]

Both uprisings reflected the unsettled conditions and fear of the assembly's acts. Inevitably, therefore, the balance of power in the assembly began to shift as debate over the proposed constitution continued. More moderate liberals in the assembly became disenchanted with the radical "*fiebres*" or "*exaltados*" led by J. F. Barrundia. This moderating trend was reflected not only in the constitution, but also in a general reconciliation with the conservatives that would eventually cause a break with the radicals. The constitution finally promulgated in November 1824 was a compromise between radicals and conservatives. José del Valle contributed heavily to formulating the final document, which blended elements of the Spanish Constitution of 1812 with the U.S. Constitution of 1789. In May 1824, Valle and O'Horan described the federal system as "one of the most profound concepts . . . ; one of the most marvelous creations of the mind," and looked forward optimistically to the representative government that it promised. They warned against fractionalization and disunion, calling on the electorate to choose their representatives wisely in an orderly fashion, "showing the entire world that if popular elections have been tempestuous in other countries, in Guatemala they are [carried out] in peace, calm and tranquility."[14]

Such was not to be the case. As a framework for government of the United Provinces, the constitution became the focus of dissension. Although it had the support of moderates led by Valle at the outset, ultimately it would become the symbol of the division between liberals and conservatives. Liberals, while accepting it as a basic framework for government, sought to modify it, while conservatives tried to replace it with a more conservative charter. As for elections, they seldom if ever met the standards called for by Valle and O'Horan.[15]

Dedicated to the protection of "liberty, equality, security, and property" (Article 2), the Constitution of 1824 also guaranteed Roman Catholicism as the religion of the state "to the exclusion of the public exercise of any other" (Article 11). It outlawed slavery (Article 13) and provided extensive guarantees of individual liberties (Articles 152–76). A complex system of indirect elections provided for selection of a president and other national officers and a unicameral federal Congress (Articles 23–54). Separate from the Congress, a senate (which had no power to initiate legislation) composed of two senators from each state, no more than one of whom could be a cleric (Article 92), had to approve all legislation before it went to the president, although the Congress could override Senate vetoes with a two-thirds majority except in cases concerning taxation, which required a three-fourths majority (Articles 78–86). Once passed the Senate, however, the president had no veto and was required to execute the law (Articles 87–88). The president, who was commander-in-chief of the armed forces, and vice-president served four-year terms. A Supreme Court, elected indirectly, had from five to seven justices serving two-year, staggered terms. (Articles 132–40). The constitution also provided for state assemblies, governors, and judicial officers, whose first duty would be to frame state constitutions compatible with the federal charter. Each state was also to have an executive council, analogous to the federal Senate, to approve legislative acts and advise state governors (Articles 177–95). This constitution went into effect immediately (Article 211), even before it was ratified by the first federal Congress in August 1825.[16]

A spirited campaign between Manuel José Arce and José del Valle characterized the first national election. A stream of political handbills and partisan newspapers document the campaign. Violence erupted in several places, even after the government threatened those who opposed the new constitutional system with death. When the new Congress convened in February 1825, presided over by Guatemalan Dr. Mariano Gálvez, liberals appeared to have triumphed, yet the election for president in April favored the more moderate Valle. Receiving 41 of 79 electoral votes actually cast, he nevertheless lacked by one vote a majority of the 82 electors authorized, and thus the election was thrown into the Congress. Arce intrigued not only to win the presidency, but also to form a broadly based coalition, which he believed would allow the federal government to succeed. To this end he gained support from some conservative members with assurances that he would not insist on a separate bishop for El Salvador. The Congress elected Arce by a solid majority vote of 22 to 5. Valle, furious, refused to accept the vice-presidency as provided for under the constitution to the second-place finisher. The liberal radical, José Francisco Barrundia, also refused the vice-presidency, the position falling finally to Guatemalan conservative Mariano Beltranena. Thus the new republic began its existence under a cloud of suspicion of betrayal of the wishes of the electorate, mistrust among the leaders, and with the extreme liberals (the Barrundia faction) already disenchanted with the liberal president, who they believed had sold out to the hated "*serviles.*" [17]

Arce had sensed the more conservative trend and had tried to accommodate himself to it. Condemned as an opportunist by his critics, he immediately became alienated from the liberal Guatemalan state government headed by Juan Barrundia, brother of José Francisco. Arce had already faced opposition from liberals in the other states and had led the army into Nicaragua early in 1825 to pacify the struggle between León and Granada there. In El Salvador, the symbolic issue of establishment of a separate bishop in the person of J. M. Delgado reflected the powerful Salvadoran desire for independence from Guatemala and led directly to San Salvador's opposition to Arce's government.

Both the Salvadoran and Guatemalan state governments pursued radical programs, offending the more conservative interests with which Arce had allied himself. The press reflected the rift between the federal and state governments in Guatemala, as there was an explosion of new, often short-lived newspapers in the capital representing many political views. Conservatives warned against the usurpation of authority by the state governments and bridled at the imposition of new taxes and forced loans by the state government. Federal troops had already checked state governments in Honduras and Nicaragua. Differences with those of Guatemala and El Salvador now prompted Arce in April 1826 to depose Barrundia and in September to place him under arrest.

The remainder of the Guatemalan state government, under Lieutenant Governor Cirilio Flores, fled first to San Martín Jilotepeque and later to Quetzaltenango. Its legislature enacted inflammatory liberal laws, declaring children of the clergy legal heirs to church property, abolishing the Consulado, and cutting the tithe (*diezmo*) in half. These laws were unenforceable for the moment. The liberals' tenure in Quetzaltenango was short lived, for in October a mob attacked Flores, tearing him literally limb from limb, and the liberal government collapsed. Federal forces led by Brigadier Francisco Cáscara soon after defeated the remnants of the state's army under the command of Colonel José Pierson at Malacatán.

Cáscara and Pierson were among several foreign soldiers of fortune who had joined the Guatemalan army. Pierson and two other foreigners in the service of the state government, Isidore Saget and Dr. J. B. Fauconnier, escaped to Chiapas, but conservative authorities later captured Pierson when he returned to Guatemala in May 1827, attempting to reach El Salvador. Governor Mariano Aycinena's order that he be immediately executed made Pierson the first to die in independent Guatemala by simple executive decree. Another liberal foreign officer instrumental in the division between state and federal governments in Guatemala was the French Bonapartist, Nicolás Raoul, brought to Guatemala from Colombia by Pedro Molina. Raoul, as the military adviser to the congressional defense committee, had refused to recognize Arce as commander-in-chief of the army.[18]

President Arce convoked a new Guatemalan state assembly in Guatemala City on the last day of 1826 and arranged for the popular election of Mariano Aycinena as governor of the state on 1 March 1827. Aycinena was a self-righteous man, moderately conservative on most issues, but an ardent defender of the clergy. As governor, however, he became inflexible and despotic. Although, theoretically, his state government was subordinate to Arce's federal government, Aycinena was in reality more powerful, for he commanded the support of the Guatemalan conservative elite in the capital and had better sources of financial support than the impoverished federal government. He established a restrictive dictatorship, limited freedom of the press, and declared Pedro Molina, Antonio Rivera Cabezas, and other leading liberals—as well as their foreign mercenaries, Pierson, Raoul, and Saget—to be outlaws.[19]

At the same time, in El Salvador the liberals forced the pro-Arce government headed by the aged and ill Juan Vicente Villacorta to step down. His successor, Mariano Prado, perhaps heavily influenced by Guatemalan refugees from the deposed Barrundia-Flores government, joined with the rebels, who now invaded Guatemala in an effort to depose Arce.

Arce stopped Prado at Arrazola, near the Guatemalan capital, on 23 March 1827, but this was but the opening skirmish in a vicious civil war. Bitterness and atrocities characterized both sides in a struggle that spread over much of Guatemala, El Salvador, and Honduras. Arce's government depended so heavily on the State of Guatemala that Aycinena soon supplanted him in importance. Antonio José Irisarri (1786–1868), a distinguished Guatemalan literary figure and the son of a leading planter-merchant, returned to Guatemala in the midst of this struggle, dismayed:

> I found myself in Central America defending a cause that wasn't mine, a federation contrary to my own opinions; but there was nothing else to defend, because all were federalists, everyone said they were armed to sustain what everyone was combatting; and I, in all that confusion, thought the most rational thing to do was to follow the standards of the federal authorities that owed their existence to the Constitution of the Republic that all invoked.
>
> With all that, I followed the party that could not triumph, for rarely does reason triumph when the recourse is to arms in human contests.[20]

Irisarri founded a weekly, *El Guatemalteco*, and served in the Guatemalan state army against the Salvadoran invaders.

A Guatemalan force under Justo Milla invaded Honduras and after bitter fighting took Comayagua, sending the captured Honduran Governor, Dionisio Herrera, a friend and relative of José Cecilio del Valle, back to Guatemala for imprisonment. Arce then ordered new elections and imposed Gerónimo Zelaya on Honduras, dismissing all liberals from office. Captured also in this campaign, on 6 June in Tegucigalpa, was the liberal leader, Francisco Morazán (1792–1842).[21]

Morazán was a creole whose grandfather had come to Honduras from Rome in the 1760s, made money in mining and acquired land at San José de Yuscarán. An intense, intelligent, and good-looking youth, Morazán began working as a clerk in a Tegucigalpa law office in 1808, where he learned rapidly and acquired some basic knowledge of the law. After independence, commissioned as a lieutenant in the Tegucigalpa army, he rose rapidly in rank and Herrera named him Secretary General of the Honduran government in 1824. He did not ingratiate himself with federal officials in this position, however, and in 1825 they accused him of "expropriating" twenty-five thousand pesos in federal funds for the State of Honduras.[22]

Milla ordered Morazán jailed in Tegucigalpa on 6 June, but after twenty-two days he gained release after pleading ill health. Jumping his bail, he fled on a mule to El Salvador and then to Nicaragua, where he organized an army with Honduran exiles and León forces. Striking back at the conservatives in Honduras, Morazán began to reverse the tide in the war at La Trinidad on 10 November 1827, when he defeated the Guatemalan forces of Generals Milla and Cáscara. Following up this victory, Morazán took over the Honduran government at Tegucigalpa two days later and captured Comayagua on the twenty-sixth.[23]

With the outcome of the war undetermined, but with bitter fighting destroying the nation, a respected Guatemalan moderate, Juan de Dios Mayorga, now called for a peaceful settlement. Philosophically, he reminded the public that there was no example in history where the form of government had been changed without suffering revolutions. "When I saw that Guatemala had done it without them," he commented, "I thought it was going to be a rare phenomenon in the annals of nations." Now that he was so unfortunately mistaken, he could see that "Central America is obeying the invariable laws of human society, but," he believed, "those who lead can reduce the horrors and length of the war," and thus he proposed a new Congress. He blamed the liberal party for failing to consolidate the nation when it had had the chance. In Mayorga's view, "The Constitution and laws they dictated in their congresses are proof of their lack of enlightenment and experience." He charged that they failed to take into account the level of civilization or the customs of the people. "They imprudently offended several classes, and they made impolitic depositions and attacks on the [religious] fanaticism of the people. In essence, they did not know how to establish liberty one step at a time, and they moved too fast and recklessly, with a political delirium that created a mass of opposition that has led to the disaster in which we now find ourselves." Yet the opposition party (the conservatives), he added, has been "neither more cautious nor more generous in their victory. It has executed people without due process, ordered many exiled, built prisons, created special tribunals, attacked the freedom of the press, and invaded the sanctity of the homes of the citizens." This, he pointed out, was bringing about another strong reaction, once more endangering the security of the country, and he warned prophetically that the bitter fighting between these two groups could destroy the republic. Thus condemning both the radical liberals and the repressive conservatives, he called for the public to elect a congress of reasonable men to deal with their differences in a civilized manner.[24]

But war decided the issue. Before the end of the year, liberal troops were invading Guatemala, threatening Chiquimula and other areas in the eastern *montaña*. The Salvadoran liberals, now seeking total victory, rejected Arce's offer to hold elections. Faced with this impasse, Arce turned over the presidency to Vice-President Beltranena on 14 February 1828 and retired disillusioned to his plantations at Santa Ana. He was not welcome in El Salvador, however, and in October Governor Juan Manuel Rodríguez exiled him from the state. Beltranena, the son of a cousin of Mariano Aycinena, named General Arzú to command the federal army and made a last effort to rally the conservative federal forces.[25]

Manuel Arzú y Delgado de Nájera (1775–1835) was a Mexican-born career military officer who had been trained in Spanish military schools and come to Guatemala in 1810 as a lieutenant colonel. After independence he accepted appointment as a colonel in the federal army and commanded the defense of León against separatists in 1824.[26] Upon returning to Guatemala, he founded the country's first military academy and, as Arce's minister of finance and war, he had ordered all men between the ages of fourteen and fifty to arms, including foreigners.

To pay for the war, the government turned to a forced loan, which fell most heavily on the Guatemala City elite, the religious orders, and on foreign merchants, the latter of which were decidedly unsympathetic. The elite and the clergy on the other hand, who now believed that they faced terrible reprisals should the liberals win, had no choice but to support the loan. The refusal of some of the foreign, especially North American, merchants to pay their quotas led to their persecution by the government, which enjoyed considerable public support in the capital. From this point on, if it was not already the case, North Americans for the most part would lean in their sympathies toward the liberals in Guatemala.[27]

Some members of the elite, as the prospect of defeat rose, may have considered separating Guatemala from the federation and reannexing it to Mexico or Spain. At least a Salvadoran government newspaper accused Governor Aycinena himself of being a leading secessionist, although there is no evidence that he or anyone else in the Guatemalan elite actually participated in a separatist movement at this time.[28]

Initially, with new funds and troops, the Guatemalans stemmed the liberal advance and pushed the enemy back into El Salvador, winning what an "Extra" of the Guatemalan official newspaper called "a complete victory" at Chalchuapa, El Salvador, on 1 March 1828. The Salvadorans suffered six hundred dead in what was certainly the bloodiest battle of the war.[29] Arzú, however, was slow to follow up the victory, and by the time his forces reached San Salvador, the liberals were safely barricaded inside the city. The federal siege of San Salvador went on for months.[30] Aycinena sent reinforcements and issued a stream of manifestos that reflected the intensity of the struggle. On 21 March, for example, he railed against "a few alienated demagogues who dare to sacrifice a valiant people to their private interests, personal vengeance, and disorganized ideas." He described the conflict as a "struggle of order against anarchy," rather than against Salvadorans, Hondurans, or Nicaraguans. He called on all Guatemalans to "listen to the voice of reason," and return to their fatherland.[31] The legislature gave Aycinena extraordinary powers to recruit troops, raise money, deal with dissidents, and support the federal army in its drive for a final victory.[32]

The failure of the Guatemalan forces to take San Salvador, however, allowed Morazán to begin his own offensive. Since his victory at Trinidad the previous November, he had concentrated on reorganizing the state of Honduras and consolidating his military forces around Choluteca. On 4 June 1828 he formally resumed command of the army and, in the name of preserving the federation, he entered El Salvador. He won an important victory at the Gualcho Hacienda near the Río Lempa on 6 July, occupied San Miguel, and caused Arzú to pull the bulk of the federal forces back from San Salvador. San Miguel had supported the conservatives and now Morazán imposed a forced loan on its inhabitants, collecting $16,000 to pay his troops and enough cotton fabric for two thousand uniforms. There was also widespread looting by Morazán's troops. Arzú had left too few troops at the siege of San Salvador, under the command of Colonel Manuel Montúfar Coronado. The Salvadorans counterattacked and defeated and captured Montúfar at Mexicanos on 20 July. Arzú's failure to come to Montúfar's aid led Aycinena to relieve him with his nephew and cousin, Lt. Col. Antonio Aycinena, but Morazán routed Aycinena at the Hacienda San Antonio, El Salvador, on 9 October. Morazán then forced the captured Colonel Aycinena to sign a humiliating surrender and march his disarmed, beaten army back to Guatemala. A few days later Morazán made a triumphal entry into San Salvador.[33]

A peace effort now failed. Costa Rica, having stayed aloof from the contest, but with a conservative government, offered its good offices. The Guatemalan assembly published an appeal to the Salvadorans to seek peace, and negotiations followed. Morazán and Prado offered peace if the former federal and Guatemalan state governments were fully restored, an offer promptly rejected by the Guatemalans. Thus, in late November Morazán invaded Guatemala. Faced with a secession movement in Los Altos, Mariano Aycinena sought once more to equip and motivate an army.[34] More than ever he cracked down on dissidents. With the cooperation of Archbishop Ramón Casáus and the legislature, he ordered that all books prohibited by the ecclesiastical authority be burned, with fines of from ten to fifty pesos on those who possessed such forbidden works. The government also depended on the church to fund the war effort. Casáus committed himself unabashedly to the conservative cause and put the church solidly behind these efforts, a policy that would soon cost the church dearly.[35]

Morazán financed his invasion by forced loans as he conquered Guatemala. Two columns advanced in early January, one from Honduras, the other from El Salvador, with Morazán at the head of the latter. Ahuachapán fell to Morazán on 1 January 1829, Zacapa the following day to the "Northern Division" commanded by the Guatemalan liberal Ramón Pacheco.[36]

Liberals in Guatemala began to take heart. The Antigua municipal government pronounced against the Aycinena government on 22 January, calling for the restoration of the deposed Juan Barrundia. A conservative detachment under Vicente García Granados quickly put down this insurgency, but it reflected waning confidence in the Aycinena government and soon thereafter Morazán reestablished at Antigua the liberal Guatemalan state government that had been dissolved in Quetzaltenango, designating Mariano Zenteno, the senior member of the 1826 government immediately available, as provisional governor. Although Morazán's forces suffered a repulse at Mixco on 15 February, he laid siege to Guatemala City and at Hacienda Las Charcas dealt the conservatives a defeat from which they could not recover. Shortages of funds and supplies and an outbreak of smallpox among his troops kept Morazán from dealing the *coup de grace*. Instead he sought a negotiated finish to the struggle, offering first to exchange prisoners, of which he held many more than he could feed. In fact, both sides were now near exhaustion.[37]

Negotiators met with the Dutch envoy, General Juan Verveer, at Ballesteros on 27 March and again on 3 April. Morazán was willing to compromise, fearing the spread of the smallpox epidemic among his troops. He offered a coalition federal government composed of himself, Mariano Aycinena, and Mariano Prado, with a federal army of a thousand men, composed equally of Salvadorans and Guatemalans, and a general amnesty for all parties. It implied, of course, recognition of the new liberal Guatemalan state government at Antigua. Aycinena found the proposal thoroughly unacceptable. The compromise appeared to offer little to the conservatives, but in retrospect it might have allowed a more gentle transition to liberal government and a less vengeful restoration of liberal rule than actually occurred.

Embittered by the haughty intransigence of the Beltranena and Aycinena governments, Morazán renewed the war.[38] On 7 April he sent Nicolás Raoul to reconnoiter the city, seeking a way to victory at the lowest cost. On the ninth his forces fought their way into the city, but could not breach the defenses at the main plaza. Yet the eventual outcome was clear, and Aycinena sought peace on the eleventh, his haughtiness still evident in the note he sent to Morazán offering to arrange a capitulation.

For Morazán the time for negotiations had passed. He immediately replied that he refused to recognize Aycinena as the chief-of-state of Guatemala and demanded unconditional surrender. Addressing Aycinena only as the "General of the forces that exist in the main plaza of this city," Morazán informed him that his position did not permit him "to lose one moment, nor to agree to anything but the surrender of the plaza," offering only a guarantee of the lives and properties of those present there. He added that further resistance would simply multiply the victims and worsen Aycinena's situation.

Yet Aycinena still refused absolute surrender and requested a meeting with Morazán to discuss "terms for turning over the plaza." He called on Morazán to "cooperate" with him in stopping the bloodshed, insisting that a "conference would be indispensable, even if the plaza is to be surrendered, and I cannot see any reason to impede it, nor can I see how to conclude [a peace] without a momentary suspension of the hostilities by both parties."

Morazán, convinced of Aycinena's hopeless position, was adamant, and insisted on unconditional surrender before any cease fire. "When you tell me that you agree to what I have proposed in my note of this date, I shall promptly meet with the commissioners that must arrange the capitulation, and only then will the hostilities be suspended at the appropriate time."

Thus the fighting continued through the night, as Morazán's fire power took its toll and caused desertions among Aycinena's troops. Finally, on 12 April, Aycinena sent a surrender note under a white flag. Without waiting for Morazán's response, he sent General Arzú and Lt. Col. Manuel F. Pavón with a note to Morazán accrediting them as commissioners. Signed the same day, the surrender called for an immediate cease fire and turning over the plaza and all arms to Morazán's forces on the following morning, with guarantees for the lives of the vanquished, including their right to join the federal army if they so desired.[39]

The immediate fruits of the war were a vindictive policy toward the conservatives and enactment of liberal legislation. Morazán occupied the National Palace on 13 April. His undisciplined troops looted the city, adding to the conservative hatred for Morazán and the liberals. Morazán invited Beltranena and other high officers of the government, including Aycinena, Arce, and most of the prominent personages of the city to the palace at 4 p.m. on 19 April, without any indication of the purpose of the meeting. Arriving in their best ceremonial dress, they expected to be burdened with a new forced loan. Instead, they were immediately arrested and marched off at bayonet point to jail. Most were released in July and sent into exile. Morazán repudiated and annulled the articles of surrender on 20 April on the grounds that Mariano Aycinena had violated its terms by having turned over only 431 of the fifteen hundred rifles that had existed at the time of the surrender. Thus Morazán began "the Restoration" with a reign of terror aimed at ridding Guatemala of conservative influence.[40]

On 11 May, Morazán began the removal of priests who had given aid "to enemies of the state," replacing them with "others who have given proof of adhesion to our cause." In July the new state and federal governments passed strong anticlerical legislation. Military forces rounded up the archbishop and about forty Dominican, Franciscan, and Recollect friars and then exiled them to Havana and New Orleans. Fifteen died from the hardships of these voyages. On 28 July the Guatemalan legislature abolished and confiscated the property of all male monastic establishments with the exception of the Bethlehemites, a hospital order that had originated in Guatemala. The federal government approved this suppression in September and applied it to all of the states. When the most violent earthquake since the 1773 destruction of the capital shook the country in April 1830, the clergy blamed it on liberal policies and especially on the banishing of Casáus and other clergy.[41]

José F. Barrundia presided over the republic until elections were held, while Morazán returned to Honduras to complete the liberal victory there. In the June 1830 election, Morazán led the field without gaining a majority over José Cecilio del Valle who, unassociated with the Arce-Aycinena government in Guatemala, now returned to politics. Valle had never been very close to the conservative elite in Guatemala City, but neither had he espoused the radical liberalism of the fiebres. J. F. Barrundia, Antonio Rivera Cabezas, and Pedro Molina also received a considerable number of votes, and in the end the federal congress decided the election in September in favor of Morazán.[42]

In the meantime, the new Guatemalan state assembly nullified all acts of the conservative government of 1826–29 and declared all officers of both the federal and state governments of that period to be traitors. It also ordered the return of all salaries paid to these officials and employed harsh measures of enforcement, resulting in confiscation of much conservative property. The Central American federal congress passed a similar act on 22 August 1829. Its resolution justified the repressive measures as necessary to preserve the constitution. It also sanctioned the perpetual exile of the high officials and military council of the conservative government of 1826–29, as well as of all military officers not born in America who had served in the federal army, all non-naturalized Spaniards who had voluntarily taken up arms in the service of that government, and judicial officers who confirmed the death sentences ordered by the military council. Many other lesser political and military officer were exiled for periods of from two to eight years.[43] In July 1829 the Guatemalan assembly granted the government extraordinary powers to deal with opponents of the state, and it was under this authority that the government dealt harshly with conservative clergy.[44] The Guatemalan state government also abolished the Consulado, the economic stronghold of the conservative merchant elite, depriving it of both its own fuero tribunal and terminating its tax support for developing infrastructure in the state.[45] The leading families, many of whose heads were now being exiled, were also called upon for forced loans in July. Fifty-six individuals provided a total of nearly $39,000, of which more than a third came from seventeen members of six elite families.[46]

From the time he took office, General Morazán planned to move the federal capital to San Salvador, freeing it from Guatemalan intimidation. The more centrally located San Salvador would also be a better place from which to deal with the separatist tendencies of the other states. Several things delayed the move, however. Earthquakes in February and September of 1831 caused great damage in the Salvadoran capital and disrupted the city's economic and political life, as many of the inhabitants fled to Cojutepeque.[47] Then Honduran conservatives, apparently with aid from the Spanish governor of Cuba, in November 1831 seized the fortresses on the north coast at Omoa and Trujillo. Honduran troops under Colonel Francisco Ferrera laid siege to these forts, and Morazán sent Colonels José María Gutiérrez and Agustín Guzmán to put down the rebellion. Guzmán, with Guatemalan troops, finally subdued the rebellion in September 1832. A firing squad in Comayagua executed the rebellion's Spanish-born leader, Ramón Guzmán, along with another rebel leader, Colonel Vicente Domínguez.[48] Morazán responded to this Spanish intervention by denying passports for travel to any Spanish-held territory and prohibiting importation of goods from Spain or its dominions.[49]

Most important in delaying the move to San Salvador, however, was resistance from the San Salvador government itself. The problem there came with the accession of José María Cornejo to the governorship of that state in 1830 and the reentry of Manuel José Arce into Central American politics. Opponents of Morazán had coordinated the pro-Spanish rebellion on the north coast of Honduras with a plan for Manuel José Arce to invade Guatemala from Mexico. Mariano de Aycinena and other leading conservatives in exile in New Orleans refused to support this plan, but Arce moved to Mexico in August 1831 and organized an army of about 400 in Chiapas among younger officers and more recent emigrés from Guatemala.

Conspiring with Cornejo in El Salvador, he then marched into Soconusco around the end of the year. Morazán sent General Raoul, who successfully stopped Arce's force at Escuintla, although Arce himself escaped back into Mexico.[50]

Morazán left for San Salvador on 29 December 1831, taking only a small force and his cabinet, seeking to avoid a military confrontation with Cornejo. He hoped to persuade Cornejo peacefully to allow the move of the capital to San Salvador, but when Morazán reached Santa Ana, Cornejo issued a strong warning to the federal president to leave Salvadoran territory. On the following day, 7 January, Cornejo's legislature declared the federal pact suspended, refusing to recognize federal authority—in effect seceding from the union!

Morazán responded with a manifesto issued in Jalpatagua on 2 February, declaring that the federal Congress had authorized him to move the capital to San Salvador, and although he recognized that some believed it inopportune or inconvenient, and that some were downright hostile to the idea, the present rebellion of the Salvadoran government against federal authority now made it essential. Having the capital in Guatemala had been a pretext, he said, for opposition from the other states, fearing the preponderance of Guatemalan power. He reminded the Salvadorans that they had been especially concerned about this, but that now they would enjoy the power that they once attributed to the Guatemalans. Challenging the authority of the Salvadoran legislature to issue orders prohibiting his entrance into the state or refusing to recognize the authority of the President and his officers, Morazán announced his intention to march on the Salvadoran capital. The attacks they made on his person, he declared, were in reality attacks on the nation.[51]

With support from the governments of Guatemala, Honduras, and Nicaragua, Morazán met and defeated the Salvadoran army at Jocoro, in the department of San Miguel, on 14 March 1832. Two weeks later, his forces entered the Salvadoran capital, where he deposed the government and legislature and imposed the same sort of repressive rule that he had previously applied to Guatemala. He sent Cornejo to a Guatemalan prison and jailed or exiled most of the other government officials, including members of the legislature. He then assumed the executive authority himself, although he soon turned it over to his friend and strong liberal, Mariano Prado. Another old liberal, Father José Matías Delgado, took over as president of a reorganized legislature. As in Guatemala, the government imposed a forced loan of one hundred thousand pesos, confiscating the property of the defeated officials and those who could not meet their assigned quotas.[52]

New acts of defiance plagued the federal government, further delaying the move of the capital to San Salvador. The Prado government fell in February 1833 and the new government attempted to secede from the federation. Morazán once more restored his authority, but more ominous was a major Indian rebellion under the leadership of Anastasio Aquino. Launching the revolt from his village of Santiago Nonualco, Aquino lashed out against both whites and Ladinos, calling for the establishment of an indigenous government in El Salvador. The revolt spread and capitalized on growing peasant resistance to the liberal policies, especially the imposition of a head tax reminiscent of the colonial tribute. The uprising terrified Salvadoran creoles and contributed to a reunion of their political interests with Morazán, with whose help they ruthlessly suppressed the rebellion. They captured and executed Aquino in San Vicente on 24 July 1834, but Indian uprisings continued in the area for several more years. In the meantime, Morazán transferred the federal Congress and capital from Guatemala to Sonsonate in February 1834, and finally to San Salvador in the following June.[53]

The government of the State of Guatemala underwent a series of changes as differences among the liberals began to surface. Morazán had reinstated Juan Barrundia on 30 April 1829 to finish his interrupted term as governor of the State of Guatemala, but Barrundia chose not to continue in that position. The state legislature elected Pedro Molina as chief-of-state in August of 1829. Molina had been a leader of the fiebres since before independence, but he had also worked with the Aycinenas and other conservatives, and he was less radical than the Barrundias or Antonio Rivera Cabezas, who now were more closely allied with Morazán. Molina proposed eliminating the expensive machinery of the federal government with a Swiss-style federation in which most of the authority would reside in the state governments or the federal Congress. Morazán fought hard against this innovation and was behind the ouster of Molina by Rivera Cabezas on 9 March 1830. Rivera Cabezas's pen had been a powerful weapon against the conservatives, as he ridiculed traditional Hispanic institutions and customs. This was part of a cultural revolution that included not only newspaper editorials, but also a great deal of poetry and theatrical performances that sought to turn the public against Hispanic traditionalism in favor of the liberals. Rivera Cabezas's brief governorship of Guatemala, with the conservatives in exile, ushered in a period of peace in Guatemala after many years of turmoil.[54] It was under the governorship of Dr. Mariano Gálvez, however, that the liberal revolution in Guatemala reached its apogee and prepared the ground for the strong reaction against it that broke forth beginning in 1837.

The election of Dr. Gálvez in 1831 represented a mild setback for the

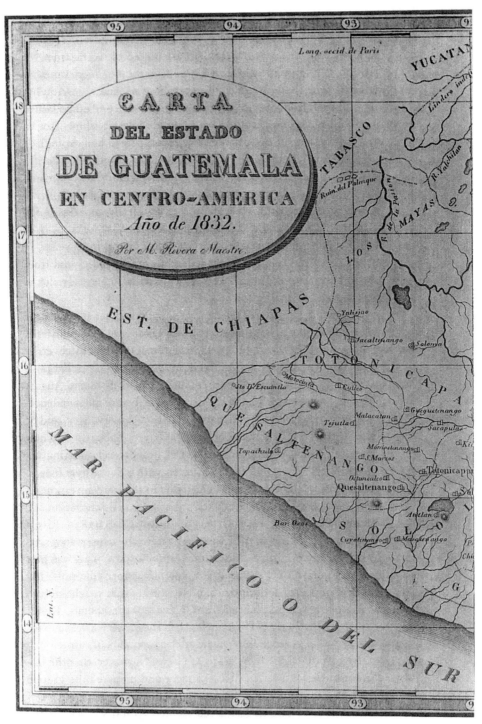

Guatemala in 1832. From *Atlas Guatemalteco*.

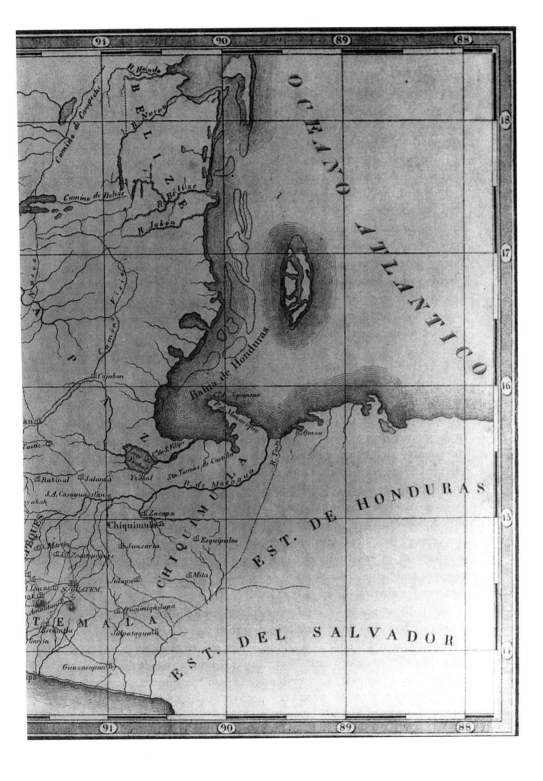

more radical liberals headed by José F. Barrundia, but Gálvez shared Francisco Morazán's liberal ideals for the economy and society. He continued and extended the sweeping reforms begun in 1829. He had broad experience in government since independence and to some degree before, and he had served as minister of finance under Barrundia in the federal government. In July 1830, in a report to the federal Congress he called for roads, immigration, and closer contact with northern Europe. Gálvez was sure that Hispanic institutions and colonialism were responsible for Guatemala's backwardness, and like many of the liberals he looked at northwestern Europe and the United States as models for the "new Guatemala."[55] As we have already seen, the Morazán government faced serious conflicts in El Salvador and Honduras, but eventually succeeded in moving the federal government to San Salvador. Gálvez, however, was able to launch his ambitious programs in a period of relative peace, which had begun during the brief Rivera Cabezas administration. The move of the federal capital to San Salvador actually relieved Guatemala of a major source of conflict and dissension. Gálvez promoted production, especially of cochineal and indigo; planned roads, ports, and other public works; promised mass education; and looked toward the flowering of Guatemala as a liberal and prosperous tropical state in the North Atlantic community.[56]

Gálvez also commissioned official histories. He called upon the conservative (although not closely associated with the hated "family") Father Francisco de Paula García Peláez to write a history of colonial Guatemala. Gálvez then asked the more liberal Alejandro Marure to chronicle the country since independence. Both works eventually appeared, and Marure's Bosquejo histórico de las revoluciones de Centroamérica, desde 1811 hasta 1834 (1877–78) is one of the major primary sources on the period. García Peláez's Memorias para la historia del antiguo reyno de Guatemala (1851–52), although informative, is poorly organized and pedestrian in style. Gálvez also ordered the publication of a periodical to be entitled Documentos para la historia de las revoluciones de Centro-América, in which important documents would be published to counter the influence of Manuel Montúfar's conservative Memorias de Jalapa (1832).[57]

Although support of federal military activities represented a drain on the state's finances, these were primarily paid for by forced loans in the areas of conflict. Military expenditures were relatively smaller in Guatemala than they had been earlier, but they still amounted to a drain on the economy. Gálvez divided Guatemala into four military districts (comandancias generales) on 30 October 1832 as a means of controlling the region. This represented something of a centralizing tendency when compared to the colonial system of corregimientos under local military chiefs.[58]

TABLE 2

Location of Federal Officers and Men, Guatemala, 25 October 1833

Ranks	Guatemala City	Antigua	San Felipe	Petén	Total
Officers					
Colonel	1				1
Lt. Colonels	4	1			5
Sergeant Majors	2				2
Captains	5	1		1	7
Lieutenants	9	1		1	11
Sub-Lieutenants	7	2	3		12
Total	28	5	3	2	38
Enlisted men					
1st Sergeants	7	2	1		10
2d Sergeants	9	5	1		15
Drummers		2	1		3
1st Corporals	2		3		5
2d Corporals	2	2	2		6
Privates	33	18	20		71
Total	53	29	28		110
Totals	81	34	31	2	148

Source: "Informe de la Inspección sobre varios puntos relativos a los puertos del Norte y estados de la fuerza federal, y sus gastos," La Gaceta (Guatemala), 9 Nov. 1833.
Note: Mathematical errors in totals have been corrected.

In addition to these state forces, a small federal force, well below the authorized peacetime level, remained in the state. A mere 38 officers and 110 enlisted men were stationed in Guatemala City, Antigua, the San Felipe fortress on the Río Dulce, and in the Petén. Tables 2 and 3 indicate the location and cost to the Guatemalan government of these forces in late 1833.

The federal government never found adequate means to finance itself and always depended heavily on the states for support, in spite of the fact that the constitution provided adequate powers for the federal government to raise revenue. Part of the problem was the liberal antipathy toward most taxes, but added to this was the structural reality that the federal government was never able to establish an effective tax collection system. The state governments continued to collect federal as well as state taxes. The principal source of government revenue in Central America was customs duties, which had been set at a maximum of 20 percent on textile imports competitive with Central American produced goods; 15 percent on clothing, gunpowder, and a few other commodities; and 10 percent on imports

TABLE 3

Salaries of Federal Forces Stationed in
Guatemala, October 1833

Number	Rank	Monthly Salary	Total
1	Colonel	$205.36	$205.36
1	Lt. Colonel	137.54	137.54
4	Lt. Colonels	108.33	433.32
2	Sergeant Majors	84.75	169.50
7	Captains	58.41	408.87
3	Adjutants	47.10	141.30
8	Lieutenants	37.65	301.20
12	Sub-Lieutenants	30.15	361.80
10	First Sergeants	15.53	155.30
15	Second Sergeants	13.58	203.70
3	Drummers	10.67	32.01
5	First Corporals	11.65	58.25
6	Second Corporals	10.67	64.02
71	Privates	10.19	723.49
Total			$3,395.66

Source:"Informe de la Inspección sobre varios puntos relativos a los puertos del Norte y estados de la fuerza federal, y sus gastos," La Gaceta (Guatemala), 9 Nov. 1833.

Note: Mathematical errors in totals have been corrected and rounded to the nearest hundredth of a peso.

not considered competitive with domestic production. Free trade sentiment was strong among the liberals, however, and they made a number of lower exceptions to these rates. In July 1832, for example, the federal rate on goods entering from Chiapas was lowered to 4 percent ad valorem, plus an additional 2 percent for the State of Guatemala.[59] Subsequently, the rate was lowered to a uniform 5 percent alcabala marítima on all overseas commerce. Although this revenue was supposed to go to the federal treasury, all of the states were keeping it, turning over little or nothing to the federal government. In an effort to gain some revenue and improve the financial relationship with the states, on 7 November 1833 the federal government proposed a compromise when it decreed that the states might keep 60 percent (3 percent ad valorem) of these revenues if they turned over the other 40 percent (2 percent ad valorem).[60] There is little evidence, however, that the situation changed much.

In Guatemala, the Gálvez government continued to tap the resources of the church to support his government, as the following communication to the vicar general early in his administration reflects:

> The Chief Executive, considering that the present exigencies demand prompt and active attention to the clothing and feeding of the forces of the State, has disposed that all funds existing in the ecclesiastical treasury for distribution to the needy are to be placed in the general treasury for the extraordinary expenses of the present time, as well as the urgent ordinary ones, with the understanding that the Government will use them conscientiously for the purpose indicated.[61]

These policies were not especially popular, and with continued difficulties in the other states, the presidential election of 1833 reflected widespread dissatisfaction with Morazán and his programs. In one of the fairest elections in Central American history, José del Valle successfully challenged Morazán's bid for reelection. Unfortunately for the moderate cause, however, Valle died before taking office, and Morazán, with the second highest number of votes, constitutionally remained as president. Morazán's victory under these terms left moderates and conservatives resentful. Their frustrations turned to hatred as grievances against the liberals mounted.[62]

In Guatemala, however, with the more extreme conservatives gone and with peace and moderate prosperity returning to the country, Gálvez won reelection in 1835. He accepted this reluctantly, for he believed in rotation in office. The Guatemalan assembly insisted on his return, emphasizing his success in restoring prosperity and peace to the state.[63]

Miguel García Granados (1809–78), a member of one of the country's prominent families and later a leading liberal, described the country in 1832 as "extremely poor," with the society in Guatemala City divided into three political parts: (1) the (liberal) conquerors, who lorded it over the rest emphasizing their supremacy; (2) the (conservative) conquered, who kept to themselves and rarely attended public functions or entertainment; and (3) those who, with little honor, favored (although only with words that did not compromise their persons or interests) the party that seemed to be most likely to win. Yet despite the general poverty of the country after a decade of turmoil, he also acknowledged the renewed economic activity, particularly the expansion of cochineal production around Amatitlán and Antigua. He noted Gálvez's conciliatory attitude toward the conservatives and that a rapprochement was occurring by 1834. Commerce had improved notably, and at the Independence Day celebrations on 15 September at Gálvez's home, for the first time since the 1829 disaster "the aristocracy" attended. He added that if a foreigner, unaware of what had happened in the country, had seen this "brilliant concurrence" at the governor's home that night, and the harmony that reigned at the fiesta, he would have believed that "an era of peace and prosperity was assured for the state, and in no way would he have suspected that we were sitting on a volcano, and on the eve of entering a terrible crisis of immense consequences for our future."[64] A number of conservatives had, in fact, quietly been allowed to return from exile by early 1837, including the third marqués de Aycinena, Father Juan José de Aycinena, after a mind-widening exile in the United States, via Havana, where he had visited Archbishop Ramón Casáus.[65]

Gálvez had devoted considerable attention to administrative efficiency, as well as to economic development.[66] The confiscation and auctioning of church properties had enabled a number of the elite, conservative as well as liberal, to gain productive new properties in the early 1830s.[67] In his report to the new assembly in 1837, he noted that the volume of trade for 1836 had doubled that for 1834. He mentioned especially the growth of agro-exports, which the government had actively encouraged, saying that "were there no other proof of the multiplication of agricultural enterprises, adequate testimony would be the fact that half of the government's time has been spent in processes for the granting and surveying of lands." Gálvez took pride in the ending of the former oppression, the establishment of religious liberty, public order, and the new judicial system recently adopted.[68]

Responding for the legislature to the above message, J. F. Barrundia noted in glowing terms the assembly's cooperation in enacting "liberal laws" for the benefit of the country. "The peace of its inhabitants," he added, "has been the result of this united effort, which by both has moved the ship of State." He attacked "the colonial regime," when "the ill-conceived and inhumane policy of the Spanish government attacked from its roots reason and morality, converting us into slaves, giving us as privileges and rights degradation and misery." But now the chains had been broken, and Barrundia emphasized the U.S. model as "one of the most fortunate circumstances on the road to free institutions." With the yoke of oppression by those who had opposed the liberal ideas broken, he declared, "We have been able to advance rapidly." This bitter attack on the conservatives stood in contrast to Gálvez's more conciliatory tone, a difference in style that would increasingly divide the two liberal leaders.[69]

Both state and federal legislation reflected the liberal intent to restructure society and economy. Gálvez shared Morazán's belief that enlightened legislation could make Central America a modern, progressive republic, according to liberal tenets. With the conservative leadership in exile and a period of peace and order established, the Gálvez government became the pilot for Morazán's liberal revolution. The influence of Jeremy Bentham on the Central American liberals was especially obvious in the Gálvez years. Following Bentham, the Guatemalan liberals placed great faith in enlightened legislation, unable to face the harsh truth that highly structured constitutions or carefully worded laws do not assure obedience to them. They fell into the trap of so many well-meaning Latin American elite leaders, that of following theory to the exclusion of the practical conditions or cultural heritage of their nations.[70]

While Gálvez gained substantial acceptance of his program among the elite, he failed to overcome widespread and growing opposition among the lower classes of the country. The Guatemalan historian Pedro Tobar Cruz has pointed to the tremendously wide psychological and cultural differences between the liberal leadership and the poor masses as a critical factor in the history of the period. Referring to this "cultural imbalance," he said that "there were select individuals of high comprehension, compared to a populace vegetating in isolation and the Indians following in the most complete ignorance." Gálvez was not only one of those well beyond the comprehension of the masses, but, according to Tobar, even worse, he made the mistake of wanting to advance the population to a higher cultural level.[71] Such reasoning, following Toynbee, perceived a Guatemalan liberal leadership too far advanced to lead its own population and therefore doomed to fall before the reaction of the masses against the liberal challenge to their sacred traditions.[72] The Guatemalan liberals were essentially calling for a capitalist revolution in a country that was in large part still feudal. In this sense they were continuing the efforts of the Bourbon reformers and in the process stimulated negative responses from all those who enjoyed some measure of security in the traditional land and labor system. In rural Guatemala, where many already lived a marginal life, threats to that existence could have explosive results.[73]

Opposition from within the elite had been substantially eliminated, although challenges from moderates occasionally surfaced.[74] It was the middle and lower sectors of Guatemalan society that now began to chafe at the liberal reforms. Liberal trade policy had damaged seriously the native weaving industry, and the federal tariff adjustments did not protect them from heavy imports of British textiles. Many suffered ruin, and as a group they were apprehensive of the liberals' talk of economic freedom.[75]

More directly responsible for the popular reaction was the establishment of a direct head tax, reminiscent of the tribute collected by the Spaniards and abolished by the Cádiz Cortes of 1812. The forced loans imposed on the wealthy citizens were not sufficient to provide for the ambitious program of the government. Governor Juan Barrundia had first established the tax at one peso (half the level of the old *tributo*) to help meet the large state deficit at the end of 1825,[76] but it had not been enforced under Aycinena's rule. Pedro Molina reinstituted it on 11 January 1830. The state assembly had passed this revenue bill on 27 November 1829 in an effort to cover the $94,033 deficit in the 1830 budget. Quotas were assigned to the seven departmental governments, according to their municipalities and number of inhabitants. While the maximum individual quota was $300, the decree specifically placed the maximum for day laborers and Indians at $1.00, and it was at that group that this tax was primarily aimed. Women without property and public employees, "in attention to their salaries having been reduced to the minimum possible," were exempted. At the same time the Molina government required that all petitions once again be on stamped paper, a requirement that had not been enforced since independence, although most legal documents had continued to have the stamp tax requirement.[77] Gálvez raised the tax to a minimum of two pesos per capita, an amount sufficient to harass the Guatemalan peasant of the 1830s who operated principally in a barter economy. In Honduras and El Salvador such a tax had stimulated widespread popular rebellion, forcing suspension of the levy there, but Gálvez maintained it in Guatemala.[78]

Gálvez's plans for an extensive network of roads and ports to complement the expansion of agro-exports resulted in heavy demands for peasant labor. The government, which had taken over the supervision of road and port development from the suppressed Consulado, frequently reminded local officials of the obligation of all residents to work on the roads three days out of every month. One could avoid this labor by payment of the low daily wage, but for the masses it meant forced labor, which could not have been welcomed. The practice was not new with Gálvez, but it was now enforced more rigorously than earlier.[79]

Another aspect of the liberal economic program contributing to rural unrest was the land policy of the government, which promoted private acquisition of public land as a means of increasing production for export. Cochineal expansion began to infringe on the land and labor of Indians and Ladinos in central and eastern Guatemala. Those with some capital acquired Indian communal lands as the trend toward latifundism increased. Gálvez himself, as early as 1826 had been trying to have Indian lands around Alotenango in Sacatepéquez declared as public land so he could acquire them.[80] Individual ownership did not have great appeal to the Indians, but the small, emerging middle class favored easier acquisition of land in early independent Guatemala and the development of a stronger capitalist system. Gálvez also believed it should be encouraged as a civilizing force, and in the end lands that were formerly used in common by local inhabitants began to pass into the hands of *latifundistas*.[81] Lands declared "tierras baldías" by the Gálvez government and claimed by private individuals led to disputes that extended into the 1860s.[82] A legislative order of 17 April 1835 provided for a commission to deal with disputes of Indians caused by the liberal land policy, but the commission did little before the political upheaval of 1837 suspended its activities.[83]

A number of large grants to foreigners caused unrest in eastern Guatemala. An integral part of Gálvez's vision of a prosperous state was his program of foreign colonization in the more sparsely inhabited reaches as a means of bringing about their development and attracting a more industrious citizenry to the state. Such plans date from the eighteenth century, but the Gálvez emphasis on northern European immigration was new. The British commercial activity at Belize had intensified traditional suspicion of foreigners by many residents.[84] Spanish colonial administrations had dealt vigorously, if not altogether successfully, with foreign interlopers, but since independence liberal policy had welcomed them, causing apprehension among those who believed themselves to be victims of foreign competition. Foreign influence was evident in many aspects of the Gálvez program, but the concessions made to mahogany loggers and the projects to populate the northern and eastern portions of the country with English colonists caused residents of those regions to regard the liberals as more favorable to foreign than to national interests. In their eyes, Gálvez was giving away what they believed to be their own resources. As the British tightened their hold on Belize, the Mosquito Coast, and the Bay Islands, and as Anglo-American colonizers in Texas threw off Mexican rule, the wisdom of Gálvez's colonization plan became increasingly dubious to many Guatemalans.[85] Between March and August 1834, the Guatemalan government ceded nearly all of its public land to foreign colonization companies. Ignoring or suppressing petitions from residents against the colonization contracts, however, Gálvez scoffed at the idea that the liberals were betraying their country to Europeans. Revolts in Chiquimula and other eastern towns in the fall of 1835, possibly linked to the uprisings against Morazán in El Salvador, focused on the foreign issue as anti-English propaganda inflamed the residents of the East. Troops suppressed the insurgency, but the inhabitants remained resentful, and the imposition of levies on the towns that revolted to pay for the military's expenses only increased the resentment.[86] Concerned over the popular reaction against the contracts, the federal government pressured Gálvez into issuing a conciliatory decree guaranteeing Guatemalan citizens full rights, but this failed to allay the inhabitants' fears. The arrival of British colonists at Izabal in July 1836 aboard the schooner *Mary Ann Arabella* aggravated the resentment, which must be considered a major factor in inflaming the populace against the Gálvez government.[87]

Central to the liberal program was the removal of the clergy from its traditional role in politics, economy, and education. Accelerating the policies begun by the Bourbon reformers in the eighteenth century, anticlericalism ran especially high after the church backed the conservative regime of 1826–29. Both federal and state governments between 1829 and 1832 exiled many clergy and confiscated the property of the regular orders. In 1832 the Gálvez government ceased collection of the tithe, ended many religious holidays, decreed religious liberty, confiscated more church property, decreed the right of the clergy to write their wills as they pleased, and legitimized the inheritance of parents' property by children of the clergy. Later, the Guatemalan legislature authorized civil marriage, legalized divorce, and removed education from church supervision. Gálvez's proposed public education aimed at westernizing the Indian and, in practice, denied Indians the paternalistic protection that the church had provided.[88] In the Indian and Ladino villages, the priests were more than just spiritual leaders. As the U.S. envoy, John Lloyd Stephens, described a typical representative of the rural clergy in 1839:

> Besides officiating in all the services of the church, visiting the sick, and burying the dead, my worthy host was looked up to by every Indian in the village as a counsellor, friend, and father. The door of the convent was always open, and Indians were constantly resorting to him: A man who had quarreled with his neighbor; a wife who had been badly treated by her husband; a father whose son had been carried off as a soldier; a young girl deserted by her lover: all who were in trouble or affliction, came to him for advice and consolation, and none went away without it. And, besides this, he was principal director of all the public business of the town; the right hand of the alcalde.[89]

Village curates could inflame their parishioners against a government that attacked their sacred institutions, brought Protestant foreigners into the country, and threatened the foundations of the society. These village priests were in the vanguard of the uprising that rocked Guatemala in 1837.[90]

Six rural priests—Padres Lobo, Sagastume, Aqueche, Aguirre, González, and Mariano Durán—were especially notable for going from village to village preaching against the liberals, accusing them of sacrilege, of plotting the extermination of the Indians and mestizos, and of being responsible for natural disasters. Mariano Durán was eventually brought before several military councils, which divided over whether he should be put to death, imprisoned, or exiled. In the end they had him shot, further inflaming the faithful against the government.[91]

None of Gálvez's reforms were closer to him than his plan to remove education from the traditionalist hands of the church and to replace it with secular schools open to all Guatemalans. An ambitious program called for establishment of public schools throughout the country, and a broad range of cultural promotions attempted to westernize the Guatemalan Indian. Trying to change long-established customs and prejudices naturally aroused the suspicions and fears of the illiterate peasants, and the government was widely perceived as intending to eliminate altogether the Indian and mestizo masses.[92]

Revision of the state's judicial system caused further opposition. Sure that the Hispanic system of private fueros and multiple courts was both unjust and antiquated, the liberals adopted the Edward Livingston Codes, which went into effect on 1 January 1837. José F. Barrundia promoted these codes, written for Louisiana in 1824, as a replacement for the system they had been abolishing piecemeal. Hailed as a progressive, model legal and penal system, the Louisiana legislature had decided that the transition from the Roman to English legal traditions would be too disruptive. Yet Barrundia had been enthusiastic about throwing off the Hispanic judicial traditions. On the day it went into effect, he praised it in glowing terms and declared that "the justice of a nation is no longer abandoned solely to the discretion of a salaried judge and to the obscure labyrinth of cruel and bloody laws."[93] Almost immediately, however, problems arose in the countryside. Where illiteracy was general and class consciousness well established, trial by jury proved difficult. Anecdotes quickly circulated ridiculing the decisions of Indian juries. The requirements of Livingston's penal code proved to be equally objectionable, as jails with separate cells for prisoners did not exist and their construction with forced labor added to the resentment of the population, who identified the codes with centralized rule from Guatemala City, and more with foreign influence and anticlericalism than with social justice. Moreover, the authoritarian manner in which the liberals introduced many of their reforms did little to ingratiate the government with the people.

Enforcement of the liberals' programs seemed to belie the liberal rhetoric about liberty and freedom. Reforms were introduced with brutality and harshness, accompanied by military repression. Such tactics had been escalating in Guatemalan government ever since the iron rule of Captain General Bustamante, and the liberals were vengeful after the harsh repression by the Aycinena government. Both the Morazán and Gálvez governments were insensitive in their efforts to develop the export economy, to regulate morality, to suppress criticism of their own policies, and to persecute political enemies through exile and confiscatory measures. Use of the military to enforce the law was becoming standard in Guatemala by 1837 and the conduct of government troops often inflamed the people of the country. The educational program provided that uneducated children might be taken from their parents and assigned to "Protectors" who would provide for their education. In practice, this often provided inexpensive personal service for the elite, and the poor classes viewed it unfavorably. The government also maintained an active propaganda campaign designed not only to promote its own program, but to discredit the opposition.[94] The liberals' good intentions, evidenced by adoption of the Livingston Codes, must have exceeded actual practice greatly, for conservatives denounced those who claimed to be "partisans of *progress* and *civilization*" as guilty of "cruel inhumanity."[95]

Into this atmosphere of bitterness came a deadly cholera epidemic. It was not unanticipated by the Guatemalan government. As early as December 1831 a Guatemalan newspaper had noted the severe cholera epidemic that was causing "terror" throughout Europe.[96] In 1833 it struck Mexico, and Gálvez warned of the danger to his state as he established sanitary cordons, opened up new water supplies and sewage facilities, and prohibited burials inside of churches. In 1836 the danger became imminent, and, despite increased precautions, cholera penetrated the cordons late that year or early in 1837, from Belize. In March and April 1837 the government began to quarantine infected areas and to tighten the sanitary cordons. These measures were undoubtedly justified, but they were poorly understood and they did not succeed. The masses, already alienated from the Gálvez government, feared the vaccines, and they believed priests who told them that the medicine that the government's health officers put into the water was poison. Panic resulted and violence broke out, particularly in the hard-hit eastern region.[97]

The scene was thus set for one of the major upheavals in Central American history. The Carrera revolt had roots at many levels. There were religious, political, economic, and social motives for those who rose in rebellion against the liberal and well-intentioned government of Dr. Mariano Gálvez in 1837. Liberal reforms had created a variety of threatened and real grievances for the rural peasants and had alienated important leaders of the people, notably the rural clergy. At the same time, division among the elite of Guatemala City into liberal and conservative factions had been a rude shock to the social homogeneity of traditional Guatemalan life and politics. The powerful Aycinena extended family faced serious challenges from other members of the creole elite, and especially from members of the upper-middle sector of the capital, often illegitimate offspring of elite families without the privileges of their legitimate brothers. Republican practices, beginning with the Cádiz Constitution, had allowed this social group to gain voice and participation to the chagrin of the elite establishment. The fracturing of the dominant class into liberal and conservative factions suddenly allowed the rural masses of the country to participate in a way not previously seen. Guatemala in 1837 was fertile ground for a blossoming popular revolution led by a charismatic man of the people.

CHAPTER THREE

The Carrera Revolt

RAFAEL CARRERA CAME into the world in the poor, Candelaria barrio of New Guatemala, probably on 24 October 1814, the son of Simón Carrera and Juana Turcios. There is a slight disagreement over the exact date of his birth, for although his baptismal certificate says that he was born on the twenty-fifth, he celebrated his birthday throughout his presidency on 24 October, the latter date also appearing on his tombstone.[1] He received holy baptism on 26 October in the parish church at the hand of Father Antonio Croquer.[2]

We don't know much about his family or early life. An anonymous pamphlet published in the 1840s argued that Carrera was the illegitimate son of Colonel Antonio Aycinena and a servant in his household, a scandal supposedly covered up by Antonio's brother, Father Miguel Aycinena, but there is no evidence to support this idea and it has been universally rejected by other historians.[3] The most thorough research on Carrera's family was done by a distant nephew of Carrera, Manuel Cobos Batres, who traced Carrera's ancestry to Captain Juan Pérez Dardón, who served with Guatemala's conquistador, Pedro de Alvarado. Pérez Dardón's great-great-granddaughter, Josefa Pérez de Palencia y López de Portillo, married a recent immigrant from New Spain, José de la Carrera in 1664 (see Figure 2). The Spanish bloodline was mixed with mestizo and mulatto blood in subsequent generations, to give Rafael a distinctly Indian appearance. Cobos argues on the basis of genealogical research that the percentage of Negro or Indian blood in his line was relatively small, but his arguments are not convincing.[4] Whatever the true percentage of mixed racial background, Carrera was a Ladino in Guatemalan terms, but, according to contemporary accounts, with rather stronger Indian physical characteristics than his older brothers. His father was a mule driver and his mother a domestic servant, who later had a small cordage shop in the main market.[5] The first-born of the family, Eustaquio Santos de Jesús (1805–?), apparently played no major role in Carrera's revolt, but by 1842 was serving him as a military secretary and aide, looking after his brother's personal financial affairs and rising to the rank of colonel by 1847.[6] More important was Sotero (1807–50), who worked as a harness maker and tinsmith in Guatemala City and in 1834 was admitted to the Literature and Arts Section of the Guatemalan Academy of Sciences (which replaced the old University of San Carlos under the liberals).[7] Sotero would join younger brother Rafael early in the revolt and remain an important military commander and corregidor throughout the 1840s. Another older brother, Laureano José (1812–38) gave his life in the revolution.[8] His sister Agueda was four years older than Rafael, and three more sisters—Juana de Jesús, María Sabina, and María Visitación—were born after him. Two older half sisters, illegitimate daughters of Simón Carrera prior to his marriage to Juana Turcios, also lived in the household, but none of these women played any known significant role in Guatemalan history.[9] This large family by modern standards was of only average size in early nineteenth-century Guatemala. It might have been normal for several to have died in infancy, but this did not occur, suggesting hardy stock.[10]

Rafael Carrera spent his early years in a disadvantaged section of the capital, where the depression of the last years of the colonial period caused an increase in suffering and crime. The diputación provincial reported in 1821 that the city had among its "40,000 souls a libertine and bloodthirsty rabble" and that its criminal records were more horrible "than those of all Europe." In 1819 the city's hospital admitted 704 wounded persons (546 men, including seventy soldiers, and 158 women), of which nineteen died. In 1820 the figure exceeded nine hundred.[11] Violence and crime were common among the rabble and were a constant concern to the elite, who legislated repeatedly against the bearing of arms by non-Spaniards to no avail.[12] Carrera grew up in this poor, violent environment, amid the turbulent political events accompanying restoration of the Cádiz Constitution in 1820, independence from Spain in 1821, annexation to Mexico in 1822, and independence from Mexico and formation of the United Provinces in the following year. Riots, armed uprisings, and street crime were a part of his boyhood experience. The rhetoric of the political factions was abundant, but it provided little tangible benefit to the working class of

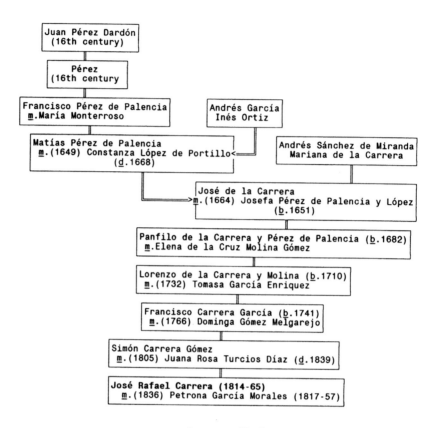

FIGURE 2. Ancestry of Rafael Carrera

the capital. Indeed, economically, things were getting worse, as English imports damaged native textile production and other cottage industries.

When civil war came in 1826, this unschooled, twelve-year-old veteran of street brawling and scavenging enlisted in the federal army as a drummer boy. He saw action at Arrazola, Chalchuapa, Mexicanos, and Agua-Escondida, rising to the rank of sergeant in Colonel Antonio Aycinena's regiment.[13]

Following the war, Carrera drifted. He worked in Amatitlán as a servant of Hertuides Díaz, a woman of dubious character, and later for a Spaniard from whom perhaps he gained a little knowledge of politics and commerce. Later he worked for a French cochineal planter named Laumonier near Antigua. Laumonier fired him when he learned of Carrera's gambling success at the expense of the other employees' wages. From Antigua he wandered eastward, along the old road to the Caribbean, where he associated with traveling merchants and lived in several different places before finally settling at Mataquescuintla in 1832. He worked on a farm for a while, then began to purchase pigs in the country, selling them in the markets of the surrounding towns. His brief career as a swineherd was profitable and helped him to become a person of some substance, but it was an occupation for which his enemies would deride him after he had become powerful.[14]

In Mataquescuintla the village priest, Father Francisco Aqueche, befriended Carrera and influenced him critically. Aqueche was a native of Chalatenango, El Salvador, but had long been the curate at Mataquescuintla.[15] Aqueche gave Carrera an ideological framework within which his rebelliousness toward the liberal regime would take shape. Moreover, the priest's friendship raised Carrera's image in the community. The padre also arranged Carrera's marriage in early 1836 to Petrona García Morales (1817–57), the daughter of an hacendado of considerable wealth for this poor rural district. Her father owned large herds of livestock, considerable land, and an attractive house on the town plaza. His handsome daughter had large brown eyes and a fine Mayan profile. Known for being as devout and prudent as she was lovely, "Toña" García was destined to play an important part alongside Rafael Carrera. Sometimes described as haughty, she was strong willed and of a jealous disposition. She both accompanied her husband in battle and looked after the administration of his property. Later, after Carrera became president, she was an important asset to his political career as first lady and hostess at his frequent dinners and celebrations, until her death in 1857.[16] A French traveler related that Madame Carrera matched her husband in courage and daring, able to handle pistol or lance effectively. She was said to have cut off the noses and ears of her husband's mistresses and she herself boasted of having mutilated many of Rafael's lovers.[17] Toña's brutality toward other females was reported in a different context by the American chargé d'affaires in Guatemala. During the revolution, he reported, after one battle she had "amputated the ears and breasts of several soldiers' wives who had been taken prisoner with their husbands, and thus mutilated sent them hither."[18]

Carrera, a drifter with an often violent, irascible, and uncommunicative disposition, was groomed by Toña and Father Aqueche, so that he soon gained favor in the community and developed the charisma that would attract the peasants of eastern Guatemala in a great crusade against the liberal government of Mariano Gálvez. He was not physically overpowering. Slim, about five feet six inches tall, he was described in late 1839 by U.S. minister John Lloyd Stephens as having "an Indian complexion and expression, without beard."[19] But in Mataquescuintla he was developing the dominant personality that would enable him to master men and situations. Although often intemperate and violent, he nevertheless gained a reputation for an intuitive sense of caution and for remaining calm when danger threatened.[20]

The first recorded appearance of Carrera in a leadership role occurred on 6 May 1837. The people of Mataquescuintla felt strongly the grievances discussed in the last chapter, and the cholera epidemic had brought fear and tension to this picturesque valley surrounded by steep, green mountains. In an attempt to stem the epidemic, the government quarantined the Mita district, including Mataquescuintla, and sent medicines to prevent and treat the disease. Carrera appeared at the head of an angry mob of more than two thousand men and women, who overpowered the officials and forced several of them to drink all the medicines, which among other things included laudanum, an opium extract. Such large doses proved fatal and convinced the mob beyond any doubt that the medicines were indeed poison. One of the government officials, however, Francisco Aqueche, was also the nephew of his namesake, the village priest, and Padre Aqueche persuaded Carrera to protect this official, who had taken refuge in the church. Carrera persuaded the mob to allow the priest to handle the matter and the crowd dispersed. Carrera later quietly released the official, who returned to the capital and reported what had happened, but with favorable words for Carrera and his uncle, who had saved his life.[21]

A few days later a health officer, Sr. Oliveros, arrived in Mataquescuintla to establish patrols for the quarantined zone. After consultation with Father Aqueche and other residents, Oliveros chose Carrera to command the patrol at La Sierra, high above Mataquescuintla on the road leading to the capital. Carrera refused, protesting that he had been married only three months and that his interests demanded his presence at home. When Oliveros insisted, Carrera again protested forcefully that he could not go, but in the end Padre Aqueche persuaded him.

After eighteen days in La Sierra, a certain Lt. Col. Ignacio Pérez summoned Carrera to a meeting in Mataquescuintla, where he offered Carrera the position of town commissioner at a salary of thirty pesos per month.[22] Carrera refused, insisting that he did not want a government career, but he agreed to continue temporarily in command of the quarantine guard, now moving to a new location at the Potrero Hacienda.[23]

The Mataquescuintla riot that had launched Carrera's new military career was but one of a wave of revolts in rural Guatemala during mid 1837. A month earlier a major protest against the Livingston Codes, and specifically the demands upon Indians to build new jails, had occurred in the Indian town of San Juan Ostuncalco, west of Quetzaltenango, a place where an earlier revolt against Spanish civil and ecclesiastical authority had resulted in bloodshed in 1815.[24] Another revolt in the Department of Quetzaltenango occurred at Zuñil in opposition to land grants made by the liberal government.[25] In fact, revolts in mid-1837 occurred in more than thirty Indian communities, opposing the Livingston Codes, the liberal land policies, the anticlericalism, and the quarantine cordons around cholera-infected areas.[26]

Indian revolts had flared in Guatemala since the Spanish Conquest, but after the Bourbon Reforms began to upset the stability and protection afforded the native villages, their was an increase in restiveness. The spirit of revolt engendered throughout the Spanish world by the Bourbon Reforms continued against the liberals after independence. The Esquilache Revolt in Spain in 1766 resulted from popular opposition to Bourbon attempts to change local customs and dress habits, especially proposed by a foreigner, the Italian Marquis de Squillace. This sort of popular reaction against the Bourbon Reforms occurred in various parts of Spain and Spanish America in defense of popular culture against the liberal changes. Referred to in some places as *comunero* revolts, this defense of traditional customs and culture, or *casticismo* as it was known in Spain, was expressed in Guatemala by nearly all classes. Among creoles it took forms that would eventually create the conservative party. Among Ladinos and Indians, it was expressed in more direct and sometimes violent terms against the liberal establishment. Peasant uprisings against Napoleonic rule in Spain were a further manifestation of this tendency. In Guatemala, they occurred after 1750 in opposition to taxation and land policies brought by the Bourbon Reforms.[27]

Although Indian revolts occurred throughout the republic in 1837, it was in eastern Guatemala that an organized rebellion arose. Unlike Los Altos, where Indians remained the dominant group, in the east Ladinos were more common. Indian villages maintained strong individual identities and often feuded with neighboring villages over land or water rights. There were linguistic and tribal differences among them. They might have traditionally recognized the government as their common foe, but they were not easily organized into a concerted revolutionary effort against it.[28]

As the priests railed against the government's policies, opposition rose in the Department of Mita. Militarism had been growing for two decades, and the government had depended heavily on this area for troops in the civil wars of the federation period.[29] In addition to the riot at Mataquescuintla, natives in Jumay had destroyed the anticholera medicines, and in Jalpatagua the irate mob had murdered every government officer in the town. In Santa Rosa, Teodoro Mejía, a small, but politically ambitious landowner organized the natives and took over the town government in protest to the head tax. The peasant communities of the East rallied to the cause, feeling threatened by the government and eager to protect their lives and land. Local landholders supported—perhaps instigated—peasants in these demands.[30]

The Guatemalan rebels were undoubtedly encouraged by the peasant uprising in adjacent El Salvador. There the principal issues were the head tax and anticlericalism. Morazán's federal government took a direct interest in that revolt, assisting the state government in its repression. Several leaders of that revolt were jailed in San Salvador on 24 April 1837, but violence persisted, especially among Indians of Zacatecoluca, San Juan Nonualco, Tecoluca, and Analco. In a violent encounter on the night of 22 May, they defeated government troops and killed several civilians, including Manuel Salas, a member of the federal congress. The state government at San Vicente was under siege by the rebels, and rioting Indians threatened to seize control in Cojutepeque. Morazán decreed martial law in San Salvador and in the departments of Cuscatlán and San Vicente as he committed federal forces to the conflict.[31]

In eastern Guatemala an Indian from Mataquescuintla, José María Zapeta, began to organize towns into a coherent rebellion. No concrete evidence proves that Carrera encouraged Zapeta in his travels throughout the region to line up support from the municipalities of Santa Rosa, Jumaytepeque, Jalpatagua, Moyuta, and Conguaco, but his Mataquescuintla origin is suspicious given Carrera's subsequent role. Carrera's own memoirs of the revolution, dictated much later, emphatically deny such an association

Eastern Guatemala and El Salvador in 1837

or any knowledge of the plot before Zapeta returned to Mataquescuintla, apparently in late May 1837, to solicit the support of the municipal government. Colonel Pérez had gone to the capital on that day, and after a long conference, the town leaders and the rebel commissioners from Santa Rosa summoned Carrera. Carrera's memoirs tell us that after discussing the plan at length, he rejected participation in the insurgency. He argued that the villagers were committing themselves with too little defense against the government's large forces. The commissioners would not be dissuaded, saying that they could no longer suffer the head taxes, the Livingston Codes, and the other grievances that oppressed the people.

Carrera went home, but at 3:00 P.M. a crowd led by the town councilmen visited him to announce that they had named him captain of the company they were going to organize. In an emotional response, he thanked them for their confidence and respect, but he would not agree to it. The crowd screamed for him to accept, some even threatening his life if he refused. His answer reflected the intense localism of the times: "I cannot go against my own country. I am a Guatemalan; and if for this you want to kill me, here I am." Carrera was referring to his Guatemala City origin, not the state of Guatemala. (Governor Gálvez, on 16 June 1837, would tell the legislature that "the enemies of the State have incited the public by suggesting maliciously that only residents of the capital are Guatemalan.")

The crowd denied any intention of taking his life, but again pleaded with him to lead them, to which he replied: "How can you want me to be against Guatemala, if that town is there as this is here. If you are oppressed, so also is Guatemala. I love you all and I am disposed to leave all my property in compensation for the consideration you have shown me. Just give me my passport, for I have decided to leave here."

A councilman answered. "Sir, we don't know how to explain. We love the Guatemalans. We are not against them, but against the bad administration that burdens us, taxes us, and wants to destroy us. And we want you to command us. You are our only hope for happiness."

Carrera said he would let them know the next day, but they persisted for an immediate answer. Santa Rosa needed aid at once. Carrera went to the church, where the aging Father Aqueche reportedly told him: "Do not vacillate in accepting, . . . for you alone will be able to argue with a mutinous people. You can do much good if you will. You will avoid much bloodshed and robberies and assassinations. You will do no evil. The cause that you shall defend is just, if you know where you are going. Try to put yourself in communication with the government, my son, and I will speak for you."

Carrera returned to the leaders of the uprising and asked, "What principals will you stand for? What weapons do you have at hand for defense? I see none."

"We put our lives and our property in your hands," they responded. "Save us however you can!"

Carrera had the commitment he had sought. He had made his decision. "I shall die for you even though you compromise me, for every people are ungrateful. At the first setback we suffer, you will abandon me and will be among those who pursue me later."

"No!" they shouted. "To death we shall be loyal to you!"

Carrera accepted the command and issued a manifesto stating the aims of the revolt and requiring the town council and the people to support him in these six demands:

1. Abolition of the Livingston Codes.

2. Protection of life and property.

3. Return of the archbishop and restoration of the religious orders.

4. Abolition of the two-peso head tax.

5. A complete amnesty so that those exiled in 1829 might return.

6. Respect for Carrera's orders as law. Anyone who robbed or harassed any honorable person, or acted arbitrarily against his disposition, would be infallibly put to death.

"If the government will accept these proposals, which we will immediately communicate to it," Carrera declared, "there will be peace." The councilmen and the people cheered their approval.

The revolution had begun! Carrera immediately organized men and arms for combat. He sent Zapeta and others throughout the valleys and hamlets of the Oriente to rally the peasants and to collect arms. There were few firearms, but they made lances and many had their own horses.[32]

Upon learning that Teodoro Mejía had formed a rebel government in Santa Rosa, Gálvez sent the district magistrate and circuit judge, Pedro José Campos, with forty cavalry and a hundred infantry to suppress it. Mejía, resolved to resist the Guatemalans, sent a call for aid to Mataquescuintla. Carrera had raised a company of thirty riflemen and thirty lancers. He quickly departed for Santa Rosa, arriving in a drenching rain at three in the morning on 9 June 1837.

Campos had already arrived with his cavalry, and battle had been joined on the plain of Ambelis, before the town of Santa Rosa. Peasants and townspeople had joined Mejía's poorly armed and disorganized forces, but it was turning into a massacre by the Guatemalan cavalry. Yet Carrera quickly rallied the defenders and turned certain defeat into a rousing victory, inflicting heavy losses on Campos's troops before the remainder fled. More important than the casualties inflicted were the twenty carbines and fourteen horses taken from the government force. Carrera became the undisputed leader of the rebellion, as Mejía willingly turned over command of the revolt to the swineherd from Mataquescuintla.[33] Exhilarated by this victory, the village leaders whom Zapeta had lined up throughout eastern Guatemala now issued manifestos denouncing the Livingston Codes, the head tax, and the government's land policy. They accused the government of trying to poison them in order to give their land to foreigners.[34]

Civil war quickly consumed much of the country.[35] Gálvez responded swiftly to the Santa Rosa defeat, seeking to crush the rebellion before it got out of hand. He acknowledged that many towns in the District of Mita were in rebellion and that violence and terror were spreading as the rebels threatened death to those who refused to participate. Gálvez called the insurgent leaders "criminals" seducing the "unhappy multitude," noting that similar commotions had arisen elsewhere and in El Salvador, where the people had falsely been led to believe that the government had caused the cholera epidemic with its medicines. He warned that "if the cholera-morbus invades the western districts, where the number of Indians is great, disorders may be feared that will victimize the other classes." To meet the crisis he decreed on 12 June 1837 that all those participating in the uprisings in any way would be tried by military courts as traitors, punishable by death. A second decree mobilized a reserve militia in each district and named the military commander in each district as special judge to try violators under the preceding decree.[36]

Warned of the approach of a large force commanded by the minister of war, General Carlos Salazar, Carrera ignored an urgent plea from the Mataquescuintla town council to return to defend that town. Instead, he withdrew into the hills with his partisans. He knew that he could not yet stand up to a major military force. On 15 June Salazar's troops swept into Santa Rosa, now left undefended, and a smaller force under Lt. Col. Manuel Carrascosa took Mataquescuintla the same day. This attack by the "División Pacificadora" was vindictive and brutal. Carrera's band offered little resistance and was driven deeper into the hills. Under this pressure some of his supporters drifted away, although the brutality of the repression drove others back to him. Avoiding contact with large government units, Carrera ambushed a small government cavalry unit, killing its commander, Lt. Col. Juan Martínez, and capturing badly need arms. By hit-and-run tactics he both survived and increased his strength in the opening stages of the war.[37]

Colonel Carrascosa interrogated Mataquescuintla residents, among them José María Batres, whose testimony revealed names of local leaders who began the revolt and elected Carrera to lead them as their "comandante general." Batres told Carrascosa that fear of the medicines and the Livingston Codes were the principal causes of the rebellion. Batres also confirmed that the revolt included both Ladinos and Indians, and he implicated Father Francisco Aqueche as a ring leader. Government troops killed several peasants and destroyed property. General Salazar immediately began trials under Gálvez's 12 June decree. The guerrilla warfare had quickly become bloody and bitter, with atrocities on both sides.[38]

Gálvez's handling of the revolt provoked sharp debate in the assembly, which Gálvez called into special session on 16 June. He reported the measures he had already taken and promised to do whatever was necessary to suppress the insurgents.[39] But opposition to Gálvez's repressive methods quickly arose among the radicals led by José Francisco Barrundia and Pedro Molina. The issue split the liberals between Gálvez's "ministerial faction" and Barrundia's "opposition."[40]

Barrundia saw these measures as repressive of the liberties that the Livingston Codes and other liberal reforms had sought to advance. Yet the majority of the assembly welcomed the recapture of Santa Rosa. Gálvez decorated Salazar and his troops for their swift action in restoring peace and order in the midst of heavy rains and the cholera epidemic.[41] On 18 June the legislature authorized Gálvez to raise the armed forces to whatever size necessary to suppress the revolt. But, reflecting the concerns of the radicals, it also authorized the government "to dictate whatever measures are needed so that the new system of judicial administration is not paralyzed" and to "decree an agrarian law to guarantee to the communities and to private individuals the security of their lands."[42] While the legislature was passing tough measures to deal with the rebellion, a clash at Gavillán, near Mataquescuintla, between Carrera's forces and those of General Salazar bolstered the government's confidence. The one-sided encounter began with an unsuccessful charge by Carrera's cavalry led by Vicente Cruz (who would become one of his most valued generals), followed by a counter charge by Salazar's forces that put the rebels into a speedy retreat.[43]

Following the government raids, the entire population of Mataquescuintla fled the town. Carrera's numbers grew as government terror drove desperate peasants to seek refuge with his guerrillas.[44] Army excesses in sacking towns and villages and the low state of military training were serious handicaps to Gálvez's efforts to snuff out the rebellion quickly.[45] Soldiers destroyed Carrera's house in Mataquescuintla and that of his father-in-law, and they reportedly raped Carrera's wife. Infuriated, Carrera joined other village chieftains in vowing never to lay down their arms while an officer of Morazán remained in the state. "He went from village to village," John Lloyd Stephens relates, "killing the judges and government officers, when pursued escaping to the mountains, begging tortillas at the haciendas for his men, and sparing and protecting all who assisted him."[46]

On 22 June Gálvez offered pardon to all but the revolt's leaders and those who had assassinated government officials. He assured all others that they might now return to their homes in peace and that any of their property that had been confiscated would be restored.[47] Yet few returned and the rebellion grew.

Carrera received constant counsel from a group of priests, notably from Padre Francisco Lobo who issued proclamations in Carrera's name condemning foreigners, doctors, and judges, while he called for the restoration of the privileges of the church and old customs.[48] The revolution became a religious crusade, with economic and social pressures bringing more peasants to the guerrillas. Carrera's forces operated in the vicinity of Mataquescuintla throughout July, with several major skirmishes deciding nothing. Carrera's "Chacurecos," as described by a twentieth-century historian, were "a confused body of political insurgents, religious crusaders, embittered peasants, and professional outlaws, all trusting in Carrera to lead them toward their respective goals."[49]

Although the government's troops almost always won these skirmishes, they were unable to deal the guerrillas a fatal blow. Short of funds, volunteers, or even sufficient conscripted recruits, on 17 July Gálvez reluctantly signed a bill authorizing the arming of prisoners. This act offered to commute the sentences, excepting only thieves and murderers, of those who would take up arms against the insurgents.[50] The high incidence of cholera in the jails of the capital provided further incentive for prisoners to volunteer. The death toll from the epidemic in the capital had reached 819 by mid July.[51]

Carrera retreated to mountain hideouts around Jutiapa, where Indians supplied him. The government moved whole communities in an effort to isolate the guerrillas, but like so many of the other government measures, this further alienated the peasants. Carrera had no regard for state boundaries, carrying his raids into El Salvador as far as Atiquisaya. In late July, on his return from El Salvador, he raided Jalpatagua and shot the departmental chief (*jefe político*). On 31 July a force under Ignacio Pérez caught up with Carrera and soundly defeated him, dispersing most of his forces. Carrera escaped to the El Soyate Hacienda with fourteen soldiers, however, and soon resumed his raiding with a reorganized guerrilla band. Once again, on 11 August at Mount Copalar, between Sañarate and Agua Caliente, government troops dealt him a defeat and temporarily dispersed his forces.[52]

In the face of popular insurgency the liberals in the capital fell to bickering among themselves. Economic interests were at least in part behind the split between the Barrundia and Gálvez factions. Gálvez had the support of merchant interests, eager to have the revolt crushed quickly and completely in order to restore security on their trade routes. Barrundia had greater landholder support, willing to pursue a more conciliatory approach to the rural revolt. Indeed, some landlords were even among the rebels. There were so-called aristocrats on both sides, but the Gálvez supporters began to call Barrundia's faction the "aristocratic party," raising the issue that had formerly been used against the Aycinenas and the conservatives.[53]

Barrundia criticized the arbitrariness of the Gálvez government and its failure to respect the people's civil rights.[54] Abandonment of trial-by-jury infuriated Barrundia, as Gálvez substituted summary justices where trial by jury didn't seem to work. In dealing with the rebellion, Gálvez couldn't trust local juries. Barrundia feared a restoration of the old Hispanic system of justice and that the reforms for which he had worked since 1812 would fall in the face of popular resistance. He argued that the resistance would not last long unless the government exercised too much authority and that the reforms must not be sacrificed. On the other hand, he predicted, "A retreat at this point, in addition to its great discredit, will open the door to the seduction of other regressions for an indefinite period, and perhaps even destroy the institution most necessary in a republic, descending to a dictatorship disguised only by liberal forms and names."[55]

On 1 September Barrundia began publication of *La Oposición*, bitterly attacking the government. A formal opposition to the government was "essential in a free regime," he claimed, and a free press was among Latin America's greatest needs. Barrundia warned against continued repressive measures and called for democratic reforms and conciliation with Carrera.[56] In his view, the government had abandoned the struggle for liberty and was sacrificing its achievements to a relatively small rebellion.[57] Pedro Molina joined the attack in a paper of his own, *El Semi-Diario de los Libres*, emphasizing natural rights, constitutional guarantees, and support of Barrundia against Gálvez.[58]

Gálvez answered the charges in speeches and handbills defending the government's hard-line policy and warning of the seriousness of the insurgency. He had, in fact, offered amnesty to those who had participated in the uprising, but the rebels neither trusted the government nor were willing simply to be pardoned.[39] On 5 October 1837 he began publication of *La Verdad*, a newspaper in which he attacked both the patriotism and the motives of Barrundia and his allies.[60] *La Verdad* rather simplistically defined the three political factions at work in Guatemala: The First Party (conservatives) owed their wealth, for which they did not work, to the old Spanish system and lived off the sweat and labor of the poor by virtue of abuses and privileges of their authority. The Second Party (Barrundia's opposition faction) were those discontented with the distribution of public power and were constant troublemakers, pursuing personal ambitions rather than the good of the nation and responsible for provoking civil war and anarchy by encouraging Carrera's revolt. And the Third Party (Gálvez's government party) were the "true patriots" without personal ambition, who served the general welfare. This faction, Gálvez claimed, included "hard working artisans, merchants, farmers and others who are for the glory and prosperity of the nation." [61]

Assassination of the respected political columnist, Juan de Dios Mayorga —who had served the federation as a diplomat, congressman, and mediator in the civil war of 1826–29—brought the government closer to anarchy. Dios Mayorga met his death near Palencia, almost certainly at the hands of Carrera's guerrillas, but *La Verdad* attributed the killing to the Barrundia faction. Barrundia responded, offended and furious, in *La Oposición*, virtually accusing the government of the assassination.[62]

To counter the opposition, Gálvez sought political allies among returning conservative exiles and merchants. Chief among these was Father Juan José Aycinena, who had spent his exile in the United States. Aycinena, although he would become firmly attached to the conservative party in Guatemala in subsequent years, had been impressed with North American democracy and at this period was eager to apply some liberal concepts that he had observed in the United States. He was particularly responsible for the Declaration of the Rights and Guarantees of Citizens and Inhabitants of the State of Guatemala, which the assembly passed on 18 August and Gálvez signed on 11 September, in large measure an answer to the criticisms of the Barrundia faction. The document has importance because it represents both liberal political philosophy, especially North American ideology, while at the same time reflecting the first conservative input aimed at checking the authoritarianism practiced by liberal governments.

The document is liberal in its preamble and in a number of its provisions, but it also is the first formal action of the legislature against abuses by the government. Article 1 repeated the basic liberal tenet that "all men are created equally free and independent, that they have certain inherent natural rights, inalienable and inviolable, that among these most especially are the defense of life, reputation, property, and the pursuit of happiness by any honest means." Article 2 declared that governments were instituted to secure these rights and "that the power and authority that they exercise are derived from the people, and are conferred with the sole object of maintaining peace among men, making everyone respect mutually their individual rights." Article 3 confirmed the right of revolution against "any Government, whatever its form," that failed to fulfill its obligations. Article 4 reminded public officials that they were trustees, not owners, of authority. And Article 5 defended the concept of natural rights. The declaration also provided for religious liberty, but recognized the right of individuals to leave their property to the state or church and defended both private and church property against confiscation by the state, a major abuse of liberal governments. Subsequent articles guaranteed other liberal legal rights and freedoms, including trial by jury, although emphasizing the necessity of a law to fix the "qualification for jurors so that justice be administered by men not only of integrity, but also of sufficient ability to meet the objectives of this institution." Article 10 guaranteed freedom of speech and press, but also cautioned that every man was "responsible before the law for abuses of this liberty." The document followed closely the principles enunciated in the U.S. Declaration of Independence, Bill of Rights of the U.S. Constitution of 1789, and French Declaration of the Rights of Man, and provided a rather complete charter of the basic rights and freedoms of western liberalism. But, subtly it put limits on these rights, and, in reality, it was part of the attack on the Livingston Codes.[63]

The entrance of Father Aycinena into active participation in the government reflected the rapprochement that was occurring between the government and the conservative elite. The growth of cochineal production around Amatitlán and Antigua was contributing to a degree of prosperity for them, and Gálvez was willingly pursuing a conciliatory attitude toward those who had been exiled or imprisoned in 1829. But the political opposition in Guatemala City preoccupied Gálvez and distracted his attention temporarily from the revolt in the montaña. Barrundia's criticisms of Gálvez's policies were singularly harsh and contributed directly to the instability that played into the hands of Rafael Carrera.[64]

Carrera's organization began to take more positive form in July, as a number of subordinate guerrilla leaders emerged in addition to Teodoro Mejía. Antonio Solares and José Clara Lorenzana were captains in the movement who later became ranking generals in Carrera's Guatemalan army. The size of Carrera's force swelled as he named local lieutenants to help recruit more men.[65] The guerrillas moved rapidly over familiar terrain, leading government troops on wild chases, but rarely to victory. On 24 August Gálvez made another conciliatory move, issuing a general amnesty to all those who had participated in the Santa Rosa and Mataquescuintla uprisings, even including those leaders who had been excluded from the 22 June pardon. He gave the rebels three days to lay down their arms. Those who refused the pardon, the decree warned, would be hunted down as traitors.[66]

In September the continuing war and criticism from the Barrundia faction led Gálvez to sign the "Declaration of Rights and Guarantees." In the countryside, Gálvez continued his repressive methods against Carrera, while in the capital he launched a relentless if futile propaganda war against Barrundia, accusing the latter of being the enemy of property and civilization and of being the ally, or dupe, of Carrera. An example of this propaganda was a handbill addressed to "Guatemaltecos" on 28 October. It cited the pretensions of the "new aristocracy," and warned property holders, merchants, and planters that "if the revolutionaries and their caudillo Barrundia get their way, soon you will have here his protege Carrera alleviating you of the burden of your interests and money as happened to the patriot Citizen Juan de Dios Mayorga." It called on artisans and soldiers to defend the government against these revolutionaries who would deprive them of their political rights.[67] By November the diatribes between Gálvez and Barrundia had reached a white heat. After *La Oposición* accused Gálvez of trying to rig elections in Antigua, *La Verdad* lashed out that Barrundia had added insult to injury: "The fury and the atrocious falsehoods of their pen reveal each time more clearly that they are moved not by the public interest, but by the hatred born of passions that poison the soul."[68]

Meanwhile, as the war went badly for the government, Gálvez sacrificed his reforms one-by-one to the rising financial demands of the military. The state's budget put into effect in September 1837 revealed that of a total of $296,032, $110,000 went to the Department of War, $57,000 to the Department of Justice, and only $12,000 to public education.[69] Having placed too much faith in advanced laws and too little in the sentiments of the people, Gálvez was paying the price. With too few troops to occupy the entire country, Gálvez sought to defeat and capture the caudillo, but the raiding and looting continued as the war became a genuine popular insurrection against the liberal policies. Carrera and his "Cachurecos" took on legendary stature as they extended their operations. In October, Carrera's raiders killed several circuit judges, releasing their prisoners from the jails to join the revolution.[70] Crying "*Viva* Religion! Death to the heretics," the rebels turned their wrath against all whites. The war became a race-class struggle, as all those of color—Indians, mestizos, mulattos, and zambos—united against the white creoles and foreigners.[71] Atrocities on both sides multiplied. The rural clergy encouraged the rebellion, demanding the return of Archbishop Casáus and the regular orders, protection of the Roman Catholic Church, and abolition of civil marriage and divorce (the "law of the dog," as they called it).[72] Hunger, misery, and disease spread as eastern Guatemala became a vast theater of guerrilla warfare.

In late October, Carrera launched another raid into El Salvador, but quickly returned to the Department of Chiquimula, where Captain Lisandro Valdés and the Sacatepéquez Squadron dealt him a defeat in November.[73] Yet the guerrillas soon reunited at Plantón and took Jalapa on 7–8 December before once more retreating into the hills.[74] Late in the year a shipment of arms reached Izabal aboard the Eastern Coast of Central America Company steamer, the *Vera Paz*. Shortly thereafter a band of Carrera's guerrillas under the command of José Dorantes raided the port, capturing most of these weapons.[75]

The insurgency disrupted commerce, making travel dangerous, and, along with the political maneuvering in the capital, contributed to a rising conservative tide in Guatemala City late in 1837. On 23 October, 250 Guatemalans led by "aristocrats" José de la Luz Larrave, Ciriaco Barrundia, and Alejo and Rafael Nájera, signed a Profession of Political Faith, which urged repeal of the Livingston Codes and the divorce law. Their petition argued that these laws were inappropriate for peoples who had not been governed under English law.[76]

Government candidates easily won elections in late October and December, but Barrundia charged fraud, claiming that Gálvez had used military forces to win the election.[77] By December Gálvez's government faced formidable opposition. Eastern Guatemala was in open rebellion and Barrundia's faction was gaining support in Antigua and western Guatemala. The government was desperately short of funds but reluctant to impose new taxes or forced loans, fearing additional loss of support. Moreover, the cholera epidemic was still taking a heavy toll. Barrundia demanded full enforcement of the Livingston Codes and an end to the restrictions on constitutional guarantees. Instead, Gálvez formed a coalition with conservative elements, seeking to isolate Barrundia's radicals against a united government more conciliatory to the clergy.

A junta of nine prominent Guatemalans met on 12 December and promulgated a plan. Eight of its ten proposals, Articles 2–9, actually favored Barrundia's point of view and restricted Gálvez's exercise of power and influence. They also removed from office those known to lack public confidence. Moreover, civil militias were to be expanded at the expense of the regular military. These militias were to maintain public order, the regular forces to be used only when absolutely necessary. Reduction in the bureaucracy would reduce government spending. The three independent branches of government were to be respected. Abuses in tax collection were to end, and there was a move toward suppression of "those taxes that are most burdensome to the afflicted classes," presumably meaning the head tax. The Livingston Codes were to be fully enforced, although facts were to be gathered regarding their application so that the next assembly could consider reforms. Articles 1 and 10, however, named Marcial Zebadúa and Juan José Aycinena as Gálvez's chief ministers and urged them to "pay particular attention to the preparations of bills for the amendment or repeal of all laws that do not conform to the letter of the Constitution and the Declaration of Rights . . . as well as all others whose execution is manifestly impracticable or against which public opinion has openly declared itself."[78] Zebadúa was a respected diplomat who had served both liberal and conservative governments at both the state and federal level, although he was regarded as moderately conservative by this date. He had come from a modest family background in Chiapas, but through the legal profession and government service had prospered in Guatemala City. He became linked to the Aycinena family through the marriage of his daughter to Manuel Francisco Pavón, a grandson of Juan Fermín, first marqués of Aycinena. Father Juan José Aycinena, the third marqués of Aycinena, was closely associated with the conservative, pro clerical faction, notwithstanding some of the liberal ideas he had brought back with him from his exile in North America.[79]

Aycinena, as minister of justice and government, and Zebadúa, as minister of finance, accepted their appointments on 15 December. The next day they issued a compassionate manifesto to "the inhabitants of the countryside" that recognized the widespread violence and the fear of the cholera epidemic. Addressing them as "friends," the ministers said that "among the cares that surround us, none weigh more heavily on our hearts than consideration of the misguided way you are being led by men who are enemies of your own welfare, who only are using you to cause the disgraces that afflict so many towns, avenging their passions, and committing excesses that horrify humanity." Aycinena's pastoral style dominated the three-page handbill that reminded the people that they had been open and friendly in their communications and trade with one another, but now their villages and small properties were destroyed, burned, and pillaged, the former peace having been destroyed by evil men. "The cholera is an epidemic which the whole world has been suffering and which finally reached us in spite of many efforts to keep it away. Elsewhere, princes and kings, every class of people, white and black, rich and poor, have died from this disease, for no one is free from a disease of this sort, just as with smallpox and other diseases that you know very well." The manifesto chastised them for rebelling in the name of a religion that taught love rather than hate and could not be used to justify the violent acts they had committed. It called on the people to submit their grievances in legitimate petitions, which, Zebadúa and Aycinena assured, would be satisfied if they were just. But, they pleaded, "Do not do it with the arms that these disorders have put in your hands for your destruction, nor in bloody turmoil that is devastating the fields and villages." The manifesto continued with a warning: "If we as friends counsel you for your own good as we become secretaries, we must also warn you that it is the obligation of the authorities to defend the peoples whose peace is disturbed, and to protect the lives and property of the inhabitants; and that we will proceed rigorously against those who do not heed this friendly plea that we make to you. And we assure you, that as soon as peace has been restored, commissioners of our confidence shall be sent to investigate the damages that have been caused by these misfortunes in the towns of Santa Rosa, Jumay, Mataquescuintla and the others that are found in the same circumstances." The appeal closed with a final warning: "Abandon, then, the caudillos that by force or deception have held you together, and return to your homes confident that if you do that there will be no proceedings against you, while on the contrary, those who continue under arms or give aid to the authors of such evil deeds will be punished severely." [80]

On the same day, General Juan José Górriz led a division of Guatemala garrison troops out of the capital toward the rebellious zone, but at Arrazola, just a few miles from the capital, they mutinied and returned to the capital. Arriving after dark and shouting, "Death to the opponents," they broke into Barrundia's house. Finding him absent, they swore to return on the next day. The new ministers heard their complaints, and far from punishing the mutinous soldiers, took no action at all against them. This act reflected the hostility that the Gálvez government had brought to bear upon the Barrundia faction and caused the latter to plot its overthrow. [81] Four days later Gálvez incorporated the district of Mita into the Department of Guatemala for the purpose of judicial administration, a response to Carrera's terrorizing of judges in the district and an effort to suppress the rebellion by bringing rebels to Guatemala for trial. [82]

Gálvez's new government now started another newspaper, *La Nueva Era*.

An editorial in the first issue claimed that a new revolutionary era had begun in 1829 and praised Gálvez's efforts to implement it. It deplored the divisions that had occurred among the liberals and called for reconciliation, which, it said, had been the motive behind appointment of the new cabinet. "A solemn pact" had been celebrated between Gálvez and his new ministers that would implement the promises agreed to by the Citizens' Junta of 12 December. *La Nueva Era* was to be the organ of this new spirit of compromise and unity that Governor Gálvez was promoting. It was, in reality, a successor to *La Verdad*, seeking a broader political base and a new image, *La Verdad* having been so obviously hostile to *La Oposición*.[83] Gálvez had recognized that Guatemala was in a class struggle and he called for unity of the elite in the face of this threat.

Barrundia's faction refused to accept the offers of conciliation and instead began to court Carrera. The liberal satirist Antonio Rivera Cabezas referred to Gálvez as a caliph, a Mandarin, and a tyrant. In late December Barrundia attempted to open talks with Carrera to bring about a negotiated settlement, but the priests advising Carrera associated Barrundia with radical anticlericalism and blocked these efforts.[84]

On 29 December, the British vice consul in Guatemala, William Hall, warned his superior that the political dissension and the rising strength of the rebels could result in the fall of the capital with accompanying pillage and bloodshed "in which foreign and British lives and interests would be the first to suffer."[85] Two weeks later the U.S. chargé d'affaires, Charles G. DeWitt, informed his secretary of state that "the roads leading from this capital have for the last six weeks been so infested by armed bands of highwaymen, that no prudent traveller, and least of all a foreigner, will venture to set out for any distant point." DeWitt said that "they are under the chieftainship of an abandoned outlaw named Carrera, whose war cry is 'down with the Livingston Codes and trial by jury' and who scruples not in the pursuit of his nefarious designs to commit the most atrocious crimes. . . . So audacious has he of late grown and so good an understanding has he continued to cultivate with the Guatemalan troops, that a band of his most daring followers penetrated into the very environs of the City."[86] Carrera's guerrillas had disrupted commerce and transit, creating serious economic problems for the government and the merchant-planter elite.[87]

What was especially distressing to the government was the popularity of Carrera among the rural inhabitants. *La Nueva Era* recognized this problem on 2 January 1838 when, in reviewing the previous year's events, it pointed to the government's achievements in spite of the cholera epidemic and the difficulties of inaugurating the new judicial system. Yet "that the mass of the society have been aroused," it conceded, "is a fact that everyone feels and that cannot be hidden from anyone with eyes!" Moreover, it added, "that this commotion must arise from a powerful cause, . . . can only be denied by he who renounces his ability to think." *La Nueva Era* attributed the cause to "a new generation" that had emerged in 1837, which after the long struggles to implement the rights gained in 1821 now thought only of itself and demanded that its interests be heard by the government. The government was listening, the editorial assured, but the answer was not a return to the old institutions. Rather, the spirit of the December compromise would bring a peaceful solution and recognize that many people were still attached to traditional ways.[88]

Whatever conciliatory sentiments the government held, however, were insufficient to bring a negotiated settlement. By January, General Juan Prem, commanding the First Division, resigned in disgust. Agustín Guzmán, the staunch liberal general from Totonicapán, replaced him and would carry the liberal banner against Carrera for several years.[89] Yet Guzmán's determination to destroy Carrera was not enough to overcome Gálvez's dearth of able military commanders or trained troops, much less the mounting opposition that Barrundia directed. *La Oposición*, opposing Gálvez's military buildup, once more accused Gálvez of betraying the revolution by restricting the liberties of the people.[90]

The radicals now enlisted the support of federal President Francisco Morazán. Pedro Molina's signature headed a list of 164 Guatemalan "patriots" who on 1 January 1838 petitioned Morazán to save Guatemala from chaos. Barrundia traveled to San Salvador to plead personally for federal aid.[91] Morazán had put down the popular uprising and conservative reaction in El Salvador. On 15 January 1838 a new periodical, *El Bien Común*, appeared in the federal capital calling for "moderation." Suggesting that the government pay more attention to the customs of the country rather than to imitation of England and the United States, it accused the liberal leaders of a lack of realism in their expectations and policies, and it blamed the failure of the Guatemalan liberals, Gálvez and Barrundia, on their extremism. It also reflected a fear that the troubles in Guatemala would spill over into El Salvador. The Salvadoran elite shared the Guatemalan elite's alarm about Carrera, whom they regarded as the enemy of civilization and moderation.[92] Morazán was not yet willing to commit federal troops to the Guatemalan problem, but he did authorize Barrundia to open negotiations with Carrera, and now began to favor Barrundia over Gálvez.

Meanwhile, Gálvez, who earlier had asked Morazán for assistance, called for the raising of a civil militia and placed the country for all intents and purposes under martial law. Utilizing a forced loan on the property holders of the capital, he had established the Concordia Battalion at the beginning of January.[93] In Antigua the Barrundia faction reacted to this by setting up an opposition government, which military commanders led by General Manuel Carrascosa and the departmental governments of Sacatepéquez, Chiquimula, and the Verapaz quickly recognized, precipitating a crisis in the government. Aycinena and Zebadúa resigned on 17 January. Morazán failed to come to the aid of Gálvez, leaving him alone. The municipal council dissolved itself, and anarchy reigned in the capital.[94]

Yet Gálvez refused to surrender. On 20 January he ordered mobilization of two thousand men within six weeks and decreed another forced loan on the property holders of the capital to cover military expenses until the legislature convened.[95] The next day he announced bravely that government forces would attack all rebel troops within eight leagues of the capital, notwithstanding the cease fire for a conference that Morazán had decreed.[96] Morazán named peace commissioners and considered coming to Guatemala himself. On 26 January the sergeants of the Concordia Battalion, associated with the merchants of the capital, declared their support for Gálvez, calling for restoration of Zebadúa and Aycinena to the cabinet, while waiting for the arrival of President Morazán to mediate all "public questions." The sergeants also demanded some changes in their officers. Gálvez agreed to all their points.[97]

Morazán sent his vice-president, José Gregorio Salazar, and foreign minister, Miguel Alvarez, to seek a solution to the crisis. After conferring with Gálvez on the twenty-seventh, they met with General Carrascosa at Guarda Vieja, where they apparently reached an agreement at 4:00 P.M. the next day. Under its terms, Gálvez was to resign and turn over the government to his lieutenant governor, Pedro Valenzuela, who was aligned with Barrundia. Barrundia's rebel force from Antigua was to occupy the capital. Gálvez believed this was the only way to prevent Carrera's forces from entering the city. Gálvez's forces, now numbering only 411 officers and men, would place themselves under Morazán's command. Upon ratification, the Guarda Vieja agreement was to be carried out within twenty-four hours. The plan broke down, however, when Gálvez, after discussing it with the Representative Council, refused to ratify and decided to hold out.[98]

Carrascosa now negotiated with Carrera through Father Mariano Durán, one of the guerrilla caudillo's advisers. Significantly, Carrascosa agreed to terms unacceptable to Barrundia, who himself had been unsuccessful in arranging a meeting with Carrera. Specifically, in return for Carrera's military alliance, Carrascosa agreed to the abolition of the Livingston Codes, to relaxation of the anticlericalism, and, most dangerous of all, to recognition of Carrera as commander of all the insurgent forces. This accord succeeded in bringing down Gálvez, but it also spelled eventual disaster for Barrundia's cause.[99]

Carrascosa's troops entered the capital on the night of 29 January, but ran into stiff resistance from Gálvez's small, but loyal, force. Barrundia reportedly then wrote a note to Carrera, requesting a meeting, to which Carrera sent the arrogant and unexpected reply, "This is no time for meetings—am rallying my troops."[100] Carrera then sent his brother, Sotero, with a detachment to assist Carrascosa. Any hopes either Gálvez or Carrascosa had of keeping the guerrillas out of the capital were dashed, and the remainder of Carrera's triumphant army marched into the capital on 1 February, Barrundia riding along side of Carrera, followed by throngs of excited peasants and camp followers. Although Carrera claimed he had only fifteen hundred troops, contemporary estimates of the size of his ragtag army ranged as high as twelve thousand. A bloody, but relatively brief reign of terror followed, as looting and murder of foreigners and the elite who failed to find hiding places occurred. John Lloyd Stephens related the scene as told to him by a gentleman who saw it "from the roof of his house, and who was familiar with all the scenes of terror which had taken place in that unhappy city":

> Choking up the streets, all with green bushes in their hats, seeming at a distance like a moving forest; armed with rusty muskets, old pistols, fowling-pieces, some with locks and some without; sticks formed into the shape of muskets, with tin-plate locks; clubs, machetes, and knives tied to the ends of long poles; and swelling the multitude were two or three thousand women, with sacks and alforgas for carrying away the plunder. Many, who had never left their villages before, looked wild at the sight of the houses and churches, and the magnificence of the city. They entered the plaza, vociferating "Viva la religion, y muerte a los etrangeros!" Carrera himself, amazed at the immense ball he had set in motion, was so embarrassed that he could not guide his horse. He afterward said that he was frightened at the difficulty of controlling this huge and disorderly mass. The traitor Barrundia, the leader of the opposition, the Catiline of this rebellion, rode by his side on his entry into the plaza.[101]

Stephens described Carrera himself as "on horseback, with a green bush in his hat, and hung round with pieces of dirty cotton cloth, covered with pictures of the saints."[102]

The U.S. chargé d'affaires reported the antiforeign sentiment of the rural mob: "The shouts of vengeance raised in the streets by Carrera's Indi-

ans were mostly directed against what are here called English foreigners."
Among the conditions for peace DeWitt recorded was a statement that
"English foreigners be destroyed, Spaniards excepted!" [103] Singing "La Salve
Regina," a religious hymn that Carrera had adopted as a war chant, mobs
roamed through the streets at will, massing at the cathedral and placing
idols from their village parishes among those in the cathedral. Priests
shielded many of the capital's residents from the excesses of the mob, and
worked to restore order. [104] Among those killed was federal Vice-President
José Gregorio Salazar, a Salvadoran and one of Morazán's closest advisers.
Barrundia worried about Carrera getting command of the army, and would
not likely have voluntarily agreed to it, but the force of events swept him
along. Carrera's dynamism and charisma carried the day. [105]

In fact, the government ceased to have any power over the country. The
departments of Los Altos, long resentful toward the failure of the Guatemalan government to pay sufficient attention to their concerns, took the
opportunity, with Barrundia's acquiescence, to secede from Guatemala and
form the State of Los Altos. Despite the absence of much real enthusiasm for Barrundia's liberal ideas, they welcomed the opportunity to claim
sovereignty in Quetzaltenango. [106]

After a wave of brutal vengeance by the peasant forces, Carrera quickly
restored order and even gained the praise of Barrundia and others for his
conduct. His troops usually respected property and the principal commercial houses. Carrera himself was obedient to the new government of
Pedro Valenzuela and maintained his troops under orders, evacuating most
of them within a few days. [107] He had toppled the government. He had
been assured that the liberals' excesses would be discontinued. He could
return to the montaña with victory and, according to some sources, with
an $11,000 bribe for himself and his associates. [108] More important, Carrera
acquired two thousand new rifles that were found stored in the basement of
the cathedral. [109]

The Barrundia faction appeared to have triumphed. Valenzuela appointed radicals to fill the vacancies left by the departure of the Gálvez
faction. Carrera, a commissioned lieutenant colonel with military command of his home district of Mita, was out of the capital with his dreaded
peasant army. Except for three hundred troops to keep order there, his
guerrilla force disbanded and returned to their homes. Pedro Molina became president of the assembly. [110]

The real situation was otherwise, however, for it was a delicate coalition
that sustained the government, and all feared a return of the guerrilla cau-

dillo. Although Gálvez was out, he still had supporters in the legislature who continued to defend actively his administration and policies.[111] In addition, the conservative faction continued to surge, having first gained from their alliance with Gálvez, and now from the proclerical reaction of Carrera and the masses. Yet the conservatives had not yet formed an alliance with Carrera as liberal historians later charged. Indeed, all classes in the capital feared a return of Carrera's guerrillas, and conservatives as much as liberals looked to the federal government for protection during the first months following Gálvez's downfall. "What wise men do now most fear," wrote Charles DeWitt, "is that the Indians, having for the first time since the conquest of the country discovered that they can by a use of their power force the whites and the Ladinos into terms, will hereafter return to repeat their atrocities upon the slightest provocation." [112] Actions by Valenzuela's government reflected Carrera's presence and the government's willingness to appease him. By 20 February, the government was addressing Carrera as "General" and processing with kid gloves complaints of *hacendados* regarding Carrera's peasants on their lands.[113] A reflection of the curious mixture of liberalism and reaction is the legislative act signed into law by Valenzuela on 27 February 1838, requiring all laws to be constitutional.[114] Under the threat of a new mobilization by Carrera, Valenzuela organized the defense of the city under Generals Carrascosa and Salazar, calling for forced loans to pay the army.

The conservatives reacted to this with a meeting of merchants and property holders on 25 February at which they, in effect, issued an ultimatum to Valenzuela, threatening to emigrate if their demands were not met. Represented by Jorge Ponce, Luis Batres, Juan Antonio Martínez, and Francisco Vidaurre, they offered to provide monthly support directly to the military (with the understanding that the funds not be entered into the general treasury) if the government would (1) organize and maintain a force adequate to keep the peace with officers appointed without respect to political parties; (2) pardon all political crimes since 1821; (3) suspend the Livingston Codes (but retain the right of habeas corpus); (4) organize a city police force from property holders and artisans; (5) immediately call President Morazán to Guatemala; and (6) organize local government consistent with public opinion and confidence.[115] Yet another newspaper, *El Observador*, appeared in mid February to defend conservative policy at home and abroad.[116] The merchants opposed appointment of the liberal Salazar as military commander, but they relented on that point when Valenzuela agreed to everything else except the amnesty. Barrundia argued eloquently in the legislature for retention of the codes, but in the end he lost. The presence of Sotero Carrera in the legislature kept the specter of Carrera's return alive and his wishes clearly present.[117]

The changing political balance became clear when Pedro Molina resigned as president of the legislature, which then enacted the forced loan at the end of February. Suspension of the Livingston Codes, restoration of government support of the church, and removal of the military governments established by Gálvez followed.[118] These decrees reflected the popular will, as voiced by the guerrilla leader. The preamble of a decree terminating all nonelected office holders illustrated the attention the legislature gave to this will when it acknowledged that "a great majority of the population of the State have armed themselves to resist the administration that violated their guarantees and the fundamental pact." It described the revolution against Gálvez as "directed toward restoring law and liberty . . . and demanded by self-preservation against tyranny, not only legitimate but consecrated by reason and justice."[119] The liberal language of this decree probably reflected the continuing influence of Barrundia, but in fact it was a manifestation of the reaction that Carrera's threat to return had prompted.

The legislature's formal and rather belated acceptance of Gálvez's resignation on 3 March stated openly the sensitivity to the possibility of renewed popular revolt:

> The Legislative Assembly of the State of Guatemala, having reviewed the resignation of Citizen Dr. Mariano Gálvez from the governorship of the State, and considering that public opinion in the country declared strongly against his administration, taking up arms to sustain their protest and not laying them down until after he had fallen; believing that Dr. Gálvez cannot return as Chief of State without immediately inciting new upheavals; and desiring that the State avoid the disasters of a popular revolution, which always extends its inflamed eruptions to incommensurate distances; has resolved to decree, and decrees unanimously that the Legislative Body accept the resignation of Citizen Mariano Gálvez from the First Magistracy of the State.[120]

The decree suppressing the Livingston Codes revealed the shifting power, giving as the principal reason "the opinion of the people, unprepared for so important an enterprise." The decree restored the preexisting tribunal system to full force and stopped all pending implementation of the codes. Only the law of habeas corpus remained in effect. The legislature repealed the codes on 13 March 1838, but it was not accepted by the Representative Council and signed by Valenzuela until the twenty-ninth. That two-week delay by the government in executing the legislature's decree contributed to Carrera's decision to mobilize again.[121]

Barrundia was slow to recognize the rising conservative strength and doubted Carrera's ability to rally sufficient force to bring down a united government. Carrera, on the other hand, annoyed with the government's progress toward his demands, prodded by new antigovernment sentiment from rural property holders, and convinced by the priests that he was being used by the liberals, began to mobilize his guerrilla force again.[122]

Carrera narrowly escaped assassination about this time. John Lloyd Stephens wrote that Carrera reported to the government, "probably supposing that the government must be interested in his fortunes," that Andrés Monreal, one of his own lieutenants, had seduced some of his men and tied him to a tree. Just as he was about to be shot, his brother, Laureano Carrera, rushed in and ran Monreal through with his bayonet. Stephens adds that this incident only incited fanatic new loyalty among most of Carrera's supporters, who revered him as a saint.[123]

In the capital the news of the mobilization caused panic. Valenzuela responded with repressive measures, not unlike those Gálvez had taken earlier. He decreed a new forced loan on 8 March and two days later called on all citizens to take up arms against the danger of a renewed attack from the "forces of Mataquescuintla."[124] He shored up the capital's defenses, as refugees from outlying areas began to pour into the city. The election of a new Representative Council—reflecting the conservative gains in public opinion and headed by conservative Mariano Rivera Paz—put Barrundia in an untenable position. He retained considerable influence in the legislature for a while longer, but the conservatives were drifting toward a natural alliance with the peasants through their clerical advisers. In the end, Barrundia fell back on his liberal ally, Francisco Morazán, and the reentry into Guatemala of the federal president with a thousand Salvadoran troops in mid-March marked a new phase of the struggle.[125]

CHAPTER FOUR

Morazán

AS EARLY AS 9 FEBRUARY 1838 the Valenzuela government had cautioned Morazán not to march into Guatemala, fearing that he would upset the recent understanding with Carrera, who had returned to Mita in peace.[1] Morazán had heeded this advice,[2] yet the resumption of warfare by Carrera in March forced Valenzuela to look to the federal government for help. After negotiators rejected Carrera's demands, Morazán launched a major offensive at the end of March to crush the rebellion. The guerrillas responded with new ferocity, particularly, although not exclusively, against foreign-owned properties. Marshall Bennett's Hacienda de San Gerónimo in the Verapaz, reportedly the largest and most valuable estate in the country, was a popular target for Carrera's raiders. This was a property formerly belonging to the order of St. Jerome, purchased by Bennett after the liberal expropriation of ecclesiastical property.[3] Bennett was Morazán's business agent in the mahogany trade of the north coast.[4] Although losing skirmishes, the guerrillas harried the government in an ever-extending area, stretching finally from the Caribbean to the Pacific and westward into the Verapaz and Sacatepéquez.[5]

Morazán escalated the military repression and atrocities multiplied upon atrocities. Morazán's execution of Carrera's father-in-law was a case in point. Occupying Mataquescuintla, Morazán captured Carrera's wife's parents after someone revealed their hiding place in the outskirts of town. Carrera had gone to the hills, but his in-laws, in custody of Carrera's infant child, returned to the town. The elder García had not participated directly

84

in the revolt, and he had even counseled Carrera against it, yet Morazán was determined to make an example of him. After personally interrogating the old man, he condemned him to death, sending word of this to Carrera and demanding his surrender. Several people tried to prevent the atrocity that followed, but Morazán ordered the sentence carried out. Troops carried the old man to the scaffold erected in the center of the plaza. His wife, the infant Carrera in her arms, was brought from the jail to watch.

García shouted to Morazán: "I am innocent of all the charges that you make against me. On the contrary, I have opposed this war against the government. But before the injustice that you are about to commit with me I ask God that my blood fall on your head and that you be gone forever." Then, turning to his wife, he ordered: "I entrust our [grand]son to you. And tell Carrera that I repent a thousand times for not having taken my place at his side to fight against these tyrants. Let the war go on until the last of them are destroyed."

Infuriated, Morazán ordered him shot immediately, and then commanded that his head be cut off and fried in a bucket of oil. It was then placed on a pole and displayed on the corner of García's house as a warning to all those who took up arms against the federal government.[6] One of Morazán's own officers conceded that this was an act "impolitic, serving only further to bathe the revolution in blood."[7]

The political disintegration of the nation continued. Chiquimula proposed to establish a separate state of the northern coastal region, a proposal that Morazán was willing to accept, just as he had accepted separate statehood for Los Altos, apparently hoping thereby to separate Carrera and isolate him to the District of Mita. Carrera, on the other hand, rejected the partitioning of Guatemala, and in the end he would become that state's unifier, if at the expense of Central American union.[8]

Within the capital, the ouster of Gálvez had not brought consensus, and conservatives continued to consolidate their strength against liberals. The *Noticioso Guatemalteco* commented sagely on 17 March on the political parties in the state, suggesting that just two great divisions struggled for control of Guatemala: On the one hand there was a great mass of oppressed plebes, hoping for improvement of their condition; on the other hand was the dominant class that had formerly controlled the country. This elite, however, was divided into two factions: one proposed to restrict the exercise of political rights and the other to enlarge it. "One is the conservator of the past, the other the promoter of the future." The editorial pointed to a hopeless financial situation, with the federal government appropriating the lucrative tobacco and import taxes, and with revenues from the populous

Los Altos departments now denied Guatemala because of their secession. The head tax could not be levied because the Indians rebelled against it, leaving only the liquor monopolies, sales taxes, stamp tax, gunpowder monopoly, the tax on meat, and the *censo*.[9] The legislature had ceased to be a viable political force, lack of a quorum forcing it to suspend its sessions for a week on 22 March.[10]

Yet Morazán had the hopeful and willing support at this point of nearly all segments of society in the capital. Even the conservatives looked to him to save them from Carrera and the guerrillas. On 9 April a group of citizens headed by moderate liberal Juan Antonio Martínez, but including prominent conservatives, addressed a petition to Morazán, relating the grim situation in the capital and urging him to come and put things right. Morazán was, they said, "the only one who can save us." They called on Morazán "to display his well-known valor, wisdom and energy, to save us from a second eruption of barbarity." They reminded the president that "masses of blood-thirsty savages, greedy for wealth," had "arisen to threaten the honor of the families, property, civilization and all that is sacred and worthy in the society." With large areas terrorized, leaving the country in anarchy, they demanded that the president himself come to put down the insurgents. Radical liberal names were noticeably absent from this petition, it clearly being a statement of the Valenzuela government's inadequacies. Their petition closed with an urgent plea: "Come then, Mr. President! Be the restorer of our liberties; take the State from the chaos of anarchy and preserve the Republic from the dissolution that threatens it."[11]

The legislature, now reconvened, echoed these sentiments and invited Morazán to Guatemala, fearful that he might return to San Salvador and leave the city vulnerable to Carrera.[12] Morazán, meanwhile, beat off a Carrera raiding party on 12 April, not a major blow, but typical of Carrera's debilitating tactics. Morazán ordered two detachments to Jalapa and Jutiapa and, responding to the legislature's invitation, entered Guatemala City with the remainder of his force on the afternoon of 14 April. The pro-Morazán *Amigo de Guatemala* reported a scene of "jubilation, great and universal, seldom seen in Guatemala." It added that "property holders, artisans, public officials, ordinary citizens, ecclesiastics, the fair sex, every class of persons, of all opinions and parties, on horseback, in coaches, on foot, came distances to greet him, the houses en route decorated with flowers and hangings, . . . an entire people who saw in his coming an end to the public evils."[13]

A new petition, signed by 187 prominent citizens, including nearly all the leading conservatives as well as several liberals, excepting only those directly associated with the Barrundia-Molina-Valenzuela faction, urged Morazán to put an end to the "horrors of the anarchy." Delivered to Morazán by Alejandro Marure, the petition argued that the constitution and the government had ceased to function. "The government that existed before 2 February was dissolved by the forces of opposing factions," it declared, and it had neither restored order nor destroyed the revolutionary movement. Los Altos had seceded. Chiquimula, the Verapaz, and Sacatepéquez had established provisional governments, and Carrera controlled the East, so that only the department of Guatemala remained under government control. Security of life and property demanded federal intervention, the petitioners pleaded. Morazán's presence alone, they insisted, could avoid a horrible and cruel war that would destroy the whole country. They urged him to take over the state's government, "ending all other authority until the [federal] Congress, at the initiative that the other states have made, convenes a special national assembly to reconstitute the Republic." [14]

Barrundia presided over the Guatemalan legislature, and with Morazán's presence, it became bolder in maintaining liberal policies. Yet it was somewhat embarrassed when Morazán, recognizing the anxiety of the Guatemalan merchants and property holders, asked it to consider carefully the citizens' demand that Morazán take over all authority. [15] The legislature acted promptly, placing Guatemala under the protection of the national government and authorizing Valenzuela to cooperate in every way with Morazán to this end, placing all military and other resources of the state under Morazán's command. [16] Then, on 21 April, the legislature resolved to move the state government and legislature to Antigua, leaving Morazán completely in charge of the capital. [17] This helped to resolve the political tension of the capital somewhat, for the Valenzuela government had not been popular owing to its complicity in bringing Carrera's troops into the capital in the first place. Indeed, the move of the state government to Antigua strengthened the hand of the conservative elite in the capital, notwithstanding their ideological antipathy for Morazán. [18] The main Guatemalan military force remaining in the capital was the Concordia Battalion supported by the merchants and headed by Luis Batres and Pedro Aycinena. It now cooperated with Morazán to defend the capital against the guerrillas. [19]

With Morazán in control, the legislature reinstated some of the liberal program that had been sacrificed earlier to appease Carrera, notably the policy of prohibiting clerics from holding office. Since this required a constitutional change, however, it did not immediately take effect and early in May the legislature recessed until 10 June. [20] In the meantime, Father

Juan José Aycinena took the lead in consolidating conservative organization and in developing the groundwork for conservative support for Guatemalan secession from the republic. Mario Rodríguez argues convincingly that Aycinena had become thoroughly indoctrinated with southern U.S. states' rights ideas during his stay in New Orleans and had been particularly impressed by South Carolina's nullification doctrine. Thus Aycinena became a leader for state sovereignty using the United States as an example. He opposed the federal constitution of 1824 as "unitary," and favored a whole new constitution.[21]

During April and May, Carrera had stepped up his raids, taking advantage of fair weather. The harvesting and shipping of cochineal around Amatitlán was a special target for his Cachurecos, and the government had to deploy large numbers of federal and state troops to protect this commerce. There was often faulty cooperation between state and federal forces. Although they repeatedly repulsed Carrera, the guerrillas kept up the raids.[22] In early May the superintendent of Belize warned a North American traveler that he might not be able to reach Guatemala City from the Caribbean, owing to "parties of factious Indians infesting the roads."[23] John Lloyd Stephens reported that the army bulletin for May and June "exhibits the track of Carrera, devastating villages and towns, and the close pursuit of the government troops, beating him wherever they found him, but never able to secure his person."[24]

The war strained the state's finances. The budget for fiscal year 1838–39 reflected the pressure. Lack of revenue forced the government to cut the budget for fiscal 1838–39 in half, to $152,982, of which $75,671.50, a 31 percent cut from the previous year, was earmarked for the War Department. To balance the budget the legislature had decreed drastic cuts in salaries, of which only part would be paid. Some positions were eliminated altogether. The Justice Department suffered a 72 percent cut, and Education's already meager budget was cut by 67 percent. Barrundia did not attend this depressing session, and José Bernardo Escobar took over the presidency of the assembly.[25]

Morazán's repeated if indecisive victories over the rebel bands led him to believe that he had greatly weakened Carrera. In the meantime, the federation over which he presided was becoming a fiction. Secession movements were alive in Nicaragua and Costa Rica. Juan José Aycinena, now a Guatemalan delegate in the federal Congress at San Salvador, led that body on 30 May to allow the states to go their separate ways.[26] A motion by Aycinena and opposed by Barrundia to dissolve the federation failed by one vote (14–15),[27] but when, on 7 July, Congress declared the states to be "sovereign, free, and independent bodies," Morazán decided it was time to return to San Salvador.[28] He would be as ineffective there in restoring the shattered Central American union as he had been in Guatemala in dealing with Carrera. The unionists were willing to compromise, but the conservatives, identifying the federation with Morazán and the liberals, were determined to dissolve the union. The federation would continue to exist in name for several years longer, but when the federal Congress adjourned on 20 July, it was never again to reconvene.[29]

Carrera's raiding increased in direct proportion to the withdrawal of Morazán's forces. Cachureco raiding parties of twenty to fifty guerrillas gained mass support through "Robin Hood" tactics of stealing from wealthy haciendas and commercial shipments, while sparing or even assisting the poor. Carrera's popularity in the countryside grew daily. The federal and state troops controlled only what land they actually occupied, and they were becoming increasingly demoralized. Desertions were frequent.[30] The British representative in Central America called it "a war for the destruction of Property, and for the concentration of all power in the country in the hands of the mulatto or coloured classes, to the exclusion of the European race."[31] The government could not stem the tide. Posters offering $1,500, two *caballerías* of land, and pardon for any crime committed as rewards for Carrera, dead or alive, reflected the impotence of the military forces.[32]

Morazán's departure left the liberals without support. Popular demonstrations called for action to forestall another sack of the capital. On 17 July the Guatemalan Council of State, headed by conservative Mariano Rivera Paz, demanded that the state legislature, still in special session but again in Guatemala City, take up immediately measures to restore peace and to suppress the "hordes of bandits headed by the rebel Rafael Carrera" that now "threaten the capital itself."[33] On the twenty-second another noisy street demonstration demanded Valenzuela's resignation. He turned over his authority to Rivera Paz at 7:00 P.M. on the following day.[34]

Mariano Rivera Paz (1804–49) was the son of a respectable, but not very prosperous creole family of the capital. Educated in traditional morals and religion, which he adhered to throughout his life, his conservative tendencies were not surprising. After dabbling in literature, he studied law, but the civil war of 1826–29 interrupted his schooling. He entered the federal army as a simple soldier, but rose rapidly to the rank of Lieutenant Colonel by 1829. Following the army's defeat at the hands of Morazán, Rivera had gone to the Verapaz, where he studied and practiced medicine, which he continued in an amateur way throughout his life. He also entered politics, representing the Verapaz as deputy to the assembly in 1833, and as a councilor for the Verapaz in 1835–37. He worked actively against the cholera epidemic in Guatemala City in 1837. Not a part of the aristocracy of the capital, he had gained economically from land he acquired during the Gálvez regime.[35] He had served that government in reconnoitering a route and a bridge over the Río Polochic in a plan to connect Guatemala City with the Verapaz and the river port of Telemán.[36] Allied with conservative interests in the recent turmoil, he had gained influence in the Marqués de Aycinena's consolidation of conservative strength. A competent administrator, he provided the firm leadership the country now demanded. He would serve as chief-of-state of Guatemala for most of the subsequent five years.[37]

Rivera's first act was to ask the legislature for a general amnesty for all political acts since 1821. Now terrified by the popular uprisings within the city as well as in the countryside, the assembly dutifully complied, welcoming back exiles and restoring all civil rights.[38] Beginning on 25 July 1838, the assembly began to undo the liberal program that had been erected over the past decade. It provided for state support of the church, formally proclaimed state sovereignty, reduced by half the direct head tax, repealed civil marriage and divorce, revoked Gálvez's municipal organization system, and restored the state government's rule in Guatemala City, ending the federal control authorized on 21 April. It also called for a convention to revise the constitution and "reconstitute the society."[39] Detailed regulations for its election were decreed on 5 August, based on a population of 311,687 for the four consolidated departments remaining in the state (see Table 4).

The conservatives also made a move to establish financial responsibility and confidence, assuring that the government would honor all obligations, contracts, loans, concessions, consignments, and other operations pertaining to the state treasury. They stressed the necessity of maintaining the government's credit and called for "nothing other than religious compliance, without modifications nor exceptions, of the agreements, transactions, transfers, and promises" of the government. The fact that the many forced loans of the liberal government were owed to these conservative property holders was, of course, a large reason for the decision not to repudiate the liberal debt.[40]

The peasants' grievances were now being met, although the government was not ready to recognize their leader. His demands of 1837 coincided closely with the policies of the conservatives, but however much their victory might owe to Carrera, they had no intention in August of 1838 of allowing him to take over, and they continued the war against him. Rivera Paz decreed special tribunals to judge those who rebelled against the gov-

TABLE 4
Election of Deputies to the Constituent
Assembly of Guatemala, 1838

Department	Number of Deputies
Guatemala, Population 87,129	
Guatemala	7
Amatitlán	2
Escuintla	1
Mistán	1
Guazacapán	1
Jalpatagua	1
Cuaginiquilapa	2
Total	15
Sacatepéquez, Population 94,609	
Antigua	4
San Lucas	1
Chimaltenango	2
Tejar	1
San Juan	3
San Martín	3
Patzún	2
Total	16
The Verapaz, Population 65,041	
Cobán	3
Cabajón	1
Petén	1
Tactic	2
Salamá	1
Rabinal	2
Total	10
Chiquimula, Population 64,908	
Chiquimula	2
Esquipulas	2
Mita	2
Zacapa	1
Acasaguastlán	1
Sansaria	1
Jalapa	1
Total	10
Grand Total	51

Source: "Tabla de elecciones de diputados a la Asamblea Constituyente del Estado que comprende de veinte y siete distritos electo-
rales, para elegir cincuenta y un representantes, por la base de seis
mil habitantes," *Boletín Oficial*, 26 July–5 Aug. 1838.

ernment. This decree kept the District of Mita under martial law, but removed the rest of the country from military rule, establishing special civilian tribunals to deal with rebels there.[41] With Morazán gone, however, Carrera made gains, especially after he defeated Colonel Bonilla's veteran federal division near Jalapa in mid August. Carrera now won new recruits and marched on Guatemala City with more than two thousand men. He defeated a government force at Petapa on 6 September and the next day occupied Antigua, where his troops destroyed the archives of the local court.[42]

The Guatemalan army was under the command of liberal General Carlos Salazar. Declaring martial law and taking over the federal tobacco revenues, he prepared the capital's defenses. Carrera moved twenty-four hundred troops to Villa Nueva, south of the capital, on 9 September. On the eleventh Salazar, accompanied by J. F. Barrundia, moved out of the capital at the head of nine hundred troops. A heavy fog covered their march and enabled them to surprise Carrera at Villa Nueva. Carrera lost nearly four hundred men, as well as a large store of arms and artillery. Carrera himself suffered a serious wound in the leg, but he was able to direct a retreat into the mountains.[43]

In the capital, liberals and conservatives alike rejoiced. Although the rural clergy continued to support Carrera, those of the conservative elite in the capital now condemned him. According to Lorenzo Montúfar, the conservative chiefs called him a "cannibal thirsting for human blood." Antonio Larrazábal, dean of the cathedral, published a seventeen-page pamphlet calling on the people to lay down their arms and abandon the revolution.[44] Bernardo Piñol, later bishop of Nicaragua and archbishop of Guatemala, on 14 September preached a sermon in the cathedral in which he attacked Carrera unmercifully and praised Salazar's victory at Villa Nueva.[45]

In the euphoria following Villa Nueva, Alejandro Marure (1809–51) wrote a pamphlet comparing the Carrera revolt with the 1790 reaction in the Vendée against the French Revolution. Marure recognized that the liberals, especially the more radical faction led by Barrundia, had alienated themselves from the masses whom they pretended to lead, and as they isolated themselves from the rest of the elite, they had became the target for a major reaction from the rural folk. Marure served both liberal and conservative governments until his death in 1851, but this work reflects a discernible turn away from the liberalism of his early and, historiographically, most important works. In it he recommended that the Guatemalan government, which he said had often imitated foreign governments where there was little applicability (a pointed reference to the Livingston Codes?), ought to imitate the French government's methods of repression of the Vendée revolt, where military units were maintained in the rebellious zones, away from population centers.[46] The following year, after Carrera's victory, Marure's conservative leanings became even more important in a pamphlet criticizing President Morazán's involvement in Guatemalan political affairs.[47]

Barrundia and Salazar, rather than following up their victory and completing the destruction of Carrera's forces, returned to the capital seeking to force a return to liberalism. Yet Rivera Paz held firm, prompting Salazar to resign his command on 5 October and precipitate a new crisis in the government when a number of military chiefs supported him. Morazán now entered the arena once more, leaving San Salvador with a large force on 10 October. On the twenty-third he dissolved the Guatemalan legislature, and on the following day he justified his intervention in Guatemala on the grounds that "the faction headed by the criminal Rafael Carrera has taken the major part of the communities that compose the State of Guatemala," especially in the Departments of Guatemala, Chiquimula, and the Verapaz, and that if the situation were allowed to deteriorate further Guatemala "would disappear from among the civilized nations." Under Article 35 of a law of 17 November 1832, he took over the civil authority in the state and declared martial law.[48]

Carrera regrouped and countered Morazán's invasion of Guatemala by striking El Salvador, occupying temporarily Santa Ana, Ahuachapán, and other towns. San Salvador braced for an attack, but Carrera turned back into Guatemala and occupied Chiquimulilla. Meanwhile, Honduras, Nicaragua, and Costa Rica all set up independent governments in early November, making the federation an illusion. Morazán had left his newly elected vice-president, Diego Vigil, in charge, but the federation was crumbling around him.[49]

The British envoy, Frederick Chatfield, recognized in early October 1838 that the future of the federation rested on Morazán's success against Carrera. "Unless he acts with talent and energy, and can reestablish peace and order in the state," Chatfield wrote to Palmerston, "his reputation is gone, and with it the only chance of preserving the small share of civilization existing in the Republic." Chatfield doubted Morazán's ability to "erect a firm superstructure on the present ruins" and he predicted that "every dollar which the government expends without contributing to the permanent establishment of Peace, is equivalent to the like sum bestowed towards the accomplishment of the aim of Carrera and his abettors, for as soon as the resources of the government are utterly exhausted, the Priests and the coloured classes may take their own way."[50]

Troops from Los Altos under Agustín Guzmán joined Morazán's federal forces. Together they forced Carrera deeper into the montaña, but they could not inflict a decisive defeat. Morazán desperately wanted to stamp out the rebellion and employed calculated terror in this effort. Hatred mounted as Morazán's atrocities failed to stem the revolt.

Rivera Paz's conservative government in Guatemala City was virtually impotent now, having little control outside the city and dependent on liberal troops for its defense. Some idea of the situation is reflected in a letter from John Lloyd Stephens, special agent of the United States to Central America. Stephens had been briefly imprisoned and explained the situation to the secretary of state late in the year.

> The Alcalde and sergeant have not been punished. The government would punish them if it could, but it is perfectly impotent. And as the Chief of the State confessed to me, does not dare intervene with local authorities. Strictly, I should have made my complaint to the central Government, but there is none, or at all events, Morazán has no more power in Guatemala than he has in New York. General Carrera, unasked, sent Mr. Catherwood a separate passport as Secretary of Legation. I left him at Copan and he will retain that letter. It is not a perfect protection but it is of very great value.[51]

Carrera may have been close to defeat by the time Stephens made this report. Wounded, and with a sharp decrease in the number of troops at his command, his predicament had become more desperate than either Rivera Paz or Morazán realized. With Guzmán's troops closing in on him in December, he sued for peace and signed a treaty at Rinconcito with the Totonicapán general, agreeing to lay down his arms and recognize the government of Guatemala in return for his restoration as military commander of Mita. Rivera Paz and Morazán both agreed, and the country enjoyed a brief interlude of peace.[52]

Morazán now reasserted his control in Guatemala City and promptly imposed a forced loan on the merchants of the capital, to be guaranteed by the sales tax (alcabala) for the coming year.[53] Rivera Paz refused to convene the legislature, where the liberals still had strength, but with Carrera apparently out of the way, the liberals now tried to recover their position and successfully staged a coup d'état. They ignored the call for a constituent convention that the conservative government had decreed in response to popular demand, and instead convened the regular assembly without government sanction. On 30 January 1839 this assembly then replaced Rivera Paz as chief of state with Carlos Salazar, who, although a Salvadoran, enjoyed some popularity in Guatemala City as the hero of Villa Nueva.[54] Rivera Paz and his cabinet protested vehemently against this coup, but they had no force to sustain themselves.[55] Rivera Paz resumed his position as president of the Council of State, but the legislative assembly, under the guidance of Morazán and Salazar, were in control. It quickly repealed nearly all the legislation that the conservatives had enacted since the previous July, including those acts passed as concessions to Carrera.[56] The new government began publication of a newspaper, *El Tiempo*, which reflected the liberal resurgence and called for national reorganization. "The age of infancy is over," it proclaimed, as it called for new reforms.[57]

While Morazán had been restoring liberal power in Guatemala, conservatives had gained power in Honduras and Nicaragua. Their allied forces invaded El Salvador in late February. Morazán had turned over the presidency of the republic on 1 February to his vice-president, responding to charges that he was continuing himself in office beyond the end of his constitutional term. Elections were impossible at this point, but Morazán, assuming the title of chief of state of El Salvador, continued the fight to restore the union.[58]

Carrera, in the meantime, had been reorganizing his forces in January. Father Francisco Lobo, one of the most important of the priests who had accompanied Carrera from the start, traveled from village to village drumming up support for Carrera.[59] The return of the liberals brought quick resumption of Carrera's guerrilla war as the cause of Carrera and the conservatives had finally become one. Both aimed at the overthrow of Morazán and the restoration of traditional institutions and policies. Salazar's government was sensitive to the threat, but sought to avoid direct confrontation. On 12 February it agreed to name Lt. Col. González Cerezo as commander-in-chief of the state's armed forces in response to the pressure from Carrera's guerillas, although in reality Salazar remained in control.[60] Carrera further demanded that elections for the constitutional convention be held and that Archbishop Casáus return to Guatemala from Cuba.[61] When this was not forthcoming, he began to conspire with the conservatives. Padre Lobo and other priests played an important role in these communications, which brought a brief cessation of hostilities. Meanwhile, Carrera was in contact with Francisco Ferrera, leader of the Honduran conservatives. Ferrera urged Carrera to break completely with the Salazar government and to join in the alliance against Morazán. Carrera resisted this at first and instead requested arms and troops from the Salazar government to defend the border against Ferrera. Salazar suspected treachery, but for the moment Carrera officially remained loyal.[62]

Morazán had returned to El Salvador to meet the threat there. Imposing a forced loan on the foreign merchants in Salvador brought him into direct conflict with Chatfield, ending the British envoy's support of the Morazán government. From this point on, Chatfield supported the conservatives and states' rights.[63]

On 11 March, Ferrera, as leader of the Honduras-Nicaragua-Costa Rica alliance, wrote to the municipal government of Guatemala City. He told the council that he was aware of the oppression the Guatemalans had suffered, "victims of a military and arbitrary regime that overthrew the administration established by the people and broke the fundamental law of that country to satisfy the illegal wishes of a tyrant," and he offered to provide all the protection and aid necessary to free them from the despot that had "trampled on your laws and annulled the sacred rights of your citizens." The municipality, in firm but polite terms, thanked Ferrera for his interest and agreed with his principles, but it rejected his offer of protection for the present.[64]

Civil war now consumed the Central American nation from Costa Rica to Guatemala. The principal theater, however, was El Salvador, where Nicaraguan troops routed a Salvadoran force at Jicaral on 19 March, forcing Morazán to return from Honduras where he had been maneuvering against Ferrera.[65] With most of the federal troops having left Guatemala to defend El Salvador, Carrera made his move. On 24 March, in a strongly worded *pronunciamento* from Mataquescuintla, he accused Morazán of cruelty toward the clergy and the people, of destroying commerce, of confiscating private property, and of terrorizing the country. Morazán, he charged, had usurped the power delegated to the assembly and had failed to convoke a constitutional convention as earlier agreed. In taking up arms once more on the grounds of defense of his country, Carrera swore before God Almighty that he would not recognize the acts of the "unconstitutional" assembly Morazán had convened, which, he said, consisted of only ten deputies.[66] Carrera's "Army of the Constitution" now marched on the capital.

The government once more prepared its meager defenses, but also named Alejandro Marure and J. J. Górriz to seek some way to end the civil war before Carrera could take the capital. Their proposal, submitted on 2 April, like so many that would follow throughout the nineteenth century, sought to establish a basis for restoration of the federal pact with provision for obviously needed reforms. They called for a cease fire between the federal government and the allied governments of Honduras, Nicaragua, and Costa Rica, while peaceful negotiations would take place at a convention that the six states would organize without reference to the present federal government, state assemblies to choose the delegates. The belligerents would agree in advance to accept the agreement reached by the convention.

The Marure-Górriz plan further called for federal Vice-President Vigil to confine his activities to the federal district of San Salvador and not meddle in the states' affairs. But this plan never went beyond considerable lip service to plans for the proposed convention.[67]

Carrera moved his forces carefully, avoiding a repeat of the disaster at Villa Nueva. In fact, there were few troops to oppose him, and when General Salazar, Mariano Gálvez, Pedro Molina, and other liberals fled the city on 13 April 1839, Carrera entered the capital without resistance at the head of an orderly army of fifteen hundred. The inhabitants barricaded themselves in their houses, expecting a repeat of the 1838 sack of the city, but no such thing happened. Carrera rode directly to the house of Rivera Paz and proclaimed him restored as chief-of-state. The troops were ordered to barracks and specifically warned against molesting persons or property in the capital.[68] There were incidents of violence, of course, and some unpleasantness. Carrera demanded peremptorily five hundred pesos from Pedro Valenzuela, who had failed to leave the city. Carrera distributed the money among his troops.[69] Stephens wrote of the insolent soldiery, which the inhabitants now had to put up with in the city:

A group of soldiers were lying at full length, so as to make everybody pass off the walk and go round them. Perhaps three or four thousand people, a large portion ladies, were turned off. All felt the insolence of these fellows, and I have no doubt some felt a strong disposition to kick them out of the way; but though young men enough passed to drive the whole troop out of the city, no complaint was made, and no notice whatever taken of it. In one of the corridors of the plaza another soldier lay on his back crosswise, with his musket by his side, and muttering to everybody that passed, "Tread on me if you dare, and you'll see!" and we all took good care not to tread on him. I returned to my house, to pass the evening in solitude; and it was melancholy to reflect that with the elements of so much happiness, Guatimala was made so miserable.[70]

Ferrera gave Carrera's peaceful takeover of Guatemala favorable press in Honduras, applauding his conduct and his restoration of legitimate authority there.[71] Ferrera congratulated Carrera on 2 May and ordered Carrera's pronunciamento of 24 March reprinted in Honduras. He urged Guatemala to name delegates to a convention with the other allied states and looked forward to "the political regeneration from which we expect so much."[72] Ferrera, however, soon faced a challenge from Morazán, who had checked the Nicaraguans on 28 March at Las Lomas, near Cojutepeque. On 5 and 6 May at Espíritu Santo, on the banks of Río Lempa near San Vicente, Morazán defeated the combined Honduran-Nicaraguan "Army of Pacification." Morazán himself suffered a wound in the right arm in this engagement, but his forces pursued Ferrera back into Honduras. They failed, however, to take full advantage of the rout. Instead, Ferrera managed to regroup his troops and repulse the invading federal forces, thus negating to some extent the victory at Espíritu Santo.[73]

Rivera Paz moved quickly to consolidate conservative control in Guatemala and to restore order, naming Carrera as supreme commander of the Guatemalan army with the rank of brigadier general. On 17 April Rivera Paz declared Guatemala absolutely sovereign and independent of the federal union and called for a constitutional convention.[74] On the same day he combined all military authority under his minister of war, Pedro N. Arriaga.[75] On the eighteenth he declared the financial independence of the state, terminating recognition of federal letters of credit in the state's customs houses and ending all federal operations in the ports.[76] At the same time Arriaga assured foreign consuls that commercial relations would not be adversely affected by the change in government. He promised that foreign individuals and property would enjoy the protection of the government and that all existing tariffs and commercial laws would remain in effect until they were revised.[77]

Arriaga also sent a communique to the other states, explaining that Carrera "and many other caudillos of the people who came to his aid" had occupied the capital on 13 April and restored the government that Morazán had deposed on 30 January. He pointed out that Carrera had taken the city ten years to the day after Morazán had taken it in 1829, "a result of a capitulation that was agreed upon and then promptly broken" by the liberals. Arriaga proclaimed that a revolution for justice, peace, security, and religion had taken place on behalf of the people. "They want, in a word, their opinions and wishes to be respected and no longer to be the plaything of the audacity and impudence of a few who have taken it upon themselves to speak for them, while exhausting their resources and increasing their suffering." The communique, referring to Morazán as "always the enemy of liberty and independence of the States," promised that the forthcoming constitutional convention would restore the rights and benefits of the people.[78]

While Manuel Francisco Pavón, the hard working secretary of the assembly and architect of much of the conservative restoration, and Frederick Chatfield sought to develop a series of alliances between Guatemala and the other states, Arriaga held open the door to a new national convention of the states to work toward a reformed federal government.[79] Arriaga emphasized, however, that first Guatemala had to hold its constitutional convention to consolidate the peace and order that had been reestablished.[80] He assured Morazán's Salvadoran government at the same time that peace reigned in the country and that commerce once more ran freely:

> Traffic runs without interruption: in the city and on the roads no one dares impede the free passage of the beasts loaded with products and effects. Supplies come in abundance. The cochineal planters are busy with their harvest. The stores are open, and the artisans' shops are active. I specify all this to refute ideas that perhaps are held very different from the reality of the facts. It will appear incredible; but it is the truth without any exaggeration.

In contrast to the suffering of the past, he said, now things were going well in Guatemala and the state was finding that it could best run its affairs independently of the federation.[81] Indeed, after so much turmoil, fear, and destruction in the state, the new government put forth a brave new front, emphasizing peace and order and launching major reorganization, in its own view, "on the basis of justice and true equality and of the strictest economy."[82]

Morazán could no longer even hold El Salvador loyal to the federal concept. That government had reincorporated the federal district (San Salvador) into the state and on 3 May declared in favor of a convention to reorganize the national government.[83] Vice-President Vigil accepted this gracefully and endorsed the idea of a convention at Santa Ana on or soon after 15 August 1839, to which all the states except Los Altos had now agreed.[84] Morazán himself was in the field, his wounds mended, still seeking to follow up his victory against Ferrera. But Ferrera had already raised new forces in Comayagua, Tegucigalpa, Yoro, and Gracias.[85]

On 11 May, Rivera Paz approved a Treaty of Friendship and Alliance with Honduras, the first in a series of treaties between May and August 1839 that would unite all of the states except Los Altos against Morazán.[86] British Consul Frederick Chatfield adjusted to the new political situation and soon saw Guatemala as his logical headquarters. Although he regarded the Guatemalan conservatives, according to Mario Rodríguez, as "retrograde," he consoled himself that "they were at least white and with some semblance of civilization."[87] Thus on 13 May Chatfield wrote Palmerston revealing his changing position:

> I freely confess that I have no predilection for any party or persons in this country. I am not a partisan of expresident Morazán, or of his friends, the existing government, first because I perceive that Morazán has no administrative ability, and secondly, because I can feel no respect for Persons, who sacrifice the publick interests and resources to their own individual emolu-

ment. With regard to the servile party, although I may lean towards them as being persons of property and reputable conduct, nevertheless on publick grounds I cannot very cordially welcome the prospect of their return to power, from a suspicion that no permanent good will accrue from the govt of a Party embued with the old Spanish prejudices, and subject to the tyrannical influence of the Romish Priesthood; however, between the two evils of only the semblance of a govt without power or principle, as has long been submitted to here, and a substantial one based on obsolete principles, perhaps the latter is best, at any rate it may be the means of leading to the establishment of such outward forms of respectability and decency, as any future rulers will find difficult to dispense with.[88]

Rodríguez argues that Chatfield was in no sense responsible for the breakup of the federation, for he abandoned Morazán only after he was clearly no longer in control of Central America. Certainly, by mid 1839, Morazán had little support left anywhere in Central America. Chatfield arranged through George Skinner, a British merchant in Guatemala, for a loan to the Rivera Paz government. From this point on Chatfield began to get favorable treatment for British interests from the Guatemalan government. Among those most important to Chatfield's cultivation of the Guatemalan government were Manuel F. "Chico" Pavón, Luis Batres, Pedro N. Arriaga, and Pedro Aycinena, all members of the conservative Guatemalan elite.

Carrera remained in the capital for only a few weeks after his victory of 13 April. He did not directly involve himself in the foreign policy that the conservatives developed during April and May of 1839, but he was a major force on their domestic policies, and one of his chief advisers, Father Joaquín Durán, became Rivera Paz's first secretary. Carrera's forces marched into the other departments, securing them and removing public officials who were not appropriately subservient to Carrera's wishes.[89] Carrera feared that a pro-Morazán faction in Chiquimula might declare that department united "to the government they call federal," and he recommended that a division should be stationed there to prevent any such occurrence.[90]

On the same day, Carrera's wife formally requested passports for her and Rafael to visit their home. She requested that a substitute be named for her husband as commandant, claiming that their "interests were suffering for lack of attention."[91] Appropriate documents, answering both requests, were forthcoming on 7 May, ordering Carrera to Chiquimula at the command of a division, with his brother, Col. Sotero Carrera, being named armed forces commandant of the Department of Guatemala. Carrera's orders were to prevent any pronunciamento of adhesion to the federal government in Chiquimula and to keep an eye on movements of federal forces in Santa Ana, although it prohibited him from actually crossing the border into El Salvador.[92] Carrera marched out of the capital on the following day in the direction of Mita.[93] As soon as news of Carrera's approach reached Chiquimula, the jefe político there, Antonio Valdés, fled to Santa Ana, fearing reprisals for his pro-Morazán position.[94]

Thus by mid 1839 Carrera and the Guatemalan conservatives had succeeded in checking Morazán. The liberals were in full retreat in every state. The Guatemalan patricians now needed only to consolidate their victory with effective organization and diplomacy to restore the peace and security they desired. Yet restoration of the power of the Aycinenas and their kinsmen was not yet assured, nor was Morazán yet down for the full count.

CHAPTER FIVE

Consolidation

THE PRINCIPAL BENEFICIARIES of Carrera's revolt were the aristocratic, conservative elite of Guatemala City. Gálvez's decree of 26 July 1838 had allowed those exiled in 1829 to return to Guatemala, and many of them had gained positions of responsibility in both the private and public sectors even before Carrera's April 1839 victory. Juan José de Aycinena led their coagulation as a political force. Like Aycinena, many were clergymen. Others headed important merchant or planter families. Discredited after their defeat by Morazán in 1829, by 1839 they had been accepted back into the social and economic life of the state, and they joined liberal members of the old elite, such as José Francisco Barrundia, Manuel Arrivillaga, and Miguel García Granados in directing the government. This class had suffered much since the beginning of the nineteenth century, but it still constituted an elite upper class.

The economic interests of this class had been represented through its fuero, the Consulado, abolished by the liberals in 1829, but now restored in 1839. A comparison of those registered with the Consulado for the years 1799, 1823, and 1839 reveals the leading merchants and planters of Guatemala. The combined lists include 168 different family surnames, but only twelve of the surnames are common to all three lists.[1] This startling statistic suggests the difficulty of economic survival during those forty years. Among the twelve families were important participants on both the liberal and conservative sides, as well as several who took no active part in the political activity, but all were major houses. On the other hand, the high rate of attrition among other merchant and landholder families illustrates the considerable dislocation of the period. Many Spaniards left the country at the time of independence. There is a notable decrease in the number of Basque names on the 1823 list. The civil disorders and wars of the 1820s and 1830s further disrupted the economy. Meanwhile, there was a small flow of newcomers to enlarge the European resident class in the capital.[2]

Both liberals and conservatives would play prominent roles in the 1840s, but the Carrera victory initiated a strongly conservative reaction. Acting Chief of State Mariano Rivera Paz and his two ministers, Pedro Arriaga and Luis Batres, were firmly committed to this reaction. The constitutional convention, or Constituent Assembly as it was called, convened on 29 May with twenty-seven delegates, with a dozen more arriving later. It had a strongly conservative flavor and roughly half the delegates were clerics. They elected Father Antonio Larrazábal as its president by a vote of 17 to 8 over Father Fernando Antonio Dávila, with 2 votes for Miguel Larreinaga, but when Larrazábal refused to accept because of his ecclesiastical duties as vicario capitular of the archdiocese, they chose Dávila by a vote of 19 to 5.[3]

Dávila, a supporter of Carrera, had only recently arrived in the capital. He called upon the representatives, the government, the armed forces, and the elite (whom he called "*los pudientes*") to cooperate in creating a constitution that would lay the foundation for a new society. Rivera Paz announced that the convening of the assembly ended the period of his temporary government, promising an account of his administration at their first session. A solemn mass in the cathedral followed the installation ceremony.[4]

Pedro Arriaga read Rivera Paz's long *memoria* to the assembly on 31 May, reviewing the past and offering a program for the future. Rivera Paz recalled how "our difficulties had brought us to the brink of the abyss," and that the passions of the first years of independence had been "the exaltation of everything new and the wish to destroy everything that existed." He said, "They banned moderation and prudence under the hateful names of servile and retrograde," so that "honorable and peaceable men fled from public affairs, persecuted by the revolutionary furor that led the country to the misery and disarray in which it is found." But now, he declared, society "by its instinct for self preservation is searching for reorganization." His review of the liberal rule suggested the emotionalism of the issues.

> There was neither personal security, nor respect for property, nor liberty, nor justice. The decrees on divorce and civil marriage produced a grand scandal, for they clashed with our customs and created misunderstandings. The honorable peasant, whose conscience had already been tortured in a thousand ways, now found insecure the honor of his daughters, even in the

confines of his poor hut, as he felt the peace of his family, the last refuge for the downtrodden, disappear. Trying violently to establish codes projected for Louisiana, the result was the immediate and sudden suspension of the administration of justice, scandalous immunity for criminals, causing fear and alarm, which the absence of justice and magistrates in a community would naturally produce.

He went on to list fiscal mismanagement, unpopular tax policy, forced labor, and military service among the causes of popular resistance. He told of the revolution of Mita and the War of the Mountain and how his efforts to convene a constitutional convention had been thwarted earlier by Morazán and Salazar. Even when the Treaty of Rinconcito had restored peace, it was the liberals who had broken it after Carrera had observed the treaty "with a religiousness of which there are not many examples in our republic." It was Morazán, he reminded the assembly, who had "defied public opinion in Guatemala and annulled with armed force the agreements of the last legislative assembly." It was Carrera who had restored peace and, as the country resumed its commerce and normal life, "inaugurated a sincere conciliation." Morazán had destroyed Guatemala's armed forces, incorporating them into the federal army or disbanding them. In Rivera Paz's view, Carrera, in alliance with Ferrera in Honduras, had become the saviour of the state and the republic.

With the federal pact broken, Rivera Paz now charged the Constituent Assembly with building lasting peace and prosperity. He informed them of the treaties being negotiated with all the other states except Los Altos. Rebuilding Guatemala, he told the deputies, would require "a great patriotic and constant effort on your part," and he urged them to began by satisfying the "religious needs and wishes of our people. . . . There is no example either in antiquity or in modern times, of a people without religion," he declared, and urged the assembly to decree "solemnly that the Government of the State professes and respects the Catholic religion," with restoration and protection of church funds. He left the door open to a restoration of the federation, at least in provisional form, but he also called for legal authority for an "energetic and expeditious executive power" that would be just, good, and maintain order and peace. He urged restoration of "the old territorial division of the state, to which the people were accustomed, and, insofar as possible, the form that the laws of Spain established for political government." He emphasized the point: "If we have not been able to establish new laws, while we give ourselves an adequate constitution, what can we do but look to the old way to pursue the peace and security that it gave us?" He advocated the same for the judicial system: Restoring the municipal courts to their old form, he argued, would give the people a defense against violence and arbitrariness.

He also called for reorganization of the treasury, in ruins, despite the ever-increasing taxes under the liberals. He favored repeal of the "unjust" taxes, but at the same time prompt recognition and liquidation of Guatemala's legitimate debt in order to insure justice and establish the public confidence in the government.

Rivera Paz also noted that public education, as he referred to the church's earlier educational system, was now in total disarray, especially outside the capital. He restated a constant conservative charge that "the wish to bring our countries the advances and improvement by enacting the legislation of enlightened nations, without being prepared to receive them, had produced nothing more than trouble and evil, missing the desired objectives. Our liberalism must limit itself to giving our people a general education and improving their habits." Despite its defects, the colonial educational system run by the clergy, he argued, provided a basis for development rather than great but impracticable projects. Above all, he insisted, it provided primary education in the small towns. While the liberal legislation had called for establishing a more sophisticated system by force, "we have seen even the few primary schools that we had before independence disappear."

He also called for protection and development of agriculture and commerce and proposed revival of the Consulado to that end. Rivera Paz closed this outline for government under conservative guidance with praise of Carrera, urging the assembly to recognize his services to the nation, as he charged the deputies to "save the state, repair its evils, and make it happy."[5] The assembly applauded enthusiastically and on the following day insisted that Rivera Paz remain in office until the assembly made other provision for the public administration. On the same day it formally authorized the government to remunerate Carrera for his distinguished service.[6]

Carrera sent a message to the assembly congratulating himself on accomplishing his two goals: restoration of Rivera Paz and convening of the Constituent Assembly. He now called on it to dismantle the liberal legislation, replacing it with "a system that will conform to our customs and especially to the religious principles that we profess. Fulfill such worthy objectives and the people will owe you their happiness." He promised to redouble his efforts to see that their just decisions were carried out and promised to "be the first to respect and obey them, as is proper."[7]

The assembly moved expeditiously, beginning with restoration of the religious orders and an invitation to the exiled Archbishop Ramón Casáus to return to Guatemala.[8] The process of returning the church's property also began.[9] Then the assembly consolidated the customs service and reorganized the treasury.[10] Carrera's religious fanaticism appeared in his congratulatory message to the assembly on behalf of the people after these acts:

> In their excessive desperation, our oppressors insult us from afar, calling us barbarians, savages, fanatics and serviles. After having failed in their own demoralizing and impious efforts, their furor is incited upon seeing that the people, with their liberty restored, are proving that all efforts to corrupt them produced nothing more than to strengthen in their hearts their love of the holy religion inherited from our fathers. On behalf of the people we armed ourselves and have triumphed, overcoming a thousand obstacles. Now that the designs of our old oppressors are exposed, we shall know how to die before once again seeing our religion insulted and our temples profaned and robbed. Firm in our resolve, and united by the same sentiments, we shall be invincible![11]

At the end of June, Rivera Paz offered his resignation again, declaring that his job was finished. Order had been restored and the assembly convened. He held no ambition for the governorship on a regular basis, he said, and asked the assembly to relieve him. But Rivera Paz now enjoyed wide popularity, supported not only by Carrera and other military chiefs, but also by the conservative elite and population generally in Guatemala City. Thus on 3 July the assembly unanimously rejected his resignation, citing the great public confidence in him and arguing that there was still a crisis situation in the state. Public confidence would be shaken and delicate negotiations in progress with the other states could be upset should he not remain in office.[12]

Municipal elections in July gave the conservatives control of the capital.[13] In August, the assembly reestablished the national mint and the Consulado, with a substantial road and port development under the latter's supervision.[14] Later it revived the office of corregidor, reflecting the consolidation of control over the country, restored education to church supervision, established a national bank, and revived the *residencia* examination for all public officials in the state.[15]

The legislators closed their first session with more decrees designed to restore Hispanic tradition. They reduced taxes on foodstuffs in another response to popular demand[16] and reinstated the former alcoholic beverage controls.[17] They abolished the head tax altogether.[18] They restored the tithe tax and provided for its enforcement.[19] They decreed a new "Declaration of the Rights of the State and its Inhabitants," which although it maintained in print many civil liberties, clearly turned the direction of the state toward authoritarianism.[20] Roman Catholicism once more became the official religion and regained its fuero and *cabildo eclesiástico*.[21] The session adjourned, having definitively terminated the liberal revolution.[22]

The new government's attitude toward the Indians is testimony to its philosophy of looking back to the Hispanic period. On 16 August 1839 the Constituent Assembly, recognizing that Indians were a majority of the state's population and that it was in the public interest not only "to protect this numerous class of the society, but also to develop and improve its customs and civilization," decreed a code for dealing with this class. Noting that the liberal program had mistreated and exploited the Indians under a system that operated under the pretext of their equality, the committee reporting the bill said that the system of the colonial era was really better. That system "compelled them to work, to provide public service on certain projects and to pay taxes; but it also gave them protection against the influential and the powerful in their land claims." It provided for their care and welfare and for their self-respect, the committee added. The liberals had abolished all that, and the Indians had consequently lost their respect for law and order. The new code reversed Gálvez's idea of incorporating the Indian into western civilization. It even called for restoration of the office of Indian interpreter and instructed departmental officials to have the decree translated into the indigenous languages. Gálvez had aimed at assimilating the Indians. The conservatives claimed this meant exploitation, with the danger of rebellion and violence. Instead, they offered paternalism and protection.[23]

Carrera's official statements in July and August were probably only mild reflections of his direct role in pressuring the assembly to hasten restoration of clerical privilege, Hispanic traditions, and protection of the rights of the peasants.[24] He also warned Morazán and the remains of the federal structure to keep their hands off Guatemala. "One of the means that the defunct federal administration often has employed to dominate and oppress," the official Guatemalan government newspaper declared, had been to "invent rumors and foment rivalry among the states and people." It accused the federal government of promoting hatred for Guatemala in the other states in order to justify a strong central power to protect them from it. "On the positive side," the paper warned, "a certain personage [presumably Carrera] has offered his sword to fight against this *fanaticism*."[25]

In the same issue a separate article attacked the "tolerance" that the liberals "talked about incessantly as a social virtue" during a period when they practiced "the most unchecked intolerance." It accused them of persecuting the population on the pretext of establishing and maintaining liberalism, which in reality only served special interests, and "with respect to religion . . . under the pretext of establishing tolerance, they allowed cults that were unknown among us, and at the same time attacked in every way the religion of the State's inhabitants." In pretending reform, the article alleged, the liberals aroused the conscience of the people in dissensions, "persecuted ecclesiastics of greater virtue, confiscated the property and revenues of the church, and more than a few times introduced the civil authority in matters that pertained solely to the internal regulation and discipline of the church itself." It derisively painted the liberals as both evil and naive, as anti-Christs and "babes in diapers." Bitter poems flourished, condemning the liberals as cowards before Carrera's lancers.[26]

Carrera charged that during ten oppressive years the village schools had disappeared, administration of justice had been neglected or entrusted to immoral and corrupt men, the welfare of the population had been abandoned, public buildings were falling into ruin, and the roads had become impassable. Now, he promised, just the opposite would happen, for "knowing our own interests, we shall work to improve our fortune and that of our children." He attacked the liberal tax and financial policies:

> The collection of exorbitant taxes to maintain a multitude of agents who worked to sustain the tyranny, and the poor use that has been made of a large part of the government revenue, not only have impoverished the state and exhausted its resources, but have burdened it with debts, so that we still must experience the ruinous consequences of so many years of suffering at the same time we double our efforts to give new life to the state under an administration formed by the free and direct vote of the people, scrupulously protecting the people's interests and zealously promoting their wealth and prosperity.[27]

In a further act, of questionable patriotism, Carrera accepted his promotion to brigadier general, but rejected the $2,000 annual salary that accompanied it. Thanking the assembly for the promotion, he said he needed no regular salary, and as long as he was in government service he would simply "request the small quantities that may be necessary for my expenses." In fact, Carrera in these days did not live extravagantly, although he made it clear that he expected the government to provide for all his desired expenditures.[28] A Quetzaltenango newspaper, apparently feeling secure in the independent state of Los Altos, attacked Carrera's action sarcastically:

> *Brigadier* Rafael Carrera has renounced the salary of 2,000 pesos annually which his compatriots and subordinates, the present governors of Guatemala, assigned him, indicating that he prefers to continue as up until now.

Wonderful! And what a good calculator is the *Brigadier*. To another dog with that bone, his Lordship thinks. What is 2,000 pesos for one who is master of lives and estates? A pittance, less than nothing. As up until now, he wants to remain the worthy patron of the nobles. And the government that owes its existence to him announces this flourish of patriotism with applause and great hand clapping. How has it served Carrera until now? Without salary.[29]

The continuing civil war in El Salvador involving Morazán against the alliance soon brought Carrera back to eastern Guatemala with a large force. His absence from the capital probably contributed to the first attempt to overthrow Rivera Paz, a movement that began in Antigua among more ardent liberals of the Barrundia faction. Led by Manuel Carrascosa, the rebels seized Antigua around noon on 3 September 1839. Heavy rains kept a force from the capital under Vicente Cruz from reaching the old city until the following evening, by which time the rebels had already fled. But on the fifth a detachment under a Captain Mejía, who had been sent from Chimaltenango, caught up with them at Patzún, killing eight, capturing one, and dispersing the rest.[30]

When Carrera returned he investigated the revolt personally. He officially concluded that the rebels had perhaps been "deceived or seduced by enemies of the State" and asked that their blood not be shed, making a "public testimony of humanity and clemency," for, he said, "nothing can consolidate more a just and popular government than generosity and moderation." Thus he called for an amnesty for the rebels, except for their leaders, who should be exiled or condemned to labor on public works. The assembly complied with this recommendation.[31]

Carrera's example in refusing his salary was followed by a general effort to reduce government expenses in the remainder of the year. Salaries of military and public officials were reduced from earlier levels.[32] Still, the government had to impose forced loans on the merchants and property holders before the year was out.[33] To emphasize Guatemala's independence from the federation, the assembly changed Rivera Paz's title to "president of the State of Guatemala" on 29 November in a long decree that detailed the attributes of the office. The assembly adjourned on 5 December, naming a provisional Council of Government to serve until it reconvened on 1 July 1840.[34] *El Tiempo*, the official government newspaper, noted that the session had "not been noisy, neither passion nor party spirit having any part in it." The government organ saw the assembly as simply enacting into law the will of the people. "It was necessary to restore them in their customs. It was indispensable to return to the principles."[35]

John Lloyd Stephens, who had only recently arrived and probably did not yet fully understand the circumstances, found this lack of passion objectionable: "The tone of debate was respectable," he wrote, "but calm and unimpassioned, from the entire absence of any opposition party."[36] Stephens met Carrera soon after. His impressions provide us with a first hand view of the caudillo at this point in his career:

> My interview with him was much more interesting than I had expected; so young, so humble in his origin, so destitute of early advantages, with honest impulses, perhaps, but ignorant, fanatic, sanguinary, and the slave of violent passions, wielding absolutely the physical force of the country, and that force entertaining a natural hatred of the whites. At parting he accompanied me to the door, and in the presence of his villanous soldiers made me a free offer of his services. I understood that I had the good fortune to make a favorable impression; and afterward, but, unluckily, during my absence, he called upon me in full dress and in state, which for him was an unusual thing.[37]

Events elsewhere in Central America occupied Carrera's attention during much of the latter half of 1839. Reluctant to involve Guatemalan troops in the civil war that continued over Morazán's efforts to preserve the federation, he was nonetheless apprehensive of threats to Guatemalan security. Morazán's victory at Espíritu Santo had gained the federal "ex-president" both time and support in El Salvador. Yet the alliance of Honduras, Nicaragua, Guatemala, and, subsequently, El Salvador against Morazán made his situation precarious. British expansionism on the Caribbean Coast further unsettled the international situation in the wake of the collapse of the federation.[38]

In July, however, Morazán regained power as head of the State of El Salvador. The Guatemalan government cautiously assured him that Carrera's troops, which were in Chiquimula, were not a threat to El Salvador and, in fact, were being pulled back to the capital.[39] But with Morazán again in control of El Salvador, Carrera had cause to worry. On 20 July, Francisco Ferrera, in command of the allied army at Nacaome, Honduras, warned Carrera that Morazán's election in El Salvador obligated the allies to "take measures . . . with resolution, firmness and persistence."[40] Ferrera then marched into El Salvador.

Morazán sought to check Guatemalan intervention by sending some of his forces to the Guatemalan border while he skirmished against Ferrera. This maneuver in turn prompted Carrera to move a force to Jutiapa.[41] The Salvadoran government formally protested on 6 September that Carrera's troops were in Salvadoran territory after it captured a courier. The Guatemalan government denied the allegation, but tension mounted.[42] In the meantime liberal federal forces under Honduran General Trinidad Cabañas defeated Honduran state forces at Cuesta Grande and took possession of Tegucigalpa on 7 September.[43]

On the same day the Guatemalan government responded to Salvadoran mobilization by reenforcing its troops on the Salvadoran frontier. Carrera issued a provocative summons to Salvadorans to rise against Morazán.[44] On 8 September an incident occurred near the border. Carrera took three hundred men into the Valley of Atescatempa when he learned that a hundred *Morazanistas* were at nearby Monte Verde. Later he received a report that these forces had entered Guatemala. At the head of a small reconnaissance patrol, Carrera came upon the Salvadorans in the middle of the night. In the skirmish that followed, a bullet struck Carrera in the chest, but the Guatemalans put their opponents to flight, without, they claimed, violating Salvadoran territory.[45]

The Guatemalan government on the tenth responded to a Salvadoran protest by saying that Guatemala desired only peace with El Salvador and that Carrera was the enemy only of General Morazán, not of the people or government of El Salvador. The solution, according to Guatemala, was for Morazán to resign.[46] Rivera Paz left the capital on 13 September to confer with Carrera in Jutiapa, where the general was recuperating.[47] His wound healed quickly, and he was back at the front by the twentieth.[48] Rivera Paz urged Carrera to exercise restraint and not to invade El Salvador, while at the same time his government maintained a strongly anti-Morazán official position. A circular from the Guatemalan government to the other states on 19 September emphasized that peace and prosperity had been restored in Guatemala along with good relations with all of the other states except El Salvador. In it Rivera Paz described "Ex-President" Morazán as the real threat to peace on the isthmus: "The remains of the federal [government], which seemed to have abandoned the idea of subjecting the states, is reanimated and threatens to conquer us again," he declared, accusing Morazán of using the state government of El Salvador to mount secretly a federal offensive.[49] Carrera himself on 20 September published a strongly worded appeal to his "Salvadoran brothers" to join him against "our common oppressors." He promised them that the people "would not be deprived of the fruits of their labors to maintain idlers and perverts!" He assured those who had resisted federal oppression and tyranny of his peaceful intentions. "I have taken up arms to defend my State and our Holy Religion, not to make war, as they have told you. You have seen that only out of respect for your territory have we not avenged the insult that was done to us on the 8th by those perverts who have been put among you to see if they can make us believe that you are our enemies." [50]

While this broadside aimed principally at rallying Guatemalan support for the inevitable struggle with Morazán, a general campaign for popular support against the federal forces seems to have been orchestrated in September 1839. Honduran President Francisco Zelaya issued an impassioned plea to his countrymen to oppose the Salvadoran invaders calling themselves *federales*.[51] And the commander of the allied forces, Francisco Ferrera, after occupying Suchitoto without resistance on 22 September, issued an audacious ultimatum to Morazán, challenging his right to the governorship of El Salvador and giving him twenty-four hours to surrender.[52]

Morazán faced serious problems within El Salvador as well, as an earthquake in San Salvador in September 1839 was followed by an anti-Morazán uprising. This forced Morazán to hasten back to San Salvador, where he restored order on 18 September.[53]

Chatfield in the meantime had lost all confidence in Morazán and had made the decision to support the allies with British gunboats if necessary.[54] The *Belize Advertiser* reflected the British position in its claim of 21 September that the majority of the inhabitants of Central America were opposed to the federation and that if Morazán could not conform to their views he should "retire to private life." [55]

Ferrera now marched boldly with twelve hundred troops into El Salvador, intending to enforce his ultimatum. Once more Morazán, with only half as many troops, stopped him, this time at San Pedro Perulapán on 25 September. Morazán's forces wounded Ferrera and at least one other senior officer, and captured eight officers and 250 soldiers. Morazán's force, by contrast, lost but a single officer and sixteen enlisted, with six officers and twenty-eight troops wounded. Moreover, the Salvadorans captured seven hundred rifles, a four-pounder cannon, and large amounts of ammunition and other military equipment, including Ferrera's sword and the personal correspondence of the Honduran and Nicaraguan commanders.[56] The defeat was a serious setback to the states' rights advocates and may have been decisive in persuading Carrera not to enter the struggle directly. Yet the fighting continued as Honduran forces managed to counterattack Morazán's army in small engagements during the weeks following their defeat at San Pedro.[57]

Morazán attempted to arrange a peace and made some headway with Nicaragua.[58] With Guatemala, his government rejected claims that Salvadoran forces had crossed the border and even questioned that Carrera had been wounded at all.[59] The Guatemalan government remained firm, called for a voluntary subscription to raise money for the army, and authorized Carrera on 21 October to "raise all the troops that he believes are necessary for the defense of the State and to borrow money in all the towns for the maintenance of the force, these loans to be secured by the government's revenues." It instructed Carrera to give receipts for all money or goods he acquired and such receipts would be recognized as debts of the state, to be paid "when the urgencies of the treasury cease."[60]

Despite the preparations for war against El Salvador, Carrera held back, concerned over Morazán's apparent resurgence after the battle of San Pedro and new victories by Cabañas in Honduras. In late November Carrera brought most of his force back to the capital, leaving small divisions at Jutiapa and Cuajiniquilapa under Colonel Figueroa.[61] The fall of the Nicaraguan government in early December was a further blow to the allied cause.[62] Carrera credited his army's defense against Salvadoran aggression for maintaining the Guatemalan peace and stability that had allowed the Constituent Assembly to accomplish so much. Yet he grew increasingly apprehensive over his allies' reverses in the neighboring states.[63]

Reassessing his strategy, he now decided to deal with the problem on his western flank. His proclamation to the troops said that the liberals had controlled only San Salvador and Cojutepeque and that the rest of the state of El Salvador was in anarchy, but that the "enemy" also still held Quetzaltenango, "buried in oppression and tyranny." These two points, San Salvador and Quetzaltenango, he told his soldiers "are the only obstacles that will delay the desired return to our homes." The State of Los Altos was not only allied with Morazán and the Guatemalan liberals, and as such a military threat on Guatemala's western flank, but the secession of those populous departments of the wesern highlands had deprived Guatemala of significant revenues.[64]

Los Altos was heavily populated by Indians, who to a large degree had continued to till their own soil and practice traditional customs in the cool highlands of western Guatemala. Regional resentment against dominance by Guatemala City had surfaced in the form of Indian revolts throughout the colonial period and during the Cortes of Cádiz, when the Quetzaltenango deputy, Father José Cleto Montiel, had called for a separate intendancy, bishopric, seminary, and audiencia.[65] The stormy years of the United Provinces increased sentiment for autonomy among political leaders in Quetzaltenango and although the Indians of the region were inherently conservative and generally proclerical, Ladino political leaders developed a strong liberal bias. The radical liberal state government of

Guatemala had moved to Quetzaltenango briefly in 1826 before being destroyed by a popular uprising there. Under the Gálvez administration there was resentment against the Guatemalan government for much the same reasons as in eastern Guatemala, but the leadership of the opposition remained in the hands of anti-Gálvez liberals rather than reactionaries. Los Altos Ladinos also felt a strong resentment against the conservative Guatemalan merchants who monopolized the trade and opposed development of a Pacific coast road and port to serve Los Altos's overseas commerce directly.[66] A Quetzaltenango newspaper in May of 1836 proposed that formation of a sixth state composed of Quetzaltenango, Totonicapán, Sololá, and Suchitepéquez, comprising more than two hundred thousand people, would provide both for greater liberty and better representation of regional interests. Quetzaltenango, the article argued, was a city capable of running a state and had experienced people to do so.[67]

The collapse of the Gálvez government thus led directly to Los Altos's secession from Guatemala on 2 February 1838. The Valenzuela government was unable to do anything about it, and the federal Congress recognized the sixth state on 5 June 1838 under a provisional junta composed of liberals Marcelo Molina Mata (1800–79), José M. Gálvez, and José A. Aguilar. General Agustín Guzmán commanded its army.[68] A Constituent Assembly, convened under the presidency of Miguel Larreinaga, in December at Totonicapán elected Molina, a distinguished jurist and a signer of Guatemala's 1821 Declaration of Independence, as governor of the State.[69] Molina addressed the convention on 27 December emphasizing the need for development of a port on the Pacific and Los Altos's close relations with the federal government in San Salvador.[70]

Guatemala's difficulties and Molina's alliance with Morazán enabled Los Altos to develop without outside interference throughout 1838 and 1839. Guzmán's forces played a significant role in checking Carrera in the latter part of 1838, leading to the Treaty of Rinconcito in December. Carrera's victory, however, and reverses to Morazán's forces jeopardized the new state's existence. On 31 May 1839 the state took action similar to that which the other states had done in declaring itself "sovereign, free and independent." It defined its territory and organization more fully, claiming Soconusco in addition to the departments of Sololá, Totonicapán, Huehuetenango, Suchitepéquez, and Quetzaltenango.[71] Official pronouncements of the Los Altos government reflected its apprehension over Carrera's intentions. In June 1839 the Los Altos leaders believed that when Carrera returned from Chiquimula it was to launch an invasion of Los Altos, and its assembly named commissioners to negotiate with the Guatemalan government, but the Guatemalans assured the federal government that Carrera had no intention of attacking Los Altos.[72]

Hardly reassured, Los Altos on 10 August signed the Treaty of Quetzaltenango with El Salvador as a check on Guatemalan pretensions. Los Altos ratified the document two days later, and Morazán ratified for El Salvador on 8 September. Los Altos joined with El Salvador in sharply denouncing British seizures on the Caribbean Coast, an item that contributed to Chatfield's increasing support of the anti-Morazán allies.[73]

Differences with Guatemala increased in correlation to Los Altos's closer relations with El Salvador. The Guatemala City merchants favored continued open trade with the other states and the Guatemalan government continued to allow Los Altos textiles to enter Guatemala without payment of tax.[74] Thus, the Guatemalans objected strenuously when on 18 July 1839 Los Altos established new tariff rates. The Guatemalan foreign minister protested formally on 2 August, denying the right of Los Altos to set its own tariffs. In this, Arriaga pointed out, he had the support of the British, French, and Belgian consuls in Guatemala.[75] A war of words was under way between the two states from July forward. *El Tiempo* accused Los Altos of having "established a political inquisition," of censuring mail, persecuting the clergy, and "circulating rumors, falsehoods and other cunning tricks" against Guatemala.[76] *El Popular*, the liberal voice of Quetzaltenango, accused the marqués de Aycinena and other members of "the family" of using Carrera to establish an ecclesiastical authority over the state.[77] Anti-Carrera jibes and letters filled its pages. Chatfield's role in the rapprochement between the English and Guatemalan governments also came in for attack, as for example the following:

> Carrera has been given a magnificent English uniform, including all the fine accouterments of an officer, a sword, helmet, barracks cap, brief case, horse trappings, etc. All adorned with English arms and insignias. We call the attention of Central Americans to this evidence which, together with the decree of the Constituent Assembly of that State which in a certain manner gives England [the territory] between the Hondo and the Javón, demonstrates sufficiently who is the person who has blown the fire of anarchy among us and indicates the designs that he has had in it.[78]

In an article entitled "Despotism of the Villains called Nobles," a diary reportedly written by one Leandro Marín documented the authoritarian rule being established by the Aycinenas, Pavóns, Piñols, and Vidaurres in Guatemala during the last days of July. The article was especially critical of Mariano Aycinena and "the savage Carrera."[79]

In fact, within Los Altos, there was growing restiveness among the Indians against the Molina government, especially against the continued head tax, which had not been abolished there. An uprising in the Indian village of Santa Catarina Ixtaguacán on 1 October 1839 was quickly put down, but other villages protested physically in the months following against both the taxation and land policies of the Los Altos government.[80]

By October 1839 the level of hostility between Guatemala and Los Altos had reached appreciable levels, and tension mounted with military movements in the area. Remnants of the abortive Antigua revolt of September, under Manuel Carrascosa, furthered the tension as they continued raiding in the departments of Sacatepéquez and Chimaltenango.[81] Rumors that General Guzmán was building an army at Sololá, with the intention of invading Guatemala, further fanned the flames.[82]

When Carrera returned from the Salvadoran front in late November, he began to make preparations to deal directly with Los Altos. Interception of a shipment of arms to Los Altos strenghtened his determination, and now British Consul Frederick Chatfield, having moved from San Salvador to Guatemala, worked actively with the Guatemalan government against Los Altos.[83] Reports of raids from Los Altos at Patzún and San Andrés hastened Carrera's preparations. He marched into the Verapaz on 6 December to provide for its security, raise troops, and collect armaments that had been stored there.[84]

While Carrera prepared for a military attack, the government pursued diplomatic avenues. On 18 December it pressured the Los Altos commissioner in Guatemala into signing a treaty of peace and friendship. This treaty offered peace, but demanded that Los Altos turn over the rifles that Carrera had delivered to Guzmán in January 1839 under the terms of the Treaty of Rinconcito. Guatemala promptly ratified the treaty on 23 December and gave Los Altos one month from that date to ratify. It was, in effect, an ultimatum.[85] Guatemala then pursued a coldly calculated timetable to bring down the Los Altos government. On the twenty-seventh, Carrera published a proclamation calling on the Indians of Los Altos to rebel against the Quetzaltenango government,[86] and in early January 1840 the Guatemalan government declared that there was widespread insurgency in Los Altos against its authorities "for the same reasons that had produced the uprisings among the peoples of this state." It suggested that the people of Los Altos now looked to General Carrera as their liberator from the oppression of the liberals, and claimed it had received a "great number of petitions and representations" to this effect.[87] There is no evidence in the Guatemalan archives of such petitions.

At noon on 20 January 1840, Carrera marched westward out of the capital with a thousand troops to wait on the Los Altos border for ratification of the treaty and delivery of the rifles.[88] That morning Carrera had published a proclamation justifying his war against Los Altos and El Salvador, claiming that his enemies had refused to cease their attacks on Guatemala. He appealed to the citizens of the other states to rise against the liberals in El Salvador and Los Altos. Praising the restoration of peace, confidence, security, liberty, and human rights in Guatemala, in contrast to the slavery he claimed existed in the states loyal to Morazán, he warned that the "oppressors of the Salvadorans were seated on a volcano that would soon explode."[89] Carrera dispatched Vicente Cruz to Jutiapa with another division, in case "El Salvador carried out its announced invasion."[90]

The Los Altos government sent an urgent message to Morazán, a communiqué that Carrera's force intercepted.[91] On the twenty-second General Guzmán published his own proclamation in Quetzaltenango, declaring war on Guatemala and warning that General Morazán would soon be marching on Guatemala City. Carrera's cavalry was in place by 23 January, when the ratification deadline expired. On the twenty-fourth he claimed that Los Altos forces from Godines had fired on his reconnaissance patrols. On the twenty-fifth he invaded Los Altos and faced Guzmán's army of six hundred near Sololá. The next day Carrera's forces routed the Guzmán force with a savage attack that achieved complete victory and captured the Los Altos general. Meanwhile, on the Pacific plain, General Doroteo Monterrosa invaded Suchitepéquez, and after suffering some initial setbacks, he defeated the Los Altos force under Colonel Antonio Corzo there on 28 January. Already faced with certain defeat, the government in Quetzaltenango collapsed before an uprising of the people, as town after town declared for Carrera. The Los Altos government sued for peace at 2:00 A.M. on the twenty-seventh. Carrera claimed to have lost but a single sergeant in the campaign.[92]

At mid day on Wednesday, 29 January, Carrera entered Quetzaltenango at the head of an army of two thousand. A large and enthusiastic crowd, just as in Sololá the day before, greeted the liberators.[93] Carrera gave the remaining Los Altos forces three days to surrender and turn in their arms, assuring the safety of their persons and property.[94]

Carrera assured the people of Los Altos that he had come "not in thirst of blood or riches, nor with a view of power or personal enhancement, but with the desire of destroying the barbaric oppression in which those calling themselves liberal patriots have held you," and in response "to the clamor of many of you who have sought the protection of my arms." He reiterated the social and economic goals of the revolution, bitterly attacking "the despot Morazán and his tyranny." He said the alliance of Guatemala, Honduras, Nicaragua, and Costa Rica was bearing fruit, and he had come to Los Altos to provide security and justice, but also to seek vengeance against the cowardly liberals, who had now evaporated into the hills when confronted by his valiant men. He promised no more "unjust and violent taxes on the peoples who obey Guatemala. They will pay no more than absolutely necessary, which is all that the government demands." There would, he also assured, be no more persecutions of the Catholic clergy, and "the religion which the false liberals have destroyed will be restored."[95]

In fact, Los Altos was dealt with as a conquered province of Guatemala, a condition that to some extent would remain throughout the Carrera era, contributing to resentment and liberal resurgence there as the center of the rebellion that succeeded in 1871. The Guatemalan government formally took Los Altos under its protection on 26 February 1840 and a decree was ratified on 13 August by the Constituent Assembly. In addition to the authority of corregidores appointed from Guatemala for the rest of the state, the corregidor of Quetzaltenango henceforth served as commandant general and superintendent of Los Altos, emphasizing a continued Guatemalan military rule over the rebellious departments.[96]

By 9 February, Carrera had put Los Altos, in his words, "back on the track to progress." Morazán now remained, in his view, the only obstacle to peace on the isthmus. Although he would have liked to have remained in Quetzaltenango to see the job of reorganization of those departments completed, he told the inhabitants in a farewell proclamation, other demands forced him to leave. "I leave you a garrison sufficient to keep order and to punish those who try to disturb it." He reminded them that their taxes had been reduced and the hated head tax had been removed, and "although you will pay sales and other taxes to which you are accustomed, no longer will there be those that they have been collecting here nor those that were collected in the time of Gálvez in Guatemala."[97]

News of Carrera's swift victory in Los Altos had been greeted with rejoicing in the capital. President Rivera Paz proclaimed the good news on 5 February, praising Carrera as the "protector" of Los Altos and then turning to blast the continued oppression in El Salvador, where the Morazán government, according to Rivera Paz, was "not only antagonizing all classes of the society, not only ruining their common resources and interests, blaspheming the Religion and attacking its Ministers, but attacking the foreigners residing in our country and offending brutally and bruskly public agents as would not even be done in Berber countries, thus compromising the credit and security of the States." He warned that Morazán's troops were now stationed on the frontier planning "to repeat in Guatemala the horrible crimes of 1829."[98]

Other presidential decrees heaped honors and medals on Carrera and his army.[99] A tumultuous welcome awaited them when they marched into the capital at noon on 17 February beneath triumphal arches decked with flags and flowers. Bands played. More than a hundred prisoners—tied together with rope and including General Guzmán, who was tied backwards on a mule—were paraded with the troops through the city, pelted with rocks and blows of machetes by the excited throng. Rivera Paz and Arriaga, along with officers of the Constituent Assembly, rode alongside Carrera in what John Lloyd Stephens witnessed as a "disgraceful triumph."[100]

A showdown between Morazán and Carrera now became inevitable. Morazán had hoped to take Guatemala while Carrera was in Los Altos, but Carrera's rapid victory had foiled that plan. Massing their troops at Ahuachapán, federal generals Morazán and Carlos Salazar received the double bad news of Carrera's victory in Los Altos and the defeat of Trinidad Cabañas's division by a combined Honduran-Nicaraguan army at El Potrero on 31 January.[101] To counter the Salvadoran threat to eastern Guatemala, on 5 February Vicente Cruz moved eight hundred troops to Jalpatagua.[102] Morazán now was desperate. He recognized that his only hope was to defeat Carrera, and he launched an offensive, combined with a campaign of terror and violence. His agents collected forced loans on property holders to raise money for the campaign, promising 10 percent annual interest on the loans.[103] Terror and hatred were characteristic on both sides. Slogans of death and bitterness filled the presses. Poems attacking the enemy reflected the tone of the conflict, such as the following anti-Morazanist ditty that appeared after Father Mariano Durán was shot for inciting peasants against the federal authorities:

> The criminal Morazán,
> The Nero, the Diocletian,
> The tyrannical assassin
> Of the innocent Durán
> Against whom are praying
> To heaven for just vengeance
> So many august victims
> That his black heart
> Has sacrificed
> With unjust felonies.[104]

Carrera, Ferrera, and the conservatives in Guatemala were painted in equally black terms by the liberals.

On 10 March 1840 the government authorized Carrera to invade El Salvador should Salvadoran forces cross the border.[105] Two days later Morazán entered Guatemala with an army of fifteen hundred. Carrera left Vicente Cruz in charge of the capital with about eight hundred men, well armed, and dug in. Carrera then withdrew with about a thousand troops to the Acetuno Plantation, about five miles from the capital.[106] Rivera Paz declared a state of siege on 16 March and on the night of the seventeenth Morazán reached the outskirts of the capital. Cruz called upon the citizens to support their "holy cause."[107]

Carrera's plan was to catch Morazán between Cruz's defenders and his own force, which would counterattack from Acetuno. But Morazán's attack, beginning at 3:00 A.M., caught both him and Cruz off guard, and Cruz's force fell back more quickly than anticipated, amid bloody street fighting. Morazán had control of most of the city before the morning was over. He freed General Guzmán and at least forty-three other liberal prisoners from the city's jails and took up defensive positions as Carrera's troops surrounded the capital. On the nineteenth Carrera stormed into the city. Savage fighting throughout the day ended in total Guatemalan victory, Morazán losing more than a thousand men killed, wounded, or captured, including many of his officers. Morazán and less than four hundred of his force managed to fight through Carrera's lines and straggle back to El Salvador.[108]

On 24 March 1840 the governor of Nicaragua, Tomás Valladares, pronounced against Morazán and invaded El Salvador, honoring the treaty of alliance with Guatemala.[109] Honduran and Guatemalan troops joined in the chase.[110] Morazán sailed from La Libertad on 5 April 1840, his officers still making efforts to enlist new support in El Salvador and Honduras.[111] He and the liberals accompanying him applied for asylum in Costa Rica, but the moderately conservative government of Braulio Carrillo denied the request for most, not even allowing Morazán and his chief officers to cross Costa Rica to take ship at Matina.[112] Morazán went on to Panama and later to Perú. He would return to Central America once more to stir the embers of the liberal-conservative fire.

In Guatemala the government made 19 March a state holiday and heaped praise and rewards on Carrera, promoting him to Lieutenant General on 22 March.[113] In the meantime, news of Morazán's initial victory on 18 March in Guatemala reached Quetzaltenango and emboldened the liberals there to attempt to seize control again. They once more declared their independence and sent a letter of congratulation to Morazán. Carrera, upon hearing of the revolt, marched immediately with his army to Quetzaltenango, where he restored Guatemalan authority and summarily executed Roberto Molina (1803–40) (Marcelo Molina's brother) and seventeen other liberal leaders in the main plaza, an act that was not soon forgotten in Quetzaltenango.[114]

Carrera was now undisputed master of Guatemala. Rivera Paz exercised power only at Carrera's pleasure and at times was clearly uncomfortable in the position. Terror reigned in the capital, as residents feared further reprisals by Carrera against anyone even remotely associated with Morazán, especially after the news of the "Quetzaltenango massacre." Some liberals left the country, although there was nothing comparable to the general exile of conservatives that Morazán had forced in 1829. Passports without Carrera's endorsement were worthless. Stephens provides a lucid description of his last interview with Carrera, commenting on Carrera's pride in signing his name. Stephens at this point judged Carrera as "honest, and if he knew how and could curb his passions, he would do more good for Central America than any other man in it."[115]

With Los Altos subjugated, order restored in Guatemala, and Morazán driven out of El Salvador, a peace conference convened in April 1840. Reflecting the totality of Carrera's prestige and power, now the government named him and his adviser Joaquín Durán as Guatemalan commissioners to meet with the delegates of the other states in San Salvador to "consolidate the peace in Central America and lay the foundations for reorganization of the Republic."[116] Antonio José Cañas had taken over the government of El Salvador following Morazán's departure. Carrera entered El Salvador with a substantial military force in early May, sending messages ahead to San Salvador of his "peaceful mission."[117] Cañas's government took every measure to avoid a clash and treated the Guatemalans with full respect when they entered the Salvadoran capital at noon on 10 May, sending word that peace talks could begin at Carrera's pleasure.[118] Three days later the commissioners signed a treaty, providing for reorganization of the Salvadoran government without any Morazanistas. Even Morazanista deserters were prohibited from serving in the government without Guatemalan permission. The treaty also provided for certain artillery reportedly taken from Guatemala by Morazán to be turned over to the Guatemalan army, and for an exchange of prisoners. Carrera imposed General Francisco Malespín (1790–1846) as military commander in El Salvador, and this Guatemalan officer dominated El Salvador as Carrera's puppet for several years.[119]

Carrera soon withdrew, but not before exacting heavy reparations, demanding another forced loan on Salvadoran property holders and merchants to cover the expenses of his army. Conservatives now reigned in both states, and the appointment of the ultraconservative Guatemalan priest,

Jorge Viteri y Ungo, as bishop of El Salvador furthered the conservative cause there.[120]

Carrera returned to Guatemala via Ahuachapán, where he signed passports for those Salvadoran troops wishing to go into exile in Mexico. He returned to the Guatemalan capital in time for the annual Corpus Christi celebration in June, dampened in 1840 by heavy rains.[121]

Morazán, meanwhile, found his way to David, Chiriquí, in the New Granadian province of Panamá. From there he wrote bitterly to his illegitimate son, Esteban:

> Carrera, who has no more worth or talent than a Chieftain of savages, and who appeared using the terrible cholera epidemic that afflicted the inhabitants of our republic, persuading the ignorant people that the Government poisoned the water, has been protected alternatively by the parties to advance their own views. First those who led the opinion in the State of Guatemala protected his entry into that city to depose Dr. Gálvez and then those who have written so much against this fact and painted Carrera in his true colors, presenting him as one of those monsters that are born and die with revolution, are today the ones that praise him for having made way over thousands of victims assassinated by his own hand to establish the Theocratic Government that four nobles without titles, without talent, and without virtue together with a handful of fanatics wish to establish in Central America.[122]

His bitterness festered in exile while through correspondence he recouped his financial affairs and tried to organize resistance. A year later he issued a biting manifesto from David, viciously attacking Carrera and calling upon the inhabitants of Central America to rise up against the conservatives.[123]

In late August 1841, he left David and sailed along with Trinidad Cabañas and other liberal leaders to Lima, where he received aid, including $20,000 from General Pedro Bermúdez. With these funds Morazán chartered the brig *Cruzador* from its owner, Robert Marshall, and, after fitting it out with armaments in early January of 1842, he sailed for Central America, returning first to Chiriquí and then arriving at La Libertad, El Salvador, on 15 February 1842.[124] This opened a new and final chapter in Morazán's career, to which we shall return in a later chapter.

For the time being the liberal threat was gone. Conservatives controlled all five states. Carrera, the peasant, the savage, the terror of 1837 and 1838, was now the exalted darling of a reaction that put a virtual end to liberalism in Guatemala for thirty years. Carrera would wield the military power, but the elite would now erect a new political structure to restore the social protection and economic privilege that had been lost with independence.

CHAPTER SIX

The Caudillo

Although caudillismo always leads to despotism and often to terror, it is still not possible to condemn outright its role in the national evolution of Spanish American countries. Caudillismo is a general social phenomenon, the result of social structures and ideologies that prevailed in all the Spanish American countries at one time, although each caudillo is a personality distinct from all the others. Thus it would be useless to sketch the portrait of the typical caudillo and paint it black or white. Latin America, which has had so many of them, has had all types. Different in their ideologies—progressive or reactionary—wise men or illiterates, some caudillos were agents of progress for their countries, others ruined them: still others, the great number perhaps, did their countries a great deal of harm but at the same time a little bit of good.[1]

The preceding statement by Jacques Lambert has particular relevance for Central America in the 1840s, a decade that was neither peaceful nor orderly, despite the promises of the conservative governments that won power following the collapse of the United Provinces. Conservatives remonstrated that this was because Morazán and his liberal allies continued to struggle violently to regain power, keeping the region in nearly constant turmoil. For the creole elite, it was a period of difficult adjustment to the emergence of popular caudillos, among whom Rafael Carrera was the most conspicuous, but certainly not the only example. The breakdown of federal authority contributed to a decentralizing trend, not only in terms of the emergence of stronger state governments exercising sovereignty, but also in terms of local authoritarian military chiefs and landholders who controlled regions either individually or collectively, through accommodations with the caudillos. Political anarchy and opportunism characterized most of the decade. Frequent efforts to restore the union floundered and the individual states drifted toward permanent status as sovereign republics.[2]

In Guatemala Rafael Carrera wielded the power in a highly personal fashion, yet he also represented the downtrodden peasants and Indians of the country against the upper class, especially against their political and economic innovations that had touched these masses. While an alliance with the conservative, clerical element led by Juan José Aycinena and other members of his clan had apparently brought Carrera under rein and restored elite rule, there was still a wide gulf of suspicion and mistrust between Carrera and the elite. It would take a decade for the alliance of the conservative elite and Carrera to become firmly established.[3] Carrera's political base remained the peasantry, who made up his ragged, ill-equipped army and provided a reserve of manpower to deal with crises, foreign or domestic. As elsewhere in Latin America, the arming of the lower classes in the period during and immediately following independence created a vast new political power that disrupted the plans of the creoles who had inherited Iberian power.[4]

Carrera was one of several notable conservative dictators of Latin America during the mid nineteenth century. Others included Juan Manuel Rosas of the Argentine Confederation, Gabriel García Moreno of Ecuador, and Antonio José Páez of Venezuela. Although each differed in peculiar ways, they all led violent reactions against liberalism and, after a period of anarchy, established strong conservative regimes restoring Hispanic institutions and a peace and order reminiscent of the colonial era. Diego Portales's Chile also had some of the same characteristics. A visitor in 1844 described Carrera's army in the following terms:

> The soldiers are a most ill-looking set of ruffians, whose appearance in the streets of London would ensure them a place in the watch-house. Carrera has adopted the British colour (scarlet) for clothing his troops, but the red jackets are few in number, and only put on upon feast days, and other extraordinary occasions; and even then, the strange figures of the men, all clothed in jackets of one size, none of which of course fit the wearer, make them look like a band of robbers who had dressed themselves in stolen clothes. The officers dress themselves, according to fancy, in strange nondescript uniforms, the most respectable resembling English footmen out of place.[5]

Even Carrera's English uniform did not fit well, according to Robert Dunlop: "He resembles a scarecrow with a coat pinned on. The dress of an

Indian chief would look natural upon him, but an European uniform is most ridiculous."[6]

Following the victory over Morazán, Rivera Paz—in collaboration with the Aycinenas, Piñols, Batres, and Pavóns—supervised reorganization of church and state, while Carrera was the actual arbiter of the country. Sometimes brutal, sometimes generous, he insisted on justice for the forgotten people in the countryside. Examples of his protection of the peasants circulated widely, along with accounts of atrocities against his enemies. The historian Antonio Batres Jáuregui related a story told to him by his father, Pedro Batres Nájera, a young man when Carrera took Guatemala City in 1839. Don Pedro had gone to the military headquarters to inquire regarding five mules the army had taken from his family's hacienda. Soldiers politely directed Batres to the caudillo, who was sitting on a staircase putting together his rifle.

"What can I do for you?" Carrera asked.

Batres explained, and Carrera promptly ordered his soldiers to note the brand on Batres's mules and to have them returned within three days. To the young man's thanks, Carrera responded: "Tell your father that from now on he may count on what is his, for I have not come here to rob, as my enemies say. Whatever you need, come to me, and my orders will be carried out."

The mules were delivered two days later.[7]

Incidents such as this cemented his relationship with the conservative landholders and ranchers. At the same time, he insisted on preservation of the communal lands of the peasants, the true base of his power. The conservative elite cooperated with Carrera in restoring colonial protection for the indigenous population. His policy toward the Indian differed significantly from the exploitive liberal attempt to westernize the Indian by removing the paternalistic protection of the colonial era.

The liberals had leaned heavily on the advice of Jeremy Bentham who, in spite of his great interest in Spanish America, virtually ignored the great mass of Indians. In his support of the Spanish American representation in the Spanish Cortes in 1821, for example, Bentham was unconcerned that the Indians were excluded from the population count on which representation would be based.[8] The conservatives, on the other hand, presented themselves as following in the tradition of Bartolomé de las Casas, the sixteenth-century Dominican priest who defended the Indians against the excesses of the Spanish conquest in Guatemala. Carrera, from the start of his revolution, took an active interest in peasant complaints. On 23 February 1838, for example, he named a committee to deal with complaints of peasants on the lands of several large hacendados.[9] On 14 July 1839 he published a strong attack on liberal social policy.[10] The assembly responded with the code mentioned in the last chapter to protect Indian interests. While this code treated them as minors, its proponents argued that it excused them from many responsibilities and, through their community funds, it provided for an elementary school in each village and for the building and maintenance of their churches and public buildings.[11]

This paternalistic attitude of the conservative creoles denied equality to the Indians, and the notion that the Indian lived well and was happy in his poverty was one of the most deeply rooted of their prejudices.[12] Yet it is undeniable that the Indians suffered greatly following the liberal revolution of 1829, and under Carrera's rule their lot generally improved. The restoration of the clerical power had important benefits for them, and the restoration of the "Laws of the Indies" protected their lands and customs, gave them security in legal matters, protection from forced labor without pay, and, of course, removed the direct head tax. Moreover, Indian villages regained some control over their affairs politically and economically.[13]

The government kept Carrera informed of its actions to defend and protect native ejidos and communal lands. Carrera often personally investigated peasant complaints and mediated land disputes himself.[14] Carrera pressured clergy as well as the government on behalf of Indian interests, as on 9 July 1840, when he informed the government that certain high church officials were neglecting the Indians' needs.[15] He also toured the country to look after the interests of the peasants, and upon his return from these visits made specific recommendations to the government to remedy grievances and complaints and to improve rural living conditions. After such a tour in the Chiquimula region in 1846, for example, he recommended the development of a much-needed water and irrigation system in and around Zacapa.[16]

An episode soon after he took the capital in 1839 reflected Carrera's personal power with both church and state. His mother, who had become a well-known vendor in the market of the capital, died in 1839. Carrera immediately requested that the prohibition against burials inside of churches, a measure Gálvez had enacted in response to the cholera epidemic, be lifted so that his mother might be buried in the Church of La Merced.[17] Burial within the major churches of the capital traditionally had been reserved for members of the elite, but the government quickly acceded to the request and arranged a grand funeral, attended by the leading citizens as well as throngs of pro-Carrera rabble.[18] This event was not merely a placating of Carrera's personal whim, which would certainly have been acceded to in any case, but it also incorporated the religious opposition to the prohibition of church burials.

Carrera enjoyed wide mass support, and fear of his peasant army gave him great power. Enthusiasm for him extended beyond Guatemala into Honduras and the other states. He had a near-divine image among the common people, who referred to him as "Angel" or "Son of God," as myths of superhuman qualities arose around the caudillo. Carrera did nothing to discourage this adulation.[19]

Despite refusing his salary, Carrera's personal finances prospered during the years following the revolution. The government imposed loans on property holders and merchants to provide for his "expenses" and for large indemnities in compensation for claimed damages to his properties during the war. Moreover, "grateful" communities assigned him the rents from plots within their community lands and Carrera and his family acquired other lands outright from the public domain or from confiscations. Carrera's wife, Petrona, was astute at managing these assets as they amassed considerable wealth during the period before he formally took the presidency in 1844.[20]

Officers loyal to Carrera were named as corregidores in each department, and they ruled as local dictators with the force of Carrera's prestige and power behind them. The Constituent Assembly, with Carrera's portrait hanging in its chambers alongside that of President Rivera Paz, dutifully fulfilled his every wish. When he offered his resignation from command in August 1840, they urged him to reconsider, declaring that his service was necessary to maintain "the confidence of the people" and that he must "consider himself as one of the greatest sustainers of the government, the courts, and other authorities, whose existence is indispensable for the good order and general welfare." Francisco Aguirre and Mariano Aycinena delivered this resolution to Carrera in the midst of a gala party Carrera gave for his officers on 17 August. That the resignation was sincere is doubtful in any case, and Carrera now withdrew it and assumed even greater power. In October the assembly restored the military fuero, which the liberals had abolished piecemeal between 1834 and 1837. Additional decrees bestowed additional funding and privileges on the military.[21]

Carrera's power reached a new high when, at the end of October 1840, the assembly recessed until the following June and allowed Rivera Paz to separate himself temporarily from the executive power during the assembly's recess. The assembly named a Council of Government, headed by General Carrera, to rule in the interim.[22]

Rivera Paz soon resumed his duties and Carrera did not actually gov-

ern the country during these last months of 1840. Rather, he made a visit
to Mita and upon returning presented a report to the government on the
problems and needs of those communities. He said the department lacked
competent judges and other public officials, with resulting abandonment
of many municipal courts. He blamed the lack of justice and uniform application of the law for widespread popular discontent and discord in the
interior. Disputes over lands and *ejidos* also caused trouble, and he mentioned specific conflicts in Jalapa. He recommended that surveyors be sent
who would be paid by the government to adjudicate claims fairly, rather
than by one side or the other as had been the custom. Whole communities
had been abandoned or decimated during the revolution, leaving many
poor widows and orphans. These needed help in rebuilding their homes
and in returning to their own villages. Crime remained a problem, and
Carrera noted the dearth of jails and prisons. In some towns no one could
read, much less write, making it urgent that teachers be sent at least to the
larger towns that could afford one. Elsewhere, Carrera demanded, parish
priests should be charged with primary instruction along with religious
education. In the villages where formal instruction was not possible, at
least one child should be sent to the capital to be taught to read, and after
two years replaced by others. He also noted the shortage of priests, "the
teachers and moralizers of the people," and he declared that it be an urgent
priority of the government to provide priests. Finally, he acknowledged
that public revenues had suffered seriously because of the defection of those
who managed them and because of low productivity in the department.

Father Basilio Zeceña, minister of gobernación, responded to Carrera's
report on 30 November. He readily acknowledged the importance of Mita,
for "those peoples . . . were the first in coming to the aid of your glorious pronunciamento against the regime of injustice and violence," and he
promised that the new corregidor, Colonel Vicente Cruz, would be leaving
immediately for Mita with instructions to implement Carrera's wishes.
The minister blamed the confusion and problems over lands on the liberal regime, and he indicated that the government had already begun to
follow exactly the procedures that Carrera had proposed, that is, sending
disinterested surveyors to resolve the disputes fairly. Zeceña also acknowledged the shortage of priests, but assured the general that the ecclesiastical
authorities were actively working to provide curates for all parishes.[23]

It was a time of violence and savagery, by no means unique in Guatemalan history, and the zeal of Carrera's forces was matched at times by the
bitterness of his enemies. One Sunday evening in August 1841, as Carrera
walked with Colonel Mariano Alvarez after a night on the town, a marimba

player by the name of José María "Chepillo" Andrade leapt from a dark corner and buried his dagger in Carrera's side. Alvarez quickly drew his sword and ran it through the assailant. Persons arriving on the scene helped carry the caudillo to his house, less than two hundred yards away. The wound was deep, but Carrera's physician, Chico Aguilar, and the surgeon general, Quirino Flores, stopped the bleeding and dressed the wound, leaving Doña Petrona with orders to keep the general perfectly still.

On the following morning Father Jorge Viteri y Ungo (1802–53), the principal government minister at this point, ordered a thorough investigation into the movements of Andrade on the previous day in an effort to identify everyone with whom he had spoken. He also issued an order over President Rivera Paz's signature that Andrade's body be brought to the central plaza. There General Monterrosa's troops quartered the cadaver and displayed the parts at the four gates of the city as an example to would-be assassins. Protests of indignation at this act of savagery from other clergy and members of the Guatemalan elite soon led Carrera, who claimed he was unaware of the act, to order the dismembered body taken down and buried, but the incident was long cited by the liberals as an example of Carrera's barbarity.

Ignoring the advice of his physicians and family, Carrera on the following Tuesday evening mounted his horse and rode through the streets, amid the cheers of soldiers and well-wishers and the tolling of church bells. Although the wound reopened and bled profusely, the general's youth and good health allowed him to recover quickly. Some wondered, quietly of course, if the wound was so serious as described by Viteri. The official accounts, meanwhile, charged that Andrade had acted as an agent of Salvadoran enemies.[24]

Public adulation was heaped on Carrera from 1840 until after his death in public displays and ceremonies at regular intervals. His birthday, 24 October, was always a major holiday, as public offices closed, bands played, and fireworks illuminated the evening sky over the Sagrario Plaza in front of his house.[25] In the departments, local chieftains were brought into Carrera's machine with opportunities for power and economic gain (but also with public manifestations of the General's appreciation of them, such as the silver medals that Carrera had the mint make up for local governors in July of 1841, with the arms of the state on one side and the figure of Carrera on the reverse along with the inscription, "RAFAEL CARRERA, LIEUTENANT GENERAL, TO THE GOVERNORS FOR YOUR SERVICES."[26]

The official press praised the peace, security, and order that Carrera had brought the country beginning in 1839. Liberal historians have argued for a century that it was a peace enforced by terror and brutality and that life and property were secure only for those close to the center of power. While liberals may have exaggerated their charges, in the manner of most Latin American oppositions, there is plenty of evidence that Guatemala in the 1840s was neither so peaceful nor secure as the government claimed. In fact, the state quickly settled into a period of political and economic stagnation that encouraged crime and lawlessness. A report from the new corregidor of Chiquimula, Francisco Cáscara, in January of 1840 contained the customary assurances that all was quiet and secure, but it went on to point out that the end of the head tax and other taxes had left the government without funds for economic development, the establishment of schools, "or other desirable things." Some public officials were not paid punctually, he admitted, and administration of justice lacked the necessary "activity and energy." But Cáscara assured the government minister that the military would "maintain personal security and the property of the citizens."[27]

Similarly, the corregidor of Chimaltenango praised the public tranquility that reigned "with few exceptions," assuring the minister of government and justice that criminals had been dealt with accordingly and noting "a considerable improvement of the population" since the new government had taken over. He acknowledged that public drunkenness had become a major problem, "but punishments have been meted out and the situation is improved, although it is still a major problem in Patzún." A new governor, recently appointed there and respected, he said, by both Ladinos and Indians, "should soon have the situation in hand." He was more sanguine about the economic situation, noting the increase in road building.[28]

Foreign visitors wrote more candidly of the situation. Frederick Crowe, for example, said that murders and assassinations were "matters of daily occurrence in Central America. They are so frequent as to excite scarcely any attention, and no signs of feeling whatever, where there is not a special interest in the parties concerned. Taught by the example of the Spaniard," he added, "every native wears in his belt a large sharp-pointed knife—most frequently of British manufacture—which is encased in a leathern sheath, more or less ornamented."[29]

Enemies of the regime accused Carrera of lawless behavior and of having no respect for government authority. Rivera Paz issued a proclamation in January 1840 specifically denying such charges and assuring that, to the contrary, he was obliged to publicly testify "to the fidelity with which this Chief responds to the confidence of the people." Rivera Paz warned that had Carrera "not obeyed the orders of the government, perhaps those ene-

mies of the State would not exist today." Carrera, said Rivera Paz, far from
disobeying the laws, had in fact restored legitimate authority and warned
enemies of the state that the "people will respect the law and authority so
long as it is just and does not oppress them."[30] It was clear who was the law!

Beyond Guatemala Carrera maintained a watchful eye on events in the
adjacent states. In Honduras, his ally Francisco Ferrera dominated until
1847. Carrera's man in El Salvador was Francisco Malespín. When liberal
resurgence appeared to threaten the government of Antonio José Cañas in
September 1840, Malespín, in command of the army, removed Cañas. His
legal successor, Norberto Ramírez, lasted only until the following January,
when he resigned over differences with Malespín. The Salvadoran assembly
then elected Juan Lindo, a moderate acceptable to conservative interests,
but Malespín continued to wield the real power in that state.[31]

Foreign pressures became very great on Guatemala during the years
following the breakup of the federation. The British, French, and Mexicans especially presented strong challenges. Great Britain, still represented
by the strong-willed Frederick Chatfield, sought satisfaction of claims by
British bondholders and pursued with gunboat diplomacy an aggressive
policy that bore the marks of territorial expansionism as well as commercial
imperialism. British seizure of the Bay Islands in 1839 touched off a storm
of anti-British protest on the isthmus, as did Chatfield's occasional use of
British naval force on the Pacific coast. Britain was establishing a protectorate all along the Mosquito Coast, and in Guatemala, after the feeling that
had developed against the English colonization scheme, anti-British sentiment ran high. Chatfield skillfully courted the conservative governments
in the several states once it became clear that Morazán's chances for survival
were slim, and from late 1839 forward more amicable relations between
Great Britain and Guatemala began to develop.[32]

Guatemala protested the British imperialism and reasserted its claim to
the Honduran coast, yet in the end the Guatemalans failed to take decisive
action against the British, as Chatfield laid the groundwork for a client
relationship between Great Britain and the Carrera regime that would last
for thirty years. Carrera's revolution had voiced a strongly anti-English
tone, but, once in power, the caudillo proved to be more reasonable. As one
English observer put it, "Although the war cry of his party was death to
strangers, he is now remarkably civil to all he meets."[33] The U.S. representative, who arrived in Guatemala on 3 December 1839, already had noted
that "at this time he could hardly be recognized as the same man who, less
than two years before, had entered Guatimala with a horde of wild Indians, proclaiming death to strangers. Indeed," Stephens elaborated, "in no

particular had he changed more than in his opinion of foreigners, a happy illustration of the effect of personal intercourse in breaking down prejudices against individuals or classes."[34]

A small but influential group of foreign merchants—notably George Skinner, William Hall, and Carlos Klée—in collaboration with Chatfield and the Belizean merchant houses linked Guatemalan commerce closely with Great Britain.[35] The colonizing efforts of the Eastern Coast of Central America Commercial and Agricultural Company, on the other hand, had been directly opposed by Carrera, and he continued to view it with distrust.[36] The Guatemalan government granted the English company an extension for its development of the port of Santo Tomás in January 1839,[37] and the company made an effort to colonize that port and an interior colony at Abbotsville, near the Río Polochic, in 1839 and 1840. Yet the grandiose hopes of the company's promoters failed to overcome the obstacles of climate and geography in the Caribbean lowlands. The colony floundered and anti-British sentiment aggravated by British actions on the Mosquito Coast—especially the takeover of San Juan del Norte (Greytown) by Belize Superintendent Alexander MacDonald in 1841—led the Guatemalan government to cancel the English concession. In the meantime, the English had sold much of the concession to a Belgian colonization company.[38]

Carrera strongly opposed all the foreign colonization programs, but Juan José Aycinena, M. F. Pavón, and other conservative members of the elite recognized the benefits of development of the lowlands and saw certain advantages in the Belgian over the English scheme. The Belgians were Catholic and represented a less threatening imperial power (although subsequent Belgian imperialism in Africa might have changed their minds on that score). The Belgian company appeared more responsible than had the English. Santos Carrera warned the Guatemalan foreign minister that General Carrera opposed granting the concession to the Belgians, saying that "the people would see the foundation of a new foreign colony as the first link in the chains of slavery."[39] Carrera had been prepared to lead an expeditionary force against any foreign colonists, yet the Guatemalan government approved the Belgian grant after rejecting another extension to the English. Obviously, Carrera had changed his mind, apparently influenced by bribes, which the Belgian company agents sprinkled among Guatemalan officials.[40] In any event, immediately after approval of the Belgian contract, the Guatemalan government awarded Carrera a land grant of a hundred caballerías adjacent to Santo Tomás on the North Coast within the area of the Belgian grant. Guatemalan government documents leave no doubt that this was a gratification to Carrera for his "services" in the matter.[41]

The French also pressed claims against the new Guatemalan government. Their representative, Auguste Mahelin, ideologically sympathetic to the liberals, created a near crisis in late 1840 when the French corvette *Indiana* arrived at Acajutla to assist him in pressing French claims. On 4 November Mahelin presented the Guatemalan government claims totaling $305,044, of which $256,463 was for the seizure by the Guatemalan government of the merchantman *Boyer*. The rest involved actions by Carrera's troops during the revolution. Guatemalan Foreign Minister Basilio Zeceña responded that most of the claims referred to actions beyond the jurisdiction of the Guatemalan government, but that the remainder would be examined carefully. The captain of the *Indiana*, at anchor off Acajutla, soon followed up the French consul's demands, vigorously protesting actions by Carrera's troops and charging that one Frenchman had been assassinated and others assaulted and robbed. Yet Captain LeCointe diplomatically applauded Rivera Paz's exemption of foreigners from the forced loans and special taxes and expressed the hope that an amicable agreement could be reached on the claims.

Successful negotiations led to dismissal of the claims, probably being used primarily as leverage for more favorable treatment of French interests generally, and on 14 December Mahelin reduced the French demand to $18,014, admitting that most of the claims were not legitimately against the Guatemalan government. The Guatemalan foreign minister, however, refused to recognize any claims, insisting that proof of Guatemalan guilt was lacking and that the damage occurred in El Salvador by troops not under Guatemalan command. Zeceña's hard line was tempered a little by a more conciliatory message from Rivera Paz to Mahelin on 20 December 1840, and on the following day Zeceña agreed to recognize a $2,000 credit made to the Guatemalan representative in Paris if proper documentation was presented, and he allowed that $34,000 claimed by a M. Jourdan in damages by Carrera's troops in Antigua could be paid if proper proof and documentation were forthcoming.[42] Negotiations dragged on for nearly four more years, but an agreement was finally signed in February 1844 and ratifications exchanged on 8 March of the following year. In the end, the Guatemalan government recognized a total of $15,650, or only 5 percent of the original claim.[43]

Troubles with Mexico involved that government's claims to the Soconusco region, along the Pacific coast. Mexican troops began to occupy the area in 1840, claiming it was part of Chiapas. Guatemala claimed it was part of Central America, but the dispute would drag on throughout the Carrera years without a satisfactory resolution.

Although it would be more than a decade before the political stability and order that Carrera promised would become a reality in Guatemala, the legal framework for the conservative regime was established early in the period by the Constituent Assembly that Carrera had insisted upon in 1839. That body completed its work in December of that year with a new Declaration of the Rights of the State and Its Inhabitants. This lengthy document revised and expanded the 1837 Declaration of the Rights and Guarantees of the Citizens and Inhabitants of the State. It became the fundamental law of Guatemala, and in it can be found much of the basic conservatism that would dominate Guatemala for the next thirty years.[44]

Its initial article declared the State of Guatemala to be "sovereign, free, and independent," while Article 2 denied the right of secession or sovereignty to any part of the state. At the same time, Article 10 addressed the question of Central American union and declared unequivocally that the "pact of union that the state recognizes with the others of Central America, be it ratified by its Constituent Assembly or its constitutional legislature, will be complied with religiously as part of the fundamental law." Article 3 declared Roman Catholicism the religion of the state and guaranteed it protection, but it also assured freedom of worship for other faiths. Subsequent articles declared that the state government existed to protect the people's rights, including "life, honor, property, and the pursuit of happiness by honest means, but by no means is it established for the private interest, personal profit, or exclusive benefit of any individual, family, or special class." Theoretically, it stated, power resided fundamentally in the people. "Public officials are not owners, but merely depositories of authority," it declared, subject and never superior to legitimately established laws and always responsible for their conduct in compliance with those laws. But it also warned that the power of the people was limited "naturally" by principles derived from rigorous reasoning. Thus the objectives of the charter were the maintenance of life, honor, liberty, property, and legitimately acquired rights, as well as "the common welfare, maintenance of good customs, repression of vices, punishment of crimes, and the maintenance and honor of the faith inherited from our fathers, the education of the young, the reward of merit, and the development of the sciences, arts, agriculture, industry, commerce and navigation." The "people's power" extended only to what was "just and appropriate for the benefit of all, and in no way could it work against the society's best interests." The declaration endorsed the sanctity of law and called for the establishment of a constitution to designate specifically the executive, legislative, and judicial powers and to fix the necessary regulations for the exercise of these powers. The document went on to prohibit either legislative or judicial ex post facto laws. The influence of Juan José Aycinena and the ideas he brought from his exile in the United States are evident in this first section, as the U.S. Constitution and Declaration of Independence are both reflected here.

A second section dealt with more immediate matters and reflected more fully the conservative reaction. Although "all men by nature have certain equal rights," declared Article 3, for example, "their condition in the society is not equal, depending on circumstances that no human power may level." Therefore, "to establish and maintain social equilibrium, the law must protect the weak against the strong, and thus all nations, even the least civilized, must especially protect all those who by their sex, age, or present capacity lack sufficient enlightenment to know and defend their own rights." Specifically, this meant that the "Indians must be protected to the extent of improving their education and preventing them from being defrauded of what they have individually or in common, and that they not be molested in the practices and habits that they have learned from their elders and which are not contrary to good customs."

The document detailed a number of other rights and responsibilities. It provided for compulsory military service and required everyone to pay taxes, "but taxes must be general and calculated in such a way so that each contributes to sustaining the administration according to his respective ability." It reaffirmed the abolition of slavery, which had been done by the federal government upon independence. More important, perhaps, all citizens of the state were declared eligible for public office so long as they had the qualifications that the law set forth. It also guaranteed freedom of the press, with the qualifying proviso that all publications "conform to the laws that must repress abuses of this liberty." Personal services demanded by the government had to be properly indemnified. No one could be persecuted for his opinions, no matter what they might be, so long as no specific law were violated, and in that case the individual remained subject only to the penalty established for the law he violated. The declaration outlawed torture, and in all criminal cases the accused had the right to be heard directly or through an attorney and to be informed of the nature and cause of the charges against him, as well as the right to confront his accusers, to see all evidence presented against him, and to bring witnesses and testimony in his own defense before a tribunal or judge in his own territory, as established by law prior to perpetration of the crime, with due process being strictly observed. It also proclaimed an independent judiciary and affirmed the right of petition to all citizens. Other civil rights included in this document were the right to bear arms as necessary for self defense, the right of habeas corpus, freedom of movement within or beyond the state's borders, and legal rights generally as provided in the U.S. Constitution and its Bill of Rights, including the sanctity of the home, prohibiting the entry of authorities without a warrant. It prohibited persecution or arrest without due process and outlawed confiscation of property as a penalty, although fines of specified sums might be established in certain cases and seizure of property was justified in cases where fraud had occurred.

All property, both communal and individual, was declared inviolable, but the state, in the public interest and with due process and only with just compensation in gold or silver or its equivalent value, could take such property in eminent domain. Individuals were free to bequeath or otherwise dispose of their property as they pleased, including leaving it to religious organizations.

The document thus contained the standard political rights growing out of eighteenth-century natural law and popular rights. It was a basic document that was conspicuously free of the glowing promises of development and progress that had characterized liberal legislation. Rather, it was intended to protect the individual from excesses of the government and to provide for a government that would preserve traditional society and the privileges of the creole elite and the rural masses. It was a document that reflected the degree to which even the conservatives had been influenced by the liberalism of the late eighteenth and early nineteenth centuries, but which also included significant modifications on the exercise of civil liberties.

In actual fact, the victory by Carrera and his Cachurecos did not immediately result in absolute conservative rule in Guatemala, nor in domination of the so-called clerical party. These conservatives had feared Carrera as much as had the liberals, a fact that was plain to Carrera. While an alliance between the caudillo and the conservatives evolved in 1839, it was neither permanent nor without mistrust. Carrera's sentiments conformed rather closely on a number of points to the ideology of the conservative elite, but he had no intention of becoming their pawn, and in the following decade he purposely remained aloof from domination by either party, often playing off one against the other. The result was that both conservatives and liberals served in the Guatemalan government for some time, and a dialogue developed that defined the issues between them clearly, a dialogue recorded in the pages of the press and in a war of pamphlets and handbills of the period.

Enemies of Carrera saw him as nothing more than a savage, hell-bent on destroying civilization and progress. A Salvadoran contemporary newspaper called him a "son of the cholera morbus," rising in power in response to the popular fear of the disease and the medicines the government dispersed. Supported by priests and peasants initially, he later gained the support of many old lawyers because of their hatred for the jury system recently established. One of Carrera's first acts, the article reported, had been to shoot a district judge and burn the Livingston Codes. It ridiculed the "peace and order" established by this "savage." A letter to the editor charged that "the only order is the will of the savage; our peace now is like that of a prisoner, buried in a stark dungeon guarded by a sentinel watching anxiously for the slightest move that might save him the work of watching in the future." Beneath this horrible dictatorship, the "marauders of Mataquescuintla" sack the city while the government is subject to the caprice of the general. Meanwhile, the marquis of Aycinena "sits vainly in his house, ignoring his debts and machinating to manipulate control, taking advantage of the anarchy like a feudal baron while atrocities are committed against his fellow citizens."[45]

Certainly there were excesses and atrocities and, in essence, much truth to the above description during the first days after Carrera's victory and again after his defeat of Morazán in March 1840. By mid-1840, however, a more substantive peace and order began to take hold. At the end of June, the Constituent Assembly reconvened, dominated by conservatives. A new cabinet was formed, with the resignations of Joaquín Durán and Luis Batres after more than a year of service. Rivera Paz thanked them for their roles in "restoring order and justice" and appointed two other conservatives to replace them. Dr. Basilio Zeceña, a priest who like Durán had come early to Carrera's support, took charge of government, justice, ecclesiastical affairs, and foreign relations, while José Antonio Azmitia, a lawyer associated with the Aycinena clan, managed the finance and war ministries.[46]

Rivera Paz addressed the assembly on 14 July, emphasizing the progress toward restoration of peace, order, and prosperity, but also noting the difficulties that faced the government. Finding funds for defense and security had been the government's largest problem, he said, given the strong public aversion to direct taxation. The head tax had been suppressed, "relieving the pressure on the poor classes," but obliging the government to rely on forced loans and special taxes, exempting only those departments that had suffered especially in the civil disorders. "And in Mita," he revealed, "we have not yet been able even to establish the internal revenue administration." But a judicial system had been restored, the Supreme Court installed, and primary jurisdiction judges appointed in the departments. The end of the war with Morazán had made this possible, and the alliance with Nicaragua and Honduras had helped to restore peace throughout the isthmus, reducing the need for defense expenditures. He alluded to broad educational advances, but specifically promised only that the (liberal) Academia de Estudios would soon disappear because "its regulations were impracticable." The return of Archbishop Casáus from his Havana exile had been a rallying point in the revolution. Casáus himself sent congratulations to Carrera on defeating Morazán, whom he called "the perfidious and impious invader that for so many years has tyrannized that unfortunate country."[47] But Rivera Paz reported that efforts by the ecclesiastical council and the government to return the archbishop to his diocese had not yet succeeded. Father José María Castilla had gone to Havana early in the year and through his efforts all obstacles to the return of the prelate had been removed by the government, but Morazán's invasion had inspired new fears in Casáus and delayed his decision to return. Rivera Paz urged the assembly to expedite the early return of the archbishop so that the churches of Central America would no longer be "widowed and desolated." Finally, the president looked toward restoration of the Central American republic, mentioning plans for a convention of the states in November, negotiations with Rome for confirmation of bishops in each state, and recognition and payment of the federation's foreign debt. He closed the message as he had begun it, with high praise of General Carrera, who had not only brought the state "glory on the battlefields, but was also the strongest supporter of the Government and its constituted authorities."[48]

The government position appeared regularly in the official newspaper, *El Tiempo*, which carried on the banner of each issue a quotation from Auguste Mignet, a moderate French historian-journalist, reflecting the government's attitude toward reform: "When a reform becomes necessary and the moment of establishing it has arrived, nothing impedes it and all second it."[49] J. J. Aycinena was highly influential in the production of *El Tiempo*, but it was edited primarily by Manuel Francisco Pavón. In August 1839 a series of articles featured an exchange of views between Pedro Molina and J. J. Aycinena on the question of federalism, the editor quite clearly slanting the articles in favor of Aycinena, as he presented questions from Molina's *Federalista*, with answers from Aycinena.[50] A characteristic of conservative political rhetoric was the denial of their existence as a "party" and general condemnation of political parties. In June 1840, for example, *El Tiempo* reprinted an article from the Salvadoran *Correo Semanario*, charging that "party spirit is the spirit in men of little spirit" and suggesting that it was "a most difficult illness to cure, for it comforts the patient and spares him the embarrassment of any examination."[51] *El Tiempo* self-righteously declared itself to be on the side of religion, morals, justice, and order, dealing with issues openly and sincerely, including its praises of the services of "General Carrera, to whose efforts we owe our freedom from the horrendous stratagems of the revolutionary system."[52]

Yet even more blatantly defending and praising Carrera were a newspaper, handbills, and pamphlets published by the Army Press (Imprenta del Ejército), in which Carrera's brother, Santos, had a strong hand. Here Carrera promoted his views among the literate population independently of the government's *El Tiempo*. Priests who had accompanied his revolutionary army since the beginning edited the newspaper, which carried forth their reactionary, proclerical views, while Carrera threatened his enemies in its pages with death or imprisonment.[53] These publications maintained a high visibility for Carrera and his clerical associates. Here could be found not only opposition to Morazanista liberalism, but also opposition to the conservative elite as well, to the "family" (the Aycinena clan). Following convocation of the new Constituent Assembly, for example, in July 1840, the Army Press published a proposition from Representative Jorge Viteri, a priest close to Carrera, challenging the aristocrat Father Bernardo Piñol as the representative from Amatitlán on the grounds that the procedural regulations of the assembly had been violated, most notably in that Señores M. F. Pavón and Mariano Aycinena, cousin and uncle of Piñol, had both voted in violation of regulations requiring relatives within four levels of kinship to abstain from such votes.[54]

Also strongly supportive of Carrera and printed by the Army Press was the proclerical *Procurador de los Pueblos*, which began publication on 12 September 1840 to defend and promote clerical and conservative views. Its first issue carried an editorial signed by "S.C." (presumably Santos Carrera) declaring that it was a paper "entirely by the people and for the people." It attacked other Guatemalan papers as representing only special interests and complained of "our singular misfortune that the governors have been enemies of the people." A brief history of the country since independence became a vehicle to blast those who had attacked the church, saying that the real victims of the civil wars and dissensions were the common people. "Can the Guatemalan recall without embarrassment the absurdities that those who have exercised power in this country have committed? Who can forget the evils to which they have submitted the people? The insurgents of Santa Rosa and Mataquescuintla finally rose up to rid the country of these self-serving leaders."[55] The second issue praised Carrera and the *montañeses* who had overcome "all the parties and injustice of the oppressors and enemies of the people." S.C. attacked both the liberals and the "party of the Nobles," both of which he said made war against Carrera and the people who were "fighting for true reforms because they wished to have their Pastor with them and to have the monastic institutions restored, so that religion is protected and can work for the good of the people." S.C. called for restoration of the Franciscan and other religious orders, an issue then before the assembly, arguing that "the people want clergymen."[56] In October the assembly complied with Carrera's proclerical wishes, as it repealed civil marriage and divorce,[57] restored the ecclesiastical fuero that had been abolished by Article 153 of the federal constitution of 1824, and began the process of restoring the clerical orders and the diezmo.[58]

On 26 September *El Procurador* entered into the debate over free trade and the role of the merchants. It began by attacking the Consulado for not wanting to pay for an annual religious festival as it had done in colonial times. It was clear that Carrera and the church were putting pressure on the merchants to support the restoration of religion in Guatemalan public life along with other colonial institutions. It chided the Consulado for its heavy spending in superfluous and unnecessary decoration of the consular building, even dressing their porter in a "ridiculous" uniform, but then being unwilling to spend twenty-five or thirty pesos on a pious event that the Consulado had formerly observed. The writer of the article hoped that the members of the Consulado "did not wish to appear impious" nor were "ashamed of having the holy Virgin as their patron." After all, he continued, Carlos III had put all Spain under her protection, as had several kings of France with that country. Even the celebrated Cortes of 1812 had made Saint Teresa a patron of the kingdom, and—clearly the most persuasive argument—"General Carrera, in our own time, has invoked and sworn as his patron and that of his army, the holy Virgin of the Rosary, thus giving an example of his piety that all should imitate, including the consulado, which owes its reappearance to this admirable Caudillo." The message was clear, and the Consulado promptly complied. The same issue attacked free trade and foreigners, especially Jews and Arabs, who brought in foreign goods. Invoking strong anti-Semitic overtones, it argued that free trade and foreign trade were injurious to the artisans and hardworking Christian people of Guatemala. This article, signed by "El Mataquescuintleco," argued that free trade had impoverished the country. It closed with a warning that the people had risen up against this economic injustice and expressed confidence that the people's interests would now be served by the government.

These appeals to the artisans of the capital helped to build urban support for Carrera to match his rural support, and it was highly significant in the formation of his powerful political machine. The Army Press published a song, reputedly dedicated to Carrera by the artisans of the city for his opposition to free trade (see Figure 3).

With Morazán defeated, Carrera needed less the alliance with the patricians—Pavón, the Batreses, Piñols, or Aycinenas—whom he did not yet trust. Some of that resentment extended toward Rivera Paz as well, although it must be said that Rivera Paz did a remarkable balancing act of maintaining the favor of Carrera while at the same time allowing the marquis of Aycinena and his cronies to consolidate their real power and influence in the country.

Carrera's domination and the conservative tone of the new government was widely recognized. Although attacked in liberal circles, the image of order and stability gained praise in conservative newspapers in both Europe and America. A New York Spanish-language newspaper, for example, in early 1842 observed:

> We know little of General Carrera, but from that little he strikes us as one of those energetic men that revolutions produce and that assure the future of the people. Dedicating his sword to defend conservative ideas, he has earned the true confidence of the masses and he can call without fear on their patriotism. Even the American traveller Stephens in spite of the slightly disguised partiality that he manifests toward the enemies of General Carrera, doesn't dare to deny his talents and we are sure that they will now be employed in defense of the honor of his country.[59]

Soon after, the official Guatemalan gazette simplified political divisions as it praised Carrera's "conservative ideas." The world, it reminded its readers, was divided between two different parties, "the conservative or moderate opinion, and the reformist or exalted." But, it added, "when peoples are oppressed with exorbitant burdens, when there is poor administration by an exclusive party or faction that is concerned only with its own personal interests, or when imprudent or insensitive reformists try to change everything without respect for customs, religious ideas and the general habits, then the opinion of the masses is against such reforms, against the breezy faction, and against the authority that they abuse." In contrast, the writer (probably M. F. Pavón) continued, "when the people are left alone except for the absolutely indispensable, when there is equal justice for all, when their will is respected, leaving them to their own ways and customs, when their religion, property and order are respected, and when each individual and family is protected in the use of their rights and in the enjoyment of their industry, of their peculiar ways and means of enjoying life, then the masses favor the order of things and give their support." The article closed

Los artesanos del Estado de Guatemala, obsequiando al Sr. General Rafael Carrera, con motivo de la proteccion que reciben de él, sobre que se restrinja el comercio libre, le han dedicado el dia 13. del actual la siguiente

CANCION.

Ya tu nombre CARRERA ha sonado,
por la fama veloz repetido:
Ya en los campos de Marte has vencido:
ya de gloria te has visto colmado.

Tú, valiente la espada blandiste
por los pueblos: por dar garantias
Generoso tu vida exponias;
pero en premio el triunfo obtuviste.

Washington su gloria inmortal,
como tú al principio adquirió.
Por la causa del pueblo lidió
y venció como buen General.

Quiso hacer á su pueblo dichoso,
y de Témis el templo instaló:
Libertad, é igualdad proclamó
y hasta verlas no tuvo reposo.

Tú esos mismos principios proclama,
que á él dieron eterno renombre:
Respetad los derechos del hombre,
y arded siempre en patriótica llama.

De partidos la voz incidiosa
no escuches; que es siempre enemiga:
La Justicia tan solo se siga
acatando su voz armoniosa.

Guatemala, Octubre 13. de 1840.

Imprenta del Exército.

FIGURE 3. Song in praise of Carrera from the artisans of Guatemala

with this apology and praise for conservatism: "It is true that conservative ideas lack the incentive of novelty, but they result in permanent happiness and the welfare of the peoples. This peace that we enjoy, this security of our persons and property, this consideration for the religion and its ministers, and the concern for not burdening the peoples, . . . this is what is called *to be conserved.*"[60]

Thus Carrera, supported by a group of military and clerical flatterers, was the arbiter of Guatemalan life as the decade of the 1840s began with a clearly conservative direction that coincided largely, but not absolutely, with the group of aristocrats who actually ran the government—a group headed by Juan José Aycinena, Manuel Francisco Pavón, Luis Batres, Mariano Aycinena, Pedro Aycinena, and Bernardo Piñol. Others close to this group, but also on good terms with Carrera, included Jorge Viteri, Basilio Zeceña, José María Castilla, and Francisco de Paula García Peláez. Other hard line conservatives who held high office during the 1840s included Fathers Antonio Larrazábal and José María Barrutia, as well as Juan Matheu, José Antonio Urruela, José Nájera, Manuel Echeverría, Andrés Andreu, and Manuel Cerezo. The issues that had divided conservatives and liberals since the Cortes of Cádiz remained, but personal animosities and opportunism had also become a major part of Central American politics. Stephens perhaps exaggerated only slightly when he contrasted Central American party politics to the United States: "We seldom do more than call men ignorant, incompetent, dishonest, dishonorable, false, corrupt, subverters of the Constitution, and bought with British gold; there [in Central America] a political opponent is a robber, an assassin; it is praise to admit that he is not a bloodthirsty cutthroat. . . . Defeated partisans are shot, banished, run away, or get a moral lockjaw, and never dare express their opinions before one of the dominant party."[61]

Carrera was subservient to no group, not even the clergy. Although he championed restoration of the religious orders and return of their confiscated lands, he refused to support complete restitution, recognizing that this might cause yet further disruption. Some of his own political allies had in fact acquired former church lands. Moreover, he had no wish for the church to become too strong an economic and political rival to his own power.[62]

The reaction was not unique to Carrera's Guatemala, for there was disgust with anticlerical and proforeign policies throughout the isthmus. In May 1844, for example, the Nicaraguan legislature decreed that no foreigner, unless he had begun naturalization proceedings, could marry a native woman, own real estate or mines, or sell at retail in the country, a law essentially revived from the *Recopilación de Indias*.[63]

Carrera's suspicion and distance from the aristocratic elite of the capital became evident in 1841, as he refused to allow the aristocratic conservatives free reign in reorganizing and developing the country. He even permitted a liberal resurgence, in effect playing off the two parties against each other, maintaining the military power himself. To some degree he was successful in using this as a device to consolidate his own personal power, but it led to substantial political intrigue, opportunism, and a failure to stabilize the country in the manner he had promised. Liberal press attacks on the conservatives began to appear late in 1840, although none was particularly effective. More important was Carrera's gradual undermining of Rivera Paz's authority and of Father Aycinena's political machine.

On 15 May 1841 Carrera called for a new Constituent Assembly to complete a constitution that would incorporate the "fundamental reforms," which he said the people wanted.[64] The Declaration of Rights of the previous assembly was considered to be only a temporary charter for the country until a more complete constitution could be written. This assembly convened in July, and Rivera Paz submitted his resignation on the sixth of that month.[65] The assembly accepted the resignation on the tenth, thanking him for his services but asking him to remain in office until a successor was found.[66] The assembly then elected Carrera as president on 12 July, but Carrera refused the appointment, and the assembly, according to custom, declined to accept his refusal. He insisted and his second refusal was accepted on 20 July.[67] Two days later the assembly named José Venacio López (1791–1863), an old political ally of José Cecilio del Valle who had played an important role in the politics of the independence movement, but had not been active politically since the 1820s.[68] Reluctantly, López agreed to serve only if Rivera Paz was incapacitated, and for the time being Rivera Paz remained at the helm. In October, however, López became president of the Council of State, although Carrera himself was the dominant member of that executive council, which once the assembly recessed actually ruled the country.[69]

López represented a moderate liberal resurgence that occurred in late 1841. The restoration of state collection of the diezmo (tithe) inevitably met some resistance, and as the government began to enforce this levy in August 1841, the liberals gained from opposition to it. The government reminded the public that defense of "religion" had been one of the major parts of Carrera's revolution, and that restoration of the orders, respect for priests, reestablishment of the church, and return of the archbishop from Havana were all under way. It warned that this was the "will of the people" and that the assembly was simply complying with that will in its measures to restore church revenues.[70]

New British aggression on the Caribbean coast also contributed to rejuvenated liberal popularity, and Carrera himself became impatient with the conservatives' refusal to take a stronger stand. On 3 November he convened a military junta, which demanded energetic measures in response to the conduct of the superintendent of Belize against the sovereignty of Central America in occupying Roatán and San Juan del Norte. The junta actually called for Central American reunification to meet the British threat, closing of all ports to British trade, and breaking of diplomatic relations until satisfaction had been gained. General Carrera presented these points to the minister of war the following day.[71] The government quickly responded that it had already strongly protested the British occupation of San Juan del Norte and sent a special commission to Belize to demand an explanation.[72] Carrera was not satisfied, and on the sixth he called the Council of State into session over the matter. Failure of the government to take what Carrera believed to be strong enough action led to a crisis in early December.[73]

These events undermined Rivera Paz's authority and the continued control of the government by the Aycinena clique. Carrera held the real power and now was cooperating with moderate liberal leaders such as López, Alejandro Marure, Mariano Padilla, and Miguel Larreinaga.[74] Appointment of José Antonio Larrave as Corregidor of the Department of Guatemala furthered the moderate resurgence, as Larrave cultivated an alliance with the military chieftain of the state and with his brother, Santos Carrera, who continued as the military commander of the department.[75]

Carrera's impatience with the conservative government, then, on a number of issues, led him to build a new base of support among moderates and liberals who hoped to use him to regain control of the country. Heated discussions in the Council of State erupted on 7 December 1841, specifically over payment of Carrera's soldiers. Jorge Viteri came to Rivera Paz's defense in the argument, announcing that he had "the force of reason" on his side. Carrera stormed out of the chamber, returning a few moments later, after his troops had surrounded the palace and brought up cannon trained on the main doorway. He then announced that his "force" was in place and demanded to know where Viteri's was! Viteri, formerly on good terms with Carrera, managed to soothe the caudillo and calm returned, but Rivera Paz and his ministers resigned, and Carrera temporarily took over the government. He still did not wish to preside, however, and a week later installed López as president. López took the oath of office on 14 December after Carrera pleaded ill health as an excuse for not continuing as president himself.[76]

There followed a stronger Guatemalan remonstrance in support of Nicaragua against the British, as another moderate, Juan José Flores, took over as foreign minister.[77] A new U.S. minister to Central America, W. S. Murphy, arrived in Guatemala City on Christmas day and soon after commented on what he saw as the political divisions in the country, reflecting Carrera's new coalition. He wrote to Daniel Webster that the "State is divided into two great political parties—Natives, against English, or the English & other Foreign Merchants in opposition to the Native inhabitants of the Country—Genl. Carrera is at the head of the Native Party, & Commands them in the shape of an armed force." He said the "British Party" had "in great measure the Secret Control of the Councils of the State, but as Genl. Carrera is also a member [of the council] . . . he is able to deter them from any open action against him." Murphy expressed concern about the British encroachments and efforts to extend the contract of the English Colonization Company, which he saw as merely a device to extend British territorial and commercial control. He expressed the fear that "Carrera is a soldier and a Patriot, but he is an illiterate man, wholly unacquainted with the 'Hooks & Crooks and Convolutions Wild' of matters of State, much less with the Wiley Cunning of British Diplomacy."[78] Murphy correctly perceived the current political alignment, although he failed to understand its transitory nature or the deeper conservative-liberal divisions in Central America. He was also reflecting, of course, the strained relations between the United States and Great Britain in the year 1842.

Carrera's alliance with the anti-British moderates and liberals put him for the moment at odds with the conservative elite who had directed the government since his revolution, but the liberals were unable to turn this situation into long-term advantage. López himself was unwilling or unable to forge a new political faction uniting the peasants with the liberal elite. The anti-British tone of Carrera's press remained highly offensive, according to the British Vice Consul in Guatemala, yet no real development of a political coalition seemed to result among Carrera's new allies.[79]

As early as 7 February 1842, López ordered his secretary to inform Rivera Paz that his two-month "leave of absence" from the presidency was about to expire and that Rivera Paz should resume his presidential duties on the fourteenth.[80] Rivera Paz responded from Escuintla, where he claimed he was trying to recover his health. Dodging the real issues, he simply said that there was little to report to the assembly and that public peace and tranquility had been maintained during their recess. "Responsible and worthy citizens," he said, had been able to carry on the function of the government during his illness. He closed the report by asking the assembly to remove the burden of the presidency from his shoulders.[81] The assembly was closely divided on the issue, but on 25 February finally accepted Rivera Paz's resignation and confirmed López as president, formalizing the moderate gains.

Viteri, in the meantime, was sent off to Rome via Havana to attempt to persuade Archbishop Casáus to return to Guatemala. He reached Havana on 8 June and found Casáus unwilling to return immediately, owing to his age and fear of "the friends of Morazán." But Casáus petitioned the pope to name auxiliary bishops for the Cathedral of Guatemala and now finally endorsed the establishment of a bishopric in El Salvador. Viteri proceeded to Rome, where he was to seek establishment of bishops for both El Salvador and Costa Rica.[82] His mission was successful, as the pope named Viteri himself as bishop of El Salvador on 27 December 1842. He returned from Rome in August of 1843 with the news also that Francisco de Paula García Peláez had been designated to become the new archbishop.[83]

Viteri took possession of the see on the following September after being confirmed in the Cathedral of Guatemala on 29 January 1843. A liberal resurgence in El Salvador, similar to that in Guatemala, had been met firmly by Chief-of-State Juan Lindo as he dissolved the legislature and exiled many of the senators suspected of Morazanista activity. Carrera showed no inclination to challenge these events, suggesting that his support of the liberals in Guatemala was more opportunistic than ideological in the early 1840s. Viteri would be a major force in Salvadoran politics until his exile from the country by a liberal government that gained power in 1846.[84]

These first years following the collapse of the federation appear chaotic, as political alliances were shifting and opportunism ran high. Yet although he was unwilling to take a firm hold of the presidency of the State of Guatemala himself, Carrera nevertheless established himself as unquestioned caudillo of the country during these years and placed himself above the factional liberal-conservative struggles of the elite. Although uneducated and lacking the sophistication of the creole elite, Carrera was proving himself to be an intelligent and skillful manipulator of the political forces in the country. The period also witnessed the beginning of the rivalry over the isthmus between Great Britain and the United States, which would become more heated later. But from 1839 to 1842, we find roots of the alliance between the United States and the liberals, which would continue well into the twentieth century. Meanwhile, alliance with the conservatives became the means by which Great Britain, at least for the present, maintained her predominant position there.

CHAPTER SEVEN

Morazán Again

WHATEVER CHANCES THE LIBERALS HAD of recouping their political fortunes in collaboration with Rafael Carrera suddenly evaporated with the return to Central America of Francisco Morazán. Following his defeat by Carrera in 1840, Morazán had gone to New Granada and Peru, where he obtained some financial backing. News of the anti-British feeling in Central America reached him in Lima, along with reports of what he was led to believe was a rising tide of opposition to Carrera's puppet in El Salvador, Francisco Malespín. Morazán decided it was a propitious time to return to El Salvador and launch a campaign to restore the federation. He landed at La Unión on 15 February 1842 and issued a manifesto, in which he said that he had intended to go on to Chile, but that his patriotism had forced him to return to defend his homeland upon hearing of the Mosquito-British invasion of Nicaragua.[1] His small force then marched to San Miguel, but he left Trinidad Cabañas in command at La Unión, where a minor incident involving Nicaraguan citizens alarmed the Nicaraguan government.[2] El Salvador's chief-of-state, Antonio José Cañas, in a carefully and politely-worded response to Morazán's manifesto, thanked the liberal caudillo for his offer to help resist the attacks on the Caribbean coast of Nicaragua. While insisting that he did not doubt his sincerity, he informed Morazán that El Salvador could not act alone in the matter, but only in concert with the other Central American states with which El Salvador was now allied.[3] Delegates of Honduras, El Salvador, and Nicaragua were at that very moment meeting in Chinandega in an attempt to restore the union under Cañas's leadership.[4]

Morazán found only about two hundred recruits for his army while becoming quickly aware of the strength of Malespín's force, which mobilized for action against the deposed caudillo. Morazán thus retreated to La Unión, sailed to Acajutla, and then marched inland to Sonsonate, continuing his correspondence with several chiefs-of-state, but finding little encouragement.[5] With no more support in Sonsonate than in San Miguel, he sailed back to the Gulf of Fonseca, where he conspired to invade Costa Rica in collaboration with opponents of the caudillo Braulio Carrillo. Landing at Caldera, Costa Rica, on 7 April 1842, with local help Morazán quickly seized power and was in command of San José by the tenth. Carrillo and his ministers fled into exile on board a ship headed for Chile two days later.[6]

In Guatemala, Carrera was quick to react to the news of Morazán's return, and he obtained from the government authorization for a loan of $40,000 for an army of three thousand "to march to the aid of El Salvador."[7] News of the fall of Costa Rica brought a wave of antiliberal sentiment in Guatemala and precipitated a return of the conservatives to power. On 13 May the assembly accepted López's resignation and restored Rivera Paz after Carrera once more declined the presidency. Sworn in on the next day, in a short address he made clear his subordination to Carrera, as he declared that he would dedicate himself, "in accord with the General-in-Chief, to the defense of the state's independence, now that it again appeared threatened by the intense enemy of Central America."[8]

Promptly, Guatemala broke all relations with the new Costa Rican regime and launched a series of bitter denunciations of Morazán.[9] The *Gaceta Oficial*, closely identified with M. F. Pavón and the conservative elite, had been silent since 31 December 1841. It resumed publication on 17 May and published a letter from Adj. Gen. Santos Carrera announcing his brother's blessing on Rivera Paz's resumption of the presidency and his pledge of the army's loyalty to the new government.[10] Guatemala reiterated its pledge of alliance with the other Central American states, especially in support of Francisco Ferrera's mobilization in Honduras. In Costa Rica, meanwhile, Morazán declared martial law and recruited an army. The lines were drawn, and a resumption of civil war seemed imminent. War fever filled the newspapers of the isthmus as hatred of Morazán replaced the anti-British tenor to some degree despite a continuing British blockade. Charges of atrocities committed by the Morazanistas in Costa Rica raised the passions of the people elsewhere on the isthmus as their governments braced for a struggle.[11]

Carrera played a direct and active role in the Council of State, now reorganized along more conservative lines. On 3 June President Rivera Paz swore in two staunchly conservative members of the elite as his principal ministers. Juan José Aycinena became minister of government, justice and ecclesiastical affairs, while Juan Matheu, a conservative merchant, became minister of war and finance. These appointments, Pavón reported in the *Gaceta*, "have satisfied the public" and guaranteed the constant zeal of the government and its ministers who had "abandoned their repose to obey loyally the call of the President, General-in-Chief, and other members of the Council." [12] Chatfield, who had returned to Central America from a trip to Britain in May of 1842 with the rank of consul general, through his close friendship with Manuel F. Pavón regained influence in Guatemalan governing circles. [13]

Carrera sounded the war cry on 6 June in a proclamation addressed to his compatriots in the other Central American states:

> The recovery of the rights of our State and of our people cost us great efforts and no few sacrifices. We have desired but to live in peace and security under the rule of law, to enjoy in tranquility the fruits of our labors. But just as we began to feel the benefits that a just and frugal Government provided us under the auspices of public peace, the enemy of our happiness appears again with the intention of reducing us to the old serfdom. Morazán returns to make war upon us and raise upon our ruins the throne of his tyranny. Can we ever forget that this impious man sacked our churches to enrich himself with their spoils, and exiled the most virtuous priests to destroy the religion we inherited from our fathers? Can we ever erase from our memory the perfidy and the scandal with which he violated all the treaties, the cruelty with which he sacrificed so many victims to his ambition, and the tricks and intrigues he always employed to crush and oppress the people, with no other law than his own whim, nor any other interest than his personal engrandizement and that of the vile satellites who always surround him? Have we forgotten the temerity with which this sacrilegious monster condemned to martyrdom clergy dedicated to the people's cause? Will those who lost their *ejidos* and were reduced to begging for not having enough land to plant and harvest nourishing grains for their poor families, thanks to the ingratitude of Morazán and his vile proselytes, be forgotten? No, it is impossible that the memory of such attacks would not excite in your breasts sentiments of horror and indignation. It is, then, these sentiments that today force us to defend ourselves from violence, and to deprecate the false promises of the tyrant.
>
> Our cause is that of our religion and our liberty; and if we abandon it, slavery shall forever be our shameful patrimony. I shall dedicate the last drop of my blood to the defense of this holy cause that I have sustained; and I do not doubt that united together to defend it, we will have the protection of the Omnipotent and will triumph over all our enemies. [14]

Ironically, the return of Morazán was a crushing blow to the Guatemalan liberals, for just as they had begun to make gains, Morazán's return led to a strong conservative reaction. José Francisco Barrundia had returned from exile and won election to the assembly as deputy from Cuajiniquilapa. He believed the downfall of Carrera to be imminent, but the conservative reaction resulted in suppression of liberal publications and precluded his taking his seat as it cut short the liberal upsurge.[15] The government clamped strict regulations on the country, and it was particularly wary of foreigners. It ordered the corregidores to report on movements of persons within their jurisdictions, tightening regulations on travel. It called on officials to "double their zeal and efficiency" in maintaining public peace and order.[16]

Morazán's return also dampened the movement toward Central American reunion. Guatemala sent delegates to the convention, but the *Gaceta Oficial* emphasized that it was a "convention of states" rather than a "National Convention" and that the priority was now on order within each state rather than national reunion.[17] In early July another editorial on the subject identified reunion with the hated Morazán. While it called for cooperation among the states into a peaceful league that could promote commerce and prosperity, it believed reunion was now impossible.[18] Delegates from Honduras, Nicaragua, and El Salvador signed a "Confederation Pact" at Chinandega on 27 July 1842, but Guatemala refused to join.[19] Morazán, meanwhile, declared Costa Rica a member of the Central American union again.[20]

The atrocities of Morazán and his associates were a constant theme in the Guatemalan press. It reprinted a Salvadoran newspaper attack on Morazán's return that told of "horrendous scene of assassinations, of the devastation of Central America in the long period of ten years that this imposter governed, and the system of persecution that constituted the essence of his administration."[21] Announcing the news that on 30 May Morazán had established martial law in Costa Rica, an "Extra" of the *Gaceta* accused him of behaving like a "hungry and carnivorous wolf," leaving a trail of blood behind him.[22] As Morazán organized his government and expressed his desire to reunify Central America, J. J. Aycinena informed foreign consuls in Guatemala that the federation no longer existed and that Morazán in no way represented Central America or Guatemala. He cited Morazán's assumption of the title "Chief of the National Army" as evidence of Morazán's illicit pretensions.[23]

The Guatemalan government decreed a $10,000 forced loan to strengthen military security. This loan exemplified Carrera's direct role in government administration. Circulars to the municipalities and corregidores emphasized that the levy was to come only from property holders and under no circumstances from those who derived their income from daily labor. More than half the loan was collected from Guatemala City residents.[24] Carrera defended the unpopular levy in a proclamation to the people on 4 August, warning of the Morazán danger and the costs of defending the state against tyranny. He reminded them that they had not suffered the forced loans as in former times until this crisis.[25] On the same day Carrera directed a note to the government indicating that justice demanded revision of some of the quotas assigned for collection of the loan, pointing out that one property holder worth more than five thousand pesos received a quota of only five pesos, equal to that assigned to an "unfortunate" with no real property.[26]

When the government did not respond quickly enough to satisfy his objections, he addressed a second proclamation to the people on 3 September, in which he lamented the continued misery and poverty in a country where "wealth and prosperity are eluded because of the lack of protection for commerce, agriculture and the arts." He promised that he had worked for everyone to benefit according to their own labors, so that the people might not "be molested by taxes, levies and assessments that are so repugnant to the liberal principles of a paternal and republican government." He said he regretted, therefore, with a frankness uncharacteristic of politicians, that he had to confess that many government orders that he had not known about, and some of which he disapproved, had circulated over his name. The assignment of quotas for the loan was such a case, and he now announced his opposition to the loan allocations and demanded a new measure. Promising to oppose all those who harass the people and that "we will triumph over arbitrariness and despotism," he called on them to remain united against the "ambitious and perverted." With their help, he concluded, happiness and public prosperity would come and the country would be compared with the most powerful of Europe.[27] The government received the message and an obedient revision soon appeared, along with a reduction in the total amount demanded.[28]

Carrera also rallied support against Morazán. In a proclamation addressed to the Costa Rican people, he reminded them that "your State was the only one in Central America, thanks to the great distance that separated it from the seat in which Morazán exercised his tyranny for ten years, that did not closely experience the terrible evils that the rest suffered." He pointed to atrocities and called on the Costa Ricans to follow the example of the Guatemalan montañeses in throwing him out. "Costa Ricans," he exhorted, "when a people fight for their liberty [and] struggle for justice, if their resolution is firm, although they may at first fight with many disadvantages, in the end their determination will triumph over the oppressors. Guatemala offers a notable example of this truth."[29]

In the meantime, Aycinena and Chatfield worked to build an alliance of the other four states against Morazán's Costa Rica.[30] Chatfield used the British naval blockade of Nicaragua and El Salvador (seeking an agreement on debt payments) to pressure those two states to go along with a plan finally agreed upon in Guatemala on 7 October 1842. This treaty agreed to the mutual recognition of their respective sovereignty with respect to their internal governance, but agreed to conduct their foreign relations as a single political body and to make common cause in case of foreign invasion. But it also agreed to "treat as treason . . . any act that tried to reestablish the Constitution of 1824."[31] A defensive treaty of military cooperation against Costa Rica followed on 17 October.[32]

Unknown at the time to the diplomats in Guatemala City, the Costa Ricans had already by this date dealt with the crisis. A movement to overthrow Morazán had begun by July 1842 under the leadership of Antonio Pinto, supported by popular uprisings in San José, Alajuela, and Heredia. After some bitter fighting, Morazán surrendered at Cartago on Sunday, 11 September, several weeks before the alliance referred to above had been concluded, reflecting the slow state of communications in Central America. A firing squad ended Morazán's life after a brief trial four days later.[33]

News of Morazán's execution did not reach the Guatemalan capital until noon on 17 October,[34] after organization of the conservative alliance had been completed except for ratification. The published decrees and proclamations of President Rivera Paz and General Carrera reflect the relief and joy they felt at this news. Congratulating the inhabitants of Costa Rica, Rivera Paz declared that "I cannot find the proper words to express to you the feelings that possess my soul. You have struggled heroically to regain your holy rights, and the triumph with which Heaven has favored you not only benefits you, but all the countries of Central America, our common fatherland."[35] Addressing his own constituents, he thanked Divine Providence for "continuing his kind protection of the peoples of Central America" and noted the appropriateness of Morazán's execution on the anniversary of Central American independence (15 September). He decreed the immediate reopening of relations with Costa Rica and ordered all civil and military authorities to attend a special mass in the cathedral to thank "the All Powerful for the extraordinary events in Costa Rica."[36]

Carrera, in his role as caudillo of the isthmus, issued his own proclamation to all the peoples of Central America for this victory of "the holy cause of the peoples," that now permitted the opportunity for peace, harmony, and general prosperity. "The death of Morazán, caudillo of depredations, should seal and put an end to this dismal chapter of Central America," he declared, printing the name upside down. "Now it is time to mend the wounds and work to forget as soon as possible past dissensions." He called for positive measures to guarantee justice, order, and security for all.[37]

Yet despite the glowing predictions of peace, prosperity, and unity, the seeds of discord continued to flower in Central America. Although all four of the allied states ratified the treaty of alliance and confederation of 7 October, the death of Morazán ended the threat, and with it, the cohesiveness of the alliance loosened. Caudillos Carrera and Ferrera, as well as the conservative cabal in Guatemala City now looked critically at their man in El Salvador, Francisco Malespín, who had given refuge to Morazanista exiles from Costa Rica. Malespín, although generally allied with Carrera, had begun to be infected, it seemed, by the recurrent liberalism in El Salvador. Thus Carrera and Ferrera moved troops to the Salvadoran frontier and began to encourage conservative elements in El Salvador against Malespín.[38]

Before new trouble broke out in El Salvador, however, Guatemala faced a new threat on its opposite frontier. Four hundred Mexican troops in August 1842 had occupied the Tonalá region of Soconusco, long claimed by Guatemala. They established a customs house at Tuxtla Chico, near the present-day Mexican-Guatemalan boundary.[39] On 11 September, General Antonio López de Santa Anna decreed that Soconusco was an integral part of Chiapas as he formally established it as a department of that state with its seat at Tapachula, which the Mexican caudillo now elevated to the rank of city. The following day in Guatemala, as yet unaware of Santa Anna's proclamation, J. J. Aycinena directed a strong protest to the Mexican foreign office, supported by documents from 1823 to 1840 supporting the Central American claim to Soconusco and accusing the Mexican government of intending to conquer all of Central America. He promised that Central American troops would immediately meet "force with force," but urged the Mexicans to avoid conflict by evacuating their troops from Soconusco.[40]

As 1842 drew to a close, war fever grew. From Mexico in October came intelligence that there was great fear in Chiapas that General Carrera might soon invade and provoke an Indian rebellion.[41] Rivera Paz published a strong protest in November, reasserting Guatemala's claim to Chiapas as well as Soconusco.[42] Carrera addressed a handbill "To the Public" on 28 November, reiterating the claim to all of Chiapas and claiming that the populations of that province "appealed daily to the Government of Central America and to General Carrera, lamenting bitterly the slavery to which these defenseless people have been subjected by the Mexican forces." The broadside, signed by "THE FAITHFUL OBSERVER OF THE RIGHTS OF THE PEOPLES THAT COMPOSE CENTRAL AMERICA" and published by the Army Press, noted that in spite of these violent outrages, the government of Central America had not employed force to repel this unjust aggression, hoping to preserve peace between the two "friendly and sister Nations," but it warned that if these peaceful efforts failed, Guatemala would defend its rights, "becoming a deserted Nation before becoming a slave to the arbitrary power that wishes to subject it."[43]

Protests and war talk persisted. The Mexicans held a plebiscite that endorsed incorporation of Soconusco into Chiapas. Guatemala charged that the plebiscite was not a true test of the people's wishes, but rather a product of Mexican bayonets. Minor border skirmishes occurred, but the Guatemalans did not directly contest the Mexican military. The dispute smoldered for decades, not finally decided in Mexico's favor until Justo Rufino Barrios came to power in Guatemala in 1871, when a solution served, in effect, as compensation for Benito Juárez's assistance to the Guatemalan liberals.[44]

President Rivera Paz's annual message to the assembly upon the opening of its sessions in late November 1842, revealed problems, but he chose to emphasize the good relations that Guatemala now had with the other Central American states, attributing his administration's success to General Carrera's "wisdom and prudence." Rivera Paz also reported vastly improved relations with Britain, taking credit for getting the blockade of Nicaragua lifted and an amicable settlement of the debt question. Acknowledging that defense expenditures had grown, he attributed the budget problem to the "commercial crisis" in which income from the alcabala had decreased with the decline in trade. He assured the legislature that proper recognition and management of the debt would improve the credit of the government, develop the general prosperity, foment commerce, and ultimately increase revenues.[45]

It was customary for the Guatemalan elite to spend the dry and sometimes chilly months of January and February in the spas of Escuintla at the foot of the Pacific slopes. Often pleading "ill health" at this time of the year, high officials relaxed in the warm, tropical surroundings and hot springs of the area between Amatitlán and Escuintla. This meant that barring major crises, little was accomplished officially during these months, although informal talks among these officials often determined the direction of specific policies. Carrera and Rivera Paz conferred several times in Escuintla during their "convalescences" in February 1843. Rivera Paz had resigned as president on 19 January for "reasons of health" and was enjoying a leave of absence until his return in early March. There was something of an air of normalcy for the first time in many years, and Carrera and Rivera

Paz turned their attention toward development of the country. Not surprisingly, they began to consider the need for a better road to Escuintla and on to the tiny Pacific coast wharf at Iztapa, which Rivera Paz visited during his vacation.[46]

Carrera returned to the capital in late February. Still pleading ill health, he immediately repeated his resignation as commanding general, a move clearly not intended to be accepted, nor was it. It merely gave the general the expected assurance of government acquiescence to his continued military buildup in the face of a reputed "Salvadoran threat."[47]

The legislature reopened its sessions on 8 March and continued the conservative reaction, turning its attention especially toward ecclesiastical affairs. Manuel Cerezo, newly appointed finance minister, on 27 March reminded the assembly of the injustices of liberal expropriations of church properties. He declared that the government was trying to rectify these injustices, but that it lacked the funds to repurchase all of the lands at once. In the meantime, a major effort was under way to reduce the large debt with which the liberals had burdened the country. He proposed guidelines for recovery of the properties for sums not to exceed the amounts actually received by the treasury from the sale of the properties, plus interest. Commissioners would be named to make such settlements without resort to the courts, except for appeals. He further proposed that funds for chaplaincies or other charitable works would be retained by the government, but that the interest would be paid from the date of confiscation and guaranteed for the future, a decision reminiscent of the Spanish Consolidation of 1804.[48]

The proclerical attitude of the legislature and the influence of J. J. Aycinena was further exemplified by the decision to allow the return of the Jesuits, specifically for the purpose of establishing a school. This decision was related to the Belgian colonization contract and reflected Belgian support of the immigration of Jesuits from that country.[49]

Notwithstanding continued financial difficulties, 1843 was a year of apparent stability and economic improvement. When the assembly convened in October, Rivera Paz reported with pride at the maintenance of domestic tranquility, improved public credit, and cordial foreign relations. The assembly recessed from November to April, leaving the country in the hands of Rivera Paz and a Council of State headed by Carrera.[50]

At the end of the year the *Gaceta* noted gradual progress in the capital city and the return to normalcy after the decline of the revolutionary years. Reviewing the urban situation, an editorial commented that "we saw after independence and until 1825 that there was a shortage of houses in Guatemala [City] and that many were divided and being expanded. This was an indication that we were growing in population and also in wealth." But later, "to the contrary, we saw property values drop, many houses without residents, and neither urban nor rural property could be sold at any price. All kinds of risky enterprises fearlessly took over priceless urban as well as rural properties, certainly an indication that the country's development was in decline." But now the situation had changed entirely, the editorial claimed. "There is not much movement, nor are grand and giant projects talked about, but everything gradually rises in value. The farms are sold at a profit and not on credit or at discounts, but for cash; repairs are constantly being made, renovations, additions, and the demand exceeds the supply of houses. This all proves that the population is increasing and that the people are improving their standard of living." The editorial suggested that this modest growth was also occurring in other towns and cities and in the rural haciendas, many of which had been formerly abandoned. Improvements could be seen everywhere, according to the *Gaceta*, reflecting the government's encouragement of development after the economic depression caused by liberal policies and the revolution against it.[51] Yet the reality of the country was that crime still was high and that both rural and urban poverty were widespread. Rural banditry continued to plague sections of the countryside, despite Carrera's frequent forays to suppress it.[52]

Carrera continued to pay close attention to events in neighboring El Salvador. On 19 May 1843 the Guatemalan foreign minister instructed its commissioner in San Salvador to assure the Salvadoran government that General Carrera had no intention of "altering the good relations between their two governments,"[53] but three days later Carrera arrived in Santa Rosa to organize military forces there "in view of the state of relations between Guatemala and El Salvador."[54] Carrera's watchful eye did not deter the liberal drift in both Nicaragua and El Salvador, however. Guatemala formally rejected the Chinandega pact on 5 July 1843 in favor of the conservative alliance promoted by Frederick Chatfield. When Nicaragua and El Salvador signed a pact on 16 August 1843 committed to replacing Francisco Ferrera in Honduras with the Morazanista General Trinidad Cabañas, they created a new crisis. The military expedition to be led by El Salvador's Malespín and Nicaraguan General Manuel Quijano meant that Malespín could no longer be trusted as the puppet of Carrera.[55] Assisted by a forced loan from the Consulado, the caudillo made hasty military preparations.[56]

In this case, however, Guatemalan military force was unneeded, for the Guatemalan conservatives now had a strong ally in El Salvador in the person of the new bishop, Jorge Viteri. While Ferrera's forces, led by Santos Guardiola and supported by Manuel José Arce, who had recently returned from exile, thwarted Cabañas's efforts in Honduras, Viteri and M. F. Pavón persuaded Malespín that the Morazanistas were simply using him. Malespín's reported ill health delayed the proposed expedition and played into the hands of Viteri. Malespín finally broke with Salvadoran President J. J. Guzmán in December 1843 and took over the presidency himself, supported by a subservient legislature on 5 February 1844. Malespín was now back in the conservative camp, with Bishop Viteri as his key adviser.[57]

The continued British presence on the Mosquito Coast and Chatfield's meddling in the internal affairs of the Central American states caused a resurgence of anti-British feeling once the Morazán crisis had passed, especially in Nicaragua and El Salvador, but Guatemala pursued cordial relations with the British consul and supported the debt settlement. Chatfield's ability to call upon British naval power allowed him to pressure these governments and thereby contributed to conservative domination, especially in El Salvador and Nicaragua.[58]

Although they had become political allies by 1844, mutual distrust remained between Carrera and the patrician clique that ran the government. These well-heeled oligarchs were mortified at having to treat the rough-hewn Carrera with respect and deference. Carrera, on his part, remembered well that the conservatives had sought his eradication equally with the liberals before 1839. Tension began to develop early in 1844 when Carrera demanded more military force and reorganization of the army. He had resigned as commander-in-chief on 5 January and again on 10 February, but agreed to remain when his demands were met on 11 February.[59] Carrera likely had a hand in the selection of three new committees. José Antonio Azmitia and other moderates figured prominently in these committees, which were officially named to "promote better administration and development." Azmitia headed the committee designated to reorganize the army and the *fuero militar*. It included another lawyer and three lieutenant colonels, including Carrera's brother Santos.[60] A second committee was charged with reforming the tariff structure to protect the country's industry and to gather statistics on crafts and employment,[61] and a third, also headed by Azmitia, was to form an agricultural company in accordance with a contract drawn up in Brussels by Bishop Viteri the previous October.[62]

The liberals now intrigued to limit the power of the conservative clergy, which had reached great proportions. They pursued this not only with Carrera but with other peasant leaders in eastern Guatemala, and they appeared to make some headway. On the same day that in Guatemala Carrera had announced his decision to continue as military commander, Sunday, 11 February, a major religious celebration had begun in San Salvador, as

Bishop Viteri consecrated Francisco de Paula García Peláez as the new archbishop of Central America. A week later Viteri and García Peláez left San Salvador on a slow, triumphal journey to Guatemala.[63] The procession reached the gates of Guatemala City on 3 March 1844 and was welcomed by Antonio Larrazábal, who had been governing the cathedral for the past four years. The new Archbishop was ushered into the city with great pomp and splendor, accompanied by President Rivera Paz, Corregidor Carlos Meany, and all the leading personages of the church, Consulado, and other corporations. But there was a notable absence. General Carrera remained in Escuintla, ostensibly "maintaining order." Major General Doroteo Monterrosa issued a statement from Villa Guadalupe praising the arrival of the archbishop on behalf of "our general [Carrera] and the rest of the individuals of the Army of the State."[64]

When Carrera did not attend the consecration of the archbishop at the cathedral on 6 March, another pompous occasion, it was clear that he was overtly snubbing the clerical party. On the following day J. J. Aycinena resigned from the cabinet, precipitating a crisis. The government immediately accepted the resignation, naming Vicente Casado, a treasury official, to replace him as acting foreign minister.[65] Suddenly, more than two thousand montañés peasants massed in Pinula and Aceytuno, near the capital, declaring their opposition to the government. Carrera hurried to the capital from the Pacific coast. He arrived on 10 March and immediately took charge of the defense, launching what was probably a mock attack against the insurgents.[66]

After a brief skirmish on the eleventh, a speedy peace accord at Guadalupe brought major changes to the government. The Convenio de Guadalupe established a new balance, bringing back considerable liberal influence in the government. Specifically, and most importantly, Carrera acceded to the reported demands of the insurgents that clergymen be barred from office. The whole affair appears suspiciously as a rigged rebellion to enable Carrera to force the clerical party from office.

The military commanders signing the Convenio protested that after five years the assembly had still failed to write a new constitution as it had been charged to do in 1839. Nor, they declared, had it met the needs of the people of Mita and other departments. They pointed out that enormous sums of money had been spent per diem for the deputies and their employees, yet the assembly had failed to solve the problems and "each day the state appears more miserable and as a ship without rudder or sail." The peace and security in the state was due "solely to our General-in-Chief." They also attacked the Supreme Court and other "defects in the government," and, claiming to have exhausted all means to get reform, said they had taken up arms rather than becoming "the toy" of the Guatemala City elite. They could have attacked the capital on the seventh, but instead had waited for the return of Carrera, and it was clear enough that they had no intention of seriously opposing Carrera.

This Convenio de Guadalupe agreed to the dissolution of the Constituent Assembly, its authority taken over by a Council of State. "This body will constitute the State," the Convenio said, and "will be popularly elected and composed of one individual from each Department." These individuals had to be natives of the departments they represented, a sharp change from the previous assembly, where the elite of the capital occupied most of the seats as representatives of the departments. This reduction in the size of the legislative body, the Convenio declared, would "result in more vigor in its proceedings, less opposition to the general welfare, more economy in the treasury, and, moreover, the disappearance of ambitious office-seekers." A second elective body, double in size, would be elected to ratify the constitution that the Council of State was to prepare. The president's powers were to be greatly expanded, with no other condition than each year submitting to a residencia by the Council of State. It placed the courts also under the direction of the council, which had the power to remove judges purely on the basis of their "good or bad administration." It called further for reorganization of the public finances, reducing the number of civil and military officials, thereby saving money and lessening the demands on the people, while making it possible for the public treasury to support the army without the necessity of bothering the property holders, who must be protected by the laws. It called for the government to promote prosperity through construction of public works, bridges and "factories for the industrious populations that are found limited to their textiles, yarns, etc." The government was also ordered to name a single land judge and surveyor for every two departments, who would be subject to prosecution and forfeiture of their fees if they did their work badly. It also demanded a surcharge on imported goods that could be manufactured within the country, reflecting the continued opposition to destruction of native industries that liberal free trade had caused. Then, reflecting the rift between Carrera and the clerical party, Article 9 demanded that ecclesiastics stay out of politics, prohibiting their election to public office, "so that the true Religion not lose its prestige and reverence." And, finally, it asked that the *fuero de guerra* be conceded to all military personnel in the state, clearly a gain for the military, which was becoming ever stronger under Carrera.[67]

The Convenio de Guadalupe, with its strong statement of popular values and attitudes toward the government, reflected the reality that neither the elite conservative nor liberal factions represented the rural masses. In this case, the military commanders rallied the peasants to defy the conservative faction with whom they had earlier allied, but the elite nature of both the liberal and conservative parties would over and over again alienate them from the masses. Certainly, it would appear that this whole rebellion was engineered by Carrera in order to curtail the clerical party. Reflecting a mix of conservative and liberal principles, it established a new balance in the government, with Carrera and the liberals gaining at the expense of the clerical party. The Convenio de Guadalupe definitively established the superiority of the military over the assembly, and it also laid the groundwork for Carrera's accession to the presidency.

On 12 March, Santos Carrera deactivated the militia in the capital, which the government had called into active duty in the face of the threatened siege.[68] At 5:00 P.M. the same day President Rivera Paz convened the assembly to "consider matters of general interest, on which the government will report." On the following day the assembly ratified the Convenio de Guadalupe, gave the government authority to implement it, and then dissolved itself in accordance with the Convenio on the fourteenth, declaring that it left the destiny of the state and its inhabitants in the hands of the government and General Carrera.[69]

As Rivera Paz began to implement the Convenio, formal and undoubtedly orchestrated notes of congratulations poured into the government from the municipalities, thanking Carrera for his action in defense of their rights, peace, and security.[70] The government set 19 May as the date for election of the delegates to the new Council of State. All gainfully employed male citizens over the age of eighteen, including soldiers, had the right to vote. This represented a considerable extension of the suffrage in Guatemala. To be elected, one had to be born in the department he would represent, be a property holder of legal age and established integrity and wisdom, and have demonstrated that he had always been "a true patriot, dedicated to the welfare of the people." Clergymen were specifically excluded, as were government employees of the department.[71]

Meanwhile, on 26 April, Rivera Paz formed a new cabinet, consisting of moderates headed by José Mariano Rodríguez as minister of government and foreign relations. After Miguel Rivera Maestre refused the finance ministry, Rivera Paz named moderate José Antonio Azmitia to that post. The new government moved into elegant, newly refurbished offices in the palace on 2 May.[72] This liberal gain in Guatemala was part of a general pattern in Central America between 1844 and 1846 as the conservative tide was temporarily checked. In the mid 1840s, former Morazanistas made significant gains in the middle states at the same time that more liberal forces gained influence in Costa Rica. British naval presence and a blockade, especially against Nicaragua, contributed to anti-British sentiment across the isthmus and checked the growing influence of Frederick Chatfield and his proconservative machinations.[73]

The election scheduled for 19 May in Guatemala did not occur, postponed indefinitely by a new crisis. Francisco Malespín, with the blessing of both Carrera and Francisco Ferrera, had taken over absolute power in El Salvador, but liberal agitation continued to keep that state unsettled.[74] In the meantime, Manuel José Arce had arrived in Antigua, an event that annoyed the Rivera Paz government, because Arce had neither asked nor received permission to reside in the state. The government kept a close watch on the former federal president, long regarded in Guatemala as a troublemaker not to be trusted politically. When Arce left Antigua and went to the Salvadoran border in early April, apparently to rendezvous with armed supporters, the Guatemalan government took quick defensive action. After the Guatemalan commissioner in El Salvador reported that an armed force had entered El Salvador from Guatemala,[75] on 2 May the government ordered General Carrera to inspect the men and arms that Guatemala maintained along the frontier and notified him that Arce had "several armed guerrillas" who were threatening peace and order in the border region.[76] Two days later Rodríguez sent a circular to the other states describing Arce's activities and justifying Guatemalan military movements to meet the threat.[77] He immediately dispatched troops from Mita to the border, while Carrera raised an army in the capital. Malespín, meanwhile, took the field quickly, and pursued Arce's band back into Guatemala.[78]

Rodríguez informed the governments of Costa Rica, Honduras, and Nicaragua on 18 May that Arce and his group had been captured and disarmed, but four days later he became aware of the presence of Malespín's troops in Guatemala and considered this as new aggression. There was suspicion that the Arce move was another plot of the clerical party, in this case against Malespín, whom the aristocrats did not trust. Malespín had met Arce's threat easily, however, and ended up strengthening his position, at least temporarily. The whole incident revived mistrust between the two governments, however.[79]

Faced with a threat of war, Rivera Paz had postponed the election, and on 23 May he simply appointed members of the Council of State, with Carrera as its head. Although it included such conservatives as Luis Batres, Manuel F. Pavón, Andrés Andreu, and José Nájera, there were none of the ultraconservative clerics on the council, and it also included a number of moderate and liberal members, such as Alejandro Marure, José Antonio Larrave, José Venacio López, José M. Urruela, José Antonio Azmitia, and José Domingo Dieguez.[80]

A week later, wearing the title of chief of the army of operations of the state, Carrera received full authority for the defense of Guatemala, and a full-fledged mobilization began, accompanied by several incidents along the border. Salvadoran troops in June advanced as far as Jutiapa.[81] Carrera's principal field commander, Vicente Cruz, issued a manifesto on 7 June, warning that the people's liberties, restored by Carrera, were in jeopardy unless they rallied to his defense.[82] Carrera himself accused Morazanistas of plotting against the peace and security of the state on 10 June in a manifesto that assured all Central American inhabitants that his army was subduing the attack and restoring peace.[83] Cruz reported on 18 June that he had driven the enemy out of Jutiapa and across the Río de la Paz.[84] Rivera Paz replaced Rodríguez on the eighteenth with Manuel Francisco Pavón as minister of foreign relations, government and war, leaving José Antonio Azmitia as finance minister.[85]

Late in the month Carrera himself marched out of the capital at the head of two divisions amid rumors that he would invade El Salvador. The government warned him on 28 June not to go beyond the borders of Guatemala, but on 7 July Carrera responded that, in accordance with the Guadalupe convention, responsibility for the security of the state was divided between the chief of state and himself, as armed forces commander, making it clear that he would determine where he would march.[86] An "Extra" edition of the *Gaceta Oficial* on 1 July carried a stinging denunciation by Rivera Paz of the atrocities committed by Malespín's forces at Jutiapa against innocent Guatemalans, and he promised that Carrera's enthusiastic but disciplined army was on its way to the border to "do justice."

Meanwhile, Santos Guardiola dealt a serious blow to the liberals in Honduras on 1 July, leading to a treaty between Honduras and El Salvador that united those two governments against the liberals in Nicaragua. With Carrera now pressing from the west, Malespín sought a peaceful solution, and Carrera agreed to a cease-fire on 26 July at the Quezada Hacienda, near El Jocote in the Department of Mita.[87] Rivera Paz initially considered sending a rather liberal delegation to the ensuing peace conference, composed of José Domingo Dieguez, José Antonio Azmitia, and Dr. Alejandro Marure, but the latter two refused to serve, so that in the end the more conservative Luis Batres and José María Urruela joined Dieguez, with Lic. Manuel Echeverría, secretary of the Consulado and another strong conservative, as secretary of the delegation.[88] In the subsequent negotiations, in which a voluminous correspondence developed, one can discern Carrera's leaning toward the liberals, even to the extent on 27 July of using the salutation "D.U.L." (Dios Unión Libertad [God Union Liberty]), long the slogan of the liberal federation, in a letter to Rivera Paz in which he detailed his military movements. Although the letter contained the usual compliments, there is a trace of coolness in its language.[89] The government responded by telling Carrera that if the Quezada meeting failed, he should maintain his army ready at the border and avoid any Salvadoran surprise attack.[90] In the meantime, Carrera's brother, Sotero, who had by now been promoted to brigadier general, maintained a force in the capital against any new attempts by the clerical party to seize power there.[91] A peace was signed at Quezada on 5 August, which essentially confirmed the caudillos Carrera, Ferrera, and Malespín, and represented a resounding defeat for the efforts of the ultraconservative clerical party in Guatemala.[92]

The military threat had turned out to be easily met by Carrera and his allies in Honduras and El Salvador, but preparations for war had precipitated another financial crisis, which Carrera used to consolidate his authority and to cement his new understanding with the moderates. Indeed, the assessment of forced loans on the propertied classes weighed most heavily against the plotting aristocratic families who were trying to oust the caudillo. In May, the Consulado had resisted a government request for $1,000 to aid the army, protesting the Consulado's lack of funds and other obligations for the public works it supervised, but in the end the Consulado loaned $2,000 to pay the troops.[93] Under Carrera's prodding the government turned to a large forced loan put under the responsibility of the departmental corregidores for collection. This levy brought grumbling immediately from Los Altos, which, although it had continued to be ruled under a military superintendent since its reincorporation into Guatemala, had been taxed less heavily. The *Gaceta Oficial* pointed that out and noted that other departments—Chiquimula, Sacatepéquez, Chimaltenango, and Amatitlán—were being called upon for quantities considerably greater than the $10,000 being collected from the departments of Los Altos.[94] The loans were also demanded from religious establishments, many of which pled poverty. When Father José Nicolás Arellano of the congregation of San Felipe Neri, however, failed to pay the $25 demanded from his community, the government slapped him with a $100 fine and demanded the full $125 immediately.[95] As the loan payments became due on 7 June, resistance stiffened. The Guatemalan corregidor protested that he could not possibly collect all the quotas in so short a time, while individuals petitioned for exemption on a variety of grounds.[96] The government advised the corregidores that the loan was urgent and told them to take whatever measures required to complete collection by the first week of June.[97]

Despite warnings of heavy fines, the loan fell far short of the demanded amount, while the military's expenses soared. On the seventh, therefore, the government demanded a new forced loan from the property holders of the capital. Warning of an imminent invasion from El Salvador, it decreed a revised sum of $60,000 (including the two previous forced loans of $10,000 each) on the capital's property holders, with a maximum assessment of $2,000 and a minimum of $200. Payments were to be made in three installments, the first immediately and the other two in a week and two weeks respectively. A commission composed of two persons from the city council, two from the Consulado, and chaired by the corregidor was named to make assessments within twenty-four hours. The loan was guaranteed by import-export duties, with bonds issued for payment of 80 percent of their face value. These bonds could be used to pay up to one-third of such duties. The decree said that foreigners were also expected to pay, and that they would be reimbursed from the treasury as soon as the present crisis was resolved, or they could accept the bonds and use them to pay up to 100 percent of customs duties. It warned that any resistance would be met by fines imposed by the same commission and enforced by the corregidor.[98]

And there was resistance! On the tenth the corregidor, in a letter to the finance minister, doubted that fines would accomplish much and asked if he could take "extraordinary measures."[99] The minister reiterated the urgency of the situation and authorized the corregidor to use fully the measures established in the decree.[100] The threat of force was real and violence occurred in some cases, but the resistance continued and in many cases it simply was very difficult if not impossible for individuals to come up with cash or liquid assets in the amounts demanded on such short notice.[101]

While continuing to pressure the citizens for loans, the government now turned to the firm of Hall, Klée and Skinner, British merchants based in Guatemala. That firm offered the government $30,000 on 17 June at 50 percent interest payable by taking two-thirds of the maritime customs revenues, until the $45,000 were collected. On the eighteenth the government called on the prior of the Consulado to try to form a consortium of capitalists in the city to procure a loan at a more favorable rate, but on the next day acting prior Juan Matheu told the government that he had solicited the merchant community and that none could make a better proposition. Thus, on the twentieth the government contracted the loan with Hall, Klée and Skinner, an indication of just how desperate the government was.[102] George Skinner promptly put up $5,000 himself, while the rest of the money was raised,[103] and while this may have relieved the immediate demands somewhat, the government continued to insist on loans from its citizens. Sotero Carrera, commanding the forces in central Guatemala, insisted that he needed money immediately to pay his troops in Escuintla and Antigua, and one can sense that the government was literally under the gun to provide payment for the military.[104] A meeting of the property holders on 1 July with the finance minister, M. F. Pavón, produced little tangible result, other than to reiterate the need for compliance.[105] On the next day the government called for a voluntary loan, in cash or horses, from the people of the state to sustain the army in their defense. It was hardly a propitious time for such a request.[106] Pavón particularly pressed the clergy of Guatemala for donations or loans for three months because of the exigencies of the defense situation.[107] The archbishop promised to convene the ecclesiastical council and to encourage individual clerics in raising a subscription as quickly as possible.[108]

A compilation of the assessments as of 9 July reveals the degree of resistance the government confronted among the capital's property holders. A hundred and seventy-two assessments, ranging from $50 to $2,000, totaled $83,295, of which only $29,301 (35 percent) had been collected by this date. Compliance was much higher at the upper levels than at the lower. Of the assessments of less than $500, only 17 percent had been paid, and among those of less than $200 (38 percent of the total number of assessments, although only 5.4 percent of the total sum), only 4 percent had been paid. By contrast, of the 23 (13 percent) highest assessments ($1,200 or more), 49 percent had been paid.[109]

That the loan fell most heavily on the property holders of the capital is evident. Of the total $90,000 loan, the capital was responsible for $83,295, or 92.5 percent. The Guatemalan government responded to the slow rate of compliance by demanding yet another loan on 10 July, seeking to raise $60,000 within three months. This offering raised the interest rate to 24 percent per annum (actually, 2 percent per month) for funds delivered within three days. As before, the loan certificates could be used to pay up to one-third of maritime duties, or they could reserve two-year certificates of $150 for each $100 paid. Those who failed to meet their assigned pledges within the three-day limit would receive no interest at all, but only the principal.[110] As funds were collected, they were dispatched immediately to the military.[111] The government quickly had no choice but to extend the three-day limit.[112] It emphasized its good credit by publishing in mid July the status of its bond issue of December 1842, when it had borrowed more than $100,000. Of the total of $111,805.84 in bonds and certificates,

$94,350.09 (84 percent) had been redeemed by the end of June 1844.[113] The corregidores meanwhile complained that they had no hope of soliciting a donativo while collecting a forced loan, with the greatest of difficulty, at the same time,[114] and on 19 July the government gave up trying to continue collections in the departments of the interior, owing to strong provincial resistance, the amount to be gained not worth the effort. It concentrated all of its effort on the residents of the capital thereafter.[115]

The government's task of collection was made all the more difficult by the military's interference on behalf of strong supporters of Carrera. On 20 July, for example, the military headquarters in the capital notified the minister of finance that Colonel José Basilio Porras and Dr. José Luna were exonerated from the payment of their quotas.[116] At the same time the army began to take a more active role in collecting the loan.[117]

After the Quezada agreement the pressure relaxed, as the military expenditures declined. Sotero Carrera, for example, the caudillo's brother, released most of the troops in the capital from service on 23 July, thereby reducing the cost of his garrison to $250 per day.[118]

The merchants of the capital supplied a significant portion of the total. Although they often found it difficult to raise the sums demanded by the government, they eventually received repayment, often at yields considerably above those that they could expect to receive from their commercial investments.[119] Meanwhile, the Guatemalan government pursued the possibility, through Young Anderson, of a loan of $100,000 to $200,000 from London bankers.[120] Shortages of funds continued into September, but whenever the troops did not get paid, Carrera applied pressure, which could include assaults by troops on commercial establishments.[121]

Such irregular means of funding the military continued to plague the city's stability, and funding came almost exclusively from the capital and Antigua. Yet under Finance Minister M. F. Pavón, the payments were regularized, and by December he could report that a large portion of the debt had been redeemed. He emphasized the need to improve and arrange Guatemala's public credit on a more stable basis. He acknowledged that the variety of kinds of notes, receipts, and paper money in circulation was a problem and admitted that there had been injustice to creditors, some being paid, others not, and that the government had to attend to the rights of all creditors equally.[122]

The return of Francisco Morazán to Central America in 1842 had been short-lived and contributed to reactionary policies throughout the isthmus, but it also set off another round of civil disturbances that kept the region in turmoil through much of the decade. The death of Morazán did not end liberal pretensions, but it did weaken the chances for reorganization of the union. The emergence of the separate state governments in the mid-1840s was accompanied by continued political unrest and military action. In the opportunistic struggles among the caudillos of the isthmus, ideological issues often became fuzzy. In Guatemala, the conservative elite had made considerable gains in restoring their hegemony following the Carrera revolt, but they had been unable to consolidate their control, and the continued liberal-conservative struggle played into the hands of the skillful caudillo, who built his military machine at the expense of the elite. The Guadalupe Convention, early in 1844, definitively established military superiority over the assembly, a reality that has not been seriously challenged since in Guatemala. While liberals were able to make virtually no progress toward their ideological goals under Carrera, they were able to share in the ruling of Guatemala and to check the dominance by the clerical elite. Yet the failure of the liberals to restore the union and to bring peace to the region meant that the continued political disorder would allow the conservatives sooner or later to consolidate and to establish a stronger hold on the state, making reunion all the more difficult. The rhetoric of Carrera's manifestos and proclamations, written by members of the elite, reflected the tone of the dialogue in the 1840s but had little to do with the caudillo's exercise of raw power.

PART TWO

The Conservative Citadel

CHAPTER EIGHT

The Republic
of Guatemala

GUATEMALA CITY, although still relatively new in the 1840s, was generally in need of modernizing. Muddy streets, partially constructed private and public buildings, and deplorable sanitary conditions characterized its appearance.[1] The center of the city appeared substantially different than it does today. The central "Plaza de Armas" was surrounded on three sides by arcades, including the city hall on the north side (where the present national palace now stands), the old national palace on the east (where today there is a park and a bandstand), and the Aycinena palace and commercial establishment on the south side (today filled with small shops, the building having been rebuilt following the earthquake of 1917). On the west side of the plaza stood the new Cathedral of Guatemala (still standing today), a neo-classical design by an Italian architect. The archbishop's palace stands on one side and the parochial school, Colegio de Infantes, on the other. The plaza itself served as the central market with its wooden stalls, a pretty fountain in the center having replaced an equestrian statue of Carlos IV, pulled down at independence. The main street was the Calle Real (today Sexta Avenida), but other important commercial streets were the Calle del Comercio (today Séptima Avenida) and Calle de Mercaderes (today Octava Calle).[2]

The restoration of peace allowed the conservative elite to pay more attention to the city's problems. Although liberal historians of Guatemala have painted the period as one of nearly complete stagnation, in fact the city grew notably during the Carrera years and experienced significant economic growth. Carlos Antonio Meany, a merchant closely affiliated with the leading families, as first alcalde of Guatemala City and as corregidor of the Department of Guatemala, in November 1842 published a new set of ordinances aimed at improving the police, security, sanitation, and appearance of the city. They outlined the obligations of property owners regarding policing of their property, disposal of trash, drainage, and so on; renewed the prohibition on carrying arms without a license; and prohibited the sale of fireworks, which had been known to start fires in the capital. These ordinances, with minor additions and revisions, were reissued periodically in the decades following.[3]

In the same year, the Constituent Assembly authorized the city to collect a half real (U.S. $0.0625) on the sale of each maquila of flour, pound of cinnamon, and bottle of aguardiente, and a quarter real per bottle of beer, wine, vinegar, oil, or any other liquor, for the purpose of providing street lighting.[4] This project dragged on for years. Julio Rosignon, one of the city's most progressive residents, proposed several times that the city install gas lights. Instead, the city implemented a complicated system of candles, changed nightly in one of three sizes, depending on the stages of the moon. Not until 1862 did gaslights finally replace the candles.[5]

With the collaboration of the Consulado, the city was able to pave the main commercial streets in 1843 and to beautify the tree-lined Paseo del Calvario with public benches.[6] In early 1844 the *Gaceta Oficial* called the municipality's attention to the need for street names and signs.[7] In the same year a British traveler observed that "the number of fine Churches, and the trees and gardens interspersed among the houses, give Guatemala a very handsome appearance when viewed from a short distance; but on entering the city the illusion is dispelled, for, although the streets are wide, straight, and very clean, the houses have a mean and dismal appearance, none having more than a ground story, and the windows being small, with iron gratings."[8] The city provided only minimal police protection and those with valuable property were for the most part obliged to provide their own security. In 1847 the municipal police department consisted of two chiefs and ten constables, chosen by and under the supervision of the corregidor of Guatemala. The chiefs received, respectively, salaries of fifteen and twelve pesos per month, while the constables received two reales ($0.25) per day, or $7.50 per month.[9]

This provincial capital was the scene of considerable pomp and festivity upon the return of Carrera's troops following the Peace of Quezada. Bishop Viteri, the Salvadoran negotiator, preceded the military forces by about a week when he arrived on 18 August 1844, and after an elaborate public reception he met with Rivera Paz on the nineteenth. Viteri remained in Guatemala for several months, claiming credit for establishing peace between Guatemala and El Salvador.[10] Following the signing of the agreement at Quezada on 5 August, Carrera assembled his army just outside the capital for a triumphal entrance, which took place finally on the twenty-sixth amid cannon salutes and throngs of people. President Rivera Paz and Bishop Viteri met them at the plaza, but the absence of Archbishop García Peláez reflected the continued coolness between Carrera and the clerical party. After a review of the troops, Rivera Paz thanked the army for its valiant service.[11] Carrera soon celebrated not only his military victory, but also the birth of a daughter, María Mercedes Carrera García, on 8 September 1844. All of the leading political, military, and diplomatic leaders in the capital attended a gala party Carrera gave after her baptism (performed by Bishop Viteri) and confirmation (by Archbishop García Peláez) on the seventeenth.[12]

Meanwhile, fighting continued between Honduras, El Salvador, and Nicaragua, with party lines often obscured in the opportunistic and feudal struggles of rival caudillos. A showdown came at Nacaome, Honduras, on 24 October 1844, when Francisco Ferrera and Francisco Malespín joined to defeat an invading Nicaraguan force.[13] Malespín and Ferrera had met during the second week of October to renew their alliance and make clear their opposition to the Morazanistas Trinidad Cabañas, Gerardo Barrios, and Joaquín Rivera. Malespín then led a combined Honduran-Salvadoran force into Nicaragua and captured León on 24 January 1845.[14] Although this did not end the fighting definitively, it brought a temporary respite. A list of the officers serving General Cabañas reveals, if nothing else, the extent to which his forces came from several states and that they did not represent regional so much as personal and ideological allegiances, or perhaps opportunistic ones. Of his twenty-four officers, there were eleven Hondurans, six Salvadorans, three Nicaraguans (León), and one national each from Guatemala, Costa Rica, France, and Santa Elena.[15]

In Guatemala, the energetic Manuel Francisco Pavón began to put some order into the Guatemalan government's finances and services. A notice he published on 7 November 1844 reflected the problems that must have accompanied more popular participation in government in the early national period:

NOTICE
In compliance with the order of the Supreme Government, the public is advised for its exact observance:

1. That all those presenting petitions or any other solicitudes will direct themselves to the chief clerk of the respective Secretariat, and present to him

the suggested resolution, without interrupting under any pretext the work of the office, serious abuse of which can no longer continue.

2. Everyone who must speak with the President will be announced by the doorman.

3. Anyone who must speak with the Secretaries of the Government on a private matter, rather than on a matter of urgent government business, will be received in the respective secretariat between 1:00 and 2:00 P.M., and at no other time.

Guatemala, 7 November 1844
Pavón. [16]

Rivera Paz labored diligently under difficult circumstances, often suffering insults and disregard for his office by Carrera and the Cachurecos. On 14 October Pavón issued an order that the president of the state was to be given the same courtesy of the use of "Excellency" as was General Carrera.[17] Public rowdiness was frequent and often involved the troops. When some of Sotero Carrera's troops wounded the British consul's secretary, Mr. Evans, Chatfield protested vehemently. Colonel Carrera ordered an "investigation," but, characteristically, no one was brought to book for the incident. Instead, the investigating committee merely made some recommendations for improving public order, and the president and General Vicente Cruz, newly named corregidor of Guatemala, issued stern manifestos warning the public against disturbing the peace.[18]

Public disorders and apparent new attempts of the ultraconservatives to regain control of the country prompted Carrera to seize full power at the end of this eventful year. The cabinet resigned on 2 December. Rivera Paz resigned on 8 December, unable or unwilling to form a new cabinet and announcing that the country needed a change in administration.[19] Pavón, upon leaving office on 3 December, had submitted a revealing report in which he pointed to the substantial reorganization of the country that had occurred and significant beginnings of construction of public works and infrastructure. Yet military costs and limited revenues had restricted greater progress. He recommended centralizing the treasury and reorganization of the financial structure of the government.[20]

The Constituent Council, later called Constituent Congress, which had been called off the preceding April, now convened on 8 December. It elected the moderately liberal José Venacio López, as its president, and under his direction on 11 December chose Carrera to succeed Rivera Paz. Two days later it appointed a liberal Supreme Court headed by Miguel Larreinaga. Carrera took office on 14 December in a ceremony that began at 11:00 A.M. in the council's meeting room. López, in administering the oath of office, compared Carrera to Bartolomé de las Casas. Carrera responded with a very short speech, promising to obey the law and work for everyone's welfare, specifically asking for the support and guidance of the clergy. Then they all went to the palace where Rivera Paz welcomed them and praised Carrera for his work in restoring peace and security. He presented Carrera to the diplomatic corps as Carrera formally took possession of the office. Rivera Paz, so long the puppet of Carrera, now retired to private life.[21]

Thus the moderate liberals had once more regained control through alliance with the caudillo, as the period of ultraconservative reaction against the Gálvez reforms came to an end. Yet what could they do? In reality they were simply the tools of the caudillo, and they soon found that they had little chance of reenacting their liberal program into law. At most, they checked the conservative reaction for a time.

Carrera quickly laid down priorities for setting the government in order, which precluded much of the legislation favored by the liberals. First of all, he sought to relieve the pressure on the public treasury through reduction in government spending, especially for public employees. On 20 December the government published these priorities for the treasury:

1. Payment of military expenses and salaries of its chiefs and officers.

2. Public employees in actual service whose salaries are $25 or less per month will receive $25 [per month]; but those with salaries of $30 to $40 are reduced to $25, and those with salaries of $50 or more are reduced by 50%.

3. Pensions to widows and retired employees will be reduced in conformity with item 2.

4. Office expenses will be paid if accompanied by the proper requisition from the General Accounting Office, otherwise they will not be paid.

5. All other obligations are temporarily suspended.[22]

The government also reduced mail service to the departments to a bimonthly schedule, as it had been before Pavón had established weekly service on the previous 1 July.[23]

The liberals wanted a constitution that would embody their principles and undo the reactionary reforms of the early 1840s. Carrera agreed to the necessity of a constitution, but he hardly endorsed liberal principals. In a public declaration on 19 December he charged the Constituent Council to write the document, warning them not to forget their mission as had the previous assembly. He made it clear that the new constitution would respect property and promote the economy, industry, science, and the arts. He promised that he and his officers were subject to public opinion and would obey the orders of the government, venerate the Christian religion, respect the independence of the judiciary, and enforce its decisions.[24] Work on this new charter, however, did not advance significantly during the Guatemalan summer. In late January 1845 Carrera left the capital, turning the executive power over to his minister of finance, Joaquín Durán. With his family, he headed for a month's rest at one of his country estates.[25]

Within a week, a small group of conservatives engineered a plot to seize the government. On the morning of 2 February a group of soldiers released some political prisoners, among them Doroteo Monterrosa, imprisoned a year earlier for attempting a coup. Monterrosa immediately proclaimed a military revolt in which officers loyal to Carrera were deposed, killed, or driven from the city. About eight hundred insurgents quickly took over the city's government and arms. Sotero Carrera rallied troops loyal to Carrera outside the city and prepared to counterattack, while within the city the insurgents celebrated by ringing church bells, firing guns, and shooting off firecrackers.[26]

Monterrosa's success, however, was unanticipated by most of the aristocratic families, for although Monterrosa's troops restrained themselves from looting and other violent acts, few people of any importance declared themselves for the revolt. Perhaps a realization that Sotero Carrera was concentrating a loyalist force in Antigua, as well as the knowledge that Carrera still commanded great popularity among the masses, had something to do with their reticence. Moreover, many of the creole elite probably considered Monterrosa to be as bad or worse than Carrera. Monterrosa soon recognized the precariousness of his position, and on 6 February agreed with Durán to vacate the city in return for 5,000 pesos to distribute to his troops. The civil authorities and merchants of the capital rounded up this sum hastily.[27]

As Monterrosa departed the capital on 10 February, Sotero Carrera and Vicente Cruz, although commanding a smaller force, surprised and routed the insurgents between San Andrés and Concepción. Cruz and Carrera disregarded, or perhaps were ignorant of, Monterrosa's agreement with Durán. Sotero Carrera reported to the government in Guatemala the following day that the "enthusiasm and valor" of his First Company of the Santa Rosa Battalion alone prevented the enemy from organizing resistance to his forces. Monterrosa suffered seventeen killed and many more wounded, while the loyalists lost only two men and captured 153 rifles, two barrels of powder, and other spoils. Pursuing the rebels, Cruz and Carrera dispersed them, preventing their rumored rendezvous with a conspiracy in Los Altos.[28]

Rafael Carrera, meanwhile, having learned of the insurgency in Escuintla, rounded up a force of two thousand mostly unarmed peasants and marched into the capital with this unwanted and unruly mob.[29] He avoided

TABLE 5
Quotas and Collections on Forced Loan, July 1845

Departments	Assigned	Collected	Remaining
Guatemala	$6,500	$500.00	$6,000.00
Sacatepéquez	2,000	1,200.00	800.00
Chimaltenango	1,500	1,494.00	6.00
Escuintla	1,200	320.00	880.00
Chiquimula	2,000	1,769.22	230.78
Verapaz	1,200	607.00	593.00
Los Altos	3,600	3,264.72	335.28
Amatitlán	2,000	1,539.00	461.00
Totals	$20,000	$10,693.94	$9,306.06

Source: Gaceta Oficial, 26 July 1845.

a direct confrontation with the conservative elite, it being unclear who had really planned or supported the coup, but he summarily shot about ten minor figures and then demanded a forced loan of twenty thousand pesos to pay the force he had hastily raised to combat the threat.[30] After paying Monterrosa $5,000, this was a bitter pill for the property holders of the capital, so they attempted to spread collection of the loan over much of the interior as well, especially Los Altos, while avoiding entirely any levy on Carrera's favored Department of Mita. Requests for collection went out to the corregidores on 3 March, with instructions to divide the "extraordinary request" among the property holders of their districts. Table 5 indicates the amounts assigned and collected by early July. Only those having in excess of one thousand pesos were to be tapped for this loan, but the government admonished the archbishop to see that the clergy paid its assignments.

A coup in El Salvador at about the same time had ousted Francisco Malespín. Bishop Viteri played a prominent role in the intrigue leading to that event, including the excommunication of his former ally. Carrera's foreign minister, José Nájera, assured the new Salvadoran government of Guatemala's nonintervention, but turmoil continued in the middle states of the isthmus and Carrera's government watched the scene carefully.[31] Heavy damage to the area around Amatitlán, Palín, and Petapa by an eruption of Volcán Pacaya in late March and early April distracted the Carrera government from affairs in the neighboring states, but a commission composed of Alejandro Marure and José M. Urruela signed a treaty with the new Salvadoran government on 4 April, ratified by Guatemala on 24 April. Carrera did not trust the moderate Francisco Dueñas, who now headed the government in San Salvador, but he also hoped to regain some influence in that state through this treaty of alliance.[32] This continuing turmoil in Central America, especially in the middle states of the old federation caused the *Mentor Costarricense* to comment: "In Guatemala General Carrera has defeated General Monterroso, forcing him to evacuate the capital. No judgment is possible regarding the disintegration that is occurring among the peoples of the Republic in the present situation. It is clear that the evils of the war continue to afflict the Central Americans of the other states, and that neither reason nor their sufferings are enough to stop them, nor to obligate the States to agree to a bond of perfect union and friendship, and to erect a Government that provides security at home and respectability abroad."[33]

The currents of internecine warfare, xenophobia toward foreign aggression and exploitation, and the inability to govern effectively at the national level continued to plague Central America, and in the middle states governments came and went with the seasons. In Guatemala, the moderate liberals held to their uneasy coalition with the caudillo against new conservative efforts to regain control. The clergy continued to attack from the pulpit. On the occasion of blessing the temple of the Recollection Fathers, for example, Antonio Larrazábal, considered one of Central America's great liberals at the time of the Cortes of Cádiz, launched a diatribe against the liberals for having expelled Archbishop Casáus and the regular orders. Barrundia, in the meantime, worked toward easing out Carrera, believing that it was only a matter of time until liberal enlightenment would once more lead Guatemala out of the darkness imposed by the Hispanic-Catholic tradition. "A savage regime in the middle of the nineteenth century cannot last in independent America," he declared. "The light comes to us from the North and from the South; only the center is overcast, and this dark night cannot be eternal."[34]

Already, of course, most of the religious orders had been readmitted to Guatemala, but now the reorganized and restored Jesuits sought to come back, and here the liberals sought to draw the line. They revoked the decree of 3 July 1843 that had authorized return of the Jesuits. A spirited debate surrounded this issue, with Father Aycinena and other clergy arguing in vain on behalf of the Jesuits. Those who had already arrived on the North Coast were reimbursed their travel expenses, and they departed once more. The liberal Constituent Assembly, in justifying its position, pointed to damage that the Jesuits had done in Europe and claimed it had no knowledge of any papal disposition to reestablish the order, despite the fact that one had been issued in 1814.[35] Carrera's direct complicity in this move to keep the clerical party in its place appears in a petition from the municipality and residents of Santa Rosa published in the *Gaceta* as evidence that the people did not want the Jesuits back. This rather simple statement, saying that wise men made the decision to expel the Jesuits in 1767 and that the order had caused much trouble elsewhere, appears contrived, and its origin in Carrera's home district suggests his approval.[36]

Joaquín Durán continued to run the government through the end of May, when Carrera decided to resume his presidency. Carrera's resumption of the presidency signified a setback for the liberals, whose influence had been growing until this point. The conservatives could take little comfort in the change, however, for it represented a more direct rule by the caudillo and his cronies, rather than a turn toward a conservative elite cabinet. Authority now resided in the hands of a triumvirate of Carrera, his brother Sotero, and General Gerónimo Paiz. Paiz replaced Durán in the ministry of finance and war on 4 June, while Sotero Carrera commanded the army. The Guatemalan elite and foreign residents regarded Paiz as a savage, perhaps worse than Carrera. Chatfield called him "a *persona non grata* among Europeans living in Guatemala, . . . pictured by them in the most derogatory colors as a drunkard, an atheist, and a man lacking *savoir vivre.*"[37] To Paiz were attributed some of the most barbaric acts of the era. It was to this period that the U.S. envoy, E. G. Squier, later referred when he wrote that the attempt to put the Indian "on a political and social footing with the white man has entailed eternal anarchy, and threatened a complete dissolution of the political body. . . . It appears that the only hope of Central America consists in averting the numerical decline of its white population, and increasing that element in the composition of its people."[38]

In the foreign ministry, José Antonio Azmitia replaced José Nájera on 5 June. Azmitia alone among Carrera's close advisers now enjoyed the respect of the creole elite. He was an enlightened moderate and may have prevented some barbaric excesses of the regime, although he had little real influence beyond foreign affairs. Despite his unsavory reputation, Paiz's brief term as minister of finance and war was not without accomplishment. Faced with the grim fiscal circumstances of the government, he followed the hard-line economic policies instituted earlier by Pavón, continuing the reduction in public employees' salaries and making other economic sacrifices to restore public credit. He reduced departmental officials, making the corregidores also the justices of original jurisdiction, and abolished the police lieutenants in that court, assigning their tasks to the municipality. This not only saved salary money, of course, but also greatly increased the local authority of the corregidores, who served at Carrera's pleasure. He gave priority to settling the foreign debt and to establishing stronger credit abroad, a factor that further alienated native creditors among the elite, but was applauded by foreign interests.[39] One foreign resident pointed out that Paiz's earlier experience as customs collector at Izabal was an asset to him in this regard, and that "he made some wise laws for the suppression of smuggling, by which he so much increased the revenue of the state that it is not only amply sufficient for the expenses of the government, but has enabled him to pay off part of the debts due to private merchants, almost a new occurrence in the government of the state."[40]

The moderately improved financial state of the country, aided by rising cochineal exports, allowed Carrera to ease up demands for forced loans. In August 1845, the government responded sympathetically to efforts of the archbishop to resist quotas assigned to two priests in the Verapaz, the government warning the finance minister that he "must always take care that the clergy not be burdened with more than justly corresponds to them" and that no one with less than a thousand pesos of wealth should be required to meet this levy.[41] In response to strong diplomatic pressure, Carrera later backed down on his cancellation of diplomatic exemptions from taxes on goods for personal use.[42] In May 1846 the government was able also to revoke its emergency measures of the previous June and July and thus to resume full payment of employees and to allow bonds in circulation to be used for payment of debts, including maritime duties.[43]

Meanwhile, Carrera put distance between himself and the Constituent Assembly as they completed a new constitution. In early August he announced his intention once more to take leave of the presidency. A committee of the assembly on 7 August urged that his resignation not be accepted, but on 1 September the assembly granted him a month's leave, requesting only that he keep them informed of his whereabouts in case anything occurred that required his attention.[44] General Vicente Cruz took over the chief executive position in Carrera's absence, signifying a more liberal leadership, especially since General Paiz now left the finance and war ministry to return to Izabal as corregidor. After the uncle of liberal historian Lorenzo Montúfar, Miguel Rivera Maestre, refused to accept that post, it was carried on by section chiefs. Azmitia also left the foreign ministry, to be replaced by another liberal, Mariano Padilla.[45] Cruz was clearly more acceptable to the liberals and was an intimate friend of Manuel Arrivillaga, who according to Lorenzo Montúfar was "then a liberal," so that José F. Barrundia once more had some influence in the government.[46]

With this shift in their favor, the liberals moved to adopt a constitution that the Constituent Assembly presented on 16 September, a document that reflected moderate liberal views. Notably, Article 90 forbade reelection of the president.[47] They also attempted to restore the liberal municipal government plan that would have eroded the substantial power of the corregidores. A committee to study the municipal reforms, however, headed by J. J. Aycinena, vehemently opposed this plan, defending the traditional system that Carrera had restored. It was a point of major difference between liberal and conservative politicians in this period as is seen in the suspension of the plan on 17 November 1847 and again on 14 February 1848.[48]

In mid-January 1846 Aycinena made a long, erudite argument opposing integration of the Indians into the municipal government system. He argued that the Spanish had done little to bring about racial homogeneity in Guatemala and that, therefore, there remained very different customs and languages among the Indians. He attacked the Cádiz Constitution of 1812, which he said was at the root of these efforts to establish a new municipal system, but which in reality caused chaos. In fact, "all the constitutions of the new Hispanic-American republics that followed the lines of the 1812" document, he said, "had fallen equally as had the Cádiz Constitution itself, after having demonstrated experimentally that, far from serving social ends, it had done no more than foment disorder and demoralize the people." He believed the municipal system was one of the greatest defects in that constitution because it tried to break down the traditional customs and securities built up over centuries, replacing it with a system that the illiterate masses, "over which only the moral force of habit has any force," could not easily comprehend. He also rejected imitation of the U.S. model, noting that the North Americans had not made major changes in their social structure nor municipal organization. The U.S. Constitution, he argued, was consistent with North American colonial tradition and organizational structure. Attempting to change the social structure in Guatemala had incited the Carrera revolution. And lest the liberals had forgotten, he reminded everyone that Carrera was dedicated to maintenance of social order and the customs of the people. In fact, Aycinena opposed the whole constitutional reform of September 1845.[49] The conservatives campaigned hard against ratification of the new constitution and debate continued throughout the remainder of the year. Meanwhile, with Cruz as acting chief of state, Mariano Padilla was able to make a few minor changes in the statutes of the University of San Carlos, although the institution remained closely under the control of J. J. Aycinena, who remained its rector and had opposed the liberal educational reforms of Mariano Gálvez in the 1830s.[50]

Carrera remained aloof from the debate until November, but when the liberals convened a new assembly to ratify the constitution, he resumed the presidency on 17 November 1845, bringing back Paiz and Azmitia to the ministries.[51] He quickly consolidated his own position, dissolved the assembly, and convened a new one that he controlled. A committee of this assembly presented a negative recommendation on 24 January 1846, concluding with a motion to reject the constitution and convene a whole new constitutional convention. After a week's discussion, the motion passed on 1 February, and Carrera signed it a week later.[52]

Guatemala was not nearly so peaceful as the government claimed in 1846 and early 1847, and a sense of instability continued. Banditry was common. Armed bands roamed certain regions, assaulting farms and towns, killing those who resisted their demands for money, food, horses, and supplies. The public treasury and customs houses were robbed on occasion. Carrera's own montaña district was the scene of much of this trouble, and it could not be blamed entirely on intrigue from neighboring El Salvador and Honduras.[53] Carrera toured eastern Guatemala in December 1845, seeking solutions to the disorder while making a pilgrimage to the shrine of the Black Christ of Esquipulas.[54] Meanwhile, his brother Santos expanded the family economic interests as he applied for permission to establish an *aguardiente* distillery, a request the government quickly granted.[55] The banditry also, of course, justified Carrera in tightening his authority and that of his corregidores. In early 1846, for example, the government imposed stringent regulations regarding the comings and goings of most foreigners and nationals.[56] Rumors of conspiracy and political intrigue continued to circulate in the capital as the conservatives sought to regain their former influence. Carrera reflected the strain of these problems in a letter he wrote to his mistress, Chepita Silva, in early April, in which he expressed his disgust with the situation in the country.[57]

The debate over the Constitution of 1845 coincided with the arrival of the news of the death of Archbishop Ramón Casáus y Torres in Havana on 9 November 1845. His advancing age, ill health, and news of the continued turmoil in Central America had deterred him from returning to his see in Guatemala even after Morazán's execution. Carrera had written him personally as recently as September, urging him to return, emphasizing the need for his leadership.[58] The news of his death reached the Guatemalan capital on 13 January 1846, at which time the double bells were rung for nine days at noon and sundown, and a funeral mass was celebrated for him in the cathedral on Monday, 19 January.[59] His cadaver was later brought to Guatemala for interment in the cathedral. The casket reached Izabal on board the royal Spanish naval schooner *Polka* on 20 May and a funeral took place in due course in the capital.[60]

A group of University of San Carlos students conspired to assassinate Carrera as he left the cathedral following the funeral. Forewarned, Carrera was well protected and nothing happened, but an investigation followed, and several students were either imprisoned or exiled. Commenting on the plot later, and on his leniency in dealing with the students, the caudillo put the blame on their teachers and parents, as he assured the "peaceful residents" of the capital that they had nothing to fear for their security. Of the students, he said that these youths, by their education, should be the hope of the country's future, but he warned parents to be more vigilant regarding their behavior, for they would be held responsible for their children's misdeeds. He warned the professors that the freedom without limits permitted these students was a cancer that devoured and damaged too many youth, and warned parents and teachers alike that his government would not tolerate such conduct, but would persist in making "Guatemala a happy country, under a rule of law, order and a rational and well understood liberty."[61]

Notwithstanding the lawlessness, by comparison with the other states of the isthmus, Guatemala began to gain a modicum of stability in the 1840s. The continual warfare among rival caudillos in El Salvador, Honduras, and Nicaragua could not be ignored by Carrera. He took steps from time to time to support his old allies, Ferrera and Malespín, with arms and supplies, but he showed little inclination to join in the efforts to restore the union.[62] Carrera was also aware of external interests in the isthmus, especially of the British on the eastern coast, highlighted by the crowning of a new Mosquito King, George Augustus, as George IV by the British at Belize in 1845.[63] There was also French and Belgian interest in an interoceanic canal, but there was especially apprehension over the designs of the United States following news of the annexation of Texas and the U.S. invasion of Mexico. Yet efforts at reunion to meet the British threat failed, in no small part owing to the influence of Frederick Chatfield. Under liberal influence, Carrera did send Mariano Padilla to El Salvador early in 1846 to try to form some sort of alliance to check the encroachment on Central American territory by its neighbors, as well as by Great Britain.[64]

Chatfield feared that the United States might support such efforts and met with Carrera on 23 May 1846, primarily to persuade him to restore the exemption from taxes on the goods of diplomatic personnel, but he also succeeded in convincing Carrera of the advantages of better relations with Britain. Chatfield tried especially to forestall General Paiz's xenophobic policies. Chatfield believed that the interview had gone well, and by the end of the year it was evident that the liberal influence of Foreign Minister Azmitia was once more waning and that the conservatives, who were closer to British interests and opposed to reunion, were regaining influence with Carrera. A distinction needs to be made here between the conservative business interests and landholding interests of the first families of the capital, who tended to favor British commercial development, as opposed to the ultraconservative, xenophobic elements such as General Paiz, Carrera, and some of the clergy, who opposed all foreign influence except Spanish. Manuel Francisco Pavón and Luis Batres were among the most important of Chatfield's friends in Guatemala, but that influence was not so great during this period of moderate liberal resurgence.[65]

Although Guatemala had declared its sovereignty and behaved independently since Carrera's victory, and there had been no federation since his defeat of Morazán in 1840, the concept of union persisted. None of the states completely closed the door to reunion. Guatemala and Costa Rica, however, especially moved in the direction of absolute state sovereignty. The Constituent Assembly of Guatemala on 14 November 1843 had emphasized Guatemala's independent course when it decreed modifications in the state's coat of arms, "in view of the dissolution of the federal pact and the independence of the State of Guatemala."[66] Yet the continual warfare since the breakup of the federation, especially in the middle states, had rekindled hopes for union among many Central Americans.[67] The liberals especially pressed for reunion, while the conservatives, encouraged by Chatfield, resisted this Morazanista idea.[68] U.S. aggression toward Mexico strengthened Chatfield's hand and had much to do with the failure of the Sonsonate Conference in mid-1846 to bring about agreement on reunion.[69]

A new plot in Guatemala in early July brought yet another shake-up to the government, with Joaquín Durán returning to the ministry of finance and war in place of General Paiz, a move generally applauded by elite liberals and conservatives alike. On 11 July the *Gaceta* assured the city that all was quiet in the state and that the plot had failed. It said that some arrests had been made, without identifying them, but assured the elite that there were "no notable persons of property" among those who would be prosecuted. Moreover, it added, the plot had no support among the honest people of the community, and it had been artisans who first reported it.[70] Suspiciously, however, the next issue of the *Gaceta* denied a charge (by unnamed persons) that the prisoners taken in the recent plot were tortured. It ridiculed the idea and said that no one believed that.[71] Further adjustments were made in the government in August, however, with the addition of a third ministry. J. A. Azmitia, formerly in charge of foreign relations, justice, and ecclesiastical affairs, continued as minister of interior (later called gobernación), while José Mariano Rodríguez, now back from the unsuccessful Sonsonate Conference, became foreign minister. And José Nájera took over finance and war following Durán's resignation after only a little more than a month in office.[72]

This capable trio of Guatemalan creoles ended the overbearing influence of Paiz. The creole elite was having great difficulty adjusting to the rising mestizo-Indian influence that Carrera had brought to power. Even now, in addition to Carrera, the military remained solidly in mestizo hands. General Vicente Cruz continued as vice-president and Sotero Carrera continued as corregidor of the Department of Guatemala.[73]

The violence continued in El Salvador, where liberals regained the upper hand and ended the influence of Carrera's man, Malespín. Jorge Viteri, the conservative bishop who had excommunicated Malespín when that caudillo had conspired with the liberals, now found himself banished from El Salvador. He continued to conspire in Guatemala, organizing support for an invasion of El Salvador by Malespín in November 1846. The effort failed, however, and in the end Malespín was murdered, temporarily diminishing Carrera's role in El Salvador.[74]

A handbill, published in December over Carrera's signature, reflected the liberal slant of the Guatemalan government at this point and its abandonment of Malespín. It argued that El Salvador had been saved from anarchy and horror and that the alliance between the two states had been preserved. The handbill justified the recent granting of freedom to political prisoners to leave the state, apparently in reference to another liberal action. It also pointed to Carrera's continuing protection of the working class and noted especially his policy of relieving them of taxation.[75] There was an especially wet rainy season in 1846, with flooding, landslides, road washouts, illness, and crop damage being the unfortunate results.[76] Carrera took care to maintain his ties to the people during such periods, aware of the potential political repercussions of natural disasters.

In matters of foreign policy Carrera could not escape the influence of Frederick Chatfield. Chatfield was wary of the rising influence of the United States in Central America. The Bidlack Treaty that the United States signed with New Granada guaranteed it rights of way through Panama as soon as it had assured its claim to Oregon (1846), and early in the war with Mexico the United States seized California, making its interest in an isthmian route all the more important. The liberals, traditionally friendly to the United States, sought to join with the United States in carving up Mexican territory. Azmitia urged Carrera to send a mission to the United States to negotiate an alliance or even to establish a U.S. protectorate over Guatemala, in return for which Guatemala would recover Chiapas and Soconusco from Mexico.[77]

British pretensions on the eastern coast of Central America had increased the tension between Central America and Britain, and Chatfield worked diligently against American influence on the isthmus from this point on. Toward this end he encouraged Carrera to declare absolute independence, hoping to make it more dependent on British protection, as he emphasized the danger of U.S. expansionism. A letter from José Mariano Rodríguez to Chatfield on 26 January 1847 reflected this influence, announcing Guatemala's intention to declare its independence, its language reading very much like that of Carrera's eventual speech declaring independence in March.[78] In any event, Chatfield claimed credit for this decision in a letter to Palmerston two days later. Chatfield was moving toward the apogee of his influence in Central America and was alarmed over U.S. rivalry. He argued to Palmerston that Britain should also dominate the Pacific coast of Central America "in anticipation of the Americans."[79]

Thus on 9 March 1847 the Guatemalan government formally notified the other Central American states of its decision to declare absolute independence. The foreign minister noted that the convention of states planned since the breakup of the federation had failed to bring about national reorganization, nor did any other proposals for reunion seem propitious, and Guatemala could no longer remain in that uncertain and difficult situation. It was, therefore, declaring its absolute independence and proceeding to form treaties and alliances with nations that recognized its sovereign independence.[80]

A week later the government named a bipartisan committee to project a new constitution. The three-member commission included Pedro Molina, a strong liberal; Alejandro Marure, a moderate liberal who had served in both liberal and conservative governments; and strong conservative Gregorio Urruela. Although the liberals still believed in Central American union, Molina's enthusiastic acceptance of this assignment suggests that the liberals accepted collaboration with the conservatives and the decision to separate Guatemala in a rare display of political unity in the state.[81]

Carrera called government and community leaders to the palace on Thursday, 18 March. In addition to the three cabinet ministers, the regent of the Supreme Court and dean of the Ecclesiastical Council were present, as were representatives of the Consulado, the Guatemala City Council, rector of the University of San Carlos, corregidor of the Department of

Guatemala, and other authorities. The minister of the interior, J. A. Azmitia, read the manifesto which, over Carrera's signature, expressed the government's motive for the proposed declaration of Guatemalan independence. Discussion, generally favorable if we can believe the official account, followed, and the meeting adjourned.

A gala celebration of the event took place that weekend, with fireworks and "general illumination" on Saturday night and a formal public declaration of independence on Sunday, 21 March. After a *Te Deum* mass celebrated by the archbishop at the cathedral, there was a splendid banquet at the palace for the dignitaries, but luncheon was also laid on for the troops in the corridors of the palace and for the public at city hall, the official account commenting on how "notable was the order which was observed at both these tables." At the main table in the palace, after enthusiastic toasts by Guatemalan officials, the British vice consul, and other diplomats and clergymen, President Carrera closed with his own: "To the Republic of Guatemala, may it always find such loyal and dedicated defenders, as I feel myself to be to it!"

At 4:00 P.M. the corregidor, with the city council seated behind him on a platform in the plaza, read the decree of independence to the public and broke out the new flag of the republic. Then he threw out doubloons especially minted for the occasion, carrying the new coat of arms and the words *República de Guatemala* on one side and the date on the other. Carrera watched these ceremonies from the balcony of the palace with other high officials. Then he and other officials walked along the Paseo del Calvario, accompanied by the firing of a salute from his battalions. Fireworks followed well into the evening.[82]

Carrera's long manifesto, undoubtedly written by Marure, but perhaps with suggestions from other officials, was mostly a historical essay tracing the failure of the federation and a statement of Guatemala's willingness to cooperate with reunification efforts and the practical difficulties that had stood in the way. It justified the erection of the new republic on these practical considerations but held out the possibility of eventual reunion.[83] Article 5 of the decree declared that "the absolute independence in which this republic is now constituted shall never be an obstacle to the reunification of Central America."[84] In actual fact the decree of independence changed nothing but the name of the country. Guatemala had been conducting itself along an independent course since 1839, and there was, of course, no federal government in existence from which to secede. Yet the unity that the act seemed to produce among liberals and conservatives came from the liberals' control of the government with the conservatives believing that this new emphasis on sovereignty offered a legal basis for reversing the liberal trend toward restructuring the state's constitutional framework. But, whatever they may have believed, the act did not immediately reverse the liberal control of the government and influence over the caudillo.

Commemorating the new era, the government newspaper changed its name from the *Gaceta Oficial* to the *Gaceta de Guatemala*, the first issue appearing on 8 April 1847. Its opening editorial referred to "the irrevocable resolution adopted by the authorities of the State" on 21 March as marking a new epoch in Guatemalan history, and promised that the new *Gaceta* would publish with greater regularity than its predecessor.[85]

Recognition of the new republic came promptly from Honduras and Costa Rica, the latter state moving quickly to imitate the Guatemalan action.[86] Costa Rica signed a formal treaty of friendship and commerce with Guatemala on 10 March 1848, and on the following 30 August declared itself a sovereign and independent republic, proclaiming a new constitution in November of the same year. Swift ratification of the treaty allowed it to go into effect in February 1849, establishing an important alliance of the two states at the extremities of the old federation.[87] The middle states continued to seek restoration of the union, but Guatemala and Costa Rica now shunned these efforts. Foreign Minister Rodríguez, on 8 July 1847, in explaining why Guatemala was not sending commissioners to the Diet of Nacaome, said that Guatemala had made its decision on 21 March, and that while it would consider collaborating in the formation of a national government if circumstances warranted, for the moment such circumstances did not exist.[88] Instead, the new republic named commissioners as diplomatic representatives in the other states in June 1847.[89] Recognition from South American and European states followed, with several treaties signed between 1847 and 1850.[90] Treaties were signed with Britain and the Hanseatic states on 25 June 1847. Bremen was the first to ratify (1 March 1848).[91]

Carrera's new constitutional commission quickly prepared a draft, which it presented on 12 July 1847. It was a conservative document, as expected, but Molina supported it, believing that any constitution was better than none. The unity between conservatives and liberals now concentrated on forming a coalition that could rid itself of the caudillo and the influence of his barbaric associates, so that the proposed constitution awaited only the convening of a new assembly.[92]

The first presidential administration of Rafael Carrera was characterized by a high degree of anarchy and instability in Guatemala, but it represents an important transition from the federation period to the establishment of the sovereign Republic of Guatemala. Carrera was inexperienced at governing and had to depend heavily on a variety of advisers from both his own military organization and from the elite of the capital. Continued rural violence and banditry was one product of caudillo government in Central America. Uncomfortable with the patrician elite and clergy of the capital, Carrera sought to keep them off balance with frequent changes in the ministries and with intrigue and collaboration with their political opponents throughout these years. He particularly worked with a number of moderate liberals, including Alejandro Marure, José Venacio López, José Antonio Azmitia, and Miguel Larreinaga, to check the clerical party's pretensions and to keep the elite off balance. Liberal participation in his government, however, did not signal any real change in the conservative tone of the régime. While there were minor victories for the liberals in these years, what is most obvious is that Carrera maintained the real power personally. He was careful not to yield on those issues that had caused the revolution of 1837 and that sustained his constituency. His playing off of the liberal against the conservative elite may have been an effective way for the guerrilla leader to maintain his control, but his failure to pacify the countryside or to satisfy the real or perceived grievances of the rural population would also move him closer to a political crisis that would temporarily bring down his government and force him into exile.

CHAPTER NINE

The Revolution of 1848

THE ESTABLISHMENT OF A GUATEMALAN REPUBLIC brought with it new problems for Rafael Carrera. Until 1847 he had been remarkably effective in playing off conservative against liberal elite interests while maintaining his army and considerable popular support as a power base of his own. Now a coalition of the center threatened that power as conditions in the country eroded Carrera's continued popular support. Heavy rains the year before had created crop shortages, and in 1847 there was growing restlessness and economic distress. Banditry plagued the countryside, especially in Carrera's own eastern district, and his prestige correspondingly dropped. A contemporary British resident in the country described Carrera's declining strength:

> His power has already endured longer than is usual in the country, but it now shows symptoms of being on the wane, for, by allying himself with the whites and mestizos, he has in a great measure lost his influence among the Indians, who say that he has betrayed them. All the other classes have never ceased to hate and fear him, and watch an opportunity to overturn his power; and though he takes great care always to keep a body of troops near his person, and has large supplies of arms and ammunition at hand, he will certainly find that the very troops in whom he trusts will betray him, and that the arms and ammunition will one day be used for his destruction.[1]

Grain shortages in May of 1847 prompted a manifesto from Carrera in which he announced that the government was buying and storing grain to allow municipalities to buy it at cost. This was, he said, working in some areas, but not in all, but steps were being taken to prevent those having monopolies on wheat from profiting at the expense of the poor. Moreover, he promised that corn harvests from the coast would soon alleviate the situation. But Carrera's own wife was among those who held such monopolies, in her case at Palencia, and this decree was an effort to stave off criticism of his own interests.[2] In June Carrera exempted imports of wheat from all taxes for six months in response to the crisis.[3] Azmitia ordered the corregidores to encourage maximum plantings of corn, wheat, yams, sweet potatoes, yucca, and other tubers. He authorized use of community funds to purchase seed for these crops, promising that the government would also provide seed if other funds were unavailable.[4] The Antigua municipal government successfully pursued a policy of buying corn in large volume at favorable prices and then reselling it to the public at the same price when the market price was much higher, but rural communities did not have the resources to purchase or store large supplies of grain.[5]

Seeking to increase further agricultural production, the government appointed a committee on 10 July 1847 to draw up measures to attract more foreigners with agricultural know-how. The consul of the Hanseatic Cities, Carlos Klée, agreed to assist this committee, composed of Luis Batres, Juan Matheu, Manuel Pavón, and Andrés Andreu.[6] In July the government blamed the increased violence and crime on the high price of grain, as bands of thieves roamed in the vicinity of Mataquescuintla.[7] The weather did not cooperate. May and June rains were even heavier than the year before, and although July and August registered levels well below normal, September and October rains were excessive, causing new washouts and crop failures. In October high water caused considerable damage in the Department of Chiquimula along the banks of the Río Motagua and at Esquipulas (see Table 6).[8]

The liberal influence in the government was alienating naturally conservative elements, although not yet to the degree that it had in the 1830s. The Consulado, for example, which the liberals had abolished in 1826 and again in 1829, complained in its 1847 annual report that, in spite of its great achievements in developing and maintaining the state's roads and ports and in expanding its trade since its restoration in 1839, there were rumors of its impending abolition. Moreover, it said, "the unfavorable opinion that the persons who are at the head of the administration certainly hold, have had no small influence on the decline of this establishment" and on the government's failure to pay the customary tax support to the Consulado to continue its work.[9] The complaint did the Consulado little good immediately, except that it correctly assessed the hostility of the liberals in

TABLE 6
Recorded Rainfall, Guatemala City,
1846 and 1847 (in Spanish inches)

	1846	1847
May	1.6174	2.6621
June	13.6142	14.0187
July	15.5957	5.4028
August	13.5759	4.1097
September	16.5200	15.7000
October	1.4830	9.1660
Totals	62.4062	51.0593

Sources: Gaceta de Guatemala, 5 July, 7 Oct., and
17 Nov. 1847.

the government toward that institution. On 25 February 1848 the government reprimanded the Consulado for not adhering strictly to its charter, suggesting that it follow its judicial procedures more carefully and that it do more to develop roads and ports.[10]

While conservative opposition to the liberal trend in the Guatemalan government was a reality, a more pressing concern for the caudillo from October 1847 forward was the insurgency centered in his own montaña district. Eastern Guatemala had been restless and lawless ever since Carrera's accession to the presidency had lessened his immediate control there, but a more active period of internal struggle in Guatemala began on the morning of 16 October 1847 when residents of the capital were awakened by the sounds of drummers calling the militia to arms. The *Gaceta* later reported that the uprising at Palencia was a surprise to the capital since the government until that point had claimed to have the disturbances in the East well under control. Yet now the storehouse of Palencia, in which Carrera's wife held the major interest, was under attack. Forty or fifty men had assaulted the town, killed the local army chief, and begun guerrilla-type raids in the area. Carrera's forces quickly recovered Palencia itself and declared order and liberty restored. In fact, this was just the beginning of a new uprising of the montañeses. By late October, it was apparent that the revolt was larger than initially admitted, for Brigadier General José Clara Lorenzana, commanding general of the Department of Guatemala, reported that since 16 October 143 rifles had been captured, 117 of them hidden in a deep ravine near the capital. The government informed the public, however, that the attack had been nothing more than a few rowdies getting drunk and that there were no political motives involved. Carrera returned from Palencia on the twenty-fifth, reporting that all was calm. He added, however, that damage in Palencia from the fighting had been heavy and would require a large public expenditure to repair. The government tightened its control over the country, including suspension of the liberal 1845 election law, while it denied rumors of new uprisings.[11]

By December, the rebel threat was serious and, despite assurances of public tranquility, Carrera was once more in the montaña hunting down armed bands. The rebels claimed to be fighting to save the region from foreign exploitation and reportedly planned to seize private lands and divide them among themselves, raising a king to rule in the East. The area of conflict stretched from Jalapa to Santa Rosa, and a mythology comparable to that which had surrounded Carrera a decade before was flowering. While the *Gaceta* emphasized that the conflict was mostly rumor and exaggeration, it is clear that there was growing concern in the capital over renewal of the War of the Mountain, and Carrera once more was recruiting new forces.[12]

The liberals continued to press for a constitution, and after Carrera returned from the field on 1 January 1848 he agreed that the elections provided for in his decree of independence of 21 March 1847 could be held in early February. This assembly was to be for the sole purpose of writing a constitution.[13]

Ten days later, however, on 22 January, as Carrera faced the reality of substantial revolution in the East, he decided to step down from the presidency in favor of his vice-president, Vicente Cruz, in order to devote all his energies to pacification.[14] His ministers, Azmitia and Nájera, also resigned, leaving General Cruz free to form a new government. On the twenty-fourth Carrera issued a stern proclamation against the rebels, and the next day formally turned over executive authority to Cruz.[15] Mariano Rivera Paz, who had remained active politically, serving as alcalde of Guatemala City and more recently as director of the Sociedad Económica, replaced Cruz as corregidor of Guatemala and issued a strong statement blaming a few troublemakers of the montaña for disturbing the peace and prosperity that Carrera had built up and calling on the public to support the government during this crisis.[16]

Liberals now seized the situation in an attempt to end Carrera's decade of dictatorship. They regarded Cruz as the most liberal of Carrera's generals, and hoped that he might be able to reach a settlement with the rebels that would result in a more liberal regime, without Carrera. A few liberals had already joined the guerrillas. There had been some foreign intrigue in these events as well. The French consul was a strong liberal and encouraged the ouster of Carrera. Chatfield attempted to counter this by assisting his conservative friends in organizing a move to restore Carrera and thereby regain some degree of influence in the government.[17] Whatever the role of these foreign diplomats, the prospect of a liberal regime under General Cruz was enough to excite the conservative elite in the capital to action. They had urged Carrera not to resign, and on 4 February the Guatemala City Council, on behalf of the property holders of the capital and meeting with other officials of the administration, urged him to resume his office. They declared their confidence in him and that "happiness and security would be assured as soon as the public is certain that you will continue at the head of the administration." Leading clergy joined merchants and the city council in this manifestation of support. "We call on you, who have elevated this Republic to the level it now occupies, to preserve it and extend it; and posterity will praise your memory." [18]

Cruz readily agreed to step down, the liberals as yet unable to make a real revolution, lacking either the arms or the popular support. Cruz himself declared that the circumstances made it urgent that Carrera resume the supreme executive power.[19] Returning to office immediately, Carrera issued a statement to the people of Guatemala blaming a few ingrates for the trouble. One senses Carrera's frustration with the political intrigues as he related how the clergy and other conservative interests pleaded with him to come back to the presidency. He called upon the army and the people to support his campaign to put down the insurrection in the montaña and to restore order and prosperity.[20]

These events during the first weeks of 1848 are important for they restored a bond between Carrera and the conservative elite, ending his flirtation with moderate liberals but also leading to a new crisis. He named conservative Luis Batres as his prime minister, and the first act of the new government, over the signatures of Carrera and Batres, suspended the elections that were to have begun on 6 February, declaring that the present emergency made it impractical to hold them in some departments, and that, moreover, the system of one deputy per department did not properly represent the population. They promised that when circumstances permitted, a truly representative body would be convened. On the eighth Batres called on the corregidores to maintain law and order, but at the same time admonished them not to abuse their authority or exact illegal monies from the people. The tone of the order emphasized the new government's desire to restore popular trust and confidence. Carrera also brought back J. M. Rodríguez and José Nájera to their respective ministries of foreign relations and finance, and on the twelfth his cabinet recommended that he form an advisory council, taking advantage of the "enlightened" in the country, for this was what was done, they said, in all nations with "enlightened governments." Carrera complied on the fourteenth, naming to it his three ministers and other persons they recommended. The president might also attend as he desired, its sessions to be held twice weekly.[21]

Meanwhile, on the tenth, some eight hundred rebels had inflicted serious casualties at the San Antonio barracks before retreating.[22] Carrera responded with both conciliation and repression. On the thirteenth, he offered amnesty to all who would lay down their arms within fifteen days, with payment of eight pesos per rifle, four per musket, and three per pistol in usable condition, and half these amounts for unserviceable arms. At the same time, he warned that he would "repress vigorously" the disorders in the departments of Guatemala and Mita.[23] He subdivided Mita into the districts of Jutiapa, Santa Rosa, and Jalapa, "for its better administration," and on 7 March Carrera led a division out of the capital to join forces already in the area between Santa Rosa and Chiquimula. This army won a major skirmish on 10 March and proceeded to penetrate the hill country.[24] Carrera moved whole villages out of the mountain areas, resettling them at new sites near Mataquescuintla in an effort to pacify the region.[25] The government defended Carrera's draconian measures as essential to restoring order, reminding the people that even great nations had difficulties with certain reactionary regions, citing the French revolutionary policy in the Vendée as an example.[26]

Yet the rebellion grew. Serapio Cruz, Vicente's brother, became a prominent rebel leader. Others included José Lucío, Francisco Carrillo, Roberto Reyes, Mauricio Ambrosio, José Dolores Nufio, León Raimundo, and Agustín Pérez. Eventually, Vicente Cruz too would join the revolt.[27] The rebellion was becoming all too reminiscent of the uprising of a decade before. There were different issues now, to be sure, but the failure of the Carrera government to satisfy all of the grievances of the montañeses and the agitation of some liberals allowed the movement to flourish. There were depredations against large landowners. Three mail runs between the capital and the port of Izabal were intercepted. Atrocities and reprisals occurred. Foreigners and their properties suffered attacks. The Gaceta, in acknowledging these disorders, called on public support for the repression. It assured the public that Carrera's troops had dispersed most of the rebels in "different directions," which explained why the area of the disturbances had seemed to widen, but it expressed confidence that "attacking the evil in its heart" would weaken the rebellion and that it would gradually disintegrate. One important difference from the uprising of 1837, of course, was the role of the clergy, which had encouraged the insurgency then. Now the clergy was nearly unanimous in its defense of the government.[28]

Carrera returned to the capital on 3 April, leaving large forces in the field at Jutiapa, Jalapa, and Sanarate. He claimed that except for some trouble in those three areas, the rest of the republic was peaceful.[29] He believed the rebellion was still serious enough, however, to cite the laws Mariano Gálvez had decreed against his own rebellion in 1837, applying military justice to all who aided or abetted the rebels.[30] Organization by Rivera Paz of a new police militia for the security of the capital further reflected the government's concern. With the normal city garrison away fighting the insurgents in the montaña, it was necessary to organize new militia companies to provide for security in the city. Rivera Paz ordered every male resident between the ages of eighteen and sixty to register within twenty-four hours. Fines and conscription into the regular forces were the penalties for noncompliance.[31]

Demands for forced loans to pay the army damaged Carrera's position in the capital as support grew for the liberal demand that a new assembly be elected. The conclusion of a commercial treaty with France on 8 March had furthered the liberal cause, for relations between the Carrera government and the French representative were less than cordial.[32] The liberals cautiously began to publish a newspaper, El Album Republicano. The initial number, on 5 March 1848, pointed out that there were only three newspapers in the republic, the official Gaceta, the Revista of the Sociedad Económica, and the Mensual of Medicine, none of which satisfied totally the curiosity of the readers. The Album promised to cover a wide range of topics and made a plea for a free press as necessary to progress. Pedro Molina was behind the Album, and he carefully avoided direct criticism of the government in the first issues. Nevertheless, by the end of the month Carrera's Advisory Council was raising questions about "abuses of freedom of the press."

The liberals had succeeded in passing a moderate free press law on 8 April 1845. On 28 March 1848 Juan José Aycinena presented a long opinion on the question, reviewing the law on the matter since 1812. In his view, "freedom of the press had been, is and should be the law of the land," and did not depend on the 1845 law. That law, he continued, contained impracticalities and failed to recognize that freedom of the press could be abused. While his discussion was extensive, his conclusion and recommendation were short and to the point. He wanted the government to suspend the 1845 law, for "it contains articles obviously contrary to the fundamental laws of the Republic."[33] The *Album* lasted eleven issues before the government closed it down on 9 May 1848, but its brief appearance heightened the dialogue, not so much for its discussion of Guatemalan politics, which was minimal, but for its discussion of politics abroad, especially in France. At the same time, the government arrested Pedro Molina. A similar order had been issued against Barrundia, but he managed to escape the country.[34]

Pressure on Carrera to convene a Constituent Assembly was rising. The Advisory Council had by April become essentially a governing council, and there was talk about it taking the place of a representative assembly. Meeting twice weekly, its members—Mariano Rivera Paz, Pedro Valenzuela, J. J. Aycinena, Marcial Zebadúa, J. J. Flores, M. F. Pavón, Alejandro Marure, Gregorio Urruela, José Coloma, and J. Matheu—represented some of the most competent minds in Guatemala and a good mix of moderate liberals and conservatives. In the face of growing impatience, the government defended the council as a more efficient system of government than that of the past, but promised that a representative body would be convened once the crisis had passed.[35]

The liberal opposition's demands in 1848, then, centered on: (1) election of a new Constituent Assembly, (2) freedom of the press, and (3) a stronger Guatemalan stand against British aggression in Nicaragua. The government justified its suspension of elections for the assembly on the montaña rebellion, and contended that the Advisory Council had been created not to substitute for a representative body, but rather to assist the government to move expeditiously toward eventual establishment of a Constituent Assembly. The government defended itself on the press issue by emphasizing its compliance with the guarantee of freedom of the press in the fundamental pact of 5 December 1839. It argued that the 1845 law was impractical. Regarding the British in Nicaragua, the government claimed it was merely maintaining its neutrality, as it was also in the war between the United States and Mexico. To intervene actively would be to declare war on Britain and that, as the *Gaceta* put it, would be foolish. Instead, Guatemala pursued "peaceful intervention." Through cordial relations with the British envoy, Guatemala could do more for Nicaragua than with a foolish military intervention.[36]

Yet in the face of spreading rebellion, on 24 May Carrera yielded on the election issue, announcing that it would be held soon for an assembly that would convene on 15 August. Carrera appeared tired of conflict as he appealed once more for support in difficult times. "Now is not the occasion to speak of my services," he said in a manifesto addressed to his fellow citizens, "but perhaps the day is not distant when they may be appreciated."

He said that although the engrandizement of the republic since his association with it was obvious, "perhaps the pain and struggle that have been
required to sustain and defend Guatemala are not known." There followed
a list of his achievements:

> To control rebellious passions in a great popular uprising, and to conciliate
> the interests created by it; to quiet the dangerous pretensions against prop-
> erty and other social rights; to restore the lost authority and subordination;
> to produce necessary public revenue from nothing; to carry the enormous
> weight of the debt of previous administrations and the foreign claims from
> the time of the federal government, and exonerating the Republic from
> it, sustaining its administration and paying nearly a million pesos to the
> government's creditors.

He promised to "someday explain my conduct," but on this occasion asked
only to "be permitted to show all the people and the distinguished property
holders of this capital, my recognition of their testimonies of affection and
confidence that so many times I have received, and to assure them that until
the National Representation is reconvened and I can deposit in its hands
the authority that I exercise, they may trust that I will be respected, suppressing vigorously the uprising that has disturbed the peace, and keeping
order by all the means at the Government's disposal." [37]

At the same time, he modified the election procedures previously provided in the decrees of 1844. The assembly would be composed of sixty
deputies in a single house, and the vote would be limited to native or
naturalized inhabitants who otherwise met the qualifications of the law of
5 August 1838. Voter registration would begin on 10 June and the elections
would begin on the first Sunday in July, continuing for ten days. [38]

A change in the cabinet followed. Carrera was in the field again by the
end of May, but he instructed Luis Batres on 29 May 1848 from Yerba
Buena that Rodríguez, who was pleading ill health, be allowed to resign,
with the president's regrets. At the same time, Carrera named Rodríguez
to the Advisory Council, so he continued to play a role in the government.
José Nájera moved from Finance and War to the Foreign Ministry vacated
by Rodríguez, and Joaquín Durán once more took over Finance and War on
1 July. Batres remained at Gobernación. [39]

As the war dragged on through May and June, the government sought
a consensus among leaders of both parties in the capital, reminiscent of
Gálvez's efforts. The *Gaceta de Guatemala* in mid April acknowledged the
existence of political parties in Guatemala as a natural phenomenon, despite the fact that the conservatives had traditionally opposed parties and

denied that they were a party. The editorial noted that parties were well-organized and recognized in France, the United States, and Great Britain, and that there was nothing bad about having parties. What was bad, however, was when parties concentrated on "old hatreds instead of recognizing that times change and that they must keep up with the spirit of the times." It was bad when parties were intolerant and exclusivist and practiced favoritism in power. In Guatemala, according to the *Gaceta*, the parties were poorly organized, but they had the worst aspects of parties and needed to acquire the advantages.[40]

The government found it hard to expand the regular army. It appointed a committee (composed of Colonels Manuel M. Bolaños and Lt. Colonels Joaquín Saenz, Cayetano Batres, Manuel Ramírez, and Miguel García Granados) in early May to investigate how best to create two new infantry battalions and a cavalry squadron composed of either voluntary or conscripted troops.[41] Carrera repeated his amnesty offer of 13 February on 7 June, referring specifically to rebels in the mountains around Jalapa, Sansur, and Jutiapa, but a rebel raid about a week later against Villa Nueva, just south of the capital, indicated that, contrary to the government's claims, the rebellion extended beyond the montaña region.[42] In July the rebellion spread to Los Altos, with forces under Serapio Cruz gaining adherents there. Cruz was conscripting troops in San Juan Sacatepéquez and other towns in central Guatemala as well as in the Department of Quiché.

Carrera repelled an attack by six hundred rebels in a five-hour fire fight at Patzún on the 14 July, inflicting heavy losses on the enemy and claiming to have wounded Cruz and killed sixty-six of his men. Carrera's losses were minor, although he himself suffered a wound to the neck. He marched on to Sololá, Quetzaltenango, and Huehuetenango, but failed to contain the revolt.[43] In the meantime the Lucío band in the East occupied Esquipulas, but left after taking a small amount of cash, four horses, and five cases of tobacco.[44]

The montaña revolt was now closely identified with the rising liberal resistance, although in fact they were not the same. As in 1837, nature did not cooperate with the government in putting down the insurgency on either front. There were grain shortages as the rainy season began, and we can speculate that the expansion of nopal cultivation for cochineal production may have been reducing wheat production, especially in the traditional wheat producing areas around Antigua and Amatitlán. As in the previous year, the government exempted imported grain from taxation for six months to help relieve the situation.[45] To make matters worse, however, the cochineal harvest appeared to be poor in Guatemala for 1848 and news from Europe showed that the market prices for the crimson dye were down.[46]

Carrera continued the military struggle while Batres ran the government and tried to keep order in the capital. At the latter's request, in early June the archbishop published a special prayer calling for order in the upcoming election and dedicated a special mass to the same end.[47] The opposition, meanwhile, continued to conspire, confident that Carrera's days in office were numbered. On 22 June an interesting pamphlet appeared, authored by "Oppressed Patriotism." Morazanista in tone, it condemned armed rebellion, but called for Carrera's resignation in favor of the enlightened opposition.[48]

The election was remarkably honest, as Carrera made good on his promise to allow a free election. Early returns indicated a liberal victory, with Pedro Molina and José Francisco Barrundia among those winning seats in the new Congress.[49]

Meanwhile, rebels took Quetzaltenango and with arms they captured there swept eastward toward the capital. But Carrera met and defeated them soundly at Patzún, and he recovered Quetzaltenango within a few days. The government charged that the rebellion in the West was "an orchestrated effort at general rebellion," but insisted, correctly, that it was unrelated to the continued fighting in the montaña. The *Gaceta* as much as accused the liberals of being behind the Los Altos insurgency, but promised that the government would "know how to deal with them." It pointed out that the president had proven his sincerity in allowing a representative body to be elected without influencing the election, and that he would peaceably turn over his power to that body, but that he would not tolerate armed rebellion.[50]

Still, the government was not pleased with the election returns. It complained that Indian masses were being manipulated by a few people, and that the intelligent people of the country, disgusted with the system, had not even bothered to register. It argued, therefore, that the returns were not reflecting true public opinion and that the new assembly would probably not have the support of the public. The threat was clear enough, and turned out to be prophetic, for in the end the elite of the capital did not support the assembly that convened in August. The *Gaceta* editorial expressing the government's position on 12 July further argued that the elections should not have been held when one of the parties was engaging in armed rebellion and putting the whole nation in danger. A week later, with the liberal electoral victory now certain, the *Gaceta* complained even more bitterly about "public functionaries" who had helped the liberals influence the election and had thus been notoriously disloyal to the very government that gave them their jobs. The spirit of conciliation with which the government had tried to conduct the election was thus betrayed by these ingrates, according to the *Gaceta*, and had resulted in the election of "radicals" who did not truly represent public opinion.[51] Meanwhile, from liberal El Salvador came charges that government officials, notably Guatemalan Corregidor Mariano Rivera Paz, had tampered with the election process. Whatever the truth regarding fraud, influence, and intimidation in this election, the results were clear: a remarkable victory for the opposition, and the government went to great pains not only to emphasize that it did not influence the election, but that certain government officials had actually helped the liberals. Moreover, Carrera made it clear that he would honor the results and turn over his power to the assembly when it convened.[52]

The unfavorable military situation was undoubtedly a more important reason for Carrera's willingness to step down than the election result. In mid 1848 montañés leader Francisco Carrillo had announced that he was willing to submit to a liberal assembly,[53] and at the end of July, the military commander of Chiquimula, Colonel José Dolores Nufio, defected to the liberals and pronounced against Carrera. He blasted the Carrera regime as tyrannical, arbitrary, and barbaric, saying that the department would place itself under the orders of the new assembly, but would separate itself from Guatemala City's administration until that body convened, allying himself with the rebels in Los Altos. He called for other Guatemalans to join in this action and for the other Central American states to support this move against Carrera. Nufio then marched to Izabal, where he imprisoned General Paiz. His control of the port and customs house made Carrera's position untenable. On 10 August Nufio announced his intention to march with his twelve-hundred-man army on Guatemala City.[54] On 1 August other rebels took Escuintla for the third time, forcing municipal officers to turn over 380 pesos before they withdrew.[55]

By 5 August, Carrera had made his decision. He had just returned from restoring his authority at Totonicapán and Quetzaltenango, but he admitted that the revolution was continuing and that he had "been unable to quiet the passions of the people." He announced that "the end of my public career is near. The very day that the Representative Body convenes, my name will cease to be the cause of misfortune. That day my obligation to sustain a fratricidal struggle will end."[56]

The liberals had triumphed after a brutal decade of struggle, turmoil, and reaction. The conservative *Gaceta* took a parting shot in an editorial that criticized the liberals' tendency to attempt to legislate change in imitation of other societies, particularly those of France and the United States. "Is the situation in Europe and the United States the same as in the Hispanic American republics? And being so different, as they are, can their ideas and institutions have here the same application that they have in those countries?" the editorial began. It went on to question the liberal effort to legislate change in the customs and habits of the people. It suggested, tongue in cheek, that perhaps dress styles should also be legislated, so that everyone could be dressed in uniform elegance. "Could we not convert by this means this mestizo-American country instantaneously into a society entirely European or North American?" It acknowledged the desirability of foreign ideas and customs, which might be adopted voluntarily and could gradually modify a country. But it argued that a nation should not abandon its own originality, except after it no longer exists or has disappeared already. "Here is the serious, most serious, question that in more than 25 years since independence these Republics have not wanted to face, and that is that we have politicians by imitation, just as we have imitation artists." This blind imitation had caused disorder and confusion and had ignored Hispanic America's originality. The editorial noted the dangers to civilized elites in America from French ideas of fraternity and equality, pointing to the situation where blacks were throwing out the whites in Martinique, and the Indians were throwing out the Spanish Americans in Yucatán.[57]

Released from prison, the aging, but still fiery Pedro Molina presided over the Representative Assembly that convened in the main salon of the University of San Carlos at 9:00 A.M. on 15 August. The galleries were full, and much celebration accompanied the event. At two in the afternoon it transmitted to the government its decree of organization.

Carrera sent back a note apologizing for not addressing them personally, but enclosed his resignation and a report on his administration. His resignation was short and contained both humility and characteristic egoism. He had accepted the presidency nearly four years earlier after turning it down several times because of the difficult circumstances in which the country had found itself. Now he had reached the end of his term. He had carried the burden of the government, "much greater than his ability," and now he deposited it in their hands. He continued:

> The circumstances in which I present this resignation are, as is not hidden from the Señores Representantes, very grave and delicate; they require me to urge you to consider it today. This period of transition cannot be prolonged

without endangering the public tranquility, for later it may be impossible to find the elements that still exist to preserve it. I am resolved to remain no longer in the capital and will move to a foreign country.

I appeal, then, to the Representatives, that in compensation for my small service, they make the sacrifice of remaining in permanent session until accepting my resignation and naming my successor.

I shall remain in my office while this respectable body continues to meet.

In response, the assembly reconvened the same afternoon, notwithstanding their earlier decree to open formal sessions on the following day. They debated whether to accept the resignation immediately and decided that such an important step should not be taken lightly, so they passed it to a committee composed of representatives Ponce and Trabanino. Molina immediately sent a note explaining this to the president. On the following morning, after hearing the committee's report, the assembly formally accepted Carrera's resignation. The resignations of his ministers—Batres, Nájera, and Durán—were all accepted by the President on the sixteenth before he left office.[58]

Carrera's accompanying report, written by his ministers as were all his reports to the legislative bodies during his years in office, contained some of his own ideas. It was primarily a review and defense of his four years in office. He began by emphasizing that the masses had suffered much and were agitated by the political discord among those who exercised the power. He said that the issues that divided government leaders were foreign to the masses, as were the interests of the elite, but their suffering was the inevitable result of the turmoil, the bad government, and "the legislative experiments that they had wanted to impose on our people." He reviewed his own efforts to keep order and promote economic progress. He pointed out that the Belgian colony at Santo Tomás continued to have difficulties, but was hanging on and still deserved government protection and support. He took particular pride in the condition of the public treasury, for it was in better shape than it had been at any time since independence and only the present insurgency had kept it from improving during the present year. He also noted the need for warehouses and wharfs in the ports to improve the republic's foreign trade and to improve the roads to Iztapa and Izabal, and he urged the legislature to find revenues so that the needed improvements could be made.[59]

The assembly now chose Juan Antonio Martínez as provisional chief of state until popular elections could be held. Carrera signed this first formal act of the assembly, his last official act before leaving the palace. He turned over the presidency to Martínez with a notable show of dignity and cordiality, and left the palace at 9:30 P.M., accompanied by his three ministers. After a day of arranging his affairs and meeting with friends, General Carrera rode out of the capital on the morning of 18 August, escorted by a section of infantry and a cavalry troop, headed for Chiapas.[60]

Martínez, immediately upon taking office, held an emergency meeting with the principal military officers on defense of the city. The appointment of Martínez had been a slight to Vice-President Vicente Cruz, who had held clear liberal leanings, and was a serious blunder on the part of the assembly in terms of the political and military realities of the country. But led by Pedro Molina, the assembly now wanted someone it could control, and it was also reflecting a genuine reaction against military rule. Martínez was a wealthy merchant whose liberalism stemmed largely from his aversion to the repeated forced loans imposed upon his firm by the Carrera government. He was elected, too, because he enjoyed support among conservatives with whom he was personally associated.[61]

The congenial Martínez immediately issued a proclamation calling on all Guatemalans to support him in attacking the problems of the state. He asked the army for its loyalty to the government in the effort to restore peace. He promised to "take care of you, your sacrifices will not go unrewarded, and it will be glorious to me to return the authority that has been placed on me once harmony has been restored."[62]

While Martínez quickly received pledges of support from the Guatemala City Council[63] and recognition from the liberal government of El Salvador,[64] the military commanders of the revolution were clearly not pleased. The revolution that had begun at Palencia on 17 October 1847 as much as anything had brought down Carrera, and the assembly, in their view, should have recognized that fact. Serapio Cruz, Roberto Reyes, José Nufio, Francisco Carrillo, and others remained in command of sizable rebel forces. On 27 August they presented their demands, which were rejected by the government with an order that they lay down their arms. They refused and the war continued.[65]

The troubles of the new liberal government were made more difficult by the rising Anglo-American rivalry on the isthmus. In late 1847 the British had begun to pursue more aggressively their alliance with the Mosquito Indians. Nicaraguan efforts to gain the support of other Central American states had not made much headway in Carrera's Guatemala, but the liberals were committed to implementing their anti-British stand. This imposed a major burden on them. On 30 June the British Foreign Office announced boundaries of the Mosquito Kingdom that extended from Cape

Honduras to San Juan del Norte.[66] While the liberal governments in Central America tended to support Nicaragua, the more conservative ones appeared to worry more about U.S. aggression. Juan Lindo, the president of Honduras, for example, went so far in July 1847 as to issue a proclamation, without consulting any legislative body, declaring war on the United States in protest of its invasion of Mexico.[67] Now the Martínez government of Guatemala took a decidedly anti-British tone.

An exchange of correspondence in early September between Frederick Chatfield and Martínez's new foreign minister, Pedro Arrivillaga, revealed one aspect of the tension. Chatfield protested that the Guatemalan government's new instructions to the corregidores suggested that he had been responsible for stirring up trouble in Guatemala. Although Arrivillaga's polite response assured Chatfield of his continued friendship, it is clear that the Guatemalan government suspected Chatfield of meddling in internal affairs and refused to retract the instructions, in the end Arrivillaga simply promising to publish the whole correspondence so that Chatfield's views and concerns would be public, along with the government's responses. Chatfield clearly disliked this and closed the exchange with the pompous proposal of laying the whole matter before Her Majesty's government. The exchange of five letters (three from Chatfield and two from the government) is interesting for it shows more than published materials might normally, the pretentiousness of Chatfield as well as the liberals' suspicion of him.[68]

Discord marked the Martínez administration almost from the beginning. The liberals, never well unified in Central America, quarreled among themselves, allowing the conservative minority in the assembly to wield greater strength than their numbers indicated. Martínez's cabinet was headed by Manuel J. Dardón, sworn in on 29 August as secretary of government, justice, and Ecclesiastical Affairs. His brother Andrés took over editorship of the *Gaceta de Guatemala*, and its dramatic change in tone from the conservatism of Pavón and Milla to strong support for the liberal measures of the Martínez government became obvious at once.[69] The *Album Republicano* resumed publication in August 1848, and Dardón was a frequent contributor.[70] The *Album*'s liberal bias was obvious, but it paid surprisingly little attention to local issues, leaving that to Dardón in the *Gaceta*. The *Album* concerned itself more with European affairs, especially the French Revolution of 1848. It did publish articles broadly supporting liberal policy, such as freedom of the press, and its focus was strongly political. Liberal poetry and reprints of the writings of Voltaire and French liberals were characteristic.

The assembly regarded its principal task as the writing of a new constitution,[71] but first José Francisco Barrundia launched a proposal in favor of a new declaration of Guatemalan independence by the assembly. Barrundia's point was a strong attack on Carrera, whom he claimed had held no authority to make his 1847 declaration of independence unilaterally. It was only for the legislature, he declared on 11 September, to make such a declaration. The new declaration could be supported by liberals and conservatives alike and served Barrundia's efforts to unite the assembly behind a nationalistic front. The bill passed the assembly on 14 September, and Martínez signed it on the following day, coinciding with national Independence Day celebrations all across Central America.[72] Only two negative votes were cast against this resolution. Conservatives regarded it as an endorsement of their own policy under Carrera, whereas the liberals, led by Barrundia, were trying to take over credit for national independence. The *Gaceta*, on 15 September, praised this "son of the people, father of his country, Citizen José Francisco Barrundia, who conceived such a happy idea." Even so, the *Gaceta* emphasized, this was not an end to federation dreams. Addressing its sister states, it said that the step the Constituent Assembly had taken "altered in no way the old fraternal relations. Sons of the same fatherland, subjects of the nation, comrades of what we formed at our independence, we have suffered the same misfortunes, but our religion, language and customs are the same. How could we break such sacred ties?" On the contrary, the editorial concluded, "we should try to strengthen the ties."

The Guatemala City Council, reflecting the conservative view, endorsed enthusiastically the "validation" of the declaration of Guatemalan independence of 21 March 1847. The tone of this declaration differed sharply from Barrundia's condemnation of Carrera. Rather, it simply applauded the assembly for endorsing what it said had been a highly popular act and one that had support throughout the country.[73] Meanwhile, liberals in other Central American states, especially El Salvador, continued to oppose the Guatemalan decision to abandon the federation.[74]

Barrundia also sponsored a strong resolution of Guatemalan solidarity with the French Republic. The assembly proclaimed its regrets for the difficulties between .the previous government and the French Consul in Guatemala and affirmed its friendship for the "great French nation." The assembly saluted the French Republic "for its social regeneration,—for its high position at the front of the free peoples of Europe,—for the latest victory which it has gained against anarchy, and its achievement of the triumphant institutions of democracy," expressing its desire "to see once more the republican flag of France in this capital, uniting its colors with those of this young republic of Guatemala, under the lofty auspices of liberty and fraternity."[75] The assembly then restored the liberal free press law of 1845.[76]

Amid this liberal enthusiasm for the revolution against what it called the "despotic" regime of Carrera, there was a delicate balance in the assembly between conservatives and liberals in which moderates held the balance. Thus, while Barrundia and Molina achieved radical expressions of their liberalism, real change was slight, and there continued to be those who trusted more in the raw power of a Carrera than in the idealism of a Barrundia. Despite the liberal polemics, therefore, we also find the assembly voting to strike a medal commemorating Carrera's service to Guatemala and to present him with an engraved sword![77]

Indeed, conservative reconsolidation began to emerge by mid September, and a new election of officers in the assembly resulted in more moderate leadership. José Bernardo Escobar replaced Pedro Molina as president, and conservative Juan Matheu replaced moderate liberal Manuel Larrave as one of the vice-presidents, with conservative José Mariano Urruela being reelected as the other vice-president. Younger liberals Marcos Dardón and Lorenzo Montúfar were reelected as secretaries, but they were less influential. Even at that, it meant the replacement of Mariano Gálvez as one of the secretaries. This legislative reorganization, in fact, signified as much the division among the liberals as the strength of the conservatives, but it was the beginning of the end of the "Liberal Revolution of 1848."[78]

Barrundia reacted fiercely, however, in a virulent attack the next day on the atrocities of the Carrera regime, calling for the restoration of individual liberties. Passionately, he pointed to the difficulties of making a peaceful transition from a society of slavery and abjection to one where the rights of the people are protected. Continuous actions of the government are necessary to complete the transition from "barbarism to liberty and civilization." He wanted the restoration of individual guarantees and pointed to the horrible conditions in the prisons, where Carrera had incarcerated the *montañeses* who had rebelled against his cruel regime, along with many other innocent people who simply suffered from his capricious atrocities. They had poured forth from those prisons upon the ouster of Carrera, and the courts had ordered their release. The assembly itself had provided for a general amnesty on 8 September, freeing all political prisoners and minor criminals, excepting only those accused of adultery, rape, homicide, and other crimes of violence.[79] But Barrundia claimed that these "prisons of death and terrible torture and suffocation are still in use" and that the atrocities continued.[80]

The government's appointment on 20 September of José Mariano Vidaurre as minister of finance and war and Luis Molina as foreign minister reflected the moderates' strength in the assembly, which on the previous day had allowed these men to continue to hold their seats in the assembly at the same time they served in the cabinet.[81]

The most immediate problem facing the Martínez government was the continuing montaña rebellion in the East and the refusal of key military commanders to recognize his government. Martínez's first decree had acknowledged the demand for land among the rebels and promised that ejidos would be restored or new communities established. The decree reflected the liberals' perception of what the rebels were fighting for. While it listed many causes for the rebellion, "the principal causes that compel the inhabitants of the Districts of Jutiapa, Jalapa and Santa Rosa and some from this department [Guatemala] to war are the lack or scarcity of lands they need for their cultivations or livestock, which reduce them to the ever sad condition of tenant farmers or renters, which in the hacienda of Palencia was grievous to them." Martínez was careful not to antagonize the clergy in this decree. He called on Francisco Carrillo, Serapio Cruz, and Agustín Pérez, offering them each the post of corregidor and comandante de armas of, respectively, Jalapa, Santa Rosa, and Jutiapa, if they would stop resisting. Otherwise, Martínez warned, they would be treated as enemies.[82]

Putting down rebellion, however, as Carrera had found, was expensive, and Martínez quickly resorted to the same means as Carrera to maintain his forces in the field. On 5 September he attempted to raise money through a voluntary loan, pledging another third of customs receipts to repayment and authorizing up to $100,000 in new bond issues. This measure gained little response, so the assembly authorized a forced loan on 8 September and also authorized use of a third of the aguardiente receipts as well as customs receipts to make the payments. Martínez signed the act into law the following day and the government proceeded to parcel the amount out to the corregidores for collection.[83] Property holders with more than 1,000 pesos of assets, the same formula as under Carrera, were subject to assignment, and the corregidores were instructed to apportion it among their "pueblos" in the following amounts:

Guatemala	$47,000
Sacatepéquez	8,000
Amatitlán	12,000
Chimaltenango	3,000
TOTAL	$70,000

The first installment was to be collected by 10 October, and a second part by 10 November 1848.[84]

Some rebels declared that they supported the new government but that they remained under arms to "protect it." For example, Mauricio Ambrosio and Roberto Reyes issued this manifesto on 8 April from the village of Arrazola, but it was undoubtedly printed by the government:

SOLDIERS OF THE MOUNTAINS!—Comrades! Upon taking up arms against the past administration, we had only the noble and natural sentiment of throwing down the reign of absolutism that weighed on our people. Our war cry shook the bloody throne of Carrera because public opinion joined it full of hopes for liberty.—Our task is finished: the monster, who with the scorn of the fatherland oppressed us for so long, has finished his abominable career. Opprobrium and remorse will corrupt his being!—Today, while a just and liberal man legitimately occupies the first magistracy and a popular assembly watches over our security and interests, we must run to throw ourselves into its paternal arms, and we that have been your comrades in danger will be proud to prove to our fellow citizens that we give our obedience to the fatherland to destroy the despotism and tyranny.—Now there are no enemies before the government to combat; all are brothers! We are not deceived by the ambitious, who try to use the turmoil and bloodshed to enslave the people. Judge men by their deeds, and note well: *that the friends and accomplices of the fallen tyrant will never be your friends.* The presidency is not hereditary.—Our holy religion preaches forgiveness of our enemies and not blood and extermination. Its ministers are respected. Oh that it had not been so much that his character has been forgotten to the point of preaching war and disobedience to the call of his virtuous prelate!—Comrades! May peace and labor return to obtain the fruits of our fertile fields! Never again raise up another despot like Carrera! And swear to always sustain the rights of the people, as we shall do until death, your friends, *Mauricio Ambrosio— Roberto Reyes.*[85]

Fighting continued in the Verapaz, however, where one Julián García had made himself "comandante" of Santa Cruz Mountain and used it as a hideout from which to raid the surrounding region. All efforts to contain him had failed, symptomatic of the situation in the country generally. Martínez ordered all dissidents to lay down their arms by the end of September or face penalties as "enemies of order."[86] He also made an effort to conciliate the commanders of the revolution. For his role in bringing down Carrera, the assembly urged Martínez to confer upon Colonel Nufio the title of benefactor with promotion to brigadier general. Nufio had remained in control of Chiquimula, effectively keeping it separated from Guatemala. Martínez was reluctant to reward this direct show of defiance, but on 10 October he yielded and announced the promotion and presentation of a sword with the appropriate "Benemérito" inscription. He also promised to promote public education in Chiquimula.[87]

Yet the rebellion continued in both East and West. Los Altos declared its independence again on 26 August 1848, an act led by the city council of Quetzaltenango. The Martínez government maintained that the Los Altos secession had no popular base, but was reluctant to attempt direct military action, hoping to bring the western departments back through negotiation. A Los Altos government, meanwhile, formally organized itself on 5 September with a junta composed of Father Antonio Dávila, Rafael de la Torre, and José Velasco. From Chiquimula, Nufio quickly recognized the Quetzaltenango government, as did the Salvadoran government, traditional ally of the State of Los Altos. Representatives of the liberal president of El Salvador, Doroteo Vasconcelos, met with Nufio in Chiquimula and hatched a plan to march on Guatemala City. Once it was taken, they planned to declare the formation of a republic composed of El Salvador, Guatemala, and Los Altos, and to invite the other Central American states to join them.[88]

Martínez appealed to Los Altos to rejoin Guatemala on 27 September, promising that the assembly would respond to their needs. He acknowledged that during this period of transition the government had not been able to do everything at once, but he assured Los Altos that it was not forgotten and that he was anxious to bring it back into the fold without violence.[89] Passive measures failing, Martínez hardened his line on 7 October, when he warned the Quetzaltenango junta that its officers must lay down their arms and submit to Guatemalan authority. He also called upon the highland deputies to the assembly to take their seats within 15 days, threatening that if they failed to comply, the army would march upon Los Altos. He reminded them that they had not consulted the two hundred thousand inhabitants of Los Altos, and that the Guatemalan army would protect those people from the illegal actions of the Los Altos junta.[90] With Salvadoran and Chiquimulan support, however, the Los Altos junta refused to submit. A publication of 14 October, ostensibly from the "Women of Los Altos" to the "valiant defenders of the sacrosanct liberty of the State of Los Altos," condemned the "unjust" and "tyrannical" aggression of Guatemala, that "always sought the slavery of Los Altos." It urged the soldiers to resist and to defend "the most precious of your rights."[91] Salvadoran and Chiquimulan aid failed to materialize, however, and Los Altos once more crumbled before a Guatemalan army that took Quetzaltenango with little resistance on 25 October. Official Guatemalan reports said the "liberation" was welcomed by the inhabitants and that the Guatemalan army was followed into Quetzaltenango by thousands of Indians from the surrounding area. Martínez installed Colonel Mariano Paredes as Corregidor and Superintendent of Finance in Quetzaltenango.[92]

If Martínez's Los Altos campaign went well, other efforts to contain the revolt were less successful. The assembly, choosing new officers monthly, reelected Escobar as president, along with conservatives Urruela and Matheu as vice-presidents on 16 October, but the division among the liberals was deepening. There was apprehension that Carrera was planning a return, and on 18 October the assembly declared him a traitor and forbade him ever to return to Guatemala.[93] Negotiations which Alejandro Marure and José Antonio Azmitia had been carrying on with agents of Serapio Cruz broke down on 20 October. Martínez continued to promise amnesty to those who would lay down their arms, while, in fact, he was suffering increasing desertions from his own forces.[94] The assembly tried to assume greater authority in the meantime by naming an Advisory Council to assist the president composed of the ministers and six additional individuals elected by the assembly and the magistrates.[95]

By early November all efforts to reach accord with the revolutionary leaders had failed. Martínez felt forced to postpone the planned elections until early December.[96] Once more he warned that the government would take stronger measures and specifically threatened that those responsible for the resistance would pay with their lives and property. The assembly authorized Martínez to take all necessary measures for the interior and exterior security of the country, including raising forces, taxes, and loans.[97]

Then, on 12 November, General Serapio Cruz declared that the Los Altos rebellion was not over when he issued a manifiesto from Palencia, dangerously near the capital.[98] The government quickly lowered the conscription age from eighteen to sixteen and demanded that every male in the capital between ages sixteen and fifty—excepting only clergy, seminarians, physicians, hospital workers, and the physically impaired (as certified by a special commission)—report for duty on 14 November at City Hall.

Martínez was now completely frustrated with his inability to restore order and with the assembly's failure to accomplish a more positive legislative record. Pedro Molina, José Barrundia, and Mariano Gálvez—the old liberal "exaltados"—had had their opportunity and produced little but rhetoric. The conservatives had been able to capitalize skillfully on liberal divisions to prevent any truly major legislation from passing. Faced with an imminent attack from Cruz, Martínez submitted his resignation to the assembly for the third time on 15 November. The assembly refused to accept it, arguing that the current crisis was an inopportune time to change administrations.[99]

The government tightened security in anticipation of attack. Then the assembly recessed until 1 January, naming to act for it in the interim a Permanent Commission composed of Pedro Molina, José Bernardo Escobar, José F. Barrundia, José Maria Urruela, and Manuel Irungaray. All were liberals except for Urruela. The recess, however, was shorter than anticipated. On 17 November, Minister of Gobernación Manuel Dardón submitted his resignation, and Martínez called the assembly back into session for the twenty-seventh. There he insisted upon acceptance of his resignation, saying that he had accepted the provisional presidency only until elections were held or until the assembly found someone more appropriate. He admitted his failure to put down the montañés rebellion and hinted that Carrera or his agents had had a hand in preventing a peaceful settlement. He cited his failing health and incapacity for the office as he begged to be relieved of the presidency. He said that the army and the people in this time of crisis needed firmer leadership than he could give. He called for a hard line policy against the rebels and chastised the assembly for not putting the army in the hands of a strong leader. The assembly had no choice but to accept the resignation and name the president of the assembly, José Bernardo Escobar, to succeed him. Escobar took over on the twenty-eighth.[100]

Escobar immediately issued a call for unity. He accepted the resignation of Martínez's ministers and quickly put together a new cabinet. Escobar was a stronger liberal than Martínez, and he made a valiant effort to make the liberal revolution work, but the odds against him were formidable. In the flowery oratory of the mid-nineteenth century, which sounds so pompous today but was probably more effective then, Escobar implored his fellow citizens to rally behind him to meet the challenge.[101] But the conservatives were gaining the upper hand in the assembly. With the resignations of Pedro Molina, Pedro N. Arriaga, and Dámaso Angulo from the assembly and their replacement on 10 December with Marcial Zebadúa, Juan José Flores, and Marcelo Molina (the first two were moderate conservatives), the balance shifted, and Juan Matheu became president of the assembly.[102]

Escobar recognized the futility of his position on 11 December. Pleading the impossibility of bringing peace because of the government's meager resources and military strength, he presented his resignation. The assembly rejected it, saying that to accept his resignation after only fourteen days in office would not look good for the country, especially after Martínez had served only a hundred days. On the following day, therefore, Escobar declared a state of siege and doggedly mobilized the remaining forces. He raised the pay of the military a half real per day and offered a new amnesty to those in Los Altos who had supported secession, as long as they were not continuing in any criminal activity. In the meantime, he unsuccessfully pursued a negotiated settlement with Serapio Cruz and the montañeses.[103]

On 13 December Mariano Gálvez reluctantly accepted appointment as Escobar's finance minister. On the same day, Escobar tried to form new military units, reviving a decree of 23 August 1823 to form a civil militia composed of four battalions organized by the districts of the city: Sagraria and Santo Domingo; Remedios; San Sebastián; and Merced and Candelaria. These battalions were solely for the defense of the city.[104] On 14 December Escobar decreed another forced loan of $50,000 among the property holders of the capital, to be administered by the Consulado. Once more customs receipts were pledged to repay the loan, but the deficits were getting larger and the property holders were not friendly toward this loan, notwithstanding the certificates of deposit the government gave them with a face value of 25 percent more than they actually contributed. Those who resisted, however, faced a doubling of their quotas, with no interest and collection assigned to the army.[105] A government manifesto the same day accused Serapio and Vicente Cruz, along with other montañés leaders, of continuing to disrupt the eastern region. In fact, by this time they were virtually at the gates of the city, with twelve hundred troops, demanding its surrender and refusing to offer any guarantees to the lives or property of its citizens. The manifesto claimed that the revolution was on behalf of the peasants. The government responded that the Cruz brothers had never had the peasants' interest at heart, as had Carrera, but had simply used them for their own purposes.[106]

Escobar sought a negotiated settlement throughout December, but the military crisis was not unrelated to economic stress. Not only were the forced loans resisted by the property holders, but the planters resisted the conscription of their workers into the military. Escobar recognized this problem on 23 December when he exempted those workers from military service during the cochineal harvest period.[107] The real position of the conservatives remained stronger than might appear at first glance. Conservatives still held key military posts and dominated the city government. Moreover, Mariano Rivera Paz continued as corregidor of the Department of Guatemala throughout the period. Martínez and Escobar both recognized that they could not ignore the conservative elite. By the end of December the liberal revolution had floundered seriously. Feuds among the liberals fueled their disunity, and cost them their control of the assembly.[108]

Escobar presented his resignation again on 29 December, citing his

ineptitude and failure to stem the violence and rebellion. His "good intentions" had not been enough. The assembly accepted his resignation on the
first day of the new year and elected Manuel Tejada, a moderate, to succeed
him, but Tejada refused. There was growing support for a military man to
bring an end to the continued rebellion.

The mantle fell upon Colonel Mariano Paredes, who took the oath of
office on 3 January. Paredes was a career officer who had a reputation for
loyalty to the government and of being relatively apolitical. He had served
as a captain under the Gálvez government,[109] but had risen in rank and
served with distinction under Carrera, without being especially close to the
caudillo, and more recently under Martínez and Escobar, as corregidor at
Quetzaltenango. He was unrelated to the contemporary Mexican president
of the same name.

Paredes astutely recognized that the liberals had lost whatever advantage
they had held earlier and that the consolidation of conservative strength in
the capital, the continuing rebellion, and the rumored return of Carrera all
argued for organizing his government along conservative lines. Yet initially
it was necessary to appoint liberals to his cabinet to maintain a satisfactory
relationship with the assembly that had installed him as chief of state. Before naming his cabinet, however, he met with the leaders of the principal
institutions in the capital to discuss personnel in the new government and
his plans for raising money to put down the rebellion. The meeting produced a list of people who would command public respect and confidence
from which a committee of property holders was named to formulate a
proposal for a new loan. On the following day (8 January 1849) Paredes
named Raymundo Arroyo as minister of government, justice, and ecclesiastical affairs; José Mariano Rodríguez as foreign minister; José Manuel
Urruela as finance minister; and Manuel Tejada as war minister. Despite
the liberal tinge to this group (only Urruela could really be classified as
conservative among them), Paredes privately was much influenced by Luis
Batres, Carrera's prime minister before his overthrow in 1848. Urruela was
sworn in on 12 January and Rodríguez on the seventeenth. Arroyo and
Tejada were away from the capital on a commission seeking settlement with
the rebels, and it was agreed that until their return Urruela would also
handle War and Gobernación. Arroyo and Tejada took office upon their
return to the capital in early February. Alejandro Marure took over editing
the *Gaceta* and continued in that influential role through October 1849.[110]

Paredes, unlike his predecessors, provided assertive leadership. On
18 January he took over full command of the military from liberal Field
Marshall Francisco Cáscara, who had resigned when Paredes became presi-

dent.[111] Paredes then decreed a forced loan that called for collection of $16,000 per month for six months from property holders to cover estimated monthly military expenses. Voluntary pledges of loans from property holders in Guatemala City covered another $10,000. Municipalities throughout the republic were made responsible for assignment and collection of quotas. Exempting the voluntary creditors from the forced loan went a long way toward improving his base of support in the capital. He also made it clear that anyone refusing to pay his assigned amount would be dealt with harshly. The capital city council made its assignments on 23 January, demanding payment within forty-eight hours.[112]

The assembly adjourned in late January. Paredes postponed the elections again, but agreed that when the assembly reconvened in May they would designate a date for a presidential election. What is clear here is that the assembly relinquished its authority to Paredes temporarily, hoping for a restoration of order, although it retained its right to reconvene sooner than 12 May should an emergency arise or if the president or Advisory Council desired it. In the meantime, a liberal commission made up of Barrundia, Luis Molina, Andrés Andreu, José Mariano Vidaurre, Luis Arrivillaga, Manuel Irungaray, and Andrés Dardón was left with instructions to write a draft constitution during the recess. In other last-day business before adjourning on 20 January, the assembly ratified the treaty of friendship and commerce with Costa Rica and ordered the establishment of a port at Champerico, Ixtlán, or some other point in the Department of Suchitepéquez, responding to one of the most important demands of Los Altos.[113] On the same day, Paredes's negotiators reached a preliminary agreement with Serapio Cruz at Palencia that promised a solution to the civil war. It essentially was part of the larger phenomenon of the return of Guatemala to military rule. Assignment of a new group of corregidores by Paredes in late January reflected his good faith to Cruz and laid the groundwork for a formal convention on 2 February. The new corregidores reflected both a more conservative trend as well as a turning to military men for these posts.[114]

The fear that Carrera would return hung over the liberals throughout their tenure. A military guard had escorted him to the Mexican border, but he remained dangerously nearby in Chiapas and in communication with his allies in Guatemala. In September 1848 Manuel Arzú Batres (1817–98), an officer whose father had commanded conservative forces in the 1826–29 civil war, joined Carrera as his personal secretary.[115] On 13 October the liberal assembly had sought to strengthen the regime against counterrevolution, declaring martial law and giving the government extraordinary powers to deal with the rebellion, including suspension of the right of habeas corpus and putting the burden of proof of innocence on the accused in cases of sedition or rebellion. Article 4 instructed the government to ask the Mexican government to intern Carrera, who was prohibited under pain of death from returning to any point within Guatemala. The next article declared as a traitor anyone who took any overt action to favor, aid, or project the return of Carrera with the object of restoring him to power. This proscriptive order, signed by Martínez on 16 October, reflected the liberals' contempt for and fear of the caudillo, but those who signed it later became the ones who were proscribed from Guatemala once Carrera returned.[116]

Carrera kept a close watch on events in Guatemala from Comitán, as he directed the liquidation of many of his assets before they could be confiscated by the government. His livestock on the Pacific coast were sold, but he lost some other property. He used receipts from these sales to finance his return. In early October he wrote to Chepita Silva of his anger over the occupation of his houses and property, but he assured her that "he was not very far away" and that it was "not very remote that she would see him again in Guatemala."[117] Soon after, Carrera moved closer to the Guatemalan border, although in November Mexican authorities escorted him back to Comitán, where he announced that he would soon leave for Europe.[118] He had no intention of going to Europe, however, and spent his time carefully organizing a plan. The news from Guatemala appeared to favor his return in January 1849, and Paredes's accession to power and the agreement with Cruz meant that he could perhaps return to a country where law and order had already been restored. Carrera wrote to Paredes from Aycitú, Chiapas, on 24 January, announcing that he was returning to restore peace and order. He agreed to place himself under the government's orders if it would apologize for the indignities he had suffered and extend him a complete amnesty. Otherwise, he warned, he could not be responsible for the consequences.[119]

Facing this challenge, on 1 February Paredes called the assembly to reconvene at noon on the following day in order to "consider affairs of great importance and gravity." He presented the assembly with a plan for national unity in the face of Carrera's return, to which it quickly agreed. Serapio Cruz agreed to it a day later. The assembly accepted the final version of the peace convention on the fifth and then recessed once more until 12 May. The main effect of these agreements was to reassert the strength of the Guatemalan military over affairs of state. Specifically, General Vicente Cerna, on 8 February became commander-in-chief of the armed forces, abrogating Paredes's assumption of that authority on 18 January.[120]

With peace agreed upon, the rebel Army of the People marched into Guatemala City on Friday, 9 February. This occurred as soon as General Cerna had taken over command of the Army. The Cruz brothers rode at the head of the Army of the People as far as Palencia. There Serapio remained with a small force mopping up dissidents in accordance with the agreement. The archbishop accompanied Vicente Cruz from Guadalupe as the rebel force was brought in and combined with the regular army in what the *Gaceta de Guatemala* referred to as a "grand and memorable act." At the plaza Paredes and Cruz appeared together in a show of unity and read proclamations. A mass at the Cathedral followed on Sunday, the eleventh, with a bullfight following in the afternoon.[121]

Paredes pursued policies designed to maintain the peace he believed he had restored. This included reconciliation with the conservative elements in the capital and creation of a coalition between moderates and conservatives. He broadened the bureaucracy and participation in government by both liberals and conservatives with a new structure of administration that was a precursor to the establishment of a large number of ministries after 1871. Specifically, on 14 February he named advisory committees for Foreign Relations, Internal Government, Ecclesiastical Affairs, Legislation and Justice, Finance, War, Education, Industry and Agriculture, Public Works, Sanitation and Health, Statistics, Land and Communal Holdings, and Pacification.[122] This coalition suggested a potential for cooperation between the two parties and a blending of the parties into a single national party, not unlike what was happening in several South American countries about this time, with the elite joining together and merging traditional conservatism and liberalism with their mutual class interests. It was also a forerunner of the increasingly corporate nature of government in Guatemala. This coalition was not to last, however, as the conservatives soon would dominate once more the regime. Although some of the more moderate liberals would continue in the government, most found it either mandatory or convenient to divorce themselves from politics or go into exile. For the time being, however, Paredes furthered the spirit of conciliation and consensus in his compliance with the terms of the peace convention as he decreed that $30,000 be appropriated for assistance to those damaged in the war. Also in accordance with the convention was a whole new slate of corregidores.[123]

Among the new appointments was Mariano Rivera Paz as corregidor of Jutiapa, which would appear to be something of a demotion from his post as corregidor of Guatemala. More probably, however, Paredes wanted a tried and trusted corregidor in Jutiapa, in the heart of the rebellious montaña area. This also made it a dangerous assignment. Rivera Paz traveled to his new post with Gregorio Orantes (the new corregidor of the adjacent district of Jalapa) with orders to complete the pacification of the region. But at Sampaquisoy on 22 February an ambush killed both officers. The elite of the capital were deeply shocked by this act, which underlined the fact that the montaña revolt had not ended.[124] The government accused the guerrilla bands of Agustín Pérez and Roberto Reyes of responsibility for the attack.

Rivera Paz, since turning over the presidency to Carrera in 1844, had developed some mines and tended to other private interests until his election as first alcalde (mayor) of the capital city in 1846. Carrera had named him as corregidor of Guatemala in January 1848 and later as a member of the Advisory Council. A credit to his reputation was that he continued in that post on through the liberal revolution. In August 1848 the Petén elected him as deputy to the assembly. For more than a decade, then, Rivera Paz had been a loyal conservative public servant, and his assassination was deeply felt in the capital.[125] The peace convention was off to a dismal start.

The government tried to solidify its position in Los Altos, accusing those who would separate Los Altos of being only a tiny group of exploiters. It cited a meeting of Suchitepéquez Indian municipalities held in Mazatenango on 20 February 1849, which had declared their preference for remaining with the Republic of Guatemala in a clear statement against the pretensions of Quetzaltenango. The Indians demanded that all representatives of the Los Altos secessionist group get out of the Department of Suchitepéquez. A long list of Indian vecinos signed the petition, delivered to the new corregidor, José Víctor Zavala, in early March.[126] The government was eager to insure the loyalty of Los Altos in the face of Carrera's announced intention to return. A manifesto of 17 February warned the public that now, just as peace had been restored, General Carrera was preparing a hostile force for the invasion of the state. It warned him that he had no right to return and that any who supported him would be treated as a traitor.[127]

Paredes made some notable progress in foreign relations. The return of conservative influence contributed to restoration of better relations with Great Britain, which formally recognized the Republic of Guatemala on 20 February 1849 and signed a commercial treaty.[128] A similar treaty followed between Guatemala and Belgium on 12 April 1849.[129] A new U.S. envoy, Elija Hise, had arrived in Guatemala in November in the midst of the crisis of the Martínez government. He presented his credentials to President Paredes on 21 January 1849 and proceeded to negotiate a treaty, signed on 3 March.[130] Even as the Republic of Guatemala moved back into conservative hands, the U.S. minister sought alliance with the ideologically more friendly liberals. This soon put Hise in better graces with Guatemala's neighbors than with the Guatemalan government. This became evident at a reception and ball held by Pedro N. Arriaga at his home in Guatemala for Hise and other dignitaries on Sunday, 10 June 1849. Arriaga had been employed by the Honduran government to try to get a commercial treaty with the United States. Hise laid the foundations for the close relationship between his more active successor, E. G. Squier, and the Honduran government a year or so later.[131]

The decline of the liberals weakened U.S.-Guatemalan cordiality, but strained relations were also noticeable with the French government. The French consul had actively promoted the liberal revolution in Guatemala, and he did not enjoy the same close relationship to Paredes that he had with Martínez and Escobar. A controversy arose regarding the rights of a group of Spanish immigrants in February 1849. Spain had not yet recognized Guatemalan independence, much less the 1847 republic, so Spanish residents there were without formal consular representation. The French chargé d'affaires, M. C. A. Challaye, had taken up their cause and was politely but firmly told by the Guatemalan foreign minister that the Spaniards were naturalized Guatemalan citizens. In essence, Rodríguez told the French diplomat to stay out of Guatemalan internal affairs. This reflected a turning away from the pro-French attitude of the previous governments. The dispute dragged on for months, until the French government named a new chargé, Dagoberto Fourcade, in late April 1849, who was received and recognized by Paredes on 3 September.[132]

The war in the montaña meanwhile continued. Generals Vicente Cerna and Vicente Cruz, both of whom had participated in the rebellion but now served the Paredes government, marched out in mid-March to deal with Roberto Reyes and Agustín Pérez, who continued to disturb the departments of Jutiapa and Jalapa. Cruz lost his life in a skirmish on 20 March with Pérez's forces.[133] General Miguel García Granados at the same time marched into Los Altos to check Carrera who, at the head of his "Army of Restoration," had begun to raid around Huehuetenango. Carrera rapidly built up support among the Indian villages of the West. At 5:00 A.M. on the morning of 5 April, García Granados beat off a force that included at least four hundred Indians, claiming to have killed at least eight and perhaps as many as thirty of the insurgents.[134] Soon after, Carrera seized a large bell from the church at San Marcos Huista in the Department of Huehuetenango and melted it down to forge two cannons. According to local legend, Carrera never returned to the village, but a few years later, Carrera sent the bell that presently hangs in San Marcos church, a bell manufactured in Paris in 1847 by order of Nicolás Larrave, "for use in Central America."[135]

As the military situation worsened, with Carrera at large in the West and the montañeses continuing their raiding in the East, Paredes took steps to protect his government. The montañeses once more were striking close to the capital, including a raid on Antigua on 9 April. Paredes called the assembly back into session for the twentieth of April, principally to ratify the treaties with Britain, the Hanseatic Cities, the United States, and Belgium, and thereby strengthen his ties to foreign governments, but the assembly balked, causing Foreign Minster Rodríguez to resign. The assembly was much more concerned with the domestic scene than with foreign affairs, and it willingly turned over strong, virtually dictatorial power to Paredes to enable him to deal with the crisis. It empowered him to raise funds internally as well as to contract a foreign loan, with future tax revenues as collateral. He could also ask for armed forces from friendly states and, finally, to take all measures necessary to establish peace in the republic, "empowered to exercise the Executive Power without any limitation whatever." This meant that Paredes could resume command of the armed forces, which he did formally on 5 May 1849. At the same time, also in accordance with the powers given him by the assembly on 26 April, he turned over executive power to a junta headed by Juan Matheu, president of the Advisory Council, allowing Paredes personally to direct the military campaign. This lasted only a week, however, and on 12 May Paredes resumed his executive power, once more reuniting the civil and military authority.[136]

During that week Paredes won an important victory when he met with General Agustín Guzmán in Antigua. Guzmán had taken command of the continuing Los Altos secession movement on 4 May as chief of state of the rebel Los Altos government, even though it had little support within Los Altos and no longer controlled Quetzaltenango. He now agreed, however, that Los Altos under his command would be reincorporated into the Republic of Guatemala and that his forces would obey Paredes's orders in common cause against Carrera. Los Altos would now elect deputies to the assembly, and Paredes promised that courts and schools would be established in Los Altos so that those inhabitants no longer would have to go to the capital for justice and education. Paredes also agreed to repeal the alcabala on overland trade with Mexico and promised full equality for the residents of Los Altos in such matters as public employment. He also assured that the majority of troops garrisoning Los Altos would henceforth be composed of its own inhabitants. Guatemala would assume the public debt of the State of Los Altos and would move toward development of the port of Champerico and repair of the roads. On 13 May the government formally approved this agreement, which offered a good statement of Los Altos' grievances. Guzmán's principal concern was that Carrera not be allowed to return.[137]

Repressive measures accompanied Paredes's efforts to check the return of Carrera in early May. Even the *Gaceta de Guatemala* was shut down for three weeks. Yet even as Paredes officially resisted Carrera, he also took steps to negotiate with the caudillo and named a commission composed of Joaquín Durán and Basilio Zeceña to "promote an arrangement respecting the person of this chief, to reestablish peace and tranquility in the pueblos that his forces have occupied," giving them wide latitude, but instructing them to try to reach a private settlement rather than some sort of formal treaty that would be "inappropriate."[138] The influence of Luis Batres as a private adviser to Paredes and his secret encouragement of Carrera's return was undoubtedly as important as several liberal historians have claimed, but also influential was the grim news of the Caste War in Yucatán, for there was apprehension that resistance to Carrera might bring Guatemala a similar sort of race war. José Urruela, who had replaced Rodríguez as foreign minister, opened negotiations with Carrera and soon was emphasizing that Carrera, far from developing a race war in Los Altos, had actually imposed order and stability there.[139]

News that the popular and dashing corregidor of Suchitepéquez, José Víctor Zavala, had defected to Carrera and that Carrera's forces had occupied Quetzaltenango greatly influenced the decision to treat with Carrera. There was bitter debate in the Permanent Commission of the assembly, with Molina and Barrundia heatedly arguing against it, urging instead that the death penalty be applied to Carrera as had been decreed by the assembly the previous October if he returned to Guatemala. Moderates led by Manuel Dardón, argued for compromise, urging that Carrera be offered a pension to return to exile. In the end, however, Luis Batres's arguments favoring a negotiated settlement with Carrera prevailed, and Paredes sent the commission named above.[140] The decision prompted resignations in the cabinet. Raymundo Arroyo left Gobernación and Manuel Tejada quit as war minister. Paredes moved Urruela from Finance to Gobernación, but Urruela also continued to manage Foreign Affairs. Francisco Cáscara became inspector general of the army. Paredes was returning to the practice of fewer ministers, as Carrera had done. Manuel Cerezo took over Finance.[141]

Paredes cracked down hard on the press on Friday, 25 May. He suspended the liberal press law of 1845 and ordered that no one could "print anything which directly or indirectly excited passions or distracted the attention of public officials." He followed this on 6 June with an edict concerning freedom of the press that recognized that "if freedom of the press is guaranteed to the citizens, it also is a dangerous weapon which is frequently abused to undermine public order," making it necessary to revoke the 1845 law as "contrary to the moral health" of the country.[142]

A further consideration, especially among the conservative merchants of the capital, in seeking a negotiated settlement with Carrera, was the avoidance of a new round of forced loans, which would be inevitable in a prolonged military resistance. On Sunday, 27 May, creditors of the government met with Finance Minister Cerezo to discuss ways to avert a new forced loan. They named a committee headed by Luis Batres to represent them with the finance minister "in this important affair."[143]

Paredes's commissioners reached Quetzaltenango on 29 May and reported that Carrera enjoyed great support there. By 5 June they had agreed that the prohibition of Carrera's return to Guatemala of the previous 13 October would be revoked and that Carrera would be recommissioned as a lieutenant general in the army.[144]

Agustín Guzmán and his followers had fled Guatemala City upon news that an accord was being arranged with Carrera. Guzmán went to Jalapa where he succeeded in negotiating a temporary truce with the rebels led by León Raimundo, Roberto Reyes, and Agustín Pérez, but the peace did not endure, and rebels sacked Jalapa on 3–4 June.[145] Guzmán went on to San Salvador where he issued a statement addressed to the "inhabitants of Guatemala," attacking "the perfidy of the immoral and always sanguinary Rafael Carrera," who had for nine years "misgoverned, [in] an era of hate and shame for the country, and of humiliation for the Guatemalans." He reviewed his efforts to defeat Carrera and explained that he had first decided to retire to San Salvador and abandon public life, for he "knew that a loyal and just heart was not enough to struggle against perfidy and evil." But then, "provoked by his enemies," he had calmly recognized that the whole country would suffer if he did not continue "in my noble, although arduous, enterprise of combatting the return of Carrera, and I decided to continue with the sons of Guatemala and the people that compose the Republic." He warned that Carrera intended to establish "a yoke yet harsher and more tyrannical than that under which Guatemala had suffered from 1840 to 1848," and he promised to continue the struggle aided by "good friends in San Salvador, Honduras and Nicaragua, as well as in Guatemala and Los Altos." This would not be the first time he had defended the territorial integrity and independence of Central America, he declared. He had fought the foreign flags in Soconusco and in Omoa, and he declared that all

Central America would rise with him against the tyrant Carrera. Indeed, Guzmán was declaring himself the successor to Morazán, not only as the enemy of Carrera, but as the unifier of a liberal Central American nation against conservative tyranny. He reaffirmed that it was not on the people of Guatemala that he was making war, but on Carrera and those who supported his return. He warned them that they were "forging the chains that will imprison you, perhaps forever." He called on the artisans of the city to join their brothers in the montaña. He called upon the military to refuse to serve the tyranny. He called upon the merchants to join in breaking the chains that were once more binding the country to Carrera.[146]

Yet Guzmán could neither rally significant support to challenge Carrera's return nor arrest the clear trend in Guatemala City toward a reconciliation with the caudillo. Paredes and his cabinet formally ended the prohibition against Carrera's return on 4 June and transmitted this news to Carrera via the Mexican minister in Guatemala. Carrera, receiving assurance of immunity from prosecution, agreed to place himself under the authority of the government, which had agreed to assume all expenses of his forces, paying the salaries of all officers and troops. Paredes appointed Ignacio Irigoyen, a Carrera supporter, as corregidor of Quetzaltenango, where Carrera remained during the negotiations. It was further agreed that he would continue to command the military forces there.[147] Carrera accepted these terms on 20 June, promising his "eternal gratitude to the supreme government."[148]

The agreement with Carrera brought peace to Los Altos, with the government even giving Carrera credit for reestablishing order there, especially owing "to the influence he exercises with the Indians." Paredes named corregidores acceptable to Carrera and firmly opposed to the separatist movement in each department. Carrera remained in Quetzaltenango for some time, consolidating his authority there, which included imposing some taxation to support his activities.[149] On 27 June he issued a proclamation justifying his return, pointing to the deterioration of things in Guatemala, with all of his good work destroyed. But now that the Paredes government had allowed him to return, he promised, he would work to restore the former peace, glory, and prosperity of Guatemala, with the help of Divine Providence.[150]

In Guatemala City, Paredes imposed a new war tax of four *reales* on flour milling (per bushel) and beef slaughter (per head), eight reales on each load (60 pounds) of cacao harvested, and eight reales on each package of foreign imports.[151] Paredes now made public his deal with Carrera, explaining that the continued war in the montaña necessitated allowing Carrera to return in order to maintain peace in Los Altos and thereby avoid complete catastrophe. He once again placed Vicente Cerna in command of the army as Paredes turned his attention to governing and to reconvening the assembly.[152]

On 7 July Marure argued vehemently in the *Gaceta* that Carrera's interest now coincided with those of the republic and that his return would contribute to pacification of the rebellion. He said that since his appearance in the republic, General Carrera had dedicated himself to the country's prosperity and had always been respectful of legitimate authority. This, and his conduct since arriving in Quetzaltenango, Marure wrote, suggested that Carrera could guarantee "prompt disappearance of the evils that afflict the Republic."[153] Ten days later Marure turned his attention to the war in the montaña, attacking those who say, "Let society perish and save the principles!" Instead, he argued, "the existence of society is the first and most sacred of principles; men know it and reject by their instinct of preservation whoever attacks it." His editorial also reflected the concern that the montañeses were getting aid from El Salvador."[154] This was part of a general campaign of the government to reinstate Carrera's image as saviour of the country against the montaña uprising. Carrera finally moved from Quetzaltenango in late July, on a slow triumphal march to the capital, holding up on 27 July at Chimaltenango, where further negotiations took place with the government.[155] The results of the Chimaltenango meeting became clear on 3 August, when Paredes named Carrera as commanding general of the Guatemalan armed forces. His brief decree acknowledged Carrera's organization of a division of Los Altos troops and authorized him to pursue pacification of the rebel communities and to direct military operations in the manner he believed most convenient to that end.[156] Extensive propaganda supporting Carrera's return appeared on the following day.[157] Paredes warned that the authority of the government would be maintained and that Carrera would enforce it.

It was clear, as Carrera marched into the capital on 7 August, that the conservative elite was back in control and welcomed his return. He assumed military command on the next day and issued a proclamation addressing squarely the problem of the montaña revolt. After crediting his return to the "invisible hand" of Divine Providence, he blamed the liberals for upsetting the society and instigating the rebellion. But he also recognized that "evils so great and suffering so prolonged cannot be conjured up by political discussions that only produce, as we have seen, division and discord." He railed against theories that tried to silence the legitimate interests and customs of the people. In effect, he was arguing that the same problems as 1837 had been brought forth by the liberals again. He called on all, but especially the clergy, to help him in this struggle. To the inhabitants of the montaña, he promised: "Soon I will be among you. My first effort will be to protect the good and peaceful farmers. Those troublemakers who return to orderly practice of their peaceful occupations will find me understanding and indulgent, but I will execute with force the authority that has been entrusted to me toward those who persist in continuing to attack the Republic and treating with its enemies." [158]

On 10 August the municipality gave a gala banquet honoring the returning caudillo. Fifty-five of the leading citizens in the city attended. The event, which began in late afternoon, went on until 11:00 P.M. It celebrated the formal end to the liberal revolution of 1848 and the resumption of Carrera's domination, now firmly allied with the conservative party. Paredes and Carrera, splendidly attired in full dress uniform, sat side by side and represented the new military power in the country. Ten days later Frederick Chatfield entertained Carrera and high government officials at the British consul's residence, symbolizing the restoration of the strong bonds between Britain and the conservative regime in Guatemala. [159]

The war in the montaña occupied Carrera most of the remainder of 1849 and throughout 1850. Before taking the field himself, he consolidated his political control throughout the country, forcing removal of many liberals from office. Some went to prison, while others he exiled or encouraged to leave the country voluntarily. The few remaining found themselves isolated from the political process. Paredes established a Permanent War Council, which had the authority to try and execute rebels summarily. [160] Carrera marched out of the capital on 23 August at the head of his Los Altos division and almost immediately began to encounter rebel attacks. General Cerna took over as corregidor of Chiquimula and carried on extensive antiguerrilla operations in that department. President Paredes frequently took to the field as well, and although the rebels continued their raids in the East, and at times in the Verapaz and even into Los Altos, the government, with a heavy military expenditure, gradually restored order to most of the country. Carrera called up all men between sixteen and fifty at the end of August, warning those who did not enlist in the new "patriot corps" that they would be conscripted into the regular army. [161] Carrera also urged the archbishop to assign more clergy to the montaña region, arguing that the teaching of the Christian religion and better customs would alleviate some of the problems contributing to the rebellion. [162] Carrera concentrated especially on the area around Santa Rosa, and claimed success there by early October 1849, but the guerrilla leaders simply moved their actions elsewhere, often using El Salvador or Honduras as sanctuary.[163]

A bold attack on the capital itself, led by Agustín Guzmán and Agustín Pérez, occurred on the night of 13 October 1849. The attack came from the north end of the city, the rebels apparently entering from the road to the Caribbean and beginning their attack in the Candelaria section. They tried to burn several houses, including Carrera's, and they nearly reached the central plaza before being stopped by Xavier Aycinena's Minerva Battalion. The rebels retreated to Palencia, where Guzmán died of a head injury.

Carrera and Paredes were both in the montaña during this attack, but Carrera hurried back to the capital on the seventeenth, accepted the resignation of the military commander of the Department of Guatemala, Ignacio García Granados, and replaced him with the corregidor, Colonel Francisco Benites. Carrera then returned immediately to Santa Rosa, where he launched a new offensive. He reported from Mataquescuintla on 24 October that the rebels were fleeing and that Colonel Bolaños and Generals Paredes and Cerna had also occupied various points where the rebels had been active. Yet on 3 November, Pérez and Reyes led a strong attack on Chiquimula, their numbers estimated at six hundred. Generals Paredes and Carrera converged on that city to repulse the attack, and from captives they learned that the rebels were taking refuge in and gaining assistance from El Salvador. By the end of the year Carrera and Paredes could claim to have diminished the rebel threat, but hardly to have ended it. They had dispersed the rebels and the montaña district was perhaps more secure, but rebel attacks in Chiquimula, the Verapaz, and occasionally Los Altos emphasized the continuation of the struggle. About four hundred rebels, declaring a new secession of Los Altos, sacked Quetzaltenango on 25 January 1850 before being routed on the next day by Serapio Cruz.[164]

The fighting continued throughout 1850, often more actively than the government admitted. Much of Carrera's time during that year was spent in the field in this frustrating struggle. One by one montaña leaders were killed, but new ones emerged. The government always won the battles, but could not conclude the war. Repeatedly, the government claimed that the rebellion had been subdued, only to once more be faced with new insurgency.[165] The government meanwhile maintained close surveillance on leading liberals who remained in Guatemala. The connection of the montaña with the liberals remained alive, and the foreign press sometimes referred to the montañeses as the republican army, fighting against conservative despotism in Guatemala.[166] By mid year, however, the rebels had suffered severe defeats. Foreign Minister Pedro Arriaga sent a circular to the other Central American states, announcing that the three-year war was over, acknowledging that his government had found it necessary to take strong measures to put down the uprising, but that the reward for these measures had been peace.[167] Yet the pockets of resistance that continued throughout the remainder of the year led Carrera to the opinion that peace depended upon elimination of the rebel refuges in El Salvador and Honduras. This would lead to Guatemalan intervention once more in those states, with Carrera becoming the arbiter of politics there as he became the most powerful caudillo on the isthmus.

In fact, the trouble in the montaña did not end completely for a long time, and Carrera was forced to march out repeatedly in the ensuing years to put down manifestations of discontent among the peoples of that region. A general amnesty was issued in April 1852 for all who had participated in the uprising, the government proclaiming that the rebellion was over. Yet a month later the government dispatched troops to Mataquescuintla to put down a new outbreak of violence.[168] Another uprising in 1855 and 1856 disturbed the peace in the Verapaz. Carrera's army finally contained it and captured its leader, Vicente Ruiz, described as one of the "worst and meanest" of the old guerrilla leaders, on 28 July 1856. Blaming Ruiz for much of the disorder that had reappeared in the region, his captor, Captain Victoriano Foronda, had him summarily shot.[169]

The violence and revolution we have called the Revolution of 1848 was the culmination of two important social movements in the country. On the one hand, it was a final effort of the liberals who had arisen with national independence to take control of the government and direct it under policies that had been put forward under Morazán and Gálvez. They temporarily ended the dictatorship of Rafael Carrera. But to do this they had allied themselves with the other social movement—the restless peasantry of the montaña and other regions of the country—that had smoldered and flamed up ever since 1837. While these two movements had some common foes, they were nevertheless largely incompatible, for the rural people remained staunchly conservative and distrustful of liberal land policy. Moreover, the liberal movement was still led by members of prominent Guatemala City families, who failed to appreciate fully the importance of regional leaders to their cause. While the 1848 movement reflected the important liberal force coming out of Los Altos, the liberals in power in 1848 were not able to consolidate their victory or to incorporate the various rebel military groups operating in the country to the extent necessary to establish a government that could hold power against the combined strength of the conservative

Guatemala City elite and the caudillo Rafael Carrera. Thus it was not sur-prising that Carrera could reorganize his forces and return to Guatemala, this time to establish a strongly conservative dictatorship that would en-dure for two more decades. Nevertheless, we see in the 1848 attempt the origins of the 1871 Liberal Reforma, when the Los Altos liberals would take the lead in ending conservative rule of Guatemala and in dominating the state for a half century to follow.

CHAPTER TEN

Arada

CONSOLIDATING HIS POWER AT HOME also involved Carrera in affairs beyond the borders of Guatemala, for a genuine fear of his liberal opponents throughout the isthmus continued to preoccupy him. The relative strength and stability of Guatemala in comparison to its isthmian neighbors gave him the ability to play an important role in the development of the entire isthmus during the remaining years of his life. It is not our intention here to detail the events in the other Central American states, except as they affect Guatemalan development, but in general, the struggles between liberals and conservatives continued, often violently, in the middle states of El Salvador, Honduras, and Nicaragua. The establishment of a moderate conservative administration in Costa Rica under Juan Rafael Mora in 1849, however, laid the foundation for a Guatemala–Costa Rica axis that would eventually help to bring a measure of unity to the whole region under conservative leadership. Costa Rican historians have often resisted the idea of Mora as a conservative, as they have developed a myth that all of Costa Rica's nineteenth-century leaders were liberals. They tend to emphasize Mora's friendliness to coffee cultivation, so long associated with the rise of the liberal party in Central America, and his willingness to allow liberal exiles from other states to reside there. Certainly his conservatism was considerably less reactionary than that of Carrera in Guatemala. Nevertheless, a closer examination of Mora's policies in Costa Rica suggests that he more properly should be classified as a moderate conservative. Certainly in foreign policy, of particular concern here, his close relations with both Great Britain and Guatemala suggest a conservative alliance at the very least.

Frederick Chatfield had, in fact, collaborated with the conservative up-surge. Chatfield cultivated the conservatives throughout the isthmus, and his role is difficult to underestimate.[1] Chatfield had been a player in Central American politics ever since he arrived in 1834, and British commercial hegemony had been rising on the isthmus since the eighteenth century. But the aggressive policy of Lord Palmerston peaked at mid-century, coincidentally with the return of Carrera to power in Guatemala. Upgrading of Chatfield's position from consul general to chargé d'affaires in mid 1849 reflected London's concern for Central America and its reaction to the sudden entrance of U.S. interests on the isthmus.[2] As Chatfield negotiated for British advantage, her majesty's naval presence became more evident on both coasts. Chatfield's aggressive machinations often exceeded his instructions and nearly brought Britain to war with the United States. Yet it is clear that Victoria's government sought to extend its commercial and strategic advantage, and hopes for an interoceanic canal heightened British interest in the isthmus.[3]

Britain's dominance in Central America following Spain's decline rested solidly on the strength of her merchant marine, her available capital, and her industrial growth. The roots of British colonialism in Central America date from the mid-seventeenth century.[4] By 1850 the British had settlements all along the eastern coast of Central America, with particular strength at Belize, the Bay Islands, and among the Miskito Indians of Nicaragua. Chatfield had furthered British ends by supporting conservatives in each state, thwarting the reorganization of the federation and building strong alliances with the elites who were coming to power. In Guatemala he developed especially close relations with a number of the local merchants and with Manuel F. Pavón.

Yet British expansionism had also engendered nationalist reaction among Central Americans, a resentment that U.S. agents encouraged after the acquisition of Oregon and California stimulated U.S. interest in the isthmus and its potential interoceanic route. British seizure of San Juan del Norte (Greytown), Nicaragua, on 1 January 1848 began several years of tense and sometimes violent confrontation between the two English-speaking powers in Central America. The British justified the seizure on the basis of their protection of the Mosquito Kingdom, but in reality they were looking toward control of the eastern terminus of the Nicaraguan transit route. Nicaraguan resistance proved inadequate, and by early February the British had driven up the San Juan River and occupied San Carlos on Lake Nicaragua, forcing the Nicaraguans to recognize British control of the mouth of the river.[5] The U.S. outcry was strong, especially after the discovery of gold in California later the same year intensified interest in a transit route. Liberals throughout Central America, but especially in El Salvador, welcomed the U.S. chargé d'affaires, Elija Hise, and he worked with them toward reunion of the five Central American states as a means of checking British expansionism.[6] His successor, E. G. Squier, intrigued even more actively to ally the Central American states with the United States in an intense rivalry with Chatfield to garner preferential privileges for their respective nations.[7] Meanwhile, Cornelius Vanderbilt and others launched ventures to capitalize on the sudden demand for transit from the north Atlantic to the California gold fields. Central America was suddenly at the center of world attention.[8]

Hise and Squier had special success with the Honduran government of Trinidad Cabañas. Chatfield sabotaged the treaty Hise negotiated with Nicaragua, which would have given the United States a protectorate there, but Squier arrived in June of 1849 and quickly arranged a treaty by which Honduras temporarily ceded Tigre Island in the Gulf of Fonseca to the United States as a means of foiling British aggression in the region. But British naval forces, in the meantime, had recently seized Tigre Island, creating a potential point of conflict. The aggressive efforts of Squier and Chatfield, however, soon led to the intervention of their superiors. The result was the Clayton-Bulwer Treaty of 1850, which defused the situation somewhat, although it did not end the Anglo-American rivalry for privilege and opportunity on the isthmus. In March 1852, for example, the British declared the Bay Islands a British crown colony, in apparent violation of the treaty.[9]

The *Gaceta de Guatemala*, reflecting Chatfield's strength with the Guatemalan government, praised the Clayton-Bulwer Treaty and cheered the State Department's decision to relieve Squier, smugly defending British policy and declaring that Squier's conduct had made that decision inevitable.[10] Meanwhile—while the Anglo-American rivalry for influence and power in Central America occupied the greatest attention—France, Belgium, Spain, and the German states were all increasing their representation and influence in an effort to gain whatever advantages were to be had.[11] Carrera, in November, was made an honorary president of the French Institute of Africa, as part of the French effort to woo him, for example.[12]

Before Chatfield himself was relieved in 1852, he busily concluded treaties with as many of the Central American states as he could. He was notably successful with the governments of Guatemala and Costa Rica, and in the process contributed to the development of a Costa Rica–Guatemala alliance against the more liberal middle states.[13] The political parties, liberal and conservative, transcended the state boundaries of Central America. There was much movement from one country to another of members of the political elites and it was not uncommon for a person born in one country to serve in high office in another. Conservatives in all the states feared collusion among liberals of the several states, and it became common for one state to allow the use of its territory by friendly exiles from a neighboring state to launch invasions. Chatfield understood this and worked to form a strong pro-British alliance among conservatives, thereby incurring the wrath of the liberals and increasing their pro-U.S. inclinations.[14]

José Francisco Barrundia reflected the liberal disdain for Chatfield in 1850 when he wrote in a Salvadoran newspaper that "the ravages of the small pox, the cholera—Civil War—bloody revolutions—tyranny—barbarism—a Malespín—and a Carrillo—all these pass away. Carrera also will pass away," he promised, "but there is an evil, horrible and interminable, there is a living curse which corrodes the vitals of Central America— and this is Chatfield, the eternal Agent of England."[15] In contrast, Pavón and Milla in the *Gaceta de Guatemala* attacked Barrundia and the liberals as the "revolutionary party" that would use any means, since it recognized no evil, to achieve their ends.[16]

The conservatives identified Central American union with the liberals, and although some looked to a distant day when reunification might be practical and desirable, they opposed it for the present. The *Gaceta de Guatemala* consistently presented that view. Before the 1848 revolution it had set the tone for subsequent editorials when it praised the "peace and prosperity" of the five small independent states of Central America in contrast to the disaster of a "united" Mexico. It criticized Mexico's liberal immigration policy, which had brought foreigners of a different culture and religion into Texas and California, and suggested that Chiapas would be better off if it established its independence from Mexico. Emphasizing that "unity wasn't everything," it pointed to the suffering of Italy in its reunification attempts, and cited disunited Germany as an example of a region that had great prosperity despite its failure to unify.[17] Upon returning to power, the conservatives renewed the theme, arguing that since its declaration of absolute independence (in 1847) Guatemala had enjoyed advances in its economic well being, public order, and foreign relations. "For the first time in 27 years," an editorial proclaimed, Guatemala was "viewed with respect and honor in its actions and progress by foreign reporters and agents."[18]

Thus, for Guatemala, the efforts of the three middle republics to reunite were dangerous. A flurry of handbills and pamphlets published in

Guatemala attacked the Salvadoran government of Doroteo Vasconcelos and his promotion of "Central American nationalism."[19] Conservatives opposed the stronger central government that the liberals advocated at the national level. The fear that such a national government might infringe on the power of the elites in the individual city states has been a recurring obstacle to Central American reunification throughout the nineteenth and twentieth centuries. Although it was strongly authoritarian, structurally the Guatemalan state was not highly centralized, and much of the power remained in the hands of landlords and local authorities. There was, of course, a nostalgia for the unity of the colonial Kingdom of Guatemala and the position Guatemala City had played in it. The *Gaceta* recognized the potential desirability of reunion, but pointed to the difficulty of restoring it once broken. It blamed the Constitution of 1824 as the origin of the difficulties and of the separation of El Salvador from Guatemala even before that. The reunification attempts, it protested, had in reality been efforts to make war on Guatemala, for any true attempt would have centered itself in Guatemala, where the diplomatic representatives were and where the capital of the old kingdom had been. The *Gaceta* concluded that party passions still prevented any true reunification. The editor continued this theme for several weeks in late 1850, blaming the separatism of other states and the aggressiveness of El Salvador for the failure of union. Costa Rica and Guatemala, he wrote, were the only states that had achieved order and control by "responsible elements." Thus, he concluded on 8 November, "We believe that in this matter we can do no more than recognize the *status quo,* and consider the separation of the states as an established fact," concentrating on economic progress rather than political reunion. A week later the *Gaceta* reiterated this opinion and again held up Costa Rica and Guatemala as models against the disintegrating situation in the middle states with their so-called national army.[20]

Three years later the viewpoint had only hardened. The *Gaceta* doubted that reunification could occur before considerable passage of time and until there had been much more commercial development. Old prejudices would have to disappear, and there would have to be "a complete transformation in the material and moral existence of these countries to restore a true nationality." It acknowledged that history provided many examples of national reunifications, citing Spain as the most pertinent case. But it emphasized that the foundations for reunion must be laid carefully to avoid rushing into the same old problems. Acknowledging that small states ran the risk of foreign domination, it thus urged that the states first work toward strengthening their ties of friendship, promising that "Guatemala will always be disposed to anything that reties the bonds with its sister states and to support whatever will promote our mutual benefit."[21]

Chatfield encouraged the Guatemalans to oppose the alliance of the middle states, while at the same time he encouraged Guatemalan alliance with Rafael Mora's new government in Costa Rica. The two countries both signed treaties with Britain in 1849, while Chatfield was unable to gain treaties at this time with the middle republics.[22] Pavón accompanied Chatfield to Costa Rica early in 1850. While there he negotiated a treaty of amity and commerce that included an improvement in the mail service between Costa Rica and Guatemala, for letters sometimes took two months between the two countries.[23] Praising Mora's accession to the Costa Rican presidency, the *Gaceta de Guatemala* published the full text of his inaugural address.[24] Costa Rica gained its own bishop at this time, negotiated in Rome by Felipe Molina.[25]

With the Guatemala–Costa Rica axis cemented, Chatfield and Pavón left San José on 12 March and visited the British Caribbean establishments at Greytown, the Mosquito Coast, the Bay Islands, and Belize. Pavón continued his attack on the liberals from Belize, issuing handbills especially aimed at the Salvadoran "Red Republicans," Doroteo Vasconcelos, and José Francisco Barrundia.[26] In another handbill published in Belize on 29 May, Pavón justified his close relationship with Chatfield, claiming that he had been guided solely by a desire for Guatemala to maintain good relations with other nations.[27] They returned together to Guatemala in late July 1850.[28]

The resurgence of liberal leadership in the middle states raised the possibility of war along Guatemala's eastern border. Rumors of troop movements and British involvement increased tension in the region throughout 1850. Guatemala's pro-British stance became more and more evident and infuriated the middle states. The continued revolt in the montaña further inflamed the situation, as the Guatemalans accused the Salvadoran government of aiding the rebels and providing sanctuary for raids against Guatemalan territory.[29]

There is no doubt that declaration of absolute Guatemalan independence and the development of a government with a strong conservative consensus contributed quickly to an improvement of Guatemalan relations with nations beyond the isthmus. Reforms in government finance and credit were partially responsible for this, but it also came from a conscious effort to develop better foreign relations and to expand overseas commerce. The treaties in the 1848–52 period regularized Guatemala's foreign relations. At the same time, however, its relations with its immediate Central American neighbors, Honduras and El Salvador, began to deteriorate seriously.

The roots of the trouble with El Salvador lay in the emergence of that state as an important economic region within colonial Guatemala and in the separatist moves dating from the late eighteenth century, which succeeded after 1821. Resentment by Salvadoran indigo planters against the Guatemalan merchant monopoly had been an important aspect of this in the late colonial period. Added to this was a desire for ecclesiastical autonomy from the Guatemala City clerical hierarchy, so that establishment of a separate diocese of El Salvador became an emotional and symbolic issue in the early national period. El Salvador had been the center of liberal sentiment since then, while Guatemala had become the stronghold of the conservatives. The enmity arising from these historical struggles had been further expanded by the role of Chatfield in applying pressure on behalf of British commercial interests in El Salvador. The election of Doroteo Vasconcelos early in 1848 brought a liberal to power there with strong anti-Guatemalan sentiments. An associate of Morazán, Vasconcelos supported the liberal Revolution of 1848 against Carrera, favored restoration of the State of Los Altos, and protected liberal exiles from Guatemala after the conservatives returned to power there in 1849. José Francisco Barrundia was especially influential among these exiles in the Vasconcelos government.[30]

Convinced that the Vasconcelos government was supporting the rebellion in the montaña, Carrera by mid-1850 had substantial numbers of troops operating close to the Salvadoran frontier. In late June the Salvadoran government accused him of arming raiders into its territory. The war of words escalated when the Guatemalans responded with vehement denials and accused the Salvadorans of supporting hostile incursions into Guatemalan territory.[31] In fact, in early August forty armed men commanded by the Pérez brothers crossed into Guatemalan territory from El Salvador. Guatemalan forces chased them to the Salvadoran border, killing four, including Lt. Col. José María Pérez, and recovering some stolen goods. The *Gaceta* charged that these Salvadorans had been attacking Guatemala for three years and supplying the montañeses.[32]

Guatemala now banned Salvadoran newspapers, charging that *El Progreso*, edited in San Salvador by Barrundia, had been published "with the sole objective of subverting order in this Republic" and preventing the pacification of the rebellious montaña region. The *Gaceta* allowed that "among judicious people" the circulation of *El Progreso* would in no way be dangerous, "but not all are intelligent . . . and this kind of publication certainly is not the best education for a society that is trying to get itself organized," thus the government had "the obligation to impede such propaganda."[33]

Carrera spent much time in the field, returning from time to time to consult with President Paredes. It is clear that Carrera often exceeded the president's instructions, especially in his refusal to keep his forces within Guatemala. Meanwhile, Chatfield stepped up his campaign against the Vasconcelos government, threatening a blockade and demanding suppression of anti-English statements in the Salvadoran press. With the arrival of the British warships *Champion* and *Gorgon*, Chatfield could increase the pressure, although his blockade was never completely effective and failed to alter the Salvadoran hostility toward England and Guatemala.[34]

Carrera marched out of the capital on 17 September 1850 at the head of a division in the direction of Mataquescuintla and Santa Rosa with the goal of completing the pacification of the montaña revolt. A second division left two weeks later under General Bolaños. By the middle of October, Carrera claimed to have cleared the rebels from the road between Guatemala and Palencia, but there continued to be trouble elsewhere. Carrera's methods were often brutal. Whole villages were destroyed, the inhabitants resettled elsewhere. When Carrera returned to the capital on Sunday afternoon, 3 November, he was accompanied by many montaña families, refugees quartered in the capital until new villages could be found for them. Torture and retaliatory raids were regular parts of the process by which Carrera gradually restored peace and security to the region.[35] The Caste War in Yucatan added an urgency to the pacification effort, for there was a fear among the elite that the Yucatecan rebellion might spread into Guatemala.[36]

Captured correspondence soon revealed that one of the principal montañés leaders, José Dolores Nufio, was preparing a large invasion force in the vicinity of Santa Ana, El Salvador, with Salvadoran assistance.[37] This undoubtedly caused Carrera to return quickly to the field. Nufio issued a declaration at La Brea on 11 November 1850, attacking Chatfield, the Guatemalan government, and the "aristocratic party," which he charged had made "common cause" with the English consul to the prejudice of Central American dignity and integrity. He claimed that it used "the barbarian Carrera to maintain the disruption of the country and to support absolutism on these unfortunate peoples" by cruel and inhumane means. Nufio's manifesto recognized the Chinandega government that El Salvador, Honduras, and Nicaragua had erected. It called on all Central Americans to unite to restore the federation and swore not to lay down their arms until they had "liberated the Guatemalan people from the oppression that buries them." Among Nufio's top commanders were Ciriaco Bran, Doroteo Monterrosa, and Agustín Pérez, the last being one of the assassins of Mariano Rivera Paz.[38]

Honduran involvement in the unionist cause exposed it to Carrera's opposition. Juan Lindo, a moderate conservative, had provided the best administrative leadership in Honduras since independence, and Lindo sought to pursue a peaceful policy of reconstruction. But Honduras was the victim of British imperialism in the Bay Islands, and feeling ran high against Chatfield and the Anglo-Guatemalan alliance, especially after Lieutenant Jolly in the schooner HMS *Bermuda* took formal possession of those islands in August 1850. Lindo had established a more conservative constitution in 1848, but Hondurans friendly to Carrera and the Guatemalan conservatives sought unsuccessfully to overturn his government behind Santos Guardiola in February 1850. These events forced Lindo to move closer to the liberals and into an alliance with El Salvador and Nicaragua.[39]

The montañeses used Honduran territory as well as Salvadoran. Nufio's "National Army" left El Salvador via Honduras before entering Guatemala and taking Esquipulas on 12 November, forcing the municipality there to place itself formally under the protection of the Chinandega government and calling upon Guatemalans to join Nufio's effort to liberate them.[40] The invading army then marched toward Chiquimula, taking Jocotán on the fourteenth. This invasion was coordinated with attempted proliberal uprisings in Antigua and Quetzaltenango. A division sent by Vicente Cerna under Lt. Col. Joaquín Solares stopped the invaders at Changüis, near Jocotán. Solares counterattacked, and captured a large quantity of supplies and mules, but most of the rebels escaped back into Honduras.[41]

The defeat at Changüis did not dissuade the unionist forces, as they quickly reorganized for a new invasion. But the Guatemalans now seized the initiative. Even before news of the Changüis victory, Foreign Minister Pedro Arriaga had notified the European diplomats in Guatemala of the invasion by a Salvadoran-Honduran army, reportedly as a response to the British blockade of El Salvador. Arriaga assured the diplomats that the Guatemalan government would take every precaution to safeguard the lives and property of their nationals in its effort to defend itself.[42] General Carrera, already operating near the Salvadoran border at the time of the invasion, issued a victory manifesto on 19 November, praising Cerna and Solares and their Chiquimula army. He warned the Salvadorans and the Guatemalan exiles to stop their hostilities, for "Divine Providence never leaves treason and perfidy unpunished."[43]

Two days later President Paredes offered his good offices to negotiate the differences between El Salvador and Great Britain, but the Salvadoran government refused, noting that a similar offer from the French consul had been rejected by Chatfield. The Salvadoran foreign minister, Francisco Dueñas, called Chatfield's demands on El Salvador so exaggerated and unreasonable that they could not even serve as a basis for discussion.[44]

Carrera now mobilized for war and sought to deal a death blow to both the montañeses and their allies in Salvador and Honduras. He asked Arriaga to extend the hand of friendship to Honduras if it would not support further incursions into Guatemalan territory.[45] Lindo's response disclaimed any responsibility for the November invasion of Chiquimula, saying he regarded it also as an invasion of Honduras.[46] The Guatemalan press accused Barrundia of being behind the whole unification scheme, including the invasion of Guatemala by the National Army.[47]

By the end of November Carrera had several divisions in eastern Guatemala engaged both in routing out the montañés rebels and in preparing for the expected invasion from Honduras.[48] Salvadoran President Vasconcelos feared a Guatemalan invasion and placed his army of about two thousand men in Santa Ana on alert.[49] Carrera waited in Chiquimula, where Corregidor Cerna and the leading citizens honored him with a ball on 1 December, but he maintained a substantial defensive force nearer the border at Esquipulas. Several skirmishes occurred as his units maneuvered in the region and encountered hostile patrols.[50]

The mobilization had been expensive. Paredes accompanied his order for a new forced loan with a manifesto, attacking El Salvador and justifying Carrera's military buildup.[51] He also appealed to Costa Rica for two thousand rifles, promising to replace them with rifles of equal or better quality within a year.[52] He sent a commission to Honduras, seeking to separate Honduras from its alliance with El Salvador and to insure its neutrality in the approaching showdown.[53] But on 6 January, Lindo issued a statement saying that despite his wish for peace, he had failed to reach accord with the Guatemalans. Thus, he declared that he would provide military aid to El Salvador. Lindo's decision was not based on ideological considerations. While expressing sympathy for conservative ideals, he also protested that he had no desire to impose on Guatemala the "old party that destroyed the Federation." His only interest, he claimed, was Honduran security. Lindo, who had served as president of both El Salvador and Honduras, felt a strong and justifiable fear of Guatemala more than he felt his conservative affinity with Carrera and Mora.[54] But his decision was even more influenced by the current military situation, in which liberal Gen. Trinidad Cabañas commanded the Honduran armed forces. Cabañas assured the Guatemalan government that he had given no aid to Nufio and had ordered him out of Honduras, where he had retreated following the defeat in November. Yet Cabañas's long loyalty to the Morazanista cause was well known, and Lindo was in no position to challenge him.[55]

Representatives of the three middle states met in Chinandega on 9 January 1851. This "National Representation" organized to resist British aggression and overturn Carrera. They chose the Salvadoran representative, J. F. Barrundia, as their president, confirming conservative Guatemalan suspicions that Barrundia was at the heart of the movement.[56] Invective in the press of Guatemala and El Salvador reached new heights, as Carrera's frustration over the continued montaña revolt was now vented toward El Salvador and Honduras.

Barrundia, Vasconcelos, Nufio, Pérez, and Gerardo Barrios, meanwhile, plotted an invasion of Guatemala. Launched from Santa Ana, their army entered Guatemala on 22 January 1851 with the intention of taking the Guatemalan capital.[57] Despite Barrundia's efforts, the Dieta in Chinandega refused to sanction officially this invasion.[58] Nicaragua gave it no support at all and Honduran support was not substantial. President Lindo, torn between his desire for peace and his fear of Guatemalan intervention in his state, was physically ill and mentally disillusioned. Thus the invading force was made up primarily of Salvadorans and Guatemalan exiles, including many from the the montaña. Paredes reported the invasion to the inhabitants of the capital in a war message on 24 January after receiving bulletins from Jutiapa. Meanwhile, Carrera, with his large force at Chiquimula, prepared to block the route to the capital.[59]

Vasconcelos wrote a long letter to the Guatemalan foreign minister on the twenty-eighth, justifying the invasion. He said that the great disorder in Guatemala in 1848 had obligated the Salvadoran government to take measures to prevent the spread of revolution into its territory and to protect the general interests of Central America. It had appeared that the liberal victory in August of that year would assure peace and order, but the return of Carrera created a security problem for Honduras and El Salvador and made efforts to restore the union more difficult. He accused the Guatemalans of encouraging disorder in the neighboring states and cited two occasions on which Guatemalan troops had penetrated Honduran and Salvadoran territory. Carrera, he said, had threatened to "exterminate El Salvador to the last village" and had sent troublemakers into the country to stir up trouble. Thus Carrera's rule in Guatemala, in Vasconcelos's view, threatened the other states and military action was Salvador's only recourse.

His ultimatum called for the resignation of the Guatemalan government and the exile of Carrera from Central American territory, but he guaranteed the lives and property of those who had served him. Furthermore, he declared that the invading army would occupy Guatemala until a provisional government could be organized there to convoke a constituent assembly to establish liberty and hold elections.[60]

Arriaga formally rejected these demands on 3 February, but Carrera had already met the enemy at San José la Arada, south of Chiquimula, a day earlier. Skillfully outmaneuvering the invaders, he easily routed them in the most stunning military victory of his career. The casualty count tells the story: Carrera lost three officers and twenty men killed, and seven officers and forty-two men wounded, compared to 528 enemy killed and an undetermined number of wounded. Nearly two hundred more were captured, and more than a thousand rifles and a large quantity of military stores were left to the Guatemalans. The remnants of the National Army straggled back into Honduras and El Salvador.[61]

While Guatemala City rejoiced at being spared another siege, Carrera followed up his advantage and marched to Santa Ana, which he occupied on 13 February. Desperate, Vasconcelos declared martial law, ordered all able-bodied men into military service, and decreed a forced loan of $20,000 per month for the duration of the war. Carrera pursued a deliberate campaign of reprisal, warning the Salvadoran government that it would continue until the government came to terms.[62]

The Salvadoran government responded bravely to Carrera's demands on 17 February, declaring that it would negotiate no treaty so long as Carrera's forces remained in Salvadoran territory, and that if he advanced further he would face "dangerous consequences." The note also chastised the Guatemalans for writing "San Salvador" instead of "El Salvador" in their communications. The regional disdain felt by Salvadorans for Guatemala was apparent when the note declared that many believed that this was not a mistake, but rather an intentional attitude of Guatemala in continuing to use the name of the colonial province rather than its independent name.[63] Carrera's response demanded an indemnity for his army's expenses and the ouster of Vasconcelos, assuring the Salvadorans that his only desire was peace and prosperity for both states, but adding, "At the same time it is my obligation to demand full satisfaction for the outrages done to my government, and indemnification for the expenses that have been incurred by the unjust and illegal invasion of the territory of my republic." Under no circumstances, he declared, would he leave El Salvador without a peace treaty, nor would he accept any commissioners named by President Vasconcelos (that is, Vasconcelos had to step down first). Symbolically, the salutations on the exchange of letters reflected the liberal-conservative conflict, as the Salvadoran notes closed with "Dios, Unión, Libertad" [God, Union, Liberty], while the Guatemalan notes carried the traditional "Dios guarde a Ud. muchos años" [God keep you many years].[64]

Five days later, however, Carrera received orders to retreat behind the border on the condition that the Salvadorans immediately send a commissioner to the capital of Guatemala to negotiate a peace. Carrera wrote the Salvadoran government of this development near midnight on the twenty-second, promising that he would be back if an honorable peace were not quickly negotiated.[65] By that time, however, the Salvadoran Congress, which had convened on the eighteenth, had impeached Vasconcelos and replaced him with J. F. Quiroz. However, the more moderate Francisco Dueñas would be the real power in El Salvador for the next couple of years. He would negotiate a satisfactory peace with Guatemala, although the commissioners did not finally sign a treaty until 17 August 1853, ratified by Carrera on 14 September.[66] In the meantime, Carrera maneuvered near the Salvadoran border where skirmishes occasionally occurred. He complained in June of 1851, after enumerating recent battles in a letter to his mistress, of the privations "of this kind of life," and apologized for neglecting her. Again in February 1852 he was in the field fighting new montañés troubles in the Verapaz and Chiquimula. A year later the East continued to be disturbed, Carrera attributing it to the continued machinations of Trinidad Cabañas.[67]

Carrera and his victorious army had returned to Guatemala City on 3 March 1851 to a triumphant celebration, capped with a promotion for Carrera to the rank of captain general, with an annual salary of 4,000 pesos.[68] Carrera responded to the honors heaped upon him in a handbill that thanked the inhabitants of the capital: "There are days that are never erased from memory. If 2 February 1851 has been such a day for our arms, 3 March of the same year, on which the demonstrations of your affection have satisfied my most ardent ambitions, will leave in my heart a memory as tender as it is indelible and lasting."[69]

Arada had long term effects. It brought Carrera enormous prestige and power, assuring his return to the presidency of Guatemala and the establishment of his authoritarian dictatorship. Defeat might well have ended his career, and Guatemala would have been returned at least temporarily to liberal rule, with the likelihood of the protracted instability and civil war that plagued the middle states. Arada dealt a death blow to the efforts of Barrundia and the middle-state liberals to reorganize the federation. Nicaragua was embroiled in its own civil war between conservatives and liberals and had disclaimed involvement in the invasion. The conservative forces of the Guatemalan-born Fruto Chamorro now gained the upper hand there, although the struggle between León and Granada continued. Salvadoran pretensions of leadership of a new federation were destroyed by Arada and Carrera's counteroffensive into El Salvador. For the time being, El Salvador was little more than a satellite of Guatemala. Reluctantly coming to terms with both Guatemala and Great Britain, El Salvador abandoned the Chinandega government, and with only Honduras remaining, the Representación Nacional moved its capital to Tegucigalpa in November 1851.[70]

Honduran President Juan Lindo had been more successful than other Central American leaders in achieving some accord between conservatives and liberals within his state, but he was disillusioned and his role as a mediator in the other states had failed as often as they had succeeded. In November 1851 he won election to a third term but then announced that he did not wish to continue and asked that someone else be elected. The result was the election of the charismatic Morazanista, Trinidad Cabañas, who succeeded Lindo on 1 March 1852. Often cited as a rare example of a peaceable and constitutional transition from conservative to liberal rule in Central America, it more accurately reflected Lindo's estrangement with the conservatives owing to his distrust of and difficulties with the Guatemalan conservatives. Moreover, Lindo recognized that Cabañas commanded the army and thereby held the real power in the state. But this reality also quickly put Cabañas into conflict with Carrera and Guatemala. If Lindo, as a conservative, had been unable to avoid difficulties with the Guatemalans, Cabañas, as the last of the old Morazanista generals in Central America, would be even less able to maintain Honduran independence. For Cabañas was not content simply to rule Honduras. In the footsteps of Morazán, Barrundia, and Vasconcelos, he sought the overthrow of Carrera, and the restoration of the union.[71]

Cabañas bitterly faced British occupation of the Bay Islands and accepted a settlement regarding financial claims with the British, the last of Chatfield's Central American successes before his departure in May 1852. Chatfield met with Carrera for the last time at noon on 29 April. Chatfield had been effusive in his praise of Carrera after the victory at Arada, and their final meeting was described as very cordial.[72] It was not long thereafter that trouble began between Guatemala and Honduras. In September the Honduran commander at Trujillo protested the British presence at Roatán, and on 9 October Cabañas launched efforts to revive the federal government from Tegucigalpa. Although Honduras was the only government supporting it, the National Constituent Congress included exiles from the other states as well. Cabañas turned down the federal presidency, to which the Congress had elected him on 13 October. The Congress then chose Francisco Castellón, a Nicaraguan, on the twenty-eighth, but in Castellón's absence, Vice-President Pedro Molina of Guatemala soon was functioning as "supreme executive authority." [73]

Carrera was determined to thwart efforts to revive a liberal union of the middle states. He arrived in Jutiapa with a large force on 10 January 1853. That night he wrote to his foreign minister, instructing him how to respond to accusations of Trinidad Cabañas that Guatemala has invaded Honduran territory. Simultaneously the *Gaceta* launched a new series of attacks on Cabañas's government and the efforts of the "liberal faction" to reorganize the federation and renew the "national" war against Guatemala. [74]

While the *Gacetas* of Guatemala and Honduras carried on a hostile dialogue, Carrera mobilized his army in Jutiapa and Chiquimula. Unwilling to risk war, Cabañas agreed to negotiate with Carrera. They met in April at the Rancho de Brea, on the Guatemalan-Honduran border near Esquipulas, and signed some agreements that were formulated into the "Convenio de Esquipulas" on the nineteenth of that month. Carrera returned to the capital after nearly three months in the East and issued a proclamation on the twentieth in which he claimed to have succeeded in maintaining peace and security against "the enemies in Honduras." [75]

But it appeared that Cabañas was only playing for time, for on 29 April the Honduran government refused to ratify the Esquipulas Convention, leaving the dispute smoldering. [76] On the same evening, in Guatemala Carrera celebrated the birthday of his wife with a private dinner party at his residence, unaware that his recent treaty success had not been ratified and that Cabañas was already plotting to invade Guatemala. [77] He had already turned his attention to domestic affairs and to establishing cordial relations with the Santa Anna government in Mexico, a conservative ally to his north, leaving General Cerna in charge of the defenses in the east. [78]

At the beginning of July, Cabañas struck swiftly at Guatemala and El Salvador, seeking to topple by surprise both conservative regimes at once. It was, as Carrera called it on 5 July, "an incredible attempt." On the following day he issued an order clamping tight security on the country, establishing martial law, and putting the country on a war footing. [79] Already, however, General Cerna had repulsed the invaders, forcing them back into Honduras, yet another disaster for the Central American liberals. [80]

Carrera now launched an invasion of his own, aimed not at the heart of Honduras, where Cabañas's army braced for the expected counterattack, but at the North Coast, where he could effectively cut off Honduran trade and thereby choke the Hondurans into a favorable treaty. On 18 August his force boarded boats at Izabal and sailed the following morning, fearing, according to Carrera, "the climate more than the enemy."[81] They disembarked at Chachaguala, Honduras, at dawn on the twenty-third. Lt. Col. José Victor Zavala led the assault on the great fortress at Omoa, gaining its capitulation at 3:30 on the following afternoon. This victory gave Guatemala a solid advantage in dealing with Honduras and resulted in a temporary cessation of hostilities. For Carrera, personally, however, the victory was hollow, for his eldest son, José, died in the battle.[82]

After burying his son at Livingston in Guatemalan territory, Carrera returned to the capital in a greatly depressed state. For several weeks he rarely came to the presidential office, although many people visited him at home. He occasionally rode out on horseback or in his carriage, and on 18 September he visited the soldiers wounded in the Omoa campaign at the San Juan de Dios Hospital. He finally met with his cabinet at his office on 23 September and gradually resumed his normal routine, but, uncharacteristically, sought peaceful means of settling outstanding differences with Honduras and El Salvador in the months that followed. He believed his military victories had opened an era of peace on the isthmus. Although there were a few skirmishes along the Honduran border, on 7 December he ordered communications reopened with Honduras.[83]

Carrera recognized the conservative government of Fruto Chamorro in Nicaragua while he maintained pressure on Dueñas in El Salvador.[84] Chamorro had crushed a liberal uprising in November 1853 and strengthened the conservatives in Nicaragua. He exiled the liberal chieftains Francisco Castellón, Máximo Jérez, and Mariano Salazar to El Salvador, where they received encouragement from Cabañas to renew the struggle.[85] El Salvador suffered a disaster in April 1854, however, when one of the worst earthquakes in its history destroyed most of the city of San Salvador. Carrera sent aid, $5,000 from the public treasury and another $5,168 from private donations. Coming on the heels of the military defeat by Guatemala, the earthquake was a serious blow to Salvadoran development and, temporarily at least, diminished its formerly active role in Central American political affairs.[86]

Maintenance of the peace required constant vigilance, for the montaña and the Verapaz were still lawless. Bandits, perhaps encouraged and financed by Cabañas as the Guatemalans claimed, were once more a problem in early 1854 and drew Carrera into the field again. His relationship with Chepita Silva had grown stronger after Omoa, and his letters to her in early 1854 reflect the depth of his emotion. "We only know what we love in absence," he wrote from Salamá in February.[87] And later, he looked forward "to bathing with her and enjoying some very good wine in her company."[88]

He was annoyed, of course, that Cabañas remained in power in Honduras and more or less openly continued to harbor plans for Carrera's overthrow. Cabañas's close relationship to the United States also concerned Carrera. And when J. F. Barrundia became the Honduran representative in the United States, there were rumors that the United States might annex Honduras, placing the power of the colossus of the north dangerously close to Guatemala.[89] Carrera thus supported the aspirations of the conservative Santos Guardiola. Earlier efforts by Guardiola had failed in Honduras, but now with Carrera's support and Cabañas's problems there was definite hope for him. Guardiola, in a manifesto to the Honduran people issued from Guatemala on the last day of 1853, attacked Cabañas and ridiculed E. G. Squier's efforts to extend U.S. influence there through his plans for a railroad across Honduras. He reviewed his own military successes and then accused Cabañas and his liberals of selling out to the Anglo-Americans, warning that the people would soon rise up to throw out Cabañas.[90]

Carrera chose to support Honduran revolutionaries rather than intervene directly, as he concentrated on mopping up remnants of the montaña rebellion and consolidating his own power. By mid-1855 Guardiola had sufficient force finally to bring down Cabañas. Important in his effort was the defection of Gen. Juan López, who had commanded Omoa against the Guatemalan assault in 1853. Liberals, furious over his subsequent joining of Guardiola and the conservatives, accused López of having turned over Omoa with insufficient resistance. In a showdown, López's army, with support from the forces of Vicente Cerna and Rafael Carrera in eastern Guatemala, routed Cabañas at Gracias on 6 July 1855.[91] Following his victory, López renounced his earlier "liberal illusions" and fought for the "cause of the people," which is "*order, peace, and security,* and not that of persecution, confiscation, seizure of *community and charitable funds* and imprisonment of the democratic." He promised to banish Cabañas so that Honduras "could dedicate itself to cementing peace and building material prosperity."[92]

Carrera returned to the Guatemalan capital on 1 August 1855. A proclamation to the Honduran people two days later accused Cabañas of fomenting and aiding the montañés rebellion in Guatemala, of invading Guatemala at the cost of the lives of many Hondurans, and of attempting to establish an evil and pernicious regime in Honduras. With Cabañas's defeat, Carrera declared, the Hondurans could look forward to progress, peace, and security, and he promised them that his "intervention in your affairs will end the day that you have established a Government that is not hostile to Guatemala."[93]

When Cabañas refused to quit and fielded another army, López once more routed him, this time at Masaguara, Honduras, forcing Cabañas to flee to El Salvador, where he would continue to plot against the conservative regime now established in Honduras. López and Guardiola remained closely in touch with General Cerna in Chiquimula and it is impossible to avoid the conclusion that Guardiola's revolution against Cabañas was Guatemalan inspired.[94] In the struggle that followed among the victors, Guardiola emerged as president in February 1856, closely allied with Rafael Carrera.[95]

In his annual message to the assembly in November 1855 Carrera could announce proudly that his efforts "to restore peace in Central America and the preservation of our own security have resulted as I promised." He admitted the Guatemalan participation in the ouster of Cabañas. Having exhausted all peaceful means to deal with the problems created by the president of Honduras, he told his Congress, "it was necessary finally to employ the Republic's armed forces to terminate a violent situation that could go on no longer. For two years we had put up with the inconveniences and supported increased expenditures purely for defense, without demanding the reparations to which we had a right." A peace had been negotiated through the good offices of the Salvadoran government, he declared, but the president of Honduras refused to accept it. Finally, "no longer able to remain mere spectators to those plots against our nationality," he had sent a section of the Guatemalan army into Honduras to unite with Hondurans who were fighting the oppression. Cabañas fell quickly and "our troops were withdrawn as soon as peace and order were restored."[96]

Carrera had thus by 1855 consolidated his control not only of Guatemala, but of the neighboring Central American states as well. He was the most powerful man on the isthmus, and with Rafael Mora of Costa Rica had begun to impose the stability on the isthmus that had for four decades been so illusive. Yet the Pax Carrera was not yet to be, for a new threat to isthmian peace and security now inflamed both the conservative-liberal and Anglo-American rivalries that would bring all five states into yet another, even bloodier civil war.

CHAPTER ELEVEN

The Conservative Citadel

THE RETURN OF CARRERA in 1849 ushered in a new era in Guatemalan history. The 1840s had been tumultuous, with shifting allegiances and much political intrigue. It was a decade of transition from liberal to conservative domination of the country. While Carrera was the dominant figure, both before and after the Revolution of 1848, the nature of government in Guatemala changed notably with the style of the caudillo. Despite the persistent trouble in the montaña and some foreign adventures in the neighboring states, it was for the most part a period of stability and peace when compared to the 1840s. Carrera no longer played one party against another or instigated mock revolts as a means of suppressing his enemies. He now aligned himself unequivocally with the conservative elite of the capital, forming a party that would rule the country for about twenty years in a strong alliance of the capital's merchant, landholding, and military interests.

It was a party forged by Carrera, dedicated to order and economic growth along traditional lines, with a strong role for the clergy. It also retained a strong role for departmental corregidores and rejected the liberal thrust of bigger government. Indeed, Carrera continued to maintain a small bureaucracy, headed by only a few ministers and an advisory council. A subservient legislature met annually to pass recommended legislation and to hear reports on the government's progress.

Carrera began to erect this new citadel of conservatism immediately upon his return from Chiapas in 1849, more than two years before resuming the presidency. His new political machine began to take shape in Quetzaltenango while he negotiated with President Paredes, who would become a leading commander in his military organization. Upon returning to the capital, he saw to the removal of the principal liberals. José F. Barrundia and the Molinas fled first to El Salvador and then elsewhere, Barrundia eventually representing Honduras in Washington, where he died in 1854. Escobar died impoverished in exile. Manuel Irungaray also fled to San Salvador, where Carrera had him shot in 1863. Lorenzo Montúfar, the youthful deputy who had served as secretary of the assembly and had become an intellectual leader among younger liberals, left for Costa Rica, his vitriolic pen continuing the fight against Carrera until he could return to serve the Liberal Reforma in the 1870s. Two companies of vigilante patrols organized in Guatemala City, ostensibly to fight crime, were part of the new regime that kept order as much by intimidating the opposition as by legitimate political action.[1]

Carrera was still the rough and ready soldier, leading his forces in the field, but he began to take on the image of a more respectable political leader as well. He had learned much of politics and protocol during his tenure as president from 1844 to 1848. Although he still sometimes appeared ridiculous to the diplomatic corps and to members of the Guatemalan elite, such occasions were less frequent. He had refined his inherent ability to manipulate power and people. Probably none of the elite truly liked him, but all feared him, and none could dispute his military talent and courage. Despite his ignorance and fanaticism, or perhaps because of it, he was thoroughly dedicated to his country. He believed that in delivering it to the clergy and aristocratic classes of the capital, he was serving the ordinary people well.

Some shuffling of ministerial posts accompanied the resumption of real power by Carrera. In August 1849 Pedro N. Arriaga became minister of the interior, replacing Raymundo Arroyo, who had served briefly following José M. Urruela's resignation. Urruela had agreed to serve only on an interim basis, claiming multiple responsibilities. Carrera named several new corregidores, all reflecting the conservative drift.[2] In September Arriaga took over Foreign Relations when José Maria Saravía resigned. At about the same time José Milla Vidaurre (1822–82), the conservative protege of Manuel Francisco Pavón, took over direction of the Gaceta de Guatemala from the ailing Alejandro Marure, thereby ending the influence of one of Guatemala's most influential moderate liberals.[3] Milla also became a chief adviser on foreign relations and secretary to the new Advisory Council, composed of cabinet officers and other prominent residents of the capital. The council reelected Juan Matheu as its president on 21 September 1849.[4]

A pro-Carrera publication defended reorganization of the government and restoration of strong authoritarian rule on the grounds of law and order. "The advance of anarchy and disorder, in consequence of the so-called principles of *Liberty* and *Equality*, poorly understood, have brought great disasters in Europe and denied to governments the most intelligent men of the old world," declared *Sucesos del Día*. It asked: "What will be, then, our risk, in this part of the new [world] in which the elements of property, order and civilization are so small with respect to the total population?" and "Who can ignore what is today happening in Yucatán?" It counseled the government to abandon abstract theories and to take each case "in a manner that reason and experience has shown to be best for the people." Such was the policy of General Carrera, the paper declared, when as a result of the Revolution of 1837 he had seized power and restored orderly government. The events since his overthrow had proven the wisdom of his policies, while the liberal ideas had proven themselves to be no more than "shadowy fantasies." It accused those who had pursued such capricious notions of not only being out of touch with reality but of committing "a true crime" against society. What was important now was to restore law and order, "so that good and peaceful men may be secure with their families, in their occupations and with their property, so that agriculture and commerce may prosper, so that there may be public works of progress and improvement, instead of ruin and destruction." This required a "strong and respectable force," which would guarantee "property and justice and guarantee the legitimate rights to all."[5] An editorial in the *Gaceta* suggested that a new political party had formed behind Carrera's leadership to bring unity, order, and peace to the country.[6]

President Paredes confirmed Carrera's return to power on 16 August 1851 when he credited him with saving the nation's independence and achieving the complete pacification of the interior.[7] A ball given in Carrera's honor at the home of the English merchant, Charles Murphy, at the end of the month further confirmed Carrera's acceptance by Guatemalan society and the British mercantile interests.[8]

The new "party" combined Carrera and his military chiefs (notably Cerna, Zavala, Bolaños, Solares, and Paredes) with the leaders of the Guatemalan church, the Guatemala City mercantile community, and the established families headed by the Aycinenas, Piñols, and Pavóns. It was a powerful consolidation of the social and economic power in the country, against which the liberal "upstarts" could muster little defense, especially when the conservatives could count on widespread popular support as well. This elite alliance established one of the most conservative regimes in the Americas.

José Milla editorialized in the *Gaceta* in December 1849, responding to the *Gaceta oficial del Salvador*, which had criticized the conservatives on the fourteenth as aristocratic oppressors. He argued persuasively that Guatemala had to develop institutions that conformed to its own customs. What was right for the United States or Great Britain was probably not right for Russia, he suggested, and the adoption of liberal institutions in Central America had brought disastrous consequences and had retarded development. "The *Gaceta* of El Salvador," he chided, can, whenever it likes, "talk about the glorious system, the order, the liberty, that reigns under elections; it can, if it thinks necessary, draw the happiest picture, not of what is, but of what should be; but who will have been deceived? Will thinking people who see and know the foundation of things, those that attend to business within the framework of reality? Doubtless not."[9]

Members of the elite families occupied most of the seats in the principal institutions of the capital, including Carrera's advisory council, the merchant guild, the bar association, economic society, and the city council, as well as the charitable boards and committees. The city council, for example, was elected by former members of the council, and while there was considerable rotation among the regidores and alcaldes, it nevertheless represented a self-perpetuating representative body of the city's elite. The members of the council were three alcaldes, ten regidores, and two syndics, normally elected in staggered two-year terms, although resignations were fairly frequent as service on the council often required considerable work with little remuneration or recognition. Characteristically, lesser members of the leading families served on the council. About two hundred men served on it during the period 1839–71, about sixty of them as one of the three alcaldes.[10]

The bar association (colegio de abogados) was restored along colonial Hispanic lines by the Constituent Assembly on 4 November 1843.[11] It defended and developed the legal profession and made some progress toward codification of the laws of the country. It was another institution where the conservative elite's views predominated, even though a few liberal lawyers remained active in it. It was reorganized again in 1852, under the direction of the supreme court. José Antonio Larrave, one of Guatemala's most prominent attorneys, played a major role in it as did Luis Batres, another key member of the conservative elite.[12]

If the civilian bureaucracy remained small and the party organization informal, Carrera's army grew substantially and became the principal institution of his regime. From a nucleus of ragged guerrillas who had brought him to power and regular forces who swore allegiance to him after he gained power, Carrera built the strongest military force in Central America. The army was his weapon and the means by which he imposed "peace and order" on the land, and he did not hesitate to use it. The army was never well outfitted during Carrera's years, but it gradually gained armaments from leftover European stocks, much of the ordnance dating from the Napoleonic wars. In 1853 he began construction of a new fort, San Rafael de Matamoros, to guard the northeast entrance to the city.[13] His troops were often barefooted, ragged, and in ill-fitting uniforms, but they were more often than not successful on the battlefield, and they built national pride and restored Guatemalan self-confidence.[14] While the liberals had also maintained a military establishment, both at the state and federal levels, the civilian government of Mariano Gálvez had sought to curtail military power and privilege. His government had begun to limit the fuero militar and had tried to maintain a relatively small peacetime force.[15] The re-emphasis on the military that began with the Carrera revolt and continued throughout the years of his domination would fasten a powerful military tradition on Guatemala, which has continued to grow to the present day.

Carrera incorporated regular officers into his army and some members of the capital's elite exercised positions of leadership there, but his most trusted generals were those who had fought with him in the montaña and were closer to the rural masses than the urban elite. John Lloyd Stephens had noted in 1840 that Carrera had no white officers in his army and wanted none.[16] This led to a certain alienation of the elite toward the military, especially embodied in a continual fear of military atrocities or outrages. After 1849 Carrera kept the military in check more closely than before 1848, and this helped him cement closer relations with the elite. Even in the 1840s Carrera often made a show of disciplining officers who abused the civilian population, although in practice such abuse was common.[17] Yet especially during his presidency of 1844–48, Carrera increased the size of the army and strengthened its fuero, extending its privileges even to officers who were not on active duty and basing Guatemalan practice on the Spanish Real Cédula of 29 March 1770.[18]

By 1847 the Guatemala City garrison consisted of 6,334 officers and men, mostly quartered in the San José de Buenaventura fortress. This represented about a sixth of the total population of the city at that time. Armaments included eighty-nine artillery pieces (with 56,185 cannon balls), 13,248 rifles and carbines, and 2,870 grenades.[19]

Carrera's army provided an opportunity for people of the lower echelons of rural society to rise to positions of importance in Guatemala, Carrera himself being the most conspicuous example. Loyalty, luck, ruthlessness, and individual merit all played a part in such cases, but achievement of a commission in Carrera's army could at least assure one of some status in Guatemalan society. It could often provide the opportunity for increased income, especially through appointment as a corregidor or post commander. The military was the major consumer of government funds throughout the Carrera period.[20]

Notwithstanding the importance of the montañeses to Carrera's officer corps, several Europeans gained high rank and power. Among the first to join the caudillo after his accession to power was Francisco Cáscara, a Sardinian who at an early age entered the French army. He left the French service in 1797, entered the Spanish army in Navarre, and came to Guatemala with Captain General Antonio González Saravía. He played an active role in the wars of the early national period, and at the time of his death in 1851 he was a field marshall, serving as Carrera's minister of war.[21]

Col. William Knoth was another important foreign adviser to Carrera. He served as a personal secretary in the early 1850s and was closely trusted by the caudillo, especially after the death of the hated General Paiz in 1851.[22] Knoth taught Carrera a little French, English, and German, but Carrera mixed them all together. His efforts at conversing with foreigners with his few phrases became a subject for ridicule.[23] Knoth later ran into difficulty when he accused Santi Antoni, the French commander of a Guatemalan naval vessel, of treason and ordered him summarily shot. Knoth received a five-year sentence in the San José prison.[24] Later, Carrera brought a French baron, Col. Paul Brun, to develop the Guatemalan artillery. Brun supervised reestablishment of the gunpowder factory in Guatemala late in 1860.[25]

While civilian members of the elite played a significant role in the government in the capital, military bosses, or corregidores, dominated the rural departments. These territorial divisions followed lines established in the colonial period for the most part. Under the federation, the State of Guatemala had been divided into seven departments.[26] A major reorganization occurred in 1836 in an effort to establish a system of judicial districts under the Livingston Codes, but upon the collapse of the Gálvez government and the secession of Los Altos in 1839, the government decreed a new territorial organization on 5 September of that year.[27] It established the departments of Guatemala, Escuintla, Sacatepéquez, Mita, Chiquimula, Chimaltenango, and the Verapaz, and, in addition, the districts of Izabal and the Petén.[28] The new Department of Mita reflected Carrera's rise to importance, and that region received special consideration throughout his administration.

The corregidores who presided over these departments had broad authority and essentially served as local dictators of their respective jurisdictions. Together with the clergy and local large landholders, they held most of the authority outside of the capital. They collected taxes and were responsible for the development of public works, as well as with maintaining law and order. They often issued detailed regulations for the commerce and daily life of the towns of their jurisdiction. Los Altos, of course, returned to the jurisdiction of Guatemala in 1840 and again in 1849. Those departments (Quetzaltenango, Sololá, Huehuetenango, Suchitepéquez, Totonicapán, and San Marcos) were treated virtually as conquered territories and were subject to more repressive government than the rest of the country. The large Indian population of that region was largely left alone, however, and the repression was principally felt by the Ladino population. This helps to explain the particular resentment of that region toward the Carrera regime and its strong support of the Revolution of 1871. The departments of Santa Rosa and Jutiapa, in the East, were formed from the Department of Mita in the 1850s in moves to increase the government's authority in those regions where rebellion had become frequent. The Carrera government also proposed organization of the Department of El Quiché between Totonicapán and the Verapaz, but this was not finally done until 1872.[29] The reports of the corregidores to the government in Guatemala City provide a vast store of information about life in the provinces during the mid nineteenth century.[30]

Among the strongest of these departmental bosses was the long-term corregidor of Chiquimula, Vicente Cerna. Cerna effectively kept order in a sometimes unruly district and played an active part in major struggles against Honduras, El Salvador, and the montaña rebels. His iron rule, loyalty to Carrera, promotion of new economic ventures, and his military successes made him among the most important of Carrera's lieutenants after 1848. Cerna and the other corregidores brooked no opposition, and they summarily gave out lengthy jail terms for sedition.[31]

On the other hand, there were rare occasions when the central government intervened to reprimand corregidores for excessive repression or abuse of their authority. Such was the case when the corregidor of Izabal, Sgt. Maj. Manuel Cano Madrazo, issued a set of draconian moral and police ordinances on 15 November 1858. A storm of criticism, mostly from merchants and foreign travelers who passed through the port, quickly reached the government in Guatemala City, which called for an explanation from Cano and ordered him to modify the regulations.[32] In general, however, the government supported the repressive policies of the corregidores. An order from the gobernación minister to the Guatemala City prisons of San José and Matamoros in 1859, for example, warned the officials there against any relaxation in enforcement of sentences, and threatened severe reprimands against any failures to apply the full sentences.[33]

Notwithstanding the importance of Carrera's army as the base of power for the dictator, it was the consolidation of the conservative elite of the capital that gave the regime its character and was important in establishing policies that made Guatemala the "citadel of conservatism." Like the regime of José Antonio Páez in Venezuela, this elite, supported by foreigners, kept the masses at bay through their alliance with the popular caudillo. While Carrera always reserved the right to make final decisions, and frequently did so, he usually allowed a small clique of well-educated and aristocratic advisers to make and execute policy.[34] The consolidation of this conservative elite in Guatemala and its control of the capital's society, economy, and political structure is what so clearly distinguishes the period 1850–71 from the 1840s.

John Lloyd Stephens had described the elite in 1840. He said they lived in aristocratic old mansions and that by their monopoly over imports during the colonial period they had acquired "immense wealth and rank as 'merchant princes.'" Led by the house of Aycinena, they had expected to inherit political power upon independence, but had been displaced by the liberals until 1839. Then, according to Stephens, "accidentally they were again in power, and at the time of my visit ruled in social as well as political life." Although Stephens could not agree with their conservative political views, he admired their life style and acknowledged that they were "the only people who constituted society."[35]

Frederick Crowe, the first Baptist missionary in the country during this decade, gave a much less complimentary account of the Guatemalan elite, suggesting that many were mentally incompetent:

> In the city of Guatemala, the unusually large number of such cases is palpable to the least observant. The wealthy are the most subject to these calamities. Scarcely a year passes but some of the most notable residents, merchants and others, are visited with temporary and often with confirmed derangement. As there are no asylums or madhouses they are kept at home, and together with idiots are constantly encountered. There is scarcely a family of note, but have the humiliating exhibition and the painful burden of one or more such objects in their own house.[36]

The high degree of inbreeding among the leading families might very well have contributed to such a phenomenon as Crowe described. A French traveler, visiting Guatemala at the height of the conservative period, described the elite as "circumspect and parsimonious" merchants dedicated to little else but the accumulation of wealth, little interested in progress and suspicious of anything that would disturb the status quo.[37]

The conservative consolidation took shape quickly after Carrera's return in 1849. From then on members of the conservative families occupied the principal ministerial posts and seats on the advisory council. That trend became obvious in September of 1849 when Paredes added Luis Batres, José Maria de Urruela, José Nájera, Pedro Aycinena, Pedro Lara Pavón, and José Coloma to the council, thereby stacking it with solid conservative voices prior to the convening of the new legislature.[38]

Soon after, José Milla defended the "aristocracy" in the *Gaceta de Guatemala*. "There are," he wrote, "profoundly marked inequities in the structure of societies. This is an undeniable, universal fact that offends the eyes of the intelligentsia, but which speaks louder than the theories of some self-styled philosophers." Moreover, he continued, these *"legitimate aristocracies, the only ones we recognize because we consider them basic to the nature of society, are indispensable to the maintenance of society."* He argued that aristocracies existed under all forms of government. He was not talking about "aristocracies of blood," but rather that in every society there were those who rose to the top and were destined to dominate. Such classes were inevitable, and in Central America, as elsewhere, they enjoyed privilege, wealth, talent, and social position, but he insisted they were the product of "virtue, labor and genius." If overthrown, he claimed, they would simply be replaced by a "new aristocracy."[39]

Manuel Francisco Pavón (1798–1855) and José Milla loomed large in the conservative consolidation. Their management of the official *Gaceta de Guatemala* was one aspect of this. Another was the organization of the ministries, beginning with the Foreign Ministry, which Milla and Pavón reorganized in 1850 and 1851, modernizing it and establishing a formal passport office.[40] Other efficiencies followed, including regularizing office procedures and requiring two copies of everything printed to be deposited in the archives.[41] Pavón had spent his exile from 1830 to 1837 in New York, Paris, and Havana, during which he gained considerable knowledge and experience. He had edited the government's *El Tiempo* from its founding in March of 1839 and the *Gaceta Oficial* that succeeded it in 1841. He had also served in a number of diplomatic positions, briefly as foreign minister in 1844, and subsequently as minister of finance and war, and he was among the most important of Carrera's advisers. Pavón died in April 1855 following a long illness, after which Milla became even more important as the principal propagandist and editor for the regime.[42] Pavón's mother was an Aycinena and his brother, Juan (1805–59), had a distinguished military career and in the 1850s served on the Guatemalan City Council.[43] Milla developed a close relationship both with traditional members of the elite and with the caudillo. His home in the capital, in fact, was a house owned by General Carrera.[44]

The Aycinena clan remained of primary importance. Mariano Aycinena, governor of Guatemala during the civil war of 1826–29, was an important adviser to the government until his death in 1855.[45] Pedro Aycinena played an even more important part in the government, especially in foreign relations, while the third marquis of Aycinena, Dr. Juan José Aycinena Piñol (1792–1865), rector of the University of San Carlos and a leading cleric, was the acknowledged intellectual savant of the conservative regime. Another member of the clan, Xavier Aycinena Micheo (1801–58), served with distinction in the merchant guild and the municipal government of Guatemala City, and also at various times as a military officer.[46] Yet another kinsman, José Ignacio Aycinena Piñol (1804–73), served as corregidor of Guatemala during the later years of the regime.

Luis Batres Juarros (1802–62), from one of Guatemala's oldest and wealthiest families and also closely related to the Aycinenas, was another major adviser and government official. Serving in both the executive and legislative branches, he was the author of much of the conservative legislation of the period.[47]

Another key member of the conservative administration, Pedro N. Arriaga (1793–1860), a Honduran by birth, had been educated at the University of San Carlos in the late colonial period. He had been involved in the turbulent politics of Honduras during the early federation period, but came to Guatemala and began to practice law there in 1830. Mariano Rivera Paz appointed him to his first ministerial position in 1838. Thereafter, he frequently served in ministerial and judicial posts under Carrera. He served briefly as minister of foreign relations but became most important as the dean of the Supreme Court from 1851 until his death in 1860.[48]

Still another major figure in the Carrera government was José Nájera (1790–1862), who served for several years as minister of finance and war. A native of the capital, Nájera had begun public service in the administration of Captain General Bustamante. He was serving as alcalde mayor of Sonsonate when independence came, and he represented that district in the

Constituent Assembly of 1823. Thereafter he served in many key positions in the capital, including first alcalde and regidor on the city council, deputy in several legislative constituent assemblies, and consul of the Consulado. After 1844 he served as councilor of state. Nájera had served briefly as foreign minister during the 1840s, but his most important role was as minister of finance and war throughout the following decade. He came from a prominent commercial and agricultural family, and he was the owner of the Hacienda el Sitio.[49]

Liberals were purged, mostly forced into exile, although some were allowed to represent Guatemala in foreign legations. A notable example was Pedro Molina's third son, Felipe Molina Bedoya (1812–55), who represented the conservative governments of both Guatemala and Costa Rica in the United States from 1851 to 1855. Molina, educated in the United States, was important in building the close relationship between the Guatemalan liberals and the United States.[50]

Under the conservatives, the church regained the powerful position that it had enjoyed in colonial times. It once more became a major landholder of both rural and urban properties and was closely connected by blood and interests to the conservative elite of the capital. Moreover, in this area more than in any other, Guatemalan influence extended over the rest of Central America as well, for Guatemalan clerics received most of the appointments to hierarchical positions in the other states as the Archdiocese of Guatemala retained jurisdiction over the entire region. Moreover, the conservatives readmitted most of the religious orders that had been terminated in Guatemala by the liberals, and these orders once more played important roles in education, agricultural production, missionary activity, and politics. Guatemala became a haven for clerics expelled by anticlerical liberal governments. The Mexican Reforma brought a wave of anticlericalism to Chiapas and religious emigres poured into Guatemala, especially after Benito Juárez's anticlerical decree of 12 July 1859. In October of that year the bishop of Chiapas, Carlos María Colina y Rubio arrived in Huehuetenango and was escorted to the Guatemalan capital in grand style.[51]

The return of the Jesuits in 1851 was especially important for the country. The liberals had blocked their return in the mid-1840s, but now the government cooperated closely with the Jesuits and other religious orders to establish schools and missions. On 31 May 1851, five Jesuits finally entered the country at Izabal, their invitation by the Guatemalan archbishop being tendered at the proposal of Carrera, the "Peacemaker of the Republic." Father Superior Joaquín Freire and four more Jesuits came from Jamaica to establish a monastery. Their arrival in the Guatemalan capital was cause for a major celebration and Carrera personally welcomed them in the national palace.[52]

In 1864 the Order of St. Vincent de Paul established a seminary in the capital. Previously, the University of San Carlos had been the principal training place for the Guatemalan clergy, and the archbishop had been complaining for years that it was not providing adequate training for enough priests.[53]

Carrera's friendly attitude toward the religious orders was part of a generally proclerical policy that the Vatican rewarded with a concordat in 1852. The clergy had long recognized Carrera as a staunch ally, although some of his political intrigues of the 1840s had pitted the clerical hierarchy against him at times. Soon after his ouster from power in 1848, Pope Pius IX formally applauded his defense of the church and clergy.[54] Upon his return to power he worked diligently for the 1852 concordat, which served as the basis of church-state relations in Guatemala until 1871. It guaranteed the church the position it had enjoyed before national independence as it required that all education, public and private, conform to the doctrines of the church, provided for ecclesiastical censorship of all publications relating to religion and public morals, and restored government collection of the tithe plus an annual payment of $4,000 by the government for the support of the cathedral as well as additional subsidies for parish churches and missionary activities. As under the *real patronato* of colonial times, the president had the right to nominate bishops and other ecclesiastical hierarchy.[55] The pope rewarded Carrera's support by naming him a Great Cross Knight of the Order of St. Gregory, a distinction he wore proudly for the remainder of his days.[56]

The head of the Guatemalan church was Francisco de Paula García Peláez (1785–1867), who had been named to succeed the exiled Archbishop Ramón Casáus in 1842 after it was clear that Casáus would not return to Guatemala. García Peláez's appointment had been a setback for the aristocracy and particularly for Juan José Aycinena, who had expected to be named. García Peláez had been born in San Juan Sacatepéquez of a Ladino family of modest means, which had nevertheless been able to assure him a solid education. Regarded as somewhat liberal in the late colonial period, he had risen in the clergy through his shrewd intellectual ability, industry, and devotion to duty. His administration as archbishop spanned the entire period of Carrera's dictatorship and ended only with his death in January of 1867. García Peláez studied civil and canon law at the University of San Carlos and received a doctorate in theology in 1819. He was a noted ecclesiastical lawyer and in 1814 had offered the first course in "political economy" at the university. In the years following he occupied a broad range of ecclesiastical assignments. Dr. Jorge Viteri y Ungo was especially influential in arranging his appointment as archbishop as part of a compromise to get papal approval of a separate diocese of El Salvador, to which Viteri had been named bishop. As a further part of this compromise, Salvadoran leaders insisted that Viteri return directly to El Salvador from Rome and that García Peláez be consecrated first in San Salvador, which was done on 11 February 1844. Formally installed as archbishop in 1846, following the death of Casáus, he was formally consecrated in Guatemala in 1851 by the priest who would succeed him as archbishop, Bernardo Piñol Aycinena.[57] In 1861 Pope Pius IX honored the Guatemalan prelate by naming him domestic prelate and attending bishop to the pontifical throne, essentially a step below cardinal.[58]

In 1859 Carrera and the Guatemalan church sought to establish two new dioceses and honor several prominent clergymen with appointments as bishops. Carrera requested on 3 January of that year that the dean of the cathedral, Dr. José María Barrutia Croquer, and the provincial of the Franciscan Order, Friar Juan de Jesús Zepeda, be named auxiliary bishops "to assist the Archbishop with the growing activities of the church in this vast and populous diocese," and that "the distinguished services of the Marquis of Aycinena be rewarded with his appointment as a bishop."[59] The pope refused to erect new dioceses in Guatemala but acceded to the request by naming the three clerics as bishops *in partibus infidelium.*[60]

The influence of the Guatemalan clergy was especially notable in Nicaragua during the conservative years. Viteri, although Salvadoran by birth, was educated in Guatemala and had become closely associated with the conservative elite. After playing a major role in Salvadoran politics during his tenure as bishop of El Salvador, he was transferred to Nicaragua at the end of 1849. Liberals in El Salvador had complained about his meddling in politics since his arrival in that state. Viteri took formal possession of the diocese of Nicaragua in June of 1850, and he found a generally more friendly political climate in Granada than in San Salvador.[61]

Another leading member of the Guatemalan elite, Bernardo Piñol Aycinena (1806–81), succeeded Viteri as bishop of Nicaragua in 1855. Piñol was actively involved in Guatemalan ecclesiastical and political life, however, and was extraordinarily slow to take up his new position. For five more years he remained in Guatemala, resisting all pressures to give up his Guatemalan political appointments. Finally, in February 1860 he resigned his seat in the National Assembly and acknowledged that it was incompatible with his position as bishop of Nicaragua. He finally arrived in the Nicaraguan capital on 9 March 1861.[62] He returned to Guatemala on several occasions thereafter, continuing to be influential in both countries, and in 1868 he succeeded García Peláez as archbishop of Guatemala.[63]

Church-state relations were close, generally cordial, and each depended on the other for important functions. In a sermon at the Cathedral of Guatemala on Central American independence day (15 September) 1851, Dr. Basilio Zeceña reflected the strongly conservative political values of the clergy when he attacked the liberal revolutions. He emphasized the importance of religion in political affairs. When Christian principles dominate governments, he said, the people benefit and love their governors with happiness and order. Governments that do not follow Christian principles, on the other hand, he said, were weak and instable. This simple rule explained Central American history since independence, he declared, as "ideas of freedom and new doctrines" caused many problems. For example, he continued,

> they permitted immoral books, full of anarchical maxims, to circulate freely, and in the hands of the ignorant and hot-blooded, but uneducated, youths, this caused more harm to the society than a sharpened dagger in the hand of the most insolent and daring assassin. They zealously propagated but poorly understood the ideas of liberty and equality, and carried them to the hut of the innocent shepherd, awakening in this way the powerful force that lay dormant in the arms of the peasants.[64]

The clergy actively regulated the moral life of the country and gave Guatemala the reputation for being a near theocracy. Soon after Carrera returned to power, for example, the archbishop objected to certain chinaware that was being imported with sacred paintings on them. The archbishop regarded this as disrespectful of religion and the government promptly ordered importation of such dishes stopped immediately.[65] All publications required the approval of the church under the concordat with Rome, and the archbishop exercised this right to prohibit the publication of anything he regarded as contrary to the proper morals and religion of the people. José Milla presented the government point of view in an 1855 editorial. After calling on the public to cooperate with Lenten services and to abstain from excesses, he closed with a defense "of the good religious and moral principles as the basis for order and, above all, as the indispensable conditions for the private and public welfare and prosperity."[66] In an independence day homily in 1856, the archbishop praised Carrera's success in checking liberal efforts to break the traditional ties between church and state in Guatemala and called for even closer relations. He emphasized the need of the government to recognize religious principles and guidance in developing the welfare of the state and society.[67] A decree of the corregidor of Guatemala, José Ignacio de Aycinena, regarding Holy Week observance in 1860 further reflects the close relation between church and state. He decreed that "anyone showing disrespect toward religious acts in churches or processions will be arrested and punished." Other provisions of the decree obligated procession directors to "keep to their schedules according to their permits," prohibited those seeking alms from covering their faces, ordered businesses closed, prohibited all traffic in and out of the city (except for foodstuffs) on Holy Thursday and Friday, and ordered all residents to keep their houses and streets neat and clean in accordance with "the solemnity of the occasion."[68] The *fuero eclesiástico,* or clerical corporation, represented one of the most powerful forces within the country and it guarded its prerogatives jealously.[69]

The church's influence extended not only into government, but also into nearly every facet of Guatemalan life. The corporate institutions of the country—the merchant guild, bar association, medical association, the artisan guilds, and other associations of professionals and craftsmen all had some sort of arrangement with the church for the celebration of patron saints, support of charitable organizations, maintenance of a cofradía, or special masses, so that the church's influence was never far away.[70]

It was a matter of considerable rejoicing when prominent foreigners publicly converted to Catholicism in Guatemala. Such had been the case with the U.S. minister, Beverly L. Clarke (1809–60), a Kentucky Democratic lawyer who James Buchanan had named to represent the United States in Guatemala and Honduras in 1858. He converted to Catholicism after his arrival, confirmed by Bishop Bernardo Piñol in Guatemala City on 14 December 1859, with Pedro Aycinena as his godfather. He was, however, already ill at that time, and the conversion did not reverse his malaise, for he died the following 17 March. Bishop Aycinena presided over his funeral at the San Francisco Church, attended by a large number of public officials and diplomats. Before they returned to their native land, Aycinena also baptized Clarke's widow and two children.[71] A year later, the conversion of a British resident, James Phillips, received great publicity. His baptism and renunciation of "the errors of the Protestant sect" took place in a two-hour ceremony in the cathedral, presided over by Bishop Piñol, who was once more back from Nicaragua.[72]

The seat of what amounted to a small kingdom by the 1850s hardly appeared as anything more than a provincial commercial center, although a few new public establishments had begun to appear to cater to the growing commerce and affluence in the city. One of the most popular was Señor Rivera's Las Variedades, which offered games of chance, musical entertainment, and refreshments. The president himself could often be found there. In November 1849 it had been the first establishment in the city to install gas lighting, hailed as a mark of advancement and progress in the country. Another establishment, Las Bolas coffee shop and confectionery store, had become a notable meeting place. Following the Revolution of 1848 General Carrera's house had been confiscated and sold, and in early 1849 it opened as the Posada de la Sociedad, providing comfortable lodgings and meals for visitors and noted for its ice creams and sweets. Later in the year, another coffee and gaming house, the Café del Comercio, opened to the public. By 1857 English ale was readily available in the city along with other imported beverages. Yet aside from the cantinas and brothels that could be found in any Spanish American capital, public entertainment was limited primarily to religious and community festivals. Bullfighting still attracted crowds, although by the 1850s interest in this spectacle had declined from colonial times.[73]

Public improvements early in the decade were headed by the establishment of a new slaughterhouse designed by the Belgian engineer, Agustín Van de Gehuchte, in 1852, and the beginnings of a national theater, which would not be completed for another decade.[74] But transportation was vastly improved as the Consulado built and maintained better roads. One Jacinto Flores began carriage service from the capital to Amatitlán in December 1849. His coach left every morning at 6:00 A.M. from the Café del Comercio. Flores also ran a horse-drawn omnibus service to Mixco on the outskirts of the capital. In 1856 he extended service to Escuintla and fares had dropped considerably, from twelve to seven reales for a Guatemala-Amatitlán passage. Also in 1856, three omnibuses began to operate within the city, charging a half real per passenger. Two stage coach companies (Tible and Lekeu) were operating from Guatemala City by 1863, their competition helping to keep fares low.[75]

The commerce of the city began to grow notably with the stability established after 1850, many shops opened by immigrants catering to the vanity of the affluent class: a fancy barber shop and perfumery by a Frenchman named Charles in 1851, for example, and a portrait shop by an Irishman named Fitzgibbon in 1852. Fitzgibbon also offered for sale attractive photographs of Guatemala's principal buildings.[76] By the 1860s the advertising pages in the *Gaceta de Guatemala* reflected the increased business activity, often running three pages or more. A decade earlier advertising had generally occupied less than a single page.

Even as late as the 1860s, however, the city was still more quaint than modern. Substantial expansion of the water system occurred in 1860–61, long overdue, with a great deal of new pipe laid.[77] Ramón Salazar, one of the leading liberal historians, recalled in 1896 that the city as he remembered it in 1861 was "even more sad than today. Few of the streets were paved and sidewalks were very rare." Houses of more than one story did not exist, except for that of Juan Matheu (which in 1896 was being used as the presidential mansion), the Piñol houses (in 1896 occupied by the Banco Colombiano), and those of Batres and Romá, which later became the Gran Hotel.[78] In 1864 the *Gaceta de Guatemala* announced that Henry Andresen's Hotel Unión was moving to the Plaza de la Victoria and would occupy the building formerly housing the British legation. The Unión's advertisement boasted that Spanish, English, French, Dutch, Flemish, German, and Danish were spoken there. Another hotel, next to Tible's stage coach terminal, opened at about the same time and advertised that French, English, and German were spoken there.[79]

Whatever modest growth Guatemala City enjoyed, change in the countryside was much less noticeable. Village markets remained the principal meeting places for the peasants and constituted a significant commercial activity. Agro-exports grew in the central part of the country, around Amatitlán, Antigua, and Nueva Guatemala. In the more remote parts of the country, especially in the western highlands, subsistence agriculture and food for domestic consumption remained the principal occupation of the inhabitants.

The conservative coalition of merchants, planters, and priests, with Carrera's army and rural popular support, consolidated its strength in the early 1850s. It supported one of the most reactionary governments in the hemisphere but also achieved a restoration of order and stability in a country that had for a half century been victimized by economic and political disruption. Although repressive, it could not stifle completely the liberal opposition, especially in neighboring countries. So Guatemala to some degree would continue to live in a state of siege for more than two decades following the 1848 revolution. For Rafael Carrera, this was a period of maturity and grandeur. While his liberal enemies would revile his near-monarchical rule, his regime would in the long run lay the foundations for elite domination of the country for a century or more to come. For it was under Carrera's rule that the creole elite was finally able to claim its inheritance from Spanish colonialism and consolidate a powerful hold on Guatemala's economic and political future.

CHAPTER TWELVE

Presidente Vitalicio

CARRERA'S GREAT VICTORY at San José la Arada gave the Guatemalan conservatives the security and peace to complete their consolidation of power.[1] The conservatives could now finally hope to enact a constitution to their liking. Philosophical discussion in the press reflected a mandate for a conservative charter that would discard the liberal legacy of 1824 once and for all. An editorial in the *Gaceta* early in 1850 had already articulated the conservative attitude. It called the new Guatemalan government "progressive" in the sense of favoring orderly development, but it blasted the liberal approaches to government, arguing that the welfare of the citizens was the real measure of progress and that peace was essential for that. "Within this framework, we are and we shall be progressives," declared the *Gaceta*. It continued:

> It is true that we have called our popular elections a farce, and if to be progressive we must think or say the contrary, then we are not. We have condemned the application of advanced political doctrines and systems, and if to be progressives we should think otherwise, then we don't deserve that name. We have defended respect for the beliefs and traditions of the people, and if to be progressive it is necessary to trample on them, then it is certain that we renounce that denomination. We have searched for guarantees in strong governments, have little or no faith in vain formulas and in institutions as quickly forgotten as written, and if to be progressive we must think to the contrary, undoubtedly we must refuse such a classification.

264

"On the other hand," the editor persisted, "we desire more than ever order and a well conceived political freedom and equality." This, however, required certain physical and intellectual prerequisites. In the *Gaceta*'s view:

> A moral and religious education and a well-founded enlightenment are in our eyes the best thing we can do for a people such as ours. To inculcate respect for constituted authority, the necessity of working to live, and the obligation of respecting the opinions of others are the surest means, although slow, of civilizing the ignorant masses. To preach to them constantly of liberty, equality, sovereignty, etc., is to lead them to insurrection and to give them arms that they will turn against us, making practical and positive the doctrines that we have carelessly taught them.[2]

Later, Milla lamented the decline in respect for authority that had occurred in Guatemala since independence, as he again emphasized the need for authority if a society were to prosper.[3] He warned against the socialist doctrines that were infecting Europe, causing misery and horror. The *Gaceta* declared its opposition to the doctrines of Pierre Proudhon, Louis Blanc, and Pierre Leroux, or "any other apostles of communism." It went on to approve conservative governments in Europe and America, praising the policies of Donoso Cortés, Narváez, Martínez de la Rosa, Mon, and Pidal in Spain; Montalembert and Thiers in France; Peel and Aberdeen in Great Britain; and Clay and Webster in the United States—"all of whom are in the highest positions and are distinguished and characterized by their conservative opinions and doctrines." After many years of the ill-fated maxims of unlimited freedom being allowed to run free, Milla added, there is now a "general effort to reconstruct solidly the power of authority, to return to the laws whose force and prestige have been reduced to a mockery, [and] to require that teaching be based on the eternal truths of religion."[4]

After the election of the Democrat Franklin Pierce in the U.S. election of 1852, the *Gaceta* lashed out at North American "democracy," charging that it had prevented the country's "great men"—Clay, Webster, Calhoun, or Buchanan—from becoming president. Clearly more favorable toward the conservative Whigs and states' rights advocates, it questioned whether such a "group of states" could truly be called a "nation."[5] The liberal *Gaceta de San Salvador* attacked this editorial, chiding that Guatemala's rulers had nothing in common with those men who professed order in other countries. The *Gaceta de Guatemala* replied that the ideas it had defended were the same as those that conservatives of many countries professed and defended, and it pointed out that it had frequently reprinted conservative articles from the leading newspapers of America and Europe, as well as the speeches of Donoso Cortés, Montalembert, and other conservatives.[6]

But the *Gaceta* appeared to be less knowledgeable about conservatives in other Latin American states. For example, in reporting the overthrow of the Rosas dictatorship in Buenos Aires, the *Gaceta* first reported that the brutal Rosas had proscribed and suppressed the "conservative party of Buenos Aires,"[7] but two weeks later an editorial sought to redress that report, pointing out Rosas's achievements in defending the Argentine against the French and in suppressing the anarchy there. In the same issue, the *Gaceta* reprinted a eulogistic discourse by Dr. D. Baldomero García from the *Gaceta Mercantil de Buenos Aires* praising Rosas and condemning the "unitario savages."[8]

In November 1850 the *Gaceta* confronted the constitutional issue directly. It acknowledged that some people favored the restoration of the Constitution of 1824 as a basis for reunification of Central America, but protested that its system of elections, "improperly called popular," precluded that. The 1824 electoral system, the *Gaceta* insisted, was not only dishonest, but it was also "detested by the masses and the respectable classes of the society," for the elections exploited illiterate Indians who knew nothing about what they were voting for. Governments thus elected, it argued, could not be as strong as was needed. The editorial also viewed the U.S. model as inappropriate, for Central America did not have the institutions of government with which the United States was born. The editor, presumably Milla, pointed to the strength of religion in the United States, where chaplains said prayers before legislative sessions and where the clergy was not persecuted, where the Jesuits had never been expelled, where ecclesiastical property was not confiscated, and where the property rights of the wealthy were protected. Moreover, he pointed out that U.S. leaders came mostly from the elite. He accused the liberals of tyranny and demagoguery and of substituting passion for good sense. He emphasized the need for a practical government that fit the circumstances of the country, one that would protect property, wisdom, religion, and the customs of the country, and promote improvements of every kind. He rejected the absolute division of powers, which the liberals made one of the principal articles of their popular creed. "We do not proclaim the sovereignty of the people," he concluded, "because this principle, in our judgment, is an absurdity of which the end result is reduced to the sovereignty of armed force; we cannot proclaim equality and liberty, because although we are not disinterested in these benefits, sorry experience has taught us that its poor understanding and worse application suggest that we can expect nothing more than anarchy and disorder." [9]

This conservative philosophy that Milla eloquently espoused favored traditional, Hispanic values. Symbolically, on 14 March 1851, the government restored the Spanish red and yellow to the Guatemalan national flag, placing it alongside the blue and white established after independence. Although there was no mention of Spain in the decree, it declared the new flag to be in accord with "public feeling in keeping those colors established at the declaration of independence [blue and white], while at the same time those adopted before that event." [10]

Shortly after the battle of Arada, the government announced that the time had come to resume orderly legislative government, suspended since 25 April 1849. A report directed to the president from his principal ministers painted a rosy picture of the political situation in the country and called for the convening of an assembly to fix the term of office for the president and to devise a procedure for his nomination. [11] A week later Paredes called for a Constituent Assembly to convene the following June. [12] Appropriate arrangements could not be completed that soon, but the assembly met on 16 August and quickly began writing a new constitution. Before the assembly convened, however, Paredes named the Advisory Council, which became highly important in directing the government along conservative lines and working with the new assembly.

This council was headed by Juan Matheu (?–1875), a Spaniard of English descent who had come to Guatemala soon after independence and had become a prominent merchant. Perhaps he had initially prospered by smuggling, but by 1829 he was well established. An act of the federal Congress that year, while it was still under conservative control in Guatemala City, granted him citizenship. Although of conservative persuasion, he remained in Guatemala City during the Gálvez years and was active as a member of the city council and as head of the commission to build a national theater, an endeavor that occupied Matheu until its completion in the late 1850s. He served in other civic posts as well. He was responsible for the installation of street lighting in the capital beginning in 1841 and served briefly in various ministerial positions during the 1840s. He was a major figure in the Consulado, where he served as consul (1847–49) and prior (1856–58 and 1867–68). [13]

The assembly, elected in a way that assured conservative control, included forty-five departmental representatives (see Table 7), plus ten more representing the five "corporations"—two each from the ecclesias-

TABLE 7

Departmental Representation in
National Assembly, 1851

Guatemala	8
Sacatepéquez	5
Chiquimula	6
Quetzaltenango	4
Suchitepéquez	2
Verapaz	4
Amatitlán	2
Totonicapán	2
Sololá	2
San Marcos	1
Huehuetenango	2
Chimaltenango	2
Escuintla	2
Santa Rosa	1
El Petén	1
Gualán, Izabal, and Santo Tomás	1

Source: Gaceta de Guatemala, 31 Oct. 1851.

tical council, the Supreme Court, the Consulado, the university, and the sociedad económica.[14]

This assembly moved expeditiously and promulgated a new constitution in October. The Constitution of 1851 was a straightforward document that provided for an authoritarian government to be headed, as everyone knew, by the caudillo Carrera. It provided for the continued representation of the "corporations" in the legislature. Suffrage was limited to citizens who had a profession, office, or significant property, and who could read and write. It further limited suffrage to heads of household over twenty-five years of age, or twenty-one if married. In addition to a House of Representatives, it provided for a Council of State (a successor to the Advisory Council), consisting of the ministers and eight additional members chosen by the House of Representatives. But the president might appoint as many additional members as he chose, thus giving him control of what amounted to an upper house. Heads of the major institutions—the archbishop and other bishops, regent of the Supreme Court, president of the ecclesiastical council, prior of the Consulado, rector of the University of San Carlos, president of the Economic Society, and the commanding general of the armed forces—also served as ex officio advisers to the Council of State.[15]

Three days after the assembly had promulgated the new constitution, it reconvened to elect the new president. To no one's surprise it elected Carrera unanimously; even the few liberals remaining in the body joined in the endorsement of the return of the caudillo to the presidency. Carrera's four-year term was officially to begin on 1 January 1852, but such was his popularity and charisma that he was installed ahead of schedule, on 6 November 1851, following a gala public celebration of his birthday on 24 October.[16]

A great show of unity and cordiality accompanied the first weeks of the new administration. Carrera rearranged his cabinet and issued a manifesto promising justice, liberty, security, and peace.[17] The institutions of the capital responded with oaths of loyalty and allegiance to the new constitution. Frederick Chatfield gave a banquet honoring the new president a week following his inauguration.[18]

Consistent with this spirit of conciliation and unity, Carrera asked the assembly to proclaim a general pardon for all prisoners awaiting trial or sentence, excepting only those accused of adultery, rape, arson, assault, homicide, sacrilege, or other crimes of violence. The assembly complied immediately. In the meantime, Carrera left the capital to join other members of the elite in the spas of Amatitlán and Escuintla, leaving the Council of State to govern.[19] In fact, Carrera traveled frequently, keeping closely in touch with the people and problems of the country, a technique that subsequent Guatemalan caudillos have usually imitated.

Carrera now thrived both in terms of his political power and his personal estate. Although his holdings would be unimpressive when compared to those amassed by the liberal dictators who followed, he nevertheless became a landowner of importance, with country estates in several places. Among the most important was one acquired from Luis Batres near the capital. Known as Lo de Batres, Carrera frequently retreated here with his family and friends, often entertaining lavishly at this location. He also acquired property within the city and in numerous locations around the country, not only in his native Mita, but also near Escuintla, and in Los Altos.[20]

Two of his early wills reflect the growth of his estate during the years immediately after his return to power. The first, executed on 15 January 1849 in Comitán during his Mexican exile, listed two houses in Guatemala City, paid for with money from his wife's inheritance, and two haciendas without liens, Buena Vista, with ten square leagues of property (more than sixty square miles) and Las Animas, with grazing livestock and seventy service horses. In addition, he declared cash assets of nearly $20,000 invested in Tabasco, Campeche, and Havana. By 1853, Carrera still had the two houses in the capital, but had added several more fincas to those at Las Animas and Buena Vista, located in Aguativia, Jalpatagua, and Suchitepéquez, all with large herds of cattle, horses, and mules.[21] His property continued to increase,[22] and in the settlement of his estate after his death, thirteen properties, headed by Lo de Batres and including agricultural, livestock, and mining properties, were offered for sale at a total value of nearly $130,000.[23]

Individual and corporate interests in the regime also prospered. The merchants of the Consulado enjoyed a monopoly on the overseas trade and received favorable treatment in their own judicial court. They were a major source of revenue for the government, often in forced loans, but the government paid high interest and the solvency of the Carrera administration meant that these loans paid good returns. The clergy had regained its former status, and perhaps was even more powerful politically, although less economically, than in the colonial period. The military too enjoyed the restoration of its fuero, and the officer corps, along with government employees, were given a pension and life insurance program beginning in 1858. The plan covered captains and above, as well as government officials. The liberals had opposed the plan as paternalistic. Miguel García Granados led the fight against it in the legislature, but after spirited debate the plan carried 24 to 16. It called for a 2 percent monthly contribution from employees, with benefits vesting after ten years of service or upon death to beneficiaries. This was essentially a return to the colonial *montepío* and is a further example of the restoration of Hispanic traditions and institutions.[24] The *Gaceta* referred to it as one of the "useful institutions destroyed by the revolutionary wave." Although not very progressive by modern standards, it is an example of conservative paternalism in contrast to the liberals, who regarded such programs as "socialistic" and emphasized laissez faire economics.

Despite political success, Carrera suffered some family tragedy after 1850. His eldest legitimate son, José, died in battle at Omoa in 1853 and his wife, Petrona, died in the cholera epidemic of 1857. His younger son, Francisco, was commissioned a captain of infantry in the Santa Rosa militia at age twelve (in 1853), intended as an honor to the president, shortly after the death of José.[25] "Panchito," as he was called, went to Belgium for his education, and as the only legitimate surviving son of the president appears to have been unduly spoiled. He was often said to have lacked good sense, and although he was good looking and often dressed as a dandy, his playboy habits were not much admired among the prudish elite of Guatemala City. A marriage with one of the leading families might have been arranged, but it was not. After Carrera's death in 1865, Panchito did not prosper. He died, poor and drunk, in an obscure post in 1871. After Toña's death, Carrera's daughters carried on the social functions of the president's household. Their marriages were unfortunate, however, in that they either went badly or their spouses died early without leaving them much wealth. Carrera's second daughter, Mercedes, in 1861 married Juan Escribá (1834–64), a young immigrant from Estremadura who had been close to the caudillo and had prospered as a result of that relationship. Escribá died of dysentery three years later, however.[26] In 1862 Carrera's eldest daughter, Ascención Concepción ("Chon"), married Ernesto Klée. Klée came from a respected German family that emigrated to Guatemala early in the national period and established a successful commercial house in collaboration with the English merchant, George U. Skinner.[27] Thus despite his great political power, Carrera would not establish a family of much permanent importance in Central America. On the other hand, he reputedly sired more than eighty illegitimate children. His sexual appetite was reportedly large, and his promiscuity widely inspired gossip, perhaps beyond the actual truth, but he carried on a long extramarital relationship with Josefina "Chepita" Silva, who bore him several children.[28]

Carrera often drank to excess, both during festive occasions and at other times. His enemies reported that he often committed unspeakable atrocities on such occasions, and there is evidence that he was at best unpredictable. He would often throw off his coat and dance in his shirtsleeves, carrying on with the young women present. On these drunken occasions he was often much more accessible than at other times, and he sometimes made generous gifts to poor or disabled persons who came into his presence. A contemporary recalls one occasion when a young man by the name of Pifaral, apparently in his cups, began to shout insults at Carrera, attacking the way he ran the country. Those present trembled at the thought of what would happen to this poor fool. Mercedes indignantly demanded that he be shot immediately for such lack of respect for her father. The caudillo, however, took it as a joke, and simply ordered that the imprudent young man be taken home and put to bed. Nor were there any later consequences of the incident.[29]

His maintenance of order and stability gained him the praise of conservative governments in Europe and America. As early as 1853, undoubtedly influenced by the close relationship that Chatfield and the British had cultivated with Carrera, the *Illustrated London News* had described Carrera in positive terms. A picture showed him as a slim and attractive military figure. The text of the article said that he came from a respectable

family and noted his marriage to a woman of "singularly energetic and decided character." Of his rule, the article ascertained that "General Carrera
takes a perspicacious and correct view of administrative subjects, and he
is wholly without prejudice and dislike toward any class of society; and
he has even shown himself superior to petty passions and the intrigues of
party." Industry was developing under his impulse, the article said. Describing Carrera as "naturally cautious and calm," it acknowledged that he
had sometimes to deal strongly with uprisings and anarchy, but that he
often pardoned his enemies. Physically, it described him as "of middling
height and of vigorous conformation; his color is dark, and his features possess considerable intelligence and expression; his manners are courteous,
and on public occasions, highly dignified; he speaks with facility and he
has the enviable faculty of converting his enemies into warm adherents; he
rarely communicates to any one his plans before the moment of executing
them," but, it added, his army had great confidence in him. Contrary to
earlier accounts, the *Illustrated News* declared that he favored foreigners and
had sought to maintain good relations with England and other European
nations, concluding that he "is one of the most remarkable amongst the
rulers of the South American Republics."[30] Similar articles appeared later
in other European and U.S. newspapers.[31]

The Carrera dictatorship, if it did not deliver absolute peace and stability
to Guatemala, did bring material benefits. The first years of the new regime
saw notable improvement in commerce and infrastructure. Roads from the
capital to Antigua and the Pacific Coast improved. Those vacationing during the season at Amatitlán and Escuintla (November through February)
benefitted especially from improvements to the Pacific road, which carried
an increased traffic of private carriages. Regular carriage service, charging
$5.00 per seat each way, was doing a brisk business by 1852. Carrera him-
self spent considerable time at Escuintla, sometimes going for weekends,
at other times spending several weeks there. There was also regular stage
coach service to Antigua, beginning in February 1851. Reflecting the improvement in prosperity and security, the largest crowd in years turned out
for the bullfights during Carnival in 1852, notwithstanding unseasonably
damp weather.[32]

This picture of stability and progress at the beginning of 1852 had limi-
tations, of course. A serious locust plague damaged cochineal production
in 1852 and 1853 and the continuing disturbances in the montaña and the
Verapaz diminished Carrera's claims of peace and stability. After Carrera
had spent several months at "pacification," beginning in late February
1852,[33] a rebellion at the San José fortress alarmed the capital on the night

of 12 August 1852, when prisoners seized the fort and bombarded the city. Carrera took charge of the counterattack on the insurgents around midnight, but he could not penetrate the fort. His forces surrounded it, however, and, with its supplies cut off, the prisoners soon surrendered.[34] Carrera dealt harshly with these rebels and warned that the same fate [death] awaited all those who threatened the peace by rebelling against the authorities and the laws.[35] Later, prisoners who had helped the army put down the insurrection had their sentences reduced by a third if they were "major criminals" and were freed if they were "minor criminals."[36]

In the meantime, the government had held elections on Sunday, 11 July, for both corporate and departmental representatives to the assembly scheduled to convene in November.[37] Returns trickled in very slowly, the final results not being known until October, but in August the *Gaceta* praised the manner in which they were conducted.[38] The conservative landslide in these elections confirmed the new regime's restoration of order and return to tradition. Praise of the Guatemalan government and the elections came from conservative opinion abroad as well, but nowhere so strongly as from the Spanish *Diario de la Marina* in Havana: "This republic, which we have frequently cited for its prudence and moderation, and with undeniable justice as the model among Hispanic American peoples," it declared on 5 December, continued "to enjoy the fruits of its prudent management, notwithstanding the grave difficulties that surround it." It reported that the elections had been carried out peacefully and that the conservative party would have near unanimity in the new assembly.[39]

The assembly that convened on 25 November confirmed the conservative sweep with the election of Juan Matheu as its president and Juan José Aycinena and Luis Batres as vice-presidents.[40] Carrera's annual report emphasized peace and prosperity, with few specifics, but promised improvements in public education and the university.[41] The assembly responded to the president in a tone that would become routine over the next decade and a half, praising the "the moral and material change . . . founded on true principles of applied justice, respect for the rights of all, protection of our religion and its ministers," and promising to cooperate with his continued good works.[42]

While Carrera accompanied the archbishop on a pilgrimage to the shrine of the black Christ at Esquipulas and made an inspection tour of Chiquimula,[43] the assembly wound up its session and adjourned on 31 January of the new year. The *Gaceta* observed that "for the first time since independence we see a [legislative] body composed of the most notable people of the country and which has met and concluded its work without the necessity of those indecorous pressures that previously have detracted from the nation's assemblies."[44]

Yet Guatemala enjoyed "peace and security" in the 1850s only in a relative comparison to the turmoil of the previous decade. Crimes of violence continued to be a problem, especially in rural areas of eastern Guatemala. Prominent citizens were sometimes murdered, especially if they ventured out after dark. Rebels were often blamed for such attacks, but it is likely that some of the assaults were carried out by common bandits, a legacy of the unruly decade of the 1840s. Long lists of wanted criminals, their offenses ranging from homicide and assault to adultery and "illicit friendship," appeared in the *Gaceta* and on posters in public places.[45]

Early in 1854 Carrera made clear that he wanted further consolidation of power, calling for reforms in the constitution that would give him authority more appropriate to a monarch than to the president of a republic. The movement was initiated in Carrera's eastern stronghold but quickly spread throughout the country. On 30 April the Municipality of Salamá, in the Verapaz, made a formal act calling for establishment of Carrera as lifetime president, and Jutiapa and other departmental capitals soon followed. Many members of the conservative elite were quick to support the movement, convinced that the strengthening of his authority would lessen the struggles for control that had plagued the early years of Central American independence. José Lara Pavón on 16 May called on the Guatemala City Council, the institution that most quickly reflected the conservative views of the capital, to pronounce in favor of Carrera as perpetual president of the republic. The council called an open town meeting to deal with the question a week later. Festivities accompanied this *cabildo abierto* of 23 May, which called upon the House of Representatives to recognize General Carrera as president of the republic for life.[46] Rockets and other fireworks accompanied the celebration, followed by a *Te Deum* thanksgiving mass in the cathedral. Although presented by the government as a spontaneous outpouring of affection for the caudillo, there can be no doubt that the movement had been thoroughly and effectively orchestrated from the start. All of the departments had formally declared in favor of the proposal by the first of June. Table 8 reflects the extent of participation, amounting to perhaps one-quarter of 1 percent of the total population.

The Council of State turned to the corporations for a final endorsement from the elite of the capital.[47] At the same time that the corporations were asked for their opinions, Carrera issued a manifesto declaring his dedication to law, order, and prosperity. "There are in the life of nations certain circumstances in which those to whom divine providence has delivered

TABLE 8
Departments that Proclaimed Carrera as President for Life

Departments	Clergy-men	Military and Govt. Officials	Munici-palities	Signa-tures	% of Total Estimated Population
Central					
Guatemala	12	20	8	374	0.5
Sacatepéquez	10	7	28	121	0.3
Chimaltenango	9	3	12	143	0.2
Escuintla	1	5	9	118	0.6
Amatitlán	3	4	4	138	0.7
Pto. San José	0	5	3	31	—
Total	35	44	64	925	
East					
Santa Rosa	3	2	14	42	0.1
Jutiapa	4	13	13	603	1.9
Chiquimula	7	24	33	157	0.3
Verapaz	3	28	17	127	0.1
Total	17	67	77	929	
West					
Quetzaltenango	6	9	15	77	0.1
Sololá	2	3	20	64	0.1
Suchitepéquez	1	14	19	50	0.1
Totonicapán	2	6	12	39	0.04
San Marcos	1	4	13	64	0.1
Huehuetenango	2	3	26	42	0.1
Total	14	39	105	336	
North					
Pto. Izabal	0	12	1	49	
Pto. Santo Tomás	0	2	1	39	
Petén	3	4	7	84	
Total	3	18	9	172	
Totals	69	168	255	2,362	0.27

Sources: "Resumen de los departamentos que han celebrado Actas proclamando Presidente perpetuo de la República al Excmo. Sr. Capitán General Don Rafael Carrera, con espresión de los prelados eclesiásticos y sacerdotes, empleados y oficiales militares que han concurrido a dichos actos, número de municipalidades y firmas que los autorizan," *Gaceta de Guatemala,* 11 Aug. 1854; see Woodward, "Crecimiento," 229, and "Population," 7–8.

Note: The figures show the number of clergy, government and military officials, municipalities, and signatories that authorized the proclamation. Percentages of population are based on contemporary estimates.

supreme authority can not remain silent," he began. He reminded the people that he had restored peace against both foreign and domestic enemies of order. Now he dedicated himself to "closing the wounds that so many years of revolution have left," and to "respecting fundamentally our religion, our people and property, to acquiring for our country the credit which it had lost, and which will give it a distinguished place in the world." His assumption of greater authority, he explained, was aimed solely at achieving these goals in harmony with everyone. "My constant efforts have been directed toward establishing union and concord," he concluded, "the only principles upon which nations can grow and prosper."[48]

Soon thereafter, the president created a new cabinet-level position, roughly equivalent to attorney general, whose purpose was to watch over all functions of government, treasury, and justice, seeing to it that the laws were upheld and violators punished. Especially important, Carrera's decree emphasized, were "cases of abuses of the press, protecting the interests of the treasury, suppressing fraud and contraband, and any other abuses observed in the public administration." It also named the new minister as "protector of the Indians" and made him a member of the Treasury Board of Directors (*Junta Superior de Hacienda*). A few days later Carrera appointed three new members to the Council of State, two of them close military supporters in Gens. Mariano Paredes and Manuel María Bolaños. Bolaños was also commanding general of the Department of Guatemala. The third new member was a liberal, Pedro J. Valenzuela, who had served briefly as president following Gálvez's fall in 1838. He was now vice-rector of the University of San Carlos and represented the university in the assembly. Valenzuela had not been politically active for some time, and he was no more than a token liberal appointee on the council.[49]

If there was little expressed opposition within Guatemala, it was not long before critics arose nearby, especially in Costa Rica, where liberal Guatemalan exiles lived in the milder ambience of Rafael Mora's conservatism. The *Gaceta de Costa Rica* criticized the movement to elevate Carrera to perpetual president and suggested that Guatemala was following in the unfortunate path of Mexico. The Guatemalan *Gaceta* retorted that it would be more accurate to say that Mexico was now finally imitating the success that Guatemala had found and that Carrera's perpetual presidency was the logical culmination of the popular revolution he had begun in 1837. It argued that the special circumstances of Guatemala made this an appropriate move and would further preserve the peace and stability that Guatemala had achieved in contrast to her neighbors.[50]

Among the corporations, only the university offered any discordant note in the process leading to Carrera's lifetime presidency. Dr. Basilio Zeceña, a distinguished ecclesiastic, was now rector at San Carlos, and his signature headed the list of faculty who signed the university's response to the question. The faculty, mostly conservative clerics related to the principal families, was careful to heap great praise on Carrera and to justify his assumption of power on the circumstances in which Guatemala had found itself. But, from the academic point of view, what was proposed was the establishment of a virtual monarchy, inconsistent with republicanism. The university argued eloquently in favor of establishment of such a monarchy, but argued that such a change could not legitimately be effected in the manner being followed. The correct procedure would require constitutional reform and should be initiated by the House of Representatives, not presently in session.[51] An editorial in the *Gaceta* challenged this interpretation, but the significant point of the editorial was that the army had made the decision and that it would not be delayed.[52]

The government did not wait for the legislature to convene in October. The process had already taken too long in the view of General Bolaños and other army leaders. The Council of State met on 23 September and decided that a general junta of the leading officials, representatives of the corporations, clergy, and military, would be convened to declare Carrera perpetual president. It named a committee headed by the archbishop to carry this out.[53] The junta convened at 10:30 on Saturday morning, 21 October, and formally confirmed Carrera as president for so long as he should live, with powers that included the right to name his successor.[54] From this day forward, if not before, until his death in 1865, Carrera ruled as a virtually unrestrained monarch.

A week later the Mexican envoy in Guatemala heaped additional honor on Carrera when he delivered the insignias of the Gran Cruz de Guadalupe, courtesy of Mexico's conservative strongman, Antonio López de Santa Anna.[55] *El Universal* of Mexico City reflected Mexican conservative opinion of Carrera's regime, calling Guatemala the only successful Central American state, the only one that had "freed itself from the havoc" of the wars and political intrigue that had plagued the isthmus since independence. It credited Carrera, a strong and energetic man, who "governed the country according to the healthy principals that the majority of its inhabitants profess."[56]

Within Guatemala, of course, there was little open criticism, but the marginal annotation of the corregidor of Sacatepéquez on an article praising the act in the *Gaceta de Guatemala* of 17 November 1854, may be more revealing of what many Guatemalan leaders really thought:

My daughters. I edit this congratulatory piece. When you read it, General Carrera and I will no longer exist, so I can say the truth. There was no glory, nor did any one believe that with the presidency in perpetuity the republic would be happy; but it is necessary to say it thus and to explain the basis for such an unnecessary, extemporaneous, and ridiculous act. He had already been proclaimed in Los Altos and we had to continue the movement so as not to offend the President. Manuel Pavón was the promoter of all this in order to suppress the House [of Representatives], which showed some strength and independence last year. This was all done in Guatemala and then sent to Los Altos, where less would have been expected were it voluntary since they don't like Carrera; but it is necessary to say it as an historical truth: that only he can command: that he deserves it by valor and prestige even though while he lives it is unnecessary that they declare him President for life because it is a fact that no one can avoid, although no one thinks so. And it is just as certain that when he loses their opinion he will fall with all his perpetuity.[57]

Carrera left the capital on 5 November for an extended visit in the eastern part of the country, leaving the government in the hands of his ministers. He headed the most absolute dictatorship in Latin America, a fact that the official newspaper readily admitted on 17 November. It conceded that Guatemala had neither a free press nor frequent elections, which it called the "true school of fiction and political immorality," and that it was certainly an authoritarian state in which assemblies had little role. "If all this is called tyranny, then doubtless there is tyranny here." But, it continued, the great economic progress and welfare of the masses that the Carrera government had promoted were more than enough compensation for their lack. Cochineal production had risen after the previous year's decline, and, in fact, 1854 witnessed the largest production of the red dye in the country's history. Commerce and agriculture were growing notably. The roads were better, urban and rural real estate values were up, the public debt was gradually declining, and there was new construction, both in the capital and in smaller municipalities as well. The *Gaceta* contrasted this progress with other Spanish American countries and singled out especially neighboring Honduras, "where each day they sink deeper into misery and backwardness."[58] The liberals under Trinidad Cabañas had regained control in Honduras, thus gaining the hostility of Carrera.

The assembly convened on 25 November and listened as Carrera's glowing message of confidence and economic progress was read to them. "The duration of my authority will depend on the benefits it produces," he promised, "for once I cease to be just and beneficent, I shall fall from God's favor and no longer have popular support, without which I could not be sustained, nor would I pretend to."[59] The assembly responded with praise for the dictator and unanimously approved the decision to make him president for life, all members of the body signing the act on 15 December.[60]

Such unanimity broke down, however, when it came to discussions of even more increase in Carrera's authority in January 1855. In endorsing Carrera's elevation to the lifetime presidency, on 15 December, the assembly had agreed that there would need to be amendments to make the permanent presidency consistent with the Constitution of 1851. The government argued that these were minor changes, but a number of representatives balked at the proposed institutionalization of Carrera's absolute power. The debate occupied most of the month of January. The House resisted a provision that gave Carrera the right to suspend its sessions or to dissolve it altogether with the concurrence of the Council of State, should he perceive it to be in the national interest. Carrera would also gain the right to initiate legislation, to name councilors of state without even the few restrictions provided in the 1851 document, and (since he was inviolable) to be free of responsibility for the acts of the government. The Consulado, representing the economic power of the merchant class, presented a negative and influential report on the proposed amendments on 11 January. While it accepted the establishment of Carrera's lifetime presidency, it opposed any changes in the constitution, arguing that things had been going so well under the present document that no alteration should be made in it. The Economic Society was less emphatic, but it, too, opposed adoption of Article 3, containing the most important changes.[61]

In the face of legislative opposition, Carrera returned to the capital from the East and made a rare personal appearance before the assembly on 15 January. Absenteeism had run high in these debates, many representatives not wanting to be counted, but most turned out for this special session and were in their seats by noon. A half hour later an artillery salute announced the caudillo's departure from the palace, en route to the House and accompanied by an entourage of army and government officials. In a long, emotional speech the caudillo thanked the assembly for its support before reviewing his rise to power, his identification with the people, and his reasoning for establishing such strong authority. The president of the assembly, Juan Matheu, responded with praise for Carrera's practical politics and his fifteen years of political success.[62]

The special committee drafting the amendments reported the proposed changes favorably three days later.[63] In the debate that followed, some additional presidential prerogatives were added and resulted in four proposed amendments to the constitution that came to a vote, article by article, on 25 to 29 January. Absenteeism again was high and a bare quorum decided each of the five votes required to enact the four amendments. They achieved the required two-thirds of those present, although the ailing Manuel Francisco Pavón had to be carried in on his sick bed to vote in order to gain passage of the last two amendments. The final act was signed on 29 January by only twenty-eight of the fifty-three representatives.[64] The amendments, which Carrera signed on 4 April, were as follows:

1. Since Carrera's authority was permanent, the ministers were made solely responsible for acts of the government, along with councilors of state who voted in favor of said acts.

2. The president of the republic was given the following prerogatives:

   a. To create honorific distinctions to reward merit and virtue.

   b. To initiate legislation on his own.

   c. To name councilors of state without the restrictions specified in the Constitution of 1851.

   d. To suspend or defer sessions of the House of Representatives by means of a message, and in grave cases with the consent of the Council of State, to call for new elections, and to call the House into special session.

   e. To name and install magistrates and judges, who would serve during good behavior, once the elected terms of the present magistrates and judges have expired.

3. The executions and edicts of the tribunals were henceforth to be executed in the name of the president of the republic.

4. The House of Representatives and councilors named by the House would serve for terms of seven years.[65]

The House closed its sessions at 3:30 P.M. on 31 January, having turned over virtually all power to the caudillo.[66]

Carrera in his later years led a more respectable lifestyle than in his early years. The nervousness and exaggerated behavior of his youth gave way to a calmer and more rational self-control once he was firmly established as dictator. He attended church regularly, dressed more conservatively, and reportedly spent much time meditating and confessing his sins. He continued to believe that he had a divine mission, which contributed to an exalted ego. Entering a house in Quetzaltenango one day, he passed a portrait of Napoleon Bonaparte on the wall. Upon seeing it, he commented to the owner, "Another me!"[67]

Most impartial observers—foreigners for the most part, for few in Guatemala were impartial regarding the government—acknowledged that

Carrera had developed considerable facility in governing during his last years. The U.S. minister, E. O. Crosby, gives that impression in one of the few contemporary descriptions of the caudillo during his later years. He noted his continued support from both the masses and the elite, as well as his ability to select able ministers and to diagnose political problems successfully.[68]

The elevation of Rafael Carrera to the lifetime presidency of Guatemala confirmed the dominance of the caudillo and the military as the most powerful elements in the coalition ruling the country. It also emphasized the weakness of the legislature. Carrera would eventually die, but the dominance of the army and the weakness of the legislature would continue to the present as grim realities of Guatemalan government. While the merchant-planter elite remained powerful and undoubtedly believed it exercised some degree of control over the government, it had embarked down a path that would, as much under the liberals as under Carrera's conservatives, make the army the dominant political force and one that eventually could determine Guatemala's destiny with few restraints. Although the liberals would later be credited with "professionalization" of the military and relying excessively on it for support, it is undeniable that it was under the conservative rule of Carrera that the army began its political domination of the state.

CHAPTER THIRTEEN

Nicaragua

BEFORE CARRERA HAD CONCLUDED his intervention in Honduran affairs, a new, more serious crisis had come to Central America, the fili-busters from the United States. The conservative-liberal struggle combined with the Anglo-American rivalry and the search for an interoceanic passage to embroil first Nicaragua and then all of the states of the old federation in a great National Campaign to expel the North Americans. The role of Carrera's Guatemala in these events has often been underestimated.

Nicaragua became a focus of attention for both North Americans and Europeans following the California gold strike. The British had been espe-cially aggressive in seizing Greytown at the mouth of the Río San Juan and in pressing the Nicaraguan government for concessions, using debts to British bondholders and other British subjects as leverage. The French, too, had their eyes on the isthmus, and the future Napoleon III had taken a great interest in the potential canal route.[1] The United States pressed the British aggressively to honor the terms of the Clayton-Bulwer Treaty of 1850. The spirit of Manifest Destiny ran rampant, and U.S. citizens looked toward the isthmus as a new frontier of opportunity for their capital, entre-preneurship, and leadership. All this occurred in a political atmosphere that had already aligned the conservative parties with Great Britain and liberals with the United States.

The intriguing story of the American filibustering expeditions to Nica-ragua has been dealt with in fascinating detail in a number of other works and will not be repeated here.[2] Pertinent here is the Guatemalan reaction to the crisis in Nicaragua. The canal projects proposed by Vanderbilt and others heightened the rivalry between conservative and liberal interests, for they strengthened their respective alliances with British and U.S. interests. E. G. Squier signed a treaty with the Nicaraguan government in León on 3 September 1849, recognizing the exclusive rights given to Vanderbilt's Atlantic and Pacific Canal Company,[3] while the British meanwhile seized Greytown and supported the conservative government in Granada. Vanderbilt successfully developed a convenient route across Nicaragua between 1851 and 1856. His Accessory Transit Company profited handsomely by providing a combination of ocean, river, lake, and ground transportation from the eastern U.S. to California via Nicaragua, but within Nicaragua the struggle between liberals and conservatives, or Democrats and Legitimists, as they respectively came to be called in the ensuing struggle, became intense.

Privately backed filibustering enterprises into Mexico, Cuba, and other Caribbean regions from the United States understandably had alarmed Central Americans. In Guatemala the *Gaceta* warned in August 1851 that Providence would punish the U.S. for its abuses in the occupation of Texas and California and its projects against Cuba. It contrasted the disorderly politics of the United States to progress in Catholic countries. It pointed to the North American sectional conflicts as an example of the result of excessive liberty, which "caused ambitious men to go too far."[4] A month later it charged that the development of California's wealth had "stimulated powerfully the Anglo-American ambition in Louisiana and other Gulf states to take over the isthmus."[5] The presence of U.S. warships along the coast of Central America and Panama, where a U.S. company was constructing a railroad, increased the danger of trouble with Great Britain. Violent incidents did occur, but after Clayton-Bulwer, cooler heads in Washington and London refused to allow them to lead to war.[6] But the struggle within Nicaragua became hotter, especially when Fruto Chamorro's conservatives began to gain the upper hand. On 28 February 1854 they decreed Nicaragua a sovereign republic in a strong step against liberal unionism. A conservative assembly that had convened in Managua on 22 January 1854 refused to seat the liberal delegates from western Nicaragua on the grounds that they had been exiled for revolutionary activities. On 21 April the Chamorro government adopted a new flag and coat of arms with the motto "Liberty, Order, Labor," and on 30 April it promulgated a conservative constitution. There were, in reality, two governments in Nicaragua, conservative at Granada and liberal at León. Trinidad Cabañas's aid enabled the liberals to continue the struggle.[7]

The situation became more complicated when North American filibusters began to arrive in Nicaragua. First, in late 1854 an expedition mounted by Col. Henry L. Kinney—a Texas politician and Mexican War veteran who intended to take over some 30 million acres along the Mosquito Coast—began to alarm conservative and British interests on the isthmus.[8] Felipe Molina (himself a liberal, but representing Mora's conservative Costa Rican government in the United States) vigorously protested the Kinney colonization scheme to the U.S. government, but the State Department rejected the protest as dealing with a purely private matter not involving the U.S. government.[9] Chamorro fell ill and died in March 1855, succeeded by José María Estrada, who issued a strong declaration against the Kinney expedition, calling for "war to the death," mobilizing all able-bodied men, and lodging a strong protest with the U.S. government.[10] Washington made an effort to stop the expedition, and the *Gaceta de Guatemala*, which followed the expedition's progress closely, reported in March 1855 that it had been frustrated as a consequence of U.S. pressures exerted in virtue of "observations made by the English government."[11]

But Kinney sailed anyway, and his "Pronunciamento" of 6 September 1855 reflected his Manifest Destiny spirit and leaves little doubt as to why he was so offensive to the Central Americans. It read, in part:

> A country without a rival in its natural capabilities and in the importance of its geographical position, yet for want of the improving hand of man, declining even in the plentitude of its resources, is to be created anew. The civilization, the arts, the stable laws and policy, the religion, the business enterprises and industry of the hardy Anglo-American race are yet to be extended over a territory ample enough for their most generous expansion. . . . I have entered upon one of the noblest enterprises of the present century.[12]

In fact, the Kinney expedition failed largely because of its own shortcomings. In the meantime, a much more serious threat to Central American sovereignty occurred in the notorious expedition of William Walker. Walker and Bryan Cole had organized this force in California directly in support of the liberals at León. Ideological issues were important for the liberal Walker, but the attraction of large land grants from the liberal government was also an incentive and attracted many recruits. Chamorro's death had weakened the conservatives, but the spread of epidemic disease, a by-product of the civil war, was taking a heavy toll on both sides by mid-1855. Efforts at a peace settlement in the spring of 1855 floundered when Gen. José Trinidad Muñoz took over command of the liberal army after Máximo Jérez was wounded. Muñoz was a capable veteran of the

Central American civil wars who had military training under Santa Anna in Mexico. This haughty, pompous, and opportunistic Nicaraguan officer who had fought on both the conservative and liberal sides attempted to negotiate a peaceful settlement first with Santos Guardiola and later with Nicaraguan President Estrada. He succeeded only in bringing Honduran troops into the conflict, including a substantial contingent commanded by Guardiola, feared widely as the "Butcher." [13]

Walker and fifty-eight North American soldiers of fortune arrived in mid-June, and in their first encounter they were mauled by Guardiola's much larger force at Rivas, leading to a falling out immediately between Walker and Muñoz, whose troops abandoned the Americans in the fray. On 18 August, however, Muñoz himself died in an action against Guardiola at El Sauce, south of León. [14] Then Cole arrived with reinforcements from California, strengthening Walker's position. His subsequent military successes and the high death toll among liberal Nicaraguan officers resulted in Walker himself becoming commander-in-chief of the liberal forces. After he captured Granada on 13 October 1855, Walker arranged a compromise peace, with conservative Patricio Rivas as president. This alienated some of the liberals, however, and by no means ended conservative opposition.

The State Department gave Walker no formal approval and Secretary of State William Marcy expressed grave doubts about the expedition. However, Walker enjoyed enormous popular support in the United States, and the U.S. minister in Nicaragua, John Wheeler, recognized the new government on 8 November 1855. Much of the U.S. press saw the episode as a continuation of the Anglo-American rivalry for control of the isthmus. [15] Ignoring the protests of the other Central American states, the government of Franklin Pierce formally recognized the Rivas government on 14 May 1856. [16] Antonio José de Irisarri, representing both Guatemala and El Salvador in Washington, protested vigorously against this decision and against Pierce's recognition of Father Agustín Vijil as the representative of the Rivas government. He called it an action "most contrary and offensive to Central American interests" and went on to attack the filibusters and the Monroe Doctrine in a long letter to the secretary of state. [17]

Walker's invasion and his rise to command of the Nicaraguan army under the Rivas government further divided liberals and conservatives across the isthmus. Some liberals regarded Walker as their only hope to defeat the conservatives, and even when new North American recruits poured into Nicaragua and became the bulk of the army, they were reluctant to oppose him. Conservatives, on the other hand, rallied to support the efforts to oust the interloper. Santos Guardiola had already brought Honduran forces into the campaign. Costa Rica's Rafael Mora took the lead in rallying Latin American opposition to Walker with a pronouncement on 1 November against the intervention and a mobilization of troops to resist Walker in Guanacaste. Some liberals joined the National Campaign against the filibusters, to be sure, but in the main it was a conservative effort aimed as much at liberal ideology and control as against the Walker invasion solely. Even Gerardo Barrios (1813–68), the liberal general who led El Salvador's forces in the war, did so under the orders of Francisco Dueñas's moderate government.

Upon hearing of the events in Nicaragua, Rafael Carrera observed that the Nicaraguans had "collared themselves with the chains of slavery that will continue to their children," but he added that the Yankees were "men just like us, and the bullets will enter them and they will die even more easily than us."[18]

An uprising in Quetzaltenango on 12 July 1855 and smaller disturbances elsewhere diverted Guatemalan attention from Nicaragua temporarily. In Quetzaltenango, Father Encarnación Domínguez, who had been ordered by his bishop to retire from his parish, rallied two-hundred-odd supporters to protest the order. They surprised the garrison, took over the fortress, and seized a large quantity of arms, which they then distributed to others who joined the insurrection. The military commander, Gen. Juan Ignacio Irigoyen, was out of town when the uprising occurred, but he hurried back when news reached him that the rebels were looting the city. A battle took place at 2:00 A.M. on 15 July at Sijá, where Irigoyen defeated the insurgents. He then marched into the city and had restored order by sunset. In the meantime, Carrera had set out for Quetzaltenango with a division, which turned out to be unnecessary. But Carrera demanded severe punishments for those involved. The leaders of the revolt—Padre Domínguez, Rudecindo de León, and José Vásquez—had all escaped, but six others were convicted of crimes connected with the revolt and promptly executed by firing squads on 19 and 20 July.[19]

There was also some trouble in the Verapaz, especially around Santa Cruz Mountain, where bandits had been raiding, a phenomenon not unrelated to the montaña disturbances further east. The corregidor of the Verapaz carried out a concerted military effort and by November had pacified the area and established several new communities to populate the rugged region. One petition to incorporate a new town asked that it be named "San Rafael" in honor of the president and his beneficent efforts to end the violence.[20]

Still another problem area was the North Coast, where the dramatic shift in Guatemalan shipping from the Caribbean to Pacific ports occasioned by completion of the Panama Railway in 1855 caused economic decline for Izabal and Santo Tomás. When municipal elections failed to establish qualified people for the municipal council and other local problems began to emerge, the Carrera government simply suppressed the municipal governments and imposed a Juez Comisionado on both communities to provide for judicial and administrative functions.[21]

In his annual message to the House of Representatives at the end of November, Carrera took pride in the continued maintenance of peace in Guatemala, without mention of the problems in Los Altos or the North Coast, but he devoted considerable attention to his peacekeeping efforts in Honduras and El Salvador and to the restoration of conservative governments there with Guatemalan assistance. He also noted with alarm the fratricidal war in Nicaragua and the threat to Nicaraguan sovereignty by the intervention of the North Americans, who had "aggravated the discord, introducing into the war interests hostile to both of its parties." He expressed the hope that the recently arranged peace would be consolidated and bring an end to the fighting there.[22]

The assembly responded with the usual congratulations on how well the caudillo was running the country, but it also raised the issue of Nicaragua as one of serious concern for Guatemala.[23] On 17 December, Representative Doroteo José de Arriola demanded to know what Guatemala was doing about the serious events in Nicaragua, calling for an expeditionary force to assist the legitimate Nicaraguan government. The interior minister assured the assembly that the president was paying close attention to events in Nicaragua and "dictating all measures that the situation demands," with Guatemalan defense and independence being the first and sacred priority. Arriola then called for formation of a volunteer army to go to Nicaragua. After lengthy discussion, there was apparently a consensus that this was beyond the competence of the assembly, and Arriola's motion was defeated. A few days later, however, the assembly approved the government's request for a special appropriation for defense, in light of the situation in Nicaragua.[24]

In early January 1856 Carrera consulted with representatives from Honduras and El Salvador. He refused to recognize or even to respond to communications from the Walker-supported government of Nicaragua, but he was reluctant to send Guatemalan forces as far as Nicaragua. Meanwhile, Salvadoran President Francisco Dueñas in January began to organize a Salvadoran expeditionary force under Gerardo Barrios's command. Carrera may well have hoped that the situation could be handled by his surrogate

Honduran and Salvadoran forces without direct involvement of Guatemalan troops. The decision to increase publication of the *Gaceta* to thrice weekly in order to provide more foreign news was a further reflection of Guatemalan concern over the situation in Nicaragua.[25]

Costa Rica formally declared war against Walker. Mora's proclamation called on Nicaraguans to rise up against the filibusters and for Central American unity against them. "All the loyal sons of Guatemala, San Salvador and Honduras are marching against that horde of bandits," he declared. "Our cause is holy; our triumph certain. God will give us the victory, and with that the peace, harmony, the liberty and union of the great Central American family."[26] With British military assistance promised, Mora now loomed as the latest caudillo to propose Central American union, but this time under conservative leadership.[27] The British press encouraged the Central American fear of American filibustering. *Blackwood's Magazine*, for example, in March 1856 observed, "Should the Americans in that country [Nicaragua] be able to maintain their position, of which, at present, there seems to be every probability, the successful filibustering of Nicaragua will be but the beginning; the end will be the occupation, by Americans, of all the Central American states, and in due course of time, of Mexico and Cuba."[28] Costa Rica's entry into the struggle, however, was felt quickly when they dealt the North Americans a major defeat at the Santa Rosa hacienda, near Liberia, providing a basis for Costa Rican acquisition of the province of Guanacaste.[29]

Carrera returned at the end of March from an extended rest at his Las Animas hacienda near Mazatenango. He sent Col. José Victor Zavala, a member of a respected conservative family who was noted as much for his quick wit as for his military ability, to discuss the situation with the Salvadoran president. They drew up plans for Guatemalan cooperation in the war against Walker.[30] On 5 May Carrera announced the formation of an expeditionary force, saying that he would go to Nicaragua himself if necessary. A vanguard of Guatemalan troops would soon unite with the Salvadoran and Honduran forces and join with the Costa Rican troops in the "honorable enterprise of liberating Nicaragua and assuring the independence of all the states." He exhorted his troops to acquit themselves with honor and confidence, recommending full cooperation with "your brothers from El Salvador, Honduras and Costa Rica, . . . eliminating those who come to meddle in our dissensions."[31]

The Rivas government sought through diplomacy to forestall the intervention of the other states. Rivas came to León to meet with representatives of the three western states, insisting that he only desired a harmonious relationship with them. "I do not want war," he announced, "much less between sister peoples and natural friends. There is no need for a rupture, and I am disposed to use all means to consolidate the peace."[32]

Rivas's mission was a total failure, but it may have had much to do with his decision to defect to the invading army in June. Walker and Rivas broke on 9 June when the latter accused Walker of attempting to take over his government by force. Rivas moved his government to Chinandega on the twelfth, and on the twenty-sixth he declared Walker an "enemy of Nicaragua and a traitor," dismissing him from the employ of the republic and calling on all Nicaraguan men ages fifteen to sixty to take up arms against the filibusters. Walker, meanwhile, established a new government in Granada, confirmed by a speedy election held on 29 June, with himself inaugurated as president of Nicaragua on 12 July 1856.[33] Walker had already issued a proclamation on 20 June, deposing Rivas, charging him with treason for moving the government secretly to Chinandega, and declaring all acts of the Rivas government from 2 June forward "null and void." Anyone, public or private, following Rivas's orders would be regarded as a traitor and treated as such by military tribunal. In effect, now, except for a few liberal hangers-on, Walker was reduced to the "American Phalanx" and faced the combined hostility of all five Central American governments and Great Britain.[34] South American aid for the allies also arrived, notably from Colombia, Peru, and Chile.[35]

The Guatemalan vanguard division left Guatemala City under the command of Gen. Mariano Paredes on Monday morning, 5 May, moving eastward to Nicaragua overland. They had reached San Vicente, El Salvador, by the nineteenth but then were delayed for several weeks awaiting transportation across the Gulf of Fonseca. Meanwhile, a flood of North Americans, mostly Mexican War veterans from the lower Mississippi Valley, poured into Nicaragua to augment Walker's ranks, lured by promises of land and wealth. Walker's attempts to Americanize Nicaragua during the lull in the fighting intensified the anti-Walker spirit within Central America. The *Gaceta de Guatemala* reprinted an article from Walker's *Nicaragüense*, obviously to inflame Guatemalans against the filibusters. Entitled "Races," it glorified the Anglo-Saxon race and its expansion over the globe. "Looking thus at what the Anglo-Saxon race is evidently destined to accomplish, how short-sighted it appears in one portion of it to throw obstacles in the path of the other. The race has already got a footing in China and Japan; it has the control of India and the islands of the Oceans, as well as nearly all of North America. Why should it defeat itself in Central America."[36] But cholera spread among the new troops on both sides, as well as among the civilian population, causing widespread economic decay and misery in the country. Paredes finally reached León on 18 July, joining with Honduran and Salvadoran troops that were converging there. Guardiola had sent a force under Juan López, while Salvadoran reinforcements had arrived under Ramón Belloso.[37] On the seventeenth, the day before Guatemalan troops reached León, Carrera's government recognized Rivas's Chinandega government, effective "from the day which he left the influence of Walker," and pledged to support it with "all the means and resources of this Republic."[38]

Honduras, El Salvador, and Guatemala signed a formal alliance on 18 July 1856 in Guatemala City "for defense of their independence and nationality." They agreed to unite their forces to "throw out the adventurers who have tried to usurp the public power in Nicaragua and which oppress that Republic, threatening the independence of the remaining states." They invited Costa Rica to join the alliance.[39] Reinforcements under Colonel Knoth left Guatemala City on the twentieth, bound for Puerto San José to board the Guatemalan coast guard schooner *Ascensión* for passage to Nicaragua. Knoth's reinforcements reached León by mid August to find fever running among the Guatemalan forces already there.[40] There had as yet been only skirmishing with the Walker army, but a struggle had emerged between the two conservative governments of Nicaragua: Rivas, who had defected from Walker, and José María Estrada, successor to the Fruto Chamorro government. After retreating into Honduras, Estrada had returned to Nicaragua with the Honduran forces and now sought cooperation from Rivas after the latter had disavowed Walker. But on 13 August assassins' bullets cut short Estrada's life and those of several of his associates. Tomás Martínez took over leadership of the Chamorro faction, but even before Walker was defeated the internecine strife in Nicaragua had resumed.[41]

Carrera remained in Guatemala, concentrating on raising troops and money for the expeditionary force. Several Spanish officers who had served Santa Anna in Mexico until his overthrow a year earlier now joined the Guatemalan army.[42] The government decreed a new forced loan on all property holders in mid-September and asked the assembly to impose new taxes to repay the loan of $120,000 at 12 percent annual interest. Half of the loan was assigned to the Department of Guatemala, with the remainder spread over the other departments.[43] The government contracted another loan of $150,000 with Guatemala City property holders in April 1857 on the same terms as the previous loan. Forty subscribers quickly covered the request, an indication of the improved economic situation in the country.[44] A new war tax on meat caused some grumbling, however, especially in eastern

Guatemala, where meat was traditionally a more common item in the diet than in the western highlands.[45] A campaign to collect patriotic donations, as had been done in the late colonial period, was also carried out to help fund the war.[46]

On Sunday afternoon, 28 September, two thousand apparently well-disciplined troops passed in review on the main plaza. Carrera intended to send a truly decisive force to Nicaragua. The allies could not afford to lose. In October Carrera repeated his willingness to go to Nicaragua himself if necessary, but in the meantime he urged the troops to join their countrymen who had already distinguished themselves at San Jacinto, northeast of Managua, where they had beaten back a contingent of Walker's forces.[47]

There had been an effort to persuade Carrera to lead the allied forces in Nicaragua. He was unquestionably the preeminent military caudillo on the isthmus, and even his enemies acknowledged his leadership and tactical abilities. Mora had suggested that Carrera should lead the expeditionary forces, but in Guatemala there was some reluctance among the local elite to see him leave, perhaps fearing his absence might threaten the peace and security he had established. The municipality of the capital had debated the issue in late September, when José Francisco Taboada and Mariano Trabanino had proposed a resolution opposing Carrera leaving the republic to head the large force opposing the filibusters. After lengthy discussion, the council deferred action on the proposal, essentially acknowledging that it was not a matter within the council's jurisdiction.[48] In late November, Gerardo Barrios encouraged Carrera to take command of the allied forces in Nicaragua, but Carrera refused in mid-December, responding that his presence was essential in Guatemala to raise funds and troops.[49] Salvadoran President Dueñas repeated the call for Carrera in January 1857, and in February Barrios again indicated that he wanted Carrera as chief of operations against the filibusters. He even made it a condition for his own command of the Salvadoran troops in Nicaragua.[50] Carrera, however, made his refusal clear, and he proposed Mora for the post, indicating that he was quite willing to place Guatemala's troops under Mora's command, as had the governments of El Salvador, Nicaragua, and Honduras already.[51]

The archbishop joined in the efforts to excite the Guatemalans for the war. In a pastoral letter of 15 October he attacked the filibusters on religious grounds, warning of the threat of Protestantism as well as the material damage by the invaders. He emphasized the Guatemalans' obligations as Catholics, noting that while many Catholic foreigners had come and benefitted Guatemala, he opposed the present growth in Protestant foreigners. This strong statement warned that if the filibusters succeeded in taking over Nicaragua, it would not be long before the entire isthmus would fall, and then "we would feel the pain of seeing Jesus Christ rejected." He called for special masses for the Guatemalan troops and three days of prayer in the cathedral beginning on 19 October, offering 80 days of indulgence to all those faithful who recited devotedly the litanies at these services in which the people and clergy would join together in a great appeal to God.[52]

Following San Jacinto (14 September 1856), the Guatemalan army began an offensive aimed at dislodging Walker from Granada. They pushed Walker's forces out of Masaya and, led by General Paredes and Colonel Zavala, entered Granada on 12 and 13 October, killing several of the Americans and seizing a large quantity of munitions. It appeared that Walker might fall there and then, but the Tennessean rallied his forces and pushed the Guatemalans back out of the city in bloody street fighting.[53] A Costa Rican offensive then took San Juan del Sur, the Nicaraguan port on the Pacific Coast, forcing Walker to move a considerable force there to retake it. The western allies repelled a Walker counterattack on Masaya on 16–19 November. The arrival of General Paredes with new troops had been crucial to the allies' victory there, but the Guatemalans suffered heavy losses—twenty-six killed and fifty-three wounded, compared to Salvadoran losses of eight killed and fourteen wounded and Nicaraguan (Gen. Tomás Martínez's division) losses of twelve killed and twenty-three wounded.[54]

The allies followed up the victory at Masaya with a fresh siege of Granada, but Walker stubbornly held out against rising odds. Dysentery and cholera began to take a frightful toll on both sides. In early December Guatemala lost Gens. Joaquín Solares and Mariano Paredes to cholera. General Belloso wrote to the president of El Salvador on the afternoon of 2 December that the resistance made by the filibusters in Granada was "undefinable." They had been reduced to a single small site and apparently numbered no more than 250, many of whom were sick, all suffering from hunger and thirst and in miserable condition. "A complete victory of our force over the enemy will take place any moment now."[55] Yet Walker not only held out but delivered a stinging counterattack on 13 December, which was especially injurious to recently arrived Honduran troops under Gen. Florencio Xatruch. José Zavala, now a brigadier general, took over command of the Guatemalans and provided dynamic leadership under the worst of conditions,[56] while in Guatemala the government heaped honors on former President Paredes and draped the city in black mourning cloth for three days.[57]

These losses were turning the war into a horrible affair, with disease and battle killing thousands of Central Americans. By early 1857, however, the British began to apply naval pressure to prevent Walker from gaining new recruits. The allies were confident, despite their setbacks, that it was only a matter of time until they would starve Walker into submission.[58]

After burning Granada, Walker finally abandoned it, but his filibusters escaped southward, digging in around Rivas to continue their dogged resistance. The allies held a war council at Granada on 21 January 1857, General Mora coming up the San Juan River and across Lake Nicaragua to meet with Generals Zavala, Martínez, and José María Cañas. Victory seemed inevitable for them now as their force of several thousand marched southward to join the Costa Ricans in the siege of Rivas, held by no more than five hundred filibusters. The ports were now blockaded, denying the Americans resupply, while a steady flow of troops and supplies were now arriving from Guatemala and El Salvador.[59]

While the allied armies closed the net on the remaining filibusters in March 1857, Gerardo Barrios paid an unusual visit to Carrera in Guatemala. Barrios had been associated with the liberals in El Salvador since the time of Morazán, and had been involved to some degree in the Chinandega effort at reunion as well as the national army's invasion of Guatemala in 1850–51. Yet he had made his peace with Francisco Dueñas and remained among El Salvador's leading military figures. Ambitious and able to make political compromises, he was now making a genuine effort to cultivate Carrera with the aim of keeping him out of Salvadoran affairs. Moreover, Carlos Antonio Meany, his sister's husband, was a leading conservative merchant in Guatemala City. The Central American unity in the face of Walker's invasion of Nicaragua gave Barrios the opportunity to promote a rapprochement with Guatemala. The Salvadoran government had named Barrios special commissioner to promote the cause of Central American union. He met with Carrera and Foreign Minister Pedro Aycinena in the National Palace shortly after noon on Thursday, 12 March. He began by reading a statement explaining his mission as liaison for cooperation in the war against the filibusters. To promote closer union among the allies, the Salvadoran government was calling for formation of another army to take the field before the filibusters could get more reinforcements. He asked Carrera to name someone to represent Guatemala in talks to form a general government that would facilitate this effort.[60]

Carrera replied that the most important thing in defeating the filibusters was to unify the Nicaraguans themselves, a clear reference to the continued division among both conservatives and liberals there. He said that they must learn "to sacrifice their diverse opinions and attend today only to their obligation to save their country." He promised that Guatemala would continue to send help, but reminded Barrios that Guatemala had already sent more than anyone else, even though it was farthest away from Nicaragua. He agreed that Central Americans needed to put their differences behind them if they were to defeat the enemy, and he named Luis Batres to represent the republic in talks with Barrios. Barrios noted that his presence in Guatemala after sixteen years of being Carrera's political adversary was proof of his cooperation in the common cause. Later Barrios was presented to other government ministers and army officers. The meeting ended cordially and Barrios remained in the city for another two weeks to confer with Batres and other Guatemalan leaders, but he gained no commitment from Guatemala beyond support of the war effort.[61] The meeting was important for Barrios, personally, however, for he succeeded in gaining the acquiescence of Carrera as he began his climb to power in El Salvador.

The final stages of the National Campaign took a terrible toll of lives in the Guatemalan and Costa Rican ranks. General Mora finally reversed his "no quarter" attitude toward the Americans and offered the beleaguered filibusters food, liquor, and passage home. Desertions from the Walker ranks followed, and, finally, on 1 May 1857 the remainder surrendered at Rivas.[62]

True to his word, Carrera continued to dispatch troops to Nicaragua right up until news had reached Guatemala of Walker's final surrender. A column of troops left Guatemala City on 16 March, embarking at Puerto San José on the twenty-fifth and disembarking at Realejo on the thirtieth. The ships returned to San José with 119 Guatemalan sick and wounded. Seven hundred more Guatemalans left the capital for Nicaragua on 31 March under the command of the aging General J. B. Asturias.[63]

Walker returned aboard a U.S. naval vessel to a hero's welcome in New Orleans and began plans for several abortive returns to Central America. The war left Nicaragua devastated and the cholera epidemic that had thrived on the war now spread to the rest of Central America with the returning troops. The legacy of the Walker episode was long lasting. It discredited the liberals in Nicaragua for decades, giving the conservatives led by Tomás Martínez control over the country and enabling them to establish the sort of desperately needed peace and stability that Carrera had applied to Guatemala. Santos Guardiola returned to provide unenlightened, strong-arm rule of Honduras for several more years. In El Salvador Gerardo Barrios returned from the war to become the center of a movement that challenged the conservative presidency of Rafael Campos. It soon resulted in Barrios's elevation to the presidency and the beginning of liberal resurgence there by 1859.[64]

In Guatemala there was rejoicing and the opportunity for Carrera to glory in yet another triumph. His victory proclamation of 14 May recounted the final battle and surrender of the filibusters at Rivas. "I congratulate myself with you and with the other peoples of Central America on the conclusion of the war. There will be no need to send more troops to Nicaragua; our valiant soldiers will soon return to their homes, and all the people of the country will now be able to dedicate themselves to uninterrupted labor toward the development of the prosperity with which Providence has favored us."[65] Public festivities and fireworks celebrating the end of the war were joined even by the earth it seemed, as Volcán Fuego, which had begun to erupt in February 1857, belched forth fire and smoke that could be seen from the capital.

The celebration was soon muted by news of the awful toll war and disease had taken on the thousands of Guatemalans who did not return from Nicaragua. It was further tempered as the effects of the cholera epidemic began to be felt in Guatemala. Not since 1837 had an epidemic brought death to so many. El Salvador felt the epidemic first, as its troops returned more quickly. By June 1857 the outbreak of many cases in that state was causing concern in neighboring Guatemala.[66]

The first large contingent of the Guatemalan expeditionary force did not embark at Puerto San José until 24 June. They marched inland to welcoming celebrations in each town, reaching the capital on 1 July to be welcomed by the president and another major public festival.[67] On 4 July the surgeon general reported to the corregidor of Guatemala that the state of public health in the capital was very good, with no sign of epidemic disease. Although there was concern over the reports of cholera in El Salvador, none had appeared in Guatemala. He added that one of the recently arrived soldiers from Nicaragua had been hospitalized supposedly with cholera, but the surgeon general had found him "perfectly healthy," suffering only from indigestion, without "any sign" of the feared disease.[68]

Nevertheless, four days later another soldier entered the hospital diagnosed with cholera. He died on 10 July. The corregidor asked Surgeon General Quirino Flores to submit reports on the city's health twice weekly, and on the eleventh Dr. Flores acknowledged the first death to cholera, but nevertheless insisted "that nothing has occurred to alter my communication to you of the 4th." Since then, he had found no other cases of cholera, although one case of yellow fever had occurred. Yet he recommended that all precautions be taken against an epidemic.[69]

More soldiers had already died in Puerto San José, however, and the epidemic had reached major proportions in El Salvador. Colonel Knoth's forces were especially hard hit with the disease. They were detained on the road from San José, and the sickness became widespread between San José and Escuintla. The *Gaceta* reported on 12 July that the soldiers' cases had not propagated the disease, but the explanation was not convincing. On the next day a surgeon who had been with the forces in Nicaragua, Lic. Manuel Padilla Durán, died in Guatemala City from an undiagnosed fever. By the sixteenth an acknowledged cholera epidemic existed in the country, and the *Gaceta* published instructions on means of preventing cholera.[70] The Antigua City Council on the same day sought permission to divert its revenues and mortgage its landholdings for expenses connected with the cholera epidemic.[71] The archbishop called on the clergy to assist in preventing the spread of the disease and in caring for the sick and dying. He said that reports from eastern Guatemala led him to believe that the epidemic was not so serious as that of 1837, but that it was nonetheless severe.[72]

In the capital the government organized a Central Board of Health and divided the city into five cantons for the purpose of dealing with the epidemic in terms of medical care and distribution of medicine. The corregidor made a concerted effort to clean up the city with fines of from one to fifty pesos for violations of his sanitation regulations.[73] Block inspectors were appointed to enforce the regulations, to see that the poor sick who could not be treated at home were taken to hospitals or to the first aid stations and lazarettos that had been established, and to make sure that cadavers were buried within four hours after death.[74] Prisoners were employed to help the sick, bury the dead, and to take over the tasks of sick workers, their sentences commuted for this service.[75] The epidemic peaked in August (see Table 9).

The epidemic showed no favoritism, striking rich and poor, strong and weak, young and old—leaving many orphans and cutting short projects and plans. The president himself suffered the loss of his wife. She had given birth on 6 May to yet another daughter, María Teresa de la Victoria, named in honor of the great victory over Walker.[76] There had been some complications with the birth, but after the first few days mother and daughter had thrived and Toña had regained her vigor and in time for the victory celebrations. But, falling violently ill on the night of 16 August, the cholera struck her down quickly, taking her life at 10:30 the following morning. The black-rimmed announcement of her death the same day also provided details of her burial in the crypt of the cathedral. The burial service was private, owing to the circumstances of the epidemic, but the government decreed nine days of public mourning.[77] The military commander of the Department of Guatemala, Major General Bolaños, also lost his wife to cholera.[78]

TABLE 9
Cholera Epidemic, Guatemala City, 1857

	New Cases	Deaths	Percent of deaths to Cases	Average no. of deaths per day
8–24 July	74	38	51.4	2.4
24–30 July	251	98	39.0	16.3
30 July–31 Aug.	2,228	950	42.6	29.7
1 Sept.–1 Oct.	180	104	57.8	3.5
Totals	2,733	1,190	43.5	14.2

Sources: El Museo Guatemalteco, 31 July–2 Sept. 1857; Gaceta de Guatemala, 23 Aug.–7 Oct. 1857.

Other prominent members of the capital's elite met the same fate. J. Antonio Larrave, a leading attorney and major figure in the Economic Society and the Colegio de Abogados died the day before the first lady. Surgeon General Quirino Flores, the principal doctor in the city for many years, died two days after Doña Petrona. Others included Manuel J. Durán (1785–1857), a Salvadoran who had come to Guatemala at an early age and had served as director of revenues of Guatemala since 1845; Lic. Juan Bautista Asturias (1774–1857), one of the wealthiest men in the country, a lawyer by training, but a merchant by vocation; Manuel Yela, another prominent merchant; Benedicto Saenz, the cathedral organist and one of the most talented musicians in Central America; several other well-known musicians; and the U.S. minister, William E. Venable, who reportedly had been sick ever since his departure from New York and, therefore, had never been able to present his credentials to Carrera. One consequence of the epidemic was the large number of new appointments the president had to make before the end of the year to replace those who had died.[79]

There were uprisings in eastern Guatemala among peasants who believed the water was poisoned, reminiscent of the revolt of 1837. Carrera left the capital on 1 September and personally supervised the round-up of rebels around Santa Rosa and Mataquescuintla, successfully ending that threat. By the end of September the epidemic had receded in central and eastern Guatemala, but it reached major proportions in the western highlands. Cuilco, in the Department of Huehuetenango, was especially hard hit, reporting two hundred cases in the first two weeks of September, with seventy-seven deaths. The corregidor of Sololá reported 803 dead in that department during the first two weeks of October.[80]

The first major event to go on as planned following the epidemic was the great annual fair at Esquipulas in January 1858. Especially large numbers attended, not only from Guatemala, but also from Honduras and El Salvador, perhaps because of the restoration of peace and end of the epidemic. The shrine of the black Christ at Esquipulas was the most important religious site in Central America and always attracted large crowds, but in recent years it had become commercially important as well as a trade fair near the intersection of the three western Central American states. Woollen cloth sold especially well in 1858, along with a variety of foreign goods. There was a shortage of livestock, however, causing abnormally high prices. The crowds attending the fair and the substandard sanitary conditions associated with it led to a recurrence of the cholera in that region. Although it was not nearly so serious as the 1857 epidemic, it was enough to cause concern. An English doctor residing at Esquipulas, Dr. Henry D. Ellery, was credited with checking the epidemic and minimizing its destructiveness.[81]

The uprisings around Santa Rosa stemming from the cholera epidemic had been subdued by the end of October 1857, but the montaña continued to be a restless area and required occasional repressive forays by Carrera's forces. They were less serious than earlier, and the political involvement of liberals operating from Honduras and El Salvador had declined. Much of the disorder that occurred after 1857 in eastern Guatemala could be classified as banditry rather than political agitation.[82]

Following the war in Nicaragua, however, Carrera maintained a standing army considerably larger than before the war and he required all men in the capital between the ages of fifteen and fifty to enlist in the reserve militia battalions. Many exemptions were allowed, and compliance was never complete, but the penalty of conscription into the regular force for those who failed to enlist in the reserves was one way that Carrera's government maintained a flow of recruits into the army.[83]

The National Campaign and the epidemic that followed had been costly to Guatemala in lives and resources. Yet the postwar period brought a degree of peace and prosperity that had not been known since colonial times. Control of the country by the small conservative elite of the capital in collaboration with the caudillo and his army had been consolidated and the war had vindicated Carrera's military strength. But liberalism would not die, and before long its resurgence in the neighboring states would again affect Guatemala.

CHAPTER FOURTEEN

The Pax Carrera

THE DEFEAT OF THE FILIBUSTERS in Nicaragua ushered in several years of relative stability and peace in Central America, in which Rafael Carrera was the most powerful caudillo on the isthmus. The conservatives enjoyed their most secure tenure in the nineteenth century, lasting until 1893 in Nicaragua and until 1871 in Guatemala. Elsewhere, where liberal resurgence occurred more quickly, Carrera took steps to check its return to power. Thus, although the late 1850s and early 1860s appear more stable than the earlier years, they were not without conflict, civil disorder, and warfare in Central America. But recognizing Guatemala as essentially a monarchy that had applied the authority necessary to bring order to the country, European observers often praised Carrera's regime as one of the most orderly in Latin America and suggested that other Latin American states might well follow the Guatemalan example.[1]

Upon the conclusion of the Nicaraguan war, Carrera's power was absolute, although he depended heavily upon the educated and prosperous conservative elite who ran the government and the economy. In a series of articles at that point, José Milla emphasized Guatemala's stability and the absence of the political intrigue that characterized less authoritarian countries. He attacked parliamentary systems where the government simply carried out the will of a legislature that he regarded as "irresponsible in fact and in law." The public looked for someone to blame for the injustices, the incompetence, and the failures, Milla charged, "and that system resulted in no one taking the blame for anything. The executive and his ministers blamed the Constitution and the laws, which tied their hands, or the Congresses which wouldn't let them govern." But, he declared, "today that doesn't happen. The government has the power for everything and is responsible for its actions. It neither flees responsibility nor shuns the judgment of public opinion, nor tries to blame others for what corresponds to itself." This made Guatemala unique in Spanish America. Guatemala, he claimed, was ruled on the basis of public confidence rather than violence. If the masses were discontented they would rebel, but instead they enjoyed increasing prosperity. Milla also pursued the argument that the form of government was of considerably less importance than its dedication to "real" progress and to carrying out the will of the people. He went on at length comparing the governments of Russia, Great Britain, the United States, and Chile, which in spite of exterior differences, all had a "conservative spirit and maintain the peculiar structure of their societies."[2]

The *Gaceta de Guatemala* had a virtual monopoly on news reporting and analysis in Guatemala, with tight government censorship and a generally negative attitude toward other newspapers. The government did not altogether prohibit them, however, and occasionally independent papers and pamphlets appeared and were allowed to exist as long as they did not criticize directly the government or the church. The liberal 1845 free press act had been under suspension since 25 May 1849, but on 30 April 1852 Carrera revoked it altogether with a decree designed to "suppress the abuses that are committed by means of the press." This decree declared that no one could use any printing press without permission of the government and without posting a bond of from five hundred to two thousand pesos, the amount to be determined by the government, which could confiscate the press if these rules were not observed. Moreover, the editor of any periodical had to post a bond of a quantity unspecified in the decree, but to be determined in each case by the government as equal to the responsibility involved. Owners or directors of printing presses were prohibited from printing anything, signed or unsigned, subversive, seditious, or contrary to the honor or reputation of any person, under penalty of six months to a year in prison or a fine of five hundred to one thousand pesos. No publication could circulate without the approval of the authorities, and two copies of any publication had to be submitted to the Ministry of the Interior for approval.[3]

It was under such restricted conditions that Luciano Luna solicited permission to begin publication of *El Museo Guatemalteco* on 15 October 1856. The *Gaceta*, the country's only newspaper at that moment, had just published a lengthy series of essays attacking the work of the French anarchist,

Pierre Joseph Proudhon (1809–65).[4] Although Luna was known to have liberal connections, his petition assured the interior minister that the *Museo* would be solely for the purpose of publishing certain works of recognized usefulness and that it would be "completely apart from politics." It would contain some "extracts of foreign news," but only to supplement the limited foreign coverage in the *Gaceta*. He offered his printing press, at a value of $1,000, as bond as required under the 1852 press law. Less than a week later the government approved the petition and, after first demanding a thousand-peso cash bond, it subsequently accepted the lien on the press in lieu of cash.[5]

Early issues of the *Museo* were innocuous enough, emphasizing Guatemalan history and literature. Published on Thursdays and selling for two reales (25 cents), it included a lot of poetry, literary articles, and a "Cedulario" section (an organized index of royal orders sent to the Audiencia of Guatemala from 1600 to 1806). Records of the first Guatemala City Council from 1524–30 also appeared, transcribed from the archival records by Rafael Arévalo, a frequent author in the new periodical. Even its only rival, the *Gaceta*, gave it a good review in early December.[6] In his first editorial, Luna disclaimed any intention to publish on political affairs, describing the venture as a purely literary journal to print prose, poetry and historical items of interest from the archives.[7] Yet articles on politics eventually appeared, albeit for the first thirty-three issues the paper was scrupulously careful to say nothing that could even remotely be interpreted as criticism of the government.

Then, on 19 June 1857, with the war over and euphoria dominating the country, an article by the leading resident liberal, Miguel García Granados, broke the political silence. The article revived the issue of federal union and attributed the filibusters' ability to come into Central America and take over a state to the failure of reunification. He said that disunion had increased the cost of government, and he made an eloquent statement on the impotence of small warring states against external aggression. He ridiculed the emergence of separate Central American states "with the pompous names of sovereign and independent republics." He argued that the first thing Central America must do was to organize a national government with sufficient funding to assure its development and strong enough to maintain internal peace and to defend the country from foreign enemies. "May these five sick and disjointed members, reunited in a single body so that the same blood circulates throughout it, recover their health and acquire new life," he pleaded. Then "the obstacles will disappear, the revenue system can be improved." He went on, "The expenses of administration will be proportionally less, immigration will be developed without compromising our independence, the army will be organized and give respectability to the country, and finally, we will be numbered among the civilized nations." The future leader of the Liberal Reforma of 1871 thus laid out the liberal goals, and while he did not directly attack the Carrera government, his rejection of the conservative, states-rights policy was obvious.[8] García Granados had been born in Spain but came to Guatemala as an infant with his parents near the end of the colonial period. Educated in the United States, England, and Europe, he had returned to Guatemala with liberal ideological tendencies but nevertheless accepted a commission in the conservative Guatemalan army during the Civil War of 1826–29. His family suffered considerable confiscation of property when the liberals triumphed. He went into exile in Chiapas, but returned to witness the rise of Carrera, whom he opposed, and from that time on championed the cause of liberalism. He was one of the few liberals who were able to continue a political career within Guatemala during the Carrera years. He would become an important link between liberals of the early independence period and the neo-liberals of the late nineteenth century in Central America.[9]

In the triumphant atmosphere after the victory in Nicaragua, García Granados's article was not challenged. All Guatemala soon thereafter became preoccupied with the cholera epidemic, but in September the *Museo* became bolder. Except for the García Granados article and a few others dealing with the war in Nicaragua and Gerardo Barrios's revolt in June of 1857 in El Salvador, the *Museo* had refrained from politics. Its silence on political matters stood in sharp contrast to the *Gaceta*'s constant adulation of Carrera. The *Museo* had not even mentioned the death of Carrera's wife. In September 1857, however, the *Museo* began to take great interest in Barrios's rise to power in El Salvador, publishing his manifestos and defending his positions.[10] On 12 September, Luna inaugurated a "Political Section." Its first article was a reprint of an article by "J.P." from the *Gaceta Oficial de Nicaragua* entitled "The People Who Want To Be Free Are Invincible." As García Granados had done in June, it emphasized the need for Central American unity to defeat filibustering attacks. On 2 October the *Museo* published a letter from Barrios that the official *Gaceta de El Salvador* had refused to publish. The letter defended his actions in June against General Belloso, whom Barrios claimed was plotting a revolution against the Salvadoran government.

This increased political coverage, especially as the *Museo* began to side against the Salvadoran conservative government of Rafael Campos, brought the axe down on the newspaper on 10 October, when the government suspended its publication. Although it appeared irregularly again between March 1858 and February 1859, it ceased to be a political force. In October of 1861, however, Manuel Pérez de Lasala received permission from the government to begin it again under a different name, *El Noticioso de Guatemala*. After its first nine numbers, in December of that year, the *Gaceta* commended the *Noticioso*.[11] But a little more than a year later the government withdrew the permission, charging that the editor had failed to honor his promise to confine the paper to commerce, literature, industry, and agriculture. Instead, the order of 4 November 1862, signed by Interior Minister Manuel Echeverría, charged that the paper had made "inconvenient comments respecting political affairs in other countries, and improper allusions on some points of internal economy and politics."

Four days later the *Gaceta de Guatemala* defended the suppression in a particularly insensitive and haughty manner, pointing out that there had been sixty-four or sixty-five newspapers published in Guatemala since 1820, with a great many during times of political excitement, yet the public remembered the names of no more than two or three of them. It emphasized the need for the responsibility of a newspaper to tell exactly the truth and not to exaggerate. Moreover, it added, few people could read in Guatemala. Papers such as *El Noticioso*, it implied, had little other purpose than to promote revolution and chaos.[12]

A *Biblioteca Centro-Americana* had begun publishing under the direction of Miguel Boada Balmes in 1858, but it kept scrupulously away from political criticism, contenting itself with poetry, literature, biography, and a section on ancient and modern morals. Well within the permissible parameters of publishing in the regime, the thirty-two-page journal formally dedicated itself to Rafael Carrera. This journal did not long survive, however, apparently unable to attract a sufficient clientele.[13] Similarly, an innocuous *Hoja de Avisos* began publication in late 1861, reportedly edited by youths who "demonstrated the praiseworthy desire to express their good dispositions." Its few issues suffered no government criticism, but it did not long survive.[14]

Thus the *Gaceta* remained the principal publication in the country, its literature section including reprints and translations from conservative and romantic European writers. In this ambience, the *Gaceta* declared on 6 May 1860 that the level of journalism in Central America had improved notably over an earlier period, a result of the decline in "the intensity of political passions," with attention directed in general "toward more noble and elevated objects." The calmer, more moderate discussions of both local and foreign issues, Pepe Milla regarded as a healthy sign.[15] Milla himself founded an independent weekly, *La Semana*, on 1 January 1864, which offered additional literature and commentary, but still strictly along conservative lines.

For three years following the war in Nicaragua, Carrera consolidated his authority amid a sense of modest prosperity in the country. He traveled widely over the country, settling disputes, adjudicating land claims, maintaining his close touch with the common people, and making certain administrative adjustments in personnel and structure. As late as 1858 he was still leading occasional forays against the montaña rebels, but in general things were going well politically, as his letter to Chepita Silva in September of that year on fine French stationery explained. The war would soon be over, so that they would once more be able to enjoy themselves together. "It's necessary to know how to live and to take advantage of the best pleasures during one's life," he added, "for it is very short." [16] The assembly met dutifully each year and passed such legislation as he recommended, applauding his continued maintenance of peace and economic growth. [17]

Carrera himself had matured and learned the ways of gentlemen, although he modestly rode a favorite black mule to his office in the capital. Still, he presented a quite different figure than that of the angry swineherd who had led the 1837 revolt. An incident involving Carrera and Manuel Arzú Batres, who had earlier served as a personal secretary to Carrera, occurred near the end of December 1860. It illustrates something both of Carrera's charisma and maturity by that date. President Carrera arrived at a ball at about 9:00 P.M., correctly dressed in a black frock. As was his custom, he chatted with the ladies and participated in the dancing, a scene that must have reflected the transition from guerrilla leader to autocratic monarch as graphically as anything. In the midst of this festive scene, Arzú, who had been drinking heavily, suddenly began to shout insults toward General Carrera. His friends tried to calm him down, but the inebriated Arzú, his anger rising, continued to launch a shower of insults on the president. Everyone present expected Carrera to order him to jail, or worse, but the general controlled his wrath, and calmly addressed Arzú: "Tomorrow I shall send you my seconds, so that this matter may have its appropriate solution, as among men of honor." He then turned away and engaged the wife of the Dutch envoy in conversation. Unruffled by the incident, he remained at the party throughout the evening.

In the morning, on a field near the capital, the two men and their seconds met and agreed to pistols before mutual friends persuaded them to abandon their duel. Neither Arzú nor Carrera were men to back down easily in the face of danger, but Arzú himself was embarrassed by his drunken behavior the previous evening. He thus offered Carrera an apology before everyone, indicating that he was unaccustomed to wine and that it had gone to his head. General Carrera graciously accepted the apology and shook Arzú's hand, saying, "We are friends as always. At the next ball, Don Manuel, I shall serve you sugar water!"[18]

Carrera's foreign relations aimed at maintaining peace on the isthmus through support of conservative governments. Guardiola in Honduras, Campos in El Salvador, Martínez in Nicaragua, and Mora in Costa Rica all enjoyed his friendship and encouragement. The *Gaceta* reflected the Guatemalan position in an endorsement of Rafael Campos at the conclusion of his term on 1 February 1858, when it observed that "fortunately, in El Salvador as in the other republics, political parties are daily losing more of their significance." Of Campos's successor, Miguel Santín, it concluded that he had been put in office by the agreement of honorable men of different factions, and whether or not he was a liberal made no difference; what was important was that he was a "man of goodness" and his election is a "step toward peace and order, a guarantee that El Salvador, under the new administration, will not abandon the system that has begun to produce such advantageous results."[19]

The Carrera government received cordially, but without enthusiasm, a Nicaraguan initiative in April 1858 proposing a Central American summit conference to discuss reunification.[20] The continued filibustering intrigues of Walker and others was a factor promoting unity, but the practical details of organization and the reluctance to surrender real authority at the state level remained serious obstacles. The Guatemalan government invited the heads of state to convene in Guatemala in November of that year on Mora's suggestion. Arrangements could not be completed in time, however, and although there continued to be discussions in support of the idea, especially in the three middle states, the overthrow of Mora in Costa Rica and the emergence of a liberal government in El Salvador in 1859 diverted attention away from unionist proposals.[21]

Guatemala's relations with nations beyond the isthmus improved steadily during the years following the National Campaign. Even with the United States a more cordial relationship developed, in part owing to Carrera's efforts to improve Guatemala's foreign relations, but also owing to the efforts of James Buchanan's ministers in Guatemala. Although his tenure in Guatemala was short, Beverly L. Clarke was especially effective in diminishing the fear of North American aggression that the early 1850s had engendered.[22]

In December 1858 Carrera sent José Milla on a special mission to the United States. Milla met with Buchanan and Secretary of State Lewis Cass just before Christmas. He remained in the United States for several weeks, not returning to Guatemala until late March of the following year.[23] In addition to his role as editor of the *Gaceta*, Milla was now serving as undersecretary and chief of staff of the Ministry of Foreign Relations. Buchanan favored reunification under the liberals, but he was willing to encourage it among conservative governments as well. Following Mora's ouster in Costa Rica, Buchanan had secretly offered Mora support in a scheme to make him president of a restored Central American federation. Mora refused, however, stating that he believed reunion would not be in the best interests of Costa Rica.[24]

Appointment of skillful diplomats by both Guatemala and the United States contributed to improved relations between the two republics. Fear of filibusterism was rekindled after Walker's ill-fated expedition to Honduras in 1860. A shipload of Americans aboard the *Mercedes,* which came to Belize and the Mosquito Coast early in 1861, especially alarmed Guatemalans. But the outbreak of the War Between the States in North America diminished the likelihood of new filibustering expeditions, and subsequently Guatemala's war with El Salvador diverted attention from such threats.

Abraham Lincoln appointed E. O. Crosby as his minister to Guatemala in March 1861. Crosby arrived in Guatemala in May and successfully cemented relations between Guatemala and the Union government. A new mail contract provided for regular mail service between the two countries beginning in July 1862, with direct service from New York and San Francisco to Puerto San José. The filibustering threats had come from the U.S. South, and many of the Guatemalan leaders, according to Crosby, believed the southerners to be "very aggressive and unscrupulous in their means of acquiring territory." Thus Carrera's government refused to recognize the Confederacy and prohibited, at Crosby's request, supplies being sent to the Confederates from Guatemalan ports.[25]

In 1862 Lincoln suggested a plan to settle emancipated slaves in Central America, following up earlier proposals by U.S. officials regarding settlement of blacks in Mexico. At a U.S. Independence Day party given by the American minister in Guatemala, Crosby mentioned the idea to Carrera. Carrera initially showed enthusiasm for the idea and even offered one of his own properties on the Pacific Coast as a site for black immigrants, but he ultimately rejected colonization of the former slaves, fearing that they would not be easily assimilated by the native population and might constitute a serious threat to native customs and institutions. Crosby had hoped such colonization might be a way to check British influence in Belize and was undoubtedly sounding out the Guatemalans on behalf of the Lincoln government.[26]

Antonio José Irisarri informed Secretary of State William Seward in August that former U.S. slaves could not be colonized in Central America without government permission. He referred to widespread discussion of the project in U.S. newspapers and formally notified the U.S. government that the two states he represented (El Salvador and Guatemala) would permit no colonization of "any species of foreigners, black or white, or of any other color, without special permission from the respective governments." Seward replied stuffily that Lincoln's statements regarding sending ex-slaves to Central America had been made to a group of private individuals, as reported in the newspaper, and did not constitute any sort of formal policy or project to establish colonies in Central America. But he added that the president had authorized him to inform Sr. Irisarri that if the U.S. government did decide to effect such a settlement in some foreign country, the first step would be to ask freely and openly the consent of the government of that country and that the project would be abandoned if such consent was not given. Irisarri responded testily that he was not trying to conduct diplomacy via newspaper articles, but only making it clear that such projects would be viewed unfavorably by the Guatemalan and Salvadoran governments. He continued, "The colonists that are wanted, as in the United States, are of a different class, having had a more liberal education than that acquired in a state of slavery." He also sent along a statement recently received from the foreign minister of Nicaragua echoing this view. Seward promptly reiterated his assurance that there would be no colonization effort without full consent of the governments concerned, and no such projects would be proposed for Guatemala or El Salvador.[27]

Ironically, toward the end of the war, a number of white southern expatriates came to Guatemala and were welcomed.[28] Among them, two French Louisianans—Auguste Fraustor and Leclaire Fuselier—in 1866 received large land grants from the local corregidor for the production of sugar and coffee around the mouth of the Río Motagua. The government in Guatemala City temporarily delayed these grants, but by the end of the year it had confirmed them. Another ex-Confederate, however, August B. Larmer (Lamar?), was denied his claim to public land in the region because it infringed on the needs of the town of Livingston.[29]

Guatemalan relations with Great Britain under the conservatives were usually cordial, especially when compared to Britain's relations with the middle states. British diplomats following Frederick Chatfield's long tenure in Central America continued to promote the close trade relations between Britain and Guatemala, but there were some points of difference between them. Most notable of the disputes was the Guatemalan claim to the British settlement at Belize.

Belize had never been occupied by Spain or Guatemala, although early exploratory expeditions in the sixteenth century gave Spain a claim on the area, which Guatemala argued it had inherited. Moreover, the British had acknowledged Spanish sovereignty in treaties of 1783 and 1786 in return for an end to hostilities with Spain and Spanish recognition of the right of British subjects to settle and cut the valuable hardwoods at Belize. British settlement had begun in the mid-seventeenth century, first as a buccaneering establishment and then as a log-cutting center. It had never been formally incorporated as British territory, but was loosely governed by local inhabitants, increasingly with the assistance of the British government at Jamaica. In the eighteenth century it became the major point of British contraband trade with Central America, and with the independence of Central America in the nineteenth century it emerged as the principal entrepôt for British commercial penetration of the isthmus. British commercial houses established themselves at Belize and developed a brisk trade with the Caribbean ports of Guatemala, Honduras, and Nicaragua.[30]

The Guatemalan claim had been made by the liberals, but without success. The Carrera government had not pressed the claim, although protests were occasionally lodged over British expansion on the Caribbean Coast. On the other hand, the Carrera government did maintain a consul at Belize to look after Guatemalan interests. The dominant position of Belize in Guatemalan trade during the first half of the nineteenth century faded rapidly, however, after the completion of the Panama Railway in 1855, allowing Guatemalan commerce to flow more economically through its Pacific coast ports. Belize began a long decline, which in some ways continues to the present.[31]

The Caste War in Yucatán worried both the Belizean and Guatemalan governments. Refugees from that destructive Indian uprising spilled into Guatemala and Belize, and the superintendent at Belize, Frederick R. Seymour, at one point feared that Carrera was trying to foment Indian uprisings all across Central America in sympathy with the Yucatecan Maya. At the very least, the Caste War contributed to a Belizean desire for closer cooperation with Guatemala.[32]

Under the Clayton-Bulwer Treaty, the British had agreed to remove their fortifications and settlements on the eastern coast of Central America, but they chose to interpret the treaty as not including the Belize settlement, which had existed since the middle of the seventeenth century. The British made a sincere effort to settle their differences with the Central American states regarding territorial rights, however, and they negotiated several treaties in the late 1850s toward this end. They withdrew from the Mosquito Coast of Nicaragua and at least began negotiations that would much later lead to Nicaraguan sovereignty over that coast. They returned the Bay Islands to Honduras, much to the disgust of the residents of those islands, who went so far as to negotiate with William Walker in an effort to stave off Honduran occupation. And they signed a treaty with Guatemala regarding sovereignty in Belize, a treaty that has clouded the issue ever since and from a Guatemalan point of view has often been regarded as a major mistake by the conservative government.

Guatemala's foreign minister, Pedro Aycinena, had strived to maintain cordial relations with Great Britain and was something of an Anglophile himself. An interesting exchange of communications between the British Consul in Guatemala, Charles Lennox Wyke, and Aycinena in early 1859 reflects the nature of their relationship. Wyke argued that children of British subjects in Guatemala should be exempted from military service, since they were British subjects by virtue of their parents. Aycinena emphasized that they were also Guatemalan citizens by virtue of their birth on Guatemalan soil and therefore subject to the obligations of Guatemalan citizenship. But Aycinena recognized the concern of the British and wished to allay their fears. He assured Wyke of his government's desire to guarantee foreigners complete confidence and security in their dealings, and to their children—Guatemalans by birth—a satisfactory social situation. But, he apologized, he "could not vainly promise to offer them in our new and still insufficiently stable country an existence so exempt from every burden and inconvenience as the children of Guatemalans enjoy in the British dominions, elevated over the course of the centuries to the highest grade of civilization and perfection possible." And in the end Carrera agreed that children of British subjects under age twenty-one were exempt from military service, and at any age they were permitted to provide a substitute, a common means of evading military service for the children of the elite in nineteenth-century Guatemala.[33] This exchange occurred during the negotiations over the Belize treaty, signed by Aycinena and Wyke on 30 April 1859.

The controversial Wyke-Aycinena Treaty of 1859 had two parts. The first six articles dealt with definitions, survey, and enforcement of the Guatemala-Belize boundary. In general, Guatemala recognized British sovereignty within a boundary that extended along the Río Sarstún from its mouth to Gracias a Dios Falls, then north to Garbutt's Falls, on the Belize River, and from that point north to the Mexican border. Each nation was to appoint a boundary commissioner within a year. Waterways on the border were open to free navigation by both parties. Article 7 provided for the building of a road from Guatemala City to the Caribbean Coast, but the details were exceedingly vague and led to difficulties later when the Guatemalans disagreed with the British as to the proper location for the road. After the liberals came to power and the British failed to build the road, the Guatemalans abrogated the treaty, and the dispute over sovereignty in Belize smolders to the present day.[34]

Carrera, who had opposed ceding the Guatemalan claim to Belize, signed the treaty the very next day, constituting Guatemalan ratification. Wyke, in a letter to the earl of Malmsbury emphasized the necessity of helping the Guatemalans build the road in order to persuade the caudillo to ratify the treaty and, further, that such a road would help Britain to regain some of the commerce it was losing to the Pacific trade and U.S. shipping.[35] Wyke left Guatemala City on 2 May to catch the English packet at Izabal with the intention of gaining ratification in London personally and leaving British merchant William Hall in Guatemala as acting consul general. Wyke returned, with the ratification, to Guatemala on 26 September 1859.[36]

Beverly Clarke immediately protested the treaty as a violation of the Clayton-Bulwer Treaty, but Guatemala coolly rejected the protest.[37] The Department of State did not follow up Clarke's protest, emphasizing instead Britain's efforts to resolve the remaining obstacles to compliance with Clayton-Bulwer by treaties with the Central American states.[38] A few days later the long-time U.S. consul in Guatemala City, Henry Savage, gave a dinner party honoring Wyke, who was staying at his house. Savage suggested that the Anglo-American rivalry was not a social problem in Guatemala at least. Dignitaries present included government ministers, Bishops Aycinena and Piñol, José Milla, several councilors of state, and other diplomats, but Carrera was conspicuous in his absence, pleading that the press of work prevented him from attending.[39]

When the assembly convened at the end of the year, there was some opposition to the treaty, but opponents failed to muster enough strength to challenge the caudillo's ratification and were defeated when the matter was brought to a vote on 10 December. In the end, the assembly's resolution, presented to Carrera on 17 December, congratulated him for bringing to an end "an old and embarrassing dispute" and approved the stipulation that the two governments would cooperate in opening a good road between the capital and the Caribbean coast. The assembly formally approved Carrera's ratification of the treaty by a vote of 21 to 12 on 30 January 1860.[40]

The boundary commission worked several years surveying the precise boundary under difficult climatic conditions, but in 1862 the British formally established British Honduras as a crown colony, naming Frederick Seymour, superintendent of the settlement since 1857, as its first lieutenant governor. For the remainder of the conservative years relations remained cordial with the British, but there was little progress on the road. At the center of the difficulty lay the British intention to build the road to the port of Belize, while Guatemalans wanted the road to go to its own port on the Gulf of Honduras. Economically British Honduras continued its decline. It also began to shift toward economic dependence on New Orleans rather than Jamaica.[41]

Although the conservatives restored Hispanic institutions and welcomed Spanish subjects, there remained a legacy of broken relations between the republic and her former mother country. Spain had not accepted the independence of Latin America with good grace and had attempted by both diplomatic and military means to recover her former empire. The Central Americans had repulsed rather easily a pro-Spanish invasion of the Caribbean Coast from Cuba in 1832, but Spanish reconquest efforts in Mexico kept Central Americans wary. Moreover, financial claims remained unresolved and Spanish subjects in Guatemala were sometimes inconvenienced by their lack of diplomatic representation there.

The accession of strong conservative rule after 1850, however, coincided with a willingness on the part of the government of Isabella II to recognize the Central American states and to negotiate treaties of friendship and commerce. Felipe Molina, a native of Guatemala but representing Costa Rica in Madrid, negotiated in April 1850 the first treaty of recognition by Spain with a Central American state soon after Rafael Mora came to power. This treaty, ratified on 6 March 1851, was quickly followed by a similar one recognizing Nicaragua.[42]

The new Spanish chargé d'affaires to Costa Rica and Nicaragua, José Zambrano, visited Guatemala in October 1852. Pedro Aycinena entered serious negotiations with the Spanish diplomat the following May, but no immediate agreement was forthcoming.[43] Following the National Campaign negotiations resumed when Zambrano again visited Guatemala for that purpose in July 1857. He succeeded in signing a treaty with El Salvador in September of that year, although ratification was delayed for several years.[44] Meanwhile, Honduras agreed to a most-favored-nations treaty with Spain in 1859.[45] Confidential negotiations continued between

Aycinena and Zambrano, who returned to Guatemala the following year. The Spanish desire for better tariff treatment than the Guatemalans were willing to yield and differences over questions of the nationality of children delayed an agreement, but it was clear that Guatemala was anxious to conclude a treaty.[46] In 1861, for example, there was a general outcry against Spain from the American republics over the Spanish reannexation of Santo Domingo. The Guatemalan official gazette approved the act, "given the circumstances and difficulties they have had there," and regarded it as consistent with continued Spanish rule in Cuba and Puerto Rico.[47]

The treaty finally signed in Madrid on 29 May 1863 was negotiated by Felipe Neri de Barrio and the marquis of Miraflores. The Guatemalan view regarding citizenship, that the laws of each country should determine the matter in their respective countries, prevailed, while Guatemala made trade concessions. The treaty confirmed Guatemalan assumption of 30 percent of the debt of the Kingdom of Guatemala and guaranteed Spaniards protection of their property under the law and a most-favored-nation clause for the commerce of both nations.[48] Isabella followed up the exchange of ratifications by naming Carrera Caballero Gran Cruz de la Real y Distinguida Orden de Carlos III.[49]

Despite the adversities of the 1850s, then, Guatemala ended the decade with optimism and confidence of growing economic prosperity and political stability. A festive celebration in the Guatemalan capital accompanied the twentieth anniversary of Carrera's capture of Guatemala City in 1839. The *Gaceta* commemorated that event by reviewing his rise to power from humble origins to restore peace, order, and prosperity to the state. "No other Hispanic American state had a similar history," it declared. Bolívar, Iturbide, Flores (Ecuador), and Rosas all lost their popularity and fell, but Carrera had endured to establish order, peace, prosperity, good foreign relations, and moral and material improvement. It repeated the conservative argument that the old parties (liberal and conservative) were losing their significance, being replaced by "a single political community, whose members, if they may dissent on some minor points, agree generally on the necessity of preserving the gains that have patiently been achieved over the narrow attitudes of routine and exaggeration. All these benefits and many more," it concluded, they owed to the chief that had "put himself at the head of our fractured republic on 13 April 1839."[50] Such adulation was repeated with increasing pomp—including balls, parades, and fireworks—on each of his succeeding birthdays (24 October).

Carrera's long rule had, in fact, begun to bear fruit in terms of the state's economy. Guatemala had achieved real economic growth, as will

Guatemala about 1860

be detailed later, and although Carrera had done little to improve the lot of most of the people, he had arrested efforts to exploit their land and labor. Furthermore, he had at least brought an end to the warfare and civil strife that had characterized Guatemala from 1825 to 1850. True, much of his administration had been spent at war, but most of the fighting had been beyond the frontiers of Guatemala. Friendly relations with Britain had brought what seemed at the time to be a satisfactory settlement of the Belize question, and in 1860 a team of British engineers began surveying the promised carriageway to the Caribbean Coast. He believed he had checked Mexican expansionism on his western frontier. He finally concluded in 1863 a treaty with Spain, and if his relations with the United States were less cordial, he had participated in successfully resisting the major Yankee incursion onto the isthmus. With generally loyal governments in Honduras and El Salvador, he intervened, nevertheless, whenever he feared liberal uprisings, as in 1859 when he stopped Salvadoran exiles from using Honduras as a base against the San Salvador regime.[51] As the decade of 1860 opened, Guatemala appeared to have achieved a political structure consistent with its colonial past and acceptable to a large majority of its population. That it was an authoritarian, intellectually stifling dictatorship, no one denied, but there was little sign that the liberal opposition could challenge it in the foreseeable future.

CHAPTER FIFTEEN

El Salvador

THE CONSERVATIVES IN CENTRAL AMERICA could not forever hold out against liberal resurgence. The moderate Rafael Mora had fallen already to a coup in 1859, an act that the Guatemalan government deplored as "an illegal and inexcusable act." Mora met with Carrera in Guatemala after going into exile on 11 February 1860.[1] Subsequently, Mora organized a force and returned to Costa Rica, but he met defeat at La Angostura on 28 September, and two days later he died before a firing squad. The governments that succeeded him appeared to continue conservative domination there, but in reality they were a transition to the liberal dictatorship of Tomás Guardia that began in 1870.[2]

But San Salvador was traditionally the liberal stronghold, and it was there that Carrera and his allies faced a more serious challenge. Gerardo Barrios had never been completely acceptable to the conservatives, although he had opportunistically cooperated with the stronger conservative forces and he had been an important commander in the campaign against Walker. Upon his return from Nicaragua, however, he involved himself in growing political intrigue. In June 1857 he failed in an attempted coup, but he gained influence in 1858 under the government of Miguel Santín de Castillo. In June of 1858 he overthrew Santín in a bloodless coup and served as acting president until September, when he returned the presidency to Santín, although keeping the real political power himself through control of the military.[3] Barrios immediately moved the capital back to San Salvador from Cojutepeque, where it had been since the earthquake of 1854, arguing that the city was sufficiently rebuilt.[4] During that period he remained nominally allied to Carrera, who sent him a "Cross of Honor" for his service in Nicaragua in July 1858. In August, however, he defiantly ordered the remains of Francisco Morazán brought to San Salvador, where they were reburied with state honors.[5] When Santín stepped down because of ill health, Barrios took over the executive power again in March 1859.[6] Carrera actually aided him by persuading Honduran President Santos Guardiola not to encourage Salvadoran exiles to use Honduran territory in efforts to oust Barrios. And he sent General Cerna to Comayagua in July 1859 to mediate the dispute between Honduras and El Salvador.[7] On 1 February 1860 the Salvadoran legislature confirmed Barrios as president, declaring him popularly elected for a term of six years and giving him the title of captain general. Barrios promised conservative policies, emphasizing order, progress, liberty, and good relations with Salvador's neighbors.[8]

Carrera congratulated Barrios on 7 February in a letter that recognized "his labor on behalf of order and progress."[9] In mid-1860 peace reigned throughout the isthmus, and the *Gaceta de Guatemala* observed that "at last the time had arrived when it was understood that the true union of the country could never be obtained by means of Congresses and even less by the use of force." The *Gaceta* asserted that it was now generally accepted that "peace, order, the increase of wealth through development of agriculture, commerce, and establishment of analogous political institutions, are the true means of slowly but surely moving toward that unity which, established on solid foundations, will benefit the entire country." [10]

Capitalizing on this new spirit of peace and unity, at the end of 1860 General Barrios made another extended visit to Guatemala with his wife and sister. The Salvadoran first family, accompanied by an honor guard, received a warm welcome in the Guatemalan capital on 23 December. Generals García Granados and Zavala had accompanied the entourage from Jutiapa, and there were small celebrations in the towns along the route. A delegation from the city council went out to meet the Salvadoran president and escort him to the entrance of the city. There Carrera and his ministers greeted the visitors, accompanied by two thousand troops. They paraded to the plaza as cannons fired salutes from the San José fortress. Barrios stayed at the home of his brother-in-law, Carlos Meany, now mayor of Guatemala City. At a luncheon that day, Barrios toasted the spirit of cooperation and extolled the virtues of union and concord, cementing the "perfect understanding that now bound Guatemala and El Salvador together." Carrera answered courteously, welcoming Barrios on behalf of the people and government of Guatemala, but he avoided the question of union, instead praising the order and stability that had made the visit possible. President and Mrs. Barrios joined Carrera and his daughters that evening for a performance at the theater, where the public saluted Barrios with extended applause. A painting by a Sr. Garibaldi was presented to Barrios, showing a seal between the flags of the two countries and emblems, alluding to the products of both and with the motto "Peace, Union and Prosperity." Barrios and his family returned to the theater throughout the week following. On Christmas Day a military review further honored the Salvadoran chief-of-state, and on New Year's Day 1861 Carrera honored him with a gala banquet. After spending several more days in Antigua, they finally returned to San Salvador in mid-January.[11]

Notwithstanding the great public displays of friendship and alliance with Carrera, Barrios's meetings with Miguel García Granados were doubtless more influential. Although we do not know the details of their discussions, it is likely that they discussed common liberal views and perhaps planned strategy. Barrios's visit to Guatemala was followed by a boisterous celebration commemorating the tenth anniversary of Carrera's victory at Arada (2 February), but in El Salvador Barrios began to pursue a liberal course that would make him the first of the neo-liberal dictators who would dominate Central America through most of the latter third of the nineteenth century.[12]

Beginnings of difficulties between Carrera and Barrios appeared in an exchange of letters between them in April 1861. Barrios challenged Carrera's practice of unilateral intervention and declared that El Salvador would not permit any neighboring state to intervene in Honduras. Carrera replied obstinately that he would answer any request for aid from the Honduran government because he was obliged to maintain the peace in Central America and to stop the use of revolution as a means of changing systems of government.[13] By January 1862 antagonism was manifest between the two, for Barrios had launched anticlerical reforms and criticized Carrera's efforts to defend the church in El Salvador. In November 1861 the bishop of El Salvador, Tomás Pineda Saldaña (1791–1875) and a large number of clergy fled El Salvador, refusing to take the oath of allegiance required by Barrios. They arrived in Guatemala City on 3 December.[14] Then, on 11 January 1862, an unidentified assassin cut down Honduran dictator Santos Guardiola. Although evidence was lacking, rumor blamed Barrios for the act, and Guatemalan-Salvadoran relations deteriorated further.[15] Adding to the speculation regarding Barrios's complicity was the fact that Guardiola's vice-president, Victoriano Castellanos, was in El Salvador at the time of the assassination, and he promptly concluded a military alliance with El Salvador shortly after taking office as the new president of Honduras.[16]

Carrera returned from summer vacation in Escuintla to confer with his ministers on the Honduran situation on 31 January. He chose for the time to honor his alliance with Barrios and to recognize Castellanos in the name of peace. Instructing Pedro Aycinena to issue a communique on the subject to the other Central American states, he returned to Escuintla the following morning, where he remained for several more weeks, keeping in touch with the situation in Honduras via regular messengers. Aycinena's statement warned that the assassination of Guardiola threatened the tranquility of all the states. He accused Francisco Montes, who had taken over provisionally until Castellanos returned from El Salvador, of complicity in the assassination and warned that the Guatemalan government would aid Castellanos if he encountered any resistance in assuming the presidency. A peaceful and lawful transition, Aycinena argued, was essential to all of the states in maintaining the peace and good credit abroad.[17]

There was also a high level ecclesiastical meeting in Guatemala about the first of February for, in addition to the presence of Salvadoran Bishop Pineda Saldaña, Bernardo Piñol of Nicaragua and Juan de Jesús Zepeda of Honduras had come to the Guatemalan capital to meet with Archbishop García Peláez and the other Guatemalan bishops. Soon after this conference of bishops, Piñol and Zepeda returned to their respective sees, committed to helping the Guatemalan government maintain peace in Honduras and in opposition to the anticlericalism in El Salvador.[18]

The Salvadoran foreign minister promptly denied that his government had any part in the murder of Guardiola. It announced on 10 February that those responsible had been apprehended in Honduras and were awaiting punishment. The following day, in Comayagua, a firing squad executed the six prisoners being held for the crime.[19] Whether or not Barrios had any complicity in Guardiola's murder, the event tipped the scales in favor of the liberals. The Salvadoran government made clear its support of Castellanos, and Trinidad Cabañas, who had been serving in Barrios's government in San Salvador, now returned to his native Honduras to become a minster in the new government.[20] Reports that the provisional president, José María Medina, who had succeeded Montes, would attempt to hold on to power proved to be unfounded when Medina met Castellanos at Santa Rosa, Honduras, and transferred the presidential authority on 5 March 1862.[21]

Guatemala's willingness to recognize Castellanos, a moderate liberal, suggested some tolerance. Castellanos, in his first weeks in office, was careful not to antagonize the Guatemalan caudillo. Upon receiving a unification proposal from the Nicaraguan minister, Pedro Zeledón, for example, the new Honduran foreign minister, Carlos Madrid, wrote Aycinena that he thought it not prudent to take steps toward union unilaterally. Union must

be agreed to by all five states, he said, not just two or three. His letter, nevertheless, carried the traditional liberal salutation, "D.U.L. [Dios,
Unión, Libertad]." Nicaraguan liberals, notably Máximo Jérez, were plotting with Barrios to restore the union of the three middle states, with the
hope of incorporating Guatemala and Costa Rica later. Honduran rejection
of this scheme was a victory for Carrera, as was his diplomatic achievement
in establishing a treaty of alliance with Tomás Martínez in Nicaragua.[22]
Later in the year, Carrera rejected a Honduran offer to mediate the dispute
between Guatemala and El Salvador.[23]

In the meantime, an alleged plot to assassinate Barrios aggravated the
situation soon after Guardiola's murder. Salvadoran liberals charged that
the Guatemalan government aided Salvadoran exiles in this plot. Leaders of
the alleged plot did indeed flee to Guatemala, where the Guatemalan government refused to honor the extradition treaty of 17 August 1853. They
joined in Guatemala with other Salvadoran exiles and, after organizing an
army in the Department of Jutiapa, raided Santa Ana on 1 April. Repulsed
there, they fled once more into Guatemala, where they received refuge with
Guatemalan military forces at Jutiapa.[24] Carrera denied any complicity in
this episode, and on the same day as the attack on Santa Ana he issued an
order to the corregidor of Jutiapa to suppress this sort of activity. Moreover,
on 5 April, once the invaders were safely back in Jutiapa, he gave the Salvadoran government permission to penetrate up to four leagues (about ten
miles) into Guatemalan territory when in "hot pursuit" of invaders such
as those who had attacked Santa Ana. This was said to be in reciprocity
for similar permission given to Guatemala in May 1859 by the Salvadoran
government.[25]

In late April, having returned from another extended stay with his family
in Escuintla, Carrera left the capital and went eastward to inspect the military forces there. While he was away, there was an incident in Guatemala
City that some interpreted as an attempted uprising. At about 10:00 P.M.
on 1 May, four men armed with pistols attacked the military commander
of the city, Maj. Gen. Manuel Bolaños. Although none of the shots hit
the general, he suffered injury in a struggle with one of the attackers. Two
hours later, a fire mysteriously broke out in the arsenal at the National
Palace. The fire was extinguished, but not before some powder exploded
and attracted a large crowd. Gen. Ignacio Irigoyen took over for the injured
Bolaños and a large number of arrests followed. Calm had been restored to
the city by 3 May and the episode had no other effect than to keep a certain
amount of tension in the capital rising as the situation with El Salvador
worsened.[26]

Carrera, increasingly concerned over renewed Mexican threats and anxious not to get himself involved on two fronts, continued to treat Barrios with respect, assuring him of his continued friendship and denying rumors of planned Guatemalan aggression.[27]

Carrera would not ignore Barrios's anticlericalism indefinitely, however, and when the French invasion eliminated the Mexican threat, Carrera turned his full attention to the annoying liberalism of Barrios. The Salvadoran press had launched an insulting attack on Carrera's regime, charging that Guatemalans lived under slavery while Salvadorans were enjoying increased liberty and prosperity under Barrios. An article on 20 November 1862 claimed that the majority of Salvadorans enjoyed a good standard of living owing to the disinterested and generous rule of President Barrios, who, far from profiting from his position (as did Carrera, the article implied), devoted his talent and fortune to public service. It defended Barrios's anticlericalism as nothing more than "insuring that the clergy observed the Constitution." Barrios, the article claimed, had done everything possible to maintain friendly relations with Carrera, but the Guatemalan administration had repeatedly attacked Barrios and supported Salvadoran exiles against him. It defended Barrios's refusal to be servile to Carrera, however, and said he would not be a puppet like Guardiola or former Salvadoran presidents (implying Campos and Dueñas). The article enraged the Guatemalan leader and was the final straw in committing him toward a hostile course of action.[28]

In his annual message to the House of Representatives, on 25 November 1862, Carrera noted that there had been new discussions on the possibility of reunification of the isthmus, but that none of the proposals had been acceptable to his government. The time had not yet come, he said, when they could overcome the inconveniences of separation, but the groundwork for reunion could be laid by maintaining peace and good faith with one another.[29] The House gave him a vote of confidence on his Salvadoran policy, and concurred that it was not a propitious time to launch a reunion of Central America, while expressing the hope that the peace which he had built would be maintained.[30]

Two days later, General Irigoyen, military chief of the Department of Guatemala, urged Carrera to act, "in view of the publications appearing in San Salvador."[31] Carrera hesitated, but on 4 December he broke diplomatic relations with El Salvador.[32] Informing the other Central American states of this decision, Pedro Aycinena reviewed the deterioration of relations, putting the full blame on Barrios. Guatemala, he pointed out, had consistently supported Barrios since his rise to power, noting that Barrios had made many enemies in El Salvador since then. Barrios had openly embraced the principles that guided Guatemalan policy, breaking with his old liberal ideas and the liberal party, even expelling some of the liberals, appearing to imitate the Guatemalan regime, Aycinena pointed out. He cooperated with Guatemala in putting down uprisings in the montaña. Guatemala had helped to mediate Salvadoran differences with Guardiola in Honduras, averting war between those two states, but, according to Aycinena, Barrios then began to change his policies. He pursued anticlericalism to a degree unacceptable to Guatemala. Then, in January 1862, Guardiola was assassinated. Since then, Aycinena charged, the Barrios government had meddled in Honduran affairs and the clergy had been forced to flee El Salvador.[33]

Concern over Barrios's anticlericalism was interrupted violently on 19 December by one of the more serious of Guatemala's many earthquakes. The trembling lasted nearly two minutes, and a second major shock followed the next day. The capital suffered only minor damage. However, the quake destroyed twenty-six houses in Antigua, and there was great damage in Amatitlán and in the western highlands. Damage stretched from Puerto San José to Sololá, and many communities in the departments of Sololá and Chimaltenango reported destruction of churches and homes. The government promised aid and immediately began a private donation fund, while the assembly voted a $25,000 appropriation for relief of victims.[34] The earthquake undoubtedly delayed Carrera's decision to invade El Salvador.

Barrios had responded to the rupture in diplomatic relations with a strongly worded manifesto attacking the Guatemalan regime for its interventionist policies ever since the breakup of the federation. Irigoyen again warned Carrera of the Salvadoran danger on Christmas Day and counseled the Guatemalan caudillo that if he didn't oust Barrios during the first six months of 1863, Barrios would attempt to do just that to Carrera.[35] Barrios, meanwhile, warned his assembly on 16 January that the state was imminently threatened by aggression from Guatemala.[36] The assembly gave him dictatorial authority to conduct the defense. In Guatemala, a rumor circulated that he had sent Lorenzo Montúfar on a mission to Europe to hire Swiss mercenaries to fight for El Salvador.[37]

Carrera responded with his own strong manifesto on 21 January 1863, declaring that the present situation was "intolerable" and that he "must put a stop to it."[38] The *Gaceta* justified "a defensive war" against the aggressions of the Barrios government, while denying that Barrios's liberalism was the cause of Guatemalan concern. A pamphlet published in El Salvador by the Cojutepeque City Council, on the other hand, saw the conflict precisely as a liberal-conservative struggle, and while the *Gaceta de Guatemala* went to some lengths to deny that it was merely a struggle between political parties, in retrospect, a different conclusion is hardly possible.[39]

A manifesto from Carrera to the "peoples of El Salvador" on 31 January promised them justice from the Guatemalan army, but warned them not to defend "the man who has done so much evil to your country and yourselves." A large expeditionary force paraded in Guatemala City on the anniversary of the Battle of Arada on 2 February. The archbishop blessed the troops, and Carrera took direct command of the expeditionary force on the following day, turning over the government to his first minister, Manuel Cerezo. At noon on 4 May the army marched out of the capital and up into the montaña east of the capital.[40]

Carrera's veteran force waited in Jutiapa for Generals Zavala, Cerna, and Cruz to bring up reinforcements. Then he massed Guatemalan forces on the Salvadoran border in answer to Barrios's threat to blockade Guatemala's Pacific ports.[41] He rejected a second Honduran offer to organize a mediation team from the diplomatic corps on 9 February with the excuse that he opposed intervention of foreign agents in internal affairs![42] A few days later Guatemalan troops crossed the border and occupied Chalchuapa, forcing the Salvadoran forces under Gen. Santiago González to retreat on 19 February.[43]

Carrera took Santa Ana with little resistance on the twenty-first, but then was unexpectedly repulsed at Coatepeque on the twenty-third. Carrera blamed the defeat on lack of water. In a hasty attempt to bring a speedy conclusion to the war, he had marched his troops into battle at Coatepeque for two days without food or water. They were exhausted. He lost eighty-three men and two pieces of artillery, but was able to retreat to Santa Ana. At the end of February he withdrew into Guatemalan territory.[44]

The Salvadorans were unable to follow up the victory at Coatepeque immediately, but a Salvadoran warship did begin a blockade of Puerto San José on 1 March and bombarded that port.[45] Another direct result of the defeat at Coatepeque was Honduras's decision to enter the war on the side of El Salvador. The Honduran foreign minister, in a terse note dated 3 March, reminded Aycinena of Honduras's efforts to mediate the dispute and blamed Guatemala for the war, warning that Carrera's interventionist policies, if continued, would have devastating results for Guatemala and that Honduras would now honor its alliance with El Salvador.[46]

Carrera returned to the Guatemalan capital on 6 March at the head of his army of three thousand. He had issued a statement to his army the day before, incorporating a humility not often seen in the caudillo, but accepting the defeat in good grace and promising to continue the struggle. In fact, the battle at Coatepeque had inflicted very heavy losses on the Salvadorans, preventing them from pursuing Carrera. Considerable desertions from the Salvadoran army followed, and on 15 March there was an unsuccessful attempt to unseat Barrios.[47]

The intensity of feeling between supporters of Carrera and Barrios was reflected following the battle of Coatepeque from an unlikely source. At the outset of the war, Antonio José Irisarri had represented both Guatemala and El Salvador in the United Sates. Irisarri, after inheriting a substantial fortune from his father, had been among those exiled by Morazán in 1829. He lived in Chile for some time and later migrated northward. An author of some note, he served in diplomatic posts for a number of Latin American nations, but had served his native Guatemala well in the United States for several years. Upon hearing of the outbreak of war, he wrote to the Salvadoran foreign minister, Manuel Irungaray, resigning as Salvadoran minister to the United States, believing his service to both governments to be incompatible under the circumstances. In accepting the resignation, Irungaray, also a Guatemalan, wrote a stern reply arguing that the present Guatemalan government deserved no support even from Guatemalans. After telling of the Salvadoran victory at Coatepeque, he said: "Guatemala, Sr. Minister, is not the source of so much trouble. It is a retrograde party, attempting to destroy the republican institutions, that is the author of the present evils. I, as a Guatemalan, must make this warning to the Plenipotentiary Minister of Guatemala in Washington, who has been away from the country more than thirty years, for it could be that exact news of events do not reach him."

Irisarri's eloquent response took note of each of Irungaray's points. He suggested that Barrios had not made every effort to keep the peace and had used insulting language in public. His response was an articulate defense of the Carrera regime from one who had not generally been counted among the conservative party. Irisarri argued that it was Barrios, not Carrera, who had acted in an uncivilized way. It was Barrios, not Carrera, who had failed to observe the common courtesy demanded in international relations. He pointed out that what was retrograde for one country was progressive for another, and it was not the place of the leader of one state to insult the leaders or political systems of another. From Irisarri's point of view, there was progress in Guatemala and El Salvador as long as there was peace. But that had changed when Barrios embarked on a bellicose policy that had brought war to the region. Thus, it was Barrios who was retrograde in Irisarri's view, not Carrera.[48]

Carrera quickly regrouped for a new offensive. A small force reentered El Salvador in mid-March and advanced to the vicinity of Santa Ana. On the twenty-eighth Col. Leandro Navas, corregidor of Jutiapa, routed the Salvadoran garrison at Ahuachapán. On 12 April Carrera ordered Cerna's division to occupy the plains of Santa Rosa, Honduras.[49] The conflict had now widened, with Guatemala and Nicaragua confronting Honduras and El Salvador. Costa Rica leaned toward Guatemala, although it was not actually involved in the combat. While Nicaraguan government forces neutralized the Nicaraguan liberal rebels who had been allied with Barrios, Cerna's forces checked the Hondurans. Carrera moved his forces cautiously this time, keeping most of them around Jutiapa. He returned to the capital in early May amid rumors of an impending revolt within the military to be led by Serapio Cruz. He delayed his major offensive until he could assure himself security at home.

New elections for the assembly were due, and Carrera issued the call for the departments and corporations to proceed with them. Much of the army was either in Honduras or mobilizing around Jutiapa, with smaller units continuing to apply pressure in El Salvador. General Cerna had been placed in command of the field units during Carrera's return to the capital. A division remained in the capital, however, under General Zavala, the hero of Nicaragua. Carrera had another division under his own personal command there. Carrera was ready to launch a new offensive against Barrios, but first he had to deal with Serapio Cruz.[50]

On Friday, 22 May, he went down to Escuintla for a long weekend. When he returned he had resolved to face the issue directly. On the twenty-ninth he issued a stirring manifesto to the troops announcing the beginning of the new offensive. General Zavala issued a similar call to his own division the following day, and on the thirty-first Zavala's division marched out of the capital, headed for Jutiapa.[51] Carrera met with Cruz early the next morning. They left the palace at about 7:00 A.M. and rode out in Carrera's elegant carriage to Los Arcos (today Parque Aurora), amid the ruins of the old aqueduct. There, Carrera told Cruz that he was aware of the plot and of Cruz's desire to take the presidency from him. Carrera reportedly said: "Comrade Serapio, I know perfectly well that you are plotting against me. I have all the details, names, and so forth. You want the presidency of Guatemala, naturally, and I am most disposed to leave it to you. But don't you think its shameful to provoke a fratricidal struggle to achieve power for one man? Shouldn't we avoid spilling so much blood?"

He opened a small wooden box he had brought with him, exposing two handsome dueling pistols. He looked at Cruz squarely and said: "We shall decide the presidency of Guatemala, comrade. Choose a pistol!"

Cruz refused, and instead took Carrera's hand and said, "Comrade, Serapio Cruz gives you his word of honor that he will take not one step more along that trail. I will order it all ended, and while you live I will do absolutely nothing against you. Take my hand as a friend and let us forget the past." They were the closest of friends thereafter, although perhaps there remained a grain of distrust on Carrera's part, for he would name Cerna to succeed him upon his death in 1865. Infuriated, Cruz would join the liberal revolt and die at the battle of Palencia on 23 January 1870.[52]

On 5 June Cerna moved deeper into Honduran territory, joining with allied Nicaraguan conservative forces in a major victory at Santa Rosa on 16 June that brought down the Castellanos government. The allies now recognized José María Medina, who moved the Honduran capital back to conservative Comayagua.[53]

On 7 June Carrera rode out of the capital at the head of his division to resume direction of the invasion of El Salvador. Arriving at Cerro Redondo at noon on the eighth, he wrote to Chepita, largely about business matters relating to his coffee fincas. He counted on an abundant coffee harvest and looked ahead to a speedy restoration of peace and prosperity.[54] He received news of Cerna's Santa Rosa victory after he had crossed into Salvadoran territory near Volcán Chingo on the twenty-second, and he now launched the offensive with vigor. On 28 June Zavala occupied Sonsonate, and in the meantime more troops arrived from Guatemala to create the largest Guatemalan expeditionary force ever. At Santa Ana, on 3 July, Carrera accepted the surrender of Santiago González, who sought to replace Barrios. A week later, however, Carrera recognized the more reliably servile Francisco Dueñas as provisional president of El Salvador at Santa Ana. The citizens of Santa Ana, now under Guatemalan protection, had pronounced against Barrios and named Dueñas as provisional president on 6 July. The capture of a large store of munitions and artillery there improved Carrera's position significantly. By the end of July the Guatemalan and Nicaraguan forces were in control of most of El Salvador and began the siege of San Salvador.[55]

Victories in the field were accompanied by a propaganda fusillade in the *Gaceta*. Continuing the claim of peace and prosperity for Carrera's regime, the *Gaceta* on 6 July 1863 explained that Guatemala had the painful necessity of making an exception to its policy of peace in Central America and went on to list six grievances against the Barrios government: (1) insults to Carrera in the Salvadoran press; (2) seizure of the Honduran government and conspiracy with it against Guatemala; (3) maneuvers to subvert the government of Nicaragua on the pretext of reorganizing the Central American union; (4) intrigues to upset Guatemala's peace and tranquility; (5) military preparations on a scale unnecessary to maintain domestic tranquility and in a dictatorial manner against the wishes of the Salvadoran people; and (6) dispatch of an envoy (Lorenzo Montúfar, a Guatemalan) to Europe in September 1862 to negotiate a loan of $2 million for public improvements, which in reality was to buy armaments and to recruit foreign soldiers to subjugate all of Central America under a national government headed by Barrios.[56]

The siege of San Salvador turned out to be more difficult than anticipated. Fearful of reports that Barrios was recruiting not only in Europe but also in the United States, the allies were eager to end his rule quickly as they massed their forces before the city.[57] Anyone suspected of sympathy to Barrios was rounded up and imprisoned in Guatemala, or worse. Supporters of Dueñas and Carrera received positions in the provisional government. In September Cerna cautioned Carrera that it was not yet time to assault the city, however, for Barrios's soldiers were beginning to desert and recruits for the allies were still arriving. Barrios and Cabañas, who was back in San Salvador after the downfall of Castellanos, led a party that defeated a detachment of Cerna's force near Soyapango on 5 September, but on the tenth Zavala took Santa Tecla, overlooking the Salvadoran capital, and soon after cut off all routes into San Salvador from the south and the west. Meanwhile, Nicaraguan General Florencio Xatruch secured the Gulf of Fonseca and the port of La Unión, in the process capturing a pro-Barrios filibuster named Thomas, who had occupied Tigre Island.[58]

With routes of supply or escape cut off, on 18 September Zavala gave Barrios forty-eight hours to surrender. The Salvadoran responded scornfully, poking fun at Zavala and Carrera. Zavala was widely known for his keen sense of humor, and Barrios suggested that this was another of his jokes![59] On the twenty-sixth Cerna launched an assault. But the victory did not come easily and bitter fighting followed. Not until exactly a month later did the last Salvadorans surrender. Barrios himself escaped and made his way to Panama.[60] He later attributed his defeat to the treason of Salvadorans rather than to the abilities of the "drunk Indian," as he described Carrera. He especially attacked Santiago González, who in 1871 would overthrow Dueñas and revive the liberal and anticlerical programs begun by Barrios.[61]

After occupying San Salvador, Carrera issued a handbill on 30 October acknowledging the assistance of Divine Providence and congratulating his troops and the Nicaraguans on their valor.[62] Carrera confiscated the artillery and other armaments of the Salvadoran army, sending them to Guatemala, while his troops looted the city and committed atrocities. They desecrated Morazán's grave. Officials of the Barrios regime who failed to escape, including Foreign Minister Manuel Irungaray and several generals, were shot. Many more were marched back to Guatemala and imprisoned in the San José fortress in the capital or in the desolate and unhealthy San Felipe prison colony on the Río Dulce near Izabal.[63] Dueñas, who would rule until Santiago González overthrew him in 1871, formally thanked Carrera for ousting Barrios in a decree posted throughout the city on 3 November, adding insult to injury to the liberal cause:

The Provisional President of the Republic of El Salvador,   Considering: That the Armies of Guatemala and Nicaragua have fought heroically for the freedom of the Salvadoran People; and that it is the obligation of the Government to give them a public testimonial of gratitude for such signal service, DECREES:

1. That the Government of El Salvador gives very expressive thanks to the Excellentissimo Captain General and President of the Republic of Guatemala Don Rafael Carrera and to the Excellentissimo Captain General and President of the Republic of Nicaragua Tomás Martínez for the unselfish and effective protection that they have given to the Salvadoran People in overthrowing the discretionary power of ex-President Gerardo Barrios.

2. A gold medal will be struck and presented to the Generals, Chiefs, and Officers of the allied armies.

3. Silver medals will be struck and presented to the Sergeants, Corporals and Soldiers.

4. A monument will be erected with the names of Carrera and Martínez and other chiefs of the allied armies, to be inscribed in gold letters to perpetuate the memory of the glorious triumph achieved on the 26th of last month against the tyranny of ex-President Barrios.

5. A portrait of Rafael Carrera will be hung in the session hall of the Legislature and another in the office of the Supreme Government in recognition of the wisdom, courage and prudence with which he directed the present campaign.

Francisco Dueñas, San Salvador, 3 Nov. 1863.[64]

Later, the Salvadoran Assembly ordered a golden sword made in Europe to honor Carrera for his services in overthrowing Barrios. Carrera died before delivery of the sword at the end of 1865.[65]

The Guatemalans did not remain in San Salvador for long, however, and their departure for Guatemala began on 12 November. Carrera himself left San Salvador on the fifteenth, and General Cerna marched out of the city the following day with the remaining Guatemalan troops. Festive celebrations welcomed them as they marched back into Guatemala, culminating in a week-long celebration as they neared the city and entered it on 29 November. Despite bad weather, huge crowds turned out to welcome the returning army.[66] The victory stimulated a broad range of songs, poems, and drama, hardly of lasting value, but reflective of the adulation bestowed upon the caudillo. The verses appeared not only in Spanish but in other languages, too, as for example the following English verse that was published as part of the Colegio Seminario fiesta in Carrera's honor:

> He that loved peace above his warrior-name
> Beyond all bound did conquer glorious fame.
> Be glorious then, great Leader! happy be:
> Thy country's love and blessings shelter thee.[67]

Upon his return to Guatemala, Carrera proudly reported that El Salvador had received him as a liberator and that Nicaragua and Honduras had enthusiastically supported his campaign. In his annual report to the assembly, which had been elected in August and September, he reminded them that twenty-five years before, "still very young and without experience in public affairs," he had found himself at the head of "the people who had risen up in defense of those great conservative principles of every society." God had given him the energy, he went on, "to dominate that victorious insurrection and to make the simple but indomitable masses, the people of the country, serve the truly civilizing labor that I have been able to continue for a quarter century."[68] The assembly responded with more than its usual praise for the caudillo, and it interpreted the president's description of the present situation of the republic as a forecast of an improving future. It proposed a full schedule of decorations and medals for the victorious forces, and appropriated $16,000 for construction of a statue of the caudillo on the Plaza de la Victoria (formerly the Plaza de San Francisco, renamed in honor of the victory over El Salvador). An amendment to this bill increased Carrera's annual salary to $12,000.[69]

Carrera spent most of December and January in Escuintla, making only brief trips to the capital during the summer months. A final war honor was bestowed on him when the inhabitants of Sonsonate, El Salvador, invited him to visit in late January. The Salvadoran ministers and General Santiago González came to meet him at Puerto San José in the steamer *Salvador* on 24 January 1864 and escorted him to Sonsonate, accompanied by Field Marshals Zavala and Cruz. President Dueñas and the bishop of El Salvador met the party in Sonsonate, where a celebration was held. Carrera returned on the steamer *Guatemala* in early February.[70] The death of his year-and-a-half-old granddaughter, the daughter of Ascención and Ernesto Klée, soon after his return saddened him greatly and left him in a depressed state for several weeks. It detracted from the pleasure he had planned with Chepita at the new, comfortable rancho near Escuintla that he had given her following the Salvadoran victory.[71]

The Salvadoran campaign of 1863 was Carrera's final military adventure, but his policy of intervention to preserve peace continued. He maintained an active correspondence with the leaders of the other states, warning against efforts to upset the peace, which he believed he had restored.[72]

Barrios, of course, did not give up. From Panama he carried on an active propaganda campaign against Carrera and the conservative elite in Guatemala. The Panama *Estrella* served as a vehicle for this effort. On 28 January 1864 it carried a letter to the editor signed by "a Guatemalan," entitled "Civilization Attacked in Its Last Refuge by Savagism." It reported that Carrera and "the nobles" of Guatemala violated the sepulcher of Morazán when they looted the city of San Salvador. The *Gaceta de Guatemala* denied the charges and suggested that far from being a "mad dog" as the letter to the *Estrella* had pictured him, Carrera had "restrained" his troops and had collected only a small portion of the expense of the war. It conceded that one Guatemalan soldier had removed the gold letters from Morazán's tomb, but that the sepulcher itself was not broken into nor the remains touched, and that, in fact, General Carrera had threatened capital punishment against any who committed such acts.[73]

Barrios entered Costa Rica late in 1864 and tried to organize an expedition to invade El Salvador. The Carrera government bristled, and on 28 January 1865 broke relations with Costa Rica because of the asylum given to Barrios. El Salvador, Nicaragua, and Honduras followed Carrera's lead and also broke relations with Costa Rica.[74] Commercial relations and mail service were only reopened in June, after Barrios had been apprehended on the Nicaraguan coast when a lightning bolt had disabled his ship, but diplomatic relations between Guatemala and Costa Rica remained broken until Miguel García Granados restored them in his first decree following the Revolution of 1871.[75] Barrios, turned over to Dueñas by the Nicaraguan authorities, died before a Salvadoran firing squad on 29 August 1868.[76]

The final years of Carrera's rule in Guatemala witnessed generally favorable foreign relations with the major powers. Guatemala's solvency, stability, and good credit contributed to this. Neighboring Mexico, however, was deep in the throes of the conservative-liberal struggle. French troops of Louis Napoleon installed the Habsburg Archduke Maximilian on the Mexican throne in collaboration with Mexican ultraconservatives. Events in Mexico had always been of major importance to Guatemalan development, and the present struggle was no exception. The Carrera government had consistently approved of conservative governments in Chiapas and Mexico City, and the ouster of the Santa Anna government by Benito Juárez and the liberals had been unwelcome among the Guatemalan conservatives.

The Carrera government gave moral and material support to conservatives in Chiapas during the War of the Reform in Mexico,[77] and it welcomed the accession of Maximilian in 1864. The *Gaceta* gave this event favorable play, while lashing out at Juárez's anticlericalism. Unlike Spanish American republics that opposed this European intervention, the Guatemalan official press saw it as the restoration of stability, order, and peace under a government dedicated to similar concepts as their own.[78] It is doubtful that there was much truth to the rumors spread by Lorenzo Montúfar in Costa Rica that the Guatemalan government was planning to establish a monarchy also and to unite with Mexico, but there was clearly a sympathy for the Mexican monarchy in Guatemala City.[79] The *Gaceta* published a lengthy defense of the Mexican Empire by E. Masseras, a Frenchman who was formerly editor of the *Courrier des Etats Unis* (New York). In essence it argued that the Mexican empire would now bring the benefits that the republic had failed to produce. Masseras also suggested that the United States was disintegrating to a point that would probably be irreparable.[80] In October 1864 Pedro Aycinena sent a circular letter to the other American republics stating clearly that Guatemala had no intention of annexing itself to the Mexican Empire, as had been widely rumored.[81] Reverses for the empire soon after, culminating in Juárez's victory and Maximilian's execution in June 1867, ended this phase of good relations between Mexico and Guatemala. The liberal victory in Mexico, however, gave heart to the Guatemalan liberals. Although Guatemala remained the citadel of conservatism in the hemisphere, and Carrera's victory in El Salvador had reenforced this, conservative regimes were now falling. Liberal resurgence was already a fact that Guatemala could not ignore. Yet already, among the conservatives of Guatemala, positivist emphasis on "order and progress" was beginning to take hold. It would provide a basis for their incorporation into the new liberalism of the late nineteenth century. Positivism, although hostile to the proclerical theocracy of the Carrera regime, would provide an ideological framework for the blending of liberal and conservative elites during the next half century.

CHAPTER SIXTEEN

The Transition to Liberalism

GUATEMALA CITY CELEBRATED Carrera's fiftieth birthday with especially great zest in October 1864. The caudillo was still hardy, although he suffered stomach upset and pain. As usual, he spent much of the Guatemalan summer of 1864–65 in the warm Pacific lowlands of Escuintla, but in March 1865 he fell seriously ill. On the thirteenth he returned to the capital, where the principal physicians of the city attended him. His own physician, Dr. Francisco Aguilar, diagnosed the illness as dysentery. Dysentery had been a major killer in Guatemala, especially in the lowland regions, but a modern champion of Carrera's has suggested that he suffered from stomach cancer.[1] Another biographer blamed alcoholism and his recurrent malaria for weakening him to the point that the dysentery became fatal. There were also contemporary rumors that he was poisoned.[2] Without an autopsy, we cannot say for certain what ended the life of the caudillo. But it is clear that he had a history of stomach ailments, and it is likely that his death was caused by a form of vascular dysentery.[3] On 17 March the archbishop administered last rites. Carrera lingered for nearly a month longer, showing signs of slight improvement, but then relapsing. Weak and exhausted, he left this world at 9:30 A.M. on Good Friday, 14 April 1865.[4] His body lay in state over the Easter weekend and he was interred on Monday in a mausoleum in the cathedral crypt. In his funeral oration, Jesuit Father José Telésforo Paul emphasized Carrera's role as defender of the church. "General Carrera returned our Holy Religion to us," he observed, and "he had no equal in America. . . . General Carrera gloried in sustaining the holy unity of Religion, which is the greatest glory of Guatemala."[5]

On his death bed the caudillo named Field Marshall Cerna to succeed him, trusting in Cerna's long record of competent and loyal service to continue Guatemala's authoritarian stability. Cerna remained in Chiquimula, however. During Carrera's illness Pedro Aycinena, as the ranking minister, had been running the government, and he continued to do so after the president's death. Making it clear that he was not a candidate for the presidency permanently, the haughty Aycinena determined to convene the assembly to choose a successor, thereby giving the new president a broader base of support.

The passing of Carrera caused both relief and consternation among the conservative elite. Carrera had built a strong government that had served their interests well, but it had been based on military charisma and great popular support, advantages possessed by none of the elite. There was also fear that moderate members of the elite would welcome more open government and liberal political and economic ideas. There was, in fact, widespread support for more liberal economic development along positivist lines, but less for opening of the political system.[6] Cerna thus became an acceptable candidate for most of the conservative elite, many of whom considered him a much better choice than the volatile Serapio Cruz, who had expected to succeed Carrera. With liberals on the rise all around Guatemala, the conservatives needed another strong man who would defend their interests.[7]

The assembly convened on 1 May, following a preparatory session on 28 April. It proceeded to constitute a General Assembly for the purpose of electing a new president.[8] This General Assembly included the voting members of the Council of State and members of the Supreme Court in addition to the assembly representatives. A secret ballot on the following day barely missed giving General Cerna a majority, with twenty-seven of the fifty-five votes cast for him. Councilor of State Manuel Francisco González, a prominent conservative merchant with some political experience in the Consulado and the government, received twenty-two; Field Marshall José Victor Zavala four; and Joaquín Durán two. Zavala withdrew and a second ballot gave Cerna the necessary additional vote:[9]

Cerna	28
González	25
Durán	2
TOTAL	55

Of the fifty-five present, fifty-two signed the acclamation. Camilo Hidalgo, a councilor of state, often noted for his independence in voting, retired without signing, pleading illness. Two lonely liberals, Miguel García Granados and Marcos Dardón, also left without signing the document.[10]

As corregidor of Chiquimula, Cerna had earned the reputation as a firm ruler dedicated to maintenance of peace, order, and economic development. Noted for efficient government and friendliness to landed interests, in many ways Cerna was more like the liberals when it came to promotion of the economy. He encouraged agro-export expansion and lacked Carrera's sympathy for the traditional rights of the Indians regarding land and labor. As a result, there had been notable growth in the agricultural production and revenues of the Department of Chiquimula during his long tenure as corregidor.[11]

Cerna arrived in the capital on 21 May and was inaugurated on the twentieth. Sworn to protect "the religion and the government," in that order, in his brief inaugural address he emphasized his authority, "because societal authority is established for the public welfare and to put a stop to abuses, wherever they may appear." But he promised to uphold the constitution, assuring that citizens would enjoy the "just and prudent liberty that they have always had under our laws and customs." He also promised efficiency and zeal in the administration of the government and the economy. "I will be tolerant of all opinions that do not violate the lines drawn by the law," he said, "but I do not believe that public officials of whatever class and category have the right to impose their personal opinions on the obligations that they have voluntarily contracted upon accepting employment." In fact, he upheld a continuation of the conservative dictatorship, but promised more economic growth, and especially noted the need for more development of the capital city. "The intelligent and energetic political philosophy that twenty-six years ago took Guatemala out of chaos and ruin, will continue to inspire the Government," he declared, "since that system has in its favor the undeniable proof of time and the eloquent sanction of accomplished facts."[12] Although Pedro Aycinena declared publicly that he would prefer to step down from Foreign Relations, he stayed on at Cerna's insistence, as did the other ministers, Manuel Echeverría at Gobernación and Manuel Cerezo at Finance and War.[13]

Cerna's attitude toward the economy became almost immediately apparent in respect to the change in protection of rural Indian labor following the death of Carrera. Cerna's support of the rapid expansion of coffee cultivation contributed directly to the accelerated alienation of Indian communal lands following the death of Carrera, a process that will be dealt with in more detail in Chapter 20, below.

On the political side, the death of Carrera caused liberals all over Central America to take heart. Liberal plots soon emerged in Honduras, El

Salvador, and Nicaragua, while Costa Rica moved more peacefully toward liberalism, especially under its liberal Constitution of 1869. The new government did not wish to present an image of tolerance toward liberal political maneuvers, however, and it quickly made it clear that the liberals were not welcome. The interior minister issued an order on 30 June declaring that political emigres were not permitted to return to Guatemala without specific government permission, whether they had emigrated voluntarily or by order of the government. Nevertheless, an editorial in the official gazette suggested a possibly more lenient policy when it declared there were only five or six such exiles. It recognized that the "past government" had often been absolutist and arbitrary and perhaps even "poco legal." [14]

The *Gaceta*, in fact, soon began to reflect a softening in the dictatorship that suggests that the Cerna regime (1865–71) can be seen as an interlude between hard-line conservative and hard-line liberal dictatorships. Cerna's first annual message to the assembly, read in the tradition of the Carrera years by Interior Minister Manuel Echeverría, had a distinctly moderate tone, although it began by reiterating his adherence to the principles established by Carrera, "the restorer of old institutions, creator of a political order that he preserved for more than a quarter century, assuring order and laying the foundations for the country's growth and prosperity." While Cerna talked of continuing to maintain that order, he also initiated policies that would become more characteristic of the liberal government to follow: professionalization of the military; development of agriculture, commerce, industry, and the arts through attraction of foreign investment; and promotion of education, a subject left to the nearly exclusive sphere of the church under Carrera. Cerna was especially active in promoting road building throughout the country, encouraging and supporting the corregidores in this area well beyond the efforts of the Consulado, as he recognized the need to connect producing regions with the ports if exports were to be significantly expanded. [15] His emphasis in this message to the assembly, however, was clear. The caudillo had died, but the system he established continued, and efficient government, peace, and order would be maintained under a firm hand. [16]

The assembly, in its response, promised to cooperate with him in promoting education and economic growth, but it lamented the continued break in diplomatic relations with Costa Rica, which "the Government of Guatemala had always treated with the fraternal benevolence that corresponds to States within a single Nation." [17] The vitriolic anticonservative publications of Lorenzo Montúfar and other Guatemalan liberals in Costa Rica, however, deterred the Cerna government from restoring diplomatic ties with that state. A year later Cerna pointed to continued peace and prosperity, as well as some reforms in the administration of government and justice. In the case of the war between Spain and Peru, he had declined Peru's request for assistance and attempted to maintain cordial relations with both Spain and her former South American colonies.[18]

Notwithstanding Cerna's tough talk, the death of the caudillo encouraged greater political dialogue even within Guatemala. Liberals began to conspire once more, and students at the Universidad de San Carlos looked to Miguel García Granados for leadership.[19] Among these younger opponents of Cerna, Justo Rufino Barrios and Marco Aurelio Soto, later liberal dictators of Guatemala and Honduras respectively, were notable. Their liberalism already had begun to be modified by the influence of positivism, first noticeable in Central America in the pages of José Francisco Barrundia's *El Progreso*, which he published in El Salvador in the 1850s.[20] Liberal opposition, although a tiny minority in the legislature, became more outspoken following Carrera's death, led by García Granados. At the end of 1865 Andrés Andreu questioned military expenditures and called for a detailed breakdown of that budget.[21] In June the legislature provided a procedure by which political rights might be restored to those for whom they had been suspended,[22] and there was reform of the rules of the assembly in January 1868.[23] There was also a more open attitude toward publication, and several new presses began to operate, generally avoiding political discourse, but expanding publication of literature, music, and other areas. But there was little real prospect of liberalization of the political structure, and the conservative elite of the capital retained its strong hold through a close alliance with Cerna.

Yet the government relaxed its xenophobic attitude toward immigration. Foreign investment accelerated quickly following Carrera's death, and foreign business multiplied rapidly under Cerna's regime. A hint of the new attitude regarding foreigners was occurring even before Carrera's death, as foreign artisans and entrepreneurs had begun to play a role in the economy of Guatemala City. The *Gaceta de Guatemala*, following the attack on General Bolaños on 1 May 1862 and rumors regarding restlessness among artisans in the capital, made the following editorial comment, suggesting that some working people resented the influx of these foreigners into the city: "The situation of our artisans and other working classes has improved considerably for some years here . . . with the establishment of so many foreign artisans and artists and by the model of other people's industry. Our artisan, a very worthy and appreciated class, is improving himself by contact with those from abroad; and all but a few consider themselves lucky to have such influence. Those few are the ones who seem to have been seduced by foolish ideas and to have given credit to absurd stories."[24]

A new immigration law drafted in 1867 won approval from the government early in 1868. It encouraged immigrants by exempting them for ten years from military service (except in case of foreign invasion), by permitting them to bring in professional or craft equipment free of duty, and by offering liberal land grant provisions with long periods to pay for the land after the harvests each year. The law established an Immigration Commission composed of a councilor of state, director of the Economic Society, prior of the Consulado, and six other unpaid members to administrate the law.[25] Concerned especially with populating the North Coast, the assembly expressed its belief that the law would favorably contribute to "the growth and civilization of the country."[26]

Among the first colonization contracts to result from this new law, a U.S. expatriate, William Goodrich, agreed to colonize the north shore of Lake Izabal.[27] Other concessions granted rights to cut wood on the north shore and opened up the region to exploitation, reminiscent of the liberal efforts of the 1820s and 1830s. Black Carib settlers—descendants of unruly slaves from St. Vincent, in the eastern Caribbean, whom the British dumped on the eastern shore of Central America in the 1790s—had received a grant at Livingston and expressed their opposition to some of the new woodcutting grants, but the local corregidor ruled that there was nothing incompatible in these grants and that the loggers were precluded only from cutting wood in the Carib town itself.[28] A couple of years later, however, the government denied a request from a British subject, Ferdinand Henry Brown, for a seven-year exclusive concession to extract rubber in the vicinity of Izabal. Earlier, the government had granted such a concession to a North American named Martin, but Martin died before acting upon the concession. In the meantime, domestic entrepreneurs had begun to extract rubber (fourteen hundred quintals in 1869), and this would seem to explain the denial to Brown. Although the corregidor of Izabal had recommended approval of Brown's petition, the Economic Society opposed it, believing it to be prejudicial to native production and to local agriculture and commerce. The government accepted the society's opinion and denied the request on 11 November 1870.[29]

At the beginning of 1867, a disgruntled Serapio Cruz launched a rebellion from the montaña region. Troops under General Solares forced the heavyset general to come to terms on 5 February, however, and in return for a safe-conduct pass to El Salvador, Cruz agreed not to return to Guatemala. Neither the Guatemalan government nor Cruz honored this agreement, however, and later in the year Cruz, after fleeing to Nicaragua, turned up in Chiapas where his brother, Francisco, had been organizing antigovernment forces.[30] The government took strongly repressive measures in the montaña region even after the 5 February agreement. It moved whole villages to new sites, evacuating the populations of disturbed regions in order to rout out rebels.[31]

Francisco Cruz launched his insurrection from Justo Rufino Barrios's hacienda, straddling the Mexican border near Malacatán. Again government forces triumphed, capturing Francisco Cruz and thirty-seven others. Cruz and several of his officers faced firing squads, while others were incarcerated in the San Felipe Prison. Barrios, however, escaped into Chiapas and emerged as the new leader of the revolution, raiding into Guatemala while seeking support from the Mexican liberal government of Benito Juárez. Barrios's less fortunate father, however, was captured and taken to the capital, where according to liberal accounts he was imprisoned and tortured.[32]

Cerna made no reference to these disturbances in his annual messages to the legislature in 1867 and 1868, declaring that both at home and abroad Guatemala enjoyed peace, stability, and economic growth. He portrayed Guatemala as a healthy political body in the midst of so much difficulty elsewhere in the Spanish-speaking world.[33] The legislature, however, in its response to his 1868 message, called attention to the "anti-progressive revolutions" that were going on, declaring that they originated in "the denial of the law of progress, the initiative and application for which Providence has trusted to the most enlightened segment of the society."[34]

Cerna sought to increase the legitimacy of his presidency on 8 January 1869 by declaring that his term would end on the following 23 May. He immediately convoked a new General Assembly for 17 January for the purpose of electing a president, whose term would run through the end of 1872.[35] This gave the liberals barely a week to organize any sort of opposition, but they rallied around the popular Gen. José Víctor Zavala and made a reasonably good showing. Zavala, of course, was not a liberal and had been a strong supporter of Carrera, but he was not especially close to Cerna and had been somewhat aloof from politics. Moreover, he was on good terms with García Granados and moderate members of the elite. The years since Carrera's death had seen many members of the elite seeking to retain their advantages under the conservative regime while at the same time incorporating liberal-positivist principles of development consistent with nineteenth-century progress. These years were thus a period of transition toward economic liberalism. Similar transitions were also occurring in Costa Rica and in Nicaragua, as well as in Mexico. These new moderates saw Zavala as one who could lead the transition from the reactionary conservatism of Carrera to a more progressive regime of economic liberalism.[36] Zavala was well-read, literate, and urbane, unlike most of the officers in Guatemala. He also enjoyed considerable support among the populace in general. On election Sunday, the streets and galleries were packed with "people of all classes," according to the official gazette, frequently shouting *"vivas* and hurrahs" for General Zavala.[37] There was also a common desire among both conservative and liberal elite to acquire land at the expense of the Indians, a practice that Carrera had checked, but that Zavala seemed even more willing than Cerna to condone in the name of economic progress.[38]

Incumbent Guatemalan presidents, however, rarely lose elections, and Cerna won by a comfortable margin when the assembly voted that afternoon:

Vicente Cerna	31
José Víctor Zavala	21
Luis Molina	3
Pedro Aycinena	1
Manuel Echeverría	1
TOTAL	57

García Granados, one of the fifty-seven, refused to sign the election act, walking out of the assembly before it was concluded. Outside, the demonstrations for Zavala continued into the night, even after Zavala, speaking to supporters in front of his house, warned them to be moderate and to recognize legitimate authority. The *Gaceta* commented on the "seditious character" of the demonstrations, caused, it presumed, by the drunkenness of many of the demonstrators. It reported that although the authorities were "very tolerant," they were forced to take some measures to restore public order and security, resulting in the death of one youth and in several arrests. Whatever support Zavala had was gone by the following morning, and the city was quiet and followed its normal Monday routine.[39]

Cerna was inaugurated for his second term on 24 May 1869 without further incident, but Barrios and Serapio Cruz had invaded from Chiapas in March. In the months that followed, they gained territory and recruits in the departments of Huehuetenango and San Marcos. Cruz gained many adherents among the Indians through his opposition to the hated liquor monopoly, a major source of revenue for the conservative government. Upon taking the town of Huehuetenango at the beginning of May, his forces destroyed the state distillery there before marching on to Momostenango and other points in Totonicapán. Once a loyal lieutenant of Carrera, Cruz now employed the guerrilla tactics of the montaña in Huehuetenango and Totonicapán, fleeing into friendly Chiapas whenever threatened by Cerna's forces. He appealed for support to both peasants and landholders against the policies of the Cerna government, and while the issues were sometimes confusing, his strength grew.[40]

Elite interests were, of course, furious with Cruz for stirring up the Indians. Milla's La Semana bitterly attacked his use of the Indians for political means as it compared him unfavorably with Carrera:

> It is well known that that segment, the most numerous and the most ignorant of our society, cannot be moved by abstract political ideas, which it cannot possibly understand. But there is an instinctive sense in many individuals of that race that makes them consider those called ladinos as usurpers; a sentiment which feeds a hatred that coalesces to cause an explosion from time to time, and almost always to cause deplorable abuses and rash acts. General Carrera was enthusiastically loved by the aborigines; he could have turned to them at that moment when the base that until then had sustained his power moved against him [in 1848]; but he knew very well the danger of such a recourse, and he preferred to separate himself from command before bathing his country in blood with a war of extermination.
>
> Without the elevated views and without the great heart of General Carrera, Cruz, as soon as he realized that he could expect little from the ladinos, undertook the seduction of the aborigines of los Altos and the Verapaz, where the indigenous element is most preponderant, both in terms of their numbers and where they have kept their life-style, tendencies, and customs of pre-conquest times. Saying he was sent from General Carrera, or was himself General Carrera resurrected to put them in exclusive possession of the land, many Indians fell into the trap and joined him as he tried to make them instruments of his designs.[41]

Unmentioned, of course, in this analysis, was the fact that Cerna had alienated the Indian by his willingness to allow coffee planters to encroach heavily on Indian land and labor since the death of Carrera. But Cruz's campaign now forced Cerna to admit openly the seriousness of the rebellion, and on 8 May he suspended constitutional guarantees.[42] Defense against the rebellion was costly, and in March 1869 Cerna turned to London financiers for a £500,000 loan.[43]

Meanwhile, in San Marcos, Barrios issued a manifesto denying charges that he was nothing more than a bandit. He declared that he was fighting to free the country from the slavery it had been in, to guarantee the rights of its citizens, and to end the monopolies. Recognizing, however, the powerful influence of the clergy, and remembering its role in raising Carrera to power three decades earlier, both Barrios and Cruz were careful not to emphasize the anticlericalism that in fact was so important to the liberals.[44]

In the capital some liberals continued to work within the system, although they clandestinely looked toward the rebellion with hope. Cerna's government became increasingly watchful of suspected ties between the liberal elite and Cruz. José Víctor Zavala appeared to be a key to their action, for although he now began to side with liberals in the assembly, he carefully took no illicit action toward the government and remained loyal to Cerna. When the assembly convened as usual on 25 November 1869, Cerna sent it an unusually short message, attacking the rebels, whom he called "a faction that without proclaiming political principles is trying to promote change favorable only to a few individual interests." He charged them with disrupting the peaceful political life of the country and destroying the economic progress. Under these conditions, Cerna argued, it was impossible for the legislature to deliberate calmly the matters that should be brought before it. He said there were no matters of urgency that could be dealt with until the rebellion had been crushed, so he asked them to adjourn until 4 April.[45]

The assembly remained in session long enough for a liberal effort to end the suspension of constitutional guarantees, sponsored by García Granados and supported by Zavala. This motion failed on 1 December by a vote of 25 to 7.[46] On the following day the obedient body chose its officers and elected representatives to the Council of State before adjourning as the president had requested, expressing to him their confidence that he would restore order to the republic.[47]

Cerna failed to contain the rebellion, although he stepped up his repressive measures and won some victories. Notably, in January 1870 Gen. Antonio Solares defeated Serapio Cruz after Cruz had led a daring raid on Palencia, only twenty miles from the capital. Cruz himself died in the battle. His head, fried in oil, was brought to the capital for public display, a testimony to the grim butchery of Central American revolution.[48] Cerna followed up this victory with a harsh crackdown on all opposition, ending the relative political freedom that had characterized the capital since Carrera's death. He ordered the arrest of García Granados, Manuel Larrave, and José María Samayoa. Larrave and Samayoa were soon in jail, but García Granados eluded Cerna's police, first protected by General Zavala, then gaining asylum in the British legation, subsequently allowed to leave the country under a $10,000 bond.[49]

Thus, when the Congress reconvened on 4 April 1870, Miguel García Granados was conspicuously absent. In fact, of the seven who had supported his motion of the previous 1 December, only Angel Arroyo was present on the fourth.[50] García Granados now joined the rebels in the West in the formation of an opposition government.

Cerna reported to the assembled legislators on 4 April that he had restored order and looked forward to a resumption of prosperous economic growth.[51] The struggle appeared to be stalemated and largely confined to the zones close to rebel refuges in Mexico. In most of the rest of the country, peace reigned and elections for the new assembly proceeded without incident in August and September 1870.[52] The assembly again elected Juan Matheu as its president when it convened in November.[53] Cerna assured the deputies that with peace fully restored, the government could promote economic growth by every means possible.[54] In fact, heavy rains in October had caused problems in production in late 1870. The destruction of considerable cochineal and coffee was less serious than the damage to subsistence crops, with reports of many milpas washed out especially in the vicinity of Amatitlán.[55]

If Cerna appeared to be holding his own in Guatemala against the liberal challenge, the same was not true with the conservative governments in Honduras and El Salvador, where the liberals were also in open revolt. Unlike his predecessor, Cerna chose not to intervene, and indeed the pressure from the Guatemalan liberals on the Mexican border precluded such adventures on Cerna's part.

With Barrios emerging as the military leader after the death of Cruz, García Granados began to issue political pronouncements early in 1871, still steering clear of anticlericalism and concentrating his attacks on the Guatemala City merchant monopoly, the liquor monopolies, and other privileged groups of the conservative regime. His manifesto of 8 May 1871 launched the formation of a government. Accusing Cerna of tyranny, García Granados appealed to the people to help him "revindicate my rights and combat an administration that oppresses the people and daily violates the most sacred rights of man." For twenty years he had waged this battle in the legislature, he declared, against an arbitrary and despotic government. He justified his futile struggle as at least serving to make known the "abuses, excesses and cruelties of the dictatorial system that ruled us." But now he had seen that it was necessary to shed his blood if need be to rid the country of the tyrants. He called for abolition of the "absurd" Constitution of 1851 "established only to maintain a dictatorship." He called for a free press, "without which good government is impossible." Consistent with the liberal desire for professional military forces, he called for the "reform and improvement of the army," so that it would no longer be "based on arbitrariness and injustice." He also called for tax reform, reform of the finance ministry, public education, abolition of "every species of monopoly" and especially the liquor monopoly as "injurious and ruinous to agriculture and commerce."[56]

The tobacco and liquor monopolies became especially important issues in the 1871 revolution, for there was widespread popular opposition to them. Liquor and tobacco production in Guatemala were unique because of the close government controls and taxes applied to these products. Establishment of a tobacco monopoly in 1766 had elicited a mild rebellion in Guatemala City (Antigua), consisting principally of an anonymous petition for which unemployed weavers were thought to be primarily responsible. The government lowered its share of revenues on tobacco while it sought to increase production in the kingdom, mostly in Costa Rica, during the remainder of the colonial period.[57] By the close of the Spanish era, the government purchased tobacco from producers at a fixed price of one real per pound and resold it for domestic consumption at six reales and for export at two reales. Government revenues were averaging more than $300,000 per year from the tobacco operation at the time of independence. Most of this production, however, was Costa Rican, and after independence that revenue was lost to Guatemala.[58]

With independence, liberals favored ending the monopoly. After separation from the Mexican Empire, which had continued it, the Central American government abolished the monopoly in 1824. State governments attempted to continue it, however, although there was considerable evasion of state control of the industry in the 1820s.[59] Continuance of the monopoly within the state of Guatemala was unpopular, and one result of Carrera's revolt was its abolition on 29 September 1840. This legislative act abolished the office of tobacco revenue and declared production and sale of the crop to be free, except for a small excise tax, exempted on tobacco for export. The decree stated that the reason for the abolition was that the monopoly system was actually costing the government more than it was receiving from production and sale.[60]

The government soon restored the monopoly, however, on 4 August 1842, citing widespread evasion of the tax as the reason. The new state controls established thirty-two legal places where tobacco could be sold, including five in the capital, two each in Antigua and Quetzaltenango, and one in each of the other principal towns. Franchises for these legal sales outlets were auctioned to the highest bidders under rather detailed regulations intended to preclude contraband.[61]

Through the 1840s the tobacco administration produced only modest revenue, and in some years it barely made expenses.[62] Contraband was common and there was probably some internal corruption as well. It appeared that the system worked effectively only in the capital.[63] On 1 January 1848 the government turned the monopoly over to an English firm, Jeffryes and Meek, but on 16 May 1849 the government charged this company with failing to fulfill its obligations and resumed control.[64]

Soon after, President Mariano Paredes once more abolished the monopoly because it was producing a deficit rather than revenue for the state. He restored the 1840 tax of a quarter real per pound on raw tobacco or cigars and added a $1.00 per thousand duty on the import of cigars and one real per pound on imported cigarettes. As before, tobacco for export was tax exempt.[65] In 1855 the government once more assigned tobacco sales to a private company, but this time to a native firm, Larraondo y Samayoa, for seven years. The company was to supervise tobacco production and sales for which it would receive the revenue, paying the government for this concession $3,000 for each of the first three years and $6,000 for each of the final four years of the contract. The contract also authorized the company to import tobacco, but it had to pay duties on such imports. The hope here was not only to produce some revenue for the government, but more especially to encourage greater production. Three years later, however, the government rescinded the Larraondo y Samayoa contract, because it had "not worked out." Thus the government restored the state monopoly on 21 September 1858, establishing the prices of tobacco at three reales per pound for good quality and two reales per pound for lesser quality, with tariffs of four reales per pound on imported tobacco. Thereafter, the government closely regulated the trade, from which it earned modest revenues through the end of the conservative regime, while it became increasingly unpopular among tobacco addicts.[66]

The liberals seized on this issue, and García Granados's second decree after forming a rebel government in 1871, even before the fall of the conservative regime, was to abolish the state monopoly on the production and sale of tobacco.[67]

Even more unpopular was the liquor monopoly. Originally established in Central America by a 1752 royal decree, it had considerable importance as a producer of government revenue. This monopoly, however, was not solely based on revenue considerations, but also on the elite's concern over alcohol abuse among Indians, peasants, and the urban poor. Liquor producing interests often clashed with these views, of course, and the terms of the monopoly often represented a compromise. In 1811, for example, the ayuntamiento of Guatemala City prevailed upon Captain General Bustamante to abolish aguardiente stands in the city, but the opposition of Spanish liquor merchants resulted in a compromise that allowed twelve controlled liquor dispensing stalls to remain. In the 1820s concern over public drunkenness led to a ten peso per month tax on *chicherías,* dispensers of the popular, fermented *chicha.* The government also ordered them closed at 6:00 P.M. This measure was probably more important as a revenue producer than as a deterrent to drinking. More importantly, it extended government control over chicha sales in the capital in a manner similar to that over aguardiente. In 1824 the government raised the tax on chicha and aguardiente and prohibited the sale of foreign liquors.[68] The Consulado protested that such a prohibition would be harmful to the national commerce, and it appears that this latter provision was not seriously enforced.[69]

Following the Carrera revolt, the conservative-oriented government restored the colonial monopoly system and sought to restrict the sale of alcoholic beverages to the masses. On 2 December 1839 the Constituent Assembly limited sales to licensed taverns and limited the capital to six such establishments, with two each in departmental seats and one each in other towns of ten thousand inhabitants or more, but none in towns where the majority of the population was Indian.[70] Subsequent legislation cracked down on clandestine manufacture and sale of aguardiente, but it is clear that enforcement was seldom very effective beyond the capital. In practice, local corregidores had wide latitude in their enforcement of the liquor laws within their respective departments, and they generally determined the number of taverns that could be established.[71]

Minor modifications occurred in the years following. On the initiative of the government, on 26 October 1843 the assembly issued new regulations for distillers, giving the government broader power to enforce the law against illegal production of aguardiente and replacing the old 4 percent alcabala collected at the city gates with a flat quarter real (about 3 cents) per bottle tax. This tax was to go directly to the public treasury except in Antigua and Guatemala City, where half was to go to the public treasury with the other half divided between the city and the hospital. The law prohibited any new distilleries outside of towns or sugar mills. Those already established elsewhere were permitted to continue, but were to be taxed $50 monthly to pay for the damages they had caused, the difficulty of controlling them, and to prevent abuses of drunkenness. Those established within towns or at sugar mills would only pay, according to their production levels, from $10 to $30 per month.[72] This did not stop clandestine production, of course, as evidenced by repeated circulars to corregidores in subsequent years calling for their active attention "to this abuse," which caused "serious damage to the public treasury, to the licensed producers, and even to public morality, because of the crimes committed in drunkenness."[73]

Again, in 1849, the assembly reaffirmed the executive's free hand in regulating aguardiente production and sales, but repeated its concern over widespread public drunkenness.[74] Regulations providing for closer control of bootleggers and moonshiners were promulgated in August 1851,[75] but these were once more revised by the Carrera government the following March, reemphasizing that manufacture and sale of aguardiente was expressly prohibited without government license.[76] Monthly licensing fees for dispensers of aguardiente and chicha for that year ranged form $10 to $270, with $17 being the most common amount, apparently based on volume and negotiations. Fifteen vendors were licensed in the capital, with six more outside the city limits but in its environs. The populous department of Sacatepéquez had a total of sixty-seven, with only fourteen of them in Antigua. There were fourteen authorized in Chimaltenango, but only three in Escuintla.[77] In an effort either to raise more revenue or limit consumption, these license fees rose to a high of $405 in the following year, but protest was apparently great, for in subsequent years they were gradually scaled downward, and by 1856 some vendors paid as little as $4 monthly for their privilege.[78] There was concern over continued smuggling of foreign liquors into the country. The law limited sale of foreign liquors at retail to "by the drink" sales in licensed taverns, but there was obviously wide violation of this provision.[79] The petition of candy merchant Pablo Wassen in late 1858 to sell fine foreign liqueurs in his establishment in the capital triggered a lengthy discussion. Wassen argued that he could not make enough money just selling sweets and pastries, and that a line of fine liqueurs, including "Rosalie and Maraschino," would be appropriate for his shop. The police chief opposed it, acknowledging that even though it was the normal thing in Europe, in Guatemala it would lead to abuses. The municipality also opposed it, and in the end the government denied Wassen's petition.[80]

To the traditional beverages of aguardiente and chicha, beer had gained popularity in the capital by 1856. Carrera decreed a new set of controls on that industry in September of that year, requiring licensing for its sales and manufacture. The government licensed six manufacturers in the capital and allowed each of them a factory and one wholesale and retail outlet, each for a $10 monthly fee. They were, however, prohibited from selling beer outside the capital until licensed vendors were established.[81] This was almost immediately revoked, because of "the great inconvenience it caused," and on 3 October the government allowed unlimited breweries to be established throughout the republic, requiring only a $12 fee from each paid to the revenue office in each department. It limited each brewery to a single sales outlet, however.[82] German influence in the beer industry was important from the beginning, and early in 1858 the brewery established by Theodor Kreitz promised to raise the quality of Guatemalan beer to German standards.[83]

A little more than a year after Carrera's death, reflecting Vicente Cerna's willingness to turn more of the economy over to private initiative and direction, the government granted the monopoly on production of aguardiente and chicha to a private Guatemalan company consisting of José María Samayoa, Pío Benito, Joaquín de la Torre, and José T. Larraondo. Their corporation claimed a capitalization of a half million pesos represented by a thousand shares. An editorial commenting on the new enterprise suggested that it was "not a monopoly delivered into a few hands, but an enterprise in which directly or indirectly nearly all those in the industry participate," and one that would make possible the distillation of liquors under the best conditions. The editorial predicted that it would mean greater revenues for the government and thereby help reduce the deficit. It retained, of course, the principal of monopoly, which still restricted the sale and manufacture of the popular beverages.[84]

The 1871 Reforma continued the trend away from the liquor monopoly tradition. Even before the collapse of the Cerna government, the president of the rebel government, Miguel García Granados, obviously seeking support in Los Altos, revoked the decree of 21 March 1860 that had specifically prohibited the importation of Chiapas aguardiente, called *comiteco*.[85] Once in power, the liberals abolished the liquor monopolies altogether.

Mexican assistance proved to be crucial to the Guatemalan liberals of 1871. With help from the Juárez government, they gained territory and confidence early in that year, forcing the government to put more and more resources into its defense. By late May the rebels controlled most of Los Altos and readied themselves for an attack on the capital. On 24 May they finally made clear their anticlerical biases with a decree expelling the Jesuits from Guatemala, a decree promptly implemented after the revolution succeeded.[86] At Patzicía, on 3 June, Barrios met with other rebel officers and drew up a manifesto formally declaring the overthrow of Cerna and establishing García Granados as provisional president, authorizing him to organize a government along the lines of his 8 May manifesto.[87]

Cerna issued his own manifesto on the same day, admitting that the rebels who had "disturbed the peace in some departments of the Republic and put in grave danger the most sacred interests of its inhabitants," had made gains in recent days. But he insisted that the people still supported the government against the "subversive" and "selfish" elements who sought to destroy the social order and prosperity the conservatives had achieved.[88] He dared not call up the power of the people as Carrera had done, however. The elite feared García Granados far less than the Indian masses, and Cerna simply lacked the charisma to pursue that course. On the contrary, he now was closely linked to the conservative elite, and his government had lost the peasant support that Carrera had commanded.

The end was near. For with the fall of Dueñas in El Salvador in April 1871, the liberals were able to launch a revolt in the East. In June insurgents took Jutiapa. General Gregorio Solares, who had broken with Cerna, entered Guatemala from Santa Ana and brought eastern Guatemala quickly into the struggle in alliance with García Granados. Although Cerna still had the larger army, the rebels were now able to outmaneuver his forces. They were also better armed, with new Winchester and Remington rifles. The climax came quickly when on 29 June Barrios routed Cerna's army near San Lucas on the heights to the west of the capital. The following day Barrios led his army into the capital without opposition. Significantly, José Víctor Zavala intervened to prevent further bloodshed and secure a peaceful transition to the new government. Cerna and most of his officers and ministers fled to Honduras.[89]

The new government quickly enacted sweeping reforms along lines similar to the Mexican Reforma, although ultimately the anticlerical reforms were carried through more completely in Guatemala than under Porfirio Díaz in Mexico. A new flag, restoring the traditional liberal blue and white tricolor in a vertical pattern, symbolized the new order beginning on 17 August. The new government would, in positivist fashion, worship economic expansion and launch a major effort to develop exports by confiscating the lands of the church and the communal lands of the Indians. García Granados would not long survive as chief of state, for his conciliatory attitude toward his relatives and friends among the elite of the capital prevented the more sweeping revolution that Barrios and others not connected to the capital elite desired. Barrios thus replaced García Granados in 1873.[90]

Mario Rodríguez has succinctly described the revolution of Central American liberals in the 1870s in these terms:

> They were determined to extract the maximum benefit from the nation's resources through a centralized and benevolent government that dispensed favors freely to both foreign and domestic entrepreneurs. Traditional values and institutions that hampered the nation's material welfare were discarded irretrievably, and the new leaders paid only lip service to constitutionalism as

a sop for the romantics in their midst. Power was for those who understood what was best for the nation.

By ignoring the democratic means that is perhaps the most basic tenet of liberalism, these new liberals in fact abandoned their earlier faith. Not surprisingly, conservatives welcomed this change of heart, as well as the program of social order and economic development, thus blurring the lines between the two historic rivals. The *personalista* age was upon Central America, and elections degenerated into a periodic fight for spoils of office.[91]

Suddenly, in 1871, liberals were in charge from Mexico through Costa Rica—except for Nicaragua, where the conservatives hung on until 1893. The conservative era was over. It would not return to Guatemala. In Guatemala, as in much of the rest of Latin America in the late nineteenth century, liberal party hegemony and consensus would replace the two-faction struggle of the first half century of independence. The conservative values that Rafael Carrera had defended did not disappear, but they were subordinated to the demands for material progress that the liberals promised. Conservatives and liberals began to join in a common effort to transform their traditional economies to capitalist enclaves dedicated to production for international markets. The alliance between conservatives and the agrarian masses that Carrera had forged died almost immediately with him, and although many conservatives nostalgically held the traditional Hispanic cultural values that had been part of the backbone of nineteenth-century conservatism, they also were becoming more aware of class ties that caused them to put greater emphasis on the material transformation of the country for their own benefit.

PART THREE

Socioeconomic Change in Carrera's Guatemala

CHAPTER SEVENTEEN

Infrastructure
Development in
Conservative Guatemala

THE THREE CENTURIES OF SPANISH RULE (1524–1821) represent a long transition from feudalism to capitalism, which was by no means complete by the end of that period. Although the sixteenth-century Habsburgs had encouraged mining and agro-exports, the conquistador generation and their creole descendants were culturally more acquainted with feudal than capitalist traditions and institutions. In the seventeenth century, declining Spanish commercial and military strength contributed to retrenchment among the creole landholding elite into self-sufficient estates and forms of labor control resembling medieval serfdom. Master-serf relationships evolved that have characterized Guatemalan rural life ever since.[1] A small capitalist element, however, existed in Guatemala throughout the colonial period, and an important segment of the economy dedicated itself to agro-exports, first of cacao and later of indigo. Yet the majority of the declining population was engaged in economic activity more akin to feudalism than capitalism.[2] The eighteenth-century Bourbons, however, put great emphasis on capitalist development and especially on agro-exports and mining in underdeveloped areas of the empire, such as Central America. Following independence the liberals continued the Bourbon emphasis on exports. Despite the theoretical liberal concept of laissez faire, from the beginning they assumed that government should play a major role in the stimulation of agricultural expansion.[3]

Paradoxically, two institutions that originated in Guatemala from the Bourbon economic policies—the Consulado de Comercio and the Sociedad Económica de Amigos del País—came to be closely associated with the conservative elite of the capital. Even though in the colonial period these institutions, especially the Economic Society, had a liberal image in that they were part of the effort to expand capitalist-oriented production and trade in Central America, their domination by the conservative interests of the capital after independence made them targets of the liberals. From 1840 to 1871 they played a key role in the economic structure and growth of the country.

The restoration of the Consulado in 1839 provided the institutional base for representation of the Guatemala City mercantile elite in the political and economic structure of the conservative state. Although this institution dated only from 1794 in Guatemala, its restoration reflected the return to Hispanic corporatism so characteristic of the reaction that swept over Guatemala in 1839. The government renewed the broad powers over commerce, transport, ports, and export production that the *real cédula* of 1793 had granted the Consulado, so that the merchants of the capital had a virtual monopoly over Guatemalan commercial development during the conservative years. The merchants also regained their exclusive tribunal, or fuero, suppressed in 1829, which gave them a privileged position in the judicial structure of the state. The Consulado was a prime example of how class privilege was an intimate component of conservative rule in the mid-nineteenth century and a strong force for the maintenance of the status quo. Not surprisingly, the Consulado was one of the first institutions the liberals abolished in 1871.[4]

The preamble to the decree restoring the Consulado reasoned that it was necessary for the protection and development of the nation's industry, agriculture, and commerce, and with government favor the institution gained in importance and power. By mid-December 1839 the Consulado had already initiated several public works projects.[5] The new Consulado regulated and supervised commerce and carried on a program of infrastructure development more extensive than any previously in Guatemala's history. Moreover, it became an important adviser to the government on economic and other matters. Acts of 1851 gave the Consulado representation in the National Assembly and made the prior of the Consulado a member of the Council of State.[6] The state borrowed significant sums from the Consulado's treasury and called on it to collect loans for the government from its constituents. The Consulado was essentially a quasi-governmental agency that reflected the corporate nature of the conservative regime. While its tribunal, composed of the prior and two consuls, maintained the merchants' fuero and represented the Consulado's position of authority within the structure of the Guatemalan state, its Junta de Gobierno carried out the economic functions.

The Consulado shared responsibility for economic development with the Economic Society, first founded in Guatemala in 1794. Efforts to revive the institution to promote new economic activity occurred in 1825 and again in 1829, with José Antonio Larrave, José Cecilio del Valle, and José María de Castilla playing prominent roles in the institution. Under Valle's leadership it remained active as an institution for the entire federation in the 1830s, seeking to promote practical educational and economic projects, with some financial support from the Gálvez government in Guatemala. It ceased to be of any importance during the bitter struggle of the War of the Mountain. The Guatemalan assembly reestablished it on 24 September 1840, and it continued to exist until a decade after the final suppression of the Consulado. The Society's stated purpose was to discover and exploit ways to increase production, to develop new industrial and agricultural products, and to raise the standard of living in the region through "scientific" development. The foundation of the Economic Society in Guatemala has been traditionally associated with the arrival of the Enlightenment among leaders of the community. As such, it always had a more liberal image than the Consulado, but both were institutions of the capital's elite, and under Carrera they became representative of the conservative, corporatist state. Its leadership shifted to conservatives such as Juan Matheu, José Milla, Manuel Echeverría, José María Urruela, Manuel Francisco Pavón, and Jacinto Rivera Paz. The fact that the society continued to be a place where liberal members of the elite participated, and occasionally even held leadership positions during the period 1850–71, gave the institution a somewhat more acceptable image to liberals after the 1871 revolution. It was not finally suppressed until 1881, its functions largely taken over by the government itself.[7]

The society sponsored a number of practical educational enterprises, with financial support from the Consulado and the government, which authorized a new lottery for the society's support in 1845.[8] In addition to a drafting and drawing school, supported by the Consulado,[9] the society gave free evening mathematics classes to artisans in the city beginning in 1843.[10] Later it offered shorthand and other business-related lessons to improve the productivity of Guatemalan workers.[11] It also encouraged new agricultural and industrial production through publication of pamphlets, and, from December 1846 to May 1848, a weekly journal; importation of seed and equipment; annual exhibitions; and advice to the government.[12] In January 1850, for example, it began lessons in weaving straw hats under the direction of José P. López and later in that year began similar lessons in the Verapaz.[13] It sponsored English, French, and German classes.[14] It also worked for establishment of a national museum, which finally opened in January 1866, and in 1862 it sponsored dramatic performances to raise money to aid victims of the recent earthquake.[15] During the Cerna administration the Economic Society published a monthly journal (*La Sociedad Económica*, 1866–70) and became more active in encouraging foreign investment, agricultural technology, and export production. In 1869 its agricultural committee, headed by an energetic Colombian immigrant, Mariano Ospina, launched a comprehensive study of agriculture in the state, seeking to determine both the present situation and future potential.[16] While the intentions and projects of the society were laudable, the impact of the institution on developing the Guatemalan economy was not great. It provided a forum for discussion, one of the few that existed in that period, but it did not provide the sort of tangible support from the elite that would have been needed to modernize more quickly the Guatemalan economy. Thus, while it was an organization that could be said to have maintained liberal economic goals and ideals, it cannot be said to have furthered them very much during the period 1840–71.

At the same time, the society did not restrict itself, as did the Consulado, to considerations of immediate profit and loss. Its economic projects, therefore, covered a wider range, including many that were not feasible. Although some of its project were certainly useful in stimulating the economy, it was closer to an academic society than a development agency in any modern sense. The Consulado formally elected two of its members to two-year terms on the Economic Society, but this gesture and the general overlapping membership of the two institutions did not guarantee close cooperation. The Consulado was primarily interested in improving existing production as a means of maintaining or increasing immediate profits, while the society was more interested in long-range development of new crops or industries that would diversify and strengthen the economy over the longer term.[17] These were, of course, complementary missions, and between 1840 and 1871 the Consulado and the Economic Society worked together more closely than they had previously, although their programs were still often uncoordinated with one another. Only for the most commercially advantageous projects, such as the development of cochineal, cotton, and coffee, was the Economic Society able to enlist more than token aid from the merchants.

Until the mid-1850s the society had little in the way of funds to carry out its projects. The government lottery provided it little income and at times ceased to exist because so few tickets were sold. Its revenues increased significantly with taxes on liquors and more enthusiastic promotion of the lottery after 1855, but most of this revenue went for construction of the handsome new building that the government assisted the society in completing in 1860, designed by the Guatemalan architect Julián Rivera Maestre (1800–86). Later, after the society's suppression, this building became the home of the national legislature.[18]

The Consulado, in fact, paid only occasional attention to promotion of new agro-exports. In 1848, for example, it published a booklet on hemp raising, and it intermittently distributed seeds for various potential crops. The merchants of the Consulado concentrated their attention primarily on a few crops that brought large profits and that they could easily control. These merchants could not ignore the capitalist philosophy identified generally with the liberals, however. Although the Consulado itself was a bastion of the conservative regime, including support for economic protectionism and limited expansion of agroexports, its merchant-members were nonetheless attracted to the agro-export emphasis that would characterize liberal Guatemala later. In effect, the economic differences between conservatives and liberals diminished during the Carrera years, as traditional conservative economic ideas were more and more out of vogue among the liberal-capitalist trends of the nineteenth century. The combining of liberal and conservative attitudes on economic policy was especially reflected in the Economic Society and helps to explain its survival beyond 1871.

The most important economic responsibility of the Consulado came to be its efforts to improve the transportation and shipping infrastructure. For thirty-two years the Consulado was the principal agency in Guatemala engaged in building national highways, ports, and other public works— until a government development ministry replaced it in 1871.[19] The Consulado managed or assisted projects on its own initiative or which were proposed to it by national, departmental, or municipal governments, by private companies and individuals, or by other quasi-autonomous corporations such as the Economic Society or the ecclesiastical council. In most cases financial aid or permission from the government was necessary to carry out a project. The income that the Consulado devoted to public works came mainly from import and export duties, port fees, and road tolls. Although Guatemala's volume of trade increased after 1839, the Consulado did not always receive more revenue, for the government sometimes lowered or rebated duties to favor a particular export or import or to encourage use of a port. The Consulado also acquired funds from fines in its tribunal, from borrowing, and from interest on loans. The government from time to time conceded it temporary revenues for specific projects. Between 1851 and 1871 the Consulado's annual income averaged about $45,000. The Consulado spent about 70 percent of this income on roads, bridges, ports, and other public works projects, but with limited funds, it had to discriminate in its choice of projects.[20] The first aim of the institution was to advance projects in the interests of the merchants of the capital, although the government occasionally forced the Consulado to use its funds for works that had no immediate commercial value.

The growth of overseas trade meant that Guatemala had to pay more attention to finding deep-water ports on both coasts. Colonial efforts had been mostly directed toward the Caribbean, although the Consulado had investigated establishment of a Pacific Coast port.[21] In the 1830s, the Gálvez government had proposed ambitious port expansion on both coasts, but it accomplished little beyond opening the little port of Livingston on the Caribbean, and Belize became Guatemala's principal entrepôt. The Belgian colonization scheme developed Santo Tomás for awhile, but the port of Izabal, on the inland Golfo Dulce (Lake Izabal) continued as Guatemala's main port, although it was used for little more than transferring cargo in skiffs to and from Belize.[22]

Guatemalans sought a Pacific alternative for their foreign trade to avoid the long, muddy trail to the Caribbean. The Consulado revived the colonial project for a Pacific port after independence, however, when the federal government in 1824 authorized Iztapa as a port of entry. Later that year the state government took over responsibility for developing the port, but complained in 1826 that it needed federal assistance to carry out the extensive improvements needed there.[23] The port had developed very little by the time Stephens described it in December 1839 as "a long sand bar, with a flagstaff, two huts built of poles and thatched with leaves, and three sheds of the same rude construction." The captain of the port, he said, "complained of the desolation and dreariness of the place, its isolation and separation from the world, its unhealthiness, and the misery of a man doomed to live there."[24] Yet by 1839 Iztapa accounted for about 15 percent of Guatemala's imports and nearly 28 percent of its exports, almost all of which was cochineal.[25]

The restored Consulado facilitated and protected the interests of the capital's merchants. Acquiring ownership of the warehouses in the ports, it arranged to be notified of the arrival of all shipments so as to coordinate their transfer and delivery, and it generally supervised commercial activity

TABLE 10

Dates of Dispatches Received in Guatemala on 10 May 1848

Source	Date	Delay
San Salvador	28 April	12 days
Chiapas	23 April	17 days
Belize	8 April	32 days
Mexico	8 April	32 days
Havana	26 March	45 days
San José de Costa Rica	20 March	51 days
León, Nicaragua	20 March	51 days
United States	18 March	53 days
London	2 March	69 days
Paris & Brussels	29 February	71 days

Source: *Gaceta de Guatemala*, 10 May 1848.

in the ports.[26] It cooperated with the Belgians at Santo Tomás, although it directed its principal efforts in the 1840s toward improving Izabal. While Santo Tomás had better access to the sea than Izabal, the absence of an adequate road to that port meant that Izabal continued to be the primary North Coast port. This continued to be the case even after the government in 1850 named Santo Tomás as the only legal port of entry on the North Coast, and the lack of a passable road resulted in the restoration of port-of-entry status to Izabal in 1852. Santo Tomás and Livingston also provided port facilities thereafter, but the amount of trade these ports handled was insignificant compared to Izabal.[27]

After the fall of Gálvez, the government had sought to shift overseas traffic from Belize to a Guatemalan port. It directly challenged Belize's reexport trade by allowing goods to pass through Guatemalan ports without payment of duties as long as they were reexported.[28] It also tried to improve the postal service among the Central American states to encourage interstate commerce.[29] Even so, mail took considerable time among the states. In 1847 the government established regular weekly service between the capital and Chiquimula, with fortnightly service on to Honduras.[30] Yet delays still encountered can be seen from the dates of dispatches that the *Gaceta de Guatemala* reported receiving on 10 May 1848 (see Table 10).

Completion of the Panama Railway in 1855 permitted more profitable use of the Pacific, nearer the Guatemalan production zones, and the Caribbean anchorages declined sharply. Although in 1853 the Consulado contributed three hundred pesos to the construction of a new warehouse at

Santo Tomás, it increasingly turned over its operations on the North Coast to local or national officials. Julio Rosignon, writing in *La Semana* on behalf of Verapaz interests early in 1865, strongly favored renewed development of Izabal and Santo Tomás, but he had no apparent effect on Consulado policy.[31] When fire destroyed most of Izabal in 1868, the Consulado took little interest in rebuilding it because the merchants had reoriented their trade to the Pacific.[32]

Because of its proximity to the producing region, the Consulado had promoted the Pacific port of Iztapa even during the 1840s, when its chief efforts had been directed toward the Atlantic. The government encouraged greater use of the port with a 2 percent tariff rebate on imports and exemption from port and anchorage fees for ships carrying exports, and by increasing tariffs on trade across the Salvadoran frontier, a move aimed at Acajutla. By 1852 the Consulado had ordered a corrugated iron warehouse from England for Iztapa when the government called for construction of a new wharf.

While making initial surveys for the construction of the wharf, the Consulado's engineer, Agustín Van de Gehuchte, concluded that a more desirable location would be at El Zapote, a few miles west of Iztapa. The merits of El Zapote had been recognized as early as 1836, when the government had moved the Pacific customs house there, but for some reason it had been abandoned by March 1837, and Iztapa was again the sole Guatemalan port on the Pacific Coast. Now, on Van de Gehuchte's recommendation, the government ordered construction of a new port at Zapote under the name of San José de Guatemala. Although it was to begin operations in January 1853, an outbreak of disease in the port delayed completion of the move from Iztapa until 13 July 1853. The first ship, the *Tres Amigos* from Costa Rica, did not arrive until the following October. The Consulado did not complete the wharf until 1857, but maintained a lighter to ferry cargo between the beach and ships anchored offshore.[33]

Profits of the Panama Railway Company soared in 1856 as establishment of fairly regular Pacific Coast steamship service greatly increased the volume of trade along that coast of Central America.[34] The Guatemalan government favored San José by excusing its workers from military service, while the Consulado maintained the port largely at the expense of its attention to the Caribbean ports. The wharf first constructed failed to withstand the weather, surf, and heavy volume of shipping, so the government began contracting for a new one in 1858. A Guatemalan, Pío Benito, finally completed its construction in 1868 after two English companies had failed.

There were demands for additional Pacific ports, especially from Quetzaltenango and the Suchitepéquez coast. The Consulado supervised some reconnaissances and the government in 1854 authorized Puerto San Luis, at the mouth of the Río Samalá, but the Consulado provided little tangible assistance in developing it. San Luis opened in March of 1855, largely as the result of the efforts of the corregidor of Quetzaltenango. By the 1860s it was the chief port on the Suchitepéquez coast, although produce, chiefly coffee, continued to be exported from Champerico, as well as from Tecojate and San Gerónimo at the mouths of the Río Coyolate and the Río Sotella in the Department of Escuintla.[35]

Exports shifted so dramatically to the Pacific that by 1865 nearly 95 percent of total exports passed through those ports. The sharpest change came between the years 1855 and 1860. The trend continued in the decade following and, although there had been some efforts to revive the Caribbean trade before 1871, the great majority of Guatemala's foreign trade still passed through the Pacific ports by that date (see Figures 4 and 5).

The failure of the government or the Consulado to provide more support for ports on the Suchitepéquez coast undoubtedly retarded the growth of agro-exports from Los Altos. Those departments were of less importance to the merchants of the capital and, moreover, rival ports threatened the monopoly of the capital merchants over the foreign commerce of the state. The failure of the Consulado to contribute materially to the establishment of a port on the Suchitepéquez coast demonstrated how the guild protected the monopoly of the Guatemala City merchants at the cost of more general development of the state. This would be a major grievance on the part of coffee planters of western Guatemala and the Verapaz, leading supporters of the 1871 Reforma to suppress the Consulado. Not surprisingly, the new government would pay considerably more attention to Champerico and ports on the Caribbean.[36]

If ports were essential to the commercial interests represented by the Consulado, no less vital were the roads and rivers that connected them with the centers of production. The merchants, of course, conceived the Consulado's road building responsibilities in terms of benefit to commerce. The Consulado also assisted the development of an interior network of roads to connect commercially important regions of the country with the capital. It thus concerned itself with roads connecting Guatemala City with Los Altos and Mexico, with El Salvador, and with the Verapaz, but it gave greater attention to connecting the capital with Antigua, Amatitlán, and Escuintla.

Highway construction in Guatemala is difficult even in modern times.

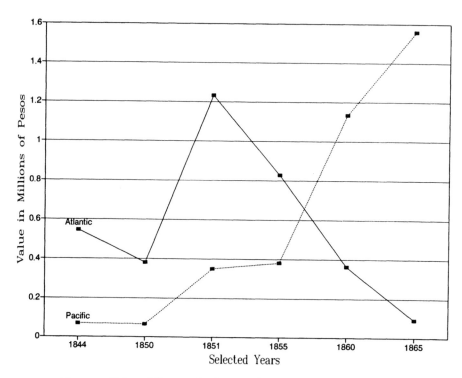

FIGURE 4. Value of Guatemalan Imports by Ports (Selected Years, 1844–1865)
Sources: Gaceta Oficial and *Gaceta de Guatemala*, 1844–1866

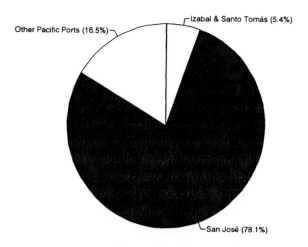

FIGURE 5. Guatemalan Exports by Ports in 1865
Source: Gaceta de Guatemala, 26 May 1866

The country's volcanic ranges and gigantic ravines, or *barrancas*, require construction of tortuous passes on very steep grades. For six months of the year heavy rains drench the land, creating bogs and turning dry *arroyos* into torrential rivers capable of washing out even the most sturdy bridge foundations and approaches. During the rain season, lowland areas of the coasts, covered with dense vegetation, often become flooded or so muddy that passage becomes impossible. Rains and earthquakes cause frequent landslides in the mountains.

For similar reasons, the rivers of Guatemala did not readily support navigation. The difficulties of road building, however, caused some to look to river and canal transport for cargo and passengers. The two river systems of greatest potential value to commerce were the Motagua and the Polochic, both of which empty into the Gulf of Honduras. The Polochic drains the Alta Verapaz and flows into the Golfo Dulce, which in turn empties into the Bay of Amatique by way of the Río Dulce. The Motagua flows from the Baja Verapaz, not far from Guatemala City, northeastward through the departments of Zacapa and Izabal. Bars that denied entrance to all but shallow draft vessels obstructed the mouths of both rivers, and similar hazards in the rivers themselves restricted their use to pirogues or dugout canoes. Even the Río Dulce could be navigated only by shallow-draft vessels. There was occasional talk of deepening the mouth of that river so that Izabal could become a true seaport, but this has never been accomplished. The Consulado, authorized to undertake this project in 1839, gave it some study and then abandoned the idea, ending the possibility of an inland deep water port.

The Río Polochic since colonial times had been a favorite route of smugglers. Efforts to construct a good road from the Guatemalan capital to the Polochic River port of Telemán had been considered several times, as the government envisioned converting smuggling to legal trade and at the same time stimulating the economy of the Verapaz. The Dominican friars of the Verapaz had expressed great interest in this route, which would have enhanced their ability to carry on trade from their agricultural enterprises. The principal geographic obstacle to the connecting road was the difficulty in crossing the upper reaches of the Río Motagua. During the dry season it was a gurgling stream, easily fordable, but during the rainy months it became a swift, raging torrent, crossed only at great hazard. In the early years of the nineteenth century the Dominicans had failed in an attempt to bridge the river; attempts by the ayuntamiento of Guatemala and the Diputación Provincial had been equally unsuccessful.[37] After independence, in the spirit of freer trade, the Guatemalan government opened the Polochic to navigation and encouraged its use, resulting in an increase in traffic via that route, but the Motagua crossing and the hazards of small craft navigation on the Polochic kept it from becoming a major route to the capital.[38] The government also renewed efforts to make the lower Motagua navigable and to develop a road connecting that river with Puerto Santo Tomás, but without success.[39]

Merely maintaining the road to Izabal consumed most of the Consulado's revenues. It deteriorated rapidly each year during the rains, and for much of the nineteenth century remained little more than the mule trail it had been in colonial times. In 1840 the Consulado brought in some eighty blacks from Truxillo and Belize and put them under the supervision of two English engineers, Robert Smith and John Baily.[40] By 1845, although there were still many difficult sections, the Consulado regarded the road as greatly improved over what had "previously caused horror to the merchant and the muleteer."[41] The Consulado completed a number of small bridges in the 1840s, but the badly needed spans over the upper Motagua and Río Chiquimula at Zacapa exceeded the resources available to the guild. President Carrera in May of 1847 ordered the Consulado to make a reconnaissance and to cooperate with the Belgians to help open a road between Santo Tomás and the Motagua, but pleading lack of funds, the Consulado did little.[42]

In 1851 Carrera personally took an interest in improving the road to the Caribbean, having acquired a fine carriage, which the existing road would hardly accommodate. The government ordered the Consulado to devote more funds to the Guatemala-Zacapa carriageway project and to complete it at least as far as El Chato, four leagues from the capital.[43] By April of 1856 the highway stretched to El Chato, but priority attention to the Pacific port after this date halted further progress.[44] The Consulado provided only minimal maintenance on the Izabal road thereafter, and the government relied principally on the corregidores or private and foreign assistance to maintain the road. Yet the improvements in the road that the Consulado had carried out brought down freight rates on the road considerably. In 1840 rates per *arroba* ranged from $2.00 to $3.50; by 1853 the same freight cost from 87 cents to $1 for the same distance.[45]

Without Consulado aid, there was little river navigation except by smugglers. In 1863, the U.S.-owned Guatemalan Canal Company proposed to dig a channel to connect the Motagua with Puerto Santo Tomás, but had given up by 1865.[46] Another Belgian engineer, Julián Marcos Deby, in 1867 received a contract from the Guatemalan government to build a road between the port and the river, but his efforts were no more successful than earlier Belgian attempts.[47] The Wyke-Aycinena Treaty of 1859 required the British to construct an all-weather road from Guatemala City to the Caribbean, but progress went little further than initial planning and survey, with no agreement on the route the road would take.[48]

The Consulado began a serious effort on the road to the Pacific port as early as 1840 and the road was passable for mule traffic by March of 1843.[49] By mid-1850 a commercial stage coach could make the run between the capital and Amatitlán in all weather. The carriageway was completed to Escuintla by the end of that year, although the treacherous and steep section between Palín and Escuintla often had to be closed after heavy rains. Yet by November 1851 the entire road had been finished and had endured in good condition through the last rainy season, with about 150 carts transporting goods along the road daily.[50] The road was not made truly passable for anything more than carts and mules, however, until the great increase in the volume of trade in the mid-1850s. In 1856 regular stage coach service extended to Escuintla and in 1858, finally, to Puerto San José. Carriage rates dropped to half their former level and completion of this road directly enabled San José to monopolize the trade of the republic.[51]

After 1855 the Consulado maintained regular work squads on this highway and increased their numbers to several hundred during severe rainy seasons. Under the supervision of the Consulado engineer this road became the finest in the country. Improvements on connecting roads with other towns also occurred, most notably on the road down to Palín from Antigua via Santa María de Jesús.[52]

The Consulado's efforts on other roads were decidedly less notable. It devoted only occasional support to the road to Los Altos, despite professions of interest in greater overland trade with Mexico. It opened a carriageway to Antigua in 1851.[53] Beyond a detailed survey of the road to Quetzaltenango, conducted by the Consulado engineer in the same year, the Consulado contented itself to subsidize, irregularly, the corregidores of the departments of Los Altos, who accomplished most of what was done on the road beyond Antigua.[54] Nor did the Consulado contribute much to the completion of the road from Quetzaltenango to the port of Champerico, which was constructed during these years largely with funds raised by the corregidores of the Los Altos departments. The Consulado supplied some survey and planning for the project only after the government ordered it to do so. What progress was made on the roads of Los Altos came largely from the initiative of local officials in building roads and bridges.[55]

Nor did the Consulado provide much support for a better land link with El Salvador. For twenty years following independence from Spain, civil disorder had disrupted life along the old *camino real* between Guatemala City and San Salvador. In 1844 the Consulado commissioned Jorge Ponce to repair the old stone bridge originally built in 1592 over the Río Esclavos,[56] but little more was done for that road until Carrera promoted the project of a carriageway to the Salvadoran border after 1850. By January 1853 the president could ride in his carriage as far as the Esclavos, but a decade later the carriageway extended no further.[57] If anything, the road seems to have deteriorated, for in December 1867 the Consulado's engineer announced that the road was passable for carriages only as far as Cerro Redondo, about twenty-five kilometers short of the Río Esclavos bridge.[58] It was later reopened as far as that river, but the Consulado never extended the carriageway beyond that point.

The Verapaz did not gain major commercial importance during the conservative years, although the Dominican estates had been productive and suggested greater economic potential for the region. The government often suggested roads stretching from the capital well into the Petén, even beyond the Río Polochic, but the Consulado, more immediately concerned with profit, had supported a road only as far as Salamá in the Baja Verapaz until it became involved in building a bridge over the upper Motagua. As a penalty for not fulfilling the terms of its contract with the Guatemalan government, the Eastern Coast of Central America Commercial and Agricultural Company purchased an iron suspension bridge in England, to be hung by the Consulado over the river on a road connecting the capital with the Verapaz.[59]

The history of this bridge is illustrative of the difficulties faced by those trying to develop the country's transportation network. In June 1842 the bridge reached Izabal from London and was transported up the Río Polochic and then overland to the bridge site on the Motagua. Under the supervision of an English engineer, the Consulado hung the bridge in July 1844 at a spot known even to this day as Puente Inglés (English Bridge). In 1847 the Consulado constructed a house at the bridge for the convenience of passengers and cargo carriers, and it continued to improve the road and approaches to the bridge as commerce with the Verapaz grew. In October 1852, however, as the rainy season reached its height, the bridge washed away. The Consulado recovered and rehung the bridge the following year, but the rains of 1855 completely destroyed it, and in 1856 the Consulado began construction of a wooden replacement. Once it was completed, in December 1858, the Consulado turned over its maintenance to the corregidor of the Verapaz. It was in such bad condition by June 1861 that the government urged the Consulado to spend some money to make it serviceable again. The structure lasted four more years before the rains of 1865 carried it away. The Consulado ordered a new iron bridge from Europe, which was in service by May 1868.[60]

The government encouraged the Consulado to extend this road to Telemán and to develop that route for international trade. The Polochic presented less of a problem for navigation than did the Motagua, and the hope was that small ships could ferry cargo from Telemán to Izabal. Modest amounts of cochineal were going out by that route,[61] but concern over the use of the port for smuggling arms into the country caused the government to close the port to international traffic in December 1851.[62] The government reopened the river to navigation in 1857. While it did not become a major commercial route, improvements in port facilities at Telemán permitted some increase in trade and facilitated coffee exports from the Verapaz.[63] In January 1866 the Consulado's Belgian-trained engineer, Salvador Cobos, presented a detailed survey of a projected highway between Telemán and Tactic at an estimated cost of $140,000 to complete the thirteen leagues of cart road at a width of about twenty-five feet. Although the *Gaceta* urged the Consulado to use its funds and local labor for the project, the Consulado did not invest further in this project.[64] At about the same time, a retired British army officer, George Douglas Harris, proposed to establish a company to provide steamboat service on the Polochic. The Guatemalan government agreed to consider ceding land to the company on which to build wharfs and warehouses at Telemán or Panzós and Tactic, as well as up to a square league of land along the proposed road between Telemán and Tactic. Nothing came of this proposal, however.[65] In the closing years of the conservative period Father José Güell y Busquets tried to establish a colonization company for the area—the Compañía Agrícola del Polochic—but he could not attract sufficient shareholders nor interest the Consulado or anyone else capable of supporting the venture. Güell lobbied actively for opening roads in the Polochic area, and he himself opened a path between the Río Hondo, Panzós, and Telemán in August 1866. He also encouraged more commerce between the Verapaz and the Chiquimula region.[66]

Guatemala was slow to begin railway construction. The Consulado never did any more than discuss that solution to Guatemala's transportation problem. The difficulty of attracting adequate capital with its limited volume of trade was undoubtedly a retarding factor. The government proposed a railway in 1858 to connect Puerto San José with Guatemala City, but the merchants of the Consulado doubted that enough capital could be raised.[67] Not until February 1868 did the Consulado seriously consider a railway

project, when it drew up a contract with Manuel García Granados for construction of a railroad between San José and Escuintla.[68] In May of the
following year, the Consulado published a detailed report on a project for
the construction of a plank road between the port and Escuintla. Its engineer, Salvador Cobos, argued that such a road would be used immediately
by carts and could also served as a base for the railroad.[69] But in 1871
the regime ended, and the Consulado was suppressed before either project
had begun. Similarly, on the North Coast, the Consulado had begun some
railroad studies, but contracted no construction.[70] The conservative nature
of the Consulado and the government's reluctance to become dependent
on foreign capital certainly contributed to Guatemala's belated start on
railroads.

The Consulado did initiate efforts to establish telegraph lines in the
republic, although it did not actively sponsor the project. It urged the
government to grant exclusive privileges for the establishment of telegraph
lines to a private Guatemalan company headed by O. du Teil, another Belgian immigrant, in 1866. In October of the following year, material arrived
in Puerto San José to begin construction of the line to the capital, and work
began shortly thereafter. However, service did not begin until after 1871
with the aid of another company and contract.[71]

While the primary concern of the Consulado was development of a transportation infrastructure for overseas trade, in effect the Consulado became
a ministry of public works under the conservative regime, consistent with
the corporative nature of the state. A French observer in 1867 may have
overstated the degree to which the Consulado was responsible for a broad
range of public works projects, but his observations reflect his impression
of the Consulado as the supervisor of public works in the country:

> These public works, which go unnoticed, would honor the most civilized
> administration and testify to the generous emulation which a successful sys-
> tem inspires. These are wooden and stone bridges, aqueducts from 2,000 to
> 10,000 meters, coffee plantations, public fountains, water tanks, construc-
> tion of cabildos and schools, highway maintenance, and repair of churches
> and government buildings. They are pursued presently in all points of the
> territory which is ordinarily estimated at 5,500 square leagues, but the sur-
> face is actually considerably more owing to its numerous and deep declivities.
> These are no longer ordered by State intervention. It is an independent asso-
> ciation, the *Consulado de Comercio*, which decrees them; the municipalities
> and private interests that accomplish them.[72]

The increased production and trade demanded more regular shipping
services, and as steam navigation began to replace the sailing vessels in

transatlantic runs, the Carrera government worked to secure regular service on both coasts. In 1838, the government had encouraged steam navigation with an exemption of tonnage taxes in Guatemalan ports.[73] By 1850 the establishment of more or less regular steam packet service between Belize and the Central American states represented an improvement over earlier uncertainties.[74] Service direct from Southampton began in 1850 and notably improved communications with Europe.[75] In 1856 the Guatemalan government began a $4,500 annual subsidy to the Guatemalan company of Francisco Camoyano to provide regular steamship service between Izabal, Livingston, Santo Tomás, and Belize, but by that time Caribbean shipping had become of secondary importance.[76] The failure of the Central American states to develop their own maritime service was characteristic of Latin America in general in the nineteenth century.[77]

From 1850 forward the Guatemalan government actively worked toward establishing regular service on the Pacific. An English company in that year began to offer service along the Central American coast to Panama and on to Valparaíso, although service was never so regular as advertised.[78] M. F. Pavón and José Coloma formed a committee to improve the Pacific ship service in 1851, and they urged the government to offer subsidies for regular service. The result was a contract in that year between the several Central American states and the company of Ducoing, Cañas, and Fernández in which each state agreed to pay the company $2,000 monthly for service by two sailing ships along the Pacific coast. The company agreed to carry the mail free and to provide monthly service in each direction.[79] This company did not thrive, but a Central American Steamship Company soon succeeded it. Its steamship *Primero* began monthly service along the Pacific coast in January 1854. Often delayed, it rarely met its scheduled arrival at Puerto San José on the fifteenth of each month, causing passengers to complain frequently. Rates from Puerto San José to Panama were $60 per ton and $75 per passenger.[80]

The addition of the Hamburg steamship *Emilie* in 1856 improved the service and included Mexican ports.[81] More reliable service came from the Panama Railway Company's Pacific steamship service. Under an 1856 contract, the Guatemalan government agreed to a subsidy of $80,000 over ten years.[82] The company's steamship *Columbus* could carry eight first-class passengers at rates of $85 between San José and Panama. It also advertised freight rates for coffee of $0.005 per pound to Panama, or an all inclusive ship-rail-ship charge of 15 cents per pound from San José to New York.[83] In the 1860s the British Royal Mail Steamship line came to provide the most reliable service along the Pacific Coast, however, with ongoing service to Europe.[84]

Other English, German, and North American ships also provided less regular service, so that Pacific Coast shipping became much easier than earlier. In 1858 the Guatemalan government agreed to a small subsidy and exemption of port charges for clipper ship service to San Francisco. The contract with Juan Serigiers and Company provided for two clipper ships of two hundred tons or more to carry Guatemalan mail free of charge. The firm was to receive a subsidy of four hundred pesos for each round trip voyage that carried Guatemalan products, to be paid from duties collected on goods exported or imported by those ships. It also provided for military and political officials to travel at half fare.[85] Similar contracts provided service under sail to Mexican ports, and in 1865 the government contracted with Crisanto Medina for steamship service with Mexico and California.[86] In 1868 Pedro N. Sánchez, with several Guatemalan and foreign associates, formed a new Central American Steamship Company and won approval of a $15,000 annual subsidy from the Guatemalan government to establish steamer service between Guatemala and San Francisco, California. Sánchez subsequently turned over his rights in September 1869 to R. Rosenberg, whose *Prince Alfred* made several trips, but the government deemed the service unsatisfactory and canceled Rosenberg's subsidy on 28 September 1870.[87] In fact, by 1870, there was sufficient service and competition among several companies so that the subsidies were no longer necessary and the government began to terminate them all.[88]

The improvement in shipping services also permitted a lowering of international postal rates in May 1866. Letters of up to a half ounce cost one real to anywhere in the Western Hemisphere or two reales to the Eastern Hemisphere. Additional ounces cost two and four reales respectively.[89] These rates were a far cry from charges of as high as $30 to $45 for a single letter in the 1820s.[90]

Although there were definite improvements in Guatemala's port and communications infrastructure during the conservative years, entrusting it to those who most directly benefited from such development had both advantages and disadvantages. The Consulado consistently failed to promote roads in areas that were not on the main existing routes of commerce, and the lack of any other agency to do so left much of the country underdeveloped and without adequate transportation facilities. The regionalism that was so prevalent in Central America may in part be attributed to the lack of communications. The concept that unity goes only as far as the means of communication can receive ample support in the history of Central America.[91] Yet the Consulado could not, with its meager resources, do much more than it did. The existing commerce did not justify large expenditures in areas that were not of proven commercial importance, nor was the Consulado large enough to provide sufficient funds to carry out widespread construction. Thus, by concentrating its effort on one or two key routes, the Consulado was able to accomplish more immediate benefit to the merchants it represented and to the state's economy than if it had undertaken a larger number of projects than its resources could support. Its consistent efforts to improve the road to the Caribbean before the shift of emphasis to the Pacific served to preserve and develop Guatemala's commercial ties with Europe, even though efforts to establish a carriageway were unsuccessful. The merchant guild's role in building and maintaining the road to the Pacific helped to make possible a relatively rapid shift from cochineal to coffee in both production and marketing. By entrusting the maintenance of highways to the merchants of the capital, the government was at least assured of supervision that had a vital interest in improvement of the roads over which the nation's foreign commerce flowed, even if it did not insure development of roads throughout the whole state.

In carrying out responsibilities that are frequently considered the legitimate functions of government, the Guatemalan Consulado reflected clearly the corporate nature of conservative Guatemala in the mid-nineteenth century. The Consulado was essentially the merchant-planter creole elite that had inherited control of the Guatemalan economy following independence. By allying itself with Rafael Carrera from 1839 forward, it was able to consolidate its economic control of the country within a framework of traditional development. As the stronghold and spokesman for the wealthy merchants and capitalists of Guatemala City, the Consulado's economic importance allowed its opinions to carry considerable weight in political councils. The Consulado typified the corporatist philosophy of the Spanish regime and of the conservatives in Central America after independence.

In allowing an exclusive group the privilege of its own court, the right to regulate its own activities even though the economy of the country as a whole was affected, and to carry on a program of public works on which the entire nation depended, the government failed, in the eyes of the liberals, to govern properly. Such a system protected a privileged class at the expense of the general welfare and therefore retarded progress and contributed unwittingly to an attitude of political separatism in outlying areas. Thus the liberals consistently opposed the Consulado and abolished it in 1826, 1829, and again in 1871. In essence, this conflict expressed the differences between the liberals, representing those denied the privilege and power of the exclusive fueros (of merchants, soldiers, or priests), and the conservatives, striving to preserve law and order through maintenance of these institutions, which protected the hegemony of the privileged few while paternalistically protecting the impoverished masses from exploitation by the more aggressive liberals.

Through the broad powers given it, the Consulado had the opportunity to launch significant and far-sighted projects that might have stimulated and diversified the Guatemalan economy. Its control over the commerce of the land allowed the institution to reduce the colonial nature of the country's economy. While the merchants probably should not be criticized severely for doing no more than their contemporaries were doing in political and social affairs, the use of the power given them for personal and class objectives alone cannot be overlooked. It poses the question whether long-range economic development in Guatemala—or anywhere in underdeveloped countries—can satisfactorily be achieved by entrusting the means of such development to a group with special class interests. The experience of the Guatemalan Consulado suggests that such a method, while useful in achieving limited goals, could not provide the more comprehensive development of the economy that was needed.

Reliance on the Consulado and the Economic Society, essentially quasi-governmental agencies, permitted the slow, ordered growth that Guatemala enjoyed. The idea that the society was a liberal institution, which has been suggested by several Guatemalan historians, was partially true, for it contributed to the liberal-capitalist spirit and emphasis on agro-exports as the salvation of Guatemala's future development, but its programs were based on a paternalistic view of development rather than on broad policies of general economic growth and improvement. The Consulado's narrow class interests and search for immediate gain made it an ineffective agency for stimulating more general economic growth, and its monopolistic position over the trade of the country prejudiced its attitude toward more widespread economic activity. The broad powers granted the Consulado, had they been employed for the benefit of the nation as a whole, could have resulted in a significant diversification of export production, which could have proven to be of more lasting value to the merchants and to the population in general.

CHAPTER EIGHTEEN

Production for
Consumption and Export

THE LIBERALS HAD PINNED THEIR HOPES for the transformation of Central America into a prosperous and modern republic on the rapid increase of exports of tropical agricultural commodities. As early as February 1824, the Guatemalan state government had called on local governments to report on the climate of populated areas, the quality of existing agricultural production, and new crops that might be introduced.[1] In the 1830s cochineal exports grew notably, but the rapid increase in trade the liberals had hoped for had not materialized before they were ousted in 1839.

The commercial policy of the conservative governments from 1839 to 1871 was carried forth in the interest of the established merchant-planter community of the capital. In general, it represented a reaction against the free-trade philosophy of the liberals and a return to protectionist and monopolistic principals learned under Spanish rule. Within this framework, the government sought to increase trade and revenues both in domestic and foreign trade. While the policy sometimes lacked consistency and was out of step with prevailing nineteenth-century liberal economic philosophy, it was consistent with the Hispanic traditionalism that so characterized Guatemala in the mid-nineteenth century. A manifestation of the preference for Hispano-traditionalism and annoyance at the rising use of British weights and measures was a call by the Guatemala City Council at the end of 1840 for standardization of weights and measures according to Castilian standards and the *Novísima recopilación de las leyes de Indias*.[2]

Damage to the native textile industry from imports had been one of the causes of resistance to the Gálvez government, and Carrera made clear his support of the weavers. It was the most important native manufacturing industry in the country, but inexpensive European factory imports had damaged it from the late eighteenth century forward. Carrera and the conservatives thus began to challenge the liberal free trade policy. On 16 September 1840 Carrera proposed to the government that it end the free importation of any goods that competed with those produced in Guatemala and thereby contributed to the decline of native industry and artisans.[3] Ten days later, a letter signed by "El Mataquescuintleco" in the reactionary, pro-Carrera *El Procurador de los Pueblos* bitterly attacked free trade as the cause of the impoverishment of the people. Supporting a recent petition to the assembly against free trade, it blamed the free-trade policy on foreigners, especially Jews and Arabs, people lacking traditional Christian values. It charged them with trying to destroy Guatemalan agriculture and manufactures.[4] In November the assembly asked the Consulado and other institutions to prepare reports on damage to native artisans and solicited opinions on the possible prohibition of the import of articles that competed with those produced in Guatemala.[5] Both the Economic Society and the Consulado recommended protective tariffs and restrictions on imports of some articles.[6]

In May 1844, however, with moderate liberal influence once more in the government, the *Gaceta* acknowledged that Guatemala should not adopt a totally protectionist system that might reduce commerce and cause serious shortages of necessary consumer goods. But it did argue that some way had to be found to "develop our products and to favor the small industries, artisans and workers of the capital and other considerable populations." It thus recommended that Guatemala develop cacao, flour, cane sugar, liquor, tobacco, and wrought iron, and prohibit imports of manufactured clothing, shoes, coarse textiles, and straw hats.[7] At the same time the government tightened its customs controls, adding an additional inspector and raising fines for fraudulent declarations.[8] Cattle raisers also clamored for protection, and in 1851 the corregidor of Suchitepéquez informed the government that municipalities in his department had requested that a tax be placed on livestock imported from Mexico and other places.[9]

By 1845 Guatemalan policy was theoretically committed to free trade among the Central American states, but to protection on trade beyond the isthmus. In practice, commercial relations with the other isthmian states were badly disturbed by the political problems already discussed.[10] Several issues of the *Gaceta* carried translations of articles by European economists questioning unrestrained free trade.[11] In August 1845 the Economic Society directed a formal statement on the question to the government, in which it called for an end to free trade, citing other nations' success with protection, notably the United States and Mexico. It added that "whatever the doctrines of the economists, the fact is that all governments protect their industry and agriculture, and promote unceasingly their advancement and protection, as the foundation and guiding principal of the prosperity of the people. — Why then, has only Guatemala been an exception to this general rule?"[12]

Continued concern over smuggling caused periodic revisions and tightening of the regulations, record keeping, and procedures regarding foreign trade.[13] The Guatemalan tariff act of 22 February 1855 reflected the trend toward protection with generally higher rates on foreign imports. The feeble liberal calls for free trade after 1850 received little notice. Miguel García Granados argued in the assembly in April 1858 for a general lowering of tariffs and freer trade and called for free transit of foreign goods destined to neighboring republics to promote commerce. He eventually withdrew his motion when it became obvious that it had no chance of passage. On 30 May he complained that his reasons for withdrawing the motion were not recorded, but the president of the assembly ruled that the minutes did not deal with reasons, but only with action taken.[14]

In March 1852 Carrera promised continued protection of the indigenous textile industry. He noted the higher quality of Guatemalan textiles over the imports, adding that the native products were especially appropriate for the working class.[15] The Interior Ministry responded immediately by making arrangements with the Economic Society to have instructions printed and distributed and to gather information on the best machinery available in the United States or England that might be brought to Guatemala to expand native production. The plan was to bring two persons from the United States or England to instruct artisans in the use of this machinery.[16] The government also published a twenty-eight-page pamphlet containing instructions for dying wool.[17]

Wool production was important in Los Altos. The corregidor of San Marcos in 1854 estimated that his department had more than one hundred thousand sheep, producing about forty thousand arrobas of wool.[18] In 1862 Carrera sent Carlos Klée to the United States to make a study of woollen manufacturing machinery, with an eye toward establishment of a factory in Quetzaltenango.[19] Carrera's attention to the textile industry would appear to have been important in insuring its survival in Guatemala in the face of growing British imports in the nineteenth century. Native textile production remained the primary source of clothing for most of the rural population throughout the nineteenth and twentieth centuries.

The British, of course, sought to restrain this trend toward protection. They instead encouraged the Central American states to increase their exports of both agricultural commodities and indigenous crafts. Frederick Chatfield, for instance, encouraged and invited each of the states to send products to London's 1851 Great Exhibition of the Works of Industry of All Nations. In Guatemala the Economic Society took responsibility for gathering and submitting articles for such exhibitions, and often pursued these projects with considerable zeal.[20]

Notwithstanding the reactionary preference for Hispanic institutions and laws, the presence of many Spanish merchants, and an antipathy toward English-speaking commercial interests, the sheer maritime and financial strength of the British Empire and the aggressive action of its Central American entrepreneurs meant that British commercial interests expanded. By 1850, according to Robert Naylor, "The commercial establishments of Guatemala had found that direct arrangements with companies in Great Britain left a better account and nearly all the import merchants now had their Liverpool and London correspondents. Only the smallest and poorest merchants confined their transactions to the Belize houses."[21] Yet a contemporary British resident, Robert Dunlop, noted that other foreigners dominated the internal trade and formed "the great bulk of the commercial class." He acknowledged that the marketing of imported articles was concentrated in the hands of a few foreigners, but said that five Spanish merchant companies controlled most of it, while four Italian, three French, three German, and two English houses held lesser prominence.[22] The enterprise of a single foreign merchant could create significant change. In neighboring Honduras, for example, in the same year, 1846, an Italian established the little port of Amapala on the leeward side of Tigre Island in the Gulf of Fonseca and made it one of the more envied commercial centers of the region.[23]

A significant difference between Central American liberals and conservatives in the nineteenth century was their attitude toward foreign capital as a means toward developing their countries. While both accepted capitalism as a means of development, the liberals were decidedly more receptive to foreign investment. Conservatives, on the other hand, while not unalterably opposed to foreign investment, tended to be more suspicious of foreigners and more often looked to, or hoped for, native investment and ownership of national resources. Thus the liberals of the 1820s had eagerly sought foreign investment, offering land, concessions, and favorable interest rates to those who would place their capital in Central American development schemes. They especially promoted the Caribbean coastal regions as places of enormous opportunity, awaiting only industrious European immigration and capital investment.[24] Early conservative opposition to liberal promotion of foreign investment succeeded in 1825 in requiring foreign corporations engaged in industry, mining, or trade to reserve a quarter of their shares for Central Americans.[25] The civil disorder and absence of adequate infrastructure limited the amount of foreign investment that the early liberals were able to attract, but a few Belize-based merchants did enter the Central American economy in Guatemala. Most important was Marshall Bennett, a business associate of Francisco Morazán, who in 1826 established a branch of his merchant house in Guatemala with Carlos A. Meany and William Hall, who both founded important families in Guatemala. Bennett also bought into mining, agriculture, manufacturing, and forest interests in Central America. He was among those who acquired church properties expropriated by the liberals after 1829, including Convento Viejo, the sugar company that the Dominicans had run in Guatemala City.[26]

Another British merchant who became important in Guatemalan commerce was George Ure Skinner (1804–67). Skinner, the son of a Scottish Anglican minister and grandson of a well-known ecclesiastical historian of Scotland, had worked for Barclay, Bevan & Company in London, and later opened a merchant house in Leeds. In 1831 he came to Guatemala and entered into a partnership with a German merchant, Carlos Klée. Investing in indigo and cochineal properties, Skinner dealt harshly with his Indian workers in forging a sizable financial estate. He also became a noted naturalist, taking an interest in insects, birds, and orchids, shipping many of the latter to England. He returned frequently to England, making thirty-nine transatlantic crossings in all. He died in Panama in January 1867 after contracting yellow fever there on his return from England. Skinner-Klée developed direct trade with Europe and became the most important single British firm in Guatemala during the Carrera years.[27]

Much of the conservative opposition to liberal policies, of course, had been rooted in fear of the growing British commercial domination that had grown illegally throughout the eighteenth century and with liberal free trade after independence. From their settlements in Belize, the Mosquito Coast, and Jamaica, British merchants were well established by 1840, and their advantages in access to capital and shipping could not be matched by Guatemalan merchants. British tariff policy gave preferential treatment to products being developed by these British entrepreneurs, especially to mahogany and cochineal, products important to the growing British industry at home.[28] Accommodation to British commercial strength was unavoidable, but the conservatives sought at least to preserve some advantage to native merchants and to prevent the country from becoming totally dependent on the foreigners. Guatemalan cochineal exports already depended on British shipping and markets, as well as on liberal free-trade policy.

Independence had brought a much-needed impetus to Guatemala's depressed foreign trade, but imports of British textiles and other manufactures competed with native production, creating severe economic problems for native weavers and other artisans, thus contributing to popular grievances against British trade.[29] Trade with Spain, mostly via Havana, did not end, but in a free-trade situation, British advantage in shipping, finance, and entrepreneurship displaced the Cádiz commercial links.[30]

The number of British merchants was not large. Naylor tells us that "by 1850 there were no more than sixteen British residents in the five Central American states who were classified as merchants, plus an additional nine who were described as small traders. But," he adds, "regardless of the nationality of the import-merchants in the Central American states, most of their trade involved Great Britain." Their imports were British, and came through Belize or Jamaica, and the exports were destined principally for the British market and depended on British shipping and credit. "Great Britain," Naylor concludes, "thus achieved commercial dominance in the Central American states by controlling factors outside the Isthmus rather than by commanding the internal situation." [31]

British domination of Guatemala's trade during the federation period is reflected in the fragmentary but conclusive statistics available for the period. For example, imports for the fiscal year 1 March 1835 to 29 February 1836 reveal that 42 percent came from Britain, with an additional 25 percent from Belize, for a total of 67 percent from British sources. Spain still accounted for 15 percent, and Havana for another 5 percent. The French supplied nearly 10 percent, while the United States and Chile each accounted for slight more than 1 percent each of Guatemala's imports.[32] Central America had officially closed its ports to Spanish shipping in 1832 as a result of Spanish reconquest efforts, but this was not uniformly enforced, and Morazán authorized the reopening of ports to Spain in mid-1836.[33] The small U.S. share of the trade would begin to grow slowly after this, as U.S. ships began to supply cargo and passenger service to North America. An advertisement placed by Cándido Pulleiro, the leading commercial agent at Izabal, for one such ship anchored at Santo Tomás appeared in mid-1837 in a Guatemala City newspaper. It announced that the new brigantine

Osage would sail for New York between 25 and 30 June, taking cargo at the rate of three pesos per hundred pounds and passengers with excellent accommodations for eighty pesos, including meals and service.[34]

Two years later imports had grown slightly, with Belize accounting for nearly 50 percent, and London and Liverpool for another 31 percent, raising the British total to 81 percent! Cádiz accounted for only 7 percent, with Havana adding another 4 percent to the Spanish total. The French now accounted for less than 6 percent of total imports, with Hamburg a little more than 2 percent and the U.S. less than 1 percent.[35] In addition to the legal trade, however, contraband continued to enter the country, some undoubtedly through legal ports of entry thanks to corrupt port officials. Also a significant, if unknown quantity came through the clandestine route via Lake Izabal and the Río Polochic. William Griffith has described the activities of Antonino Sotela, the leading practitioner of this Polochic trade before 1840 and an original settler at the British colony at Abbotsville. He worked in cahoots with Pedro Oliva, a resident and local power in Telemán, on the Polochic. These men operated an extensive contraband trade in aguardiente, tobacco, arms, and gunpowder.[36] The government made Telemán a legal port of entry in 1840 and statistics for the following year reveal exports of $60,640.50 (of which $57,000 was cochineal) and imports of $13,549.50.[37]

With the restoration of peace following the defeat of Morazán in 1840, Guatemala looked forward to a growth in commerce and prosperity. An editorial in *El Tiempo* closed the year 1840 optimistically, noting increased interstate trade, the presence of more goods in Guatemala City, and the lowering of many prices. About thirty thousand head of cattle had arrived from Nicaragua and Honduras, making meat more plentiful and cheaper. Foreign trade had also picked up, especially at the Pacific port of Iztapa.[38] In fact, for fiscal 1840 (1 Oct. 1839–30 Sept. 1840), foreign trade had increased by about 9 percent over the previous year, with Iztapa accounting for about 16 percent of the total. And this did not include additional exports, perhaps to a value of $50,000, exported via Acajutla, El Salvador.[39] In December 1841 the Guatemalan government raised the ad valorem tax on imports through Salvadoran ports from 3 to 15 percent, but repealed this increase the following October in the interest of maintaining good relations with El Salvador and supporting free trade among the Central American states.[40] In June of 1843, however, after the Salvadorans had in March imposed a 10 percent tax on goods entering from Guatemala, Guatemala reimposed its 15 percent rate.[41] In fact, interstate trade was not great, reflecting the political difficulties between the states, and in practice the

Guatemalan government showed more interest in collecting taxes on inter-state trade than in promoting free trade with its neighbors.[42] In November 1851 the Guatemalan president prohibited altogether imports of any merchandise disembarked at Acajutla.[43] Growing concern over contraband and evasion of taxation was cited for this decree, and a month later all commerce on the North Coast was limited solely to the ports of Izabal and Santo Tomás for the same reason.[44]

Guatemala's declaration of absolute independence in 1847 resulted in more direct commercial ties with its European and North American trading partners. Both the French and the Germans sought to increase their Central American trade after 1850, but neither gained more than a tiny percentage of that carried by the British. Nor did Central America represent a significant part of their total Latin American trade.[45] In 1852, for example, Guatemala imported only 2 percent of total French exports to Latin America, and accounted for only 1.2 percent of Latin American exports to France in that year.[46] And it was growing much slower than French trade with the major Latin American states. By 1856 French trade with Guatemala represented only a half of 1 percent of total French trade with Latin America.[47]

Indigo had been the principal export of colonial Central America, but it came mostly from El Salvador. The civil wars of the first decades of independence had disrupted the earlier close relationship between the Guatemalan merchants and the Salvadoran planters, and while indigo remained El Salvador's principal export, its importance to the Guatemalan merchants disappeared.[48] Guatemala continued to produce indigo, but it was a minor export by 1850. Efforts to revive it by the Economic Society had little success, even after the government in 1868 conceded it special incentives and encouragement, including a new annual indigo fair in Jutiapa and a promise to build a new port on the Pacific Coast near Chiquimulilla once production and exports merited it.[49] Although exports soared from a value of 4,200 pesos in 1865 to 57,510 pesos (or about 2.5 percent of total exports) by 1869, the Consulado resisted pressures to proceed with establishment of the new port. Nor would it give material aid to encourage the industry further, and after 1869 exports of the dye leveled off and declined again.[50]

Far more important during the conservative years was another natural dye, cochineal. Produced from dried female cochineal insects harvested from the nopal cactus, this dye had been produced in Guatemala since pre-Columbian times. As a potential agro-export, however, it had been promoted by Captain General Bustamante about 1811, and nopal cultivation around Antigua and Amatitlán spread fairly rapidly thereafter. By 1821 Guatemala had already exported some cochineal to Spain, and beginning in

TABLE 11

Guatemalan Exports of Cochineal, 1827–1890

Year	Pounds	Value	Year	Pounds	Value
1827	15,000		1861	1,539,780	$788,650
1830	45,000		1862	1,659,185	837,986
1831	105,000		1863		855,838
1835	539,250	$605,757	1864		688,080
1838	851,007	851,007	1865		975,933
1840		665,662	1866		957,132
1842		413,275	1867	1,525,782	1,068,047
1843	721,800	541,350	1868	1,273,591	891,513
1845	1,024,950	896,831	1869	1,862,667	1,266,614
1846	1,068,450	943,270	1870	1,443,357	865,414
1848	1,525,800	1,186,475	1871	1,460,082	876,025
1849	1,543,930	994,444	1875	688,608	241,013
1850	1,605,000	892,690	1876	615,844	246,338
1851	2,041,050	1,231,730	1877	363,386	181,683
1852	680,100	568,150	1878	45,368	22,684
1853	323,450	312,850	1879	100,595	65,387
1854	2,587,200	1,757,300	1880	48,789	32,193
1855	1,210,360	985,780	1881	90,100	45,077
1856	1,782,550	1,381,240	1882	23,737	11,868
1857	1,470,440	1,017,270	1883	18,401	9,200
1858	2,018,440	1,407,410	1884	812	
1859	1,786,670	1,222,680	1888	2,400	1,248
1860	1,676,160	1,274,240	1890	0	0

Sources: Chester Lloyd Jones, *Guatemala, Past and Present* (1940), 385; *Gaceta de Guatemala*, 1850–71; Solórzano Fernández, *Historia*, 261; and Manuel Ruboi Sánchez, "Historia de la grana cochinilla en Guatemala" (1982).

Note: There is some disagreement among these sources, although these differences are slight and the figures shown here represent an effort to resolve such differences. Figures for the years 1827–54 are for fiscal years, running 1 Oct.–30 Sept. or from 1 June–31 May.

1822 it sent a growing quantity to Great Britain via Belize. Soon cultivation spread to the area around Nueva Guatemala, into eastern Guatemala, and the Verapaz. The liberal state government appointed a commission to promote cochineal exports in 1824 and cultivation of the crop expanded and surpassed indigo as the state's leading export before 1829. The government prohibited the export of live cochineal or of nopal plants, fearing especially competition from neighboring Belize. Henry Dunn estimated production in the neighborhood of seventy to ninety thousand pounds of the dye in the mid 1820s, but exports were not that high.[51] The rapid growth in legal exports of the dye for years for which data is available appears in Table 11.

Cochineal planters often leased lands from communities and municipalities, rather than owning them outright.[52] This was a step toward eventual private takeover of these lands, justified on the grounds that it allowed the poorer segments of the population to participate in the growth of cochineal cultivation. Much of the cochineal was, in fact, produced by small farmers or communities.

Great Britain encouraged cochineal imports through favorable tax legislation on behalf of its textile industry and became the principal consumer for Guatemalan cochineal. This was a powerful determinant in the close relations between Guatemala and Britain after 1840.[53] Production varied rather markedly from year to year, but in good years profits could be as high as 300 percent of investments in the crop, and the value of the exports were important to both individual and collective prosperity from the 1830s through the 1860s. By 1840, some two hundred thousand manzanas (about 350,000 acres), valued at $1,000 per manzana, were in nopal cultivation. The government burdened this trade with a heavy export tax in 1845, making it the single most important source of revenue, but the quality of the Guatemalan product was exceptionally high, so it continued to sell well.[54] The following year, the *Gaceta Oficial* estimated that the state's cochineal producers would realize a profit of $738,437.50 on gross sales of $1,035,937.50 for 1,275,000 pounds of the crimson dye.[55] A group of producers wrote the *Gaceta*, protesting that it had underestimated and overlooked many expenses, and alleged that the net profits would only amount to $188,062.50[56] In the London market, Guatemalan medium grade cochineal consistently brought a better price than the best Mexican product, as Guatemala became Britain's principal supplier of cochineal after 1842, accounting for 75 percent of British imports of the dye by 1850.[57]

The value of Guatemalan cochineal exports averaged more than a half million pesos per year in the 1840s. Years of high production did not necessarily mean higher profits, for prices usually fell, and in general (see Table 12), prices generally declined over the period as the supply grew.

The discovery of mauve aniline dye by Sir William Henry Perkin in 1856 assured the continued decline in cochineal prices and the eventual obsolescence of the crimson dye.[58] By 1860, Perkin's coal tar dyes had begun to cause considerable alarm in Guatemala. The Consulado warned of the danger of falling prices. It recommended excusing cochineal workers from military service to maximize production, but also to encourage production of other crops. The government enacted this recommendation as prices continued to fall.[59]

There were a few who optimistically argued that the chemical dyes would

TABLE 12

Mexican and Guatemalan Cochineal
Prices in London, 1846–1858

1 Jan. Year	Guatemala "mediana"	Mexico "buena"
1846	5s 4d	5s 4d
1847	5s 4d	none
1848	4s 8d	4s 4d
1849	4s 1d	3s 10d
1850	4s 4d	4s 2d
1851	3s 10d	3s 7d
1852	2s 10d	2s 7d
1853	4s 0d	3s 10d
1854	4s 8d	4s 6d
1855	3s 8d	3s 6d
1856	3s 8d	3s 5d
1857	3s 10d	3s 9d
1858	3s 8d	3s 6d

Source: Gaceta de Guatemala, 28 Feb. 1858.

not destroy the Guatemalan industry. A series of letters to the *Gaceta* from Felipe Tible, who ran a stage coach service in Guatemala City, emphasized that the quality of the Guatemalan dye would ensure a continued demand for it over the artificial substitutes. He was sure that the new dyes were imperfect and expensive and could never produce the fine color and permanency of cochineal.[60] The early aniline dyes were often uneven in quality, so that the drop in cochineal prices was slight for a while, and the government tried to calm the fears of producers and merchants.[61] But prices fell more sharply in 1861, and by 1865 prices and imports by the principal London buyers had fallen off considerably from the highs of the 1850s. Near panic resulted as land prices fell and the number of *nopalero* plantations for sale rose. Increased litigation in the tribunal of the Consulado reflected the financial difficulties of both merchants and planters.[62] Yet, the bottom did not drop out for several more years, and as late as 1867 a French traveler could write, "It is cochineal, still . . . on which is founded the prosperity of Guatemala."[63]

The stamina of cochineal exports together with diversification into cotton, coffee, and indigo in the 1860s actually resulted in an overall increase in Guatemalan exports during the last decade of conservative rule, with new prosperity for the merchant-planter elite. Far from paralyzing the economy as had been feared, the cochineal crisis actually turned Guatemala more rapidly toward coffee production.

Costa Rica had pioneered Central American coffee production, and small amounts had also been produced in the Nicaraguan highlands.[64] Some coffee may even have been produced in colonial Guatemala, for in 1805 the colonial government had exempted coffee production from payment of alcabalas and the tithe in an effort to stimulate its production,[65] but there was no significant production of coffee in early nineteenth-century Guatemala. In 1835 Governor Mariano Gálvez asked Alfonso Basire to acquire coffee seed in Havana, London, and Paris,[66] but not until the 1840s did it become more widely cultivated, when the Consulado and the Economic Society appropriated funds to guarantee a fixed minimum price for the beans.[67]

These two institutions promoted coffee export by publishing articles and instructions, giving seeds and seedlings to people all over the country, and generally encouraging its cultivation.[68] The government cooperated by awarding some modest subsidies and tax incentives. On a proposal by Juan Matheu, in January 1843 the government agreed to pay planters $25 for each thousand coffee trees planted that reached productivity, up to a total of $250. It also promised a subsidy of $2 per quintal of coffee exported and of two reales ($.025) per arroba of sugar exported. These subsidies were originally for ten years, but the government later extended the coffee subsidy at $1.00 per quintal to 1868.[69] The government exempted coffee production from the alcabala for twenty years in March 1857 and at about the same time the Catholic Church reduced the tithe on coffee profits to 1 percent.[70] In the 1850s these efforts began to show results, but not until the following decade was coffee an important export.

While soaring coffee exports after 1871 dwarfed these export volumes, it is nonetheless obvious that the shift to coffee was well under way before the liberals took power. Areas formerly producing cochineal were important first in coffee production; new areas in the Verapaz and Los Altos also became important, often developed by individuals not represented in the conservative elite that controlled the government. Eventually, these coffee producers, especially in the western highlands (Los Altos), became associated with the liberal opposition to the Guatemala City elite that had, in their view, failed to give sufficient support to expansion of coffee cultivation and infrastructure development.

Community lands were used for production of coffee to a great extent. This was often the beginning of conversion of these lands to private ownership. This was especially promoted in the Verapaz, a relatively under-

TABLE 13
Value of Guatemalan Coffee Exports, 1852–1871

Year	Coffee Exports in Pesos	Percent of Total Exports	Year	Coffee Exports in Pesos	Percent of Total Exports
1852	690	0.05	1864	192,762	12
1856	1,500	0.1	1865	265,404	17
1857	1,700	0.1	1866	384,936	23
1859	4,680	0.3	1867	415,878	22
1860	15,350	1	1868	788,035	36
1861	53,110	5	1869	790,228	32
1862	119,076	9	1870	1,132,298	44
1863	199,830	13	1871	1,312,129	50

Sources: Boletín Oficial, 11 Aug. 1871 and 15 Mar. 1872; Ciro F. S. Cardoso, "Historia económica del café en Centroamérica (siglo XIX): Estudio comparativo," Estudios Sociales Centroamericanos 4, no. 10 (1975):9–55; Gaceta de Guatemala, 13 Oct. 1869 and 24 May 1870; Sanford Mosk, "The Coffee Economy of Guatemala, 1850–1918: Development and Signs of Instability," Inter-American Economic Affairs 9, no. 3 (1955):6–20; and Manuel Rubio Sánchez, "Breve historia del desarrollo de café en Guatemala," Anales de la Sociedad de Geografía e Historia de Guatemala 27 (1953–54):185.

developed area until the rise of coffee cultivation. The Dominican Order had dominated it in the colonial period and had allowed the continuance of much community ownership of land. The municipality and corregidor of Cobán made special efforts to promote coffee and sugar production using these communal lands beginning in 1859. On 30 May the Carrera government approved a plan for the Cobán municipality to loan up to $500 per single individual, at 6 per cent annual interest with terms of up to five years, for the protection and development of agriculture. With collateral of real property, planters could borrow double that amount. The government also authorized, as it had done elsewhere, municipalities of the Verapaz to rent community lands for coffee cultivation at the rate of one real per cuerda per year. Rentals not paid for two years could be repossessed by the government, and the corregidor was designated to enforce these rules. By providing both land and capital for development, the Verapaz authorities claimed that it was opening the way for "the poor classes" to become coffee planters.[71] By the end of October seven coffee planters had obtained municipal funds under this arrangement, and by June 1860 the policy had stimulated considerable coffee planting. The Verapaz became one of the leading coffee-producing regions within a few years.[72] An 1862 Consulado report on the Alta Verapaz written by Julio Rosignon called for continued development in northern Guatemala, including the Petén.[73] As of 1 March

TABLE 14
Coffee Cultivation in Guatemala, 1862

Department or District	Number of Fincas	Trees Producing	Total no. of plants
Amatitlán	92	238,278	710,604
Escuintla	n/a	569,849	n/a
Jutiapa	n/a	70,800	197,500
Sacatepéquez	n/a	69,155	119,835
Santa Rosa	95	74,292	263,533
Suchitepéquez	86	568,001	1,087,006
Verapaz	75	69,230	2,071,789

Source: Incomplete and unclassified reports, Archivo del Ministerio de Gobernación, AGCA. Some but not all of these reports appear in the Gaceta de Guatemala, March–June 1862.

1862 there were thirty-nine coffee fincas in Cobán, with thirty-two more in nearby San Pedro Carchá, and four in San Miguel Tucurú. The corregidor reported that nearly seventy thousand coffee plants were now producing in the department, with two million more in early stages of development.[74] Juan José Aycinena, noting the remarkable growth of coffee culture in the Verapaz by 1865, urged the government to encourage even more use of community lands. Completion of a new road to Salamá, he pointed out, would soon allow easier marketing of Verapaz coffee.[75]

Escuintla was another area where there was considerable emphasis on coffee cultivation. There the Belgian du Teil brothers built a prosperous coffee finca known as "La Concepción." The du Teils also owned a major import-export house in Guatemala and operated a maritime shipping and insurance agency. The corregidor of Escuintla reported in August of 1861 that there were nearly six hundred thousand coffee producing plants in his department.[76]

Other corregidores reported expansion in both eastern and western Guatemala. Among those developing coffee in the west, near the Mexican border, was Justo Rufino Barrios, the eventual caudillo of the 1871 revolution. From corregidores' reports of 1862, the government estimated that there were about 2 million coffee trees producing in the state with another 4.5 million trees planted or in seedling stage. The principal plantations were in the Verapaz, Chimaltenango, Sacatepéquez, Suchitepéquez, Escuintla, Amatitlán, Santa Rosa, Jutiapa, and Chiquimula.[77]

While many of those developing coffee production were Guatemalans, foreigners played a significant role in this development even before the Liberal Reforma, when German involvement became very important. The most important coffee finca in the 1860s was said to be Las Mercedes, in Suchitepéquez, owned by the Colombian firm of Ospina, Vásquez, and Jaramillo. Julio Rosignon, active in Verapaz production, had come to Guatemala with the Belgian colony at Santo Tomás, as had the Baron du Teil. In all, 144 Belgians from the Santo Tomás colony accepted Guatemalan citizenship and settled in the interior. Several went into coffee production, among whom Bramá and Zollikoper were especially successful. Others practiced their trades or professions in the capital, where they made noticeable contributions to the city's progress. Thirty-three more settled in the other Central American states.[78]

The Carrera government recognized the need to diversify and to avoid dependence on a single crop subject to fluctuations over which Guatemala had no control. In his annual messages to the assembly at the end of 1861 and 1862, Carrera had declared that the wealth of a country should not rest on a single commodity. He called for diversification, new exports, and specifically emphasized coffee, cotton, and silk.[79] The Consulado and the Economic Society were institutions through which the conservative elite promoted such diversification, but much of the actual production of new crops was developed by entrepreneurs outside the elite of the capital. The department of San Marcos, for example, in the mid to late 1860s became an important producer of both coffee and cotton, as well as wool and sugar.[80]

Cotton and indigo exports helped to provide foreign exchange during the transition from cochineal to coffee. The U.S. Civil War (1861–65) provided an unexpected opportunity for Central American cotton exports as a Confederate embargo and Union blockades curtailed exports from North America. The rise in demand and prices provided immediate markets for Central American producers. Central Americans had long cultivated cotton and, although they had exported little since colonial times, it was still important in domestic trade. A substantial cotton textile industry existed in colonial Guatemala, employing Indians who worked looms in small shops or at home. Imports of inexpensive British cloth after independence severely damaged this industry, and cotton cultivation had correspondingly declined after 1821.[81]

An inadequate transportation network had been a major obstacle to the growth of Guatemalan cotton exports. Climatic and terrain conditions confined most of the country's cotton production to the Pacific watershed, far from Caribbean ports reached only by mule trains along terrible roads. The completion of the Panama Railway in 1855 and improvements to the roads on the Pacific slopes made export via the south coast feasible. Not until the North American War Between the States, however, did Guatemalan cotton producers benefit significantly from the new routes.

Even before the Civil War, the growing demand for cotton occasioned by expansion of British textile manufacture had caused the British to encourage Guatemalan production of raw cotton. Having nearly destroyed Guatemala's textile manufacturing, the British now in classic mercantilist fashion were glad to make Guatemala a supplier of raw materials in exchange for its purchases of the finished product. English emancipation societies also encouraged manufacturers to use cotton produced by free labor.[82] In 1858 a Manchester association began to provide free seed and instructions to Guatemalans who would "seriously dedicate themselves to the cultivation of that plant."[83]

Carrera's government responded to British encouragement. Guatemalan interests supported the establishment of a cotton spinning mill in Quetzaltenango under the direction of Gustavo Savoy in 1860. Prominent Guatemalans—Luis Batres, Juan Matheu, and Manuel Larrave—worked with Savoy to raise capital for the venture after the Consulado gave its blessing to the project. This enterprise played an important role in the rise of Guatemalan cotton production during the War Between the States. Savoy's mill received exclusive privileges for the spinning of cotton produced in the departments of Los Altos and the Suchitepéquez coast for fifteen years. In 1858 Savoy had made extensive recommendations regarding types of cotton and methods of cultivation that would be most successful in the region.[84] The government subsequently granted similar concessions to José María Samayoa for the departments of Guatemala, Sacatepéquez, and Chimaltenango.[85] These spinning mills were important not only in encouraging cotton production, but also in reviving the native cotton textile industry so that Guatemala was not merely a supplier of raw cotton to British mills.

The *Gaceta de Guatemala* extolled the advantages of cotton cultivation and urged farmers to plant the crop. Similar articles appeared in the semi-independent *El Noticioso*. The Economic Society had promoted cotton cultivation by importing seed from the United States and Egypt as early as 1831.[86] However, in the late 1850s it joined the Consulado in more aggressively supporting the government policy by distributing seed and instructional pamphlets, importing seedings and bailing machinery, which it sold at cost, and in encouraging cultivation of unused land in the Verapaz.[87] In 1862 the government began to offer a subsidy of one peso per quintal on cotton exports during the next six years, similar to what it had earlier offered for sugar and coffee exports. Moreover, the government sought to

TABLE 15
Value of Guatemalan Cotton
Exports, 1862–1868

Year	Value in Pesos	Percent of Total Exports
1862	1,230	0.1
1863	16,240	1.1
1864	240,600	15.4
1865	351,425	19.2
1866	77,875	4.6
1867	114,934	6.0
1868	20,485	0.9

Source: Woodward, Class Privilege, 52.

speed up exports by offering prizes of $4,000, $3,000, and $2,000 respectively for the first three export shipments of more than a thousand quintals.[88] Meanwhile, a New York–based company, J. A. de Brame & A. Marié, gained an exclusive privilege for cotton ginning in the republic for twenty years beginning in May 1862.[89]

Cotton exports before 1862 in Guatemala were negligible, in some years nonexistent. Beginning in 1862, however, exports surged upward. The Guatemalan cotton was of high quality. On the London market it received prices as good or better than North American cotton, and only the finer grades of Egyptian cotton earned higher prices than the best Guatemalan product.[90] Table 15 shows the value of Guatemalan cotton exports and its percentage of total Guatemalan exports.

Hopes for further growth of cotton exports suffered a serious setback at the end of 1864, when a variety of worms and insects began to damage the crops in eastern Guatemala. The destructive insects marched westward in the years following. Not until the introduction of pesticides in the twentieth century did Central America again compete seriously in world cotton markets.[91]

The development of cotton exports in Guatemala, although short-lived, helped to sustain the economic stability of Carrera's regime and demonstrated the advantage of a more diversified export base. Falling cochineal prices were driving planters out of business, particularly the smaller farmers.[92] Even while the volume of cochineal exports increased in the 1860s, profit margins declined steadily, permitting only the largest producers to continue. Coffee, and to a lesser extent sugar, eventually found markets, but the cotton market created by the U.S. Civil War provided quick markets at a critical time. While some farmers suffered losses when insects invaded the Guatemalan cotton fields, the ruin to Guatemalan planters would have been substantially greater had a large British cotton market not been available. Even had insects not damaged Guatemalan cotton, it is doubtful that Guatemalan cotton could have competed successfully with peacetime exports from the United States, owing to the more efficient operations and transportation that were developed in the northern republic.

The Consulado exerted similar, if less successful, efforts on behalf of several other agro-exports. In the case of tobacco, it financed a sample shipment of Guatemalan leaf in 1845 to John Carmichael, a Liverpool merchant, in an effort to establish markets. Most of the tobacco eventually found buyers in Hamburg, but its poor quality discouraged further development.[93] The French consul, Raymond Baradére, offered to bring in French varieties and instructions to improve the Guatemalan product,[94] and the government removed the tax of a quarter real (about 3 cents) per pound in 1853.[95] Most of the Guatemalan tobacco came from the Chiquimula and lower Río Motagua region, relatively convenient to Caribbean ports, but it did not compete successfully with Cuban or even other Central American varieties. Thus most Guatemalan tobacco remained in the country for domestic consumption, favored by heavy taxes on imported tobacco. There was also encouragement for sugar production during the 1850s and 1860s. In response to the needs of the rapidly expanding California population, exports increased impressively to a value of 138,000 pesos in 1863. After that, however, exports slumped and a declining production was principally consumed locally.[96]

A frequent, but not very successful, interest of the Economic Society since colonial times had been the development of the silk industry. A small amount had been produced in Guatemala, and it often found its way into native textiles, but the society had hopes of developing a larger export potential. Efforts by Juan José Aycinena in the 1830s and 1840s to promote its production had also not been very successful.[97] In 1862 the government chartered a company to develop silk production in the republic. The firm of John Samuel (Guatemalan consul in London), George Skinner, and Gustavo Arlés Dufour (of Arlés, Dufour & Company of León, Nicaragua) in September 1862 planned to raise a half million French francs, but very little silk ever resulted from its activities.[98] In reality, Guatemalan law regarding such activities was primitive, and there was little protection to such companies in terms of enforcement of contracts or protection of their property.

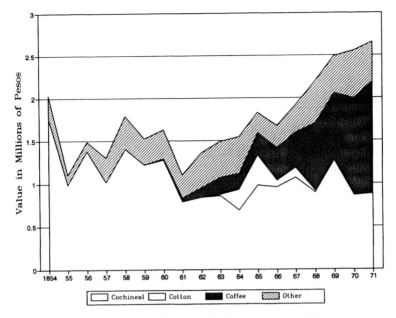

FIGURE 6. Value of Guatemalan Exports, 1854–1871

Not until June 1864 did Guatemala even have a modern patent law, and then it offered protection to inventors and authors for only ten years.[99]

The conservative governments after 1838 were less enthusiastic than their liberal counterparts about rapidly expanding exports, and the growth in the total exports during the Carrera years was quite modest before 1865 (see Figure 6). They nonetheless took substantial interest in production for domestic consumption as they sought to maintain adequate supplies of foodstuffs, especially during bad crop years, and were sensitive to the danger agro-export production might pose to food production. Accurate production and consumption figures are rare for the first half of the nineteenth century, but fragmentary evidence does suggest adequate food supplies for most Guatemalans during the Carrera regime. Beef consumption in the capital, for example, based on slaughterhouse tax reports, averaged about fifty to fifty-five pounds per year per capita, with little change in this amount between 1850 and 1865.[100] Contemporary travelers were often impressed by the great variety and abundance of foodstuffs in native market places, and while primitive living conditions were often noted, hunger or malnutrition did not seem to be a problem.

Prices of basic commodities provide something of an index to standards of living in mid-nineteenth-century Guatemala, although data is

TABLE 16
Commodity Prices, Guatemala City, 1853–1866

Commodity	Unit	Range		Annual Average	
		Lowest	Highest	Low	High
Wheat flour	fanega	2.50	11.75	4.93	6.10
Corn	fanega	0.50	10.00	2.22	3.58
Beans	fanega	1.25	9.00	3.00	3.77
Rice	arroba	0.625	2.875	1.26	1.48
Salt	quintal	2.00	9.00	3.93	4.54
Sugar	arroba	1.00	5.00	1.99	2.73
Cacao	60 pounds	13.00	50.00	20.02	22.18

Source: *Gaceta de Guatemala*, March 1853–May 1866.
Note: Figures represent pesos equal to U.S. dollars.

too fragmentary to be precise. Moreover, price fixing by municipal and state governments was traditional since the conquest, so that prices do not accurately reflect supply and demand. Weekly price currents published irregularly in the *Gaceta de Guatemala* confirm the instability of life and economy in Carrera's Guatemala, even though data is missing for many weeks. High and low weekly prices for the major items of consumption in Guatemalan diets—wheat flour, corn, beans, rice, salt, sugar, and cacao—appeared for 180 weeks between March 1853 and May 1866, 97 percent of these in the decade 1853–62.[101] These prices, although fragmentary, tell us something about life in the Guatemalan capital and probably the country as whole. The most obvious feature of these price currents is the great fluctuation that occurred both across the whole period and within any single year. Taking the decade as a whole, there is no constant trend of rising or falling prices. Seasonal and annual fluctuations are very great, however, and major disasters drove prices up frequently. For example, wheat flour prices, which averaged during the period from $4.93 to $6.10 per fanega (1.58 bushels), ranged from a low of $2.50 to a high of $11.75. The annual average weekly low price for corn was $2.22 per fanega, with an average high of $3.58, but weekly prices ranged from as low as 50 centavos to as high as $10.00 per fanega. Other commodities show similarly wild fluctuations.

Seasonal fluctuations, reflecting growing cycles and weather conditions are illustrated in Table 17, in which prices have been converted to indexes for comparison with each other, 100 equaling the average annual price of each commodity. While there are some differences in seasonal patterns, the

TABLE 17
Monthly Commodity Indexes, Guatemala City, 1853–1866

Month	Wheat Lo	Wheat Hi	Corn Lo	Corn Hi	Beans Lo	Beans Hi	Rice Lo	Rice Hi	Salt Lo	Salt Hi	Sugar Lo	Sugar Hi	Cacao Lo	Cacao Hi	Adj. WCI[a]
Jan.	90	92	62	65	86	94	87	91	106	108	93	95	97	98	85.1
Feb.	88	92	70	74	75	79	82	82	95	97	95	101	101	105	86.5
Mar.	88	91	81	87	80	81	81	84	76	79	92	94	106	112	87.5
Apr.	89	98	78	82	83	83	80	84	90	93	92	99	105	110	88.9
May	110	114	122	123	103	108	97	100	97	99	97	102	100	104	109.0
June	123	127	140	143	107	110	117	118	109	113	97	99	97	98	120.8
July	101	105	126	140	93	99	147	149	97	103	100	101	99	99	116.8
Aug.	111	113	158	164	105	106	132	140	105	105	105	110	94	97	126.7
Sept.	115	118	103	108	114	117	126	128	95	97	104	109	93	94	111.7
Oct.	93	96	85	94	125	126	96	103	101	107	100	107	86	90	97.9
Nov.	77	78	71	80	127	129	86	93	120	122	95	106	102	107	86.8
Dec.	84	86	64	65	88	91	75	82	93	97	100	101	101	104	82.1

Source: Woodward, "Population and Development," 12–13.

Note: 100 = annual average for each commodity throughout period.

[a] Adjusted wholesale commodity index.

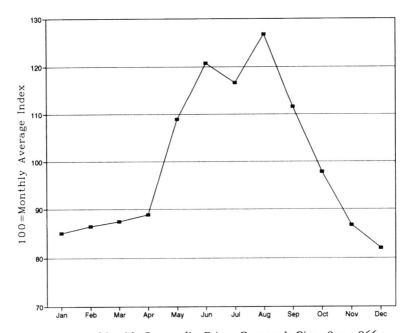

FIGURE 7. Monthly Commodity Prices, Guatemala City, 1853–1866

seven commodities follow a more-or-less similar price pattern throughout the year, with the result that the cost of basic food staples ran more than 30 percent higher in the winter months of May to October than in the more abundant dry months of December through March. Alcabala records, showing the volume of produce brought into the capital, reveal the relative importance of these commodities. Based on these reports, published for several years between 1853 and 1865 in the *Gaceta de Guatemala*, the consumption of these commodities in the capital approximated the following percentages, in terms of the units of measure indicated:

Wheat flour (fanegas)	29.0 percent
Corn (fanegas)	26.1 percent
Beans (fanegas)	0.5 percent
Rice (arrobas)	15.2 percent
Salt (quintales)	4.4 percent
Sugar (arrobas)	22.5 percent
Cacao (arrobas)	2.3 percent

These percentages have been used to determine the wholesale price indices in tables 17 and 18.

A survey of the annual price fluctuations, despite the deficiencies caused by missing data for many weeks, nevertheless reveals that the most serious economic crisis of the period was that caused by the locust invasion of 1854. Wheat, corn, and other prices soared to their highest levels in the decade. The hardships of 1854 probably had much to do with the greater assumption of authority by Carrera at the end of that year, when he became president for life. Carrera met the food shortage crisis during the year by attempting to control prices through government purchase and resale of much of the production of the items in short supply. The effort was not altogether successful, but may have prevented prices from soaring even higher. He also stimulated increased imports and insisted that villages plant more corn, with a resulting oversupply and corresponding plunge in prices during the next two years. The cholera epidemic of 1857, with its concomitant labor shortages, brought a restoration of corn prices to higher levels in 1857.[102]

Lesser fluctuations can also be explained in terms of climatic and man-made disasters, including wars and insurgencies, over these years. Heavier-than-normal rainfall often caused washouts of both crops and roads.[103] The Carrera government took measures to mitigate these problems and was not insensitive to the sufferings of the masses. It sent relief money and food to disaster victims and in times of shortages exempted grain imports from taxes, purchased large quantities of grain for resale to maintain lower

TABLE 18
Annual Commodity Indexes, Guatemala City, 1853–1866

Year	Wheat		Corn		Beans		Rice		Salt		Sugar		Cacao		Adj. WCI[a]
	Lo	Hi	Lo	Hi	Lo	Hi	Lo	Hi	Lo	Hi	Lo	Hi	Lo	Hi	
1853	86	94	62	64	96	96	79	80	87	87	73	93	80	82	79.4
1854	145	151	153	164	110	113	127	133	84	84	107	109	90	91	134.6
1855	101	104	39	46	116	123	69	79	55	62	151	179	94	101	94.5
1856	82	90	34	37	83	90	60	60	50	56	92	102	78	84	70.3
1857	96	100	90	102	48	48	112	113	78	87	105	126	83	95	102.5
1858	85	86	108	117	83	84	110	111	115	120	116	121	118	120	105.9
1859	68	68	74	76	124	125	90	94	126	130	120	123	80	85	88.8
1860	85	85	111	118	97	100	96	100	100	113	108	109	91	95	101.6
1861	96	98	59	64	92	101	84	89	81	96	84	88	140	147	84.3
1862	113	115	100	104	111	114	96	94	97	98	72	90	116	118	99.9
1863	104	117	79	84	135	161	101	105	92	99	75	78	76	80	97.6
1866	82	89	68	87	97	111	69	76	106	117	84	89	86	90	82.6

Source: Woodward, "Population and Development," 12–13.
Notes: 100 = annual average for each commodity throughout period. Data for 1864–65 is not available.
[a] Adjusted wholesale commodity index.

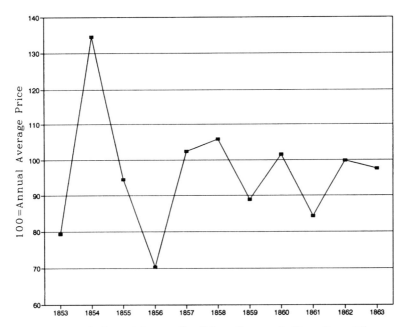

FIGURE 8. Annual Commodity Prices, Guatemala City, 1853–1863

prices than the market would ordinarily dictate. It encouraged, sometimes forcibly, planting of additional crops. As in 1854, the latter measure sometimes resulted in oversupply the following year, depressing food prices.[104]

The government had fixed the price and weight of bread since colonial times. Since 1771 the price of French loaves (*baguettes*) had been fixed at a real ($0.125) each, and they were to contain 16 ounces. A government inspection of the thirty-four bakeries in Guatemala City in 1854, however, revealed that in the thirty-one bakeries having baguettes for sale, they averaged only 14.5 ounces, and ranged in weight from 11 to 16 ounces. Only eleven bakers had bread that met the 16-ounce standard. This year saw wheat prices hit their high point for the entire period, of course, so that normally more bakers might have complied with the regulations, which the government once more reissued in October 1854.[105]

The three decades between the rise of Rafael Carrera and the Liberal Reforma was a period during which agro-exports expanded modestly, despite traditional liberal descriptions of the period as retrograde and stagnant. The rapid expansion of cochineal production accounted for most of the rise in Guatemalan exports and financed the growth in imports. But coffee, cotton, indigo, sugar, and a variety of other minor exports also contributed to the rise, which accelerated more rapidly after 1865. Although Guatemala's eventual heavy dependence on coffee exports would be associated closely with the liberals after 1871, it is clear that its beginnings occurred under conservative leadership and encouragement. By 1871 Guatemala was already becoming highly dependent on agro-exports and had developed a commercial community that was increasingly involved in overseas commerce. The commercial infrastructure for Guatemala's more substantial entry into the international economy was already in place by 1871.

That growth of the international economy under Carrera developed considerably more slowly than under liberal leadership is also obvious, for it is clear that Carrera and the conservative elite had some reservations about transforming Guatemala rapidly into an export-dependent economy. Carrera's own xenophobia was an important element in this, but there were also limits to the amount of domestic resources the conservative elite was willing to commit to development of the infrastructure necessary to increased exports. And there were social costs in converting subsistence land and labor to export production, which had erupted in the civil war of 1837–40, a memory fresh in the minds of the elite during the Carrera years.

CHAPTER NINETEEN

Currency and Government Finance

RESTORATION OF PEACE AND STABILITY, combined with rising prices in Britain during the early 1850s, contributed to a sense of prosperity among Guatemalan merchants and undoubtedly whetted their appetite for further expansion of exports. The shift among conservative landholders toward greater export production brought conservative economic thinking closer to the liberal emphasis on agro-exports. Only the powerful caudillo prevented them from expanding more rapidly as he continued to protect Indian land and labor.

By 1855 Guatemalan commerce had grown notably. Carriages, pianos, furniture, chandeliers, mirrors, porcelain, jewelry, decorative wall papers, fine clothing, and European footwear were among the luxury items available in Guatemala City, stimulating the elite to favor more exports to balance the trade. The *Gaceta de Guatemala* even noticed an increase in consumption of foreign merchandise among the working classes and interpreted it as a sign of an improvement in their standard of living.[1] Notwithstanding the rise in imports and the threat to cochineal exports from aniline dyes, however, Guatemala's official trade statistics report favorable balances of trade throughout the Carrera years, a situation that continued well into the liberal period that followed and helped maintain Guatemala's strong currency and credit (see Figure 9). These figures must be viewed with suspicion, given the tendency for Latin American imports to be notoriously underreported. Nevertheless, they do suggest that during

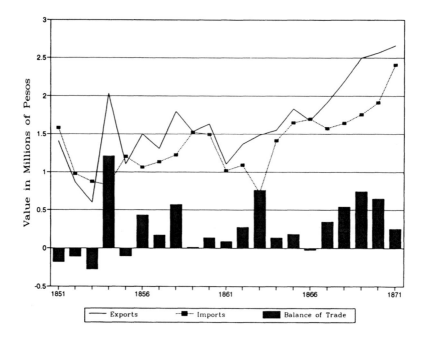

FIGURE 9. Guatemalan Balance of Trade, 1850–1871
Source: Import and export figures were published regularly in the
Gaceta de Guatemala, 1851–1871
Note: More extensive trade statistics, confirming the favorable balance
of trade but based on European and U.S. trade statistics with Guatemala,
have been assembled by Thomas and Ebba Schoonover, "Statistics for an
Understanding," part 3.

the conservative years Guatemala was able to avoid the serious negative
balance of trade that caused currency difficulties for many Latin American
countries.[2]

Shortages of currency had been a chronic problem in Guatemala. The
Spanish government had ordered establishment of a royal mint in Guatemala City in 1731. From 1733 forward this mint produced standard coinage,
principally in silver, but there continued to be complaints of a shortage of
hard currency, especially after the growth of commerce later in the century.[3]
Upon independence the mint served the federal government, continuing to
mint Spanish pesos for a time until new dies could be cast. G. A. Thompson
reported that this mint produced 156,591 marks of silver and 925 marks of
gold between 1820 and 1825, for a combined value of U.S. $1,456,857,

in that period of transition from royal to republican rule, but production following independence was declining.[4]

Following the breakup of the federation, the mint continued to produce federal currency, at least until 1842, but the small amount of mining in the country meant that there was never sufficient currency. Foreign currency of many different types—especially Mexican, South American, British, and U.S.—circulated freely in the country. The Gálvez government had in 1836 legalized this practice in response to the shortage of national currency.[5] There was also a large amount of *macaco,* or clipped coinage, which became increasingly a problem for merchants and the government, demanding the use of paper currency or more minted specie.[6] The depreciation in value of a number of South American currencies further complicated the problem as a report of the prior of the Consulado, Manuel F. Pavón, emphasized in mid-1840. It was especially coins of minor denomination (less than a peso) that were of uncertain value, the report said, as it called on the government to appoint a commission to standardize the currency and to increase the volume of coinage minted.[7] The government responded by prohibiting certain Peruvian and Bolivian silver coins as legal tender, but there continued to be confusion and complaints regarding the use of foreign coinage in the country, as well as an inadequate money supply.[8]

The Guatemalan government reorganized the mint in 1842, placing it under the direction of Marcial Zebadúa, dean of the Supreme Court of Guatemala, but the volume of coinage continued to fall short of the country's commercial needs. The government thus began to issue paper currency early in 1843, secured against customs and other revenues, in denominations of $5, $10, $20, $50, and $100. These paper notes were issued specifically to meet operational expenses, including salaries, pensions, the University of San Carlos, and per diem for members of the assembly. The paper, although sometimes discounted by merchants, entered into the currency system of the country and soon became widely accepted.[9] This practice increased the public debt, of course, but the governments during the Carrera years were sensitive to the good credit of Guatemala, and they successfully maintained the peso on a par with the traditional Spanish piece of eight reales (or U.S. dollar). Thus, for example, in 1845 it rejected, on the recommendation of both the mint and the Consulado, a proposal of Benito Pérez to establish a company with English and French capital that would introduce a million pesos in silver currency over the next five years. Specifically they propsed to bring in Spanish pesetas at the rate of four to one, instead of the normal rate of five to one. Pérez argued that although it would devalue the Guatemalan currency, it would greatly increase the amount of silver in the country, which was so badly needed. The mint proposed instead a temporary prohibition on the export of silver coinage and a permanent ban on export of silver bullion.[10]

The conservatives in control of the government from 1850 forward continued to defend the value of the Guatemalan peso, while seeking ways to increase the currency supply. In 1851 the government formally declared its peso of eight reales equal to the U.S. dollar and took steps to establish a national currency to replace the variety of foreign currency in circulation.[11] Although the mint had issued one-real coins under the seal of the Republic of Guatemala since 1847, it was not until 1853, when the mint was formally reorganized, that it began to mint substantial coinage.[12] The coinage act of 26 April 1853 provided for the minting of gold and silver coins in the same weights as formally minted under the Central American republic seal. The new coins would carry the coat of arms of the republic on one side and the bust of Christopher Columbus on the reverse, along with the date and value.[13] In 1857, however, the bust of Rafael Carrera replaced Columbus, and Carrera coins continued to be minted until the liberal Revolution of 1871.[14] In 1866 the inscription on the coin referring to Carrera was changed from "President of the Republic of Guatemala" to "Founder of the Republic of Guatemala." This change was debated at considerable length in the assembly before finally passing by a vote of 23 to 14, reflecting attitudes toward the deceased caudillo and the presence of some liberal and moderate representatives.[15]

It was still necessary to accept foreign coinage, and the California gold strikes now made available more U.S. coinage, notably U.S. $20 and $50 gold pieces. Chilean $10 gold coins also were authorized to circulate at a value that ranged from $9.00 to $9.50.[16] The government continued to prohibit the export of silver,[17] and took steps to encourage mining, resulting in a modest increase in the production of silver by 1865.[18]

Another reorganization of the mint occurred in 1859 under the direction of Luis Batres, after which the ban on export of silver was dropped.[19] During its first seven months of operation (1 June–31 December 1859, the mint issued 153,889 coins valued at nearly $60,000. A large part of this was in gold, with 37,885 pieces of one peso and an additional $6,200 in two-peso gold pieces, and the remainder in silver coins of 1 peso, 4 reales, 2 reales, 1 real, ½ real and ¼ real.[20] In 1860 the mint also began to produce gold 4-real coins.[21]

The *Gaceta* responded angrily to a charge appearing in the Panama *Star & Herald* and the *Noticioso* of New York in 1860 that the new Guatema-

TABLE 19
Guatemalan Currency Equivalents, 1869

Currency	Gold	Silver
U.S. (dollar)	1.00	1.00
Chile (peso)	0.925	1.00
New Granada (peso)	0.9875	
Great Britain (pound)	5.00	5.00
France (franc)	0.1938	0.20
Piedmont (franc)	0.1938	0.20
Germany (guilder)	0.3875	
Spain (doubloons of 100 rs.)	5.00	
Spain (peseta)		0.1875
Peru (sols)	0.9875	1.00

Source: Gaceta de Guatemala, 3 Apr. 1869.

lan coins contained low-quality silver from President Carrera's mines at Chiantla. The *Gaceta* insisted that both the silver coins and the new four-real gold "Carrera" contained metal of the proper weight and quality, and in any case, that "not a single real" had been minted from the Chiantla silver to date. Far from any difficulties with the new coins, the article continued, they were circulating freely and without problem.[22] As no further objections of this sort surfaced, the charge apparently came from political enemies of the caudillo rather than being based on the quality of the coins. The encouragement of mining allowed the mint to increase its production of silver coins during the 1860s significantly, although currency shortages continued to hamper the country's commerce and new gold coinage dwindled considerably. In 1862, for example, the mint produced $137,446 in silver coins, and only $8,320 in gold.[23] By 1869, however, the mint's output of $893,115 in gold coins and $228,954.53 in silver coins totaled $1,122,069.53.[24] Thus the Guatemalan peso held its value throughout the conservative period. Foreign coins by the end of the regime circulated in Guatemala at the values indicated in Table 19.

Guatemala revised its currency laws slightly on 9 June 1869 to conform to the Monetary Convention of 1865, which established standard weights for European and Latin American nations. Guatemala set its silver peso as equivalent to the French five-franc and its five-peso gold piece as equivalent to the French twenty-five-franc gold coin. The new law also established the decimal system, dividing pesos into centavos instead of reales, although this was slow to be adopted in actual practice.[25]

Near the close of the conservative era, the Finance Ministry commissioned Enrique Palacios to study the monetary system. Palacios's report emphasized that the major problems were not unlike those of thirty years before, the clipping of coins and the multiplicity of moneys—state, national (Central American), and foreign—circulating within Guatemala. The report recommended amendments to the 1869 law that would create a unified national decimal system of currency in the country. Palacios estimated the amount of coinage in circulation in Guatemala in 1870 at $2.7 million in national and $1.5 million in foreign currency. Included in the foreign amount, however, was an estimated $1 million in clipped macaco.[26]

If Palacios's estimates were correct, it meant that national coinage amounted to less than 65 percent of the total in circulation. Palacios also estimated that a large part of the national currency was not in the new decimal form, and that much of it was of less intrinsic value than its face value. The silver content of the currency varied, he pointed out, because there were basically three standards of national currency in circulation: the Spanish standard dating from the colonial period and consisting of 24.38 grams of silver to the peso had been kept through April of 1859; the peso adopted in 1859 and minted through June of 1869 contained only 22.18 grams; while the new 1869 metric peso, conforming to the Monetary Union, contained 22.5 grams per peso. In each case, there had been no demonetizing of the previous pesos, which continued to circulate. Moreover, many of the foreign coins in circulation, on a par with national money, contained only 19.76 or 20.93 grams of silver. The situation in gold was less serious, for the 1869 law providing for 1.45 grams of gold per peso was a reduction from the 1.48 contained in the Spanish peso, although a number of foreign gold pesos of varying content also circulated in the country. The problem was that the higher content coins tended to leave the country while smaller value coins remained, amounting to an export of specie for which Guatemala received nothing. Palacios called for a complete remonetization of Guatemalan money to make it all standard and conforming to the Monetary Convention of 1865. The result was a new monetary law in 1870 that sought to unify the currency along the lines of the Palacios proposals.[27]

More serious than the currency problem for the development of commerce was the absence of adequate banking facilities. The liberals of the 1820s had planned banks but had been unable to attract sufficient capital to develop the sort of capitalist financial institutions that a developing country needed. Financing of the agro-export production and trade remained primitive, provided principally by merchant houses or individuals, with the church continuing to play a role in rural land exploitation. President Rivera Paz had tried to facilitate establishment of a national bank in October of 1839 in collaboration with an English company, but the political turmoil that followed had prevented its success. Throughout the Carrera years, Guatemala lacked the adequate credit and financial services that were being developed in the major Latin American states, another reflection of the slower pace of conservative economic development.

Before the caudillo's death, however, a change in the attitude of the Guatemalan conservative elite began to occur, leading to a more serious effort to establish national financial institutions that could provide credit for expanding production. On 17 September 1864 Carrera granted a Swiss banking firm a concession to form a National Bank in Guatemala. Although this plan did not come to fruition because of the lack of sufficient local capital, it was a step toward establishment of a national bank.[28] Under Cerna and with the growth of exports in the latter half of the 1860s the project gained momentum. A group of Guatemalan citizens, including both liberal and conservative members of the elite and foreign immigrants, proposed a plan toward the end of 1866, which the government accepted and which Cerna strongly supported. These citizens sought to raise $200,000 to $300,000 to fund the bank. Initial organization of the bank occurred in 1867, although the bank would not become a significant financial institution until after the liberal revolution, when one of its founders, Miguel García Granados, became president of the republic.[29] The same period saw the beginning of savings banks. The government authorized *montes de piedad,* or mutual aid societies, on 29 August 1866, allowing such institutions to make loans of up to $100 per year. Both the Consulado and the Economic Society cooperated with efforts to create savings banks in the capital and in Antigua.[30]

Although minuscule in comparison to contemporary Third World debts, the nineteenth-century conservatives regarded their government debt as a serious impediment to greater economic development. A sizable debt had been carried over from the colonial kingdom, and liberal borrowing in the 1820s and 1830s had increased the burden, which the conservative governments of mid-century sought to reduce and manage.

A state bank, the Banco Nacional de Guatemala, erected in 1827 with the assistance of the Consulado also sought investment from abroad, but had little success and did not long survive.[31] The most well known foreign investment of the 1820s was the loan to the Central American federal government from the London firm of Barclay, Herring, and Richardson, which became the source of much dissension between the British government on behalf of the Corporation of Foreign Bondholders and the Central

American states following the breakup of the federation.[32] This loan became the most frequently cited example of the general failure of foreign investment to accomplish much in the early national period. It also was an example of how the British used debt to gain influence and land in the country, and it contributed to the strong antiforeign feeling discussed earlier that helped Carrera rise to power.

The Central American federal government's debt had reached nearly 5 million pesos by 1831, and in 1836, before the outbreak of the Carrera revolt, the Central American states owed British creditors alone $835,000 in principal plus $250,000 in back interest.[33] Arrangements worked out by Frederick Chatfield succeeded in dividing that amount—stemming principally from the ill-fated Barclay, Herring and Richardson loan of 1824—among the several states, among which only Costa Rica, with the smallest share (one-twelfth), was able to pay quickly.[34] Guatemala carried the largest share (five-twelfths, or £67,900), which Frederick Chatfield used to extract favorable commercial treatment for British subjects.[35] The Guatemalan government was slow to recognize its share (30 percent) of the colonial debt and a third of the federal debt, but by 1858 it had agreed to this.[36] In 1847 Chatfield and Rodolfo Klée helped to arrange a loan with Reid Irving & Company of London for the new Guatemalan republic to pay off British bondholders.[37] By 1850 these bonds were selling well in London, and as Guatemala's foreign credit strengthened, their value rose steadily from around 35 percent of face value in 1850 to around 60 percent by 1857.[38] By August of that year the growth of cochineal exports and strong harvests of domestic staples had improved the country's economic condition and confidence in the government so that its bonds were selling well.[39] The government subsequently negotiated a new loan of £100,000 with the London firm of Isaac & Samuel to pay off the old one. It provided that Guatemala acknowledge liability for a third of the entire federal loan of 1825 (£54,433) and for the interest in arrears (reduced and estimated at £45,567), and Guatemala pledged 50 percent of her customs receipts to guarantee the loan.[40]

The demands of Carrera's military forces remained a steady drain on the national treasury as well as on the principal corporate bodies making up the Guatemalan establishment. As early as September 1839, for example, only a month after the restoration of the Consulado, the government asked it for a voluntary contribution for the support of General Carrera's army. Thus the Consulado almost immediately became an institution that raised money for the caudillo from its constituent merchants and hacendados.[41]

The new government had moved rapidly, in August 1838, to assure that all obligations would be met, as it sought to establish the credit of the government. Fiscal responsibility and an aversion to the liberal willingness to borrow from abroad became a strong point with the conservative elite that now ran the government. An editorial in *El Tiempo* a year later called for Hamiltonian measures, noting the disorder of the past and congratulating the Rivera Paz government for restoring public credit. It recognized the Barclay & Herring debt as a major obligation, calling for its division among the states, but it also called for equal recognition of the domestic debt in order to restore the full credit of the government. Later it praised the colonial administration for its prudent fiscal policy as it blasted the liberals' mismanagement during the federation period.[42]

The government slashed expenses substantially, discharging some public employees and cutting the salaries of all of those receiving more than 25 pesos per month by 25 percent. At the same time, the government published a budget for fiscal year 1838–39 totaling only $153,000, half of which was earmarked for the military. The reduced budget reveals the new priorities of the Guatemalan government, as it reduced the size and cost of the state government, putting greater emphasis on security and order than on infrastructure or education. It also reflects the semi-autonomous situation regarding the departments of Los Altos, which continued to pay most of their own officials with their own revenues.[43] This budget was not far in excess of an estimate that had been provided earlier in the year, showing net state income (not including Los Altos) of $146,703. Projected net loss revenue from Los Altos was about $32,000. The bulk of the income came from the alcabala, collected at 5 percent on all transactions. An additional 1 percent alcabala was designated for the federal government, but after this date it remained with the state as well.[44] This budget represented substantial cuts, however, reflecting the new government's goal of restoring the state's credit and reducing taxation on the elite. The hated forced loans and levies that had become regular in Guatemala since the late colonial period would not end here, but there was an effort to reduce expenditures to make them less likely.[45] By the end of 1839 the government had made considerable progress in liquidating the government's debt. While the assembly authorized the government to borrow money, it specifically provided that any loans from foreign capitalists had to stipulate that they could not be a justification for intervention by any foreign government or authority, a clear reaction to the growing threats of British creditors and their government.[46]

Salaries paid to government employees offer an additional indicator of the relative development of the state during the Carrera years. At the

TABLE 20
Guatemalan Military Salaries, 1839

	Former	New
Commanding General	$2,000.00	$2,000.00
Colonels	1,800.00	1,200.00
Lieutenant Colonels	1,400.00	960.00
Majors	1,128.00	700.00
Captains	700.50	600.00
Lieutenants & Surgeons	451.50	451.50
Sub-Lieutenants	365.50	365.50

Source: El Tiempo, 7 Jan. 1840.

beginning of the nineteenth century, Spanish colonial officials in Guatemala had gained notable salary increases under the Bourbons. In 1800 the Captain General's annual salary was 5,000 ducats, or about $6,875, but various allowances and emoluments he received brought his total to more like 10,000 ducats or nearly $14,000.[47] In 1811 justices on the audiencia received $3,300. The chief accountant at the Royal Treasury received $3,000. Other officials received considerably less. The third officer at the Royal Treasury for example, received only $500, but up from $300 in 1777. Scribes at the Treasury also received $500 annually. The first officer received $800 and the second officer $600 annually. The average rural worker, by contrast, in 1810 received about $50 per year, or an average of 1.34 reales per day, excluding Sundays and holidays.[48]

After independence and the organization of stronger state governments, the decentralization and exigencies of the times forced salaries lower, although the liberal governments attempted to keep them near their colonial levels. Following the Carrera revolt, the new conservative government in November 1839 revised the salary schedule, with notable reductions in both civilian and military salaries. These cuts reduced the total salaries paid to the government's officials from $92,427 to $67,583, a reduction of 27 percent. Substantial savings ($12,132) came by removing the salaries of the Representative Council.[49] Additional savings came by reducing Treasury salaries from a total of $56,919 to $26,566. With the president's salary trimmed to $2,500 and two ministerial secretaries to $1,400 each, minor savings were made in the executive branch and in the Secretariat of the Assembly, while increases in total salaries occurred in the ministries of Justice and Interior.[50] There were also cuts in military salaries (see

Table 20), especially at the field grade level, perhaps aimed particularly at the higher proportion of such officers in the army carried over from the previous regime.

Of course, many of the functions of government in Carrera's regime were carried out by the church or by quasi-governmental agencies, whose officers were paid by private funds or by revenues assigned to those agencies. The government had some control over these salaries as well, and it sought to prevent those salaries from rising out of line with those paid by the government itself. In 1843, for example, when the Consulado voted to increase its secretary's salary by $100 to $500 annually, the government refused to approve the increase until the Consulado's prior provided a detailed statement justifying the raise.[51]

Salaries of both public and private agencies gradually improved in the quarter century following, concomitant with the increase in general prosperity and government revenues, but they remained at modest levels throughout the period. Still, they contrasted sharply with those received by working-class people. Even skilled laborers rarely made as much as a peso per day.[52] Moreover, as has already been mentioned in Chapter 12, in 1858 the government established a pension and life insurance plan for the officer corps and government employees.[53]

With the collapse of the federation, the state took over completely taxation on overseas trade, the largest source of revenue by far, and this enabled more progress on the foreign debt. At the same time, the Carrera revolt and the secession of Los Altos brought an immediate reduction in government revenues.[54] The figures in Table 21 do not include import and export duties. These were estimated at an additional $200,000, giving the state (not including Los Altos) an annual income of more than $300,000, with estimated expenses at $273,000. Only $37,000 remained for debt service. Of the estimated expenditures of $273,000, $130,000 was for the military, but the hope was expressed that this could be reduced to as little as $100,000 or even $80,000 if the war could be ended, thus making possible a substantially greater payment on the debt. In fact, however, the continued war against Morazán required keeping more than three thousand men under arms and forced the government to borrow additional funds during 1840. Moreover, Morazán had pledged a considerable portion of the duties on foreign trade (*alcabala marítima*) to payment of the federal debt.[55]

The government published a detailed statement of the debt in May 1840, along with a sharp criticism of the Morazán government's abuses in committing the customs revenues. During 1838–40, it reported, the federal government had issued bonds and made other commitments for nearly

TABLE 21

Income of the State of Guatemala, 1839

Administration	Alcabala		Meat Tax	Aguar-diente	Chicha	Papel Sellado	Land Sales	Totals	Percent
	4%	2%							
Guatemala	18,531	12,310	9,076	12,841	2,236	3,231	1,817	60,042	46.8
Antigua	10,265	—	6,337	9,589	7,276	1,682	—	35,149	27.4
Chimaltenango	535	—	1,203	5,092	2,941	56	—	9,827	7.7
Escuintla	1,281	—	2,019	5,600	1,552	312	—	10,764	8.4
Chiquimula	943	170	1,132	2,239	—	1,552	—	6,036	4.7
Gualán	280	468	192	324	—	211	—	1,475	1.1
Verapaz	1,216	75	660	1,844	—	205	—	4,000	3.1
Petén	529	—	—	424	—	15	—	968	0.8
Totals	33,580	13,023	20,619	37,953	14,005	7,264	1,817	128,261	100.0

Source: El Tiempo, 7 Jan. 1840.

Note: Figures are rounded to the nearest peso.

$300,000 against receipts at the Guatemalan customs houses. A considerable portion of that sum had now been paid from customs receipts, but there remained $72,170.89 of those obligations yet to be paid, and the total state debt was $368,900.[56]

The acquisition of the customs returns greatly expanded the size of the Guatemalan budget, and when final figures were in for fiscal 1839–40, total income reached nearly $600,000. Of this amount, about $275,000 went to creditors of the state with another $256,000 going to the military.[57] The customs receipts were by far the largest source of revenues for all the Central American states, and taking over of these receipts by Guatemala was undoubtedly a major factor in its reluctance to work more constructively toward the restoration of the federal union. As Mario Rodríguez has pointed out, the liberal financial reform and tariff act of 1838 had much to do with the growth of separatist feeling among the elites throughout Central America.[58] The Noticioso Guatemalteco had reflected concern over the paucity of funds to support the state government in March 1838:

On what revenues can the state count? On tobacco? No, for the Federation has appropriated that. On the 5 percent import tax? No, because the Federation denies us that and if we were permitted to collect it, it would have to be dedicated exclusively to amortization of the debt. On the head tax? No, also, for that weighs on the indigenous classes and they resist paying it. Then what's left? The monopolies of chicha and aguardiente, the states sales tax, the stamp tax, gunpowder, the meat tax, and the censo.[59]

Recall that the Carrera revolt had in part been stimulated by strong popular opposition to the two-peso head tax imposed by the Gálvez government, reminiscent of the hated tributo of colonial times. For the Guatemala City elite, however, that tax appeared not only fair, but it represented a major source of revenue that they were reluctant to give up. Specific recommendations of a finance committee of the Constituent Assembly in October 1839, in attempting to find sources of revenue for the new government, thus included the imposition of the $2 levy on all males between the ages of eighteen and fifty. It also recommended a very modest real property tax of $2.50 on property valued from $500 to $1,000, five pesos on property valued from $1,000 to $5,000, and ten pesos on that of a value greater than $10,000. At the same time it recommended suppressing the alcabala on most internal commerce, ending the liquor monopoly as a revenue source, and adding protective tariffs to stimulate native industry, while abolishing export duties altogether. Attacking the liberal free trade policy, the committee declared that the "tax system adopted by the previous government . . . appeared to have been calculated intentionally to demoralize and destroy the population." The report blamed the liberals' liquor monopoly for producing so much drunkenness in the country, because the government encouraged the Indians to buy liquor in order to increase revenues, thereby, the report concluded, contributing to the decline of the state. It advocated, therefore, abolition of the liquor monopoly, and strong government enforcement against drunkenness, putting the state against liquor consumption instead of for it. At the same time, it argued that aguardiente production should be closely controlled by the government, while *chicha* should be abolished altogether. The liquor question would continue to be important throughout the conservative years.[60]

Carrera, of course, refused to allow restoration of the head tax, and it survived only in an extremely watered down fashion in the tax bill of 5 December 1839, when the assembly authorized the government to impose a direct tax for one year to raise up to $40,000 only if the government could not raise that amount in loans. This head tax, however, to be collected by the municipalities in each department, would be divided only among property holders, in proportion to their wealth, and it specifically excluded from this tax "all other classes."[61] Far from being a restoration of the old *capitación*, this tax, which was not imposed at all at this time, was actually a forerunner of the war tax that the government imposed regularly after 1849. In fact, for most of the Carrera period, the government relied most heavily upon commercial taxes, principally import duties and the internal sales tax. Collection of both these taxes was substantially tightened after 1842.[62] The resistance to direct taxation was strong, and even made difficult the reimposition of the tithe for support of the church, which was done only at a greatly reduced level from colonial times.[63]

Civil disorder and war continued to be a heavy burden on government finances, forcing repeated loans and retarding efforts to restore the government's solvency. Although the initial effect of Carrera's revolt was to reduce or eliminate taxes, particularly those that the peasants had objected to, and thereby reduce government revenue, after 1841 the government increased taxes, especially on imports. The government regularly issued bonds to cover deficits in its domestic spending, but these amounts were not excessive, and by 1850 the credit of the government had been well established as these bonds were regularly either paid or replaced by new bonds. The government's budget for fiscal 1841–42 was significantly larger than that described above for 1838–39, with a total projected disbursement of $263,428, not including service on the foreign debt. A breakdown by categories in Table 22 reveals that the military still consumed more than half of the receipts.

The manner in which accounts were kept makes accurate comparison year to year difficult, especially because customs receipts were often paid for with *vales* representing a portion of the debt. A rough determination of income and expenditures can be gained from the national accounts of the period, however, as published in the government gazettes. Since much of the customs receipts were consumed by debt service, even before they entered the national treasury, the official treasury expenditures and receipts are somewhat misleading by themselves. What is clear from the statistics is that there was a steady increase in government revenues after 1850, with the military getting the lion's share after debt service, which regularly took a third to more than half of the income of the government. Total government debt had reached $441,224 by 1851. Although this was reduced to under $300,000 a year later, it rose thereafter and had reached $461,337 again by the end of 1853, owing to the war with Honduras.[64]

Table 23 presents a summary of available data on government revenues and expenditures during the mid-nineteenth century. Some of this information is incomplete or presented in inconsistent form, and it includes estimates that have often been made on the basis of incomplete data. Thus this table is intended only as a general approximation of total expenditures. Its purpose, along with Figure 10, is to provide a general idea of the

TABLE 22
Projected Government Expenditures, 1841–1842

Assembly	15,000
Its Secretariat	1,744
Executive Department	8,680
Judicial Department	13,690
Judges	5,040
Interior Government	11,800
Police	1,440
Finance Department:	
Chief Accountant	1,860
General Treasury	2,300
Public Credit	500
General Admn.	4,896
Post Office	996
Mint	2,150
Customs houses	6,100
Security	10,700
Pensions	3,180
Interest on capital	5,000
Public Education	7,192
Ecclesiastical benefits.	1,560
General expenses	19,600
Armed forces	140,000
Total	263,428

Source: Gaceta Oficial, 5 Nov. 1841.

percentage of government revenues expended, not to provide an accurate record of government expenditures. But this table does give us an approximate indication of the amounts available to the Guatemalan government and the relative amounts of military versus civilian expenditures. Many of the modern functions of government were carried out by the corporations (Consulado, church, and so on) outside the framework of government, so that the military was the one major institution that drew on the public treasury. Table 23 also shows us a significant increase in debt service in the 1860s, especially after the death of Carrera.

The practice of imposing forced loans on property holders was not unique to Guatemala. While it was hated, it was a by-product of the strong aversion of Central American elites to taxation. In the turbulent times of the 1830s and 1840s, these forced loans were often not repaid and amounted to sudden and unexpected taxes.[65] The Carrera government relied repeatedly on this method as well as special war taxes, which continued

TABLE 23
Revenue and Expenditures of Guatemalan Government, 1833–1871

Year	Gross Revenue	Military		Civilian		Debt Service	
1833–34[a]	157	60	(38)	97	(62)	0	(0)
1838–39[b]	153	85	(55)	64	(42)	4	(3)
1839–40[c]	589	256	(43)	59	(10)	274	(47)
1841–42[d]	263	140	(53)	117	(45)	6	(2)
1845[e]	—	—	(51)	—	(28)	—	(21)
1846–47[f]	316	117	(37)	83	(26)	116	(37)
1847–48[g]	482	260	(54)	105	(22)	117	(24)
1848–49[h]	806	298	(37)	122	(15)	386	(48)
1849–50[i]	499	307	(61)	54	(11)	138	(28)
1851–52[j]	592	273	(46)	91	(15)	228	(39)
1852[k]	501	230	(46)	62	(12)	209	(42)
1853[l]	673	285	(43)	123	(18)	265	(39)
1854[m]	869	313	(36)	205	(24)	351	(40)
1855[n]	775	293	(38)	189	(24)	293	(38)
1856[o]	826	356	(43)	182	(22)	288	(35)
1857[p]	939	386	(41)	194	(21)	359	(38)
1858[q]	897	294	(33)	238	(26)	365	(41)
1859[r]	1030	231	(22)	284	(28)	515	(50)
1860[s]	950	239	(25)	288	(30)	423	(45)
1861[t]	824	246	(30)	215	(26)	364	(44)
1862[u]	1019	248	(24)	216	(21)	555	(55)
1863[v]	1109	527	(47)	197	(18)	385	(35)
1864[w]	887	278	(31)	232	(26)	377	(43)
1865[x]	957	246	(26)	190	(20)	521	(54)
1866[y]	1084	243	(22)	235	(22)	606	(56)
1867[z]	1257	282	(22)	240	(19)	735	(59)
1868[aa]	1082	210	(20)	196	(18)	676	(62)
1869[bb]	1963	293	(15)	304	(15)	1366	(70)
1870[cc]	1546	366	(24)	425	(27)	755	(49)
1871[dd]	987	475	(48)	270	(27)	242	(25)

Notes: Figures represent thousands of pesos. Figures in parentheses are percentages.

[a] Noticioso Guatemalteco, 17 Mar. 1838.

[b] Based on budget for fiscal 1838–39, Boletín Oficial, 10 June 1838.

[c] El Tiempo, 26 Aug. 1840.

[d] Based on proposed budget for fiscal 1841–42. These figures do not show income from loans that were used to roll over the debt. Gaceta Oficial, 5 Nov. 1841.

[e] Based on fragmentary figures from Gaceta Oficial, 21 Oct. 1845.

[f] Gaceta de Guatemala, 12 June 1847.

[g] Ibid., 14 June 1848.

[h] Ibid., 18 June 1849.

[i] Ibid., 7 June 1850.

[j] Ibid., 18 June 1852.

[k] 1 June–31 December only. "Estado de Valores y Distribución de los Ramos de Hacienda Pública en los

into the 1860s. Eventually, though, it gained a better record of repayment of the forced loans, as the credit of the government improved notably after 1850 as a result both of the imposed stability and the increased exports of cochineal. Faced with a considerable increase in the debt by the war with El Salvador in 1863, the assembly, after a long debate, authorized by a vote of 18 to 11 property and income taxes for one year beginning in 1864. The bill would have provided for a direct tax of two pesos per thousand dollars of property value, exempting those with property of less than $2,000, and an income tax of 3 percent on annual incomes of $200 or more. The government, however, refused to implement the act, and it did not go into effect.[66]

Heavy dependence on import taxes throughout the period meant that as trade fluctuated considerably during the period, so also did the government's receipts. Taxes on alcoholic beverages were the second most important source of revenue after 1850, and together these two sources normally accounted for more than 60 percent of revenues. The internal sales tax rarely produced more than 10 percent of total revenue after 1850, the special war taxes about 6 percent, and a variety of minor taxes relatively little after expenses.[67] The Guatemalan aversion to direct taxation, which remains a strong characteristic even to the present day, meant that drops in trade or serious crises inevitably forced the government to turn to loans,

TABLE 23 Notes continued

siete meses corridos de 1 de junio a 31 de diciembre de 1852," ibid., 24 Feb. 1854. This is a table for the treasury and probably does not show some debt payment made directly at the customs houses or internal revenue service before funds were transferred to the treasury.

l *Gaceta de Guatemala*, 24 Feb. 1854.

m Ibid., 19 Feb. 1856.

n Ibid., 11 Jan. 1856.

o Ibid., 8 Jan. 1857.

p Ibid., 14 Jan. 1858.

q Ibid., 15 Jan. 1859.

r Ibid., 11 Jan. 1860.

s Ibid., 15 Jan. 1861.

t Compiled from monthly accounts reported in ibid., Feb. 1861–Jan. 1862.

u *Gaceta de Guatemala*, 23 Jan. 1863.

v Ibid., 30 Jan. 1864.

w Ibid., 13 Jan. 1865 and 3 Jan. 1866.

x Ibid., 29 Jan. 1866.

y Ibid., 28 Jan. 1867.

z Ibid., 26 Jan. 1868.

aa Ibid., 16 Jan. 1869.

bb Ibid., 13 Jan. 1870.

cc Ibid., 26 Jan. 1871.

dd *Boletín Oficial*, 19 Jan. 1872.

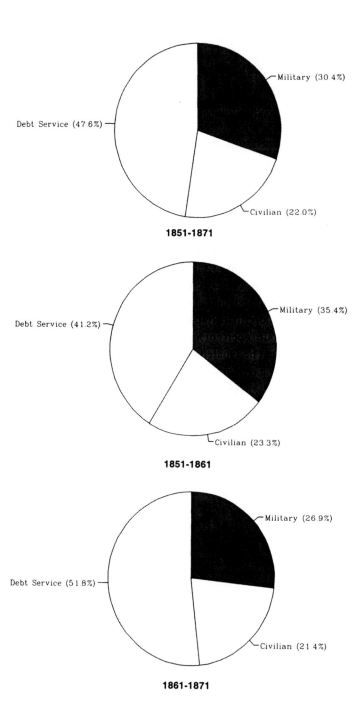

Military (30.4%)

Debt Service (47.6%)

Civilian (22.0%)

1851-1871

Military (35.4%)

Debt Service (41.2%)

Civilian (23.3%)

1851-1861

Military (26.9%)

Debt Service (51.8%)

Civilian (21.4%)

1861-1871

FIGURE 10. Guatemalan Government Expenditures, 1851–1871

which accounted for one-quarter to one-third of the state's revenues in the mid-1850s.[68]

Guatemala was a relatively poor country, and, although the cost of living was low by European standards, most of its inhabitants could not afford luxuries. There was little credit available, for there was little native capital or savings. Miguel García Granados had reported that as of 1832 a family of six or seven could live comfortably on a hundred pesos per month, and with two hundred they would live luxuriously. The only thing expensive was money, because of it shortage. Interest rates, he said, were never below 2 percent monthly and often rose to more than 3 percent, even then only with good collateral.[69] This was, of course, well above usual rates in Europe at the same time, and the reduced emphasis on rapid development after the overthrow of the liberals brought down the rates somewhat. A usury law of October 1840 limited private interest rates to 6 percent per annum. Anyone attempting to charge more than that would lose their rights to all interest, receiving only the principal in repayment. This law did not apply, however, to the government nor to commercial loans as long as their terms did not exceed one year. Annuities were regulated at 5 percent of their endowment by the same law.[70] This law probably had little to do with lowering actual interest rates, but by the 1860s the stability and solvency of the Carrera government had greatly improved Guatemala's credit and brought interest rates down closer to those of the industrial world, although they could not match the one-digit percentage rates on European bonds of the 1860s.[71] By the close of the conservative period prime Guatemalan interests rates were in the 10-to-12-percent range, about the same as for the rest of Central America, but several points higher than prevailing European rates.[72]

After the rise of Carrera, although foreign investment did not end, it was much less the subject of active government promotion. Development as did occur came largely from creole Guatemalan initiative. They were often assisted in their enterprises by resident foreigners, and the shortage of native capital meant that these foreigners continued to be among the most important entrepreneurs and investors in the country. For example, following his presidency Mariano Rivera Paz staked out several mines around Alotepeque and requested titles to them on 30 January 1847. Approved the same day, the titles revealed that he was in partnership with Miguel Midence, Carlos Meany, and Young Anderson.[73] In the same year Edward Klée gained exclusive rights for eight years for his iron foundry, for which he promised to import modern machinery and raw materials from Europe.[74] Mechanized cotton weaving, on the other hand, was first developed under government license beginning in May 1848, by a Guatemalan,

José María Samayoa, an entrepreneur later involved in several economic activities under government charter.[75]

The Carrera government in the 1850s frequently borrowed money from European financial sources, supplementing domestic loans and taxation, but it was careful not to become excessively indebted to foreigners. Loans for road building, for example, were more often arranged through the Consulado from local sources. Even when foreign funds were obtained, the government required the merchant guild to guarantee the loan.[76]

Establishment of peace and government solvency encouraged expansion of commerce in the capital and new foreign investment in Guatemala after 1850. The government entertained petitions to open an ice cream shop and a new iron foundry in 1852.[77] A German general merchandise store, Springmühl and Gaedechens, opened on Commerce Street next to the Internal Revenue building in 1855.[78] The following year two local women opened a chocolate factory on Calle de la Libertad (formerly Calle del Correo Viejo) featuring a newly acquired European candy-making machine. Its product was sold in shops around town at prices ranging from two to three reales per pound.[79] Upon the recommendation of the Economic Society, the government in 1865 granted Doña María del Tránsito Santa Cruz and her sisters the exclusive privilege to make ice in the departments of Guatemala, Amatitlán, Sacatepéquez, and Escuintla. Doña María proposed to import Carré ice-making machines and to begin production within eighteen months.[80] These symbols of modernity were part of the awakening of the Guatemalan capital as it changed from a quiet, provincial town with muddy streets and few amenities to the bustling center of commerce and export activities which it would become under liberal rule a few years later. A Chilean life insurance company began operations in Guatemala in October of 1857[81] and thereafter a growing number of Guatemalan agents appeared for foreign insurance and other financial services, reflected in the expanded advertising section of the *Gaceta de Guatemala*.

A list of the commercial establishments for the year 1854 suggests that most of the 788 businesses registered at that time were small shops, but it also reflects the beginnings of a more complex business community:[82]

210	clothing stores	2	tanneries
29	warehouses (almacenes)	15	fireworks shops
5	taverns	11	pharmacies
28	sugar mills	6	silver shops
5	breweries and distilleries	34	carpenters
3	billiard halls	10	chairmakers
4	cafés	16	barbers

70 shops and booths on the plaza	12 cobblers
35 shops in the arcades	12 hatters
172 mixed shops	7 paint shops
19 woollen shops	15 blacksmiths
28 bakeries	15 tailors
21 public houses or bars	4 tinsmiths

A significant number of the Belgian colonists to Santo Tomás wound up in Guatemala City in various commercial enterprises. Agustín Van de Gehuchte opened a successful civil engineering office in the Guatemalan capital. Van de Gehuchte did a great deal of the surveying and planning for the Consulado in its road, bridge, and port building efforts, as well as for other government projects. He made noteworthy contributions to mapping much of Guatemala, and his work served as the basis for the major map developed by Maximilian Sonnenstern under contract with the Guatemalan government in 1858. Sonnenstern, another foreigner, received an exclusive privilege for the manufacture of paper in the republic in 1858, as well as the contract for producing the first modern map of Guatemala, a task he had already performed for the government of El Salvador.[83] Other Belgians in business in Guatemala City were the du Teil brothers, for whom the visit of their father, the Baron du Teil, in July 1858, brought tragedy and reminds us of the continuing problems in the city of inadequate sanitation and health care. The baron died of typhoid fever soon after his arrival in the Guatemalan capital.[84]

By the end of the decade there were a number of foreigners in business in Guatemala City, and they represented an important part of the commercial class. They had been attracted to the country largely because of its stability and opportunities, rather than by government appeals. Their operations, by later standards, were small and did not appear to be taking over the resources of the country, thus they elicited no strong reaction from native interests. Yet they represented an important part of the country's capital and entrepreneurial resources. Moreover, native capitalists were also present and remained important leaders in the country's economy. While they sometimes employed foreigners for their expertise, control remained Guatemalan.

Under the aegis of the Economic Society there were a variety of native industrial and agricultural projects that reflected a gradual recognition of Guatemala's need for more economic development with a predilection for native management. A small, but illustrative example was the enterprise of one Antonio Barreda, Guatemalan inventor of a machine to manufacture cotton wicks. Carrera awarded him a prize of a hundred pesos for this invention on 27 May 1862, and subsequently, after the Economic Society had awarded Barreda its First Class Medal and recommended approval of his project, granted him the exclusive right to manufacture such wicks in the republic for five years.[85] In another case, Pablo Edelman established a small factory to produce farm implements, including cotton gins and coffee skinning machines that sold for $200 each, and a variety of other machines useful to planters.[86] In 1869 a Prussian resident of Guatemala, Francisco Fischbach, won the approval of the Economic Society and an exclusive right to manufacture for eight years his invention of a coffee skinning machine. Its energy source could be, he claimed, "men, horses, oxen, water, or steam."[87]

By the close of the conservative period, a business community of considerable vitality had emerged in Guatemala City, composed of both native Guatemalans and foreigners. In an interesting study of the political and economic activities of some 175 families during the 1860s, Gustavo Palma Murga has revealed the extent of this community and its activities, concluding that although most continued their economic activities after the 1871 revolution, there was a significant reduction in the political participation of many of them. His list of the principal commercial houses in Guatemala during the 1860s appears below in the Appendix.[88]

Conservative economic policy laid the foundation for the subsequent rapid conversion to a dependent agro-export economy. Conservative economic growth was slow, however, when compared to the post-1871 period, and although it contributed to the prosperity of a small elite, the economy remained for the most part subsistence-oriented. Yet it was the increased foreign trade that provided most of the revenues for the Guatemalan government. The expenses of this highly decentralized government were not great, for it did not share the ambitious public works and development goals of either its liberal predecessors or successors, and although paternalistic, the government spent little on social or educational development. Much of the expenditures associated with modern governments were in Guatemala carried out by corporate institutions outside the framework of government finance—including the Consulado, church, charitable institutions—or by local municipalities and departmental governments. Thus the army and the small bureaucracy were the principal burdens on the public treasury, along with service on the debt. The government inherited a substantial debt from the federation and the civil war of 1837–39, to which was added considerable military expenditure in the 1840s. With most taxes abolished, the government was forced to depend upon import and export duties, the liquor and tobacco monopolies, and minor taxes, with loans from the Consulado, the church, and private individuals, including a number of forced loans on the property holders. Never popular, these forced loans were nevertheless tolerated by the elite, and in the long run turned out to be good investments. Military expenditures prevented the conservative governments from coming closer to balancing the budget and eliminating the debt altogether.

Thirty years of conservative rule in Guatemala had, in fact, witnessed considerable growth in Guatemala City. The modernization of the country along capitalist lines had advanced significantly during these three decades and especially since 1850. This process expanded the elite and brought it closer to acceptance of liberal economic values and procedures, even as it clung to conservative politics. Thus, while Guatemala had real economic growth during the conservative years, it was much less impressive than in those countries that had accepted more fully liberal economic tenets. At the same time, because of its slower pace of growth and emphasis on maintaining traditional social relationships, it had not yet sacrificed the stability of its social or economic structure or begun the destruction of its rural peasantry that would become so much a part of liberal economic policy after 1871. The maintenance of a favorable balance of trade throughout the period, especially when compared to other Latin American countries, was testimony to the soundness of conservative fiscal policy and its resistance to the temptations of liberal trade policies. Indeed, the fiscal responsibility of the Guatemalan government from 1850 to 1871 was exemplary when compared to nearly all later administrations.

CHAPTER TWENTY

Conservative Social Policy

As with economic development, during the Carrera years the social development and control of the population fell largely to institutions outside the government bureaucracy. This chapter is not a comprehensive social history of the period. Instead, it looks at several aspects of the government's policy regarding health care and rural land and labor as indicators of the social concerns of the oligarchy and its treatment of the population in general. The following chapter continues this examination with a study of educational and cultural development in Carrera's Guatemala.

As in the colonial period, the welfare of the population was a matter more for the concern of the clergy and the elite than of the state. Health care is an obvious example of this, and for the most part the state was not involved in medical services or health care. Nuns ran the principal hospital, San Juan de Dios, directed by a board of prominent residents of the capital. Yet the state could not ignore the problems created by epidemic diseases and the need to provide better sanitation and water services. With urban growth, these problems became more acute. Especially in the area of epidemic disease, the conservative governments of the mid-nineteenth century took steps that laid the foundations for later government programs of health care and disease prevention.

Smallpox was a disease that had taken heavy tolls in Guatemala since the conquest. Yet in the late eighteenth century, the Guatemalan surgeon general (*protomédico*), José de Flores, had been a pioneer in seeking ways to check epidemics. He enjoyed some success through inoculations from 1780

418

forward. Once Edward Jenner perfected the cowpox vaccination method, Guatemala was one of the first places in the Spanish world to apply it actively, establishing a Vaccine Center in 1805. The first successful vaccination had occurred the year before and the practice spread quickly, first among the elite and then to the population in general.[1] By 1815 vaccination of rural communities had gone forward and smallpox as a major killer had been arrested, contributing directly to the more rapid population growth that the country experienced.[2]

The tumultuous times following independence led to neglect of public health, and the government failed to maintain the earlier emphasis on vaccination. An epidemic at the beginning of 1840, however, forced the government to look back to the colonial experience in yet another way. Rivera Paz on 17 January ordered boards of health established in each department to aid in controlling smallpox and in getting people vaccinated. Later in that year the government reestablished the Vaccine Center and through vaccination effectively stopped the epidemic.[3] Again in 1855–56, when smallpox threatened, a vaccination campaign averted an epidemic. Children in the capital received vaccinations more or less regularly thereafter, and a new outbreak of the disease in Escuintla in July of 1861 was quickly checked by a vaccination campaign there. The disease persisted in 1862, but the vaccination campaign prevented it from becoming the major killer it was in some other areas of Latin America.[4]

Cholera, as we have already seen, proved to be more difficult to control and caused much loss of life in 1837, 1851, 1857, and 1858. The Gálvez government had attacked poor sanitation and water contamination, but had met stiff resistance in rural areas where superstition and fear were powerful deterrents to science.[5] Improvements in sanitation and quarantines were the methods used by the Carrera government against this disease, under the direction of local health boards (*juntas de sanidad*). The tendency, however, was to focus attention on these matters as an epidemic approached, but to pay too little attention to more long-term improvements in public sanitation.[6]

The recurring cholera epidemics and the growth of Guatemala City put added strains on limited medical facilities. As in colonial times, during the Carrera years medical services were under the supervision of the protomédico. New government regulations issued on 7 December 1840 reorganized this office. Serving one-year terms, the protomédicos took their responsibilities with varying degrees of dedication, but several were diligent in trying to improve health care with limited resources. They made recommendations regarding sanitation and public health, and they inspected

TABLE 24
Hospital de San Juan de Dios, 1842

	Number	Died	Days in hospital
Medicine			
Ecclesiastics	4	1	19
Men	467	111	7,451
Women	639	138	12,596
Surgery			
Men	243	11	5,045
Women	145	20	8,513
Injuries			
Men	149	14	2,460
Women	58	1	1,012
Military	431	7	8,678
Totals	2,136	303	45,774

Source: Gaceta Oficial, 13 Jan. 1843.

the pharmacies in the capital. After Dr. Quirino Flores, who had been re-appointed for many years as the protomédico, died in the cholera epidemic of 1857, the government extended the term of office to four years.[7]

San Juan de Dios was the only formal hospital in the country. Although primitive by modern standards, it enjoyed a good reputation in its own time and provided care for several thousand patients annually. In 1842, for example, it admitted 2,136 patients, and provided a total of 45,774 patient-days of care, individual hospital stays averaging more than twenty days. Death took 303 of the patients. The hospital's annual reports provide only limited indication of medical services. They reveal treatment of patients under the categories of "medicine," "surgery," and "injury," and classified the sex and military or ecclesiastical status of the year's patients (see Table 24).

Hospital admissions grew in the years following and considerable expansion of the hospital occurred in 1845, when more than fifty beds were added.[8] The annual report for 1849 revealed an annual budget of about $25,000. The hospital served 3,245 patients in that year, of which 339 died. It provided a breakdown of the origins of the patients (see Table 25).

These statistics reflect the relative lack of growth in the institution since the late colonial period, however. In 1813 the annual budget had been nearly $27,000, and the hospital had cared for 3,515 patients for 78,634 patient-days.[9] Yet British resident Robert Dunlop had considerable praise for the hospital in 1844: "Adjoining the cemetery is the hospital, the only

one in Central America, and which is kept up in a manner not inferior
to the best in London, having four large rooms well ventilated, neat and
clean, for the poor, and separate apartments for those who can afford to
pay,—a plan which might well be copied in more advanced countries." [10]
The hospital also managed the city cemetery, and the 1849 report revealed
that only about a third (339) of the people buried there during the year had
died in the hospital. Of the 987 buried, there were 554 charity cases; 615
adults (including "three clergy and two Protestants"), and 372 children. [11]

In 1854 Carrera authorized taxes on billiard halls and foreign liquors
to provide additional financial support for the hospital. Soon after, he
established a new charitable institution to care for orphans and other unfortunates. This poorhouse, known simply as the Hospicio or Casa de Misericordia and founded under the direction of Rafael Ayau, formally opened on
15 March 1857 in a new building erected at a cost of more than $30,000.
The government provided a small monthly subsidy to the institution, increased to $50 per month in 1859, but most of its funds had to be secured
from private donations and bequests. [12] A report on its operations in 1860
reviewed its first three years of operation, during which 305 unfortunates
were admitted (see Table 26). It takes little imagination to suppose it was a
dreary place, but Ayau, who died in 1868, was applauded for his success in
developing this necessary institution.

While patterns of urban health care provide some insight into the social
policy of nineteenth-century Guatemalan conservatives, of more general
significance was their policy toward exploitation of the land and labor of the
rural population. There is no question that from the arrival of the Spanish

TABLE 25
Residences of Patients in Hospital
de San Juan de Dios, 1849

Guatemala City	1,533
Dept. of Guatemala	346
Rest of the Republic	1,062
El Salvador	162
Honduras	25
Nicaragua	25
Costa Rica	9
Foreigners	59
Unknown	24
Total	3,245

Source: Gaceta de Guatemala, 15 Feb. 1850.

TABLE 26
Casa de Misericordia, 1860

	Admitted	Released	Escaped	Died	Continuing
Men	24	6	6	8	4
Youths	108	11	11	6	80
Pensioners	14	5	1	0	8
Women	88	21	2	27	38
Children	71	7	3	29	32
Totals	305	50	23	70	162

Source: Gaceta de Guatemala, 11 July 1860.

in the early sixteenth century, a pattern of exploitation of the Indian population characterized Guatemalan history. Yet because of the destruction of much of the Indian population at the time of the conquest and its continued decline well into the eighteenth century, and because of a more humane imperial policy in reaction to the abuses of the conquistadors and their successors, a body of legislation and custom had evolved in colonial Guatemala that allowed substantial Indian survival in highland Indian communities. That is not to say that the European residents (creole and peninsular) did not continue to live off the labor and resources of the Indians, for they did. But the imperial laws nevertheless provided a degree of protection against excessive abuse. They created the opportunity for many Indian communities to preserve their communal lands, folk customs, and social structure.[13] The Bourbon Reforms began to challenge this protection, and the nineteenth-century liberals, under the guise of egalitarian philosophy, would seek to end the special protection that Spain had granted Indian lands and labor. This very issue had been at the center of the Carrera revolt in 1837.

In earlier chapters we have shown how the rise of Rafael Carrera arrested the liberal attack on Indian protection. Moorhead, Miceli, Rodríguez, and others have also shown how especially in the 1840s the colonial protection of the Indian masses was restored under Carrera as he checked the trend toward alienation of Indian land and labor. It has been less clear what happened after Carrera returned to power in 1849. Miceli and Moorhead, as well as Julio Castellanos Cambranes, have implied that Carrera was less concerned with the peasant masses after 1850 and that he essentially allied himself with the capital elite in exploiting the rural poor. The present work has explained in some detail how Carrera did, in fact, join with the conservative elite in the capital after 1849 to form a strong authoritarian dictatorship, which primarily benefited the commercial and landholding elite of the capital. The growth of agro-exports began to put increasing pressure on rural land and labor, and this came as much from small Ladino farmers as from the creole elite. Yet Carrera himself served as a powerful obstacle to an unrestrained attack on peasant land and labor.

The Carrera years are properly classified as a period of reaction, a return to the Hispanic heritage in reaction against the seemingly radical liberal reforms of the 1820s and 1830s, and in the broader sense, even a rejection of many of the Bourbon Reforms. In no aspect of Guatemalan life is this more apparent than in patterns of land and labor. The continued expansion of cochineal production did not require great amounts of land for the nopaleros, and infringement on Indian land and labor was certainly curtailed while Carrera exercised leadership in the country. For a quarter of a century, the process begun in the late eighteenth century—converting Guatemala from largely a subsistence economy to a dependent agro-export state—was arrested, or at least slowed.

The expansion of coffee, however, begun under conservative rule, once more emphasized the need for land and labor of the Indians, as both members of the elite and upcoming Ladinos sought to expand production. The full impact of this change would not be felt until the 1870s, when, as Doug Madigan has succinctly explained in his study of the Santiago Atitlán region, "not since the thirty years following the conquest had such major change taken place in Guatemala."[14] Yet pressure was already building up against Carrera's protective policies, and upon his death there was a rapid increase in encroachment on Indian lands.

Indian labor was not so plentiful as it became later, either, for the community structure of the colonial era was still largely intact. Wages were low (about 2.5 reales or 31 cents per day), but workers had some bargaining power and also received wages for their travel time. They often received their pay in advance. There was considerable variation in wages, however, as low as one real (12.5 cents) per day in Los Altos and only around 1.5 reales (19 cents) per day in the area around Antigua Guatemala. But most Indians were still free to contract for their labor, and under Carrera they enjoyed a modicum of protection from the government against unfair treatment.[15] The exploitation of the Indians by the medium and small Ladino coffee planters would characterize the rise of that export industry and would usher in the modern period of Guatemalan social history after 1865.[16]

Carrera repeatedly expressed concern for the rights of the Indians, and the conservative governments that held power following 1849 reenforced this by their decrees. In October 1851 the minister of government pointed to the demoralized state of the Indians of the Verapaz as he urged the Supreme Court to make sure that all the laws protecting the Indians were observed. He recommended a new law to protect the Indians, a law that would halt the "complete demoralization of the Indians, by means appropriate to their customs, knowledge, and needs." He alleged that since adoption of the system of regulating the Indians by the same laws as for other classes in the society, the result had been the dispersal of their populations, the disappearance of good police protection, and a society that was dangerously threatened.[17] The concern was undoubtedly related to the continued disorders in the montaña region, which had spread into the Verapaz, but it also reflected a sincere social philosophy that favored the colonial practice of segregating and protecting the Indian, while at the same time exploiting his labor. The resulting decree, signed by Carrera on 8 November 1851, "in favor of the aboriginal class," emphasized that the *Recopilación de Indias* (the Spanish Laws of the Indies), providing protection of the Indians, remained in force except where they were contrary to Guatemala's independence or its constitution. It specifically instructed judges and corregidores to protect the rights of the Indians in legal procedures and judicial cases, specifically prohibiting authorities from using injurious language, striking the Indians in custody, or otherwise maltreating them. At the same time, corregidores were to take special pains to combat Indian drunkenness and idleness, while insuring that those ordered to work for private citizens (*mandamientos*) were well treated and paid punctually, not only for their work time, but also for their travel to and from their villages. In case of illness, where there were no hospitals, those employing the Indians were responsible for caring for and curing them. Corregidores, in collaboration with village priests, were also to guard the Indian community funds and to see to their wise use, so that Indian community buildings, schools, churches, and jails were kept in good condition. Where facilities did not exist, they were to establish schools that would teach the Indians the Spanish language and Christian doctrine. The corregidores were specifically charged to insure that the Indians were not deprived, even under the pretext of sale, of their communal lands, and that they not be required to serve in the armed forces. A further important feature of the law was, again as in the colonial period, the requirement that the Indians not be permitted to leave their villages to live in the mountains or to become vagrants. If that happened, the authorities were to capture and return them to their own communities. Such provisions had often been used to exploit the Indians, but this decree warned the corregidores that in no case should these regulations, intended to help the Indians, be turned against them:

If they have to be detained, it should be done by officials of their same class; if their punishments exceed that which customarily are applied, those officials should be restrained, reprimanded, and themselves punished; if it is necessary to proceed against some Indian or a group of Indians, or an action must be begun or continued when the public attorney is unavailable, an official protector must be appointed to assist them, but with care that they not be abused by their ignorance and subjected to fraud or extortion.

And finally, the corregidores were ordered to keep a copy of the *Recopilación de Indias* in their departments and to observe its rules in all cases involving Indians in their respective departments and courts.[18] This decree did not, of course, end abuse or exploitation of the Indian population of Guatemala and, as in the colonial period, it also served to keep the Indians congregated in communities where their labor could more easily be exploited by the creoles and Ladinos. Indian rights did not extend to idleness. But it did reflect the will of the government to protect the indigenous classes in the paternalistic manner that had evolved over three centuries of colonial experience, and it established firmly a policy that at the very least slowed the alienation of Indian lands and the excessive exploitation of their labor.

The expansion of private agro-export land tenure was a process that began in the late eighteenth century and was accelerated after independence. The expropriation of church lands was an important step in this direction early in the independent period, but later, especially after 1865, it became more serious for Indian lands. Julio Castellanos Cambranes has documented the process of encroachment on Indian communal lands especially well,[19] and only a few examples are needed here to illustrate that trend.

Just as the coffee industry originated during the Carrera years, so also did some of the labor practices that would eventually become general during the liberal era that followed. Debt peonage and the use of vagrancy laws to exploit cheap labor, for example, were practices that were not widespread until the latter third of the nineteenth century in Guatemala, although they occurred considerably earlier in Mexico. We find their beginnings, nonetheless, in Guatemala as early as the 1840s. In August 1847, perhaps reflecting the temporary liberal strength in the government at that moment, the state imposed a vagrancy law. Reflecting the labor shortages in the country, this law sought to put more people to work on both private farms and public works. It prohibited anyone being without an occupation and required those moving from one place to another to have a certificate from their alcalde or employer. Vagrants could be put to work on public works. The preamble to the act specifically noted the losses that hacendados "frequently suffered" when they paid in advance workers who failed to appear for the work. The law required workers changing from one employer to another to carry a certificate of recommendation from the previous employer, and those working for the first time had to have a certificate from their alcalde stating that the person was known to them. The certificate was also to indicate any sum of money owed the previous employer, and that account had to be settled before the employee was paid any money by the new employer.[20] The concern over Indians wandering away from their village and becoming vagrants was a recurrent one, reflecting the elite's interest in maintaining the Indian labor supply. The government repeatedly warned the corregidores to take care to keep the Indians from drunkenness and other vices, and particularly to pay attention to enforcing the *Recopilación de Indias* with respect to seeing that the Indians did not abandon their villages.

Temporary liberal accession to power in the mid and late 1840s raised the apprehension of Indian communities in Los Altos and elsewhere regarding protection of their community lands. After the 1848 revolution, Carrera insisted that Indian grievances regarding land be dealt with promptly and fairly. A number of Indian uprisings had occurred directly related to land tenure, and Carrera reaffirmed his commitment to protecting the Indians' rights and lands. A report from Totonicapán in February 1852 told of insurrections in several Indian communities, but also indicated the nature of the encroachment that was taking place. Corregidor Rosendo García Salas said that the Indians were best behaved where Ladinos were present, as in Totonicapán and San Cristóbal, with the most serious uprisings occurring in the Indian communities of Momostenango, San Bartolo, and the ranchería de Calel. This report is disparaging toward the Indians and it reflects the resistance of the Indians to Ladinos who were moving into formerly Indian towns. The report also reflects the dismal condition of roads and development in the Department of Totonicapán.[21]

This report prompted Carrera to make a major inspection tour of Los Altos, ostensibly to assure that Indian interests were being properly cared for. He took along the surveyor and councilor of state, Juan José Flores, and announced that this *visita* would deal with "questions of lands between villages and Indians, roads, bridges, public buildings, churches, and schools." Carrera began his tour in Chimaltenango on 22 March 1852 and continued on to Sololá, Totonicapán, and Huehuetenango. He personally resolved numerous disputes and left Flores and a team of surveyors and officers to carry out his dispositions, which in some cases involved resettling Indians to new locations and surveying considerable land. Flores fell ill and died in Huehuetenango on 24 May 1852, but the work continued under the supervision of Col. Juan Ignacio Irigoyen. While the primary motive of this activity may well have been to put down Indian insurrections, it was successful in fostering a better image of the Carrera government among many of the Indian communities of Los Altos.[22]

Upon his return to the capital, Carrera decreed on 4 May 1852 another law to improve the Indians' social welfare. It provided that those unable to care for themselves, the sick and disabled, were to be exempted from forced labor or other levies and were to be provided with certain social services. Parish priests and village governors were specifically required to see that such people, as well as homeless orphans and widows, were provided with food, clothing, and shelter at community expense. This decree also required each community to make an annual charity report to the corregidor.[23] This apparent concern for the poor and unfortunate did not necessarily bring major changes, for Indian communities generally provided for such people themselves, but it did put the force of the government behind community efforts and thus assisted the survival of Indian communities at a time when Ladino agrarian interests were beginning to encroach upon them. This paternalistic policy of the Carrera government on behalf of the Indians did not exempt them from continued exploitation for their labor by the Ladinos, but it did protect them from some of the abuses that came later under Justo Rufino Barrios and his successors. Emphasizing separation and protection of the Indian peoples, this policy differed notably from Barrios's policy of openly regarding the Indian as an inferior class and actively encouraging its assimilation with the Ladinos. Compare the Carrera decrees, for example, with Barrios's circular of 3 November 1876 to the jefes políticos (successors to the corregidores in Barrios's Guatemala), in which he says:

> If we abandon the farmers to their own resources and do not give them strong and energetic aid, they will be unable to make any progress, for all their efforts will be doomed to failure due to the deceit of the Indians. You should therefore see to it: *First:* that the Indian villages in your jurisdiction be forced to give the number of hands to the farmers that the latter ask for, even to the number of fifty or a hundred to a single farmer if his enterprise warrants that number. *Second:* when one set of Indians has not been able to finish the work in hand in a period of two weeks, a second set should be sent to relieve the first, so that the work may not be delayed. *Third:* the two weeks' work shall be paid for ahead of time by the mayor of the Indian town, thus avoiding the loss of time involved in paying every day. *Fourth:* above all else see to it that any Indian who seeks to evade this duty is punished to the full extent of the law, that the farmers are fully protected and that each Indian is forced to do a full day's work while in service.[24]

Government surveyors, important under liberal rule for delineating land for private acquisition, continued to be sent out by the Carrera's government to assure that Indian community lands were protected.[25] A petition from the Indians of Santa Maria Toyabá in the Department of Sololá in December 1856 is illustrative. They requested surveyors to be sent to establish definitively their boundary with the Hacienda Choacorral of Manuel Pérez, whom they claimed was encroaching upon their corn fields and grazing lands. Pérez, they claimed, was trying to establish his landmarks to the edge of their village, and his livestock was destroying their corn and other crops, causing them great damage and endangering their food supply. They asked the president to send surveyors to establish the landmarks according to their ancient title. The government quickly responded favorably, requiring only that the Indians pay the surveyors for their services.[26]

By the 1860s, however, and sometimes even earlier, we find the Ministry of Gobernación sometimes siding with Ladino coffee planters encroaching on Indian ejidos. Such was the case, for example, in the Department of Suchitepéquez in 1862 when the Indians of San Felipe complained that Ladinos who had rented their lands to plant coffee were not paying the rent into the Indian community fund. The ministry's view was that the planting of coffee would enrich their lands and provide lucrative work to the community, implying that they should be grateful for this development.[27] The liberals had begun to encourage private planters to use communal lands to develop export agriculture soon after independence, providing in the land law of 5 August 1835 for such users to pay an annual rent of up to 3 percent of its assessed value to the Indian communities.[28] This law continued in effect during the conservative years and was, in fact, reaffirmed in an executive order of 6 November 1862, accompanying greater encouragement of coffee planting on such lands.[29] But for most of the Carrera years, the government defended the right of community officers to approve or reject such rentals. There were exceptions. In one case Rafael Carrera himself seized 57 caballerías from the community of Santa Lucía Cotzumalguapa and sold it to the creole Manuel María Herrera,[30] but in general the Indians were able to protect their communal lands and to count on the caudillo's active intervention on their behalf. Castellanos has presented considerable evidence showing the success of the Indians in resisting encroachment on their lands during most of the Carrera period, but he also shows rising encroachment on their lands after 1860, and especially after the death of the caudillo in 1865.[31]

On 31 January 1863 the assembly passed an agriculture law that limited the size of communal ejidos to one square league, defined more clearly public lands, and made their acquisition by Ladinos easier. While the law appears not to have been actively publicized by the Carrera government, it would in many respects appear to mark the beginning of a new phase of Guatemalan socioeconomic history in which the interests of the Indian communities would be increasingly sacrificed to those of the coffee planters and exporters.[32] At the same time, as the population of the Indian communities had been growing, competition for these lands among the Indians themselves had become increasingly sharp, resulting in some cases in fighting between villages over disputed ejido lands.[33] Thus, although there was a sympathetic government policy toward the Indians, and the pace of encroachment slowed, it is obvious that continued alienation of those lands occurred. Carrera himself acquired several ejidos during his administration, and although his accumulated wealth was small compared to later Guatemalan presidents, he joined the elite practice of acquiring land as the principal symbol of power in the country.[34] Significantly, after his death, Ladino encroachment on Indian lands accelerated rapidly and the documented record of Indian complaints correspondingly increased.[35]

Evidence in the archives of the Ministry of Gobernación reveals that the administration of the renting of community lands of the department was subject to abuses and corruption, and the indigenous population often suffered from such abuses by Ladinos. Accusations against the political commissioner in Carchá, Miguel Molina, in 1866, for mismanagement of community funds derived from coffee production suggests one form of common abuse of the Indian communities.[36] Castellanos has demonstrated in some detail the trend that began during the conservative years, that of community lands being claimed by coffee planters. Castellanos's evidence, however, drawn principally from the Ministerio de Gobernación archive, is almost entirely from the period following the death of Carrera. While alienation of Indian community lands by Ladinos may be said to have begun earlier, it was not widespread until after 1865. What is remarkable is how quickly the trend accelerated following the death of Carrera, supporting the idea of the Cerna administration being a transition and forerunner to the liberal era. Castellanos documents the pressure on Indian community lands from the 1850s forward. A number of important coffee fincas, including those of Justo Rufino Barrios, developed on land rented from indigenous communities. It is of further significance that although this development occurred during the conservative years, actual ownership of this land did not pass to private hands until after 1871.[37]

Cerna's socioeconomic policy became almost immediately apparent in respect to the change in protection of rural Indian labor following the death of Carrera. A series of articles entitled "Indígenas" in the *Gaceta de Guatemala*, beginning 28 January 1867, reflected the change in tone from

Carrera's protective policy. Although reiterating earlier concern for protection of the Indians, these articles emphasized the need to keep them in their pueblos and not allow them to wander about as vagrants or into the woods or mountains. While the author insisted that his main point was the application of Spanish and Guatemalan laws that protected the Indians, the series nevertheless concluded that the protection of the Indian should "not extend to tolerance of his faults." Real protection of the Indian, the *Gaceta* concluded, meant keeping them in their pueblos and seeing that they met their obligations under the law. "This may mean punishing some of them, but always with the prudence and consideration that the law requires."[38]

In April 1866, the municipality of San Felipe made a particularly revealing statement, in which the Indians complained of encroachment by Ladinos over the past nine years. They requested that no further grants be made to those "empresarios," that unpaid rents on the lands be paid into the community funds, and that those funds be outside the control of the political governor.[39] The coffee planters argued that the lands were unused, while the Indians usually argued that the lands were essential to their livelihood and that the planters failed to pay the annual rents required. Indian practice of leaving a third of their lands fallow, ecologically sound, perhaps gave the appearance of lands being underutilized. One Indian community in Verapaz in 1866, for example, complained that its people were being "tyrannized" and dispossessed of their best lands, which they cultivated and used for pasture. They complained especially of foreigners who were coming to establish fincas, despite what "the late President Rafael Carrera told us, that only natives of the country would be granted rights to them." Moreover, they complained that the *finqueros* were making them pay too much for damages caused by their livestock in the coffee fincas because their fences were not good.[40] The corregidor's report on the matter, representative of the attitude toward the Indians from this time forward, was not sympathetic. It said that the amount of land conceded to coffee planters was insignificant in comparison to the amount the pueblo possessed, emphasizing that the municipality was free to grant away their land for income if they wished.[41]

Already, in the more heavily populated zones near the capital, the transition to export agriculture was beginning to cause shortages of food and force emigration of peasants, a problem that would assume gigantic proportions in the present century.[42] As a government official in Ciudad Vieja noted on 31 December 1866, "The harvests of corn, beans, and cochineal have been abundant . . . but the *ejido* is very small and is limited to the skirts of Agua volcano, whose lands are worn out from being worked too much." Thus much of the population "lacks sufficient land for their subsistence." The result, he said, was that a growing number of families were emigrating, many of them forming a new community at Santa Catarina Siquinalá, in the Department of Escuintla, where some eight hundred former natives of Ciudad Vieja lived.[43]

The coffee entrepreneurs were aggressive following Carrera's death, not only in encroaching upon the land of the Indian communities, but also in exploiting their labor. The Indians did not easily give up their subsistence agriculture for low-wage work on the coffee fincas. A request from a group of coffee planters on the San Agustín hacienda in Sololá in August 1867 mentioned their "great difficulties in procuring enough people to work for them, because these lands are very isolated from any population." Needing workers "to sustain the large fincas that they were forming," the planters asked to establish a new town to congregate some four hundred Indian families from the Los Altos departments they would bring for that purpose. The planters were prepared to provide these Indians with plots for their own cultivation of food, as well as to build a church, a school, and a hospital in the town, advantages they claimed the Indians did not have in their previous location. Their petition sought permission for the town as well as support from local authorities in moving the families, who the planters argued did not presently have even enough land for their own subsistence. They also asked that the new community be exempted from military and municipal responsibilities, since the planters had no other communities to draw upon for labor. The government responded favorably to these requests on 17 September of the same year.[44]

Late in the same year (1867), Indians of Carchá, in the Alta Verapaz, complained formally to the government that they had been despoiled of their lands and homes to make way for coffee production. In their appeal to President Cerna, they said that they were native sons and leaders of the community who had built their homes and ranchos with hard work, that local officials had told them that the president himself has ordered them to move, but that they knew that "that can't be so." Moreover, they said that they had been ordered by the commissioner in Panzos to plant coffee in their cornfields in the mountains, while to do so "would seem to have no other intention but to exterminate us." Contradicting the Indians, the corregidor's report stated that they had migrated voluntarily.[45] By 1868 it was obvious that the corregidores of the highlands were facilitating the organization of Indians to work on the coffee fincas, in some cases clearly exceeding the limits of the law.[46] Regulations issued by Gabriel Burbano,

TABLE 27

Daily Wages Expressed in Terms of
Corn at Current Prices

Years	Pounds of corn
1853–66	7–12
1870–89	7.5
1890–99	10
1900–1917	2.5–4.5
1917–21	5.5
1920–39	4–4.5

Sources: Woodward, "Population and Development,"
12–13; David J. McCreery, "Debt Servitude in Rural
Guatemala, 1876–1936," Hispanic American Historical
Review 63 (1983), 748–50. This table was first com-
piled for Ralph Lee Woodward, Jr., "Economic De-
velopment and Dependency in Nineteenth-Century
Guatemala," in Crisis in the Caribbean Basin, edited by
Richard Tardanico, p. 73, in vol. 9 of Political Econ-
omy of the World-System Annuals, edited by Immanuel
Wallerstein (1987).

the corregidor of San Marcos, at the end of 1870, in effect provided a
means to impose debt slavery on coffee workers in San Marcos and San
Pedro Sacatepéquez.[47]

Expansion of agro-exports thus began to take land formerly producing
the local food supply and ultimately drove food prices up. The prices of
basic staples fluctuated considerably, as we have already shown, but the
conservative governments had made sincere efforts to maintain a plentiful
supply of food. Average prices increased only slightly during the period.[48]
It appears certain that the Liberal Reforma resulted in lower standards of
living for many, if not most, Guatemalans. Although data is fragmentary
for both wages and prices, available data suggests a decline in real wages
in terms of current corn prices, a trend that became more obvious in the
twentieth century than the nineteenth (see Table 27).

Much of the evidence presented in this chapter is fragmentary, and more
comprehensive conclusions must await the detailed social history being
written by Professor Julio Pinto Soria of the University of San Carlos.
Nonetheless it is clear enough that conservative social policy under Rafael
Carrera reflected a paternalistic concern for the welfare of the working
masses. As during Spanish administration of the Kingdom of Guatemala,

and spurred by the special concern for the rural masses exhibited by the caudillo Carrera, the Guatemala City elite provided a little care for those who could not provide for themselves. In their Indian labor policy they restored the Laws of the Indies with the rationale that although this enabled them to utilize Indian labor, it also protected that class. It is undeniable that these elites—conservative or liberal—exploited the Indian in Guatemala, but there was a qualitative difference in attitude between the two. The conservatives, in turning back to Hispanic traditions, provided some degree of protection for the natives against the liberal tendency—under the guise of egalitarianism—to subject them to a process of proletarianization, which would deprive them of their land and their culture in return for a lower standard of living in the name of modernization and progress.

At the same time, the conservative protests that their laws were solely for the protection of the Indian cannot be taken at face value, and even Carrera himself joined the elites in enriching himself at the expense of the rural masses. There was a significant difference between the letter and the observation of the laws regarding Indian land and labor, and it is clear that the trend toward alienation of Indian lands did not end with the rise of Rafael Carrera. We can simply say that the trend significantly slowed. During the period 1840–65, Indian communities and their communal lands seem to have been strengthened as an institution, contributing to their survival, in some cases even to the present day. Those who were perhaps most aggressive in seeking to alienate Indian lands and convert Indian labor from subsistence to agro-export were middle-sector Ladinos, rather than the patrician elite of the capital, who to a large degree already owned substantial amounts of land. It is also apparent that in the latter years of the Carrera regime, protection of Indian land and labor began to fade. His death signaled a major assault on these lands, which accelerated into the liberal period.

The conservatives reduced the size and scope of the central government of Guatemala even as it became more strongly authoritarian. There was a strong reaction against the ambitious policies of the Gálvez government in both economic and social policy. It is ironic that the liberals, theoretically favoring laissez-faire and private sector development, pursued substantial state intervention in social and economic development in their eagerness to bring it about. By contrast, the conservatives sought to limit the role of the government. Nevertheless, in turning back to the colonial model, they could not avoid the Hispanic corporate tradition of very substantial regulation of social and economic life. Thus, even though the conservatives reduced the size and scope of the bureaucracy, the government continued to have a large regulatory role. Moreover, the church, as a virtual agency of the state, also played a major role in regulating society. Thus, in fact, the strong role of the state in society would continue to be one of the most powerful characteristics of Guatemalan history.

CHAPTER TWENTY-ONE

Education and Culture

GOVERNMENT POLICY TOWARD EDUCATION AND CULTURE offers one of the clearest areas of difference between liberal and conservative philosophy in nineteenth-century Guatemala. Spanish policy had largely left education to the church, and conservatives in Guatemala held to that tradition. It theoretically favored at least minimal education for all under clerical guidance. It intended to preserve and develop Christian morals, good work habits, and the use of Spanish so that the masses could better serve the elite. In practice education of all but the elite and a small middle sector was ignored in much of the colonial period. Early efforts at educating the Indians had faded by the seventeenth century. For the most part, except for the modest efforts of some parish priests, there was little general education in the country. Eighteenth-century liberalism, however, reflected in Bourbon policy, emphasized the importance of mass education as one of the keys to modernization and general prosperity, and nineteenth-century Guatemalan liberals argued in favor of public education for all. In their view education had to be wrested from the reactionary control of the church and provided by the state or community to all, at least at the elementary level, in order to develop a civilized citizenry and to train more productive workers. In practice, the liberals did not come near to achieving their goal in the nineteenth century. It must be admitted that a strong elite fear of education of the masses persisted among both conservatives and liberals. Indeed, it persists to the present day among the Guatemalan elite. Just as the Guatemalan elite has been slow to realize that higher wages contribute to greater productivity and prosperity, they have also been reluctant to assign education the priority that would bring about a population able to develop a more advanced civilization.

At the elementary level, the conservative educational policy differed very sharply from that of the liberals. Theoretically, during the colonial era, the church was responsible for providing basic education in every parish, and a number of royal orders had emphasized that. In practice, however, there had been little in the way of general education for the population, and formal education had been largely limited to a small elite. The liberals proposed a much broader system of public education, widely perceived as part of their anticlericalism in the 1830s. While they began a public education system, in practice—like the conservatives—they provided little in the way of real instruction for anyone but the elite. Some of the children of the elite were sent abroad for their early education, but most were educated in Guatemala, and nearly all received their higher education at the University of San Carlos.[1]

In the late colonial period, the Bourbons had encouraged the establishment of schools in each community. In 1799 the royal government in Guatemala had specifically ordered establishment of public schools in all communities of more than a hundred taxpayers. The schools were to teach Spanish reading and writing and were part of the current trend toward integrating the Indians into the community. This idea would find favor with the liberals later and had as its goal the training of the Indian populations to labors that would increase their productivity.[2] Immediate results were few, but by 1815 some communities were complying and had begun the process of establishing regular schools.[3] Although they could be seen as the beginning of a public education system, in most cases these schools were run by the clergy, so that the church continued to be the principal institution involved in education.

After independence there was considerable impetus for public education in both the federal and state governments of Central America. Behind the leadership of José Cecilio del Valle, the federal government gave at least lip service to a broad program.[4] In Guatemala the legislative assembly on 1 July 1826 ordered a school to be established in each town, using municipal funds. Where community funds were inadequate, it authorized a school tax of 3 reales (37.5 cents) per person. The liberal government of Juan Barrundia, which supported this, soon collapsed, but when liberals returned to power in 1829 they resumed their effort to support public education and restored this law on 29 April 1834.[5] Guatemala had only three primary schools and the university in 1821, but by 1830 the numbers had grown to forty primary schools, two secondary schools, the university, and five private schools. Standards were low in the primary schools, and there was little instruction in the natural sciences, economics, or political economy. But there was optimism that further educational expansion would follow.[6] Governor Mariano Gálvez perceived educational reform as a major part of his plan to bring European modernization and civilization to Guatemala. Thus he established schools, museums, a national library, and the academy of sciences, often utilizing expropriated church properties for this purpose.[7] Federal President Francisco Morazán supported Gálvez and emphasized the key role of education in "breaking the chains of slavery." Morazán told the federal Congress in 1836 that he was not talking about advanced culture, or higher education in the sciences, but simply teaching the humble youth to "read, write, and count," for "a few moral and political concepts and a little knowledge in other subjects, that facilitate the crafts and vocations, is all that a people need for their happiness and liberty; and this is the kind of instruction that the government provides the inhabitants under its rule with the greatest success."[8]

Public education suffered greatly during the Carrera revolt, however. With the church's role reduced, the conservatives charged that under the liberals, education had actually declined rather than improved. In August 1839 the church was again operating the three principal primary schools for boys in Guatemala City. With a total enrollment of 321, they were Belén (161), San Casiano (100), and San José (60). In addition, there was a primary school for girls at Los Beaterios, but one that El Tiempo reported was in "great decadence." All these schools, it said, had miraculously survived owing only to the spirit of charity. These schools all provided free education. The Belén school received a small subsidy of twenty-five pesos per month from the municipality. There were also a few small private schools that charged tuition. According to El Tiempo, the liberal government had passed many laws and talked with lofty ideals, but the results had actually been a decline in educational quality and quantity. Formerly, it said, there had been schools in convents throughout the city, but now, as a result of the liberals' policies, the children had nowhere to learn their letters, "this being the progress of the great defenders of the armed civilization."[9]

The conservatives thus sought to restore the church to its exclusive position in elementary and secondary education. A conservative editorial made this clear in September 1840:

Public instruction has never received the attention it deserves in Guatemala, but it has had the greatest disrespect during the last nineteen years. . . . Where are the schools which even in the poorest hamlet were there in the time of the Spanish Government? What will the poor do to teach their children the principals of the holy religion and of morals? What happened to the schools that all the regular orders had in their convents and where parents could be assured that their children would receive a good education? Painfully, we say that all that has disappeared, all gone. Even in the capital there exist but three free public schools.[10]

This comment probably had a more sanguine view of colonial education than was justified, but it is undoubtedly true that at least in the capital there had been a real decline. Even in rural areas, the formal and informal educational efforts of rural priests and of the schools begun near the close of the colonial period had suffered greatly during the liberal years. Thus the proclerical *Procurador* chastised the assembly for not moving faster in restoring the university and the traditional educational system.

While the rhetoric in the debate over state versus ecclesiastical control of education was heated, the truth was that neither provided nearly adequate instruction for the youth of Guatemala. Conservative education was perhaps somewhat more comprehensive than what the liberals had actually provided, but it still was far behind recognized standards in the more developed nations of Europe and North America in the early nineteenth century. Frederick Crowe provided one of the most depressing descriptions of Guatemalan education in the 1840s. He said the few schools were in miserable shape. Cruel teachers taught few children, with more emphasis on religion than letters. In his view: "The schools of Central America are worse than inefficient. The injury done to the flexible minds and tender hearts of the children who are subjected to such a process must be great indeed, and in some respects irreparable. The cruelty which is most apparent is far surpassed by that which does violence to the moral susceptibilities, and refused aliment to the soul."[11] Another Briton with less of a personal interest in the matter, Robert Dunlop, concurred in this bleak picture, as he charged that there was little intellectual activity in Guatemala. Guatemala City lacked even a single bookstore, for "reading is rarely resorted to in Guatemala." In the towns outside of the capital, he contended, "not one in ten can read or write, and in many parts of the country, not one in a thousand. In many villages containing some thousand inhabitants, no person is to be found who can read, and, when a traveller is compelled to show his passport to the alcalde, who is the first civil and criminal judge, he is generally requested to read it."[12]

Crowe, a Baptist missionary distributing Bibles and various prohibited Protestant religious pamphlets, sought to open a primary school in Guatemala City. His petition to open such a school created a notable stir in the city in 1844. The archbishop urged denial of the petition, which the municipality would have undoubtedly done, but in the meantime the Supreme Court intervened and ordered Crowe out of the country. Instead of leaving, however, Crowe began his school without authorization in January 1845. Again ordered to leave, he nevertheless persisted. He was repeatedly denied permission and eventually forced to leave Guatemala.[13]

There was, of course, a highly literate element among the tiny elite in the capital, to whom most education in the country was reserved. Nearly all had been educated at the University of San Carlos, and there was considerable intellectual dialogue among members of this class during the 1840s. Some of these men recognized the need for expansion of educational opportunities, among them especially Manuel F. Pavón, who in the *Gaceta Oficial* in 1843 would argue for more public instruction, quoting Alexis de Tocqueville regarding "ignorance putting liberty in danger."[14] In the following year, Pavón wrote the archbishop urging him to speed reopening of the parochial schools of the country. Emphasizing the strong role of the church, Pavón said education should be developed within the context of the "Laws of the Indies and many other dispositions that should be considered in force, that recommend to and even impose upon the parish priests the obligation of providing public instruction." Acknowledging that the turbulent times had not permitted this development, he urged the archbishop to promote education and to issue the necessary orders so that parish priests would take up this responsibility.[15]

Very modest progress followed. By 1846 most of the highland departments had a few schools. In the Department of Sololá, for example, there were twelve schools, all supported by community funds except in the town of Sololá, where a half-real-per-fanega tax on wheat flour milling supported the school there. These twelve schools taught 145 Ladino and 90 Indian students in grades one through six. Sixty-nine (59 Ladinos and 10 Indians) of these were in the town of Sololá. Course enrollments are revealing. All took "religious principles," and 83 were in beginning reading. Fifty-two were reading Cato. But only 5 each were enrolled in Spanish grammar or handwriting, 7 in music, and 20 in arithmetic.[16] A similar pattern could be found in the East, where in the District of Santa Rosa there were 354 pupils in the primary schools.[17]

With the temporary return of the liberals to influence, on 6 December 1847 the Ministry of Gobernación revived the 1826 law referred to above,

TABLE 28
Courses Taught in Guatemala City Schools in 1848

Subject	Boys	Girls	All
Christian doctrine	98.6	100.0	99.2
Reading	94.9	100.0	97.1
Writing	75.6	21.6	51.9
Arithmetic	64.5	17.2	43.7
Algebra	4.9	0.0	2.7
Spanish grammar	26.9	6.2	17.8
Geography	12.1	0.0	6.8
Sewing	0.0	84.6	37.2
Embroidery	0.0	27.5	12.1
Bookkeeping	3.7	0.0	2.1
Flowers	0.0	9.2	4.0
Music	1.9	1.2	1.6
Drawing	7.0	2.4	4.9

Source: "Estado de las escuelas de primeras letras de ambos sexos de esta capital, con expresión del número de alumnos y genero de instrucción que reciben," Gaceta de Guatemala, 11 Mar. 1848.
Note: Figures represent percentages of students taking each course.

calling upon the corregidores to require all property owners between the ages of eighteen and fifty to contribute three reales annually for the schools in settlements where community funds were inadequate. A school board was to be established in each department to manage the schools. While this move reemphasized the state's role in public education, it did not attempt, as had been done earlier, to remove the clergy from education. Village priests, it said, should necessarily serve on these boards.[18]

The situation in the capital had advanced by early 1848 to the point that there were eleven schools for boys with 431 pupils and thirteen schools for girls with 338 pupils. Virtually all pupils took Christian doctrine and reading. Most of the boys also took writing, with a scattering of other subjects (arithmetic, algebra, Spanish grammar, geography, music, and drawing). Most of the girls took sewing or other household arts, but relatively few (73, compared with 326 boys) learned to write. Percentages of the pupils taking each subject are shown in Table 28. Teachers were scarce, but much was expected from them for very little pay. An advertisement for the school in Totonicapán in 1850 sought someone to teach Spanish grammar, elementary geography, writing, reading, and Christian morals for a salary of $25 per month.[19]

With the restoration of conservative rule, the government took steps to improve and expand primary education under church supervision. The president in November 1851 appointed Dr. Basilio Zeceña to inspect the school system, and his report led directly to the educational act, or *Ley Pavón*, of 16 September 1852.[20] A survey of the existing system in 1852 revealed that there were a total of 206 primary schools in the country with 6,286 pupils. They spent a total of $24,451.75 annually, or an average of $3.89 per pupil.[21] In the eastern departments the average annual expenditure amounted to only about $2.50 per pupil. Thus in September of 1852 Carrera authorized a special tax on commerce in Santa Rosa and Jutiapa to improve education in those departments. As an editorial in the *Gaceta* indicated, an alarmingly small number of children were being educated in a population of nearly a million. The editorial attributed this to the "resistance of the aborigines," who constituted the majority of the population.[22]

The new educational law of 16 September 1852 was drawn up by Carrera's first minister, Manuel F. Pavón, and it was a reaction against the liberal efforts in 1848–49 to secularize and centralize education. The *Ley Pavón* put primary responsibility for education of the republic's children on the parish priests. It required each parish to establish a school for boys and another for girls and outlined a curriculum with strong emphasis on religious instruction, morals, and manners. It also provided reading, writing, and arithmetic for boys, with more emphasis on sewing, embroidery, and household crafts for the girls.[23]

A number of specialized schools were established in Guatemala after 1850. The Consulado helped found a School of Agriculture under the direction of José María Aguirre. The plan provided that a young orphan from each department would be enrolled free, with the hope that in a short time the school would train agriculture teachers for the whole country. It especially looked toward promoting coffee cultivation.[24] It also supported classes in bookkeeping, French, and English.[25] Also in 1854, the Jesuits opened an Academia de Literatura y Bellas Artes. This school had a strong religious orientation, with religious literature emphasized.[26] The corregidor of Chiquimula, Vicente Cerna, meanwhile, succeeded in establishing a new school of arithmetic, Latin, and Spanish grammar in Zacapa in the same year, with support from the central government, the archbishop, and the rector of the university.[27] Father Mariano Navarrete founded the San José school in Antigua in May 1856, and in the same month, Sr. José Sevilla opened his dancing academy in the capital.[28] At the beginning of 1858 Alejandro Arrué converted his small Liceo San Ignacio primary school into the Academia Comercial Centro-América. He promised to soon publish a commercial arithmetic text.[29] This coincided with the opening of a new primary school by the Immaculate Conception order. This school, headed by José Mariano Andrade, began with eighty-three pupils, including ten part-time. Twenty-five pupils boarded at the schools, with the remainder living at home.[30] New primary schools were opened in the capital later in the year by José León Valdés and the Spaniard Alejandro A. Alvarez.[31] By 1860 there was a considerable variety of special schools and lessons for European languages and music lessons, mostly taught by teachers of European origin.

Near the end of the conservative period, in 1868, a Colegio Científico-Industrial opened in Antigua under the direction of Pastor Ospina, with an annual tuition of $200 including room and board, or $100 without room and board. Claiming to offer the most advanced instruction in Central America, it offered courses for farmers, merchants, miners, and surveyors.[32]

The enthusiasm that accompanied the Pavón law for improvement in the country's education was followed by not much real advancement, especially in rural areas. A report from the corregidor of Santa Rosa, for example, revealed that there were then only seven primary schools in his department, compared with nineteen according to the report of 1852. He complained that the parish priests were not paying sufficient attention to education and were not following the 1852 law.[33]

Only in the capital was there real expansion of instruction, and even there most children were not educated. A few religious orders were making an effort to rectify that situation. Notably, the Bethlemite nuns opened the Colegio de Belén for girls in 1860. This school had considerable difficulty during its first years of operation, but by 1864 it had achieved considerable importance in the city. It had by that date thirty-five tuition-paying pupils who lived in the school and another forty who lived at home, plus another thirty on half-tuition waivers, and more than two hundred poor girls who paid nothing.[34]

Yet a survey conducted in 1861 revealed that there had been relatively little progress during the previous decade in developing primary education in the country as a whole. A table published in the *Gaceta* indicated a total of 280 schools in the country, public and private, including music schools and lyceums, with 8,125 pupils. Expenses for the 200 public schools, which served 6,038 pupils, amounted to $27,620, or an annual average of only $4.57 per pupil. For all 280 schools, the average was only $3.75. These expenses apparently consisted only of the salaries paid to the teachers by the municipalities, and there is no mention of any additional expenses for maintenance or construction of schools. A note to the table, however, indicated that in addition to the sums in the table, teachers often also received free housing and meals. While improvement over 1852 is noteworthy in a few departments, especially Chiquimula and San Marcos, the table reflects a depressing lack of substantial primary education in the country, even though it does represent considerable improvement over the situation at the outset of independence.[35]

The liberals had established a local school tax on 1 July 1826 and again on 29 April 1834, to be collected by municipalities for the support of primary education, but there is evidence that under conservative rule this tax was not always collected or that it was not always put to the use intended. In 1865 an editorial in the Gaceta lamented that over the years some communities had confused this tax with the ordinary community funds and diverted it to other uses. The tax was to be paid by all individuals from eighteen to fifty in age, except for the very poor or handicapped. A government order of 6 December 1847 had detailed collection of this tax, and the Gaceta noted also that the military was not exempt as had sometimes been pretended. The editorial urged the corregidores to enforce this tax so that education could be improved.[36]

The last years of the Carrera dictatorship did see some expansion of primary education, with several departments increasing the number of primary schools and pupils. By 1865 there were thirty-one schools with 133 teachers in the Department of Guatemala teaching 1,435 boys and 902 girls.[37] A report published in February 1869 for Guatemala City provided an overview of all education in the city. It listed a total of 1,438 boys (1,201 in the colegios and escuelas and 237 in the university) and 913 girls. There were 120 teachers for these 2,351 students.[38]

The reports of the corregidores for 1865 indicate that some of the other departments had increased the number of schools and pupils significantly since 1861, although everywhere the number was tiny relative to the population. In others, however, there was a decline. Chimaltenango, for example, dropped from fourteen to twelve schools and from 556 to 366 pupils.[39] On the other hand, there was significant growth in Suchitepéquez. Schools increased from nine to seventeen, but with only a very modest increase in the number of pupils. The corregidor's report noted, however, that an additional 340 boys and 106 girls "should have been attending."[40] San Marcos increased the number of schools from twenty-one to twenty-two, but showed a drop in enrollments from 650 in 1861 to 611 in 1865. The San Marcos report indicated that there were nine schools for Ladinos, eight for Ladinos and Indians, and five for Indians.[41] Jutiapa showed fairly substantial growth, increasing its schools for boys from fifteen to twenty and their enrollments from 396 to 514. Jutiapa had also finally established a girls' school with thirty-six pupils.[42] The corregidores' reports for 1865 also indicated that teachers' salaries ranged from nothing to $25 per month. Outside the capital they were more often in the range of $10 to $15 per month, with considerable variation. The average in Jutiapa, for example, was only $6.47 per month for the boys' schools, although the mistress of the girls' school received $40 per month. In Suchitepéquez the average teacher's wage was $10.13 for the men and $8.00 for the women (although if the woman who received nothing is discounted, the average goes up to $10 for the remaining school mistresses). In Chimaltenango the average was $12.50 for the public schools, but the five music teachers in that department were paid in a range of $6 to $20, with an average of $14.80, and, including them, the average for all seventeen teachers rises to $13.18. On the other hand, in Chiquimula, where there were thirty schools in twenty-seven communities (twenty-eight for boys and two for girls), the average was only $8.84.[43] The corregidores' reports for these departments also reveal that there had been no revision in the curriculums of the schools, with Christian doctrine, morals, reading, writing, arithmetic, and Spanish grammar being taught in most.[44]

While support for education in the conservative years was obviously meager, and Guatemala failed to endow its youth with the sort of system that more modern development required, it was nevertheless sensitive to criticism of this failure. The *Gaceta de Guatemala* bristled at an 1866 comment by the *Gaceta de Costa Rica* that Guatemala spent $25,107.69 monthly for the military and only $175 for public education. The Guatemalan gazette declared that such a statement was "entirely false," for the Guatemalan primary and secondary schools had their own income that they managed themselves, and which was only in part provided by the government. According to the *Gaceta de Guatemala*, the primary schools spent more than $20,000 monthly and the secondary schools more than $15,000, from public funds. Since they have their own funds (from municipal and private sources), the *Gaceta* continued, the state's treasury provides only an annual subsidy of $7,000, in monthly allotments, "and if there is a month in which only a part of it is paid, as surely happened in May, which the *Gaceta de Costa Rica* took as a regular standard, the amount due is made up in other months." By the same token, the Guatemalan gazette said that the $25,000 for the military was not an average month, but was higher than usual because of some back payments being disbursed.[45]

Conservative rule in Guatemala also meant a restoration of the colonial

University of San Carlos. Tracing its roots to the first bishop of Guatemala, Francisco Marroquín, and sanctioned as a university in 1676, the third oldest university in Spanish America had formally opened its doors in 1681. It had made remarkable contributions in many areas of learning during the colonial period.[46] In the late eighteenth century, however, the university had become a target of the liberals for its tradition-bound curriculum and strong clerical domination.[47] The Baptist missionary Frederick Crowe reflected the worst view of the colonial university:

> Under the Spanish regime the education of the most highly favoured was confined to a few ill-selected subjects, in which they were imperfectly instructed by monks and friars, at private houses, in their own cells, or under the auspices of the more ostentatious university of San Carlos. From such teachers, the sons of Spanish Dons, who were probably the least eager to be taught, received that amount of tuition which would entitle them to the degrees of 'Bachiller' 'Licenciado,' or 'Doctor,' in philosophy, in laws, in theology, and in canons.
>
> The only professions open to them were the ecclesiastical, the legal, or the medical. All their studies were, of course, more or less tinged with the gloom of the cloister, and infested with the leaven of hypocrisy.[48]

While this view was not altogether fair, it was one shared by liberal, anticlerical politicians of the 1820s, who refused to provide government revenue for the university, replacing it with more "modern" lyceums and academies. In 1832 the Gálvez government suppressed the university altogether, replacing it with an Academy of Sciences that emphasized a new curriculum, academic freedom, and a well-paid faculty made up of the state's best minds. Gálvez's reforms removed education from clerical influence and placed it under state control, incurring bitter opposition from the clergy. Gálvez also converted some of the expropriated properties of the religious orders into schools and other public institutions, further enraging the clergy.[49]

Following the Carrera revolt, it was not surprising that the government moved quickly to restore the church to its former position in education. President Rivera Paz formally restored the university on 26 February 1840. His decree provided for a rector, a secretary, and a librarian with annual salaries of $200 each, and, interestingly, a treasurer whose salary was set at 5 percent of the income he collected for the university. The decree established professorial chairs at salaries ranging from $200 to $400 in law, canons, Latin, medicine, surgery, theology, philosophy, and mathematics. Notably absent were positions in modern languages, political economy, or other social sciences that the liberals had emphasized.[50] The government

TABLE 29

University Salaries in Arrears, 1840

Employees	Amount due	Received to date	In arrears
President	$4,189.53	$3,291.03	$898.50
Vice-President	83.38	0.00	83.38
First Director	997.25	560.06	437.19
Secretary	2,942.00	2,118.88	823.12
Treasurer	3,996.72	1,889.69	2,107.03
Second Librarian	166.62	0.00	166.62
Total	12,375.50	7,859.66	4,515.84
Professors			
José M. González	5,896.97	3,359.22	2,537.75
José Venacio López	1,436.69	838.66	598.03
Buenaventura Lambur	2,799.66	2,196.59	603.07
Dr. José Luna	5,373.00	3,338.50	2,034.50
Alejandro Marure	4,938.28	4,247.25	691.03
Presb. Mariano Herarte	3,110.12	2,060.00	1,050.12
Presb. Fco. Sánchez de León	803.78	639.00	164.78
Pedro Saenz	903.00	424.66	478.34
Miguel Larreinaqu	1,564.91	648.75	916.16
Eusebio Murga	2,809.28	1,990.37	818.91
Andrés Andreu	4,281.75	2,572.31	1,709.44
Francisco X. Urrutia	1,479.56	892.81	586.75
Total	35,397.00	23,208.12	12,188.88
Summary			
Salaries owed			$47,772.50
Paid			31,067.78
In arrears			$16,704.72

Source: Presented by José Cleto Peralta and Miguel Rivera Maestre on 6 Aug. 1840. *El Tiempo*, 17 Nov. 1840.

then suppressed the Academy of Sciences. A separate medical school faculty was established later in 1840, consisting of medicine, surgery, and pharmacy departments.[51] A listing of the academy's unpaid accounts in Table 29 suggests the higher pay that the liberals had assigned to academics. It covers the period from the academy's establishment in 1832 through its suppression on 7 March 1840, but apparently does not include academy employees, if any, who received the full amount due them.

A ceremony at the Capuchin Church on 4 December 1840—a day chosen because it was the fiesta of the university's patron saint, San Carlos Borromeo—formally inaugurated the restored university.[52] The appointment of Juan José Aycinena as rector of the university exemplified not only the return of the clergy to power over higher education in the country, but also the return of the conservative, aristocratic elite to prominence. Aycinena held the office until 1854 and from 1859–65, and continued as vice-rector from 1854–59. He was the dominant individual shaping the university throughout the conservative period, as well as the leading spokesman for Guatemalan culture and learning in the era of Carrera.[53]

While it received some government money, the university depended primarily on private gifts, ecclesiastical support, and a modest tuition charged the students. The university frequently complained of insufficient funds, as in 1845, when Aycinena presented an especially bleak report. He complained not only of the lack of funds, but also that political disturbances disrupted its operations. He said the university's library was a century and a half behind and mentioned its need for English and French literary and scientific journals in order to keep up with the enormous scientific advances of the period. He went so far as to declare that the restoration of the university had not resulted in improvement of higher education in the country, but rather the situation had worsened because of financial stringency. The university building was unfurnished. He especially bemoaned the decline in the study of Latin, but seemed unaware of the need for curriculum reform.[54] Yet Aycinena's bleak report stimulated the Guatemalan assembly to decree twenty-three articles of reform on 20 September 1845 in an attempt to modernize the university and bring it more into the study of contemporary affairs. It divided the university into three equal divisions: (1) moral and political science, (2) natural science, and (3) ecclesiastical sciences and preliminary studies. The medical faculty had already been established separately. Moreover, the university was given responsibility for directing all public education in the state. There were some rather vague provisions about future tax support, although in the end funding was left in doubt. This reform, in fact, brought the university more closely under the control of the state, although it continued to be run largely by clergy and one provision of the reform emphasized the academic freedom of the faculty.[55] The university continued to be seriously in debt, primarily to its professors and other employees.[56]

By 1843, notwithstanding these problems, the University was well established. In that year it granted sixty-seven bachelor's degrees (fifty-one in philosophy and mathematics, nine in law, two in canons, and five in surgery), one doctorate in laws, and one surveying certificate. A total of 301 examinations reflected a curriculum that was heavily weighted toward theology, philosophy, law (civil and canon), Latin, and mathematics. Compared with forty-one exams in Latin grammar and seventeen in Latin literature, there were but three in Castilian and one in French.[57] In 1846 it granted ninety bachelor's degrees (fifty-five in philosophy and mathematics, eight in surgery, twenty-three in laws, one in canons, and three in moral theology), and a licenciatura and a doctorate in moral theology. The following year the number of bachelor's degrees increased to 106, but slacked off somewhat during the turmoil of the 1848 revolution, dropping to eighty degrees in 1849 and sixty-seven in 1850.[58]

In 1845 the university began a branch in Antigua, offering classes in Spanish grammar, Latin, and philosophy, with two chairs for this branch of the university. The alcalde of Antigua hailed the event on 15 July as one of major importance, reflecting the literary and scientific revolution that had been taking place since 1812, but which had been delayed in Central America for lack of resources and classrooms. He said it opened the sciences to the most important parts of the society, which had been closed to them owing to the "aristocratic spirit that dominated the Spanish cabinet prior to the Constitution of 1812." Even for many of those who had the means, the offering of instruction "exclusively in the capital has always presented serious obstacles." Parents had been reluctant to send their children away to school at that age, fearing that they might be perverted or get into trouble, "paternal love preferring ignorance to ruin for their beloved children." Now they would be able to live at home and begin the preparatory studies for many professions. Even though it was not a full-fledged university with all of the major subjects being taught, he acknowledged, it at least provided a beginning in which students would learn to read and write correctly and to know the Latin authors.[59] The university established a similar extramural center in Quetzaltenango the following year.[60]

Liberal resurgence in 1847–48 brought greater support from the government, allowing for a considerable reduction of the university debt. At the same time, the liberals established an Academy of Practical and Theoretical Law to encourage study and application of modern legal principals. Its founders envisioned the academy as a forum for enlightenment and legal training.[61] Later in the same year, liberal deputies, including Mariano Padilla, Lorenzo Montúfar, and Vicente Dardón, complained that the University Reform Act of 20 September 1845 had not been implemented. A long report by the minister of public instruction, Manuel J. Dardón, explained that the government had offered additional funds to implement the reorganization called for in those reforms, but the cloister of doctors in the university had balked and refused, so the government had allowed the reforms to be postponed. In Dardón's view, the government had allowed the university's faculty to resist successfully efforts to make the university curriculum conform to republican institutions.[62]

Criticism of the university during the liberal resurgence of 1848 also appeared in the government press. The *Gaceta de Guatemala* acknowledged on 10 November that "the only literary institution that exists among us is the University, which unfortunately is found in a state of decadence that can only sadden those interested in the propagation of enlightenment." The statutes of the university, the editorial continued, "are not in consonance with the spirit of the century, a defect that directly prejudices the sciences that it ought to promote." It urged the faculty to at least comply with the 1845 reforms, which the "bachelors" and "licenciados" supported. But the restoration of absolute conservative power by 1850 included a reaffirmation of faith in the traditional university. General Carrera himself donated a thousand pesos that year toward construction of the university's new building, which was nearly completed under the direction of Francisco Castillo Larriva, whom Carrera had recommended for the job.[63]

In his annual address opening the university in October of 1850, Aycinena emphasized the necessity of traditional education and discipline, warning against corruption and too much dependence on the sciences.[64] Two years later Aycinena headed a committee to reorganize the university along conservative lines, as the government charged the committee "to recognize as fundamental the ancient statutes on which the institution was founded and which had earned it in its time so much credit and good reputation, making those modifications which time and circumstances demand; and also proposing whatever is needed to assure it adequate revenues and good administration."[65]

The number of bachelor's degrees granted by the university remained small during the 1850s, ranging from about sixty to seventy-five each year, with an occasional licenciatura or doctorate in medicine or law.[66] After a brief tenure as rector by Basilio Zeceña, Aycinena's kinsman Bernardo Piñol succeeded him as rector in 1855 and continued the conservative leadership until 1859.[67] Aycinena once more served as rector until his death in 1865, being succeeded at the end of that year by José Farfán.[68]

Thus, under conservative rule the university was restored to its colonial status, the final abolition of the Gálvez reforms coming in 1855 when the government emphasized that the fundamental statutes of the university were those established by Carlos II on 20 February 1686. This reform act of 22 September—signed by Carrera and Manuel Echeverría, the minister of public instruction who was also serving as Carrera's prime minister and minister of justice and ecclesiastical relations—provided a lengthy set of regulations with detailed chapters on faculty, curriculum, salaries, administration, and students. It assured clerical control of the institution and emphasized its religious orientation. The university would be one of those institutions targeted for substantial reform after the Liberal Reformation of 1871.[69] The strongly conservative and traditional flavor of the university was reflected in the renovations to its building in 1856, where the coat of arms of Spain hung alongside reliefs of Bishop Francisco Marroquín and Captain Pedro Crespo Suárez, colonial benefactors of the university.[70] Carrera emphasized his support of the institution not only with personal gifts, but also by providing it with some government revenues. In 1856 that support was set at $4,000 per year, but he also provided a one-time tax on 17 July of that year to provide the university with additional funds. It placed a 2 percent tax on annual salaries in excess of $300 for all government employees except the military and placed a 1 percent tax on property rents and a 12 peso surcharge on all professional titles (lawyers, surveyors, notaries, scribes, pharmacists, physicians, surgeons, and engineers).[71] Some modest increases in faculty followed, but the university remained a relatively small institution throughout the conservative years.

Apart from the formal educational structure of Guatemala in the time of Carrera, the popular culture of the country was also closely connected with the church. Formal entertainment in early nineteenth-century Guatemala was limited. Public fiestas celebrating patron saint days provided the principal spectacles for most communities, and in some Indian areas native dancing survived from the colonial period.[72] Other forms of folk culture, such as storytelling and religious pageantry, provided inspiration and relief from the daily labors of the Indian masses. Only in the capital was there more formal theater, following European models. Visiting troupes from Europe brought occasional drama and circuses to Guatemala City, and bullfights at the Plaza de Toros often accompanied festive celebrations, although bullfighting was much less popular than in Spain, Mexico, or Colombia. The bull fights were held from the end of December through Carnival, just prior to the Lenten season. Carnival Tuesday was the scene of considerable merrymaking, in costume parties, and with large crowds at the final bull fights and theatrical productions of the season.[73] In many rural communities, however, "corridas de toros" were much less formal affairs and involved only bull riding and running, as the young men of the town chased bulls (or vice versa) through the streets or around the plaza of the town. Much drinking and merrymaking usually accompanied these affairs, along with the occasional and inevitable tragedies.[74]

In the capital, Mariano Gálvez had emphasized European dress and culture as part of his program to "civilize" Guatemala, although he had commissioned Miguel Rivera Maestre (1806–88?) to make a thorough study of ancient Maya ruins in the country as early as 1834.[75] In an effort to promote music composition and performance, in 1833 he ordered the cathedral choir reestablished at government expense. He also promoted theater and attempted to have the old municipal slaughterhouse remodeled as a theater. What was probably the first operatic performance in Guatemala occurred on 28 August 1833, a production of *Adolf and Clara*, before, reportedly, "a large and enthusiastic audience." Considerable opposition arose, however, to the social criticism that came with the theatrical performances that Gálvez promoted in Guatemala. An incident involving the first professional actor to come to Guatemala, Carlos Fedriani, occurred in 1834, when in some of the plays in which he starred were obvious attacks on clerical abuse. When Fedriani gave performances during Lent, the clergy became further annoyed with him. Then, when the actor refused to remove his hat before a Corpus Christi procession, a priest named Perdomo knocked it off for him. This incident sparked a small riot, with several persons jailed. The conservatives used the incident as an example of liberal irreverence and blasphemy.[76]

Establishment of conservative rule did not end theatrical productions in Guatemala, although the tone changed notably. On 25 December 1839 one Tiburcio Estrada opened a theater at his house on Calle Belén. The total absence of any such entertainment in Guatemala prompted him to do this, he said, encouraged by, "among others," President Rivera Paz and Brigadier General Carrera, who, in addition to providing financial aid, stationed police at these performances to provide for public security. Estrada's first performance, "La Zayda," was advertised as an "excellent tragedy," and was to be preceded by the orchestra's rendition of a famous Beethoven symphony, "never before heard in this city." Estrada's home theater provided two hundred seats in his patio, plus several boxes and a gallery on the side. Admission was two reales (25 cents), with an additional two reales charged for the patio seats and three pesos for boxes. A season ticket for the boxes, however, was available for twenty pesos for ten performances.[77]

There is no evidence that Estrada's theater thrived, but there were sporadic efforts to provide the capital's population with classical theater and music during the decade following these opening performances. The Economic Society organized a Philharmonic Society toward the end of 1841. Few concerts resulted, and it periodically reorganized this group, in 1859, 1860, and again in 1864, with only modest success.[78] An editorial in the

Gaceta in mid-1846 praised the theater as an institution and Rafael Carrera for his promotion of it. It was at this time that Carrera began to support the idea of constructing a great national theater, and the architect Julián Rivera Maestre was charged with drawing up some model plans and cost estimates.[79] Rivera Maestre turned the task over to his younger brother, Miguel, who completed plans for the theater in September 1847 and was then commissioned by the government to direct its construction for a salary of a hundred pesos per month.[80] A committee, on which Juan Matheu played the prominent role, supervised the project and sought private contributions to support the work. Although the government guaranteed funds for the project, it depended on these substantial contributions as shortages of funds delayed progress as several points.[81] This Gran Teatro de Carrera was finally completed in 1859 at a total cost of more than $110,000, one of the most important monuments of the Carrera regime.[82]

Even before completion of the Carrera theater, there was a gradual increase in operatic and other theatrical performances during the 1850s. These ranged from classical opera to popular burlesque, ballet, and circuses, but there was a great burst of new activity with the opening of the new theater in 1859. This monument to Carrera was richly decorated inside with murals by a Swiss painter named Wirtz, with much marble, and chandeliers imported from Europe. The government commissioned the impresario Manuel de Lorenzo to bring the Italian opera company of Pedro Iglesias from New York for the first season. He agreed to provide a series of thirty-four lyrical performances, but he actually exceeded that number.[83] The opening performance took place on 23 October 1859, although a private, miniperformance was given for Carrera and sixty-eight guests on the twentieth, to which many more people were allowed to come in.[84] Featuring six operas by Verdi, Donizetti, and Bellini, each performed seven times during a triumphant first season, the theater was repeatedly cited as evidence of the advance of civilization in Carrera's Guatemala.[85] Admission to the orchestra or boxes was 50 cents, with an additional 25 cents for seats in the orchestra or $2.00 for boxes seating seven to ten people. Admission to chairs or benches in the balcony and the gallery were only 25 cents. It was free altogether in the gallery for those willing to sit on the floor or stand, providing an opportunity for even the poor to enjoy the performances.[86]

The first season ended with the beginning of Lent on 21 February 1860. The *Gaceta* reviewed the year in glowing terms. Nearly fifty performances had been given since 23 October (forty-two operas, plus several other concerts). It acknowledged that this was more frequent than a city the size of Guatemala could support, "for few cities of Europe even can have opera three times per week." The company had grossed more than $20,000, much of which had been reinvested in local musicians, artists, and other employees. People from Antigua, Amatitlán, and the other Central American states were also visiting the city because of the opera, so that the *Gaceta* predicted that the city was on the threshold of a great boon to its economic as well as its cultural life.[87]

The theater resumed its performances on Easter Sunday, 8 April 1860, and enjoyed several years of successful operation with a series of Italian opera companies, but after the initial enthusiasm, its popularity waned, so that after 1865 there were fewer performances than during its early years.[88] Following the 1871 Reforma, the theater was renamed the Teatro Nacional and later the Teatro Colón, but it never quite achieved the glory of its early days, perhaps in part because of its association with Carrera. Earthquakes damaged the building, and after the 1917 earthquake the building had to be abandoned. In the meantime, motion pictures replaced opera in the early twentieth century as the principal form of spectacle.[89]

Among the men of the capital, the most common leisure time activities were drinking, gambling, and womanizing. Members of the elite commonly kept mistresses and casual relationships were generally accepted and even expected. Robert Dunlop observed in 1847 that "concubinage is common among all possessed of any wealth; nor is this, as in other countries, done secretly, if at all; but even wives will publicly speak of their husbands' mistresses, and express their approbation and disapprobation of their taste."[90] As in the colonial period, gambling was also common, despite the formal disapproval of it by the conservative assembly of 1840, excepting only raffles and the lottery favoring charitable works and the Economic Society. The government reiterated this law from time to time, but while it remained in effect throughout the conservative years, it was not rigidly enforced.[91] Cockfighting and games of chance were thus widespread. Efforts to curb heavy public drinking were equally lax in enforcement, and drinking and gambling often led to violence in the bars and streets of the city. This seemed to be a characteristic of all classes. The prevalence of murder and other violent crime during the Carrera period belied somewhat the conservative claim of stability and tranquility, but these problems were not unique to these years in Guatemalan life.[92] A government decree of April 1855 reflected the concern with such abuses and imposed strict regulations regarding youths and liquor in pool halls, cafés, hotels, and other public establishments. It warned of the grave damage to the morals and upbringing of youths and children who frequented such places, and complained that daily drunkenness was increasing.[93]

In the latter years of the Carrera administration, the establishment of at least a veneer of European culture and the increased prosperity of the small class of merchants and planters allowed for an increase in elite leisure time pursuits. This was reflected in an increase in the issuance of passports for foreign travel. Escuintla and Amatitlán, meanwhile, became more popular summer resorts for the elite, although Chinautla, much nearer the capital but at a considerably lower altitude, also gained some popularity as a vacation spot.[94]

It is easy to conclude that academic learning and literary activities were largely limited to the small elite class and upper-middle urban sector of the capital during the conservative years. There were few bookshops, and except for occasional translations of European writers, there was little literary production until near the very end of the period. José Milla represented something of an exception, although even he published little beyond his articles in the *Gaceta* until after 1860.[95] Historical and literary works were very few in number during these years, and what little there was tended to pursue romantic themes with emphasis on other times and places than Guatemala under the Carrera dictatorship. The press was limited largely to the government *Gaceta* or to occasional periodicals friendly to the government. The tiny amount of literature in these papers consisted mostly of translations of European romantic fiction or essays, in both cases reflecting conservative thought. There was little book publishing, except for an occasional school text, and few books were imported.

This review suggests that educational and cultural activity in mid-nineteenth–century Guatemala was generally unimpressive. Although there was a notable expansion of primary and secondary education over the previous period, it still left most of the youth of the country illiterate and without the knowledge or intellectual training necessary to develop a stronger economy or a more politically sophisticated electorate. Education was still, in fact, the preserve of a small elite that was committed to traditional values and it was increasingly out of step with the march of progress in the nineteenth-century Western world. Thus, while by the 1860s Guatemala had improved its educational system over that of the 1830s and in the capital there was a thin veneer of European cultural attractions, in relative terms, Guatemala had slipped further behind the standards of the developed nations of the north Atlantic. The restored University of San Carlos had not begun to develop a curriculum suitable for the times, and was in fact a bastion of outmoded values and attitudes.

The failure of the conservatives to place a higher priority on educational and cultural development for the population undoubtedly contributed to the survival of folk culture and Indian communities in general to a greater extent than in much of the rest of Latin America, as Bradford Burns has suggested in his *Poverty of Progress*. It also reflected the doubts and skepticism of the elite regarding the wisdom of rapid change along liberal-capitalist lines, as the patricians of Guatemala City jealously and self-righteously held on to traditional ways of life. Indeed, with Spanish governors gone, this class had risen to the top of the society and controlled its economy. They were reluctant and resistant to change.

Yet by 1860 a new generation was emerging. Younger conservatives, especially, could not ignore the progress of the Western world any more than they could resist the economic gain that could come from expanded agro-export production. There were few to carry on the extreme conservative patterns of Carrera's Guatemala. Conservatives were, in essence, becoming liberalized by the world around them. Guatemalan liberalism, on the other hand, had lost much of the idealism of its youth. Conservative repression and popular resistance had made a powerful impression on a rising generation of liberals, causing them to lose faith in liberal tenets of popular democracy and representative government. In effect, the differences between conservatives and liberals began to fade, a process that would not be complete until the early twentieth century, as domination by the Liberal Party (1871–1944) became institutionalized. Although the liberals would again espouse expanded public education, in fact their educational policy would serve only the narrow interests of an expanded elite and middle class. As with the conservatives, they left most of the population uneducated.

CHAPTER TWENTY-TWO

Conclusions

No single individual dominated the first half century of Guatemalan national independence more than Rafael Carrera. Although uneducated, his native intelligence and personal energy enabled him to overcome the intrigues of the "enlightened" creole elite and enforce a unity on the country that had eluded it since the beginnings of the disintegration of the Spanish empire in 1808. Although undisciplined, his intelligence, good judgment, and ability to recognize and command trustworthy advisers served him well. His revolution rode the crest of a strong rejection of liberalism by people of all classes as it restored Hispanic tradition and institutions and established the independent Republic of Guatemala. Although contemporaries and subsequent critics would often poke fun of his lack of education and his crude manners, few could deny his military genius, charismatic appeal to the masses, or ability to get to the core issues of a problem quickly.

The grievances of the rural masses against the liberal governments of both the State of Guatemala and the federation had become numerous by 1837. They reflected the insensitivity of liberal leaders to the social and psychological security of the general population as well as their inexperience in republican politics. In their enthusiasm to create a modern, republican state, they had looked to the countryside for the land and labor that their economic ambitions required. They encouraged development of mining and export agriculture with little understanding of the effect on the welfare of the majority of the population. In attempting to break the power of the Roman Catholic Church and to seize its lucrative properties, they made powerful enemies among the influential parish priests as well as the ecclesiastical hierarchy, who were so influential with the conservative elite. They exacted forced labor levies to build roads, bridges, jails, and other public works. And the quixotic adoption of the Livingston judicial reforms also alienated influential lawyers, always a dangerous step. Committed to free trade and a minimum of taxes on the entrepreneurial and landholding classes and thus having abolished most of the taxes of the Hispanic period, they burdened the rural masses with a direct head tax reminiscent of the hated tribute. Indian rebellion in eastern El Salvador and highland Guatemala had already reflected indigenous restlessness with liberal reforms, but the liberals, confident of the wisdom of their development model, failed to comprehend the potential power of popular resistance. Placing their faith in military strength and hopes for rising prosperity from their trade policies, they refused to abandon their course until it was too late.

The cholera epidemic of 1837 has generally been acknowledged as the straw that broke the camel's back, leading to the Carrera revolution. Frustration over the grievances mentioned above had certainly reached a breaking point when the cholera added to the misery and created panic in some communities. The rural clergy blamed it on the government and attacked efforts of public health officers to ameliorate the disease's spread. But even at that, had it not been for the leadership of Carrera and his ability to rally the peasants into a crude but sustained military resistance, the government in Guatemala might have survived the 1837 cholera crisis. It is doubtful, however, that the liberals could have survived for much longer against the rising conservative reaction to the liberal experiments, a rising tide all across Latin America after 1830. What made Guatemala somewhat unique, however, was that the conservative reaction came in the wake of a successful popular rebellion led by a man of humble origins, a man of the people. This injected elements of class warfare into the reaction. With the accession of the caudillo, advised by many of the rural priests and those who had suffered under the liberal policies, the Guatemalan conservative reaction became more extreme than that in much of the rest of Latin America. In some ways it represents an aberration or caricature of the general conservative reaction that characterized the region.

A leading Guatemalan historian, David Vela, attributed Carrera's victory in 1838 to the alliance between the Barrundia faction and the conservatives in what he called "suicide liberalism."[1] For the conservatives, the alliance with Barrundia achieved the ouster of Gálvez, and then they were able to turn on Barrundia and Valenzuela. Yet in the long run that alliance probably didn't make much difference. It may have even postponed conservative victory, prolonging the influence of Barrundia in the government. It reflected, however, the fear of Carrera and his rural horde shared by both the liberal and conservative elite families of the capital. Carrera's ability to harness the indignation of the peasants terrified them, and their willingness to put aside their political and economic differences in an effort to forestall Carrera was an early indicator of future cooperation among rival factions of the elite in the face of popular opposition. But Carrera would not disband his forces until the liberal programs had been dismantled, thus assuring the accession of the conservatives. This became evident under the government of Pedro Valenzuela, and it was only then that we find the beginnings of the reluctant alliance of the conservative opposition with Carrera.

The split between Barrundia and Gálvez, of course, was damaging to the liberals, but it was endemic of the problem the liberals had had throughout the federation period. Repeatedly bickering among themselves, they could not present a unified front. Disunity would continue to be a liberal defect throughout the nineteenth century.

Carrera's overthrow of Gálvez was just one episode in the broader regional opposition to the national government in Central America. Carrera's victory, however, was especially deadly to the federation, and his defeat of Morazán in 1840 sealed its doom. The hatred and violence engendered in the 1824–29 period bore bitter fruit by 1840, and in Guatemala it ultimately brought a military force to power that was not led by members of the capital's elite. This triumph of an army of the people under Ladino leadership brought a new force into the Guatemalan political arena, which has had profound implications to the present day.

Carrera's rout of Francisco Morazán at Guatemala City in March 1840 effectively terminated the liberal experiment in Guatemala for more than thirty years. Liberals continued to have some influence in the 1840s and briefly regained full control of the government in 1848, but until the death of the caudillo, they could not reverse the powerful reaction that restored Hispanic customs and institutions. The collapse of the Central American federation by 1840, although not fully recognized at the time, insured the fragmentation of Central America into five city-states in which local oligarchies would dominate the economic, political, and social life of each of the provinces. The creole elite of Guatemala City had been the most powerful of these local groups, but the destruction of the capital city in 1773, the economic decline of the late colonial period, and the frequent political disorder after 1821 had diminished its strength considerably. The emergence of these city states as sovereign republics was a lasting and unfortunate result of the Carrera period. Balkanizing the isthmus, this fragmentation denied Central Americans a more progressive national leadership and deprived the people in each state of a defense against the local tyrants and interest groups that have characterized the region ever since.

Historical debate over Carrera's place in Central American history began even before he died. The vitriolic pens of Lorenzo Montúfar and other liberals condemned his regime as retrograde and savage. Defenses came from official apologists, notably Manuel Francisco Pavón and José Milla, and occasionally from other Central American literary figures, such as Antonio José Irisarri, and a few foreigners who had benefited from the stability imposed by the caudillo. During the liberal age that followed—in Guatemala extending from 1871 to 1945 and in some ways even to the present—the liberal view of the period became standard and was written into the textbooks and public consciousness. They ridiculed Carrera as an illiterate buffoon or savage. Serious study of the period was neglected for nearly a century.

There were early revisionists, however. In Nicaragua, where conservatives remained in power for two more decades following the Liberal Reforma in Guatemala, an extended dialogue in *El Diario Nicaragüense* in 1888 revealed the heat between liberals and conservatives on the subject. Enrique Guzmán attacked as "intemperate and false" Montúfar's accusations, which he said had already become a part of the popular mythology of Guatemala:

> The concept of Carrera that my countrymen have was formed by the lying liberal legends, copied from the curious *histories* of Doctor Lorenzo Montúfar, passionate and fictitious libels which Clio views with shame and indignation. . . . Vested with absolute authority, like all Guatemalan governors, lifetime president by the will of the people he governed, he abused his power less than the majority of his predecessors, and much less than the *liberal* chieftains produced by the ill-fated revolution of 1871.

Guzmán painted Carrera as the restorer of law and order and as the founder of the Republic of Guatemala, as a phoenix that rose from the ashes of liberal misrule during the federation period. While he acknowledged Carrera's brutality, he argued that the circumstances of that time and place required strong, authoritarian rule, an argument often repeated in Guatemala to justify military rule even to the present. For Guzmán, Carrera compared with the conquistador Hernán Cortés and the Liberator, Simón Bolívar, as a founder of Latin American nations. He downplayed the "myth" of Carrera's savagery. He attacked Carrera's critics unmercifully. Barrundia was "a theoretical pedant for Guatemalan liberalism, with a head full of absurd ideas on the subject of government," while, he reminded his readers, Montúfar had himself admitted that he lacked impartiality and that his methodology was unscientific. In Guzmán's view, Carrera was honest and had provided Guatemala with the best government it had enjoyed since independence. He contrasted Carrera's critics with the highly respected literary giant, José Milla.[2]

José Gámez responded with the liberal version, ridiculing Guzmán's defense of Carrera and expressing the liberal contempt for the "uncivilized Indians" and the retrograde quality of Carrera and his followers. He defended Morazán and the other liberals. Just as Domingo Sarmiento had described the struggle in the Argentine, it was European civilization against the barbarism of the indigenous races. Both views were elitist and reflected the interests of nineteenth-century upper class liberals and conservatives.[3]

These exchanges and those that followed in the pages of Central American newspapers reiterated the arguments of Montúfar and Milla as they highlighted the differences between liberals and conservatives without shedding much new light on Carrera or the conservative era. The absence of personal papers of the caudillo limited the depth of his biographies. They are based for the most part on official papers written by his ministers or other advisers, and on anecdotal sources, compiled in large part by his enemies. The intensity of the liberal-conservative struggle, with its bloody wars and revolts and religious undertones, made it inevitable that Carrera would be at the center of historical attacks as well as praise.

In the twentieth century, Manuel Cobos Batres, a distant kinsman of Carrera, in the first full-length biography of the caudillo went to great lengths to prove that Carrera was not an Indian, but a Ladino, perhaps making him more acceptable to the Ladino and elite classes. More recently the works of Clemente Marroquín Rojas, Pedro Tobar Cruz, Luis Beltranena Sinibaldi, and Manuel Coronado Aguilar have emphasized Carrera's role as the first great Guatemalan nationalist, not only for his separating Guatemala from the federation, but for his preventing the further fragmentation of Guatemala and his establishment in 1847 of Guatemala as the first sovereign republic on the isthmus after the collapse of the federation.

All of these conclusions have validity and are supported by the present work. In addition, Max Moorhead concluded a half century ago that Carrera's foreign wars consumed energies and funds that might have been more usefully applied to domestic projects.[4] While that is certainly true, it is hard to see how Carrera could have avoided the struggles, so much was he the target of both Guatemalan and other Central American liberals. In retrospect, it may be said that he showed remarkable restraint in his dealings with the other states, especially in comparison with the liberal caudillos later in the century.

Carrera's military adventures, however, allowed him to build up the army as the most powerful of Guatemalan institutions, with a Ladino officer class separate from the creole elite that dominated political, economic, and social power. This emergence of Ladinos in the military and political leadership of the country is certainly one of the most lasting legacies of the Carrera period and one that has persisted to the present. The era of independence all across Latin America witnessed the rise of the armed forces to greater importance in the political evolution. In Guatemala, this process was evident already in the late colonial period under Captain General Bustamante, and it is impossible to blame the rise of militarism as a salient Guatemalan institution on a single political leader or party. During the first decade of independence, military leaders played an important role in suppressing uprisings and enforcing the law. Especially after 1825, they were involved in repressive activities on both the conservative and liberal side, at both state and federal levels. Arce's government resorted to military solutions to subordinate state interests to federal policy, and under Morazán the army was already becoming the political arbiter in Central America, especially in the middle states.

Although Guatemalan governor Mariano Gálvez resisted the rise of the military, the Carrera revolt forced him to increase his dependence on it. Carrera brought a new army to power, but combined his peasant guerrillas with the regular army. Under his leadership the military began to take on the institutional form that has characterized it in Guatemala ever since. By restoring Hispanic authoritarian traditions and the military fuero, the institution was strengthened. At the same time, the building up of the army as a people's institution, with Ladino officers, began its role as a challenger to the creole elite that had formerly monopolized the power. The army enforced the will of the caudillo, who claimed to rule in the name of the people. Indeed, his widespread popular support was essential in allowing him to counter effectively the power of the capital's elite.

Carrera's revolution was thus a successful uprising of the rural masses against the elite of the capital. Through Carrera and his peasant army, their grievances against the liberals received attention. The caudillo protected their lands against encroachment and distribution to foreigners. They could once again concentrate on feeding their families and retaining their corporate community structure.[5] Although the trend toward more agro-exports continued, its pace of growth was slowed, and the peasants felt less threatened.

While the peasants were responsible for elevating Carrera to power, however, they hardly came to power themselves. The conservative elite of the capital skillfully learned to cooperate with Carrera, and the army and thereby managed to retain operational control of the government in its own interests. While ultimate power was in the hands of the caudillo and his army and he protected the peasants from the excesses of the liberal development schemes, there was no positive program for the improvement of their lives. They did not really participate in the government. At best, perhaps, their folk culture survived and indigenous communities continued to exist. They managed their own local affairs, although under the watchful eye of the departmental corregidor.[6] Carrera delayed the process of proletarianization for a generation as feudal relationships remained to delay the rise of agrarian capitalism. Indigenous survival under conditions similar to the colonial period, with continued population growth, resulted in the enlargement of indigenous society in Guatemala, but the condition of the rural masses probably did not noticeably improve under Carrera. It may be said, though, that their deterioration was arrested and that the native textile industry was possibly saved from total destruction. Yet the political turmoil, violence, and political intrigues of the first half century of independence disrupted their lives and left them vulnerable for the liberal assault on their land and labor that would resume as soon as Carrera died, even before the Reforma of 1871.

The uprising that Carrera led in 1837—the War of the Mountain— never quite ended. Once armed and aware of their power, rural brigands continued to raid and to organize resistance to the government. Much of the disorder in the East and in the Verapaz was little more than common banditry after 1840, but it continued a pattern of guerrilla warfare started under Carrera that would continue intermittently to the present. Much of Carrera's efforts as caudillo were spent in quelling these recurring uprisings. They contributed to his fall in 1848 and delayed his return to the presidency after his return in 1849.

Carrera's policy toward the rural population continued the Spanish policies in effect since the conquest. He resettled troublesome Indian communities elsewhere, and his corregidores exercised dictatorial authority in the countryside. Thus, while Carrera was protector and champion of the indigenous peoples, once in power, he soon became a perpetuator of the Spanish conquest that had subjugated the Indian and that kept him in a subservient role. This paternalistic attitude toward the Indians, promoted equally by the conservative elite, may have been more benign than the liberal effort to modernize the Indians for the purpose of exploiting their lands and labors more extensively, but it should not be confused with a genuine effort to liberate or bring the Indians to power.

The Indians, of course, were neither "liberals" nor "conservatives." They were interested in preserving their land and in being left alone. Just as they had supported Carrera in 1837 against the liberals, when they felt his government threatened them, some of them supported the opposition to Carrera in 1848, and even more supported Cruz in 1869. The Indians, thus, became the tool of Ladino and elite political and military chieftains. Carrera set a pattern for manipulating the Indians that his liberal successors would copy. His trips into the rural areas to gain favor among the peasant masses, especially when he took steps to reward loyal communities or to curtail encroachment by Ladino planters, became a model that later Barrios would cynically copy to rally popular support. Estrada Cabrera, Ubico, Ydígoras, and the military caudillos followed him with the same. Unlike Carrera, however, these caudillos did little to protect indigenous interests. In the final analysis, for both Carrera and his liberal and neo-liberal successors, the principal base of support came to be the army, ironically made up principally of ragged Indians. Beginning with Carrera, the army became a place where young Indian men could escape their villages or urban slums and make a transition to Ladino life under the leadership of Ladino officers who could now aspire to high political office and economic opportunity.

The emergence of the dual power structure between the Ladino military and the creole elite became obvious with the Convenio de Guadalupe in March 1844, a clear victory for the army over the assembly. As an institution, the Guatemalan legislature has never really recovered from its diminished importance under Carrera and has remained a relatively weak branch of government ever since. The legislative branch had been of considerable importance in the federation period, but it was another casualty of the Carrera years. Carrera yielded to the assembly in 1848, representing somewhat of a comeback for the institution, but that victory was temporary. Ultimately the army once more asserted its superiority under Carrera's leadership in 1849 and 1850.

The 1848 revolution, largely neglected in Guatemalan historiography because of its short duration and ultimate failure to bring a more lasting return to liberalism, is significant nevertheless. It reflected the continuing struggle between the liberal and conservative factions and the struggle between the elite and the military. It provided a temporary victory for the liberal elite and reflected Carrera's eroding power as a result of the continuing montaña war and his inability to control the divided elite completely. Ultimately, though, it fell to the superiority of the military as the most powerful institution in Guatemalan society. Thereafter, the legislature represented little more than a rubber stamp for the executive in Guatemalan history. With the emergence of Mariano Paredes and the return of Carrera, the firm alliance between the military and the conservative faction resulted in the establishment of the conservative citadel that lasted beyond the death of the caudillo in 1865.

The rise of the military as the predominant institution in Guatemalan politics was not solely a result of its internal repression, but also of its success against the liberal challenges from the neighboring states. In this context the Battle of Arada in February 1851 was especially significant, for it established Carrera and his army not only as the defender of the interests of the conservative elite and the peasants within Guatemala, but also as the defender of Guatemala's national sovereignty. Guatemalan nationalism was not yet highly developed, but the celebration of Guatemala's declaration of independence as a sovereign republic in 1847 and the Battle of Arada in 1851 were symbolic steps in that direction. The major Guatemalan role in the defeat of William Walker furthered that trend and greatly enhanced the prestige of the army, as did its dominance over Honduras and El Salvador in the years following the Nicaraguan intervention.

The role of the major imperial powers cannot be ignored from the process of Central American political disintegration and the rise of caudillo conservatism. Mario Rodríguez and Robert Naylor have shown especially well how Great Britain closely influenced the course of events in Central America before 1850. Belgium, France, the United States, and the German states also played a role in the internal development of the isthmus, as Thomas Schoonover's work has been demonstrating.[7] For the first thirty years of Central American independence, Britain replaced Spain as the predominant power in the foreign trade of Central America, a role that the United States would ultimately inherit. Without diminishing the importance of this foreign influence on the economic history of Guatemala, however, the peculiar political development of the country appears to be primarily related to the emergence of the creole elite and the Ladino-led army following independence as the dominant political forces in the country.

The division of the Guatemala City creole elite into liberal and conservative factions had arisen from differences among them from the late colonial period forward. These differences sharpened and intensified during the violent federation period, and although formal political parties did not organize until much later, these factions had been recognized by the time Carrera came to power. The conservative faction consolidated its power behind the leadership of Father Juan José Aycinena in collaboration with Carrera and his army, notwithstanding some differences with the caudillo in the 1840s. The liberal opposition referred to this faction simply as "the family," because of the close relationship of its members to the Aycinena clan. They also called it the "Clerical Party" because of the numerous clergy among its leaders. While clerics certainly constituted a high percentage of this oligarchy, it more broadly represented the merchant-landholder elite of the capital, especially those committed by both economic and psychological influences to traditional Hispanic customs and institutions. The institutions that represented this conservative elite were the church, including a number of its dependencies such as the university and various charitable institutions, the Consulado, the Economic Society, the National Assembly, and the Guatemala City Council. The other major institution, of course, was the military, which under Carrera did not represent the elite so much as Carrera's own interests, mostly with Ladino officers and Indian troops.

Nineteenth-century Central American conservatism played an important role in checking the dominance of liberalism that clearly has been the primary ideological force on the isthmus from the late eighteenth century to the present. But the conservative years not only checked the rise of liberalism, but also greatly modified it. Vestiges of conservative thought remain an important part of elite rule in Central America long after the conservative faction has faded as a political organization, except in Nicaragua, where even today the successor to the nineteenth-century conservative party has returned to power.

At its roots, the differences between conservatives and liberals in Central America went deep into the colonial experience and reflected both economic and spiritual divisions. Conservatives reflected a reverence for Hispanic traditions dating from the sixteenth century, with strong allegiance to the Habsburg political tradition and to Catholic philosophy dating from medieval times. While distinctly unprogressive by nineteenth-century capitalist terms, it emphasized security, order, mutual trust, and obligation between master and serf, and strong authority exercised by church and state. Inevitably, those most attracted to this reverence for the past tended to be those who were most comfortably established in the social and economic structure of the country. Central American liberalism, by contrast, grew out of Enlightenment intellectual currents, especially as espoused by the Spanish Bourbons and their advisers, and the reforming impulse at the Cortes of Cádiz. Inevitably, liberalism was more attractive to those newly arrived peninsulares and elements of the Guatemalan elite or upper-middle sectors who were eager to improve their economic and social situation.

These differences intensified during the early years of independence as the liberals sought to make specific reforms that challenged the structure of the economy and society, particularly of the ecclesiastical establishment and the subsistence nature of the economy. The creole elite had only limited experience in governing, but the liberal political ideals of more open representative political institutions, including legislatures and a stronger role for the city councils, brought the issues out into the open. Bitter and often violent struggle between the two factions followed. It is easy to blame the liberals for attempting to impose institutions alien to the Hispanic or indigenous tradition on Guatemala in the period 1810–37. As Colin Mac-Lachlan has recently suggested, the Bourbon Reforms were at the root of much of the political disturbance following independence and the disasters of the new republics of Latin America.[8] Nowhere was this more obvious than in Guatemala, where the rejection of Bourbon-initiated liberalism led to the strong reaction to restore "Hispanic legitimacy" in an effort to recover the heritage that the liberals had so denigrated. Liberal notions of progress were derisive both toward the Hispanic and indigenous traditions to the extent that they alienated a very large portion of the population, but they established the issues that would divide the elite for a century or more. Central to these differences was the role of the Roman Catholic Church, and liberal anticlericalism became the most visible difference between the two factions.

There were also economic differences that were as important in the long run. The liberals were strongly committed to the development of capitalist institutions and particularly the promotion of agro-exports as the means to greater prosperity and progress. To this end their programs promoted foreign immigration, investment, reduction in taxes, infrastructure development by the state, incentives to production, and free trade. They began the liberal economic model for Central America that continues to be prominent. Conservatives expressed skepticism and outright opposition to some details of this plan, although it cannot be said that they were totally opposed to the concept of increasing exports. But they shared traditional Hispanic xenophobia toward outsiders and resisted the speed with which the liberals sought to transform the economy.

There was a fundamental difference in their attitudes toward the rural masses, although in both cases it reflected selfish interests of their own. Both viewed the indigenous population with contempt while at the same time depending on their labor and personal service. But the conservatives favored retaining the colonial system that offered paternalistic protection to that class through their continued segregation and with special laws for them. The liberals on the other hand, in general contemptuous of everything about the colonial past, favored egalitarian laws and practices that would in effect allow them to exploit even more the labor and lands of the Indians without their traditional protection. This difference came to be important in the Carrera period, as the conservatives cooperated with the caudillo in restoring the colonial protection for the rural masses and checking Ladino encroachment on their lands and labors.

In several respects, the differences between the two factions diminished after 1850 as many conservatives began finally to accept the liberal-capitalist development model and to become more interested in agro-export production themselves. From 1850 forward the positivist concept of "order and progress" begins to show up frequently in their writings. In fact, positivism began to influence both liberals and conservatives, bringing them closer together and effectively causing them to look more to economic than political issues. For the conservatives, it brought them closer to liberal economic thinking, while for the liberals it brought them closer to accepting the authoritarian political traditions that the conservatives defended. Positivism became the unifying intellectual force that transformed nineteenth-century liberalism and conservatism into the so-called new liberalism that would characterize the Guatemalan dictatorships from 1873 to 1944. The rise of positivism becomes especially notable in the Cerna years following the death of the caudillo, opening the way for the full-speed transformation of feudal Guatemala into capitalist dependency. "Order and Progress" became a conservative slogan that the liberals could incorporate into their own philosophy after 1871. Further evidence of the blending of liberal and conservative economic philosophies via positivism appears in the principal commercial houses and families of the conservative era. The Aycinenas, Pavóns, Batreses and others survived very well under liberal rule and continued to be important economically, although largely staying out of politics.

This left anticlericalism as the major difference between the two factions as the Carrera years closed. The war with El Salvador especially reflected this division, as Gerardo Barrios had been remarkably effective in reaching rapprochement with Carrera following the war in Nicaragua, and Carrera showed little inclination to interfere with Barrios's liberal economic reforms. But when he began to tamper with the power of the church, Carrera intervened. And it would be in this area that the liberals would move rapidly against the "Clerical Party" after 1871.

The conservatives' economic interests largely survived the Revolution of 1871, as they adjusted to working within the liberal structural framework. Their principal institution of the conservative years—the Consulado—was among the very first to fall to the revolution. The Consulado had been the interpreter, spokesman, and protector of the monopoly of merchants in the capital, extremely influential in determining the direction of infrastructure and production in the country. The Carrera revolt permitted the conservative merchants to regain their favored position over foreign trade.

The Economic Society was the other institution closely linked to economic development during the Carrera period. Although associated with liberal political and economic development in the late colonial period, after independence its political identification became less absolute in the shifting political allegiances of many members of the elite and in the fragmentation of the provinces. Reliance on these two institutions for production and transportation development by the conservatives would contrast with the more active role the liberals would subsequently give the government in this area. It was at the heart of traditional conservative philosophy, which, while supporting a strongly authoritarian government, left the supervision of the society and economy to corporate institutions such as the church or the Consulado. The policy of turning responsibility for development of transportation and port facilities over to those who benefited most from them was not without its advantages. On those projects in which the interests of the capital merchants were dependent, some admirable work was completed, especially in the development of a Pacific Coast port and highway. Money was often spent more carefully than on projects over which government officials were given responsibility, and the limited funds available were spent for their intended purposes. Nevertheless, the opposition of the Consulado to increased taxes on commerce shows less than a wholehearted commitment by the merchants to constructing or maintaining good roads throughout the country. Furthermore, the concession of this work to the Consulado was used not for general development of the country, but only for development along those lines necessary to maintain the capital merchant monopoly. It tended, therefore, to maintain a status quo that was not conducive to the expansion of production, prosperity, or the general welfare of the nation. Removal of this monopoly allowed new elite interests, especially coffee interests from Los Altos, to join and expand the economic elite of the capital and to take political precedence over it after 1871.

Thus the new liberalism blended nineteenth-century liberalism with conservatism and positivism to create the modern "neo-liberal" elite, which has dominated the country for more than a century. It was an elite considerably more complex and larger than the old "family" of the conservative years, and it included a strong element from Los Altos, finally bringing a degree of unity to the country. Despite elite rhetoric, political liberalism was largely abandoned and the tight control of the press and free expression that had characterized the Carrera dictatorship if anything was intensified under the liberal dictatorships that followed. The liberals talked of expanded public education, but in destroying the church's monopoly over education under the conservatives, they created a system that served primarily the elite and middle sectors of the capital. Education of the rural masses became even worse. And in economic policy, while emphasizing capitalist enterprise and investment, in practice they built a stronger state and used its apparatus to protect and enhance the economic interests of the new elite.

Both the liberals and conservatives represented the continuing European conquest of Guatemala's indigenous population. Carrera, however, was neither conservative nor liberal. He represented a reaction against both, injecting a rural vision into Guatemalan events. In defending the rural masses from the economic exploitation of the creole elite, Carrera arrested the rapid destruction of indigenous culture that had already begun to occur by 1837. It also, of course, delayed Guatemala's entrance on a large scale into the North Atlantic economic system and the dependency that accompanied that under liberal rule after 1871. In contrast to Benito Juárez, who sought to represent the rural masses through application of liberal principles, Carrera allied with the conservatives. Instead of incorporating them into the European tradition, Carrera allowed them to preserve traditional values and their community life. In this sense Carrera stood outside the traditional liberal and conservative political parties and represented a unique historical force rooted in indigenous custom and interests. In protecting Indian land and labor from creole and foreign exploitation for nearly thirty years, Carrera was responsible for preserving much of Guatemala's native culture and uniqueness. This contrasted sharply with what happened elsewhere in Latin America and what would happen later in the century even in Guatemala.

Nevertheless, conservative Guatemala was a paternalistic, corporativist state that sought to retain for a small elite the comfort and security that the Hispanic regime had provided. Conservatives were not opposed to capitalist economic development, but they favored gradual expansion rather than the rapid change that they feared would cause violent social upheaval. It was therefore unprogressive by contemporary standards, only mildly interested in developing the sort of economy that the nineteenth-century was demanding of the former colonial world. At the same time, it developed authoritarian and militaristic patterns that would become ingrained in the country's political tradition, especially to prevent the emergence of stronger populist and peasant movements in the Carrera tradition. The emergence of the Republic of Guatemala during the first half century of national independence was thus accompanied by the crystallization of many of those institutions and patterns that have given modern Guatemala its unique and often tragic character.

Principal Commercial Houses
During the Decade 1860–1870:
Their Proprietors and Activities

THIS LIST is translated and reordered alphabetically from Gustavo Enrique Palma Murga's history licenciatura thesis, "Anexo No. 4," *Algunas relaciones entre la iglesia y los grupos particulares durante el período de 1860 a 1870. Su incidencia en el movimiento liberal de 1871* (Guatemala: Universidad de San Carlos, Escuela de Historia, July 1877), 225–30. Palma cites as his source the *Gaceta de Guatemala*, 1860–1870.

Enrique Andresen—Hotel, stage coach service between Antigua, Guatemala, and Amatitlán
Salvador Arévalo—Warehouse for wines and preserves; crystal shop
E. Ascoli—Unspecified business proprietor
José Avila—Cotton merchant
Manuel Ayau—Unspecified business proprietor
Rafael Ayau—Commercial house
Pedro José Barros—Unspecified business proprietor
Benito, Novella & Company—Commission house
Gustavo Bernoulli—Physician and surgeon
Bertholin & Currier—Import-export
Bertrand & Perrot—Unspecified business proprietor
Pablo Blanco—Bookstore and retail merchandise
Pedro Boisard—Bookstore and stationery store
Bramma Brothers—Importer of agricultural machinery
A. de Brug—Unspecified business proprietor
Francisco Camacho & Company—Unspecified business proprietor

Andrés Castanet—French hatter

Coloma Brothers—Bookstore

Compañía de Agencias—Freight transport, domestic and overseas

Adolfo Delfis & Carlos Buisson—Agent of the Caja Universal de Capitales General Mutual Life Insurance Company

José Descalzi—Unspecified business proprietor

Du Teil Brothers—Import-export; maritime agency; marine insurance

Emeterio Echeverría A.—Drug store

Pablo Edelman—Importer of machinery for coffee, wheat, rice, and cotton

P. Fashen—Unspecified business proprietor

Fitzgibbon, Spann & Company—Commission house; general agents; import-export

V. Foncea—Unspecified business proprietor

Fuchs & Donzell—Agents of the Swiss Central Bank

Juan García Moreno—Unspecified business proprietor

Goethals & Vandeputte—Unspecified business proprietor

Gomar & Kroeger—Commercial house; import-export; fruit dealer; commission agent

Emilio Goubaud—Bookstore and retail merchandise

Pedro Guirola—Grocery warehouse

Hall Brothers—Variety store

E. Herbruger—Unspecified business proprietor

Hockmeyer & Rittscher—Import-export; commission agent; maritime agency

Gabriel Jubín—Dentist

Keller, Nieder & Company—Warehouse for wines, preserves, and other articles

Guillermo Kuhsick—Unspecified business proprietor

José Lara—Drug store and perfumery

Mateo LeKeu—Stage coach company

Julio Lowenthal—Variety store

David Luna—Unspecified business proprietor

Santiago R. MacDonald—Agent for English Royal Mail Steamship Company

Federico Matheu & Company—General commercial house

Juan Matheu—Commercial house; agent of the General Maritime Insurance Company (Vienna), La Tutelar Insurance Company (Madrid), and Lloyds (London)

F. Minondo & Company—General commercial house

Mariano Montis—Unspecified business proprietor

H. Morales & Company—Unspecified business proprietor

Morales, Muñoz & Company—Commission house

Mariano L. Morales—Miscellany; buyer of grain, coffee, etc.

Tomás Ortiz & Company—Export house

Carlos T. Penin—Retail merchandise and perfume shop

Agustín Pinajel—Unspecified business proprietor

Porta, Peña & Company—Import-export; consignees

José Revello—Commercial house; import-export; commission agent; and unspecified business proprietor

J. Rheiner—Unspecified business proprietor

Rieper, Augener & Company—Import-export agent and consignees; maritime agents

Santiago Robles—Stage coach company

Juan Miguel Ruiz—Unspecified business proprietor

Miguel Ruiz—Unspecified business proprietor

Pedro Sáenz de Tejada—Unspecified business proprietor

Samuel, Skinner, & Arlés—Compañia Agrícola de Guatemala

Dionisio Sánchez & Company—Import-export agent and consignees

Salvador Saravía—Pharmacy

Gustavo Savoy—Grocery warehouse; sales and service of spinning and weaving machinery

Juan Serigiers & Company—Import-export; maritime agency of the British Pacific Mail Steamship Company

Sres. Sinibaldi & Company—Unspecified business proprietor

Santiago H. Thompson—Machinery shop: coffee cleaners, sugar mills, sawmills, cotton gins

Felipe Tible—Stage coach company

Roderico Toledo—Machinery agent: sugar refining mills, coffee equipment, and agricultural tools

Urruela Brothers & Company—Commercial house; commission agent

Francisco Urruela—Unspecified business proprietor

Luis Valdés & Company—Import-export agent and consignees

Luis Vanhaels—Stagecoach company

Carlos H. Van Patten—Dentist

Vasconcelos & Silva—Commercial house; import-export; commission agent

Vásquez & Jaramillo—Agricultural and industrial company

Viteri, Everall & Company—Import-export agent and consignees

Pablo Wassen—Candy shop; import-export

F. Widmer—Unspecified business proprietor

Wunderlich & Alejos—Commercial corporation; coffee exporter

Notes

Preface

1. Joanne Weaver, "Liberal Historian or Conservative Thinker? Alejandro Marure and Guatemalan History, 1821–1851" (M.A. thesis, Tulane University, 1975); Oscar Guillermo Peláez Almengor, "Alejandro Marure, la historia y el proyecto político" (1989).

2. Daniele Pompejano, *Centro America: La crisi dell'ancien régime (Guatemala 1840–1870)* (1990); Juan Carlos Solórzano F., "Rafael Carrera, ¿reacción conservadora o revolución campesina? Guatemala 1837–1873," *Anuario de Estudios Centroamericanos* 13(2)(1987):5–35. For a fuller discussion of the historiography on the period, see William J. Griffith, "The Historiography of Central America since 1830," *Hispanic American Historical Review* 40 (1960):549–63, and Ralph Lee Woodward, Jr.'s bibliographical essay "Central America from Independence to *c.* 1870," in *The Cambridge History of Latin America*, vol. 3 (1992), 471–506, 874–79; and his "The Historiography of Modern Central America since 1960," *Hispanic American Historical Review* 67 (1987):473–84.

1. The Colonial Burden

1. Carlos Guzmán Böckler and Jean-Loup Herbert, *Guatemala: Una interpretación histórico-social* (1970), 9–10.

2. See William L. Sherman, *Forced Native Labor in Sixteenth-Century Central America* (1979). For a detailed discussion of the relationship between Spaniards and Indians in Guatemala, see Severo Martínez Peláez, *La patria del criollo* (1970), 535–57, and Carol A. Smith, ed., *Guatemalan Indians and the State, 1540 to 1988* (1990).

3. See Severo Martínez Peláez, "Los motines de indios en el período colonial guatemalteca," in Congreso Centroamericano de Historia Demográfica, Económica y Social, I, Santa Barbara, Costa Rica, 1973, *Ensayos de historia centroamericana*. Colección Seminario y Documento, 17(1974), 27–47.

4. W. George Lovell, *Conquest and Survival in Colonial Guatemala: A Historical Geography of the Cuchumatán Highlands, 1500–1821* (1985); Christopher H. Lutz, *Historia sociodemográfica de Santiago de Guatemala, 1541–1773* (1982).

5. Stephen A. Webre, "The Social and Economic Bases of Cabildo Membership in Seventeenth-Century Santiago de Guatemala" (1980); Martínez Peláez, *La patria del criollo*; Murdo J. MacLeod, *Spanish Central America, A Socioeconomic History, 1520–1720* (1973), especially 235–389; Franklin D. Parker, *The Central American Republics* (1964), 61. For a vivid description of the country in the last decade of the seventeenth century see Francisco Antonio de Fuentes y Guzmán, *Recordación Florida*, 3 vols. (1933).

6. Wilbur E. Meneray, "The Kingdom of Guatemala during the Reign of Charles III, 1759–1788" (1975), gives a fairly thorough account of Guatemalan economic development for the period with which it deals. For broader descriptions of the Bourbon Reforms in Central America, see Miles L. Wortman, *Government and Society in Central America, 1680–1840* (1982); and Ralph Lee Woodward, Jr., *Central America, a Nation Divided*, 2d ed. (1985), 61–91.

7. Manuel Rubio Sánchez, *Historia del añil o xiquilite en Centro América*, 2 vols. (1976); Jorge Alberto Escobar, "El añil en la economía de El Salvador," *Economía Salvadoreña* 11 (1962):23–36; MacLeod, *Spanish Central America*, 176–203; Miles L. Wortman, "Bourbon Reforms in Central America, 1750–1786," *The Americas* 32 (October 1975):222–38; Troy S. Floyd, *The Anglo-Spanish Struggle for Mosquitia* (1967), 119–90; and Frances Armytage, *The Free Port System in the British West Indies: A Study in Commercial Policy* (1953).

8. Thomas M. Fiehrer, "The Barón de Carondelet as an Agent of Bourbon Reform: A Study of Spanish Colonial Administration in the Years of the French Revolution" (1977), 96–365.

9. Alberto Herrarte, *La unión de Centroamérica (tragedia y esperanza)*, 2d ed. (1963), 104; Mario Rodríguez, *The Cádiz Experiment in Central America* (1978), 92–112. On the development of the state in Central America, see Julio C. Pinto Soria's excellent *Raíces históricas del estado en Centroamérica*, 2d ed. (1983).

10. Ralph Lee Woodward, Jr., *Class Privilege and Economic Development: The Consulado de Comercio of Guatemala, 1793–1871* (1966), xi–xiii, 107–14; Carlos Meléndez Chaverri, *La ilustración en el antiguo Reino de Guatemala* (1970), 115–25; Troy S. Floyd, "The Guatemalan Merchants, the Government, and the *Provincianos*, 1750–1800," *Hispanic American Historical Review* 41 (1961):90–110; Ciro F. S. Cardoso and Héctor Pérez Brignoli, *Centro América y la economía occidental (1520–1930)* (1977), 87–110.

11. Diana Balmori, Stuart F. Voss, and Miles Wortman, *Notable Family Networks in Latin America* (1984), 52–78; David L. Chandler, *Juan José de Aycinena, idealista conservador de la Guatemala del siglo XIX* (1988), 3–10.

12. Alberto Lanuza Matamoros, *Estructuras socioeconómicas, poder y estado en Nicaragua, de 1821 a 1875* (1976), 87–88.

13. A series of articles by Manuel Remacha in the *Gazeta de Guatemala*, 5 May–

4 Aug. 1800, tell of the improvement to commerce, agriculture, and industry that regular navigation of the Río Motagua would stimulate.

14. A royal order of 17 Jan. 1803 confirmed this exemption. *Gazeta de Guatemala*, 1 June 1803.

15. The role of Juan Bautista Irisarri was especially important in this development on the Pacific coast. See his series of articles, written under the pseudonym Chirimía, in the *Gazeta de Guatemala*, 2 Mar.–13 July 1801. Irisarri worked especially to develop the port of Acajutla. *Gazeta de Guatemala*, 15 Feb. 1802.

16. Ralph Lee Woodward, Jr., "Economic and Social Origins of the Guatemalan Political Parties (1773–1823)," *Hispanic American Historical Review* 45 (1965):544–66.

17. Antonio Batres Jáuregui, *La América Central ante la historia* (1915–49) 2:380; Eduardo Arcila Farías, "Evolución de la economía en Venezuela," in *Venezuela independiente, 1810–1960* (1962), 366–67. Robert S. Smith, "Indigo Production and Trade in Colonial Guatemala," *Hispanic American Historical Review* 39 (1959):201–5, shows the indigo prices fixed in Central America between 1758 and 1810. These prices were somewhat more stable than those paid in Europe, but they were not necessarily the actual price paid by merchants to producers. Rather, they were assessed values established by the government for tax purposes.

18. Brian R. Hamnett, *Politics and Trade in Southern Mexico, 1750–1821* (1971). An unsigned article in the *Gazeta de Guatemala*, 23 Aug. 1802, describes French efforts to develop cochineal in Saint Domingue.

19. See Floyd, *Anglo-Spanish Struggle*, 119–90.

20. Sergio Villalobos R., "Problemas del comercio colonial," in *Temas de historia económica hispanoamericana* (1965) 1:57–62; D. S. Chandler, "Jacobo de Villaurrutia and the Audiencia of Guatemala, 1794–1804," *The Americas* 32 (1976):407–13. See also Jacques Barbier and Allan Kuethe, eds., *The North American Role in the Spanish Imperial Economy, 1760–1819* (1984). For a report by sixteen Guatemalan merchants who opposed the trade with the United States, see Archivo General de Centro América (hereinafter cited as AGCA), A.5.8(4), leg. 6 (Honduras), exp. 110, fol. 1–4; see also the "Informe" of the Consulado, 19 May 1810, in AGCA, B, leg. 32, exp. 783.

21. Robert J. Shafer, *The Economic Societies in the Spanish World, 1763–1821* (1958), 130.

22. AGCA, A, leg. 50, exp. 1253, fols. 75–91; see also leg. 266, exp. 5832; and leg. 2397, exp. 18180, for the 1799 donativo of $15,000, which was credited toward the 1800 donativo of $100,000.

23. AGCA, A, leg. 51, exps. 1262–63.

24. It called for 30 percent of the amount from peninsular consulados and the remainder ($140,000) from the consulados of Mexico, Lima, Buenos Aires, Veracruz, Havana, Caracas, and Cartagena. Royal order of 13 Apr. 1800, Germán Tjarks, *El Consulado de Buenos Aires y sus proyecciones en la historia del Río de la Plata* (1962), 2:316–17.

25. Geoffrey A. Cabat, "The Consolidation of 1804 in Guatemala," *The Americas* 28 (1971):20–38. See also Romeo R. Flores, "Las representaciones de 1805," *Historia Mexicana* 17 (1968):469–73; and Asunción Lavrin, "The Execution of the Law of *Consolidación* in New Spain: Economic Aims and Results," *Hispanic American Historical Review* 53 (1973):27–49.

26. Rodríguez, *Cádiz Experiment*, 43.

27. See the royal order of 10 Oct. 1805 prohibiting this practice, an empty threat given Spain's maritime weakness by this date, in AGCA, A, leg. 2317, fol. 109. Records in Belize also reflect the growth of privateering in the Gulf of Honduras in 1805–9. John Burdon, ed., *Archives of British Honduras* (1931–35) 2:88–107; and Robert A. Naylor, "British Commercial Relations with Central America, 1821–1851" (1958), 4–7. A Spanish version of this dissertation has been published: *Influencia británica en el comercio centroamericano durante las primeras décadas de la Independencia (1821–1851)* (1988).

28. AGCA, A, leg. 2317; A, leg. 1745, exp. 11716. fol. 685.

29. *Gazeta de Guatemala*, 3 Nov. 1809; Louis Bumgartner, ed. "Demostraciones públicas de lealtad que ha hecho el comercio de la ciudad de Guatemala," *Anales de la Sociedad de Geografía e Historia de Guatemala* 38 (1965):69–70. The majority of the $1,066,996.25 donativo was sent in silver specie, the remainder in indigo and in "libranzas contra Holanda." In addition to the $100,000 from the merchants, another $100,000 came from the Indian community funds. Ramón A. Salazar, *Historia de veintiún años: La independencia de Guatemala* (1928), 114.

30. *Gazeta de Guatemala*, 14 Sep. 1809 and 10 Nov. 1810. Jorge Mario García Laguardia details the political events during the period 1808–15, based on research in Guatemalan, Spanish, and Mexican archives, in his *Orígenes de la democracia constitucional en Centroamérica* (1971).

31. Martínez Peláez, *La patria del criollo*, 296–97; Héctor Humberto Samayoa Guevara, *Los gremios de artesanos en la ciudad de Guatemala (1524–1821)* (1962), 49–51.

32. Pedro Pérez Valenzuela, *La Nueva Guatemala de la Asunción; terremoto de Santa Marta; fundación en el llano de la Virgen* (1934); Inge Langenberg, *Urbanisation und Bevölkerungsstruktur der Stadt Guatemala in der ausgehenden Kolonialzeit: Eine sozialhistorische Analyse der Stadtverlegung und ihrer Auswirkungen auf die demographische, berufliche, un soziale Gliederung der Bevölkerung (1773–1824)* (1981), 94–394; a Spanish condensation of Langenberg's work is "Urbanización y cambio social: El traslado de la ciudad de Guatemala y sus consecuencia para la población y sociedad urbana al fin de la época colonial, 1773–1824," *Anuario de Estudios Americanos* 36 (1979):351–74, and in slightly different form, "La estructura urbana y el cambio social en la ciudad de Guatemala a fines de la época colonial (1773–1824)," in *La sociedad colonial en Guatemala: Estudios regionales y locales*, edited by Stephen Webre (1989), 221–49.

33. Francisco de Solano, "Tierra, comercio y sociedad: Un análisis de la estruc-

tura social agraria centroamericana durante el siglo XVIII," *Revista de Indias* 31 (July–December 1971):329–30.

34. Roberto Molina y Morales, "El Barón de Carondelet, intendente-corregidor de la provincia, 1789–1793," in Miguel Angel García, ed., *San Salvador desde la conquista hasta el año de 1899*, vol. 1 of *Diccionario histórico enciclopédico de la República de El Salvador* (1952–58), 234–36; Hubert H. Bancroft, *History of Central America* (1886–87) 3:563–64; *Gazeta de Guatemala*, 26 Oct. 1809–21 Feb. 1810.

35. Smith, "Indigo Production," 183; José del Valle, *Instrucción sobre la plaga de langosta; medios de exterminarla, o de disminuir sus efectos: y de precaber la escasez de comestibles* (1804). The AGCA holds an enormous store of records relating to the locust invasion. The most illustrative of these documents are found in A, leg. 37, exps. 4305–12, 4328, and 4333; leg. 171, exp. 5438; leg. 1977, exp. 13473; leg. 2185, exp. 15728; leg. 2354, exp. 17796; leg. 2450, exp. 18878; leg. 2769, exp. 24070; leg. 5458, exp. 46827; leg. 6091, exp. 55306; and leg. 6106, exp. 55874.

36. Woodward, *Class Privilege*, 39–40.

37. "Realejo: A Forgotten Colonial Port and Shipbuilding Center in Nicaragua," *Hispanic American Historical Review* 51 (1971):295–312; see also Manuel Rubio Sánchez, *Historia de El Realejo* (1975).

38. Solano, "Tierra, comercio y sociedad," 330. See also Henry Dunn, *Guatimala* [sic], *or, The Republic of Central America, in 1827–8* (1829), 208–9.

39. Cardoso and Pérez, *Centro América*, 117–26; Martínez Peláez, *La patria del criollo*, 399, 727.

40. "Government Revenue and Economic Trends in Central America, 1787–1819," *Hispanic American Historical Review* 55 (1975):251–86.

41. Martínez Peláez, "Los motines," 27–47.

42. For a discussion of the emerging economic and political interest groups among the elite in the late colonial period, see Woodward, "Economic and Social Origins," 544–66.

43. Samayoa Guevara, *Gremios*, 53–85, 205–09; Webre, "Social and Economic Bases;" Woodward, *Class Privilege*; Robert S. Smith, "Origins of the Consulado de Guatemala," *Hispanic American Historical Review* 26 (1946):150–61; and Manuel Rubio Sánchez, "El real consulado de comercio," *Antropología e Historia de Guatemala* 19 (July–December 1967):59–73.

44. The Montepío de Cosecheros de Añil is described in some detail in Smith, "Indigo Production," 181–211 passim, and idem, " 'Statutes of the Guatemalan Indigo Growers' Society' by M. de Gálvez," *Hispanic American Historical Review* 30 (1950):336–45.

45. Fiehrer, "Carondelet," 315–27. Smith, "Indigo Production," 194–95, says that the indebtedness of the Montepío had risen from $434,861 in 1800 to a peak of $848,897 in 1818 before recovering slightly to $662,250 by 1820. The number of borrowers rose from 131 in 1791 to 196 by the end of 1820, but Smith believed that there were probably more than 250 in 1818.

46. Julio C. Pinto Soria, *Guatemala en la década de la independencia* (1978), 4–43. Patricia Brady Schmit has also reassessed the political activity and interest groups surrounding Central American independence in "Guatemalan Political Parties: Development of Interest Groups, 1820–1822" (1977).

47. Rodríguez, *Cádiz Experiment*; see also John T. Reid, *Modern Spain and Liberalism: A Study in Literary Contrasts* (1937), 10–21.

2. Conservatives and Liberals, 1821–1837

1. Mario Rodríguez, *The Cádiz Experiment in Central America, 1808–1826* (1978).

2. An excellent biography of Valle is Louis Bumgartner, *José del Valle of Central America* (1963); see also *El Editor Constitucional* (1820–21) and *El Amigo de la Patria* (1820–22).

3. J. Antonio Villacorta Calderón, *Historia de la capitanía general de Guatemala* (1942), 496–516; Bumgartner, *José del Valle*, 134–43, 155–59; Rodríguez, *Cádiz Experiment*, 146–49; Salazar, *Historia de veintiún años*, 226–55; Susan Strobeck, "The Political Activities of Some Members of the Aristocratic Families of Guatemala, 1821–1839" (1958), 144–515; Andrés Townsend Ezcurra, *Las provincias unidas de Centroamérica: Fundación de la República* (1973), 21–22; Martínez Peláez, *La patria del criollo*, 330–32; Lorenzo Montúfar y Rivera, *Reseña histórica de Centro-América* (1878–88), 1:7; AGCA, B, leg. 46, exp. 950.

4. Rodríguez, *Cádiz Experiment*, 149–61; Bumgartner, *José del Valle*, 162–67, 232; Alejandro Marure, *Efemérides de los hechos notables acaecidos en la República de Centro-América desde el año 1821 hasta el de 1842*, 2d ed. (1895), 1–4; Bancroft, *Central America*, 3:46–51.

5. Strobeck, "Political Activities," 21–22; Antonio Batres Jáuregui, *El Doctor Mariano Gálvez y su época*, 2d ed. (1957), 53–54; and Bumgartner, *José del Valle*, 166–67.

6. Marure, *Efemérides*, 5; Bancroft, *Central America*, 3:49–57; Bumgartner, *José del Valle*, 165–77; Strobeck, "Political Activities," 29–30; Rodríguez, *Cádiz Experiment*, 151–68; Thomas L. Karnes, *The Failure of Union, Central America, 1824–1960* (1961), 23–24; Schmit, "Political Parties," 257–302; L. Montúfar, *Reseña*, 1:6; Salazar, *Veintiún años*, 13–14; Rafael Heliodoro Valle, ed., *La anexión de Centroamérica a México (documentos y escritos de 1821–1828)*, (1924–49), 1:10–3:280; and Gordon Kenyon, "Mexican Influence in Central America, 1821–1823," *Hispanic American Historical Review* 41 (1961):175–205.

7. R. H. Valle, *Anexión*, 3:94–4:124; Marure, *Efemérides*, 5–8; Bancroft, *Central America*, 3:57–65; Bumgartner, *José del Valle*, 207; Rodríguez, *Cádiz Experiment*, 169–93.

8. Marure, *Efemérides*, 9–11, 22; Rodríguez, *Cádiz Experiment*, 184–90; *Incorporación de Chiapas a México: discursos* (1922); Valle, *Anexión*, 5:11–44; *Exposición*

sobre el derecho que tiene la Provincia de Chiapa para pronunciar libremente su voluntad, y el que tiene Goatemala para ser independiente (1823); Consulado Nacional de Guatemala to Supremo Poder Ejecutivo, 20 Sep. 1824, AGCA, B, leg. 32120, exp. 1391.

9. George A. Thompson, *Narrative of an Official Visit to Guatemala from Mexico* (1829), 71–72; see also Rodríguez, *Cádiz Experiment*, 176.

10. Both liberal and conservative Guatemalan publications frequently quoted Bentham in the early nineteenth century. Rafael Heliodoro Valle, *Cartas de Bentham a José del Valle* (1942); Miriam Williford, *Jeremy Bentham on Spanish America: An Account of his Letters and Proposals to the New World* (1980), 26–30, 96–98, 114–141; Elmer L. Kayser, *The Grand Social Enterprise: A Study of Jeremy Bentham in his Relationship to Liberal Materialism* (1932), 84; and Ricardo Palomares, "Jeremy Bentham in Spanish America" (1978), 149–50.

11. The unpublished theses of Strobeck and Schmit are among the most useful analyses of the political activities of the elite during the first years after independence.

12. Marure, *Efemérides*, 11–12; Rodríguez, *Cádiz Experiment*, 195; Isidro Menéndez, comp., *Recopilación de las leyes del Salvador en Centro América*, 2d ed. (1956) 1:20, 126; AGCA, B, leg. 1391, exp. 32107.

13. Karnes, *Failure of Union*, 40–41; Rodríguez, *Cádiz Experiment*, 195; Marure, *Efemérides*, 13–14; José Joaquín Castilla to Asamblea Nacional Constituyente, 21 Sept. 1823, AGCA, B, leg. 100, exp. 2706.

14. *Manifiesto del Gobierno Supremo de los Estados del Centro de América* (Guatemala, 20 May 1824), copy in Collection 20, Central America Political Ephemera, Latin American Library, Tulane University, New Orleans, Louisiana (hereinafter cited as LALTU). Arce, who was absent from the city at the time, did not sign this manifesto.

15. Karnes, *Failure of Union*, 39; Ramón Salazar, *Manuel José Arce (hombres de la independencia)* (1952), 30–31; L. Montúfar, *Reseña* 1:8.

16. "Constitución Federal de 1824," in Ricardo Gallardo, *Las constituciones de la República Federal de Centro-América* (1958) 2:703–38.

17. Woodward, "Central America from Independence to *c.* 1870," 482; Manuel José Arce, *Memoria*, edited by Modesto Barrios (1959), 26–29; Philip F. Flemion, "Manuel José Arce and the Formation of the Federal Republic of Central America" (1969), pp. 121–44.

18. Marure, *Efemérides*, 24–41; Rodríguez, *Cádiz Experiment*, 227–28. Pierson was a creole from Saint Domingue, while Cáscara (1777–1851) was a Sardinian who had served with Napoleon. See Manuel Rubio Sánchez, *Los Mariscales de Campo: I—Francisco Cáscara* (1984) for a documentary biography of Cáscara's long career in Guatemala. Most of the other foreign officers played a role only in the 1820s. Jean Baptiste Fauconnier had been a physician and professor of chemistry at the University of Paris before coming to Guatemala, where, on the recommendations of J. F. Barrundia and Pedro Valenzuela he had been granted a chair in chemistry at the Universidad de San Carlos in January 1825(AGCA, B, leg. 196, exp. 4358;

leg. 3563, exp. 81253; and leg. 3479, exp. 79472). He proposed to establish a glass factory in 1826 (leg. 1147, exp. 26241), and asked for a twenty-year concession, but in 1827 he was accused of murdering José Eufracio Ordoñez (leg. 1254, exp. 30638). Santos Carrera testified in this case against Fauconnier, Saget, and Pierson, claiming they had ordered Ordoñez killed when Pierson's force attacked the town of Saleajá. On Raoul, see Adam Szaszdi, *Nicolás Raoul y la república federal de Centroamérica* (1958). See also Miguel Angel García, *Gral. Don Manuel José Arce* (*Diccionario histórico enciclopédico de la República de El Salvador*) (1945) 3:417–22. Pierson's capture is dealt with in the *Gaceta Estraordinaria del Gobierno* (Guatemala) no. 21 (2 May 1827):171.

19. Other liberals declared as outlaws by Aycinena included Molina's son, Pedro Esteban Molina, Miguel and Cleto Ordoñez, Antonio Corzo, Juan Rafael Lambur, and Juan Vendaña. L. Montúfar, *Reseña*, 1:9, 25; Marure, *Efemérides*, 38–41; Marure, *Bosquejo histórico de las revoluciones de Centroamérica, desde 1811 hasta 1834*, 2d ed. (1960), 2:418–19.

20. Ricardo Donoso, *Antonio José de Irisarri, escritor y diplomático, 1786–1868*, 2d ed. (1966), 127.

21. Marure, *Efemérides*, 41–42; L. Montúfar, *Reseña*, 1:9–13; Bancroft, *Central America*, 3:161–63.

22. Manuel del Apartado, "Vida de Morazán" (unpublished manuscript, San Salvador, 1959), 3–25 in LALTU.

23. Marure, *Efemérides*, 41–44; Bancroft, *Central America*, 3:92–93; Apartado, "Morazán," 29–30, 42–43, 282.

24. Juan de Dios Mayorga, *Manifiesto sobre el decreto de nuevo convocatoria que expidió el Supremo Gobierno en 5 del corriente* (Guatemala City, 25 Nov. 1827), 3–6, Collection 20, Central America Political Ephemera, LALTU.

25. Marure, *Efemérides*, 24; Bancroft, *Central America*, 3:94; Apartado, "Morazán," 52.

26. Arzú married into the Batres family in Guatemala and sired a large family that figured prominently in the conservative party in the nineteenth century. Edgar Juan Aparicio y Aparicio, "La familia de Arzú," *Revista de la Academia Guatemalteca de Estudios Genealógicos, Heráldicos e Históricos* 3–4 (1969–70):77–79.

27. Szaszdi, *Raoul*, 141–42.

28. Strobeck, "Political Activities," 63, citing *Diario de Guatemala* 1, no. 39 (2 Mar. 1828):170, and Joel R. Poinsett to Henry Clay, Mexico, 30 Dec. 1828, in William Ray Manning, ed., *Diplomatic Correspondence of the United States Concerning Independence of Latin American Nations* (1925) 3:1672.

29. *Gazeta del Gobierno* (Guatemala), "Estraordinario" al no. 45 (3 Mar. 1828).

30. Clemente Marroquín Rojas, *Francisco Morazán y Rafael Carrera* (1965), 23.

31. Mariano Aycinena, *Guatemaltecos* (Guatemala, 21 Mar. 1828), Collection 20, Central America Political Ephemera, LALTU.

32. Legislative Decrees of 16 June and 23 August 1828, Guatemala, Collection 20, Central America Political Ephemera, LALTU.

33. *Aviso* (Guatemala, 23 July 1828), Collection 20, Central America Political Ephemera, LALTU; Apartado, "Morazán" 44–49, 52, 276, 287; Bancroft, *Central America*, 3:95. Antonio Aycinena was among those exiled by Morazán in 1829. He went to the United States, where he settled, never returning to Central America. Ramiro Ordóñez Jonama, "La familia Varón de Berrieza," *Revista de la Academia Guatemalteca de Estudios Genealógicas, Heráldicas, e Históricos* 9 (1987): 644.

34. Marure, *Efemérides*, 48–49; "La Asamblea del Estado de Guatemala a los Pueblos," Guatemala, 20 Oct. 1828, Collection 20, Central America Political Ephemera, LALTU. See also in same collection, Mariano Aycinena's decrees on security (24 Oct. 1828) and discipline (3 Nov. 1828), and his "Proclama" to the Quetzaltenango inhabitants, Guatemala, 27 Oct. 1828.

35. Marure, *Efemérides*, 49; Marure, *Bosquejo histórico*, 2:533–34; Mary P. Holleran, *Church and State In Guatemala* (1949), 91–102.

36. "Morazán [Comandante jeneral de los ejércitos aliados protectores de la ley] to Jefe Político de este Departamento," in Rómulo E. Durón, *Album morazánico* (1942) 1:37; Marroquín Rojas, *Morazán y Carrera*, 21.

37. Marure, *Efemérides*, 50–51; Szaszdi, *Raoul*, 142; Bancroft, *Central America*, 3:96–98; Apartado, "Morazán," 57–58.

38. Marure, *Efemérides*, 52; Apartado, "Morazán," 59, 284–85.

39. L. Montúfar, *Reseña* 1:66–77; Manuel Montúfar Coronado, *Memorias para la historia de la revolución de Centro América* (1832), 132–33.

40. Marure, *Efemérides*, 53–54; Apartado, "Morazán," 64–67, 295; Arce, *Memoria*, 183–92; L. Montúfar, *Reseña*, 1:110; Szaszdi, *Raoul*, 153–54. Many of those arrested were held prisoner in the monastery of Belén, including many of the most important conservatives of the capital: Miguel González Saravía, Jorge Ubico, Juan Chavarría, Antonio Villar, Juan Emeterio Echeverría, Luis Pedro Aguirre, José Piloña, Juan Ignacio Yrigoyen, José Petit, José Velasco, Francisco Solivera, Pedro Menocal, Juan Monge, Blas García, Angel Trevillas, José Bernardo Sagaceta, Mateo Subieda, Rafael García Sirtiaga, Miguel Nistal, José Vicente García Granados, Juan del Valle, Agustín Prado, Luis Basagostia, Domingo Payes, Ramón Pacheco, Juan Francisco Lanruaga, Francisco Quevedo, Manuel Arzú, Antonio Batres Asturias, Juan Piñol, Antonio Batres Nájera, José M. Beltranena, Francisco Valdez, Pedro Aycinena, Manuel Pavón, Juan Pavón, Luis Batres, Manuel Beteta, Francisco Vigil, Juan Ernesto Milla, José S. Milla, José Justo Milla, Mariano Córdova, Francisco Beteta, Manuel Zea, Fernando Prado, Francisco Cáscara, José Antonio López, Manuel Mesa, Manuel Bargas, John Baily, Manuel González, Mariano Asturias, José Antonio Ariza, Juan de Dios Castro, Manuel Ramírez, Basilio Porras, Pedro González, Pedro Arrasola, and Calisto Sánchez. Morazán to the Ministro General del Gobierno del Estado de Guatemala, Guatemala, 26 May 1829, Apartado, "Morazán," 299.

41. Marure, *Efemérides*, 57; *El Tiempo* (Guatemala) 1, no. 14 (5 July 1839): 54; Holleran, *Church and State*, 100–113; Hubert J. Miller, *La iglesia y el estado en tiempo de Justo Rufino Barrios* (1976), 24–25, 102; Bancroft, *Central America*, 3:103, 154;

Apartado, "Morazán," 81, 326–28. Apartado reproduces, 468–75, Morazán's defense of his suppression of the regular orders, "La expulsión de los regulares en Centro América."

42. David Vela, *Barrundia ante el espejo de su tiempo* (1956–57) 1:190; Marure, *Efemérides*, 36, 54; Bancroft, *Central America*, 3:112.

43. Apartado, "Morazán," 301–6. Those sentenced to perpetual exile included Federal President José Manuel Arce, Vice-President Mariano Beltranena, Foreign Minister José Francisco Sosa, Secretary of War Manuel Arzú, and their secretaries, Francisco María Beteta and Manuel Zea, federal army commanders Francisco Cáscara, Manuel Montúfar, and José Justo Milla; Mariano Aycinena, "who titled himself Chief of the State of Guatemala," and secretaries Agustín Prado, José Francisco Córdoba, Antonio José de Irisarri, José Velasco, Vicente Domínguez, and Vicente de Piélago.

44. Bancroft, *Central America*, 3:101–2; Marure, *Efemérides*, 58; Holleran, *Church and State*, 104–5.

45. Woodward, *Class Privilege*, xv–xvi, 31, 121–22.

46. Strobeck, "Political Activities," 85, citing *La necesidad de consolidar el gobierno después de un trastorno jeneral* (Guatemala, 21 July 1829).

47. Bancroft, *Central America*, 3:564.

48. Marure, *Efemérides*, 65–71; Szaszdi, *Raoul*, 189–97; Miguel García Granados, *Memorias del General don Miguel García Granados* (1877–93) 2:35–36; Apartado, "Morazán," 104–05.

49. Decree of Francisco Morazán, 30 Aug. 1832, *Gazeta Federal* (Guatemala), 3 Sept. 1832.

50. Szaszdi, *Raoul*, 177, citing Matías Romero, *Bosquejo histórico de la agregación a México de Chiapas y Soconusco y de las negociaciones sobre límites entabladas por México con Centro-América y Guatemala* (Mexico City: Imprenta del Gobierno, 1877), 736–46; Apartado, "Morazán," 104–5; Bancroft, *Central America*, 3:113–16.

51. "Manifiesto del Presidente de la República federal de Centro-América," Jalpatagua, 2 Feb. 1832, *Gaceta de Guatemala*, 6 Dec. 1850.

52. Marure, *Efemérides*, 66–69; García Granados, *Memorias*, 92–93; Durón, *Album morazánico*, 1:90–95; Apartado, "Morazán," 109–10, 345–51.

53. Mario Rodríguez, *Central America* (1965), 68–69, gives a succinct description of the exaggerated localism that led to rivalries between municipalities, regions, and the federal government. See also Marure, *Efemérides*, 74–85; García Granados, *Memorias*, 2:95–114; Robert Dunlop, *Travels in Central America* (1847), 185; Apartado, "Morazán," 110–16, 355–59; David Browning, *El Salvador, Landscape and Society* (1971), 142; Julio Alberto Domínguez Sosa, *Ensayo histórico sobre los tribus Nonualcos y su caudillo Anastasio Aquino* (1964); on the continued Indian uprisings in El Salvador, see Morazán's decree of 27 May 1837, in *Boletín Oficial* (Guatemala), 2d part, 26 June 1837.

54. Bancroft, *Central America*, 3:152–53; Ephraim G. Squier, *Travels in Central America, Particularly in Nicaragua* (1853) 1:372n; Carlos C. Haeussler Yela, *Diccio-*

nario General de Guatemala, (1983) 1:212; and Federico Hernández de León, *El libro de efemérides: Capítulos de la historia de la América Central* (1925–66) 7:27–31.

55. William J. Griffith, *Empires in the Wilderness; Foreign Colonization and Development in Guatemala, 1834–1844* (1965), 5–9, 93.

56. Pedro Tobar Cruz, *Los montañeses*, 2d ed. (1959), 44–45.

57. Miriam Williford, "Las Luces y La Civilización: The Social Reforms of Mariano Gálvez," in *Applied Enlightenment: 19th Century Liberalism* (1972), 38–39; see also the theses of Weaver and Peláez Almengor.

58. The four districts and their commandants were (1) Department of Guatemala, Gen. Carlos Salazar; (2) Departments of Sacatepéquez and Sololá, Gen. Juan Prem; (3) Departments of Chiquimula and Verapaz, Gen. Juan José Górriz; and (4) Departments of Quetzaltenango and Totonicapán, Gen. Agustín Guzmán, Marure, *Efemérides*, 74. These military governments lasted until 23 February 1838.

59. Robert S. Smith, "Financing the Central American Federation, 1821–1838," *Hispanic American Historical Review* 43 (1963):490; *Gazeta Federal* 1, no. 56 (12 July 1832):446–47.

60. *La Gaceta*, 23 Nov. 1833.

61. Holleran, *Church and State*, 120.

62. Valle died on Sunday, 2 March 1834, at 10:00 A.M. near the Corral de Piedra, Guatemala. *A la muerte del Ciudadano José del Valle* (Guatemala, 7 Mar. 1834) Collection 20, Central America Political Ephemera, LALTU; Bumgartner, *José del Valle*, 265–69; Robert S. Chamberlain, *Francisco Morazán, Champion of Central American Federation* (1950), 32–33; Marure, *Efemérides*, 81–82. See also Franklin D. Parker, *José Cecilio del Valle and the Establishment of the Central American Federation* (1954).

63. L. Montúfar, *Reseña*, 2:175–80; Tobar Cruz, *Los montañeses* (1959), 45–46, 86–87.

64. García Granados, *Memorias*, 2:53–54, 180.

65. Strobeck, "Political Activities," 92.

66. See, for example, Mariano Gálvez, *Documentos sobre arreglar un plan de administración antes de encargarse del Ministerio de Relaciones el Ministro nombrado Ldo. Marcial Zebadúa* (Guatemala, 1833).

67. Strobeck, "Political Activities," 85, notes a number of cases where important conservatives, including José M. Urruela, Luis Batres, and his brother José Antonio Batres, among others, acquired valuable ecclesiastical properties between 1829 and 1837. She also notes (p. 90) that a tax census taken on 20 October 1836 indicated that nearly forty "aristocrats representing a dozen of the oldest and most respected families" were residing in Guatemala City. Many of these had taken little or no part in politics, "yet their very presence in the city indicates that as a social class they were not feared by the Liberals. The fact that so many other aristocrats are known to have been in Guatemala and holding official positions would lead one to the conclusion that at least the members of the aristocracy with liberal sympathies were welcomed in politics. Nor were pressures exerted to prevent vari-

ous members from purchasing confiscated church property and thus accumulating even greater economic power. The exile of conservative and aristocratic leaders in 1829 apparently was intended as a warning rather than as an attempt to completely break this potentially powerful group."

68. "Mensaje del gefe de estado, Doctor Mariano Gálvez, al abrir sus sesiones ordinarias de Asam. Lej. de 1837," *El Editor: Periódico de los Tribunales* (Guatemala), 4 Mar. 1837. There is also a copy of this address in Collection 20, Central America Political Ephemera, LALTU.

69. "José Barrundia al mensaje del gefe del estado, Asam. Lejislativa," 20 Feb. 1837, *El Editor: Periódico de los Tribunales*, 24 Feb. 1837.

70. Williford, *Jeremy Bentham*, 137–41.

71. Tobar Cruz, *Los montañeses* (1959), 42.

72. Arnold Toynbee and Eaisaku Ikeda, *The Toynbee-Ikeda Dialogue: Man Himself Must Choose* (1976), 75.

73. Tobar Cruz, *Los montañeses* (1959), 148, 160; Rodrigo Facio, *Trayectoria y crisis de la federación centroamericana* (1949), 82.

74. See, for example, Juan de Dios Mayorga's early attack on Dr. Gálvez in his *Observaciones sobre la conducta política del Dr. C. Mariano Gálvez con respecto a los horribles males que con ella ha causado a Centro-América* (1831).

75. Naylor, "British Commercial Relations," 154; Smith, "Financing," 506–7; Tobar Cruz, *Los montañeses* (1959), 48.

76. Rodríguez, *Cádiz Experiment*, 227.

77. Decreto de Pedro Molina, Guatemala, 11 Jan. 1830, Collection 20, Central America Political Ephemera, LALTU.

78. Marroquín Rojas, *Morazán y Carrera*, 116; Rafael Carrera, *Memorias del General Carrera, 1837 a 1840*, edited by Ignacio Solís (1906), 15, 24; Marure, *Efemérides*, 55, 73–74; García Granados, *Memorias*, 2:93–95.

79. For examples, see AGCA, B, leg. 1191, exps. 28983 and 28991; see also Manuel Pineda de Mont, comp., *Recopilación de las leyes de Guatemala* (1869–72) 1:772–74; Max Leon Moorhead, "Rafael Carrera of Guatemala: His Life and Times" (1942), 145–46.

80. Juan Gavarrete to Min. de Gobernación, Guatemala, 4 May 1866, AGCA, B, leg. 28607.

81. Robert A. Naylor, "Guatemala: Indian Attitudes toward Land Tenure," *Journal of Inter-American Studies* 9 (October 1967): 626–29, 634; Pineda de Mont, *Recopilación*, 1:658–86; William J. Griffith, "Juan Galindo, Central American Chauvinist," *Hispanic American Historical Review* 40 (1960):28–31; Ignacio Solís, *Memorias de la Casa de Moneda de Guatemala y del desarrollo económico del país*, edited by Julio Castellanos Cambranes, 3 tomes in 4 vols. (1978–79), 3A:663–71; Martínez Peláez, *La patria del crillo*, 410; "Mensaje del gefe de estado de Guatemala, Doctor Mariano Gálvez, al abrir sus sesiones ordinarias de Asam. Lej. de 1837," *El Editor: Periódico de los Tribunales*, 4 Mar. 1837.

82. See for example José Guardiola to the Corregidor of Suchitepéquez, no date,

AGCA, B, leg. 28607, relating to an 1865 case in Suchitepéquez involving ejidos that had been declared "tierras baldías" in 1835 by the "Gefe de Estado."

83. This commission was reactivated, under the direction of surveyor Juan J. Flores, in March of 1850, under a government more sympathetic to Indian interests. *Gaceta de Guatemala*, 19 Apr. 1850.

84. Dunn, *Guatimala*, 24–45.

85. The most complete work on the liberals' encouragement of foreign colonization is Griffith, *Empires*. See also his "Attitudes Toward Foreign Colonization: The Evolution of Nineteenth-Century Guatemalan Immigration Policy," in *Applied Enlightenment: 19th Century Liberalism* (1972), 71–110. For the colonization contracts see Solís, *Casa de Moneda*, 3A:677–706. See also Vela, *Barrundia*, 1:229; Naylor, "British Commercial Relations," 4–7, 13–15, 25, 90–96, 159–61, 183; Robert A. Naylor, "The British Role in Central America Prior to the Clayton-Bulwer Treaty of 1850," *Hispanic American Historical Review* 40 (1960), 364–67; Burdon, ed., *Archives of British Honduras*, 2:150, 179–80, 184–88, 209–14, 224, 239, 255, 259, 266–75, 282; Wayne M. Clegern, *British Honduras, Colonial Dead End, 1859–1900* (1967), 7–9, 167–68; Virgilio Rodríguez Beteta, *La política inglesa en Centroamérica durante el siglo XIX* (1963), 15–18, 22, 48; Thompson, *Narrative*, 71–72, 419–21; and Szaszdi, *Raoul*, 54.

86. Griffith, *Empires*, 32–52, 84–113. Belize merchant Marshall Bennett was most active in pursuing concessions to the extent of curtailing the rights and opportunities of Guatemalan citizens. Bennett was also in partnership with Francisco Morazán in a mahogany cutting scheme between Omoa and the Patook River on the Honduran coast. Mario Rodríguez, *A Palmerstonian Diplomat in Central America, Frederick Chatfield, Esq.* (1964), 127; and Frederick Chatfield to Lord Palmerston, 19 Aug. 1837, Great Britain, Public Record Office, FO 15/19, f. 127, and Chatfield to Palmerston, 5 Nov. 1837, CO 123/54.

87. Griffith, *Empires*, 114–19, 138–50; AGCA, B, leg. 164, exp. 3428, fol. 6; Pineda de Mont, *Recopilación* 1:822–23; Marure, *Efemérides*, 89; *Semanario de Guatemala*, 16 July 1836.

88. Marure, *Efemérides*, 57, 70–71, 80–83, 93; *Boletín Oficial*, 10 Oct. 1837; Holleran, *Church and State*, 121–22; Miller, *La iglecia*, 26–27; Williford, "Las Luces," 35–36.

89. *Incidents of Travel in Central America, Chiapas and Yucatan* (1841) 1:170–71.

90. García Granados, *Memorias* 2:154–61, 177; Dunlop, *Travels*, 185–86, 343; Carrera, *Memorias*, 16; Arlene Eisen, "The Indians in Colonial Spanish America," in Magali Sarfatti, *Spanish Bureaucratic-Patrimonialism in America* (1966), 104; Holleran, *Church and State*, 118–22; Moorhead, "Rafael Carrera," 8.

91. Apartado, "Morazán," 142.

92. Miriam Williford, "The Educational Reforms of Dr. Mariano Gálvez," *Journal of Inter-American Studies* 10 (1968):461–73; Williford, "Las Luces," 35–40; Marure, *Efemérides*, 62, 65–66, 72–73, 87; and Tobar Cruz, *Los montañeses* (1959), 43–44.

93. Speech of J. F. Barrundia, Guatemala, 1 Jan. 1837, in the Biblioteca Nacional de Guatemala, Collection of Hojas Sueltas, cited in Mario Rodríguez, "The Livingston Codes in the Guatemalan Crisis of 1837–1838," in *Applied Enlightenment: 19th Century Liberalism* (1972), 14. Rodríguez's work is an excellent survey of the establishment of the Livingston Codes in Guatemala.

94. Bancroft, *Central America*, 3:102; Williford, "Las Luces," 35–39; García Granados, *Memorias*, 2:92–93; Tobar Cruz, *Los montañeses* (1959), 161; Griffith, *Empires*, 97.

95. A letter published in *El Tiempo*, 11 Aug. 1839, 91–92, told of the horrible liberal prisons, many of them having been established in the confiscated monasteries of the regular religious orders. This letter is reprinted in Ralph Lee Woodward, Jr., "Social Revolution in Guatemala: The Carrera Revolt," in *Applied Enlightenment: 19th Century Liberalism* (1972), 53.

96. *El Siglo de Lafayette*, 15 Dec. 1831.

97. Williford, "Las Luces," 37–40; Tobar Cruz, *Los montañeses* (1959), 54–57; Griffith, *Empires*, 153–54; Rodríguez, *Palmerstonian*, 121; *Semanario de Guatemala*, 6 Oct. 1836; *Boletín Oficial*, 19 Mar.–29 Apr. 1837; "Mensaje del gefe de estado de Guatemala, Doctor Mariano Gálvez, al abrir sus sesiones ordinarias de Asam. Lej. de 1837," *El Editor: Periódico de los Tribunales*, 4 Mar. 1837; subsequent issues of *El Editor* detail statistically the toll the epidemic took in Guatemala; L. Montúfar, *Reseña*, 2:348–54; Carrera, *Memorias*, 16.

3. The Carrera Revolt

1. AGCA, B78.25, leg. 729, exps. 17024, 17026, 17040, and 17046; leg. 739, exp. 17276; *Relación de las exéquias del Excmo. Sr. Presidente Capitán Gral. D. Rafael Carrera, celebrada en la S. I. Catedral de Guatemala el día 17 de abril de 1865* (1865).

2. "José Rafael Carrera: Año del Señor de mil ochocientos catorce, el 26 de Octubre, yo el Doctor Don Antonio Croquer, Cura Rector de la Paroquía de los Remedios y encargado de esta de Candelaria, baptize subcondicione a un niño a quién le echó el agua una persona que no conozco y nació a 25 de este mes, a quién puse por nombre José Rafael hijo legítimo de Simeón Carrera y Juana Turcios, fue su madrina Manuela de la Cruz Carrera, a quién le advertí lo necesario y lo firmó: *Antonio Croquer*. Registrada para la Comandancia General. Diciembre 13 de 1844. *Navarro*," in Carrera, *Memorias* (1906), 19.

3. M. M., *Origen y nacimiento de Carrera*; Moorhead, "Rafael Carrera," 10–11.

4. Manuel Cobos Batres, *Carrera* (n.d.), 10–48. Cobos Batres concludes that Carrera was 10.5 percent Indian, 17.5 percent Negro, and 72 percent Spanish (p. 48); Ramiro Ordóñez Jonama, "Familias fundadoras en el Valle de la Ermita," *Revista de la Academia Guatemalteca de Estudios Genealógicas, Heráldicas e Históricos* 2 (1968):183–86, 223.

5. García Granados, *Memorias*, 2:169; Moorhead, "Rafael Carrera," 13–14; Cobos Batres, *Carrera*, 44–46; and Tobar Cruz, *Los montañeses* (1959), 63.

6. Santos Carrera to Ministro de Relaciones Exteriores, 16 Feb. 1842, AGCA, B, leg. 1395, exp. 32354; Corregidor del Departamento de Suchitepéquez al Ministro de Hacienda, 27 Apr. 1847, AGCA, B, leg. 3633, exp. 85421.

7. Poder Ejecutivo al Presidente de la Dirección de Estudios, Guatemala, 30 Oct. 1834, AGCA, B, leg. 1075, exp. 22758, fol. 2.

8. In 1839 Carrera referred to losing two brothers in the revolution, suggesting that he may have also had a younger brother. Rafael Carrera, "El Brigadier y Comandante General de las Armas del Estado a los Pueblos," *El Tiempo* (Guatemala) 1, no. 18, 22 July 1839.

9. Cobos Batres, *Carrera*, 45–48; Moorhead, "Rafael Carrera," 13–14.

10. Studies on Guatemalan family size in this period are lacking, but large families were common as is evident from the genealogies published in the *Revista de la Academia Guatemalteca de Estudios Genealógicos, Heráldicos e Históricos.*

11. Diputación Provincial to Capitán General Carlos Urrutia, Guatemala, 12 Feb. 1821, *El Editor Constitucional*, 21 Feb. 1821.

12. Martínez Peláez, *La patria del criollo*, 293.

13. Carrera, *Memorias*, 27; Moorhead, "Rafael Carrera," 14, who also cites George Washington Montgomery, *Narrative of a Journey to Guatemala in Central America, in 1838* (1839), 143, as saying that Carrera never rose higher than a corporal in the federal army. But Antonio Batres Jáuregui claims not only that he made the rank of sergeant by 1828, but that he was a captain by 1830, *América Central* 3:168.

14. Moorhead, "Rafael Carrera," 15–16; Alfred de Valois, *Mexique, Havane et Guatemala—notes de voyage* (1861), 321–24; Tobar Cruz, *Los montañeses* (1959), 62–63; Stephens, *Incidents*, 1:224–25.

15. *El Tiempo* 1, no. 30, 11 Sept. 1839, 120. Aqueche suffered harassment at the hands of the Gálvez government after the outbreak of rebellion. Never convicted of any charges, he was released under bond, but arrested and imprisoned later by Morazán, leading to a prolonged illness and death on 4 Sept. 1839.

16. Luis Beltranena Sinibaldi, *Fundación de la República de Guatemala* (1971), 87; Stephens *Incidents*, 1:250; Carrerà, *Memorias*, 18; Dunlop, *Travels*, 195; Tobar Cruz *Los montañeses* (1959), 64; Moorhead, "Rafael Carrera," 16; Miguel Angel García, "Carrera," *Diccionario histórico-enciclopédico de la República de El Salvador* (1948) 11:180–82. García Granados, *Memorias*, 2:169, incorrectly identifies Petrona's father as Pascual "Chúa" Alvarez, an error that a number of subsequent authors have repeated. I can find no basis or corroboration for this error, and, unfortunately, the parish records in Mataquescuintla for this period have been lost. It is possible that her father was named Pascual García Alvarez, but I have found no evidence of this.

17. Valois, *Mexique*, 327–28. Valois adds, "Toutes les dames de la ville vont faire leur cour a madame la présidente, et, pour la distraire, elles lui racontent avec beaucoup de verve les petits scandales de la ville."

18. DeWitt to Forsyth, Guatemala, 24 Oct. 1838, doc. no. 799, Manning, *Diplomatic Correspondence* (1925) 3:154.

19. Stephens, *Incidents*, 1:247.

20. *Illustrated London News*, 26 Feb. 1853.

21. Carrera, *Memorias*, 16–20; see also Moorhead, "Rafael Carrera," 20; Tobar Cruz, *Los montañeses* (1959), 62; Marroquín Rojas, *Morazán y Carrera*, 117; Batres Jáuregui, *América Central*, 3:163.

22. Pérez had been ordered to organize the garrisons that formed the sanitary cordons in the District of Mita on 12 April 1837. Previously, he had been the jefe político of the District of Jalpatagua and Cuajiniquilapa. AGCA, B, leg. 1103, exp. 24508.

23. Carrera, *Memorias*, 19–21; Tobar Cruz, *Los montañeses* (1959), 62.

24. For a more detailed account of this revolt see Marure, *Efemérides*, 91–92; *El Editor: Periódico de los Tribunales*, 16 Mar. 1837; and Dunlop, *Travels* 192–93. The 1815 revolt reportedly resulted from efforts to suppress natives from worshiping traditional deities. For more than two years, according to the corregidor of Quetzaltenango, these Indians and those of San Martín and Concepción had been practicing their pagan religion "opposed totally to our Holy Religion." A newly elected alcalde had arrested some Indians committing idolatrous acts in San Martín on 30 April 1815. A riot resulted, forcing the alcalde to take refuge in the convent. An estimated four thousand Indians then massed on the plaza. Armed with clubs and stones, they assaulted the convent. Apprised of the situation by the village priest, the corregidor sent fifty troops from Quetzaltenango to put down the uprising. Corregidor de Quetzaltenango to Capitán General José de Bustamante, 4 May 1815, AGCA, A, leg. 5502, exp. 47450. The 1837 revolt also had religious overtones. The Indians left at the scene of the conflict a small idol and jug of stones from the nearby stream. They believed that these items with the help of their ancient gods would strike the soldiers with lightning and venomous snakes would come forth from the surrounding woods to attack their enemies. Marure, *Efemérides*, 91–92.

25. A document entitled, "Los principales de Zuñil, Quetzaltenango, al Presidente de la República," no date (c. 1866), relates the history of this community, including the 1837 revolt. AGCA, B, leg. 28606.

26. Rodríguez, *Palmerstonian*, 138–39.

27. Martínez Peláez, "Los motines," 27–47. For a discussion of the development of casticismo and the Esquilache Revolt in Spain, see Jaime Vicens Vives, *Approaches to the History of Spain* (1967), 116–19.

28. Michael Fry, "Política agraria y reacción campesina en Guatemala: la región de La Montaña, 1821–1838," *Mesoamerica* 15 (June 1988):40–42. Native peasant rebellion against Hispanic rule, of course, was not limited to Guatemala, but occurred widely throughout the Spanish Empire. It was common for there to be a strong mystical or religious quality to these revolts, along with their concern for control of community lands. Nineteenth-century peasant rebellions in the Philippines, for example, had characteristics remarkably similar to those in the Carrera revolt of 1837. David R. Sturtevant, *Popular Uprisings in the Philippines, 1840–1940* (1976), 27–40. See also Carol A. Smith, ed., *Guatemalan Indians*.

29. Tobar Cruz, *Los montañeses* (1959), 27.

30. Carrera, *Memorias*, 20–22; Moorhead, "Rafael Carrera," 21–22.

31. Francisco Morazán, "Decreto de 27 de mayo de 1837, San Salvador," *Boletín Oficial*, part 2, 26 June 1837.

32. This account of Carrera's actions is taken from his *Memorias*, 22–23, dictated intermittently to his secretary, Mariano Chaves, mostly in 1863, following his defeat at Cojutepeque while he was reorganizing his army. They were not discovered until near the turn of the century, by Ignacio Solís, who published them with some explanatory notes, in 1906. It may be supposed that the account is not altogether accurate factually, having been dictated a quarter century after the events, and there are some errors of dates in the work, which is clearly confused in places and not always coherent. Yet the basic facts are corroborated by other sources, and Carrera's *Memorias* provide detail and insight into the motives and organization of the revolt.

33. Marure, *Efemérides*, 95–96; Carrera, *Memorias*, 25–29; García Granados, *Memorias*, 168; Moorhead, "Rafael Carrera," 23; Marroquín Rojas, *Morazán y Carrera*, 118–19; Tobar Cruz, *Los montañeses* (1959), 64–65.

34. L. Montúfar, *Reseña*, 2:361, 370–75, 421, reproduces several of these manifestos and relates the actions of the peasants in Santa Rosa, Jalapa, Jalpatagua, Chiquimula and elsewhere. Regarding Carrera's manifestos against foreigners as early as June 1837, see Vela, *Barrundia*, 1:229.

35. Hazel M. B. Ingersoll, "The War of the Mountain, a Study of Reactionary Peasant Insurgency in Guatemala, 1837–1873" (1972) provides a detailed account of the military actions of this struggle.

36. *Boletín Oficial*, Tercera Parte, 12 June 1837.

37. Carrera, *Memorias*, 30–31; Tobar Cruz, *Los montañeses* (1959), 56–57; Marure, *Efemérides*, 97.

38. Carlos Salazar to C. Secretario Jeneral del Supremo Gobierno, Sta. Rosa, 16 June 1837, *El Editor, Periódico de los Tribunales*, 24 June 1837; Tobar Cruz, *Los montañeses* (1959), 55–57.

39. *El Editor: Periódico de los Tribunales*, 1 July 1837.

40. Marure, *Efemérides*, 97; "El Doctor Pedro Molina," *Gaceta de Guatemala*, 29 Sept. 1854.

41. "A los defensores del orden en Santa Rosa el 15 de Junio de 1837," *Boletín Oficial*, part 3, 19 June 1837.

42. *Boletín Oficial*, 21 June 1837. See also the legislature's "Contestación al Mensaje del Gefe del Estado," Guatemala, 21 June 1837, *El Editor: Periódico de los Tribunales*, 1 July 1837.

43. Carrera, *Memorias*, 31–32.

44. Manuel Carrascosa to Carlos Salazar, Mataquescuintla, 18 June 1837, *El Editor: Periódico de los Tribunales*, 24 June 1837.

45. See José Yañez to Carlos Salazar, Mataquescuintla, 19 June 1837, AGCA, B, leg. 16268, exps. 53371 and 53408.

46. Stephens, *Incidents*, 1:226.

47. *Boletín Oficial*, part 3, 23 June 1837.

48. Antonio Larrazábal to Secretario del Gobierno, Guatemala, 11 Feb. 1839, AGCA, B, leg. 1114, exp. 25153; Stephens *Incidents*, 1:178. Although he was widely known simply as "Padre Lobo," this was in actuality Pbo. Francisco González Lobos.

49. Moorhead, "Rafael Carrera," 24.

50. *Boletín Oficial*, 17 July 1837. The Assembly had passed this bill on 22 June.

51. *El Editor: Periódico de los Tribunales*, 13 July 1837, and *Alcance al No. 15*, 20 July 1837. The disease had also spread into the western highlands (Los Altos) by this date, Quetzaltenango having recorded 161 deaths from cholera between April and July.

52. *Boletín Oficial*, part 3, 27 July 1837; Tobar Cruz, *Los montañeses* (1959), 69; AGCA, B119.2, leg. 2522, exp. 57100.

53. Strobeck, "Political Activities," 98, citing *El cuadro veterano del segundo batallón moviliares, a sus compañeros de armas y conciudadanos* (Guatemala: Imprenta del Gobierno del Estado, 26 October 1837), Biblioteca Nacional de Guatemala, Colección Valenzuela, 1837. García Granados, *Memorias*, 2:183, wrote that "el antiguo partido conservador, vencido en [1]829, y destruído con la espulsión de todos los principales miembros de él, con muy pocas excepciones, no tomó parte en la contienda entre opositores y ministriales. Algunos pocos, como los Arrivillagas, Zepedas (parientes estos de Barrundia), mi hermano Joaquín . . . y yo nos afiliamos á la oposición. Otros pocos, especialmente si eran comerciantes, sostenían a Gálvez, condenado a la oposición como inoportuna, injusta, y aún anárquica. En los departamentos, la opinión contra el Gobierno se fué haciendo general."

54. He accused Gálvez of violating articles 171 through 174 of the constitution. *La Oposición*, 12 Sept. 1837.

55. "Voto de oposición a la facultad dada al gobierno para establecer jueces de hecho y de derecho," *La Oposición*, 23 Sept. 1837.

56. *La Oposición*, 1 Sept. 1837. There is a considerable literature on the 1837 split among the liberals in the face of Carrera's revolt. See especially Vela, *Barrundia*, 1:210–51; Batres Jáuregui, *El Doctor Mariano Gálvez*, 75–76; Tobar Cruz, *Los montañeses* (1959), 73–87; García Granados, *Memorias*, 2:183–89; Herrarte, *La unión de Centroamérica*, 125–26; Charles DeWitt to John Forsyth, Guatemala, 13 Jan. 1838, Doc. no. 793, William Ray Manning, ed., *Diplomatic Correspondence of the United States, Inter-American Affairs, 1831–1860*, vol. 3, *Central America, 1831–1850* (1933), 145–46, 148; Marure, *Efemérides*, 97–99; and Rodríguez, "Livingston Codes," 3, 8, 20–22.

57. *La Oposición*, September–December 1837, 1–70, passim.

58. (Guatemala), Prospectus, 8 Nov. 1837 and 3 Jan. 1838, especially reflect these views, although they are evident in other issues as well.

59. García, "Carrera" 10:412.

60. *La Verdad*, 5 Oct. 1837. *La Verdad* was officially edited by Felipe Mejía and Manuel J. Jáuregui, but it regularly published articles by Gálvez and reflected the government position. García, "Carrera" 10:413.

61. *La Verdad*, 29 Nov. 1837.

62. L. Montúfar, *Reseña*, 2:455–57; and Tobar Cruz, *Los montañeses* (1959), 77–79.

63. *Boletín Oficial*, 13 Sept. 1837; L. Montúfar, *Reseña*, 2:425–35.

64. *El Editor: Periódico de los Tribunales*, 1 July 1837 and 13 July 1837.

65. Tobar Cruz, *Los montañeses* (1959), 68. See also the "Informes del Magistrado Ejecutor del Distrito de Chiquimula," of 9 Nov. 1837, AGCA, B, leg. 2522, exps. 57059 and 57060, regarding Carrera's recruiting activities. For a biography of Lorenzana, with many documents of his career, see Manuel Rubio Sánchez, *El Mariscal de Campo José Clara Lorenzana* (1987).

66. *Boletín Oficial*, part 3, 24 Aug. 1837.

67. Coll. 20, Central America Political Ephemera, LALTU.

68. *Alcance al Núm. 7 de La Verdad*, 14 Nov. 1837.

69. *Boletín Oficial*, 30 Oct. 1837.

70. *La Verdad*, 19 Oct. 1837; AGCA, B, leg. 2522, exp. 57104. Hazel M. B. Ingersoll, "The War of the Mountain, a Study of Reactionary Peasant Insurgency in Guatemala, 1837–1873" (1972), 129–42, provides detail on Carrera's growing strength during October through December 1837. See also Carrera, *Memorias*, 40–44.

71. A U.S. racist later observed that race was at the root of the problem. Ephraim G. Squier, *Notes on Central America* (1855), 58, believed that "the only hope of Central America consists in adverting the numerical decline of its white population, and increasing that element in the composition of its people. If not brought about by a judicious encouragement of emigration or an intelligent system of colonization, the geographical position and resources of the country indicate that the end will be attained by those more violent means, which among men, as in the material world, often anticipate the slower operation of natural laws."

72. García Granados, *Memorias*, 2:176–77.

73. AGCA, B, leg. 2522, exps. 57056, 57065, and 57111.

74. AGCA, B, leg. 2522, exps. 57064 and 57068.

75. Griffith, *Empires*, 163, citing Young Anderson to Frederick Chatfield, 28 Oct. 1838, FO 252/6, PRO, London.

76. Strobeck, "Political Activities," 100, citing *Profesión de fé política* (Guatemala: Imprenta del Gobierno, 23 Oct. 1837), in Biblioteca Nacional de Guatemala, Colección Valenzuela, 1837.

77. Rodríguez, "Livingston Codes," 20.

78. Ibid., 22–23, citing the Junta Consultativa, Guatemala, 12 Dec. 1837, in Hojas Sueltas Collection, Biblioteca Nacional de Guatemala. Mariano Gálvez, "El Gefe del Estado a los habitantes del mismo," Guatemala, 13 Dec. 1837, Coll. 20, Central America Political Ephemera, LALTU; and DeWitt to Forsyth, Guatemala, 13 Jan. 1838, Doc. no. 793, Manning, ed., *Diplomatic Correspondence* (1925) 3:145–46.

79. Marure, *Efemérides*, 98–99; García Granados, *Memorias*, 2:189; Tobar Cruz, *Los montañeses* (1959), 87; Chandler, *Aycinena*, 13–23.

80. Marcial Zebadúa and J. J. Aycinena, "Los Secretarios del Gefe del Estado a los habitantes del campo," Guatemala, 15 Dec. 1837, Coll. 20, Central America Political Ephemera, LALTU.

81. García Granados, *Memorias*, 2:190–91.

82. *Boletín Oficial*, part 3, 23 Dec. 1837, 102.

83. *La Nueva Era*, 22 Dec. 1837.

84. Tobar Cruz, *Los montañeses* (1959), 88.

85. Rodríguez, *Palmerstonian*, 141, citing Hall to Frederick Chatfield, no. 8, 29 Dec. 1837, FO 252/18, PRO, London.

86. DeWitt to John Forsyth, Guatemala, 13 Jan. 1838, in Manning, ed., *Diplomatic Correspondence* (1933), Doc. no. 793, 144–45.

87. Griffith, *Empires*, 163–64.

88. *La Nueva Era*, 2 Jan. 1838.

89. Tobar Cruz, *Los montañeses* (1959), 91.

90. *La Oposición*, 4–13 Jan. 1838.

91. E. Martínez López, *Biografía del General Francisco Morazán*, 4th ed. (1966), 196–98.

92. *El Bien Común* (San Salvador), 15 and 31 Jan. 1838.

93. *Boletín Oficial*, part 3, 15 Jan. 1838; García, "Carrera" 10:415.

94. L. Montúfar, *Reseña*, 2:377–559, provides much detail and numerous documents on this period. See also Moorhead, "Rafael Carrera," 26–27; Marure, *Efemérides*, 100; Tobar Cruz, *Los montañeses* (1959), 88–92; and Batres Jáuregui, *América Central* 3:138–40.

95. *Boletín Oficial*, part 3, 20 Jan. 1838.

96. *Boletín Oficial*, part 3, 15 [*sic* 25] Jan. 1838.

97. García Granados, *Memorias*, 2:204–5.

98. L. Montúfar, *Reseña*, 2:561–70; Bancroft *Central America*, 3:128–29; Tobar Cruz, *Los montañeses* (1959), 91–94.

99. Moorhead, "Rafael Carrera," 27; Tobar Cruz, *Los montañeses* (1959), 95–99; L. Montúfar, *Reseña*, 2:572–73; García Granados, *Memorias*, 2:192–93; Full details of the "División de Reforma," signed by Carrera, appear in García, "Carrera" 10:416–17.

100. García, "Carrera" 10:417.

101. Stephens, *Incidents*, 1:231–32.

102. Ibid., 1:231.

103. DeWitt to Forsyth, Guatemala, 10 Feb. 1838, Doc. no. 794, in Manning, ed., *Diplomatic Correspondence* (1933), 148.

104. For other accounts of Carrera's occupation of the capital, see Moorhead, "Rafael Carrera," 28–29; Carrera, *Memorias*, 54–58; Tobar Cruz, *Los montañeses* (1959), 94–99; and Bancroft, *Central America*, 3:130–32.

105. DeWitt to Forsyth, Guatemala, 10 Feb. 1838, Doc. no. 794, in Manning, ed., *Diplomatic Correspondence* (1933), 147; Bancroft, *Central America*, 3:131; Tobar Cruz, *Los montañeses* (1959), 94.

106. L. Montúfar, *Reseña*, 3:9–23; Marure, *Efemérides*, 101; on the Los Altos secession, see Jorge González, "Una historia de Los Altos: Origen, desarrollo y extinción de un movimiento autonomista regional" (1989).

107. García Granados, *Memorias*, 2:219–21; Tobar Cruz, *Los montañeses* (1959), 99.

108. Stephens, *Incidents*, 1:234–35; Bancroft, *Central America*, 3:132, cites Stephens, but also says, "The facts appear in the records of the asamblea."

109. Tobar Cruz, *Los montañeses* (1959), 100–101.

110. Marure, *Efemérides*, 101; "Secretaría de la Asamblea del Estado de Guatemala al Secretario del Gobierno," Guatemala, 4 Feb. 1838, *Boletín Oficial*, 30 Feb. [*sic*] 1838.

111. See, for example, *Alcance al Número 11 del Apéndice*, 4 June 1838.

112. DeWitt to Forsyth, Guatemala, 10 Feb. 1838, Manning, ed., *Diplomatic Correspondence* (1925) 3:148.

113. AGCA, B, leg. 1962, exp. 45282.

114. *Boletín Oficial*, 18 Mar. 1838.

115. *Noticioso Guatemalteco*, 2 Mar. 1838.

116. *El Observador*, 15 Feb.–1 Mar. 1838.

117. García Granados, *Memorias*, 2:228–37; L. Montúfar, *Reseña*, 3:81–82; *Boletín Oficial*, part 3, 28 Feb. 1838.

118. *Boletín Oficial*, 30 Feb. [*sic*] and 18 Mar. 1838.

119. Decree of 12 March 1838, *Boletín Oficial*, 17 Mar. 1838.

120. *Boletín Oficial*, 18 Mar. 1838.

121. Ibid., 30 Mar. 1838; Marure, *Efemérides*, 90; Rodríguez, "Livingston Codes," 24–28.

122. Vela, *Barrundia*, 1:231; Moorhead, "Rafael Carrera," 31–32; *Boletín Oficial*, part 3, 7–15 Mar. 1838; *El Observador*, 1 Mar. 1838; L. Montúfar, *Reseña*, 3:50–51.

123. Stephens, *Incidents*, 1:237.

124. *Boletín Oficial*, part 3, 7 and 15 Mar. 1838; *El Observador*, 16 Mar. 1838.

125. *Boletín Oficial*, 23 Mar. 1838.

4. Morazán

1. Secretario Gral. del Gobierno del Estado de Guatemala al de la Federación, Guatemala, 9 Feb. 1838, AGCA, B, leg. 166, exp. 3470.

2. *El Observador*, 1 Mar. 1838.

3. Montgomery, *Journey to Guatemala*, 174; for requests by the British consul for indemnification for damages from these attacks, see AGCA, B, leg. 1405, exp. 32888; see also Griffith, *Empires*, 152.

4. William J. Griffith, ed., "The Personal Archive of Francisco Morazán,"

Philological and Documentary Studies 2, no. 6 (Middle American Research Institute Publication No. 12, 1977):223–68.

5. García Granados, *Memorias*, 2:246–59, 262–63; AGCA, B, leg. 166, exp. 3470; leg. 3600, exp. 82790; leg. 3618, exp. 84635; Manning, ed., *Diplomatic Correspondence* (1925), 3:151; *Boletín Oficial*, 23–24 Apr. 1838; Carrera, *Memorias*, 39–91; Moorhead, "Rafael Carrera," 32–33; Tobar Cruz, *Los montañeses* (1959), 108–10; L. Montúfar, *Reseña*, 3:105–9.

6. "La muerte del suegro del General Rafael Carrera," *Revista del Departamento de Historia y Hemeroteca Nacional* (San Salvador) 2, no. 3 (August 1939):27–29. This anonymous article mistakenly repeats the error of García Granados, *Memorias*, 2:169, 246, regarding the name of Carrera's father-in-law.

7. García Granados, *Memorias*, 2:246.

8. Tobar Cruz, *Los montañeses* (1959), 162.

9. *Noticioso Guatemalteco*, 17 Mar. 1838.

10. *Boletín Oficial*, 23 Mar. 1838; *El Amigo de Guatemala*, 29 Mar. 1838.

11. Among the leading conservative signers were Mariano Rivera Paz, Manuel Beltranena, M. F. Pavón, José Batres, Bernardo Piñol, M. J. Piñol, Miguel Matheu, Carlos Meany, Rafael Batres, and Miguel Larreynaga. The full petition, with all forty-nine signatures, is in Martínez López, *Morazán*, 198–99.

12. *El Amigo de Guatemala*, 18 Apr. 1838.

13. *El Amigo de Guatemala*, 18 Apr. 1838; Tobar Cruz, *Los montañeses* (1959), p. 111.

14. The full petition, with signatures, is in Martínez López, *Morazán*, 199–201. Among the most prominent conservatives signing this petition were Luis Batres, Pedro Aycinena, Juan J. Piñol, M. J. Piñol, Juan José Echeverría, Carlos R. Kleé, Juan Matheu, Mateo Beltranena, Juan José Aycinena, Cayetano Lara Pavón, J. Rafael Ayau, Xavier Aycinena, Juan Nájera, José Nájera, Francisco Pavón, Tadeo Piñol, and Carlos A. Meany. A number of moderate liberals who had been associated with the Gálvez administration also signed, led by Alejandro Marure.

15. Francisco Morazán a los Ciudadanos Diputados Secretarios de la Asamblea Legislativa, Cuartel General en Guatemala, 17 Apr. 1838, in ibid., 158–59.

16. Decree of 17 Apr. 1838, ibid., 159–60.

17. *Boletín Oficial*, 24 Apr. 1838.

18. DeWitt to Forsyth, Guatemala City, 30 June 1838, Doc. 795, in Manning, ed., *Diplomatic Correspondence* (1925), 3:151.

19. García Granados, *Memorias*, 2:248.

20. L. Montúfar, *Reseña*, 3:96, 131. Actually, it never went into effect, since Carrera subsequently abrogated it before it was implemented; *Boletín Oficial*, 25 May 1838.

21. Rodríguez, *Palmerstonian*, 156–57; García Granados, *Memorias*, 2:260–61.

22. García Granados, *Memorias*, 2:249–63; Ingersoll, "War," 172–75; Tobar Cruz, *Los montañeses* (1959), 111–12.

23. Montgomery, *Journey to Guatemala*, 35.

24. Stephens, *Incidents* 1:241.

25. *Boletín Oficial*, 25 May and 10 June 1838.

26. *Boletín Oficial*, 16 July 1838. This Congress was presided over by Gerardo Barrios, one of the most important long-term Morazanistas in El Salvador. Rodríguez, reflecting Chatfield's sentiments, believed this act was intended to bring Nicaragua back into the union, but it failed to do so. Rodríguez, *Palmerstonian*, 157.

27. Strobeck, "Political Activities," 103–4.

28. Pineda de Mont, *Recopilación*, 1:69.

29. Rodríguez, *Palmerstonian*, 159.

30. AGCA, B, leg. 2523, exp. 57171; L. Montúfar, *Reseña*, 3:135, 204; Tobar Cruz, *Los montañeses* (1959), 133; Montgomery, *Journey to Guatemala*, 147–48; DeWitt to Forsyth, Guatemala, 24 July 1838, Doc. no. 797, and Guatemala, 6 Oct. 1838, Doc. no. 799, in Manning, ed., *Diplomatic Correspondence* (1925), 3:153–54.

31. Chatfield to Palmerston, No. 50, 16 Aug. 1838, FO 252/19, quoted in Rodríguez, *Palmerstonian*, 149.

32. Stephens, *Incidents*, 1:242.

33. *Boletín Oficial*, 16 July 1838.

34. AGCA, B, leg. 3610, exp. 84142, fol. 1v; *Boletín Oficial* 16 July 1838; Marure, *Efemérides*, 105–6.

35. "El Sr. D. Mariano Rivera Paz, Apuntes biográficos," *Gaceta de Guatemala*, 13 June 1851.

36. AGCA, B, leg. 1417, exp. 33137; leg. 3618, exp. 84623.

37. Edgar Escobar Medrano, *Mariano Rivera Paz y su época* (1982).

38. Mariano Rivera Paz, *Memoria que presentó a la Asamblea Constituyente en su primera sesión el Consejero Gefe de Estado de Guatemala, por medio del Secretario del Despacho de Relaciones* (31 May 1839); *Boletín Oficial*, 26 July 1838.

39. *Boletín Oficial*, 26 July–5 Aug. 1838.

40. Ibid., 24 Dec. 1838.

41. Ibid., part 3, 22 Aug. 1838.

42. Marure, *Efemérides*, 106–7; AGCA, B, leg. 3607, exp. 83853.

43. DeWitt to Forsyth, Guatemala, 6 Oct. 1838, Doc. no. 799, Manning, ed., *Diplomatic Correspondence* (1933), 155; AGCA, B, leg. 3652, exp. 86106; Ingersoll, "War," 186–87.

44. *Exhortación cristiana que el Vicario capitular de este arzobispado, dirije á los pueblos que engañados y deducidos hacen al guerra a sus hermanos; y á los demas pueblos pacíficos del Estado.* Different portions of this pamphlet were reprinted in L. Montúfar, *Reseña*, 3:212–13, and Tobar Cruz, *Los montañeses* (1959), 150–51.

45. "Oración fúnebre que en las solmnes exéquias que se hicieron el dia 14 de setiembre en esta S. I. C. por todos los valientes militares que fallecieron en la accion de Villa-Nueva, librada contra Carrera, dijo el presbítero Bernardo Piñol y Aycinena," L. Montúfar, *Reseña*, 3:216–21. Montúfar, pointing to the contradic-

tions among the clergy, also published a sermon praising Carrera given from the same pulpit a month later by Father José Telésforo Paul, later bishop of Panama.

46. *Memoria sobre la insurrección de Santa Rosa y Mataquescuintla en Centro América, comparada con la que estalló en Francia, en el año de 1790, en los departamentos de la Vendée* (1838). This rare pamphlet was reprinted in serial form in *La Revista, Organo de la Academia Guatemalteca de la Lengua*, 3d series, 1, nos. 24 and 25, (16 June and 1 July 1889):425–28, 441–44; 2, nos. 1–3, (1 and 16 Aug. and 1 Sept. 1889):13–16, 30–32, 46–47.

47. *Observaciones sobre la intervencion que ha tenido el ex-Presidente de Centro-América, General Francisco Morazán, en los negocios políticos de Guatemala, durante las convulsiones que ha sufrido este Estado, de mediados de 837 á principios de 839* (1839). For studies of Marure's career, see Weaver, "Liberal Historian," and Peláez Almengor, "Marure."

48. Martínez López, *Morazán*, 167.

49. Marure, *Efemérides*, 109–10; Rodríguez, *Palmerstonian*, 160, 171.

50. Rodríguez, *Palmerstonian*, 169, quoting Chatfield to Palmerston, 4 Oct. 1838, FO 15/20.

51. Stephens to Forsyth, Guatemala, 25 Dec. 1838, Doc. no. 800, Manning, ed., *Diplomatic Correspondence* (1933), 157.

52. AGCA, B, leg. 153, exp. 3260, fol. 14; leg. 1412, exp. 33009; leg. 3607, exp. 85853; leg. 3652, exp. 86106; L. Montúfar, *Reseña*, 3:204; Marure, *Efemérides*, p. 111; Carrera, *Memorias*, 86–87; Pedro Zamora Castellanos, *Vida militar de Centro América* (1924), 167; Bancroft, *Central America*, 3:135–37.

53. *El Tiempo*, 26 Aug. 1840.

54. AGCA, B, leg. 2437, exp. 51825; Víctor Jérez, "General Don Carlos Salazar," in *San Salvador y sus hombres*, 2d ed., edited by Academia Salvadoreña de la Historia (1967), 98.

55. Statement signed by Mariano Rivera Paz, Pedro Nolasco Arriaga, and Francisco Javier Aguirre, Guatemala, 30 Jan. 1839, AGCA, B, leg. 2437, exp. 51821.

56. Moorhead, "Rafael Carrera," 37–38; L. Montúfar, *Reseña*, 3:240–41.

57. *El Tiempo*, 9 Mar. 1839. A negative response by J. J. Aycinena appeared in the same issue.

58. Chamberlain, *Morazán*, 37–38; Rodríguez, *Palmerstonian*, 176–78.

59. AGCA, B, leg. 1114, exp. 25153.

60. AGCA, B, leg. 1196, exp. 29349.

61. AGCA, B, leg. 214, exp. 4941. fol. 722.

62. Rodríguez, *Palmerstonian*, 181; Jefe Político de Chiquimula, 6 Mar. 1839, AGCA, B, leg., 2524, exp. 57215.

63. Rodríguez, *Palmerstonian*, 178.

64. Francisco Ferrera to Municipalidad de Guatemala, Gracias, 11 Mar. 1839; Municipalidad de Guatemala to C. Francisco Ferrera, General en Gefe del ejército aliado pacificador de Centroamérica, Guatemala, n.d., *El Tiempo*, 27 Mar. 1839.

65. Apartado, *Morazán*, 155.

66. *Pronunciamiento del General Rafael Carrera y del ejército de la Constitución*

del Estado de Guatemala (1839), in Coll. 20, Central America Political Ephemera, LALTU.

67. *El Tiempo*, 23 Apr. 1839; Rodríguez, *Palmerstonian*, 181–86.

68. *El Tiempo*, 2 June 1839; *Disposición de Rafael Carrera, Comandante de los Pueblos de Mita* (Guatemala, 13 April 1839), Coll. 20, Central America Political Ephemera, LALTU; Carrera, *Memorias*, 87; Moorhead, "Rafael Carrera," 39; L. Montúfar, *Reseña*, 3:398–403; Tobar Cruz, *Los montañeses* (1959), 102, 125.

69. AGCA, B, leg. 3600, exp. 82810.

70. Stephens, *Incidents*, 1:220.

71. "La verdad desnuda," *El Informador* (Comayagua), 1 May 1839, reprinted in *El Tiempo*, 12 June 1839.

72. Ferrera to Carrera, Yoro, 2 May 1839, *El Tiempo*, 21 June 1839.

73. Chamberlain, *Morazán*, 38; Rodríguez, *Palmerstonian*, 181–82; Marure, *Efemérides*, 113–14; Arturo Mejía Nieto, *Morazán, presidente de la desaparecida república centroamericana* (1947), 153–54.

74. Moorhead, "Rafael Carrera," 42; Marure, *Efemérides*, 114. The assembly subsequently approved Carrera's commission. AGCA, B, leg. 214, exp. 4941, fols. 244–45; *Actas de la Asamblea Constituyente y Acuerdos Oficiales del Gobierno*, no. 5 (19 Oct. 1839), 23.

75. Decreto no. 4, Guatemala, 17 Apr. 1839, in Coll. 20, Central America Political Ephemera, LALTU.

76. Decreto no. 5, 18 Apr. 1839, Coll. 20, Central America Political Ephemera, LALTU; AGCA, B, leg. 1183, exp. 28515.

77. *El Tiempo*, 3 May 1839.

78. "Circular mediante la cual se informó a los gobiernos de los Estados de Los Altos, Honduras, Nicaragua y Costa Rica, que el día 13 el Comandante de Mita, Rafael Carrera, quien se pronunció en armas el 24 de marzo, ocupó la capital e inmediatamente restableció en el poder al Consejero-Jefe de Estado Mariano Rivera Paz, quien había dispuesto el 30 de enero, por el Gral. Francisco Morazán," AGCA, B, leg. 2437, exp. 51825; *El Tiempo*, 3 May 1839.

79. *Gaceta de Guatemala*, 1 June 1855; Rodríguez, *Palmerstonian*, 182–84.

80. "Circular dirigida a los gobiernos de los Estados del Salvador, los Altos, Honduras, Nicaragua y Costarrica por el Secretario del de Guatemala, en que se inserta la contestación dada al vice-presidente de la República á la última invitación que ha hecho para que se reuna la Convención," 30 Apr. 1839, *El Tiempo*, 14 May 1839.

81. Arriaga al Secretario General del despacho del Supremo Gobierno del Estado del Salvador, Guatemala, 26 Apr. 1839, *El Tiempo*, 14 May 1839.

82. "Tranquilidad pública," *El Tiempo*, 14 May 1839.

83. Marure, *Efemérides*, 86; *El Tiempo*, 24 May 1839.

84. Rodríguez, *Palmerstonian*, 182.

85. *Alcance al Número 6 de El Tiempo*, 4 May 1839.

86. AGCA, B, leg. 1413, exp. 33005; Marure, *Efemérides*, 114. Guatemala

signed similar treaties with El Salvador on 4 July, Nicaragua on 24 July, and Costa Rica on 1 August. They were all ratified within the year. Pineda de Mont, *Recopilación*, 1:382–94. Similar treaties were signed among the other states, including a treaty between Los Altos and El Salvador. *Convención provisional de los Estados de Centro-América, formada a concecuencia de la disolución del Gobierno Federal y en virtud de los convenios y tratados que se publican reunidos y por su orden, para mejor conocimiento del público* (1839).

87. Rodríguez, *Palmerstonian*, 190–91.

88. Ibid., 191.

89. AGCA, B, leg. 2525, exp. 57308.

90. Carrera to Durán, Guatemala, 4 May 1839, AGCA, B, leg. 2437, exp. 5187.

91. Petrona García de Carrera to Durán, Guatemala, 4 May 1839, AGCA, B, leg. 2437, exp. 51828.

92. Arriaga to Carrera, Guatemala, 7 May 1839, AGCA, B, leg. 2437, exp. 51828.

93. *El Tiempo*, 14 May 1839.

94. Valdés to Durán, Santa Ana, 13 May 1839, AGCA, B, leg. 2525, exp. 57308. Valdés left Chiquimula the night of 9 May.

5. Consolidation

1. Arrivillaga, Asturias, Aycinena, Barrundia, Batres, Cambronero, Nájera, Pavón, Piñol, Tejada, Urruela, and Váldez. Six other surnames—Benítez, Gorriz, Romá, Rubio, Taboada, and Vidaurre—appear on the 1799 and 1839 lists, but not on the 1823 list. Eighty-six individuals, representing seventy different family surnames, appeared on the 1799 list; 115 individuals, representing seventy-nine family surnames, appeared on the 1823 list; and 119 individuals, representing eighty-one family names, appeared on the 1839 list. Twenty-one of the family surnames appear on both the 1799 and 1823 lists, and thirty-six on both the 1823 and 1839 lists. There are forty-four different family surnames that appear only on the 1799 list; thirty-four appear only on the 1823 list; and forty-two appear only on the 1839 list. AGCA, Lista de Comerciantes y Hacendados de esta Capital, 12 June 1799, A, leg. 6, exp. 110, fols. 8–9; Lista de los Yndividuos Comerciantes y Hazendados que componen el gremio consular, 22 Dec. 1823, B, leg. 1391, exp. 32111; Lista de los comerciantes y hacendados que á juicio de los que suscriben pueden ser nombrados por el Supremo Gobierno para efectuar la reorganización del Consulado Mercantil, 25 Aug. 1839, B, leg. 214, exp. 4941, fols. 200–206.

2. Dunlop, *Travels*, 317, 334–35.

3. *Actas de la Asamblea*, 7 Aug. 1839, 1; *El Tiempo*, 5 June 1839. Juan José Aycinena was elected first vice-president and Miguel Larreinaga second vice-president. José Mariano Vidaurre, Manuel F. Pavón, José Domingo Estrada and Manuel Sala-

zar were elected secretaries. For a table of political officials of the state see *El Tiempo*, 28 June 1839, supplement.

4. *Discurso pronunciado en el acto de la instalación de la Asamblea Constituyente del Estado, por su primer presidente el Sr. Presbítero Fernando Antonio Dávila* (1839).

5. Rivera Paz, *Memoria* (31 May 1839).

6. *El Tiempo*, 5 June 1839; AGCA, B, leg. 214, exp. 4941, fols. 11, 242; and *Actas de la Asamblea*, 27 Aug. 1839, 8–9.

7. "Felicitación del General de Brigada Rafael Carrera a la Asamblea Constituyente del Estado," AGCA, B, leg. 1411, exp. 32977; *El Tiempo*, 14 June 1839. The message was read to the assembly on 13 June. *Actas de la Asamblea*, 19 Oct. 1839.

8. *Dictamen de la comisión de negocios eclesiásticos de la Asamblea Constituyente, sobre el reestablecimiento de las Ordenes Regulares* (1839), Coll. 20, Central America Political Ephemera, LALTU. A petition with more than eight hundred signatures had been presented to the assembly on 11 June requesting these actions. *Actas de la Asamblea*, 27 Aug. 1839, 10, and 19 Oct. 1839, 21–22; *El Tiempo*, 21 June–15 July 1839; Pineda de Mont, *Recopilación*, 1:242–43, 273.

9. *Actas de la Asamblea*, 19 Oct. 1839, 24.

10. *El Tiempo*, 10 July 1839, supplement. See also the editorial "Crédito Público," on 11 Aug. 1839, calling for Hamiltonian measures and annual budgeting to restore the public credit, policies generally followed during the Carrera years. See also *Actas de la Asamblea*, 19 Oct. 1839, 21–22.

11. "Rafael Carrera, General de Brigada de las armas del Estado, á los pueblos que lo componen," *El Tiempo*, 18 July 1839.

12. AGCA, B, leg. 214, exp. 4941, fols. 15–16; *El Tiempo*, 10 July 1839.

13. Those elected, all by easy margins over numerous other candidates, were: Damaso Angulo, first alcalde; Pedro Aycinena, second alcalde; Manuel Rubio, third alcalde; Felipe Prado, eighth regidor; José Nájera, ninth regidor; Alejo Vaca, tenth regidor; and José María Palomo, síndico. *El Tiempo*, July 1839.

14. *El Tiempo*, 15 Aug 1839; Woodward, *Class Privilege*, xvi–xvii, 55–127 passim. Regarding problems of currency, see Manuel F. Pavón, "Informe del Consulado sobre las monedas del Sur en circulación," Guatemala, 20 de junio de 1840," *El Tiempo*, 28 June 1840 and 5 Dec. 1840, and Chapter 20, below.

15. Pineda de Mont, *Recopilación*, 1:504–11; *El Tiempo*, 11 Oct., 3 Nov., and 14 Nov. 1839.

16. AGCA, B, leg. 214, exp. 4941, fol. 607; *Gaceta Oficial*, 10 June 1842.

17. *El Tiempo*, 11 Dec. 1839.

18. Pineda de Mont, *Recopilación*, 2:263.

19. *Gaceta Extraordinaria*, Guatemala 14 Aug. 1841.

20. *El Tiempo*, 21 Dec. 1839. This declaration is discussed in the following chapter.

21. L. Montúfar, *Reseña*, 3:381–82; *El Tiempo*, 26 Nov. 1840.

22. See *El Tiempo*, 7 Dec. 1839, for a review of the assembly's accomplishments.

23. Members of this commission were F. Vidaurre, José Orantes, Alejandro

Marure, Andrés Andreu, and M. F. Pavón. "Dictamen á la Comisión de organización provisional sobre establecer un régimen de protección y fomento en favor de los indios," *El Tiempo*, 2 Aug. 1839; the decree of 16 Aug. appeared on 30 Aug. 1839; Jorge Skinner-Klée, *Legislación indigenista de Guatemala* (1954), 18–30. Another comparison of the liberal and conservative approaches to the Indians of Guatemala is found in Rodríguez, "Livingston Codes," 30.

24. R. L. Woodward, Jr., "Liberalism, Conservatism, and the Response of the Peasants of La Montaña to the Government of Guatemala, 1821–1850," *Plantation Society in the Americas* 1 (1979):109–29; and Keith Miceli, "Rafael Carrera: Defender and Promoter of Peasant Interests in Guatemala, 1837–1848," *The Americas* 31 (1974):72–95.

25. "Chismes," *El Tiempo*, 5 July 1839.

26. "Tolerancia," *El Tiempo*, 5 July 1839. An example of such poems is found in ibid., *Alcance al Num. 14*:

> No toman la lanza, dices:
> dices que no son valientes
> los moderados. Pues mientes
> por ojos, boca y narices!
> Voto á tal, que no me atices,
> que todos los liberales
> como niños en pañales
> tenies de morir de miedo,
> con solo mover un dedo los lanceros nacionales.

27. "El Brigadier y Comandante General de las Armas del Estado: Á los pueblos," *El Tiempo*, 22 July 1839.

28. Carrera to Secretario General del Gobno. del Estado de Guatemala, Guatemala, 15 July 1839, AGCA, B, leg. 214, exp. 4941, fols. 246–47.

29. "Desinterés," *El Popular*, 3 Aug. 1839.

30. *El Tiempo*, 11 Sept. 1839.

31. Rafael Carrera to Joaquín Durán, Antigua, 10 Nov. 1839, ibid., 20 Nov. 1839; 27 Nov. 1839.

32. *Colección de las ordenes de observancia general emitadas por la Asamblea Constituyente del Estado de Guatemala en los años 1839, 1840, 1841 y 1842* (1842): 9; *El Tiempo*, 7 Jan. 1840.

33. AGCA, B, leg. 214, exp. 4941, fols. 118–20; Ernesto Chinchilla Aguilar, *Historia y tradiciones de la ciudad de Amatitlán* (1961), 98.

34. *El Tiempo*, 6 Dec. 1839. The Council was composed of Francisco Xavier Aguirre, Mariano Aycinena, José Mariano Vidaurre, Marcial Zebadúa, Miguel Larreinaga, and Rafael Urruela. *El Tiempo*. 7 Dec. 1839.

35. *El Tiempo*, 7 Dec. 1839.

36. Stephens, *Incidents*, 1:203.

37. Ibid., 1:249.

38. Rodríguez, *Palmerstonian*, 179–84.

39. AGCA, B, leg. 1411, exp. 32978, fol. 37v.

40. AGCA, B, leg. 2437, exp. 51843, fol. 7.

41. AGCA, B, leg. 2524, exp. 57287.

42. AGCA, B, leg. 1411, exp. 32981, fol. 92.

43. Marure, *Efemérides*, 119. For a detailed account of the role of Trinidad Cabañas in these campaigns, see José Reina Valenzuela, *José Trinidad Cabañas: Estudio biográfico* (1984), 73–95.

44. AGCA, B, leg. 1411, exp. 32981, fols. 1v and 38.

45. Carrera to Rivera Paz, 9 Sept. 1839, AGCA, B, leg. 2437, exp. 51855; Ministro Gral. del Gobno. de Guatemala al Gobno. de Honduras, Guatemala, 14 Sept. 1839, AGCA, B, leg. 1411, exp. 32981, fol. 35; *El Tiempo*, 18 Sep. 1839; *Circular a los Gobiernos de los Estados*, Guatemala, 19 Sep. 1839, Coll. 20, Central America Political Ephemera, LALTU.

46. AGCA, B, leg. 1411, exp. 32981, fol. 36v.

47. Rivera Paz to Joaquín Durán, Jutiapa, 16 Sept. 1839, AGCA, B, leg. 221; exp. 50009; *El Tiempo*, 14 Sept. 1839.

48. *El Tiempo*, 25 Sept. 1839.

49. *Circular a los Gobiernos de los Estados*, Guatemala, 19 Sep. 1839, Coll. 20, Central America Political Ephemera, LALTU.

50. "Rafael Carrera á los salvadoreños," General Headquarters, Jutiapa, 20 Sept. 1839, *El Tiempo*, 9 Oct. 1839.

51. "El Presidente del Estado de Honduras á sus habitantes," Juticalpa, 21 Sept. 1839, reprinted in *El Tiempo*, 7 Nov. 1839.

52. *El Tiempo*, 4 Oct. 1839.

53. Marure, *Efemérides*, 63, 119–20.

54. Rodríguez, *Palmerstonian*, 202–4.

55. *El Tiempo*, 16 Oct. 1839, quoting (in translation) the *Belize Advertiser* of 21 Sept. 1839.

56. Apartado, "Morazán," 177, 420.

57. AGCA, B, leg. 2437, exp. 51843.

58. Rodríguez, *Palmerstonian*, 205–6.

59. AGCA, B, leg. 1411, exp. 32981, fol. 42; leg. 1413, exp. 33006, fol. 11.

60. Joaquín Durán to Rafael Carrera, Guatemala, 21 Oct. 1839, with decree of Rivera Paz of same date accompanying it, AGCA, B, leg. 2437, exp. 51843, fol. 31; *El Tiempo*, 24 Oct. 1839 and 7 Nov. 1839.

61. *El Tiempo*, 30 Nov. 1839; Mónico Bueso, Ministro de Relaciones Interiores y Exteriores del Sup. Gobno. del Estado de Honduras, to Sr. Secretario del Supremo Gobno. del Estado de Nicaragua, Juticalpa, Honduras, 18 Dec. 1839, *NRO. 15* (Ministerio General del Supremo Gobierno del Estado de Nicaragua, León, 8 Jan. 1840), in Coll. 20, Central America Political Ephemera, LALTU; Marure, *Efemérides*, 121.

62. Rodríguez, *Palmerstonian*, 213.

63. "Proclama del General Carrera á sus soldados," Guatemala, 5 Dec. 1839, *El Tiempo*, 11 Dec. 1839.

64. Ibid.

65. Rodríguez, *Cádiz Experiment*, 126.

66. Woodward, *Class Privilege*, 96–97, 126.

67. "Opinion pública," *El Ciudadano*, Quetzaltenango, 21 May 1836.

68. AGCA, B, leg. 4126, exp. 92817, fol. 12; Marure, *Efemérides*, 101; *Boletín Oficial*, 30 Feb. 1838; L. Montúfar, *Reseña*, 3:9–23; Ingersoll, "War," 208–22.

69. Marure, *Efemérides*, 111.

70. *Mensaje del Gobierno Provisional a la Asamblea Constituyente de Los Altos al abrir sus sesiones en la Ciudad de Totonicapan 26 de diciembre de 1838* (1838), Arturo Taracena Collection, Casa de Cultura, Quetzaltenango.

71. Apartado, "Morazán," 399–401.

72. AGCA, B, leg. 1411, exp. 32977, fols. 4–16.

73. Ratifications were exchanged in Quetzaltenango on 6 November 1839. *Gaceta del Gobierno de Los Altos*, Quetzaltenango, 7 Nov. 1839; Rodríguez, *Palmerstonian*, p. 185.

74. *El Tiempo*, 15 Aug. 1839.

75. Pedro N. Arriaga to the Secretario Gral. del Gobno. de Los Altos, Guatemala, 2 Aug. 1839, *El Tiempo*, 11 Aug. 1839; the Los Altos government declared its right to set its own tariff rates on 10 July, and on 18 July its assembly decreed certain changes in the tariffs. *El Tiempo*, 29 July 1839 and 2 Aug. 1839.

76. *El Tiempo*, 19 July 1839.

77. Ibid., 3 Aug. and 11 Aug. 1839.

78. *El Popular*, 11 Aug. 1839.

79. Ibid., 14 Sep. 1839. From Guatemala, *El Tiempo* kept up a constant attack on Los Altos sovereignty and answered the attacks of *El Popular* in kind.

80. Marure, *Efemérides*, 120; Ingersoll, "War," 217–20.

81. Manuel Gálvez, Jefe Político of Chimaltenango, to Ministro de Gobernación del S. G., Chimaltenango, 12 Oct. 1839, *El Tiempo*, 16 Oct. 1839.

82. *El Tiempo*, 31 Oct. 1839.

83. Rodríguez, *Palmerstonian*, 215–24.

84. *El Tiempo*, 11 Dec. 1839.

85. Mariano Rivera Paz, *Informe dado a la Asamblea Constituyente por el Presidente del Estado de Guatemala, sobre los sucesos ocurridos desde que la misma Asamblea suspendió sus sesiones, y sobre el estado en que se halla la Administración Pública* (14 July 1840), 2–3; the treaty is published in *El Tiempo*, 28 Dec. 1839.

86. Rodríguez, *Palmerstonian*, 221.

87. Rivera Paz, *Informe* (14 July 1840), 3.

88. Rivera Paz, *Informe* (14 July 1840), 3; *El Tiempo*, 16 Feb. 1840; AGCA, B, leg. 2437, exp. 51912.

89. "Proclama del General R. Carrera á sus conciudadanos de los otros estados," Guatemala, 20 Jan. 1840, *El Tiempo*, 31 Jan. 1840.

90. AGCA, B, leg. 2437, exp. 51912; *El Tiempo*, 22 Jan 1840.

91. Rodríguez, *Palmerstonian*, 222.

92. AGCA, B, leg. 1413, exp. 33014; B, leg. 1192, exp. 29053; *El Tiempo*,

31 Jan. 1840; *Parte Oficial*, 28 Jan. 1840, in Coll. 20, Central America Political Ephemera, LALTU; Rivera Paz, *Informe* (14 July 1840), 3–4; Marure, *Efemérides*, 122; Doroteo Monterrosa to Secretario del Sup. Gobno. del Estado, Santo Domingo, 29 Jan. 1840, *Noticia Interesante* [Guatemala, 1839], Arturo Taracena Collection, Benson Latin American, Collection, University of Texas, Austin (hereinafter cited as BLAC), no. 9021.

93. *El Tiempo*, 4 Feb. 1840.

94. Decree of Rafael Carrera, Quetzaltenango, 29 Jan. 1840, *El Tiempo*, 7 Feb. 1840.

95. "El General en Gefe del Ejército del Estado a los Pueblos de los Departamentos de Los Altos," Quetzaltenango, 31 Jan. 1840, *El Tiempo*, 16 Feb. 1840.

96. *El Tiempo*, 4 Mar. and 20 Aug. 1840; *Gaceta Oficial*, 5 Oct. 1842.

97. "Rafael Carrera a los pueblos de los departamentos de Los Altos," Quetzaltenango, 9 Feb. 1840, *El Tiempo*, 25 Feb. 1840.

98. *El Presidente de Guatemala a los Habitantes del Estado*, Guatemala, 5 Feb. 1840, *hojas sueltas* collection, Hemeroteca of the AGCA.

99. *El Tiempo*, 21 Feb. 1840.

100. Stephens, *Incidents*, 2:108–9; *El Tiempo*, 21 Feb. 1840.

101. Marure, *Efemérides*, 123; Rivera Paz, *Informe* (14 July 1840), 5; Reina Valenzuela, *Cabañas*, 87–91.

102. Cruz to Sr. Ministro del Supremo Gobierno, Jalpatagua, 5 Feb. 1840, in *Aviso al público*, Guatemala, 7 Feb. 1840, *hojas sueltas* collection, Hemeroteca of the AGCA.

103. Decree of Francisco Morazán, Cojutepeque, 14 Jan. 1840, *El Tiempo*, 7 Feb. 1840.

104. Apartado, "Morazán," 142:

> El criminal Morazán
> Al cielo venganzas justas
> El Nerón, el Dioclesiano,
> Tantas víctimas augustas
> El asesino tirano
> Que ha inmolado la ambición
> Del inocente Durán
> De su negro corazón
> Contra quien pidiendo están
> Con felonias injustas.

105. AGCA, B, leg. 2437, exp. 52018.

106. Tobar Cruz, *Los montañeses* (1959), 137; Rodríguez, *Palmerstonian*, 229, notes that Carrera's "plans bear the mark of a professional" and suggests that Chatfield may have "worked out the defense strategy," although there is no documentary evidence to support that contention.

107. *El Coronel V. Cruz a los Guatemaltecos*, Guatemala, 17 Mar. 1840, *hojas sueltas* collection, Hemeroteca of the AGCA.

108. L. Montúfar, *Reseña*, 3:461–64; Ingersoll, "War," 242–44; Stephens, *Incidents*, 2:109–13; Tobar Cruz, *Los montañeses* (1959), 137–39; Chamberlain, *Morazán*, 40. For Carrera's own accounts of the battle, see AGCA, B, leg. 2438, exps. 52064 and 52092; Carrera, *Memorias*, 88–90; and in the *hojas sueltas* collection, Hemeroteca of the AGCA, *Parte circunstanciado de la acción de los dias 18 y 19 de marzo, que ha sido dirigido al Gobierno por el General en Gefe del Ejército del Estado* (Guatemala, 23 March 1840); Joaquín Durán, *Parte Oficial*, 19 Mar 1839; *Listas de los individuos actuados, que estaban presentes el 17 de Marzo en estas cárceles, y fueron sacados por la tropa de Morazán*; and *Colección de algunos de los interesantes documentos que se encontraron en los equipajes tomados en la acción de los días 18 y 19 de marzo. Se publican de orden del gobierno para conocimiento del público de los Estados aliados* [1840]; Mariano Rivera Paz, Proclamation, Guatemala, 21 Mar. 1840.

109. *El Senador que ejerce el S.P.E. del Estado de Nicaragua, a los habitantes del mismo*, León, 24 Mar. 1840, and M. Quijano, *A los valientes vencedores en el Potrero*, León, 30 Mar. 1840, *hojas sueltas* collection, Hemeroteca of the AGCA.

110. Francisco Zelaya, "Proclama del Presidente del Estado de Honduras a las tropas del mismo," Tegucigalpa, 31 Mar. 1840, in Apartado, "Morazán," 185–86.

111. See, for example, the letter from Máximo Orellana to Francisco Ferrera, Libertad, 2 Apr. 1840, *Redactor* (Comayagua) 15 Sept. 1840, reprinted in *El Tiempo*, 20 Oct. 1840.

112. The list submitted by Morazán in his request for asylum included many of the leading liberals of the isthmus: Pedro Molina, Carlos Salazar, Diego Vigil, Miguel Alvarez Castro, Joaquín Rivera, Gerardo Barrios, Doroteo Vasconcelos, Antonio and Bernardo Rivera Cabezas, Felipe Molina, José Trinidad Cabañas, Agustín Guzmán, Nicolás Angulo, José María Silva, José Miguel Saravía, Manuel Irungaray, Máximo Orellana, Isidro Menéndez, Enrique Rivas, Indalecio Cordero, Máximo Cordero, Manuel Antonio Lazo, José de Jesús Osejo, Domingo Asturias, José María Tacho, Manuel Merino, Rafael Padilla, Guillermo Quintanilla, José Antonio Milla, Dámaso Sousa, José María Prado, José Rosales, José María Cañas, José Molina, Juan Orozco, Felipe Bulnes, José Antonio Ruiz, and Francisco Gravil. Apartado, "Morazán," 187–89.

113. Min. Gral. del Gbno. de Guatemala to Asamblea Constituyente, 3 Aug. 1840, AGCA, B, leg. 225, exp. 5082, fol. 3.

114. Stephens, *Incidents*, 2:203–9; García, "Carrera," 10:445; J. Antonio de la Roca and Efraín Arriola Porres, *Los que fueron . . . (de viris illustribus) 1777–1951 (Biografías mínimas de varones ilustres)*, no. 4 (1955), 1–2.

115. Stephens, *Incidents*, 2:134–39.

116. AGCA, B, leg. 1407, exp. 32903, fol. 3; leg. 2438, exp. 52239.

117. Carrera to Gobno. de El Salvador, Santa Ana, 4 May 1840, AGCA, B, leg. 1407, exp. 32903, fol. 6.

118. Manuel Barberena to Ministro Gral. del S. G. del Estado de Guatemala, 18 May 1840, in *Para conocimiento y satisfacción del pueblo se imprimen de orden del Gobierno los siguientes documentos* ([n.p. [Guatemala], n.d.]), in Coll. 20, Central

America Political Ephemera, LALTU; AGCA, B, leg. 1407, exp. 32903, fol. 11.

119. Joaquín Durán and Rafael Carrera to Secretario del S. G. del Estado de Guatemala, 13 May 1840, in *Para conocimiento y satisfacción del pueblo*, Coll. 20, Central America Political Ephemera, LALTU; AGCA, B, leg. 1407, exp. 32903, fol. 16; Philip Flemion, *Historical Dictionary of El Salvador* (1972), 83–84.

120. Manuel Barberena to Ministro Gral. del S. G. del Estado de Guatemala, 18 May 1840, in *Para conocimiento y satisfacción del pueblo*, Coll. 20, Central America Political Ephemera, LALTU.

121. *El Tiempo*, 26 June 1840.

122. Francisco Morazán to Esteban Travieso, David, N.G., 14 Aug. 1840, in Griffith, ed., "Personal Archive of Morazán," Doc. 54, 276–77. This letter goes on to review his struggle against Carrera's rise.

123. *Manifiesto al pueblo centro-americano* (1841).

124. Apartado, "Morazán," 198; Reina Valenzuela, *Cabañas*, 98.

6. The Caudillo

1. Jacques Lambert, *Latin America: Social Structures and Political Institutions* (1969), 610.

2. Eric B. Wolf and Edward C. Hansen, "Caudillo Politics: A Structural Analysis," *Comparative Studies in Society and History* 9, no. 2 (1967):168–79, provide a perceptive description of this process in Latin America. Although not dealing specifically with Central American cases, their analysis helps to explain the period very well.

3. See Lambert, *Latin America*, 163–64, for a discussion of the frequent tendency of caudillismo to be associated with movements opposed to the upper class.

4. Wolf and Hansen, "Caudillo Politics," 168–69; Richard M. Morse, "Toward a Theory of Spanish American Government," *Journal of the History of Ideas* 15 (1954):71–93; Tulio Halperín-Donghi, *The Aftermath of Revolution in Latin America* (1973), 10–25.

5. Dunlop, *Travels*, 83.

6. Ibid.

7. Batres Jáuregui, *América Central*, 3:179.

8. Williford, *Jeremy Bentham*, 139–40.

9. AGCA, B, leg. 1962, exp. 45282.

10. "El Brigadier y Comandante General de las Armas del Estado: Á los pueblos," *El Tiempo*, 22 July 1839.

11. *El Tiempo*, 2 and 30 Aug. 1839; *Gaceta de Guatemala*, 28 Jan. 1867. See also Rodríguez's commentary on the differences between conservative and liberal policy toward the Indians in his "Livingston Codes," 30.

12. Martínez Peláez, *La patria del criollo*, 222.

13. Moorhead, "Rafael Carrera," 145; Miceli, "Rafael Carrera," 72–95;

Douglas G. Madigan, "Santiago Atitlán: A Socioeconomic and Demographic History" (1976), 7.

14. See, for example, AGCA, B, leg. 1419, exps. 33274–82. For examples of his mediation in land disputes in San Luis Jilotepeque, San Pedro Pinula, and Jalapa in April 1843, see ibid., exp. 33326.

15. AGCA, B, leg. 3594, exp. 82514.

16. *Gaceta Oficial*, 30 Jan. 1846.

17. AGCA, B, leg. 1155, exp. 26948.

18. Stephens, *Incidents*, 1:246.

19. Thomas Young, *Narrative of a Residence on the Mosquito Shore, During the Years 1839, 1840 & 1841, with an Account of Truxillo and the Adjacent Islands of Bonacca and Roatan* (1842), 143–44; *El Tiempo*, 3 June 1840.

20. See AGCA, B, leg. 2367, exp. 48745; leg. 1922, exp. 44192; leg. 3633, exp. 85421; leg. 716, exp. 16045; Stephens, *Incidents*, 1:248–50; Dunlop, *Travels*, 88.

21. *El Tiempo*, 24 Aug. and 29 Oct. 1840.

22. AGCA, B, leg. 212, exps. 4783 and 4881. Other members of the council were Venacio López (regent of the Supreme Court), Luis Batres, Joaquín Durán, Francisco X. Aguirre, Father Jorge Viteri, Father José Mariano Herrarte, and Dámaso Angulo. *El Tiempo*, 17 Nov. 1840.

23. Carrera to Sr. Ministro del Supremo Gobierno del Estado, Guatemala, 25 Nov. 1840, and Basilio Zeceña to Rafael Carrera, Guatemala, 30 Nov. 1840, in *Para conocimiento del público, y del orden del Presidente del Estado, se imprime la siguiente comunicación del Sr. General Carrera, con la contestación correspondiente*, in *hojas sueltas* collection, Hemeroteca of the AGCA.

24. *Gaceta Oficial*, August 1841; L. Montúfar, *Reseña*, 3:541–48; *Niles Register* (Washington, D.C.), 20 Nov. 1841; Hernández de León, *El libro de efémerides*, 3:259–64; AGCA, B, leg. 1078, exp. 23031.

25. *El Tiempo*, 12 Nov. 1840.

26. Superintendente de la Casa de Moneda to Ministro de Gobernación, Guatemala, 26 July 1841, AGCA, B, leg. 3617, exp. 84548.

27. Cáscara to Sr. Secretario del Gobierno del Estado, Chiquimula, 13 Jan. 1840, *El Tiempo*, 6 Feb. 1840.

28. M. Gálvez to Ministro de Gobernación y Justicia, Chimaltenango, 30 Jan. 1840, *El Tiempo*, 27 Feb. 1840.

29. Frederick Crowe, *The Gospel in Central America* (1850), 295.

30. Mariano Rivera Paz, "Proclama del Presidente del Estado," Guatemala, 21 Jan. 1840, *El Tiempo*, 24 Jan. 1840.

31. Marure, *Efemérides*, 125; Bancroft, *Central America*, 3:170, 285–86; *El Tiempo*, 29 Jan. 1841; Basilio Zeceña to Secretario del Supmo. Gob. del Estado del Salvador, Guatemala, 23 Oct. 1840, in *Contestación que el Presidente del Estado de Guatemala dirige al Gobierno del Salvador, con motivo de haber pedido éste explicaciones sobre los alistamientos de tropas que se hacen en el estado*, in Coll. 20, Central America Political Ephemera, LALTU.

32. Rodríguez, *Palmerstonian*, 90–251, has described these efforts in great detail.

33. Dunlop, *Travels*, 89.

34. Stephens, *Incidents*, 1:247.

35. Naylor, "British Commercial Relations," 14–16.

36. For a detailed study of this company and the English colonization efforts in Guatemala, see Griffith, *Empires*. See also his "Attitudes Toward Foreign Colonization," and his *Santo Tomás, anhelado emporio del comercio en el Atlántico* (1959).

37. Acuerdo Gubernativa, 3 Jan. 1839, AGCA, B, leg. 1395, exp. 32352.

38. On the Belgian experience in Guatemala, see Ora-Westley Schwemmer, "The Belgian Colonization Company, 1840–1858" (1966); and Nicolas Leysbeth, *Historique de la colonisation belge a Santo-Tomas Guatemala* (1938).

39. Santos Carrera to Ministro de Relaciones, Guatemala, 16 Feb. 1842, AGCA, B, leg. 1395, exp. 32354, fol. 5.

40. Griffith, *Empires*, 242–44, documents charges that, among others, the president of the assembly, Alejandro Marure, Minister General Juan Flores, and Carrera's personal physician all received bribes from Belgian agents.

41. The assembly formally approved the land grant to Carrera on 6 May 1842. AGCA, B, leg. 212, exp. 4815; leg. 218, exp. 4990.

42. The correspondence on this affair appeared in the *Gaceta Oficial*, 4–20 March 1841.

43. *Gaceta Oficial*, 8 Feb. 1844 and 11 Mar. 1845.

44. "Ley 13, llamada generalmente de garantías, expedida en forma de constitución, por la Asamblea Constituyente, en 5 de diciembre de 1839, firmada por todos los diputados concurrente a su emisión," Pineda de Mont, *Recopilación*, 1:230–35.

45. The letter to the editor was signed by "E.C." *El Atleta*, San Salvador, 25 Dec. 1839.

46. *El Tiempo*, 12 June–6 July 1840; *Gaceta de Guatemala*, 30 Apr. 1856.

47. Fr. Ramón, *Arzobispo de Goathemala y Administrador de la Havana to Sr. Gen. del Egército Triunfante del Estado de Guatemala, Ciud. Rafael Carrera, Habana, 1 July 1840*, printed as a broadside by the Imprenta del Ejército, in *hojas sueltas* collection, Hemeroteca of the AGCA (1840).

48. Rivera Paz, *Informe* (14 July 1840).

49. François Auguste Marie Mignet was a liberal historian of the French Revolution, but he made his peace with the monarchy and served as director of the French foreign ministry archives, 1830–48. His studies of sixteenth-century Spain had made him more widely known in the Spanish world and given him an appeal to conservative creoles.

50. *El Tiempo*, 11–30 Aug. 1839.

51. Ibid., 3 June 1840, quoting from "Espíritu de Partido," *Correo Semanario* (San Salvador), 15 May 1840.

52. *El Tiempo*, 16 Sept. 1840.

53. Moorhead, "Rafael Carrera," 52.

54. Jorge Viteri, *Proposición, Guatemala, 17 July 1840* (Guatemala: Imprenta del Ejército, 1840), in *hojas sueltas* collection, Hemeroteca of the AGCA.

55. *Procurador de los Pueblos*, 12 Sept. 1840.

56. 10 Sept. 1840.

57. These laws had only been suspended on 26 July 1838. *El Tiempo*, 24 Oct. 1840.

58. Marure, *Efemérides*, 71, 126.

59. *Gaceta Oficial*, 8 July 1842, quoting from *Noticioso de ambos mundos* (New York), no date.

60. "El General Carrera," *Gaceta Oficial*, 20 July 1842.

61. Stephens, *Incidents*, 1:306.

62. Dunlop, *Travels*, 214; and AGCA, B, leg. 858, exp. 20678.

63. *Archivo Americano y Espírituo de la Prensa del Mundo* (Buenos Aires), 28 Feb. 1845.

64. AGCA, B, leg. 3600, exp. 82821.

65. Mariano Rivera Paz to Asamblea Constituyente, Guatemala, 6 July 1841, AGCA, B, leg. 21, exp. 5012–14.

66. AGCA, B, leg. 213, exp. 4888.

67. Decreto no. 212, AGCA, B, leg. 213, exp. 4889; leg. 221, exp. 5015–17.

68. Decreto no. 213, 22 July 1841, AGCA, B, leg. 213, exp. 4890.

69. Asamblea Constituyente, Decreto no. 141, AGCA, B, leg. 213, exp. 4902.

70. *Gaceta Extraordinaria*, 14 Aug. 1841.

71. Carrera to Ministro de Guerra, Guatemala, 4 Nov. 1841, AGCA, B, leg. 2498, exp. 55290; Rodríguez, *Palmerstonian*, 248–49.

72. AGCA, B, leg. 2498, exp. 55293.

73. AGCA, B, leg. 2498, exp. 55294.

74. Other moderate liberals who cooperated with Carrera during the 1840s included Miguel García Granados, Felipe Molina, José Mariano Vidaurre, Pedro José Valenzuela, J. Domingo Diéguez, Raymundo Arroyo, Buenaventura Lambur, José María Samayoa, Francisco Albúrez, Doroteo Arriola, and José Antonio Larrave. Even extreme liberals continued to function politically in Guatemala, including José Francisco Barrundia, Pedro Molina, Mariano Gálvez, Juan Barrundia, Antonio Rivera Cabezas, Bernardo Escobar, Manuel Irungaray, and Lorenzo Montúfar. Many of these would later go into exile and become bitter foes of the Carrera regime. Moorhead, "Rafael Carrera," 46–47; Cobos Batres, *Carrera*, 116–17.

75. *Gaceta Oficial*, 17 Dec. 1841.

76. AGCA, B, leg. 3610, exp. 84,195; leg. 3612, exp. 84391; leg. 3617, exp. 84550; Bancroft, *Central America*, 3:266–67; Moorhead, "Rafael Carrera," 56–57. Various versions of these events are provided by L. Montúfar, *Reseña*, 3:536–37; Marure, *Efemérides*, 129; Dunlop, *Travels*, 88–89; Crowe, *Gospel*, 154; and Squier, *Travels*, 2:433–34.

77. Rodríguez, *Palmerstonian*, 249.

78. W. S. Murphy to Daniel Webster, Guatemala, 4 Feb. 1842, in Manning, ed., *Diplomatic Correspondence* (1933) 3:173.

79. William Hall to Alexander MacDonald, Guatemala, 15 Feb. 1842, National Archives of Belize (hereinafter cited as NAB), 10R452–53.

80. Draft of a note from the Secretario del Gobierno to Mariano Rivera Paz, Guatemala, 7 Feb. 1842, AGCA, B, leg. 3606, exp. 83761.

81. Rivera Paz to La Asamblea Constituyente, Escuintla, 13 Feb. 1842. This message, read to that body on 15 Feb., was then printed as a handbill. In *hojas sueltas* collection, Hemeroteca of the AGCA.

82. *Gaceta Oficial*, 3 and 28 July 1842.

83. Ibid., 4 Sept. 1843; Gregorius PP. XVI to Mariano Rivera Paz, Rome, 11 Mar. 1843, copy in *hojas sueltas* collection, 1843, Hemeroteca of the AGCA.

84. Marure, *Efemérides*, 129, 134; L. Montúfar, *Reseña*, 4:171–85.

7. Morazán Again

1. Morazán to the Presidents of the States of El Salvador and Honduras, on board the Brigantine *Cruzador*, Bahía de la Unión, 16 Feb. 1815, Apartado, "Morazán," 43–46.

2. Morazán to Srio. General del Sup. Gobno. del Estado de Nicaragua, San Miguel, 20 Feb. 1842, in Apartado, "Morazán," 207; Reina Valenzuela, *Cabañas*, 101–3.

3. Cañas to Morazán, San Vicente, 18 Feb. 1842, Apartado, "Morazán," 437.

4. The Chinandega Convention was signed on 11 Apr. 1842. *Gaceta Oficial*, 10 and 17 June 1842; Marure, *Efemérides*, 130.

5. L. Montúfar, *Reseña*, 4:47–55, 145.

6. Bancroft, *Central America*, 2:216–22; *Gaceta Oficial*, 17 May 1842.

7. AGCA, B, leg. 2369, exp. 48942.

8. AGCA, B, leg. 213, exp. 4910; *Gaceta Oficial*, 17 May 1842.

9. Executive Decree no. 38, 16 May 1842, AGCA, *El Libro Verde*, item no. 77, vol. no. 4148 (microfilm copy, LALTU), and "El Presidente de Guatemala a los habitantes del Estado," Guatemala, 16 May 1842, *hojas sueltas* collection, Hemeroteca of the AGCA.

10. Santos Carrera to Ministro Gral. del Supremo Gobierno del Estado, Comandancia General del Estado, Guatemala, 17 May 1842, in *Gaceta Oficial*, 17 May 1842.

11. The *Gaceta Oficial*, 28 May–28 Oct. 1842, is full of such attacks by Carrera, Rivera Paz, and other Guatemalan leaders. It also reprinted many of the stories from other Central American papers.

12. *Gaceta Oficial*, 10 June 1842.

13. Rodríguez, *Palmerstonian*, 250, 361.

14. Rafael Carrera, "Proclama . . . a los Estados aliados y a los pueblos que componen el de Guatemala," *Gaceta Oficial*, 17 June 1842.

15. Vela, *Barrundia*, 2:205–8.

16. *Gaceta Oficial*, 23 June 1842.

17. Ibid.

18. "Centro-América," *Gaceta Oficial*, 3 July 1842.

19. *Registro Oficial*, San Fernando (Masaya), Nicaragua, 15 Feb. 1845; *Proyecto de la Confederación Centro-Americano entre los Estados del Salvador, Honduras y Nicaragua acordado en la Ciudad de Chinandega a 27 de Julio de 1842* (1842).

20. Marure, *Efemérides*, 110, 131. This decree, dated 21 July 1842, is given in its entirety in Apartado, "Morazán," 211–12.

21. "Artículo interesante," *Gaceta Oficial*, 23 June 1842, citing *Correo Semanario del Salvador* 1, no. 85.

22. *Apéndice al Num. 49 de la Gaceta Oficial*, 9 July 1842.

23. E.g., Aycinena to Chatfield, Guatemala, 11 July 1842, *Gaceta Oficial*, 13 July 1842.

24. J. J. Aycinena, "Circular a Municipalidades de Guatemala," 14 July 1842, *Gaceta Oficial*, 18 July 1842; J. J. Aycinena, "Circular to Sr. Corregidor de ———," Guatemala, 8 Aug. 1842, Coll. 20, Central America Political Ephemera, LALTU; and Municipalidad de Guatemala to the citizens of the city, Guatemala, 25 July 1842, in *hojas sueltas* collection, Hemeroteca of the AGCA.

25. "Rafael Carrera, Teniente General y General en Gefe del Exército del Estado de Guatemala, a los habitantes que lo componen," Guatemala, 4 Aug. 1842, *Gaceta Oficial*, 9 Aug. 1842.

26. Carrera to Aycinena, Guatemala, 4 Aug. 1842, AGCA, B, leg. 2369, exp. 48917.

27. "Rafael Carrera, Teniente General y General en Gefe del Exército del Estado de Guatemala, a los habitantes que lo componen," 3 Sept. 1842, *hojas sueltas* collection, Hemeroteca of the AGCA, 1842.

28. Mariano Rivera Paz, Decreto no. 43, Guatemala, 23 Sept. 1842, Coll. 20, Central America Political Ephemera, LALTU, also printed in *Gaceta Oficial*, 28 Sept. 1842.

29. "Rafael Carrera, Teniente General y General en gefe del Ejército del Estado de Guatemala, á los habitantes del de Costarrica," *Gaceta Oficial*, 13 Aug. 1842.

30. J. J. Aycinena, "Circular del Gobierno de Guatemala a los del Salvador, Honduras y Nicaragua," *Gaceta Oficial*, 18 Aug. 1842.

31. "Confederación Centro-Americana: Pacto de Unión entre los Estados de Guatemala, Honduras, Nicaragua y el Salvador," *Gaceta Oficial*, 14 Oct. 1842.

32. *Gaceta Oficial*, 28 Oct. 1842. For Chatfield's role, see Rodríguez, *Palmerstonian*, 254–58. The treaty was ratified by Guatemala on 7 October 1842, by Honduras on 31 October 1842, by Nicaragua on 23 November 1842, and by El Salvador on 6 January 1843. Costa Rica, which had already deposed Morazán by 7 October, unknown to the diplomats in Guatemala City, was subsequently invited to sign the treaty. *Gaceta Oficial*, 26 Jan. 1843.

33. Facio, *Trayectoria*, 84; Mejía Nieto, *Morazán*, 187–89; see also the proclamation of Antonio Pinto, General en Gefe de Costa Rica, San José, 16 September 1842, in *hojas sueltas* collection, Hemeroteca of the AGCA, 1842; and *Gaceta Oficial*, 25 Nov. 1842.

34. Montúfar, *Reseña*, 4:15–16.

35. Mariano Rivera Paz, *El Presidente del Estado de Guatemala, a los habitantes del de Costarrica*, (Guatemala: Imprenta de la Paz, 21 October 1842), *hojas sueltas* collection, Hemeroteca of the AGCA.

36. Rivera Paz, "El Presidente del Estado de Guatemala, a sus habitantes," *Gaceta Oficial*, 28 Oct. 1842; L. Montúfar, *Reseña*, 4:16–18.

37. *Rafael Carrera, Teniente General y General en Gefe del Exército del Estado de Guatemala, a los Pueblos que lo componen, y a los demas de Centro-América*, Guatemala, 21 Oct. 1842, *hojas sueltas* collection, Hemeroteca of the AGCA.

38. F. Ferrera, *Memoria presentado a la Cámara Lejislativa por el Ministro de Guerra que suscribe* (1846), 2; Bancroft, *Central America*, 3:218–19, 224, 287–88; Rodríguez, *Palmerstonian*, 256.

39. *Gaceta Oficial*, 17 Sept. 1842, *Apéndice*.

40. Mariano Rivera Paz, Proclamation issued by the President of the State of Guatemala under the letterhead of the "Confederación de Centro América," Guatemala, 17 Nov. 1842, reprinted in Juan José Aycinena, *Reclamación y protesta del Supremo Gobierno del Estado de Guatemala, sobre la ocupación de Soconusco, por tropas de la República mexicana, con los documentos en que se fundan* (1843), 12–18; "Unos Centroamericanos," in *Soconusco (territorio de Centro América) ocupado militarmente de orden del gobierno mexicano* (Guatemala: Imprenta de la Paz, 17 Oct. 1842), Item no. 65 in *El Libro Verde*, AGCA, vol. 4148.

41. Encargado de Negocios de Guatemala en México to J. J. Aycinena, México, 8 Oct. 1842, AGCA, B, leg. 1412, exp. 33000, fol. 22v.

42. Proclamation of 17 Nov. 1842, in Aycinena, *Reclamación*, 12–18.

43. Rafael Carrera, *El fiel Observante de los Derechos de los Pueblos que Componen Centro-América, AL PUBLICO* (1842).

44. For a discussion of Mexican-Guatemalan relations, see John E. Dougherty, "Mexico and Guatemala, 1856–1872: A Case Study in Extra-Legal Relations" (1969); for the colonial background to the dispute and the tradition of Guatemalan rule of Soconusco, see Peter Gerhard, *The Southeast Frontier of New Spain* (1979), 147–72. For additional correspondence regarding the dispute in 1842–43, see AGCA, B, leg. 1412, exp. 33000.

45. Mariano Rivera Paz, *Informe del Presidente del Estado de Guatemala a la Asamblea Constituyente sobre los sucesos ocurridos desde que ésta suspendió sus sesiones: sobre el estado de la administración pública, y medidas dictadas para su mejoramiento. Leydo en las sesiones de los dias 23 y 24 de noviembre de 1842* (1842).

46. AGCA, B, leg. 3605, exp. 83621; *Gaceta Oficial*, 3 and 10 Mar. 1843. See Chapter 17, below, for a fuller discussion of the development of Pacific coast roads and ports.

47. Carrera to Supmo. Gobno., Guatemala, 24 Feb. 1843, AGCA, B, leg. 3604, exp. 83303.

48. M. Cerezo to los Sres. Secretarios de la Asamblea Constituyente, 27 Mar. 1843, *Gaceta Oficial*, 1 Apr. 1843.

49. Miller, *La iglesia*, 38; *Gaceta Oficial*, 23 May 1845; Juan José Aycinena,

Exposición que hace al público el Presbo. Dr. Juan José de Aycinena sobre el asunto de la llamada de los padres de la Compañía de Jesús por la intervención que en ella tuvo como Ministro de relaciones, justicia y negocios eclesiásticos del Estado de Guatemala en el año de 1843 (1845), in *El Libro Verde*, vol. 2, item 102, micofilm copy in LALTU.

50. *Gaceta Oficial*, 10 and 18 Nov. 1843. The other members of the council, all members of the conservative elite, were José Nájera, Luis Batres, José Antonio Larrave (the least conservative among them), and José Coloma. Decreto de la Asamblea Constituyente, no. 188, AGCA, B, leg. 213, exp. 4936.

51. "Prosperidad," *Gaceta Oficial*, 9 Dec. 1843.

52. See, for example, the circular of J. J. Aycinena to the corregidores of 22 June 1844, in *hojas sueltas* collection, Hemeroteca of the AGCA.

53. J. J. Aycinena to Juan Antonio Alvarado, Guatemala, 19 May 1843, AGCA, B, leg. 412, exp. 33000, fol. 98.

54. Carrera to Aycinena, AGCA, B, leg. 2491, exp. 55121.

55. Rodríguez, *Palmerstonian*, 262–64.

56. Manuel de Yela to Manuel Cerezo, 25 Aug. 1843, AGCA, B, leg. 3612, exp. 84417.

57. L. Montúfar, *Reseña*, 4:222–25; Bancroft, *Central America*, 3:288–90; and Rodríguez, *Palmerstonian*, 264.

58. Rodríguez, *Palmerstonian*, 246, 261–66.

59. Carrera's notes to the government, Guatemala, 5 Jan., 10 Feb., and 11 Feb. 1844, in AGCA, B, leg. 1186, exp. 28793; leg. 3604, exp. 83338.

60. The other members of this committee were Lic. Raymundo Arroyo and Lt. Cols. Dr. Eusebio Murga and Francisco Benites. *Gaceta Oficial*, 13 Feb. 1844.

61. Headed by Supreme Court Chief Justice Marcial Zebadúa, a moderate who had served liberal as well as conservative governments, this committee also included Luis Batres, José Antonio Larrave, Manuel Cerezo (chief accountant for the government), and Julián Rivera. *Gaceta Oficial*, 13 Feb. 1844.

62. This was a contract with L. H. C. Obert in connection with the Belgian Colonization Company, designed to attract Belgian capital to Guatemala. Other members of this committee were liberal Manuel Arrivillaga and moderate Manuel Rubio. *Gaceta Oficial*, 13 Feb. 1844, and 4 Nov. 1843, Apéndice.

63. *Gaceta Oficial*, 24 Feb. 1844.

64. Ibid., 13 Mar. 1844.

65. Ibid., 18 Mar. 1844.

66. "Tranquilidad," *Gaceta Oficial*, 13 Mar. 1844.

67. *El Teniente General Rafael Carrera, General en Gefe del Exército del Estado de Guatemala, y los Gefes de las dos divisiones de los pueblos aliados que operaban hostilmente sobre la capital, hemos convenido en obsequio de la paz pública y de la sangre centro-americana, en que atendiendo á las peticiones racionales de los Gefes y los intereses del Estado, bajo los puntos siguientes* (Villa de Guadalupe, 11 Mar. 1844), *hojas sueltas* collection, Hemeroteca of the AGCA; also published in *Gaceta Oficial*, 18 March 1844; original in AGCA, B, leg. 213, exp. 4939. The military commanders signing the conve-

nio were Rafael Carrera, Antonio Solares, José Clara Lorenzana, Manuel Figueroa, Pedro León Vásquez, Manuel Solares, and Manuel Alvarez.

68. "Santos Carrera, Teniente Coronel del Exército, y Comandante General del Departamento de la Corte, a los gefes, oficiales y tropas de las milicias de ella," Guatemala, 12 Mar. 1844, *Gaceta Oficial*, 18 Mar. 1844.

69. *Gaceta Oficial*, 18 Mar. 1844. For an enlightened liberal version of these events, see Vela, *Barrundia*, 2:209.

70. *Gaceta Oficial*, late March through May 1844.

71. Ibid., 4 May 1844.

72. Ibid.

73. Rodriguez, *Palmerstonian*, 266.

74. Ferrera, *Memoria*, 4.

75. Juan Antonio Alvarado to Rodríguez, San Salvador, 23 Apr. 1844, *Gaceta Oficial*, 25 May 1844.

76. AGCA, B, leg. 1414, exp. 33028, fol. 103.

77. José Manuel Rodríguez, "Circular al Sr. Secretario del Supremo Gobierno de _____," Guatemala, 4 May 1844, and Rodríguez to Alvarado, Guatemala, 4 May 1844, in *Gaceta Oficial*, 25 May 1844.

78. *Rafael Carrera, Teniente General, y General en Gefe del Exército del Estado de Guatemala, a los pueblos que lo componen, a las fuerzas de estas guarnición y a las milicias que forman el exército*, Guatemala, 18 May 1844, in *El Libro Verde*, item no. 75, AGCA, vol. 4148.

79. *Gaceta Oficial*, 25 May 1844. See also Rodríguez to the governments of Honduras, Nicaragua, and Costa Rica, 18 May 1844, *Gaceta Oficial*, 20 June 1844; and Bancroft, *Central America*, 3:190–91.

80. Other members were José Coloma and José Alvarez Piloña. *Gaceta Oficial*, 20 June 1844.

81. AGCA, B, leg. 2491, exp. 55149.

82. "Vicente Cruz, Coronel vivo y efectivo, y Comandante General de la División Vanguardia de la derecha del Exército del Estado de Guatemala, a los pueblos que lo componen," Cuajiniquilapa, 7 June 1844, in *Gaceta Oficial*, 20 June 1844.

83. *Manifiesto del Teniente General Rafael Carrera, General en Gefe de las Armas de Guatemala, a los habitantes del estado y demas de Centro América*, Cuartel General en Guatemala, 10 June 1844, in *hojas sueltas* collection, Hemeroteca of the AGCA, also in *Gaceta Oficial*, 20 June 1844.

84. "Vicente Cruz, Coronel vivo y efectivo, y Comandante General de la primera división Vanguardia de la derecha del ejército del Estado de Guatemala. A los pueblos que lo componen," Cuajiniquilapa, 18 June 1844, in *Gaceta Oficial*, 1 July 1844.

85. *Gaceta Oficial*, Apéndice, 21 June 1844.

86. Carrera to Ministro de Relaciones del Supremo Gobierno del Estado, AGCA, B118.19, leg. 2491, exp. 55176. *Gaceta Oficial*, 1 July 1844.

87. This large hacienda of some eight hundred caballerías belonged to Salvador

de Quezada, who later sold it to the Vidaurres. It eventually came into the possession of José Milla y Vidaurre. In 1882, after Milla's death, it was broken up, with portions sold to private buyers and the remainder divided among the *colonos* of the hacienda. During Carrera's time it produced large amounts of sugar and grazed large herds of cattle and horses. Peter C. Wright, *The Role and Effects of Literacy in a Guatemalan Ladino Peasant Community* (1965), 43–47.

88. AGCA, B, leg. 1414, exp. 33028, fol. 47; Bancroft, *Central America*, 3:193. Narciso López to Rafael Carrera, Santa Anna, 20 July 1844, and Carrera to "los Señores de la Legación Confederal," Jutiapa, 26 July 1844, in *Gaceta Oficial*, 7 Aug. 1844.

89. Carrera to Rivera Paz, Jutiapa, 27 July 1844, in *Gaceta Oficial*, 7 Aug. 1844.

90. AGCA, B, leg. 1414, exp. 33028, fol. 135.

91. Sotero Carrera to Ministro de Relaciones y Guerra, Guatemala, 30 July 1844, in *Gaceta Oficial*, 14 Aug. 1844; *Sotero Carrera, General de Brigada y Comandante General del Departamento de Guatemala, a sus habitantes*, Guatemala, 1 Aug. 1844, Arturo Taracena Collection, BLAC.

92. *Convenio ajustado entre los Gobiernos de Guatemala y El Salvador para restablecer entre sí la paz, relaciones y buena inteligencia*, Hacienda de Quezada, 5 Aug. 1844, *hojas sueltas* collection, Hemeroteca of the AGCA.

93. AGCA, B, leg. 1392, exp. 32234; leg. 2370, exp. 48172.

94. *Gaceta Oficial*, 14 Aug. 1844.

95. AGCA, B, leg. 2370, exp. 49133 and 49141.

96. AGCA, B, leg. 2370, exp. 49135; leg. 2371, exp. 49380 and 49411. Members of the diplomatic corps argued that they were exempt. See for example, Corregidor del Departamento de Guatemala to Secretaria de Hacienda, Guatemala, 4 June 1844, AGCA, B, leg. 2371, exp. 49371; Juan José Aycinena protested the quota assigned him, as a clergyman, arguing that his brother, Pedro Aycinena, was head of the family firm (leg. 2370, exp. 49145); José de Ortiz simply complained that the seven hundred pesos assigned him was an impossible sum for him to pay (leg. 2370, exp. 49146).

97. AGCA, leg. 2371, exp. 49369 and 49408. Legajos 2370 and 2371 contain a large volume of records regarding attempts to collect this forced loan.

98. Mariano Rivera Paz, Decreto no. 62, 7 June 1844, *Gaceta Oficial*, 20 June 1844.

99. Corregidor of Guatemala to Ministro de Hacienda, Guatemala, 10 June 1844, AGCA, B, leg. 2371, exp. 49366.

100. Ministro de Hacienda to Corregidor of Guatemala, Guatemala, 11 June 1844, ibid.

101. The municipal government of the capital acknowledged on 28 June that in "rare cases" violent means had been used against those who refused payment of their quotas. AGCA, B, leg. 2370, exp. 49177.

102. The text of the agreement and correspondence relating to this loan was

published in the *Gaceta Oficial*, 1 July 1844. See also the decree of Rivera Paz of 29 June 1844 regarding the issuance of the bonds in *Gaceta Oficial*, 10 July 1844.

103. AGCA, B, leg. 2370, exp. 49186.

104. Sotero Carrera to Ministro de Hacienda, Antigua, 27 June 1844, AGCA, B, leg. 2370, exp. 49175.

105. AGCA, B, leg. 2370, exps. 49182 and 49183.

106. Decreto no. 66, AGCA, B, leg. 2370, exp. 49185; also in *Gaceta Oficial*, 10 July 1844. See also the "Aviso" of the Municipality on this new "donativo voluntario" issued by Joaquín Calvo on 3 July 1844, *hojas sueltas* collection, Hemeroteca of the AGCA.

107. Pavón to Archbishop Coadjutor Dr. Don Francisco García Peláez, Guatemala, 2 July 1844, in *Gaceta Oficial*, 10 July 1844.

108. García Peláez to Pavón, Guatemala, 4 June 1844, *Gaceta Oficial*, 10 July 1844.

109. The assessments are not a precise index to the wealth of the city but probably provide some guide to assessed property. The five firms assigned $2,000 payments were Juan Bautista Asturias (acknowledged the wealthiest merchant in the city); Manuel Olivera, for son and brother; Ysidro Ortiz; Rafael Urruela; and Joaquín Valdés. Five $1,600 assessments went to Manuel Tejada; Dámaso Angulo; Estrada y Piloña; Larraonda y Rubio; and Juan Antonio Martuier. The full list is found in AGCA, B, leg. 2370, exp. 49196.

110. AGCA, B, leg. 2370, exp. 49192; *Gaceta Oficial*, 19 July 1844.

111. See, for example, the list of receipts and disbursements for the period 9–11 July 1844, AGCA, B, leg. 2370, exp. 49195, in which of 2,577 pesos collected, 2,572 pesos and 6.5 reales were dispatched to various military purposes. The documentation on these collections is very rich in legajos 2370 and 2371 and includes many solicitudes for lowering quotas, statements of who has paid and who has not, pleas from villages and corregimientos that cannot meet payment, warnings from the government, and orders to corregidores to enforce. Several separate loans are involved.

112. *Gaceta Oficial*, 19 July 1844.

113. "Estado de los vales expedidos a virtud del Decreto de 29 de diciembre de [1]842, de las certificaciones que se ha extendido, admisibles como vales, por órdenes del Supremo Gobierno; y de las cantidades amortizadas hasta fin de junio próximo pasado," *Gaceta Oficial*, 19 July 1844.

114. See, for example, AGCA, B, leg. 2370, exps. 49197–201, and leg. 3605, exp. 83632.

115. Ministro de Hacienda to Administrador de Rentas, AGCA, B, leg. 2370, exp. 49214.

116. Porras had been assigned a quota of nine hundred pesos of which he had paid all but $125. Luna had paid $100 of a $600 quota. AGCA, B, leg. 2370, exp. 49229.

117. On 21 July 1844 the Comandante General del Estado (Carrera) was given instructions to make effective the loan decreed by the state. AGCA, B, leg. 2370, exp. 49231.

118. Sotero Carrera to Ministro de Hacienda, Guatemala, 23 July 1844, and "El Coronel Sotero Carrera, Comandante General del Departamento de Guatemala a los Señores Gefes, oficiales y tropa que se retiran del servicio de la guarnición de esta plaza," Guatemala, 23 July 1844, *Gaceta Oficial*, 27 July 1844.

119. See the list of merchants who were participating in the loan submitted by the prior of the Consulado to the government on 30 July 1844, AGCA, B, leg. 2370, exp. 49256. In seeking to improve the general financial situation, a commission revised some of the loan schedules and interest rates; AGCA, B, leg. 2370, exp. 49262, and leg. 2404, exp. 50224. Some of the loans of Klée, Skinner, Juan Matheu, and other leading merchants were extended over eight years. These loans were often made half in specie and half in merchandise at current prices, further allowing the merchants to profit.

120. Sec. del G. de Guat. to Young Anderson, 16 Aug. 1844. AGCA, B, leg. 1395, exp. 32376. It also pressed the church for additional loans, although the archbishop resisted. AGCA, B, leg. 3590, exp. 82258, and leg. 2371, exp. 49309.

121. On 20 Sept. 1844, the battalion in the capital revolted because of arrears in pay and raided the commerce of the city. Carrera restored order the next day, and had six men shot, but not before considerable damage was done to commerce, making the point. L. Montúfar, *Reseña*, 3:531, 538–39 (who offers evidence that Carrera himself instigated the revolt); Dunlop, *Travels*, 244; Zamora Castellanos, *Vida militar*, 231; and Bancroft, *Central America*, 3:266.

122. M. F. Pavón, *Informe sobre los diferentes ramos de la administración pública presentado al Exmo. Señor Presidente, por El L. M. F. Pavón, al dejar la secretaria del despacho* (1844), 1–2, 11.

8. The Republic of Guatemala

1. Horacio Espinoza Altamirano, *El libro del ciudadano* (1930), 36.

2. Szaszdi, *Raoul*, 53–54.

3. The ordinances were published broadside and posted around town. They also appeared in the *Gaceta Oficial* on 23 Feb. 1843 and again on 12 Apr. 1845.

4. *Gaceta Oficial*, 28 July 1843.

5. *Gaceta de Guatemala*, 8 Nov. 1849, 22 Apr. 1862, and 16 May 1862.

6. *Gaceta Oficial*, 14 Sept. 1843, 6 Oct. 1843, 13 Feb. 1844; Consulado de Comercio, *Memoria leída por el secretario del Consulado . . .* (1844), par. 22.

7. *Gaceta Oficial*, 12 Apr. 1844.

8. Dunlop, *Travels*, 78.

9. The regulations of this force appeared in the *Gaceta de Guatemala*, 19 June 1847.

10. *Gaceta Oficial*, extra, 22 Apr. 1844. See Viteri, "Circular del Obispo de San Salvador a los parrocos de la diócesis," Palacio Arzobispal de Guatemala, 10 Nov. 1844, *Gaceta Oficial*, extra, 16 Nov. 1844.

11. *Gaceta Oficial*, 31 Aug. 1844; AGCA, B, leg. 727, exp. 16977.

12. AGCA, B, leg. 743, exp. 17431; *Gaceta Oficial*, 20 Sept. 1844.

13. Bancroft, *Central America*, 3:194–96; L. Montúfar, *Reseña*, 4:576–79.

14. Ferrera, *Memoria*; Reina Valenzuela, *Cabañas*, 120–21.

15. Salvador Mejía to General Espinoza, Minister of Finance and War of El Salvador, San Miguel, 8 Sept. 1844, *Gaceta Oficial*, 12 Oct. 1844.

16. *Hojas sueltas* collection, Hemeroteca of the AGCA.

17. AGCA, B, leg. 590, exp. 10616, fol. 1.

18. See *Gaceta Oficial*, extra, 16 Nov. 1844, and for the correspondence with Chatfield, 22 Nov. 1844. This was a particularly aggressive period for the British on the eastern coast, and, following the death of the Mosquito King, Robert I, in 1844, the British established their protectorate over the Mosquito Kingdom. Rodríguez, *Palmerstonian*, 246.

19. *Gaceta Oficial*, 14 Dec. 1844.

20. Pavón, *Informe*.

21. *Gaceta Oficial*, 19 and 28 Dec. 1844; *Consejo Constituyente* (Guatemala, 14 Dec. 1844), copy in possession of the author.

22. *Gaceta Oficial*, 28 Dec. 1844.

23. Ibid., 19 Dec. and 10 July 1844.

24. Rafael Carrera, "El Presidente Interino y General en Gefe del Ejército del Estado de Guatemala, a los pueblos que lo componen," *Gaceta Oficial*, 28 Dec. 1844.

25. AGCA, B, leg. 2506, exp. 56174.

26. Dunlop, *Travels*, 110.

27. Ibid., 109–11; L. Montúfar, *Reseña*, 4:663–69; Bancroft, *Central America*, 3:268; Moorhead, "Rafael Carrera," 62–63; and AGCA, B, leg. 2547, exp. 59446.

28. Sotero Carrera to Ministro de Relaciones del Supremo Gobierno del Estado, Cuartel General en marcha, Argueta, 11 Feb. 1845, Coll. 20, Central America Political Ephemera, LALTU. An attachment to this communication, from General Cruz, dated 12 Feb. 1845, reports on his reconnaissance following the battle and gives the following details on spoils and casualties: "153 rifles, 115 bayonets, 19 steel helmets, 2 cornets, 1 war chest, 1 case of provisions, 2 barrels of powder, 17 horses, 30 prisoners, 5 wounded, 17 dead, 22 more prisoners taken in the municipality of Sololá, 19 taken at Tecpán, 8 by the Governor of Chimaltenango, and others taken in San Martín, the government division suffering no more dead than a sergeant and a soldier."

29. R. Carrera to J. Durán, Escuintla, 9 Feb. 1845, AGCA, B, leg. 2547, exp. 59446.

30. Dunlop, *Travels*, 111.

31. Nájera to Gobno. del Salvador, no date, *Gaceta Oficial*, 11 Mar. 1845; Bancroft, *Central America*, 3:201–4.

32. *Gaceta Oficial*, 12 Apr., 26 Apr., and 10 May 1845.

33. *Mentor Costarricense*, (San José), 22 Mar. 1845.

34. L. Montúfar, *Reseña*, 5:4, 9.

35. *Gaceta Oficial*, 23 May 1845; Joaquín Durán, Decreto no. 13, 8 May 1845, items no. 100–103, AGCA, *El Libro Verde*, LALTU microfilm no. 985, roll 2; Miller, *La iglesia*, 38–39.

36. *Gaceta Oficial*, 13 June 1845.

37. Rodríguez, *Palmerstonian*, 270–71, quoting from Chatfield to Palmerston, no. 21, 21 July 1846.

38. Squier, *Notes on Central America*, 57–58.

39. *Gaceta Oficial*, 13 June and 11 July 1845; Bancroft, *Central America*, 3:268.

40. Dunlop, *Travels*, 247.

41. *Gaceta Oficial*, 14 Aug. 1845.

42. On 20 Oct. 1846, in response to complaints from the consuls of France, Britain, the Hanseatic cities, Prussia, Hanover, and Belgium, Carrera revoked his order of 3 March 1846 that had denied them that privilege. *Gaceta Oficial*, 6 Nov. 1846.

43. Ibid., 20 May 1846.

44. Dictamen of a Special Committee of the Asamblea Constituyente, 7 Aug. 1845, AGCA, B, leg. 221, exp. 5024, fol. 2; congressional resolution of 1 Sept. 1845, leg. 3605, exp. 83681; Rafael Carrera, *El General Presidente del Estado de Guatemala a sus habitantes*, Guatemala, 7 Sept. 1845, Coll. 20, Central America Political Ephemera, LALTU.

45. *Gaceta Oficial*, 25 Sept. 1845.

46. L. Montúfar, *Reseña*, 5:9–11.

47. Item no. 129, AGCA, *El Libro Verde*, LALTU microfilm no. 985, roll 2; *Gaceta Oficial*, 25 Sept. 1845.

48. *Gaceta Oficial*, 31 May 1846; *Gaceta de Guatemala*, 23 Nov. 1847 and 18 Feb. 1848.

49. "Informe al Sr. Ministro de Relaciones del S. G. del Estado," *Gaceta Oficial*, 31 May 1846; continued in 6 June 1846.

50. L. Montúfar, *Reseña*, 5:12; Williford, "Educational Reforms," 461–73.

51. AGCA, B, leg. 3605, exp. 83641 and 83642; leg. 3610, exp. 84286; L. Montúfar, *Reseña*, 5:12.

52. *Gaceta Oficial*, 6 Feb. 1846; a long discussion by the committee justifying its decision, appeared in *Gaceta Oficial*, 13 Feb. 1846, and the decree itself on 27 Feb. 1846.

53. Pedro Tobar Cruz, *Los montañeses, facción de los Lucíos* (1971), 33.

54. AGCA, B, leg. 2535, exp. 58175.

55. AGCA, B, leg. 1852, exp. 42762; leg. 3604, exp. 83365; *Gaceta Oficial*, 8 and 21 Oct. 1845, and 23 Apr. 1846.

56. Restoring a liberal 1831 decree, on 9 Feb. 1846, the government required

all foreigners to register with the corregidor of the first district or department they entered. This included residents of other Central American states. *Gaceta Oficial*, 20 Feb. 1846; L. Montúfar, *Reseña*, 5:15–16.

57. Carrera to Chepita Silva, 2 Apr. 1846, William J. Griffith Collection, Spencer Library, University of Kansas, Lawrence (hereinafter cited as GCUK).

58. Rafael Carrera to Archbishop Ramón Casáus, Guatemala, 4 Sept. 1845, GCUK.

59. *Gaceta Oficial*, 14 Jan. 1846; a fuller description of the mass may be found in *Gaceta Oficial*, 6 Feb. 1846, with an extended biographical sketch of Casáus following.

60. *Gaceta Extraordinaria* (Guatemala), 30 May 1846.

61. "El Presidente del Estado de Guatemala a sus habitantes," *Gaceta Oficial*, 24 July 1846; Moorhead, "Rafael Carrera," 64.

62. Karnes, *Failure of Union*, 116–36; the newspapers of the period are full of the maneuvering of the rival forces, their manifestos, and correspondence among their representatives. Regarding Guatemalan aid to forces in the neighboring countries, see, for example, *Gaceta Oficial*, 26 June and 26 July 1845; *Registro Oficial* (León), 24 Jan. 1846. See also Ralph Lee Woodward, Jr., "La política centroamericana de Rafael Carrera, 1840–1865," *Anuario de Estudios Centroamericanos* (Costa Rica) 9 (1983):55–68.

63. Patrick Walker to Aberdeen, 9 Jan. 1845, Great Britain, FO 53/2, fol. 20, PRO London (microfilm copy in LALTU).

64. *Gaceta Oficial*, 30 Jan. 1846.

65. Rodríguez, *Palmerstonian*, 270–75.

66. Decreto no. 176, AGCA, B, leg. 28576. The coat of arms resembles closely the national seal adopted in 1821.

67. See Ferrera, *Memoria*, 1–2, in which the Honduran caudillo describes much of the fighting in the recent war and accuses the Morazanistas of fomenting revolution and violence in Guatemala and Honduras from bases in El Salvador and Nicaragua.

68. Rodríguez, *Palmerstonian*, 273–76.

69. See the report of Guatemalan representatives José M. Rodríguez and Alejandro Marure to the Guatemalan Ministry of 18 July 1846 in the *Gaceta Oficial*, 31 July 1846.

70. *Gaceta Oficial*, 11 July 1846.

71. Ibid., 19 July 1846.

72. Ibid., 3 Sept. 1846.

73. Ibid., 3 Sept. 1846.

74. E. Aguilar, *El Presidente del Estado del Salvador para conocimiento de todos los centro-americanos publica los documentos que comprueban la complicidad que el Sr. Obispo Viteri ha tenido en las facciones que vinieron armadas de Honduras para trastornar el orden de este estado el 1 de noviembre último* (1846); Parker, *Central American Republics*, 149; and Bancroft, *Central America*, 3:293.

75. *Rafael Carrera General y Presidente del Estado de Guatemala a sus conciudadanos*,

10 Dec. 1846. Coll. 20, Central America Political Ephemera, LALTU.

76. *Gaceta Oficial*, 6 Nov. 1846.

77. Rodríguez, *Palmerstonian*, 278.

78. Ibid., 279. The letter is in FO 15/45, 49–61, with a translation. It is also found in *Gaceta Oficial*, 29 Mar. 1847.

79. Rodríguez, *Palmerstonian*, 282.

80. José Mariano Rodríguez, "Circular a los Gobiernos de los Estados de Centro América," 9 Mar. 1847, *Gaceta Oficial*, 20 Mar. 1847.

81. Tobar Cruz, *Los Lucíos*, 104–5.

82. *Gaceta Oficial*, 29 Mar. 1847.

83. Rafael Carrera, *Manifiesto del Exmo. Señor Presidente del Estado de Guatemala, en que se exponen los fundamentos del Decreto expedido en 21 de Marzo del presente año, erigiendo dicho Estado en república independiente* (1847).

84. Pineda de Mont, *Recopilación*, 1:73–76.

85. It continued the numeration begun earlier with the *Gaceta Oficial*, however. Thus, the first issue of the *Gaceta de Guatemala* was vol. 3, no. 1.

86. Honduras recognized the new republic on 8 Apr., Santos Guardiola to José Mariano Rodríguez, Comayagua, 8 April 1847, *Gaceta de Guatemala*, 24 May 1847; Costa Rica recognized it the following 4 June, Joaquín Bernardo Calvo to Rodríguez, San José, 4 June 1847. Ibid., 20 July 1847.

87. *Tratado de Paz, Amistad y Comercio entre las Repúblicas de Guatemala y Costa Rica* (San José, 8 Feb. 1850). *Gaceta de Guatemala*, 14 Oct. 1848; Rodríguez, *Palmerstonian*, 295; and Parker, *Central American Republics*, 80, 260.

88. J. M. Rodríguez to the Commissioners of Honduras, Nicaragua, and El Salvador at the Dieta de Nacaome, 8 July 1847, *Gaceta de Guatemala*, 21 Sept. 1847.

89. José Montúfar to El Salvador, Ignacio González to Honduras, and Nasario Toledo to Costa Rica. Naming of a Commissioner to Nicaragua was awaiting a Nicaraguan response to Guatemala's declaration. *Gaceta de Guatemala*, 12 June 1847.

90. Woodward, "La política centroamericana," 59–60; *Gaceta de Guatemala*, 12 June 1847, with its translation of an article from the London *Morning Chronicle* welcoming establishment of Guatemalan independence from Central America and looking forward to increased British-Guatemalan trade.

91. *Gaceta de Guatemala*, 10 July 1847 and 7 Sept. 1849.

92. Ibid., 20 July 1847; Bancroft, *Central America*, 3:271.

9. The Revolution of 1848

1. Dunlop, *Travels*, 90.

2. "El Presidente de la República á sus habitantes," L. Montúfar, *Reseña*, 5:306.

3. Decreto no. 18, *Gaceta de Guatemala*, 9 June 1847. The decree was reestab-

lished again for six months beginning on 15 May 1848 because of continued grain shortages. Ibid., 18 May 1848; AGCA, B, leg. 2548, exp. 59703 and 59752.

4. *Gaceta de Guatemala*, 5 July 1847.

5. Ibid., 22 Oct. 1847. A table shows the exact amount and prices paid and sold, but, in essence, the municipality was able to sell the corn to residents at an average price of $5.74 per bushel of corn purchased beginning 25 July, at a time when the price in the market was eight to ten pesos per bushel. The municipality claimed that, as a result of this policy, by late August the price in the market had fallen three to four pesos.

6. *Gaceta de Guatemala*, 20 July 1847.

7. Ibid., 14 Aug. 1847.

8. Ibid., 27 Oct. 1847.

9. *Memoria leída por el secretario del consulado de comercio de la República de Guatemala*, . . . (1847), 7.

10. *Gaceta de Guatemala*, 3 Mar. 1848.

11. Ibid., 27 Oct., 23 Nov., and 2 Dec. 1847.

12. Ibid., 5 Jan. 1848; Rafael Carrera to Chepita Silva, Agua Caliente, 24 Dec. 1847, GCUK.

13. Decree of 12 Jan. 1848, *Gaceta de Guatemala*, 28 Jan. 1848.

14. *Gaceta de Guatemala*, 28 Jan. 1848.

15. "Rafael Carrera, Teniente Jeneral, Presidente de la República de Guatemala y Jeneral en Jefe del Ejército: a sus habitantes," *Gaceta de Guatemala*, 28 Jan. 1848.

16. "Mariano Rivera Paz, Corregidor de Guatemala, a los habitantes del Departamento," Guatemala, 24 Jan. 1848, *Gaceta de Guatemala*, see also ibid., 10 Nov. 1847; and Escobar Medrano, *Rivera Paz*, 22–23.

17. This is the position of Rodríguez, *Palmerstonian*, 292–93.

18. *Gaceta de Guatemala*, 11 Feb. 1848.

19. Vicente Cruz, Decreto no. 26, *Gaceta de Guatemala*, 11 Feb. 1848.

20. "Rafael Carrera, Teniente General, Presidente de la República de Guatemala, á sus habitantes," Guatemala, 4 Feb. 1848, *Gaceta de Guatemala*, 11 Feb. 1848.

21. *Gaceta de Guatemala*, 11 Feb., 18 Feb., and 3 May 1848.

22. *Algunas reflexiones sobre la última sedición, artículos publicados en los números 37, 38, y 39 de La Semana*, 9.

23. Decreto no. 28, *Gaceta de Guatemala*, 18 Feb. 1848.

24. *Gaceta de Guatemala*, 25 Feb. and 11 Mar. 1848.

25. "Relativa a litigio de tierras en Santa Rosa . . . ," AGCA, B, leg. 28627. In 1870 the government was still refusing to allow some of these people to return to their homes because it would be contrary to the public peace.

26. *Gaceta de Guatemala*, 11 Mar. 1848.

27. Tobar Cruz, *Los Lucíos*, 145–285; María Eugenia Morales, *Movimiento de los Lucíos: un acercamiento histórico sociológico* (1983).

28. *Gaceta de Guatemala*, 16 Mar. 1848. See the appeal of the archbishop in

June: "Nos el Dr. Francisco de Paula García Peláez, por la gracia de Dios y de la Santa Sede Apostólica, Arzobispo de esta Santa Iglesia Metropolitana de Santiago de Guatemala a nuestros amados diocesanos los fieles del distrito de las parroquías de Santa Rosa, Jutiapa, Sansaria y Jalapa, salud en Nuestro Señor Jesu-Cristo," Palacio Arzobispal de Guatemala, 19 June 1848, ibid., 28 June 1848.

29. *Gaceta de Guatemala*, 31 Mar. 1848 and 6 Apr. 1848.

30. Decreto no. 33 of 5 April 1848 declared the obligation of the government to maintain peace, order, and security for both natives and foreigners, and since an armed rebellion still existed in the departments of Guatemala and Mita, "in observance of the decrees of 12 and 18 June 1837, having heard the recommendation of the Advisory Council, and in conformity with it," Carrera decreed: "1. All who supply war materials or any other aid to the insurgents, and those who advise, or maintain correspondence with them, will be judged and punished as guilty of armed rebellion. 2. All who by whatever means foment the insurrection and publish writings by the press, which directly or indirectly incite the insurgents against the authorities or against the security of the peaceful inhabitants of the Republic, whether they be natives or foreigners, will be judged and punished as guilty of the same crime. 3. The cases of those who are arrested for the crimes to which this decree refers will be judged in accordance with the Ordinances for Military Tribunals." *Gaceta de Guatemala*, 6 Apr. 1848.

31. *Gaceta de Guatemala*, 31 Mar. 1848.

32. Carrera signed the treaty on 8 Apr. 1848. There is a copy of this long treaty in the Arturo Taracena Collection, BLAC, and it is reprinted in the *Gaceta de Guatemala*, 21 Mar.–26 Apr. 1850.

33. *Gaceta de Guatemala*, 26 Apr. 1848.

34. Bancroft, *Central America*, 3:272–73.

35. *Gaceta de Guatemala*, 18 Apr. 1848.

36. Ibid., 3 May 1848.

37. "Manifiesto que el Presidente de la República de Guatemala dirije a sus conciudadanos," Guatemala, 24 May 1848 (item é183, *El Libro Verde*, AGCA, leg. 4148), also in *Gaceta de Guatemala*, 2 June 1848.

38. Decreto no. 35, Ministerio de Gobernación, 24 May 1848, Coll. 20, Central America Political Ephemera, LALTU; *Gaceta de Guatemala*, 2 June 1848. The 1838 law is found in the *Boletín Oficial*, 9 Aug. 1838.

39. Nájera took over the Foreign Ministry immediately on 31 May. Durán was not actually sworn in as the new minister of finance and war until 3 July 1848. *Gaceta de Guatemala*, 6 June and 5 July 1848.

40. *Gaceta de Guatemala*, 18 Apr. 1848.

41. Ibid., 3 May 1848.

42. Ibid., 21 June 1848.

43. Rafael Carrera to Chepita Silva, Patzún, 14 July 1848, GCUK; *Gaceta de Guatemala*, 12 and 19 July 1848; *Boletín de Noticias del Ejército* (Guatemala) 17–18 July 1848.

44. Juan J. Sagastume, Alcalde 1o. de Esquipulas, to Corregidor y Coman-

dante Jeneral del Departamento, Esquipulas, 24 July 1848, *Gaceta de Guatemala*, 10 Aug. 1848.

45. *Gaceta de Guatemala*, 10 May 1848.

46. Ibid., 21 June 1848.

47. Batres to García Peláez, Guatemala, 4 June 1848, and García Peláez to Batres, Guatemala, 7 June 1848, *Gaceta de Guatemala*, 14 June 1848.

48. "El patriotismo oprimido," *Observaciones sobre la revolución en Guatemala* (Guatemala: Imprenta del Estado, 22 June 1848), *El Libro Verde*, item no. 189, AGCA, leg. 4148.

49. *Gaceta de Guatemala*, 12 and 19 July 1848.

50. "Derota que sufrieron los sublevados en Patzum," *Gaceta de Guatemala*, 19 July 1848.

51. *Gaceta de Guatemala*, 19 July 1848. Among the liberals who had won election, in addition to Barrundia and Molina, were José Mariano Vidaurre, José Bernardo Escobar, Pedro N. Arriaga, Mariano Padilla, Mariano Gálvez Irungaray, Miguel García Granados, Luis Arrivillaga, and Luis Molina. There were also, of course, some notable conservatives elected, including José María and Juan Francisco Urruela, and Juan Bautista Asturias, but some of the most important conservatives were defeated. A point worth mentioning here is that representatives did not have to live in the districts they represented. Almost all of the representatives, officially representing the various departments and districts of the republic, were residents of the capital. A complete list of those elected is given in the *Gaceta de Guatemala*, 10 Aug. 1848.

52. *Gaceta de Guatemala*, 2 Aug. 1848.

53. Bancroft, *Central America*, 3:273.

54. "Acta del pronunciamiento del Departamento de Chiquimula, desconociendo al Gobierno actual del Estado de Guatemala, por las razones que en ella se espresan," *Gaceta de Guatemala*, 25 Aug. 1848.

55. Toribio Rodríguez, 10. Alcalde de Escuintla, to Ministro de Hacienda y Guerra, Escuintla, 1 Aug. 1848, *Gaceta de Guatemala*, 10 Aug. 1848.

56. "El Presidente de la República a los habitantes de la capital," Guatemala, 5 Aug. 1848, *El Libro Verde*, item no. 187, AGCA, leg. 4148.

57. *Gaceta de Guatemala*, 2 Aug. 1848.

58. Ibid., 25 Aug. 1848.

59. Rafael Carrera, *Informe que dirigió el Presidente de la República al Cuerpo Representativo, en su instalación el día 15 de Agosto de 1848* (1848), 2, 6–8.

60. *Gaceta de Guatemala*, 25 Aug. 1848.

61. L. Montúfar, *Reseña*, 5:555–644; Bancroft, *Central America*, 3:274.

62. *El Presidente interino de la República a sus habitantes* (Guatemala, 17 Aug. 1848), also in *Gaceta de Guatemala*, 25 Aug. 1848.

63. "Felicitaciones que la Municipalidad de esta capital dirijió a la Asamblea Constituyente del pueblo libre y soberana de Guatemala," Guatemala, 18 Aug. 1848, *Gaceta de Guatemala*, 25 Aug. 1848.

64. Doroteo Vasconcelos, "El Presidente del Estado del Salvador, a sus conciu-

dadanos," San Salvador, 23 Aug. 1848, *Gaceta de Guatemala*, 2 Sept. 1848.

65. Rodolfo González Centeno, *El Mariscal de Campo Don Serapio Cruz, sus notables campañas militares* (1982), pp. 20–42.

66. Rodríguez, *Palmerstonian*, 283–88.

67. Bancroft, *Central America*, 3:312.

68. *Gaceta de Guatemala*, 14 Sept. 1848; Chatfield's pretentiousness is, of course, evident in much of his correspondence, as indicated by Rodríguez, *Palmerstonian*.

69. *Gaceta de Guatemala*, 2 Sept. 1848. The new editor took over beginning with this issue, so that the switch to liberalism is not noticeable before that date.

70. Dardón, upon resigning as editor of the *Gaceta* on 28 Nov., following Martínez's resignation, claimed authorship for the following articles in the *Album* during the period August through November: no. 2, "La Revista refutada por sí misma"; no. 4, "Observancia de la ley"; no. 6, "Estar en todo"; no. 9, "Denuncia al público contra los Editores de la Revista"; no. 11, "Ley de imprenta"; and no. 14, "La muerte." *Gaceta de Guatemala*, 28 Nov. 1848.

71. *Gaceta de Guatemala*, 14 Sept. 1848.

72. *Alcance de la Gaceta de Guatemala*, 16 Sept. 1848.

73. *Gaceta de Guatemala*, 22 Sept. 1848.

74. *Gaceta de Guatemala*, 28 Sept. 1848 and 5 Oct. 1848, refuting the article in no. 78 of the *Gaceta del Supremo Gobierno del Salvador* in which the Salvadoran government had criticized the Guatemalan assembly's action.

75. *Gaceta de Guatemala*, 12 Sept. 1846.

76. Passed by the assembly on 29 Sept. and signed by Provisional President Martínez on 5 October. *Gaceta de Guatemala*, 14 Oct. 1848.

77. Report of Miguel Rivera Maestra, who headed the commission to produce the sword, 16 Oct. 1848, in AGCA, B, leg. 2405, exp. 50347; Bancroft, *Central America*, 3:208, mentions the medal.

78. *Gaceta de Guatemala*, 22 Sept. 1848.

79. Ibid., 14 Sept. 1848.

80. "Proposición que hizo el Ciudadano Representante José Barrundia a la Asamblea Constituyente en la sesión de 17 del que rije," *Gaceta de Guatemala*, 22 Sept. 1848.

81. *Gaceta de Guatemala*, 22 Sept. 1848.

82. Decree no. 1, 3 Sept. 1848. *Gaceta de Guatemala*, 8 Sept. 1848.

83. Ibid., 8 and 14 Sept. 1848.

84. Executive Decree no. 3, of 22 Sept. 1848, *Gaceta de Guatemala*, 28 Sept. 1848.

85. Item no. 13, *El Libro Verde*, vol. 3, AGCA, leg. 4149 (LALTU Microfilm).

86. *Gaceta de Guatemala*, 28 Sept. 1848.

87. AGCA, B, leg. 229, exp. 5137, fol. 4; *Gaceta de Guatemala*, 20 Oct. 1848. A long report appeared in the *Gaceta*, specifically emphasizing Nufio's loyalty to the assembly.

88. *Gaceta de Guatemala*, 22 Sept. and 14 Oct. 1848; L. Montúfar, *Reseña*, 5:588–89; a copy of the Los Altos declaration of 5 Sept. 1848 is in Coll. 20, Central America Political Ephemera, LALTU.

89. J. Antonio Martínez, "El Presidente Interino de la República a los pueblos de los Altos," Guatemala, 27 Sept. 1848," Coll. 20, Central America Political Ephemera, LALTU, also in *Gaceta de Guatemala*, 28 Sept. 1848.

90. *Gaceta de Guatemala*, 14 Oct. 1848.

91. *El Libro Verde*, vol. 3, item no. 36, AGCA, leg. 4149. Also in the *Gaceta del Gobierno Supremo del Estado del Salvador en la República de Centro-América* (San Salvador), 27 Oct. 1848.

92. *Gaceta de Guatemala*, 3 Nov. 1848.

93. Ibid., 20 Oct. 1848; Bancroft, *Central America*, 3:274n.

94. *Gaceta de Guatemala*, 28 Oct. and 17 Nov. 1848.

95. Ibid., 3 Nov. 1848. The assembly formally named the six nominees to the council on 12 Nov.: Lic. José Antonio Azmitia, Dr. Pedro Molina, Dámaso Angulo, Juan Matheu, José Francisco Barrundia, and Lic. Pedro Nolasco Arriaga. *Gaceta de Guatemala*, 28 Nov. 1848.

96. Decreto no. 15, *Gaceta de Guatemala*, 3 Nov. 1848.

97. *Gaceta de Guatemala*, 10–17 Nov. 1848.

98. Serapio Cruz, *El Jeneral en Jefe del Ejército de los Pueblos Aliados del Estado de Los Altos y sus compatriotas y amigos* (Palencia: Imprenta del Estado, 12 Nov. 1898), *El Libro Verde*, vol. 3, item no. 59, AGCA, B, leg. 4149.

99. *Gaceta de Guatemala*, 17 Nov. 1848.

100. Ibid., 28 Nov. and 7 Dec. 1848.

101. José Bernardo Escobar, *El Presidente interino de la República á los habitantes de la capital*, Guatemala 28 Nov. 1848, Arturo Taracena Collection, BLAC, no. 9456; and "El Presidente de la República á sus habitantes," Guatemala, 28 Nov. 1848, *Gaceta de Guatemala*, 7 Dec. 1848.

102. *Gaceta de Guatemala*, 30 Dec. 1848.

103. Some of the correspondence between the rebels and the government is published in *Gaceta de Guatemala*, 23 Dec. 1848. The Paredes government repealed the pay raise on 10 Feb. 1849, once the crisis had passed; *Gaceta de Guatemala*, 2 Mar. 1849.

104. *Gaceta de Guatemala*, 23 Dec. 1848.

105. Ibid., 30 Dec. 1848.

106. *Algunas reflexiones*, 10; and "El Presidente Interino á los habitantes de la República," 14 Dec. 1848, *Gaceta de Guatemala*, 23 Dec. 1848.

107. *Gaceta de Guatemala*, 30 Dec. 1848.

108. Ibid., 23 Jan. 1849.

109. Ibid.; Tobar Cruz, *Los montañeses* (1959), 93.

110. *Gaceta de Guatemala*, 23 Jan. and 8 Feb. 1849 and 4 July 1851.

111. Rubio Sánchez, *Cáscara*, 132–33.

112. *Gaceta de Guatemala*, 23 Jan. 1849.

113. Ibid., 31 Jan. 1848. The government authorized the Consulado to open the port of Champerico on 31 Mar. 1849, AGCA, leg. 28547, exp. 842.

114. The following were named corregidor and comandante de armas: Sacate-péquez, Lt. Col. Lic. Manuel Ramírez; Verapaz, Lt. Col. José Montúfar; Chimal-tenango, Lic. Salvador Saravía, who would serve as judge of original jurisdiction; Chiquimula, Hermenejildo Morales; and Izabal, Capt. Francisco Sigui. *Gaceta de Guatemala*, 31 Jan. 1849.

115. *Gaceta de Guatemala*, 7 July 1854.

116. Ibid., 20 Oct. 1848; Bancroft, *Central America*, 3:274, 279.

117. Rafael Carrera to Josefina Antonia Silva, Comitán, 2 Oct. 1848, GCUK.

118. Mariano López to Ministerio de Hacienda y Guerra, Comitán, 20 Nov. 1848, AGCA, B, leg. 2405, exp. 50348.

119. Crowe, *Gospel*, 177–78; L. Montúfar, *Reseña*, 5:746–47.

120. *Gaceta de Guatemala*, 8 Feb. 1849.

121. *Gaceta de Guatemala*, 16 Feb. 1849, gives a detailed description of these events.

122. While some notable liberals were among those named, conservatives dominated the nominations:

Relaciones Exteriores: Lic. Manuel Ubico, Lic. Manuel Echeverría, and José Milla y Vidaurre.

Gobernacion: Presb. José María Barrutia, José Coloma, and Manuel Joaquín Dardón.

Negocios Eclesiasticos: Dr. Bernardo Piñol, Presb. Pedro Diez, Presb. Anselmo Llorente.

Legislacion y Justicia: Lic. Andrés Andreu, Manuel Ubico, and Lic. Manuel Cruz.

Hacienda: Dr. Pedro Molina, Luis Batres, and Pedro Aycinena.

Guerra: Col. Manuel María Bolaños, Lt. Col. Joaquín Saenz, and Lt. Col. Miguel García Granados.

Instruccion Publica: Juan José Aycinena, Dr. Alejandro Marure, and Lic. Ignacio González.

Industria, Agricultura y Comercio: José María Vidaurre, Juan Matheu, and Pedro Lara Pavón.

Obras Publicas: José Nájera, Antonio Zirión, Marcos Dardón.

Policia y salubridad: Dr. José Luna, Buenaventura Lambur, and Francisco Xavier Aguirre.

Estadisticos: Narcisco Payés, Buenaventura Lambur, and Juan Piñol.

Tierras y Ejidos: Juan José Flores, Juan Andreu, and Juan de Dios Morales.

Pacificacion: General Vicente Cruz, Rafael Urruela, and Pedro Diez.

Gaceta de Guatemala, 24 Feb. 1849.

123. Decreto no. 32 detailed how the $30,000 would be administered. *Gaceta de Guatemala*, 24 Feb. 1849.

124. *Gaceta de Guatemala*, 2 Mar. 1849.

125. "El Sr. D. Mariano Rivera Paz, Apuntes biográficos," *Gaceta de Guatemala*, 13 June 1851.

126. *Gaceta de Guatemala*, 16 Mar. 1849.

127. Manifesto signed by R. Arroyo and Manuel Tejada, Guatemala, 17 Feb. 1849, *Gaceta de Guatemala*, 24 Feb. 1849.

128. Pineda de Mont, *Recopilación*, 1:317–25; Palmerston to J. M. Rodríguez, London, 16 June 1849, in *Gaceta de Guatemala*, 31 Aug. 1849. The treaty appeared in *Gaceta de Guatemala*, 21–28 Feb. 1849.

129. Pineda de Mont, *Recopilación*, 1:339–52; Guatemala ratified this treaty on 26 Apr. 1849, and ratifications were exchanged in Brussels on 3 July 1850. The treaty was printed in *Gaceta de Guatemala*, 11–25 Oct. 1850. Seven additional articles were agreed to on 10 Nov. 1858. *Gaceta de Guatemala*, 18 Mar. 1860.

130. U.S. ratification of the Hise-Rodríguez Treaty was delayed for some time; ratifications were not finally exchanged in Guatemala until 13 May 1852. *Gaceta de Guatemala*, 28 Nov. 1848, 31 Jan. 1849, and 12 Nov. 1852.

131. *Gaceta de Guatemala*, 18 June 1849.

132. Exchange of correspondence between Rodríguez and Challaye in *Gaceta de Guatemala*, 16 Feb.–22 Mar. 1849; Unos Españoles, *Documentos relativos a la cuestión sobre los españoles, que ha pasado al conocimiento de la Asamblea Constituyente el Sr. Ministro de Relaciones* (1849); and E. Drouin de Lhuys to Rodríguez, Paris, 25 Apr. 1849, *Gaceta de Guatemala*, 7 Sept. 1849.

133. V. Cerna, "Proclama a los pueblos," Aguacaliente, 18 Mar. 1849, and "Necrología," *Gaceta de Guatemala*, 30 Mar. 1849; Bancroft, *Central America*, 3:277.

134. García Granados to Cerna, Huehuetenango, 21 Mar. 1849. *Gaceta de Guatemala*, 30 Mar. 1849; García Granados to Cerna, Huehuetenango, 5 Apr. 1849, "Boletín de Noticias, No. 5," *Gaceta de Guatemala*, 10 Apr. 1849.

135. I do not know where the bell was originally destined to hang, or if it even had a specific purpose. It carries only the inscription: "Para el Uso en Centro-América por Orden del Señor Nicolás Larrave, Fabricada en Paris, Enero 10, 1,847." After the bell cracked, the village purchased a new, larger bell in 1949, but the cracked 1847 bell still hangs there also. Anita Cox de Collins, "San Marcos Huista: Unas notas," *Guatemala Indígena* 5(1970):134.

136. *Gaceta de Guatemala*, 10 and 18 Apr. and 19 May 1849; "Informe presentado por el Sr. Ministro de Relaciones Exteriores a la Asamblea Constituyente," 20 Apr. 1849, *Gaceta de Guatemala*, 2 June 1849.

137. *Gaceta de Guatemala*, 19 May 1849.

138. José M. Urruela to Joaquín Durán, Guatemala, 16 May 1849, *Gaceta de Guatemala*, 7 July 1849.

139. Nelson Reed, *The Caste War of Yucatan* (1964); Clegern, *Colonial Dead End*, 10–11; and José M. Urruela to Felipe Neri del Barrio, 15 June 1849, *Gaceta de Guatemala*, 7 July 1849, which helps to explain this fear of the Caste War and why Paredes agreed so quickly to Carrera's return.

140. Moorhead, "Rafael Carrera," 74–75; L. Montúfar, *Reseña*, 5:767–75.

141. *Gaceta de Guatemala*, 19 and 29 May 1849.

142. Ibid., 29 May and 18 June 1849.

143. Other members of the commission were Juan Matheu, Juan B. Asturias, Joaquín Valdez, and José María Samayoa. *Gaceta de Guatemala*, 2 June 1849.

144. Ibid., and 8 June 1859, where Paredes's Decreto no. 35 of 5 June is published, in which the Mexican minister in Guatemala was designated to notify General Carrera of this revocation.

145. *Gaceta de Guatemala*, 18 and 26 June 1849.

146. "Agustín Gusman, Jeneral de Division de la Federacion de Centro-América, a los habitantes de Guatemala," San Salvador, n.d. (San Salvador: Imprenta de L. Romero, [1849]); *Gaceta de Guatemala*, 26 June 1849.

147. Urruela to Carrera, Guatemala, 15 June 1849, *Gaceta de Guatemala*, 7 July 1849.

148. Carrera to Urruela, Quetzaltenango, 20 June 1849, *Gaceta de Guatemala*, 26 June 1849.

149. *Gaceta de Guatemala*, 18 June 1849; AGCA, B, leg. 28547, exp. 851.

150. Rafael Carrera, *El Teniente Jeneral Rafael Carrera a sus compatriotas guatemaltecos, Quetzaltenango, 27 June 1849*, Coll. 20, Central America Political Ephemera, LALTU, also in AGCA, B, leg. 28547, exp. 853.

151. These taxes, decreed on 26 June, went into effect on 1 July and were to last for six months. *Gaceta de Guatemala*, 7 July 1849.

152. *Gaceta de Guatemala*, 7 and 17 July 1849.

153. Ibid., 7 July 1849.

154. Ibid., 17 July 1849.

155. AGCA, B, leg. 753, exp. 17755.

156. *Gaceta de Guatemala*, 11 Aug. 1849; L. Montúfar, *Reseña*, 5:784–85.

157. See, for example, the pamphlet, *Sucesos del Día*, (4 Aug.) 1849.

158. Rafael Carrera, "El Teniente General Rafael Carrera, Comandante Jeneral de las armas de la República, a sus conciudadanos," Guatemala, 8 Aug. 1849, *Gaceta de Guatemala*, 23 Aug. 1849.

159. AGCA, B, leg. 728, exp. 16991; *Gaceta de Guatemala*, 23 Aug. 1849.

160. *Gaceta de Guatemala*, 11 Aug. 1849.

161. Ibid., 31 Aug. 1849.

162. Carrera to García Peláez, Guatemala, 10 Sept. 1849, *Gaceta de Guatemala*, 4 Oct. 1849; see also 21 Sept. 1849.

163. Rafael Carrera to Chepita Silva, Sta. Bárbara, Oct. 1849, Palencia, 16 Nov. 1849, Mataquescuintla, 3 Sept. 1850, and Plan Grande, 21 Oct. 1850, GCUK. The *Gaceta de Guatemala* gives running accounts of the skirmishes and battles that Carrera and the other generals fought against the "*facciosos*" during 1849 and 1850.

164. *Gaceta de Guatemala*, 18 and 26 Oct., 2 and 14 Nov., 21 Dec. 1849, and 1 Feb. 1850.

165. The *Gaceta de Guatemala* carried regular reports on the continued fight-

ing and the manifestos of Paredes, Carrera, and other generals calling on the montañeses to lay down their arms.

166. See, for example, the report of the Mexican *Monitor Republicano* in the *Gaceta de Guatemala*, 23 Aug. 1850.

167. "Circular a los gobiernos de Costa-Rica, Honduras y Nicaragua," Guatemala, 5 July 1850, ibid., 12 July 1850.

168. L. Montúfar, *Reseña*, 6:291; *Gaceta de Guatemala*, 28 May 1852.

169. *Gaceta de Guatemala*, 6 Aug. 1856; see also 4 and 18 May 1855, and 24 Apr. 1856.

10. Arada

1. Rodríguez, *Palmerstonian*, is the definitive work on Chatfield's Central American career.

2. Palmerston to Minister of Foreign Relations of Guatemala, London, 16 June 1849, *Gaceta de Guatemala*, 31 Aug. 1849.

3. Naylor, "British Role in Central America," 361–82; and, for more detail, his *Influencia británica en el comercio centroamericano durante las primeras décadas de la independencia (1821–1851)*.

4. R. G. Albion, "British Shipping and Latin America, 1806–1914," *Journal of Economic History* 11 (Fall 1951):361–62.

5. Rodríguez, *Palmerstonian*, 84–86, 291–97; James T. Wall, *Manifest Destiny Denied: America's First Intervention in Nicaragua* (1981), 5–8, 21.

6. A handbill entitled *Cuestión del Día. Nacionalidad de Centro-América y sistema esclusivo, sin influencia de los gobiernos monárquicos europeos* (San José, Costa Rica, 9 Feb. 1850), in Coll. 20, Central America Political Ephemera, LALTU, advocated unification under U.S. protection and aid, reportedly offered by Zachary Taylor.

7. Rodríguez, *Palmerstonian*, 294–302; Charles L. Stansifer, "E. George Squier: Yanqui versatil en Centro América," *Revista Conservadora del Pensamiento Centroamericano* 15, no. 73 (October 1966):13–20; and Stansifer, *Ephraim George Squier: Diversos aspectos de su carrera en Centroamérica* (1968).

8. Albert Z. Carr, *The World and William Walker* (1963), 42–43; William O. Scroggs, *Financiers and Filibusters: The Story of William Walker and his Associates* (1916), 71–81.

9. Rodríguez, *Palmerstonian*, 300–326; Reina Valenzuela, *Cabañas*, 153–60.

10. *Gaceta de Guatemala*, 12 July 1850; and "El nuevo gobierno de los Estados-Unidos y el Sr. E. George Squier," *Gaceta de Guatemala*, 29 Nov. 1850.

11. José Rodríguez Cerna, comp., *Colección de Tratados de Guatemala*, (1939–44), 3:5–13, 38–49, 100–110, 137–51; Woodward, "Política centroamericana," 66; Thomas Schoonover, "Metropole Rivalry in Central America, 1820s–1929: An Overview," in *Central America: Historical Perspectives on the Contemporary Crises*, edited by R. L. Woodward, Jr. (1988), 24–28, 36–38.

12. *Gaceta de Guatemala*, 15 Nov. 1850.

13. Pineda de Mont, *Recopilación*, 1:304–15; Chatfield to Minister of Foreign Relations of Guatemala, *Gaceta de Guatemala*, 3 Aug. 1848.

14. Karnes, *Failure of Union*, 119–47.

15. Rodriguez, *Palmerstonian*, 316–17, citing *El Progreso* (San Salvador), 9 May 1850, as translated by Chatfield in his dispatch, no. 43, to Palmerston, FO 15/64 (25 June 1850).

16. "Analogías," *Gaceta de Guatemala*, 12 July 1850.

17. *Gaceta de Guatemala*, 25 Feb. 1848.

18. Ibid., 17 July 1849.

19. See, for example, Unos Guatemaltecos, *La Prensa del Estado del Salvador, Num. 3*, 12 July 1849, in Coll. 20, Central America Political Ephemera, LALTU.

20. "La nacionalidad de Centro-América," *Gaceta de Guatemala*, 23 Oct.–6 Dec. 1850.

21. "Nacionalidad de Centro-América," *Gaceta de Guatemala*, 10 June 1853.

22. Rodriguez, *Palmerstonian*, 269, 280–81, 309–10; Naylor, "British Role in Central America," 372; Bancroft, *Central America*, 3:209, 230–37.

23. Manuel F. Pavón to Ministro Trato. de Despacho, San José, 18 Feb. 1850, Archivo Nacional de Costa Rica (hereinafter cited as ANCR), Serie Relaciones Exteriores, Caja no. 21, Año 1850.

24. *Gaceta de Guatemala*, 21 Feb. 1850.

25. Molina presented his request on 9 Nov. 1849 and on 2 Feb. 1850 received news of the pope's favorable decision of 16 Jan. 1850. Bishop Anselmo Llorente y Lafuente took up his see on 10 Apr. 1851 and remained bishop of Costa Rica until his death in 1872. *Gaceta de Guatemala*, 10 May 1850; Victor Sanabria Martínez, *Anselmo Llorente y Lafuente, primer obispo de Costa Rica: Apuntamientos históricos*, 2d ed. (1972).

26. Rodríguez, *Palmerstonian*, 317–20.

27. M.F.P., "Impreso suelto," reprinted in the *Gaceta de Guatemala*, 28 June 1850.

28. *Gaceta de Guatemala*, 26 July 1850.

29. Pedro N. Arriaga to Minister of Foreign Relations of Costa Rica, Guatemala, 13 Sept. 1850, ANCR, Sección Histórica, Serie Rel. Ext., Caja no. 23, Año 1850; and *Gaceta de Guatemala*, 12 July, 16 Aug., 23 Aug., and 15 Nov. 1850.

30. Bancroft, *Central America*, 3:294–97; the *Gaceta de Guatemala* reflects the deteriorating state of relations between Guatemala and El Salvador from mid–1849 forward.

31. R. Pino to Pedro N. Arriaga, San Salvador, 27 June 1850, and Arriaga to Pino, Guatemala, 5 July 1850, in *Gaceta de Guatemala*, 12 July 1850.

32. *Gaceta de Guatemala*, 9 Aug. 1850.

33. Decree of 14 August; *Gaceta de Guatemala*, 23 and 30 Aug. 1850.

34. Rodríguez, *Palmerstonian*, 322.

35. *Gaceta de Guatemala*, 19 Sept., 4 Oct., 18 Oct., and 8 Nov. 1850; see also the correspondence in 1850 between Gerónimo Rosales et al. and Padre Nicolás

Arellano, transmitted to the archbishop, regarding the government's methods and rebel demands that the government forces stop destroying their milpas, in AGCA, B, leg. 28551, exp. 155. See also the demands of Roberto Reyes, in AGCA, B, leg. 28549, exp. 37.

36. AGCA, B, leg. 28549, exps. 941–43.

37. *Gaceta de Guatemala*, 6 Dec. 1850.

38. Estados de Centro-América, "Pronunciamiento del Ejército Nacional," *Gaceta de Guatemala*, 29 Nov. 1850.

39. Bancroft, *Central America*, 3: 312–20; *Gaceta de Guatemala*, 28 June 1850.

40. "El General en Gefe del ejército nacional, a los individuos que lo componen y a los habitantes del Estado de Guatemala," *Gaceta de Guatemala*, 29 Nov. 1850.

41. Joaquín Solares to Vicente Cerna, Jocotán, 16 Nov. 1850, and Cerna to Minister of War, Chiquimula, 19 Nov. 1850, *Gaceta de Guatemala*, 29 Nov. 1850.

42. Arriaga, "Circular a los Sres. Encargados de Negocios de la Gran Bretaña y Francia y Consul Jeneral de las Ciudades anseáticos, Prusia y Hanover," *Gaceta de Guatemala*, 16 Nov. 1850.

43. "Rafael Carrera, Teniente Jeneral en Jefe del Ejército de Guatemala a lo Habitantes de la República," Jutiapa, 19 Nov. 1850, *Gaceta de Guatemala*, 29 Nov. 1850.

44. *El Presidente de la República de Guatemala hace saber* (Guatemala, 21 Nov. 1850), which includes letters from Arriaga to Dueñas, Guatemala, 29 Oct. 1850, and Dueñas to Arriaga, San Salvador, 4 Nov. 1850, Arturo Taracena Collection, BLAC.

45. Carrera to Arriaga, Esquipulas, 26 Nov. 1850, *Gaceta de Guatemala*, 14 Dec. 1850.

46. *Gaceta de Guatemala*, 20 Dec. 1850.

47. Ibid., 29 Nov. 1850.

48. "Boletín de Noticias, Guatemala, Dic. 2 de 1850," *Gaceta de Guatemala*, 6 Dec. 1850.

49. Bancroft, *Central America*, 3:279; AGCA, B, leg. 2439, exp. 52260.

50. *Gaceta de Guatemala*, 14 Dec. 1850; Rafael Carrera to Chepita Silva, Cipala, 22 Nov. 1850, and Santa Catarina, 15 Jan. 1851, William J. Griffith Collection, GCUK.

51. *Gaceta de Guatemala*, 20 Dec. 1850.

52. Pedro N. Arriaga to Secretary of Foreign Relations of Costa Rica, Guatemala, 20 Dec. 1850, ANCR, Sección Histórica, Serie Rel. Ext., caja no. 22, Año 1850.

53. Arriaga to Minister of Foreign Relations, Guatemala, 26 Dec. 1850, *Gaceta de Guatemala*, 18 Jan. 1851.

54. "El Presidente de Honduras a los pueblos del Estado y los demás de Centro-América," Ocotepeque, 6 Jan. 1851, *Gaceta de Guatemala*, 25 Jan. 1851 (originally published by the Imprenta del Triunfo, San Salvador).

55. Cabañas to Jesús Maria Gutiérrez (Father Gutiérrez was one of the com-

missioners Paredes had sent to Honduras), Ocotepeque, 6 Jan. 1851, *Gaceta de Guatemala*.

56. Karnes, *Failure of Union*, 136–38 Rodriguez, *Palmerstonian*, 323, 344; Bancroft, *Central America*, 3:210.

57. *Gaceta de Guatemala*, 10–31 Jan. 1850; José N. Rodríguez, *Estudios de historia militar de Centro-América* (1930), 219; Bancroft, *Central America*, 3:279–81.

58. The Dieta passed a resolution on 21 Jan. warning Salvador and Honduras not to invade Guatemalan territory, but this news did not reach Guatemala until 19 Feb., brought by the British warship *Gorgon*, and it did not likely reach the invading army in time to have any influence with it either. *Gaceta de Guatemala*, 22 Feb. 1851. The resolution is published in the following issue of the *Gaceta*, 28 Feb. 1851.

59. Ibid., 25 Jan. and 1 Feb. 1851.

60. Vasconcelos to Arriaga, Metapán, 28 Jan. 1851, *Gaceta de Guatemala*, 12 Feb. 1851.

61. Mariano Paredes, "El Presidente de Guatemala a los pueblos de la República," and Rafael Carrera to Ministro de Guerra, Ipala, 6 Feb. 1851, *Gaceta de Guatemala*, 12 Feb. 1851; Rodríguez, *Palmerstonian*, 344; Rubio Sánchez, *Lorenzana*, 47–64; and the battle map in J. N. Rodríguez, *Estudios*, 219–20. The engineer of the Consulado, Agustín Van de Gehuchte, in March reconnoitered the battleground and drew a detailed map of the battle, dedicated to General Carrera. It was described by the *Gaceta de Guatemala*, 28 Mar. 1851, "for its exactness and precision, it is an important work, destined to preserve the memory of one of the most glorious military actions of our armed forces."

62. *Gaceta de Guatemala*, 15 Feb.–28 Mar. 1851; AGCA, B, leg. 753, exp. 17776; Bancroft, *Central America*, 3:280.

63. José A. Jiménez to R. Carrera, San Salvador, 17 Feb. 1851, *Gaceta de Guatemala*, 7 Mar. 1851.

64. Carrera to Jiménez, Santa Ana, 20 Feb. 1851, *Gaceta de Guatemala*.

65. Carrera to Jiménez, Santa Ana, 22 Feb. 1851, *Gaceta de Guatemala*, 7 Mar. 1851.

66. Bancroft, *Central America*, 3:299. The text of this treaty is in Pineda de Mont, *Recopilación*, 1:431–33.

67. Rafael Carrera to Chepita Silva, Cerro Redondo, 12 June 1851; San Francisco, 29 June 1851; Salamá, 23 Feb. 1852; San José, 29 Feb. 1852; Aranalpa, 9 Jan. 1853; and Chiquimula, 21 Jan., 17 Feb., and 19 Mar. 1853, GCUK. There was ample evidence that Carrera was correct in suspecting Cabañas of conspiring against him in eastern Guatemala. Reina Valenzuela, *Cabañas*, 175–80.

68. Paredes ordered the promotion on 8 Feb.; the Constituent Assembly confirmed it on 27 Sept. 1851. AGCA, B, leg. 2439, exps. 52477, 52478 and 52573.

69. "Rafael Carrera a los Guatemaltecos," Guatemala, 4 Mar. 1851, *Gaceta de Guatemala*, 7 Mar. 1851. Carrera's triumphal entry into the city is described in detail in this issue.

70. Rodríguez, *Palmerstonian*, 348.

71. Reina Valenzuela, *Cabañas*, 143–52; Medardo Mejía, *Trinidad Cabañas, soldado de la República Federal* (1971); Francisco Solano Astaburuaga y Cienfuegos, *República de Centro América, o idea de su historia i de su estado actual* (1857), 70–71; Bancroft, *Central America*, 3:319–21; Parker, *Central American Republics*, 185–86.

72. *Gaceta de Guatemala*, 15 Feb. 1851, 30 Apr. 1852, and 28 May 1852. Rodríguez, *Palmerstonian*, 353, contends that Chatfield continued to have influence in Central America even after his return to England through his friends in Guatemala, M. F. Pavón and Marcos Idígoras, as well as through Edward Wallerstein, the Guatemalan minister in England.

73. *Gaceta de Guatemala*, 19 Nov. 1852; Reina Valenzuela, *Cabañas*, pp. 162–63; Medardo Mejía, *Historia de Honduras*, (1988), 4:66–119.

74. Carrera to Ministro de Relaciones, Jutiapa, 10 Jan. 1853, B, AGCA, leg. 2460, exp. 54348; *Gaceta de Guatemala*, 14 Jan. 1853.

75. *Gaceta de Guatemala*, 14 Jan.–22 April 1853; Reina Valenzuela, *Cabañas*, 166–67.

76. R. Mejia to Jesús María Gutiérrez, Sinnapa [*sic*], Honduras, 29 Apr. 1853, *Gaceta de Guatemala*, 6 May 1853; Reina Valenzuela, *Cabañas*, 169.

77. *Gaceta de Guatemala*, 6 May 1853.

78. Antonio López de Santa Anna to Rafael Carrera, México, 25 Apr. 1853, and Carrera to Santa Anna, Guatemala, 6 June 1853, *Gaceta de Guatemala*, 10 June 1853.

79. Rafael Carrera, Proclamations of 5 and 6 July 1853, in *Gaceta de Guatemala*, 8 July 1853.

80. "Boletines de Noticias" nos. 7 and 8, *Gaceta de Guatemala*, 15 July 1853; Reina Valenzuela, *Cabañas*, 175–79.

81. *Rafael Carrera, El Presidente de la República, Capitán Jeneral del Ejército, a División de Operaciones*, Chiquimula, 2 Aug. 1853, in Coll. 20, Central America Political Ephemera, LALTU; AGCA, B, leg. 2460, exp. 54477 and 54485; Rafael Carrera to Chepita Silva, Chiquimula, 8 Aug. 1853, Gualán, 15 Aug. 1853, and Yzabal, 18 Aug. 1853, GCUK.

82. Zavala to Carrera, Omoa, 24 Aug. 1853, AGCA, B, leg. 2460, exp. 54479, and Carrera to Manuel María Bolaños, Omoa, 24 Aug. 1853, exp. 54481. Details on the battle also appeared in "Boletines de Noticias" nos. 15 and 16, *Gaceta de Guatemala*, 9 Sept. 1853.

83. Carrera's decree of 6 July 1853, following Cabañas's invasion of Guatemala, had prohibited all communication and commerce with Honduras. *Gaceta de Guatemala*, 9 Dec. 1853.

84. *Gaceta de Guatemala*, 9 Sept.–28 Oct. 1853.

85. Bancroft, *Central America*, 3:259.

86. *Gaceta de Guatemala*, 28 Apr. 1854 and 19 May 1853; Bancroft, *Central America*, 3:300, 564; Browning, *El Salvador*, 153.

87. Carrera to Chepita Silva, 15 Feb. 1854, GCUK.

88. Carrera to Chepita Silva, Guatemala, 2 Sept. 1854, GCUK.

89. *Gaceta de Guatemala*, 4 Aug. 1854. As early as 8 August 1851, the *Gaceta de Guatemala* had expressed the fear that the United States wished to establish protectorates over Central America and Hispaniola.

90. Santos Guardiola, *Manifiesto a los pueblos de Honduras por el que suscribe*, Guatemala, 31 Dec. 1853, in Coll. 20, Central America Political Ephemera, LALTU.

91. Leandro Godoy to Cerna, Gracias, 7 July 1855, *Gaceta de Guatemala*, 20 July 1855; Reina Valenzuela, *Cabañas*, 190–96.

92. "El General en Gefe del Ejército Constitucional de Honduras a sus Habitantes," Gracias, 20 July 1855, *Gaceta de Guatemala*, 17 Aug. 1855.

93. *El Presidente de la República de Guatemala a los pueblos del Estado de Honduras* (Guatemala, 3 Aug. 1855), Arturo Taracena Collection, BLAC.

94. "Boletines de Noticias" nos. 21 and 22, *Gaceta de Guatemala*, 19 Oct. 1855; Reina Valenzuela, *Cabañas*, 185–88.

95. Bancroft, *Central America*, 3:281, 322. A formal peace treaty between Honduras and Guatemala was signed on 13 Feb. 1856 and included a provision that political refugees were to be kept away from the border, as had the Guatemalan-Salvadoran treaty of 1853. This treaty may be found in Pineda de Mont, *Recopilación*, 1:433–36, or the *Gaceta de Guatemala*, 9 Apr. 1856.

96. Rafael Carrera, *Mensage dirigido por el exelentisimo señor Presidente de la República de Guatemala, Capitán General don Rafael Carrera, a la Cámara de Representantes, en la apertura de sus cuartas sesiones, el dia 25 de Noviembre de 1855* (1855), 2.

11. The Conservative Citadel

1. *Gaceta de Guatemala*, 1 and 22 Sept. 1854; Bancroft, *Central America*, 3:279; AGCA, B, leg. 28457, exp. 858.

2. Juan José Piñol to Escuintla, Manuel Arango to Sololá, Rafael Arévalo to the Verapaz, and J. B. Yudice to Totonicapán. *Gaceta de Guatemala*, 23 Aug. 1849.

3. Weaver, "Liberal Historian," 8–29; "Apuntes Biográficos," *Gaceta de Guatemala*, 4 July 1851. Marure died on 23 June 1851.

4. *Gaceta de Guatemala*, 27 Sept. 1849.

5. "Adición," *Sucesos del Dia*, 24 Sept. 1849.

6. *Gaceta de Guatemala*, 23 Aug. 1849.

7. Mariano Paredes, *Informe dirijido por el Presidente de la República al cuerpo representativo, en la apertura de las sesiones el dia 16 de agosto de 1851* (1851), 1–2.

8. *Gaceta de Guatemala*, 5 Sept. 1851.

9. Ibid., 29 Dec. 1849.

10. Results of the annual elections, normally held in December, for the ayuntamiento, were reported in the government gazettes. See also the list of vecinos convoked by the municipality of the capital for 2 Dec. 1860, in *hojas sueltas* collection, Hemeroteca of the AGCA.

11. *Gaceta Oficial*, 5 Dec. 1843.

12. *Gaceta de Guatemala*, 12 Nov. 1852, 18 Dec. 1858, 19 Dec. 1859. The junta of the colegio was established 1852 with José Antonio Larrave as decano, and José Venacio López, Francisco X. Urrutia, Pedro Aycinena, and José Mariano González as deputies, Manuel Dardón as fiscal, and Arcadio Estrada as secretary. *Gaceta de Guatemala*, 18 Dec. 1858, 19 Dec. 1859. For a list of the country's lawyers as well as other professionals and officials in 1853, see *Guía de forasteros de Guatemala para el año 1853*, 33–38.

13. Manuel Rubio Sánchez, *Historial del Fuerte de San Rafael de Matamoros* (1982), 29–47.

14. Mariano Zeceña, *La revolución de 1871 y sus caudillos: Estudios políticos*, 3d ed. (1957), 33.

15. *El Editor: Periódico de los Tribunales*, 14 Oct. 1837.

16. Stephens, *Incidents*, 2:111.

17. *El Tiempo*, 22 Jan. 1840, published an account of an officer, Juan Barillas, who had demanded seven pesos from the alcaldes of the village of Mixco, apparently without authorization or justification. The government in that case reprimanded Barillas, ordered him to refund the money, and warned other post commanders not to abuse their authority.

18. *Gaceta Oficial*, 20 Nov. 1846. On the colonial military fuero, the standard work is Lyle N. McAlister, *The "Fuero Militar" in New Spain, 1764–1800* (1957), but also useful are Christon I. Archer, *The Army in Bourbon Mexico, 1760–1810* (1977), and Allan J. Kuethe, *Military Reform and Society in New Granada, 1773–1808* (1978).

19. *Gaceta de Guatemala*, 13 Oct. 1847. A report on the Guatemala City garrison here includes a table listing the amounts of all sorts of military equipment in the capital.

20. Carrera's army fits rather closely the description of nineteenth-century military development in Latin America by Lyle McAlister, "The Military," in *Continuity and Change in Latin America*, edited by John J. Johnson (1964), 139–40. See Table 23 and Figure 12 below, for detailed statistics on the military's share of government revenues.

21. Rubio Sánchez, *Francisco Cáscara*. See also Cáscara's obituary, *Gaceta de Guatemala*, 4 April 1851, and a much more detailed "Apuntes Biográficos" in the 11 Apr. 1851 issue of the *Gaceta*.

22. José M. Palomo to Ministro del Interior, Antigua, 28 Dec. 1851, AGCA, B, leg. 28554, exp. 1253.

23. S. A. Lazardi, "El Excelentísimo Señor Gral. Don Rafael Carrera," *El Progreso Nacional* (Guatemala) 2, no. 34 (7 May 1895):73. Knoth was promoted by Carrera from Lieutenant Colonel to Colonel in June 1854. Also serving at this time as a personal secretary to Carrera was Manuel Arzú, who had entered Carrera's service as private secretary in 1848. *Gaceta de Guatemala*, 7 July 1854.

24. This incident occurred in March 1857 and brought a strong protest from the French consul. Knoth was tried by the military fuero, and a board presided

over by General Bolaños heard his case on 14 Jan. 1858, sentencing him to five years. Knoth's appeal to the Supreme Court, heard in April, was denied. The court reviewed the case on 10 July and ordered Knoth to serve his sentence in the Castillo de San José, declaring that although it appreciated the circumstances of the act, Knoth should have given Antoni due process as provided under Guatemala law. *Gaceta de Guatemala*, 16 Jan. and 18 July 1858.

25. *Gaceta de Guatemala*, 25 Aug. 1860. AGCA, B78.24, leg. 16396, leg. 719.

26. Guatemala, Sacatepéquez, Verapaz, Chiquimula, Sololá, Quetzaltenango, and Totonicapán. "Decreto. El Jefe de Estado de Guatemala, 24 de mayo de 1828," in Coll. 20, Central America Political Ephemera, LALTU.

27. Marure, *Efemérides*, 31.

28. *El Tiempo*, 5 Sept. 1839.

29. Rafael Carrera to Ministro de Gobernación, and accompanying documents, AGCA, B, leg. 28574, exp. 2398, Archivo del Ministerio de Gobernación (hereinafter cited as AMG), Exps. Sololá, Año 1857; and Manuel J. Urrutia, "Apuntamientos estadísticos del Departamento de Jutiapa," *Gaceta de Guatemala*, 8 Aug. 1866; Mariano de Anguiano, Corregidor de Totonicapám, to the Ministro de Gobernación, 18 July 1870, in AGCA, B, leg. 28623, exp. 117. Francisco Gavarrete's three little *geografícas* (1860, 1868, and 1874) reflect the changes in departmental jurisdictions.

30. Many of these reports were published in the *Gaceta de Guatemala*, especially when, as was usual, they were favorable. Many more, unpublished, are in the AGCA.

31. See, for example, Cerna to Ministerio de Gobernación, Chiquimula, 16 Sept. 1857, regarding seditious conduct in the village of Cuviletes. AGCA, B, leg. 28574, exp. 2399, AMG, Exps. Zacapa, Año 1857.

32. AGCA, B, leg. 28578, exps. 100–101, AMG, Comunicaciones, Izabal, Año 1859.

33. *Gaceta de Guatemala*, 9 June 1859.

34. See Lewis Snow, "The Páez Years: Venezuelan Economic Legislation, 1830–1846" (1970), 64–65.

35. Stephens, *Incidents*, 1:304.

36. Crowe, *Gospel*, 305–6.

37. Arthur Morelet, *Travels in Central America* (1871), 399. For an especially useful study of the principal Guatemalan families during the federation period, see Strobeck, "Political Activities."

38. Executive Decree no. 40, *Gaceta de Guatemala*, 13 Sept. 1849.

39. "Aristocracia," *Gaceta de Guatemala*, 18 Oct. 1849.

40. Ibid., 19 Sept. 1850 and 21 June 1851.

41. Ibid., 25 Aug. 1851.

42. *Gaceta de Guatemala*, 20 Apr. 1855; a detailed biographical sketch of Pavón appeared in the *Gaceta de Guatemala*, 30 May–14 June 1855. The government displayed its gratitude to Pavón following his death by granting his widow an annual

pension of $900, the largest pension to that date authorized by the Guatemalan government. Ibid., 18 Jan. 1856. On Milla, see Walter A. Payne, *A Central American Historian, José Milla (1822–1882)* (1957), and Mario Alberto Carrera, *Breve biografía de Pepe Milla* (n.d.).

43. *Gaceta de Guatemala*, 15 Jan. 1859.

44. AGCA, B, leg. 630, exp. 12805.

45. Ramón A. Salazar, *Mariano de Aycinena* (1952); biographical sketch in *Gaceta de Guatemala*, 26 Jan. 1855.

46. *Gaceta de Guatemala*, 19 Aug. 1858; see also the long biographical sketch on Juan José Aycinena published in the *Gaceta*, 12 March–8 April 1865; and Chandler, *Aycinena* (1988).

47. *Gaceta de Guatemala*, 18 June and 17 Aug. 1862; the latter article was reprinted as a pamphlet: *Noticia biográfica del Señor Don Luis Batres, Consejero de Estado y Vice-Presidente de la Cámara de Representantes* (Guatemala, 1862). Following Batres's death, on 17 July 1862, Carrera ordered that his portrait be hung in the Council of State chamber as a reminder of his great services. AGCA, B, leg. 28590, AMG, Comunicaciones, Guatemala, Año 1862. The municipality of the capital actually paid for the portrait (AGCA, B, leg. 754, exps. 17808–09), and it was later hung in the city council chamber. It was removed following the liberal revolution of 1871, but on the motion of Regidor Agustín Girón on 24 Dec. 1872, it was replaced, a credit to Batres's reputation. AGCA, B, leg. 754, exp. 17835. This was done after Batres's family had solicited on 13 Dec. to be given the portrait that had been taken down. AGCA, B, leg. 699, exp. 15223.

48. *Gaceta de Guatemala*, 20 Aug. 1849 and 27 July 1860.

49. Ibid., 8 Jan. 1863; Manuel Octavio Zea Carrascosa, *Semblanzas: Ministros de la Guerra y de la Defensa Nacional de Guatemala* (1971), 95.

50. *Gaceta de Guatemala*, 20 Apr. 1852. Theodore S. Creedman, *Historical Dictionary of Costa Rica* (1977), 125–26.

51. *Gaceta de Guatemala*, 10 and 24 Sept., 22 Oct., and 31 Dec. 1859. After several months in Guatemala, Colina went to Europe, but he returned to Guatemala in December 1860. Ibid., 6 May and 21 Dec. 1860.

52. A formal decree allowing them to return was dated 7 June 1851. Pineda de Mont, *Recopilación*, 3:272; the Guatemalan legislature approved the restoration of a Jesuit Institute on 29 Oct. 1851. See *Gaceta de Guatemala*, 6 and 13 June and 8 Oct. 1851, and 1 May 1861, regarding support of Capuchin and Jesuit missions in northern Guatemala; Miller, *La iglesia*, 39; Holleran, *Church and State*, 133–45; AGCA, AMG, leg. 28552, exp. 1091.

53. Pineda de Mont, *Recopilación*, 3:289; *Gaceta de Guatemala*, 11 Nov. 1864; Francisco de Paula García Peláez to Ministro de Gobernación, Guatemala, 1853 AGCA, B, Leg. 28599, exp. 1490, in which the archbishop emphasizes the urgent need for more priests and calls for philosophy classes at the university to be taught in Latin to improve the training of priests. Later, in 1859, the archbishop began positive planning for a seminary, which culminated in the establishment of the

seminary by the Order of St. Vincent de Paul in 1864. Francisco Arzobispo de Guatemala to Ministro de Gobernación, AGCA, B, leg. 28577, AMG, Comunicaciones, Año 1859.

54. Pius IX to Rafael Carrera, Rome, 11 Nov. 1848, *Gaceta de Guatemala*, 31 Aug. 1849.

55. Pineda de Mont, *Recopilación*, 1:353–60; Rodríguez Cerna, *Colección de Tratados*, 3:250–55; Miller, *La iglesia*, 40–41. Carrera ratified the concordat on 31 Dec. 1853, and the pope ratified the document in Rome on the following 13 March. *Gaceta de Guatemala*, 7 July 1854.

56. *Gaceta de Guatemala*, 28 Apr. 1854. Carrera attended a solemn mass at the Cathedral of Guatemala on 23 Apr. 1854 where the concordat was formally published, and at the same time the archbishop announced Carrera's decoration as Caballero Gran Cruz de la Orden de San Gregorio Magno (dated 20 Dec. 1853). *Gaceta de Guatemala*, 28 Apr. 1854.

57. See the biographical sketch on García Peláez in the *Gaceta de Guatemala*, 27 June–25 Aug. 1867; Francisco Fernández Hall, "Historiadores de Guatemala posteriores a la independencia nacional: El Doctor don Francisco de Paula García Peláez," *Anales de la Sociedad de Geografía e Historia* 15, no. 3 (March 1939):261–78; and three articles in the *Anales de la Sociedad de Geografía e Historia* 40, no. 1/2 (January–June 1967):15–36, commemorating the hundredth anniversary of the death of García Peláez: Francisco Gall, "En el centenario del fallecimiento de García Peláez," 15–19; Valentín Solórzano Fernández, "García Peláez: Cátedra prima de economía política en el Reino de Guatemala," 19–29; and Jorge Luis Arriola, "García Peláez, uno de los precursores del liberalismo económico en Guatemala," 29–36.

58. AGCA, B, leg. 28587.

59. Carrera to Pius IX, Guatemala, 3 Jan. 1859, *Gaceta de Guatemala*, 27 May 1859.

60. Naming clerics as bishops of lands held by the infidels was a means of honoring clergymen for whom there were no dioceses immediately available. Barrutia was named bishop of Camaco, Zepeda (who served in the Diocese of Comayagua, Honduras) bishop of Arindele, and Aycinena bishop of Trajanapolis. The first two were named auxiliaries of Archbishop García Peláez. Pope Pius IX to Rafael Carrera, Rome, 21 Mar. 1859, *Gaceta de Guatemala*; and 23 June 1859. Carrera named Barrutia as cantor of the cathedral shortly thereafter, replacing Bernardo Piñol, who had left to take up his position as bishop of Nicaragua. *Gaceta de Guatemala*, 13 Aug. 1859.

61. *Gaceta de Guatemala*, 15 and 21 March and 19 July 1850.

62. Ibid., 2 Mar. 1855, 22 Feb., 13 and 21 Dec. 1860, and 10 Apr. 1861.

63. Piñol's conservative views and activities did not sit well with the liberals who came to power in 1871. Accused of plotting a counterrevolution after the liberals expelled the Jesuits in that year, Piñol himself was exiled soon after. He died in Havana on 24 June 1881. Bancroft, *Central America*, 3:630.

64. Basilio Zeceña, *Oración pronunciada en la Santa Iglesia Catedral en el aniversario de la independencia; por el Sr. Presb. D. Basilio Zeceña, Doctor en Sagrada Teologia, Cura de San Juan Sacatepéquez* (1851), 2–7, 9.

65. *Gaceta de Guatemala*, 23 Oct. 1850.

66. Ibid., 2 Mar. 1855.

67. Francisco de Paula García Peláez, *Discurso pronunciado el 15 de septiembre de 1856 XXV aniversario de la independencia de Guatemala* (1856), 7–8.

68. Decree of José Ignacio Aycinena, Corregidor of the Department of Guatemala, Guatemala, 31 Mar. 1860. Alcaldes and Regidores were charged with enforcement. *Hojas sueltas* collection, Hemeroteca of the AGCA.

69. The regulations for this important institution were published in full in the *Gaceta de Guatemala*, 1 Mar. 1860.

70. For examples of these sorts of activities, see the *Gaceta de Guatemala*, 27 Aug. 1857 and 29 Sept. 1858.

71. Clarke's wife, Zenobia, had already been taking instruction in Catholicism before her husband's death. She and her two children were baptized on 23 Mar. and departed for San José on the following day, her godmother being Susana Bayley de Piñol. *Gaceta de Guatemala*, 25–29 Mar. 1860.

72. *Gaceta de Guatemala*, 6 July 1861.

73. *Gaceta de Guatemala*, 29 May and 8 Nov. 1849, 1 Jan. 1857, and 7 Jan. 1858.

74. Ibid., 25 Feb. 1852.

75. Woodward, *Class Privilege*, 55–80; *Gaceta de Guatemala*, 21 Dec. 1849, 6 June 1850, 15 Aug. 1851, 14 Feb., and 19–24 Apr. 1856, and 15 Jan. 1863.

76. *Gaceta de Guatemala*, 28 Mar. 1851, 24 Dec. 1852, 21 Feb. 1856.

77. "Informe" of Jorge Ponce to Ayuntamiento, 5 Feb. 1861, *Gaceta de Guatemala*, 17 Feb. 1861.

78. Ramón A. Salazar, *Tiempo viejo, recuerdos de mi juventud*, 2d ed. (1957), 9.

79. *Gaceta de Guatemala*, 21 Mar. 1864.

12. Presidente Vitalicio

1. *Gaceta de Guatemala*, 15, 21, and 28 Mar., and 30 Aug. 1851.

2. Ibid., 21 Feb. 1850.

3. Ibid., 26 July 1850.

4. Ibid., 13 Sept. 1850.

5. Ibid., 14 Jan. 1853.

6. *Gaceta de Guatemala*, 18 Nov. 1850. See also 20 and 27 Dec. 1850, and 18 Jan.–15 Feb. 1851. Montalembert's strong Catholic version of liberalism presumably made him attractive to the Guatemalan conservatives.

7. *Gaceta de Guatemala*, 4 June 1852.

8. Ibid., 18 June 1852. The Unitario party in Argentina reflected liberal philosophy and had bitterly opposed Juan Manuel Rosas.

9. "Nacionalidad de Centro-América. Artículo 2," *Gaceta de Guatemala*, 1 Nov. 1850.

10. Decree no. 55, *Gaceta de Guatemala*, 21 Mar. 1851. The assembly approved this change on 3 Dec. 1851. Ibid., 19 Dec. 1851. A modification of this flag, making it appear even more like the Spanish ensign, occurred on 1 May 1858. AGCA, B, leg. 28576; *Gaceta de Guatemala*, 31 May 1858; María Albertina Gálvez G., *Emblemas nacionales* (1958), 153–55.

11. Pedro N. Arriaga and José Nájera, "Exposición dirigida al Exmo. Sr. Presidente de la República por los Sres. Secretarios del despacho," Guatemala, 8 May 1851, *Gaceta de Guatemala*, 16 May 1851.

12. Decreto no. 57, *Gaceta de Guatemala*, 16 May 1851. Paredes based his call on Carrera's decree of 24 May 1848.

13. AGCA, B, leg. 627, exp. 12580, fols. 12, 13 and 58; leg. 715, exp. 15987; leg. 736, exp. 17206; leg. 863, exp. 21128; leg. 2362, exp. 48043; leg. 2436, exps. 51819–20; leg. 3560, exp. 81169; leg. 3591, exp. 82403; leg. 3633, exp. 85397; leg. 4126, exp. 92809, fol. 69; see also the column by Juslongo Orsini (pseudonym for Julio Rosignon) in *El Progreso* (Guatemala) 27 July 1875; and Woodward, *Class Privilege*, 131–32. Other members of the Advisory Council included the ministers of government (Pedro N. Arriaga, José Nájera, and M. F. Pavón), the secretary of the Consulado (Manuel Echeverría), Camilo Idalgo, Juan José Flores, Luis Batres, the chief accountant (Manuel Cerezo), and head of the Revenue Department (Manuel J. Durán). *Gaceta de Guatemala*, 8 Aug. 1851; *Guía de forasteros de Guatemala para el año 1853*.

14. Representatives were not required to be residents of the departments that they represented, so most of them were members of the elite of the capital. *Gaceta de Guatemala*, 31 Oct. 1851.

15. "Acta Constitutiva." *Gaceta de Guatemala*, 25 Oct. 1851; Pineda de Mont, *Recopilación*, 1:79–87; Moorhead, "Rafael Carrera," 78–81.

16. "Acta de elección del Presidente Constitucional de la República de Guatemala," *Gaceta de Guatemala*, 31 Oct. 1851; AGCA. B78.25, leg. 738, exp. 17276.

17. M. F. Pavón replaced the ailing Arriaga as prime minister, in charge of interior government, justice, and ecclesiastical affairs. José Nájera remained from the previous administration as minister of finance and war, while José Mariano Rodríguez took over the Foreign Ministry, which Pavón now vacated. *Gaceta de Guatemala*, 8 Oct. [*sic* Nov.] 1851; "Manifesto del Exmo. Señor Presidente de la República de Guatemala á sus conciudadanos," Guatemala, 10 Nov. 1851, *Gaceta de Guatemala*, 14 Nov. 1851.

18. *Gaceta de Guatemala*, 14–21 Nov. 1851.

19. Ibid., 28 Nov. 1851–2 Jan. 1852.

20. AGCA, B, leg. 717, exps. 16134, 16159, 16164, 16180; leg. 718, exp. 16224.

21. AGCA, B, leg 2460, exp. 54341.

22. AGCA, B, leg. 604, exps. 11694, 11698, 11725; leg. 717, exp. 16134; leg. 719, exp. 16322; leg. 720, exps. 16411, 16452; leg. 28590.

23. A summary description of the properties appeared in the *Gaceta de Guatemala*, 19 Dec. 1865. A much more detailed inventory of the properites can be found in "Inventarios del mortual del Capitán Gral. Don Rafael Carrera, 1865," AGCA, Juzgado Civil, leg. 25, fols. 10–74.

24. The assembly passed the bill on 19 Apr. 1858, and it was signed by Carrera on 7 May following. The full text of the *Montepío Civil y Militar* appears in the *Gaceta de Guatemala*, 13 May 1858.

25. *Gaceta de Guatemala*, 23 June 1854.

26. Ibid., 29 June 1861 and 24 Dec. 1864.

27. AGCA, B, leg. 720, exp. 16411; *Gaceta de Guatemala*, 13 Jan. and 28 Feb. 1862.

28. A number of letters between Carrera and Silva are found in GCUK.

29. Lazardi, "Carrera," 74.

30. *Illustrated London News*, 26 Feb. 1853.

31. See, for example, the New York *Observer*, 3 June 1864.

32. *Gaceta de Guatemala*, 13 and 27 Feb. 1852.

33. Ibid., 27 Feb.–12 Nov. 1852, 20 May 1853.

34. Ibid., 13 Aug. 1852.

35. Rafael Carrera, "El Presidente de la República, Capitán General del ejército, a los habitantes de la capital," *Gaceta de Guatemala*, 20 Aug. 1852.

36. Rafael Carrera, Decreto no. 89, 27 Sept. 1852, *Gaceta de Guatemala*, 1 Oct. 1852.

37. *Gaceta de Guatemala*, 16 July 1852.

38. Ibid., 27 Aug. 1852. Final selection was in part delayed by the fact that the same representatives were elected by several different departments, prohibited by the new constitution and requiring in some cases new elections. See the *Gaceta de Guatemala*, 29 Oct. 1852, for a complete list of the new representatives.

39. Reprinted in the *Gaceta de Guatemala*, 14 Jan. 1853.

40. *Gaceta de Guatemala*, 2 December 1852.

41. Rafael Carrera, *Informe dirijido por el Exmo. Señor Presidente de la República de Guatemala a la Cámara de Representantes, en el acto de su instalación, el día 25 de noviembre de 1852* (1852).

42. *Gaceta de Guatemala*, 17 Dec. 1852.

43. Ibid., 17–24 Dec. 1852.

44. Ibid., 4 Feb. 1853.

45. See, for example, the list of ninety fugitives from Juzgados 1 and 2 in Guatemala in the *Gaceta de Guatemala*, 18 Mar. 1853; and the list of 237 fugitives from the Antigua Juzgado on 22 Apr. 1853.

46. "Acta de la sesión que a cabildo abierto, celebró la municipalidad de la capital, resolviéndose solicitar a la Cámara de Representantes la reforma del Acta

Constitutiva y sea reconocido el Teniente General Rafael Carrera como Presidente Vitalicio de la República," AGCA, B, leg. 753, exp. 17788.

47. *Gaceta de Guatemala*, 26 May–9 June 1854. Formal requests for the opinions of the ecclesiastical council, the supreme court, the university, the consulado, and the Economic Society went out on 20 June. Ibid., 23 June 1854.

48. Rafael Carrera, "Manifiesto," (Guatemala, 22 June 1854); also in *Gaceta de Guatemala*, 23 June 1854.

49. *Gaceta de Guatemala*, 4 Aug. 1854.

50. *Gaceta de Costa Rica*, 22 and 29 May 1854, quoted in "La autoridad vitalicia y la Gaceta de Costa Rica," *Gaceta de Guatemala*, 21 July 1854.

51. "Informe del Claustro de Doctores sobre la aclamación de Presidente perpetuo hecha en los departamentos de la República en favor del Exmo. Sr. Capitán Jeneral D. Rafael Carrera," *Gaceta de Guatemala*, 15 Sept. 1854; AGCA, B, leg. 1069, exp. 22447.

52. "La cuestión del día," *Gaceta de Guatemala*, 22 Sept. 1954.

53. *Gaceta de Guatemala*, 29 Sept. and 6 Oct. 1854.

54. *Acta de la Junta General de autoridades, funcionarios públicos, prelados eclesiásticos, gefes militares y diputaciones de las corporaciones, en que se aclamó presidente perpetuo de la República de Guatemala, al Exmo. Señor Capitán General Don Rafael Carrera*, (1854), also published in the *Gaceta de Guatemala*, 27 Oct. 1854, along with an article, 3–4, detailing the events of the day's proceedings. See also Enrique del Cid Fernández, *Origen, trama y desarrollo del movimiento que proclamó vitalicia la presidencia del General Rafael Carrera* (1966).

55. *Gaceta de Guatemala*, 6 and 20 Oct. 1854.

56. Reprinted in *Gaceta de Guatemala*, 5 Jan. 1855.

57. Arturo Taracena Flores, "Biografías sintéticas de guatemaltecos distinguidos," *Revista de la Academia Guatemalteca de Estudios Genealógicos, Heráldicos e Históricos* 3–4 (1970):380–81.

58. "Situación," *Gaceta de Guatemala*, 17 Nov. 1854.

59. *Mensage dirigido por el Exmo. Sr. Presidente de la República de Guatemala, Capitán General Don Rafael Carrera, a la Cámara de Representantes, en la apertura de sus terceras sesiones, el día 25 de Noviembre de 1854* (1854), pp. 1–2.

60. Juan Matheu, "Contestación de la Cámara de Representantes al Mensaje dirijido por el Exmo. Sr. Presidente de la República al abrirse las sesiones," *Gaceta de Guatemala*, 22 Dec. 1854 and 19 Jan. 1855.

61. Francisco Benites, 1o Consul, to Juan Matheu, Presidente de la Cámara de Representantes, Guatemala, 11 Jan. 1855, *Gaceta de Guatemala*, 16 Feb. 1855.

62. "La sesión del 15," *Gaceta de Guatemala*, 19 Jan. 1855.

63. "Dictamen de la Comisión Especial de la Cámara," *Gaceta de Guatemala*, 16 Feb. 1855.

64. The votes on the key issues were 20-8 (25 absent), 21-7 (25 absent), 19-9 (25 absent), 19-9 (25 absent), 17-8 (28 absent). Miguel García Granados and Juan Andreu led the small active opposition, but the high number of absences was more

revealing than the few courageous "nay" votes. Summaries of the debates appeared in the *Gaceta de Guatemala* 2 Feb.–13 Apr. 1855.

65. "Acta en que se reforman algunos artículos de la ley constitutiva de la República de Guatemala," *Gaceta de Guatemala*, 13 Apr. 1855.

66. *Gaceta de Guatemala*, 2 Feb. 1855.

67. Lazardi, "Carrera," 73–75.

68. Moorhead, "Rafael Carrera," 177, citing "Statement of events in California as related by Judge E. O. Crosby," MS., Bancroft Library, University of California, Berkeley, 1874.

13. Nicaragua

1. N. L. B. [Napoleon Louis Bonaparte], *Canal de Nicaragua, or a Project to Connect the Atlantic and Pacific Oceans by Means of a Canal* (1846).

2. Most of the facts regarding the Walker episode were carefully set down by Scroggs in 1916, yet more recent volumes continue to add details and shades of interpretation. Carr's attempt at psychohistory in *The World and William Walker* is especially useful. Frederick Rosengarten, Jr., *Freebooters Must Die!* (1976) is an attractive popular history, with many illustrations and maps. Robert E. May, *The Southern Dream of a Caribbean Empire, 1854–1861* (1973) places the Walker episode in the larger context of southern U.S. expansionism, while Wall, *Manifest Destiny Denied*, deals not only with the Walker episode, but also with Walker's less–well–known rival filibuster in eastern Nicaragua, Henry Kinney. David Folkman, *The Nicaragua Route* (1972), is useful for its detailed description of the development of the interoceanic route closely related to the filibustering activity. Probably no one has done more voluminous research on the Walker episode than the retired Nicaraguan physician, Alejandro Bolaños Geyer, who in the 1970s edited *Diario de John Hill Wheeler, Ministro de los Estados Unidos en Nicaragua, 1854–1857* (1974); *Documentos diplomáticos de William Carey Jones, agente especial de los Estados Unidos ante Costa Rica y Nicaragua, 1857–1858* (1974); *El testamento de Scott* (1975); *La guerra de Nicaragua según* Frank Leslie's Illustrated Newspaper *y* Harper's Weekly (1976); *El filibustero Clinton Rollins* (1976), and *Con Walker en Nicaragua* (1977). More recently he has begun the publication of a multivolume biography of Walker with his *William Walker, The Gray-Eyed Man of Destiny. Book One: The Crescent City* (1988). See also Walker's own account, *The War in Nicaragua* (1860).

3. The Nicaraguan Assembly in León quickly ratified the treaty, but U.S. Secretary of State Clayton refused to accept it because of the direct challenge to the British that it implied. Rodríguez, *Palmerstonian*, 302; Stansifer, *Ephraim George Squier*, 13–15.

4. "La exposición universal.—Progresos del Catolicismo—La América y su porvenir," *Gaceta de Guatemala*, 15 Aug. 1851.

5. *Gaceta de Guatemala*, 19 Sept. 1851.

6. Jamie Woods, "Expansionism as Diplomacy: The Career of Solon Borland in Central America 1853–1854," *The Americas* 40 (1984):399–417.

7. Bancroft, *Central America*, 3:257–59; Reina Valenzuela, *Cabañas*, 217–19.

8. Kinney was born in Wyoming Valley, Pa., in 1814, but moved to Chicago at age fourteen and was wealthy by age twenty-one. He served in the Black Hawk War and later was a merchant in Havana. He moved to Corpus Christi, Texas, in 1839 and served in the Texas legislature from 1841 to 1855. Along with eighteen other North American capitalists, he obtained the huge grant, 22.5 million acres, that the Miskito king had made to Peter and Samuel Shepherd, long-time British residents of the Miskito Coast, to colonize the region. Wall, *Manifest Destiny Denied*, 111–52.

9. Felipe Molina to William L. Marcy, Washington, 13 Dec. 1854, and Marcy to Molina, Washington, 19 Dec. 1854, in *Gaceta de Guatemala*, 2 Mar. 1855.

10. Wall, *Manifest Destiny Denied*, 118, citing John Priest (U.S. consul in San Juan del Sur) to Marcy, 1 June 1855, U.S. National Archives T152, 1, and John H. Wheeler to Marcy, 1 June 1855, M219, 11/19.

11. *Gaceta de Guatemala*, 23 Mar. 1855.

12. New York, *Weekly Post*, 6 Sept. 1855, quoted by Wall, *Manifest Destiny Denied*, 111.

13. Bancroft, *Central America*, 3:258–60; Rosengarten, *Freebooters*, 80.

14. Francisco Ortega Aranciba, *Cuarenta años (1838–1878) de historia de Nicaragua*, 3d ed. (1974), pp. 221–38; Andrés Vega Bolaños, *Gobernantes de Nicaragua: Notas y documentos* (1944), 157–209; Carr, *Walker*, 122–28; Marco A. Soto V., *Guerra Nacional de Centroamérica* (1957), 31–39; Walker, *War in Nicaragua*, 68–85.

15. Wall, *Manifest Destiny Denied*, 252–53, citing Marcy to Wheeler, 8 Nov. 1855, and Wheeler to Marcy, 12 Nov. 1855.

16. Carr, *Walker*, 182. See Pierce's message to Congress of 15 May 1856, in James D. Richardson, comp., *A Compilation of the Messages and Papers of the Presidents, 1789–1902* (1900–1903) 5:368–74.

17. *Gaceta de Guatemala*, 12 July 1856.

18. AGCA, B, leg. 2499, exp. 55314.

19. *Gaceta de Guatemala*, 20–27 July 1855.

20. Ibid., 7 Dec. 1856.

21. Ibid., 24 Aug. 1855.

22. *Mensage . . . 25 de noviembre de 1855*, 1–2.

23. *Gaceta de Guatemala*, 28 Dec. 1855.

24. *Gaceta de Guatemala*, 4 Jan. 1856.

25. AGCA, B, leg. 2499, exp. 55333, *Gaceta de Guatemala*, 4 Jan.–12 Feb. 1856; Bancroft, *Central America*, 3:300.

26. "El Presidente de la República de Costa Rica a todos sus habitantes," San José, 1 Mar. 1856, *Gaceta de Guatemala*, 11 Mar. 1856.

27. Carr, *Walker*, 173.

28. Reprinted in *Littell's Living Age* 13, no. 621 (9 Aug. 1856), and quoted in Wall, *Manifest Destiny Denied*, 2.

29. *Gaceta de Guatemala*, 19 and 26 Apr. 1856.

30. Ibid., 10 May 1856.

31. Rafael Carrera, "El Presidente y Capitán General de Guatemala, á los habitantes de la república y á la vanguardia de las fuerzas espedicionarias," *Gaceta de Guatemala*, 7 May 1856.

32. Patricio Rivas, "El Presidente de la República a los Nicaragüenses," León, 30 Mar. 1856, *Gaceta de Guatemala*, 19 Apr. 1856.

33. *Gaceta de Guatemala*, 19 Apr.–12 July 1856.

34. "William Walker, General en Gefe del Ejército de Nicaragua, Granada, 20 de junio de 1856," *Gaceta de Guatemala*, 12 July 1856, reprinted from *Boletín de Noticias*, Cojutepeque, El Salvador.

35. *Gaceta de Guatemala*, 9 Nov. 1856; Cleto González Viquez, *Capítulos de un libro sobre historia financiera de Costa Rica* (1977), 57–71.

36. *El Nicaragüense*, 3 Aug. 1856, reprinted in Spanish translation in the *Gaceta de Guatemala*, 16 Oct. 1856.

37. *Gaceta de Guatemala*, 7 and 24 May, 2 and 16 July, and 2 Aug. 1856.

38. Pedro Aycinena to Pedro Zeledón, Comisionado del Gobierno provisorio de Nicaragua, Guatemala 17 June 1856, *Gaceta de Guatemala*, 19 July 1856.

39. *Convención de liga y alianza entre las repúblicas de Guatemala, Honduras y El Salvador*, published by order of Rafael Carrera in Guatemala, 18 July 1856; also published in the *Gaceta de Guatemala*, 30 Aug. 1856.

40. *Gaceta de Guatemala*, 24 July 1856 and 24 Aug. 1856.

41. See the editorial on this problem in the *Gaceta de Guatemala*, 21 Sept. 1856.

42. There were six in all sworn into the Guatemalan service by President Carrera on 22 August 1856: Col. Luis Pérez Gómez, Capt. Luis Martínez, Capt. Tomás Suárez, Capt. Pedro Lesaca, Lt. José María de los Ríos (all infantry officers), and artillery Captain Agustín López. *Gaceta de Guatemala*, 24 Aug. 1856.

43. *Gaceta de Guatemala*, 2 Oct. 1856.

44. Subscriptions ranged from $750 to $10,000 per subscriber. *Gaceta de Guatemala*, 7 May 1857.

45. Evasion of this tax was so widespread that Carrera authorized closer control over cattle slaughtering by the corregidores on 28 Feb. 1857. AGCA, B, leg. 28574, AMG, Santa Rosa, Año 1857.

46. *Gaceta de Guatemala*, 2 Oct. 1856. Notices of the amounts donated throughout the republic are found in the *Gaceta*.

47. "El Presidente y Capitán General de Guatemala a los gefes, oficiales y soldados de la división expedicionaria," Guatemala, 14 Oct. 1856, *Gaceta de Guatemala*, 16 Oct. 1856.

48. J. F. Taboada y M. Trabanino to Municipalidad de Guatemala, 24 Sept. 1856, AGCA, B, leg. 753, exp. 17799.

49. Barrios to Carrera, San Miguel, El Salvador, 25 November 1856, AGCA, B, leg. 2499, exp. 55430.

50. Dueñas to Pedro Aycinena, Cojutepeque, 22 Jan. 1857, and Barrios to Carlos Antonio Meany, Cojutepeque, 20 Feb. 1857; AGCA, B, leg. 2499, exps. 55454 and 55474.

51. *Gaceta de Guatemala*, 5 Mar. 1857.

52. Ibid., 19 Oct. 1856.

53. Ibid., 2 Nov. 1856; Carr, *Walker*, 205.

54. *Gaceta de Guatemala*, 4 and 7 Dec. 1856; *El Museo Guatemalteco*, 11 Dec. 1856.

55. Pedro Cardenal to Pedro Aycinena, León, 5 Dec. 1856, *Gaceta de Guatemala*, 19 Dec. 1856.

56. *Gaceta de Guatemala*, 25 Dec. 1856.

57. "Acuerdo de S. E. el Presidente en que se dispone ciertos honores a la memoria del S. General Paredes," *Gaceta de Guatemala*, 21 Dec. 1856; Paredes's funeral is described in ibid., 18 Jan. 1857, and a detailed biographical sketch ran 8–22 Jan. 1857.

58. Carr, *Walker*, 215–20.

59. *Gaceta de Guatemala*, 30 Jan. and 5 Feb. 1857; Walker, *War in Nicaragua*, 313–400.

60. *Gaceta de Guatemala*, 15 Mar. 1857. While Dueñas had a liberal background, as did Barrios, under the pressure of Carrera he had restrained his liberalism and pursued more moderate policies in El Salvador.

61. *Gaceta de Guatemala*; see also ibid., 26 and 29 Mar. 1857; and the anonymous pamphlet published by order of the Guatemalan government in 1857, which emphasized the new unity, *Guatemala y El Salvador*, in Coll. 20, Central America Political Ephemera, LALTU.

62. Carr, *Walker*, 216–18. Among the Guatemalans killed in the final campaign was Lt. Col. Joaquín Cabrera, an officer who had made his reputation fighting against the montañeses in the Verapaz and who had fought valiantly in Nicaragua since the previous May. *Gaceta de Guatemala*, 9 Apr. 1857.

63. *Gaceta de Guatemala*, 2 Apr. and 16 Apr. 1857, and 14 Jan. 1858; *El Museo Guatemalteco*, 9 Apr. 1857.

64. *El Museo Guatemalteco*, 19 June–21 Aug. 1857; *Gaceta de Guatemala*, 18–21 June 1857.

65. "El Presidente y Capitán General de Guatemala a los Habitantes de la República," *Gaceta de Guatemala*, 17 May 1857.

66. *El Museo Guatemalteco*, 1 July 1857.

67. *Gaceta de Guatemala*, 4 July 1857.

68. Quirino Flores to José Ignacio de Aycinena, Guatemala, 4 July 1857, *Gaceta de Guatemala*, 9 July 1857.

69. "Informe del Protomédico sobre santidad pública," *Gaceta de Guatemala*, 12 July 1857 and 21 Jan. 1858.

70. *Gaceta de Guatemala*, 16 July 1857; Juan M. Echeverría to Ministro de Gobernación, 19 July 1857, ibid., 23 July 1857.

71. The government approved the request on 22 July 1857. AGCA, B, leg. 28574, AMG, Exps. Sacatepéquez, Año 1857.

72. Dr. Francisco de Paula García Peláez al Venerable clero secular y regular del Arzobispado, Guatemala, 16 July 1857, *Gaceta de Guatemala*, 23 July 1857.

73. *Gaceta de Guatemala*, 19–26 July 1857 and 21 Jan. 1858.

74. "Expediente del cólera morbus," AGCA, B, leg. 1109, exp. 24621. This document contains thirty-eight sheets of materials dealing with the epidemic, including such things as closing of schools, postponing of festivals, lists of those who died. These pages reflect the misery, suffering, and, to some degree, panic, that the epidemic brought.

75. AGCA, B, leg. 1109, exp. 25621, fol. 37; *Gaceta de Guatemala*, 25 Sept. 1857.

76. *Gaceta de Guatemala*, 7 May 1857 and 16 Jan. 1858; the baby was baptized by Father Nicolás Arellano on 17 May and immediately afterward confirmed by Archbishop García Peláez in the palace chapel.

77. *Boletín Extraordinario*, Guatemala, 17 Aug. 1857, AGCA B, leg. 1109, exp. 24621, fol. 33; further detail in the *Gaceta de Guatemala*, 20 Aug. 1857.

78. Perfecta Obregón to Bolaños, Guatemala, 22 Oct. 1857, *Gaceta de Guatemala*, 27 Oct. 1857.

79. *Gaceta de Guatemala*, 23 July–23 Aug. and 10 Dec. 1857; 2 Sept. 1858. Other musicians who fell to the cholera included the two best flutists in the city, Leandro Andrino and Domingo Gutiérrez, and the clarinetist in the Second Battalion Band, Trinidad Andrino.

80. *Gaceta de Guatemala*, 3 Sept., 7 and 30 Oct. 1857.

81. Ibid., 21–25 Jan. 1858. Four years later, Vicente Cerna, the corregidor of Chiquimula, proposed hiring an English doctor, Richard Ellery, trained at the Faculty of Medicine in London, as the surgeon for the garrison at Chiquimula, at an annual salary of $456. Dr. Ellery would also be allowed to carry on a private practice. I have not been able to ascertain whether this was a relative of Dr. Henry Ellery or perhaps the same man with a confusion of names, or if he was actually contracted in Chiquimula. AGCA, B, leg. 28587, AMG, Comunicaciones, Chiquimula, Año 1862.

82. *Gaceta de Guatemala*, 27 Oct. and 16 Nov.–2 Dec. 1857.

83. These urban militias were composed of two battalions of six hundred men each. *Gaceta de Guatemala*, 29 Sept. and 13 Nov. 1857.

14. The Pax Carrera

1. See, for example, the reprint of an article from the Brussels *Emancipation* in the *Gaceta de Guatemala*, 4 May 1855.

2. "La situación," *Gaceta de Guatemala*, 29 Mar., 2 Apr. and 19 Apr. 1857.

3. *Gaceta de Guatemala*, 7 May 1852.

4. The serialized article was a translation of the work of the French conservative Eugene de Mirecourt. It ran in the *Gaceta de Guatemala*, 18 Sept.–2 Oct. 1856.

5. *El Museo Guatemalteco*, 31 Oct. 1856.

6. *Gaceta de Guatemala*, 7 Dec. 1856.

7. *El Museo Guatemalteco*, 31 Oct. 1856. "Centro–América, su situación actual y medios de mejorar su porvenir," *El Museo Guatemalteco*, 19 June 1857.

8. "Centro-América, su situación actual y medios de mejorar su porvenir," *El Museo Guatemalteco*, 19 June 1857.

9. José A. Mobil, *100 personajes históricos de Guatemala* (1979), 201–6.

10. See especially *El Museo Guatemalteco*, 2 Sept. 1857.

11. *Gaceta de Guatemala*, 21 Dec. 1861

12. Ibid., 8 Nov. 1862

13. Ibid., 6 Sept. 1858.

14. Ibid., 21 Dec. 1861.

15. Ibid., 6 May 1860.

16. Rafael Carrera to Chepita Silva, Chiquimula, 24 Sept. 1858. GCUK.

17. The *Gaceta de Guatemala*, 1857–60, records the details of this process and Carrera's movements throughout the country.

18. This account is based principally on that of Fray José Paul, as he recalled it in the *Diario del Salvador* of 23 Nov. 1907, reprinted by García, "Carrera," 11:83–84.

19. *Gaceta de Guatemala*, 11 Feb. 1858. For a more detailed discussion of Carrera's policy toward the other Central American states, see Woodward, "Política centroamericana."

20. Rosalio Cortez to Pedro Aycinena, Managua, *Gaceta de Guatemala*, 13 Aug. 1858.

21. V. Bosque to R. Cortez, San Salvador, 14 Sept. 1858, and G. Barrios to P. Aycinena, San Salvador, 1 Oct. 1858, *Gaceta de Guatemala*, 10 Oct. 1858; P. Aycinena to R. Cortez, 20 Sept. 1858, *Gaceta de Guatemala*, 24 Sept. 1858; and *Gaceta de Guatemala*, 5 May 1859, citing *Gaceta Oficial de Honduras*, 10 Apr. 1859.

22. Clarke presented his credentials to Carrera on 13 July 1858 and died in Guatemala on 17 March 1860. *Gaceta de Guatemala*, 15 July 1858 and 25–29 March 1860.

23. *Gaceta de Guatemala*, 1 Feb. and 31 Mar. 1859.

24. Dana Munro, *The Five Republics of Central America* (1918), 181, citing Mora's nephew, Manuel Argüello Mora, *Recuerdos e Impresiones*, 60.

25. Moorhead, "Rafael Carrera," 113, quoting Crosby, "Statement," Bancroft Library; *Gaceta de Guatemala*, 14 Mar., 22 Apr., and 30 May 1861, and 17 Sept. 1862.

26. *Gaceta de Guatemala*, 9 July 1862; Moorhead, "Rafael Carrera," 130, citing Crosby, "Statement," Bancroft Library, 95–100; for a fuller account of U.S. efforts

to settle ex-slaves in Central America, see Thomas Schoonover, "Misconstrued Mission: Expansionism and Black Colonization in Mexico and Central America during the Civil War," *Pacific Historical Review* 49 (1980):607–20.

27. Irisarri to Seward, Brooklyn, 26 Aug. and 9 Sept. 1862, Seward to Irisarri, Washington, 5 and 15 Sept. 1862, *Gaceta de Guatemala*, 2 Nov. 1862. English versions of this correspondence appear in U.S. Department of State, *Papers Relating to the Foreign Relations of the United States, 1862* (1863), 883; Schoonover, "Misconstrued Mission," 616.

28. Clegern, *Colonial Dead End*, 37.

29. AGCA, B, leg. 28604, AMG.

30. See Robin A. Humphreys, *The Diplomatic History of British Honduras, 1638–1901* (1961), and José Antonio Calderón Quijano, *Belice 1663?–1821: Historia de los establecimientos británicos del Río Valis hasta la independencia de Hispanoamérica* (1944), for the respective sides in the dispute, and Naylor, "British Role in Central America," pp. 361–82, and his *Penny Ante Imperialism: The Mosquito Shore and the Bay of Honduras, 1600–1914* (1988) for British commercial development of the settlement in the early nineteenth century. On British diplomacy in Central America during the decade following the departure of Chatfield, see Richmond Brown, "Friends and Relations: Charles Lennox Wyke and the Central American Diplomacy of Great Britain, 1852–1860," (1986).

31. Clegern, *Colonial Dead End*; "Comercio por las vías de Panamá y Belice, estracto de una carta dirijida de Panamá por el ajente comercial del ferro-carril de aquel Istmo, á una persona de esta Capital, y fechada el 16 de enero próximo pasado," *Gaceta de Guatemala*, 18 Feb. 1858.

32. Reed, *Caste War*, Clegern, *Colonial Dead End*, 14–15.

33. Wyke to Aycinena, Guatemala, 4 Jan. 1859, Aycinena to Wyke, 17 Jan. 1859, Resolution on the subject by Carrera, Guatemala, 5 Apr. 1859, *Gaceta de Guatemala*, 10 Apr. 1859; Wyke to Aycinena, Guatemala, 10 Apr. 1859, *Gaceta de Guatemala*, 14 Apr. 1859.

34. Clergern, *Colonial Dead End*, 99–104; see Clegern's "Guatemalan Defense of the British Honduras Boundary of 1859," *Hispanic American Historical Review* 40 (1960):570–81.

35. Wyke to Earl of Malmsbury, Guatemala, 30 April 1859, in Mario Rosenthal, *Guatemala, the Story of an Emerging Latin-American Democracy* (1962), 137–38.

36. *Gaceta de Guatemala*, 29 Sept. 1859.

37. Clarke to Aycinena, Guatemala, 1 Oct. 1859, *Gaceta de Guatemala*, 18 Aug. 1860; Batres Jáuregui, *América Central* 2:452–56.

38. See Buchanan's comments in his third annual message to Congress, 19 Dec. 1859, in Richardson, comp. *Messages*, 5:561–63; and the comment on this speech in the *Gaceta de Guatemala*, 26 Feb. 1860.

39. *Gaceta de Guatemala*, 22 Oct. 1859. Wyke went on to negotiate treaties with Honduras and Nicaragua before being promoted to chargé d'affaires in Mexico in March 1860; *Gaceta de Guatemala*, 7 Apr. 1860. He was succeeded as Consul

General in Guatemala by George Fagan, who had been Secretary of the British Legation in the Argentine Confederation; *Gaceta de Guatemala*, 28 May 1860.

40. Opposing the treaty were representatives Aguilar, Jose Maria and Francisco Aguirres, Asturias, Arrivillaga, A. Andreu, García Granados, Murga, Padilla, Samayoa, Urruela and Valdez. Representatives Alburez, Peralta, and Idalgo had opposed the treaty during the discussions in December, but did not vote on the final resolution. Dardón had also opposed it in December, but voted in favor on 30 January. *Gaceta de Guatemala*, 15–23 Dec. 1859 and 12 Feb. 1860.

41. Clegern, *Colonial Dead End*, 59–61.

42. *Gaceta de Guatemala*, 28 June 1850; Bancroft, *Central America*, 3:230, 253.

43. *Gaceta de Guatemala*, 22 Oct. 1852 and 17 May 1853.

44. *Gaceta de Guatemala*, 16 July 1857; "Memoria leída el día 28 de enero de 1859, por el Señor Jefe de Sección encargado del Ministerio de Relaciones Esteriores, D. Manuel Irungaray, al Cuerpo Legislativo," San Salvador, 28 Jan. 1859, *Gaceta de Guatemala*, 17 Feb. 1859.

45. *Gaceta Oficial de Honduras*, 30 June 1859.

46. See *Gaceta de Guatemala*, 1 Aug. 1858; and the letter by Manuel P. de Salas, reprinted from *Península Española* in the *Gaceta*, 26 Apr. 1860, in which he calls for Spanish rejuvenation and alliance with Guatemala against the United States: "España, que gloriosamente se eleva de nuevo entre las naciones europeos a reconquistar su antigua preponderancia, y que cuenta ya con una respetable marina de guerra, debe ante todo tender su escudo fraternal sobre estos débiles restos de su poderosa raza, alentarlos moralmente con su alianza y defenderlos con su espada, si necesario fuera, de la ambición destructora y voraz del avaro del Norte, el más inveterado enemigo de nuestra raza."

47. "Reincorporación de Santo Domingo á la España," *Gaceta de Guatemala*, 14 July 1861. Even after the treaty had finally been ratified in 1864, Guatemalan foreign minister Pedro Aycinena responded cautiously to a message from the Chilean foreign minister regarding Spanish attacks on the Chincha Islands. Aycinena said that, while Guatemala deplored the act, it must have been a purely personal act of the officers involved, for he was "confident that it would not receive Her Majesty's government's approval." Manuel A. Tocornal to Pedro Aycinena, Santiago de Chile, 4 May 1864, and Aycinena to Tocornal, 14 July 1864, *Gaceta de Guatemala*, 1 Aug. 1864.

48. Carrera ratified it on 1 Dec. of the same year and ratifications were exchanged in Madrid on the following 20 June. Pineda de Mont, *Recopilación*, 1:375–81; *Gaceta de Guatemala*, 14 Sept. 1864.

49. *Gaceta de Guatemala*, 7 Oct. 1864.

50. "Aniversario," *Gaceta de Guatemala*, 14 April 1859.

51. Carrera, *Mensage . . . 25 de noviembre de 1859* (Guatemala, 1959 [*sic*, 1859]).

15. El Salvador

1. *Gaceta de Guatemala*, 12–17 Feb. 1860.

2. *Gaceta de Guatemala*, 2 Sept. 1859; Pedro Aycinena to Ministro de Relaciones del Gobierno de la República de Costa Rica, Guatemala, 21 May 1860, ibid., 28 May 1860; Bancroft, *Central America*, 3:375–76.

3. Gerardo Barrios, "El General Gerardo Barrios, Senador Encargado del Supremo Poder Ejecutivo a los Salvadoreños," Cojutepeque, 24 June 1858, *Gaceta de Guatemala*, 3 July 1858; Gerardo Barrios, "El General Barrios á los Pueblos del Salvador," San Salvador, 22 Sept. 1858, *Gaceta de Guatemala*, 2 Oct. 1858, 1–2. The best biography of Barrios is Italo López Vallecillos, *Gerardo Barrios y su tiempo* (1967).

4. *Gaceta de Guatemala*, 8 July 1858.

5. José Nájera to Gerardo Barrios, Guatemala, 12 July 1858, and Barrios to Nájera, San Salvador, 2 Aug. 1858, *Gaceta de Guatemala*, 7 Aug. 1858; López Vallecillos, *Barrios*, 1:297–302. The remains had been brought to El Salvador in 1849, but had remained in Sonsonate. L. Montúfar, *Reseña*, 5:650–52, 664–67.

6. "Gerardo Barrios, General de División, Senador en Ejercicio del Supremo Poder Ejecutivo, á los Salvadoreños," San Salvador, 12 Mar. 1859, *Gaceta de Guatemala*, 26 Mar. 1859.

7. Cerna signed a convention with Francisco Cruz in Comayagua on 9 Aug., subsequently ratified by Carrera on 20 Sept. and by Barrios on 30 Sept. *Gaceta de Guatemala*, 18 Apr., 10 and 22 July, 25 Aug., 2 Sept., 7 and 11 Oct. 1859, and 13 Apr. 1862; Carrera to Barrios, Guatemala, 16 and 18 Apr. and 30 June 1859, AGCA, B, leg. 2480, exps. 54813, 54814 and 54841.

8. *Gaceta de Guatemala*, 4 and 12 Feb. 1860.

9. Carrera to Barrios, Guatemala, 7 Feb. 1860, AGCA, B, leg. 2480, exp. 54671.

10. "Situación de la América Central," *Gaceta de Guatemala*, 17 June 1860.

11. *Gaceta de Guatemala*, 30 Dec. 1860, 5 Jan., and 15 Jan. 1861.

12. Ibid., 7 Feb. 1861.

13. Carrera to Barrios, Guatemala, 15 Apr. 1861, in response to Barrios to Carrera, San Salvador, 8 Apr. 1861, AGCA, B118.14, leg. 2480, exp. 54886.

14. Barrios to Carlos Antonio Meany, San Salvador, 9 Jan. 1862, AGCA, B, leg. 2440, exp. 52579; *Gaceta de Guatemala*, 6 Dec. 1861.

15. See the anonymous pamphlet, *Guatemala y El Salvador* ([December 1862]), 27. This collection of documents relating to the controversy between Guatemala and El Salvador was obviously published in defense of the Guatemalan government and specifically in response to a 20 Nov. 1862 article in the *Gaceta Oficial del Salvador*. Copy in Coll. 20, Central America Political Ephemera, LALTU.

16. Bancroft, *Central America*, 3:303, 324–25; Francisco Montes, "Senador Propietario y President Provisorio de la República de Honduras, a sus habitantes," *Gaceta de Guatemala*, 24 Jan. 1862.

17. Pedro Aycinena, "Circular á los Gobiernos del Salvador, Nicaragua y Costa-Rica, relativa a los asuntos de Honduras," Guatemala, 31 Jan. 1862, *Alcance al No. 23 de la Gaceta de Guatemala*, 6 Feb. 1862; *Gaceta de Guatemala*, 1 and 9 Feb. 1862.

18. *Gaceta de Guatemala*, 9 Feb. 1862.

19. Ibid., 22 and 28 Feb. 1862.

20. Manuel Irungaray to Pedro Aycinena, San Salvador, 14 Feb. 1862, *Gaceta de Guatemala*, 28 Feb. 1862; Reina Valenzuela, *Cabañas*, 222–23.

21. *Gaceta de Guatemala*, 15 Mar. 1862; see also 22 Feb. 1862, and Aycinena to Irungaray, Guatemala, 24 Feb. 1862, in ibid., 28 Feb. 1862.

22. Madrid to Aycinena, Santa Rosa, Honduras, 27 Mar. 1862, *Gaceta de Guatemala*, 27 Apr. 1862. Aycinena's reply of 19 Apr., agreeing with Castellanos, is found in the same issue. Additional coverage of the Nicaraguan unification initiative is in the *Gaceta de Guatemala*, 4 Oct. 1856, and Bancroft, *Central America*, 3:303–4.

23. Carrera to Castellanos, Guatemala, 8 Nov. 1862, AGCA, B, leg. 2440, leg. 52603.

24. "La prensa de Guatemala," *Gaceta Oficial del Salvador*, 20 Nov. 1862, reprinted in *Guatemala y El Salvador*, 5–6; M. Irungaray to Pedro Aycinena, San Salvador, 31 Mar. 1862, *Gaceta de Guatemala*, 22 Apr. 1862.

25. *Gaceta de Guatemala*, 13 Apr. 1862; Aycinena to Irungaray, Guatemala, 5 Apr. 1862, *Gaceta de Guatemala*, 22 Apr. 1862.

26. *Gaceta de Guatemala*, 27 Apr., 7 May 1862, and 14 June 1862.

27. Carrera to Barrios, Guatemala, 23 May 1862 and 25 July 1862, AGCA, B, leg. 2440, exps. 52580 and 52588; Carrera to the Vice President of Honduras, Guatemala, 8 Nov. 1862, AGCA, B, leg. 2440, exp. 52603.

28. "La Prensa de Guatemala," *Guatemala y El Salvador*, 7–10, citing *Gaceta Oficial del Salvador*, 20 Nov. 1862; Antonio José Irisarri to Manuel Irungaray, Brooklyn, 21 May 1863, *Gaceta de Guatemala*, 16 June 1863.

29. Carrera, *Mensaje . . . 25 de noviembre de 1862*, 1–2.

30. AGCA, B, leg. 28587, AMG, Comunicaciones, Asamblea, Año 1862.

31. Irigoyen to Carrera, Guatemala, 27 Nov. 1862, AGCA, B, leg. 2440, exp. 52611.

32. Pedro Aycinena to Secretaries of the Cámara de Representantes, Guatemala, 6 Dec. 1862, *Gaceta de Guatemala*, 8 Jan. 1863.

33. *Guatemala y El Salvador*, 12–30; *Gaceta de Guatemala*, 6 December 1862.

34. *Alcance al Núm. 67 de la Gaceta de Guatemala*, 22 Dec. 1862; *Gaceta de Guatemala*, 23 Jan. 1863; AGCA, B, leg. 28590, AMG, Comunicaciones, Guatemala, Año 1859; Ygnacio Saravía, Corregidor de Sololá to Ministro de Gobernación, Sololá, 27 Dec. 1862, AGCA, B, leg. 28587, AMG, Comunicaciones, Sololá, Año 1862.

35. Irigoyen to Carrera, Guatemala, 25 Dec. 1862, AGCA, B, leg. 2440, exp. 52624.

36. *Gaceta de Guatemala*, 15 Jan. 1863.

37. According to a note in the *Gaceta de Guatemala*, 29 Sept. 1863, which cited "the Honduran press," a letter written from Paris on 14 Jan. 1862 by a "well known person" contained the following paragraph: "Don Lorenzo Montúfar is found here on a mission of the President of El Salvador, and I have heard indirectly that he is in search of a Swiss military colony, an idea that seems very good to me for the respectability that a thousand of these men would give to El Salvador, and I assure you that then the chicaneries from Guatemala would cease."

38. *Gaceta de Guatemala*, 21 Mar. 1863.

39. Ibid., 23–30 Jan., 14 Feb. 1863.

40. A manifesto to his troops charged that the Salvadorans were about to make war on them and urged them to fight for the defense of the most sacred rights of Guatemala, assured that God was on their side. *Gaceta de Guatemala*, 7 Feb. 1863. Carrera marched out on the fourth, with Generals Zavala and Cruz remaining in the city to organize more troops. They left on 10 Feb. Ibid., 14 Feb. 1863.

41. Carrera to P. Aycinena, Sacualpa, 7 Feb. 1863, AGCA, B, leg. 2440, exp. 52688.

42. Carrera to P. Aycinena, Jutiapa, 9 Feb. 1863, AGCA, B, leg. 2440, exp. 52699.

43. *Gaceta de Guatemala*, 4 Mar. 1863; Carrera to P. Aycinena, Santa Ana, El Salvador, 22 Feb. 1863, AGCA, B, leg. 2440, exp. 52746.

44. Carrera to P. Aycinena, Santa Ana, 22 and 24 Feb. 1863, and Yupiltepeque, 26 Feb. 1863; Carrera to Cerezo, Jutiapa, 25 Feb. 1863; Carrera to Irigoyen, Jutiapa, 28 Feb. 1863, AGCA B, leg. 2440, exps. 52746, 52748, 52753, 52806, 52760; *Gaceta de Guatemala*, 4 Mar.–10 Apr. 1863.

45. Pedro Aycinena, circular letter to the diplomatic corps in Guatemala City, *Gaceta de Guatemala*, 31 Mar. 1863.

46. J. A. Milla to P. Aycinena, Comayagua, 3 Mar. 1863, *Gaceta de Guatemala*, 21 Mar. 1863. A haughty response from Aycinena appeared in the same issue of the *Gaceta*.

47. *Gaceta de Guatemala*, 13–21 Mar. 1863.

48. Irisarri to Irungaray, Brooklyn, 11 Mar. 1863; Irungaray to Irisarri, San Salvador, 12 Apr. 1863; Irisarri to Irungaray, Brooklyn, 21 May 1863, *Gaceta de Guatemala*, 16 June 1863.

49. *Gaceta de Guatemala*, 21 Mar., 10 and 25 Apr. 1863; Carrera to Cerna, El Oratorio, 12 Apr. 1863, AGCA, B, leg. 2440, exp. 52825.

50. *Gaceta de Guatemala*, 22 Feb.–9 June 1863.

51. Ibid., 31 May–9 June 1863.

52. García, "Carrera," 11:182–83.

53. *Gaceta de Guatemala*, 16–27 June 1863 and 24 June 1864.

54. Carrera to Silva, GCUK.

55. *Gaceta de Guatemala*, 9 June–8 Aug. 1863; Carrera to P. Aycinena, Fraijanes, 5 Mar. 1863, El Oratorio, 12 Apr. 1863, Jutiapa, 27 Apr. 1863, Cerro Redondo,

8 June 1863, AGCA, B, leg. 2440, exps. 52778, 52825, 52865; leg. 2442, exp. 52924; and Carrera to Chepita Silva, Santa Ana, 21 July 1863, GCUK.

56. *Gaceta de Guatemala*, 6 July 1863.

57. Father José Güell y Busquets wrote to Carrera on 3 Aug. 1863 from Jutiapa that a New York newspaper of 30 June had reported that on 19 June the Salvadoran Minister had called upon President Lincoln in an effort to get U.S. aid. He urged a quick victory over Barrios to avoid U.S. intervention. Direct U.S. intervention in the midst of the Civil War was unlikely, of course, but the Walker episode had created a paranoia among many Central Americans regarding the United States, and indirect aid was certainly possible. AGCA, unclassified.

58. Carrera to P. Aycinena, Santa Tecla, 12 Sept. 1863, AGCA, B, leg. 2440, exp., 53115; Ramón Solís to Carrera, N. Guatemala, 3 Aug. 1863; José Güell y Busquets to Carrera, Jutiapa, 3 Aug. 1863; Vicente Cerna to Carrera, Tonacatepeque, 1, 3, 4, 5, 6, and 23 Sept. 1863; Manuel M. Ramos to Carrera, 7 Aug. 1863; P. Aycinena to Carrera, Guatemala, 5 and 8 Aug. and 13 Sept. 1863, AGCA, unclassified; *Gaceta de Guatemala*, 25 Aug.–20 Sept. 1863.

59. *Gaceta de Guatemala*, 25 Nov. 1863; the foreign minister advised that his correspondence not be published until after the complete victory over Barrios, thus the delay in publishing it until November. Aycinena to Carrera, Guatemala, 25 Sept. 1863, AGCA, unclassified.

60. *Rafael Carrera, President de la República de Guatemala y General en Jefe de los Ejércitos Aliados, a los Jefes, Oficiales y Soldados del Ejército Expedicionario* (San Salvador, 30 Oct. 1863), Arturo Taracena Collection, BLAC; Cerna to Carrera, Tonacatepeque, 23 Sept. 1863; Aycinena to Carrera, 25 Sept. 1863, AGCA, unclassified; *Gaceta de Guatemala*, 29 Sept.–10 Nov. 1863, contains details of the siege, including occupation of the plaza of San Salvador on 26 Oct.

61. Barrios to Col. Domingo Fagoaga, New York, 2 Jan. 1864, typescript from original in possession of Col. Luis Lovo Castelar, in Archivo General de la Nación, San Salvador.

62. *Rafael Carrera, President de la República de Guatemala. . . .* (San Salvador, 30 Oct. 1863) Taracena Coll., BLAC.

63. Carrera to Aycinena, San Salvador, 9 Nov. 1863, AGCA, unclassified; Bancroft, *Central America*, 3:306

64. Published by the Ministerio de Hacienda y Guerra del S. G. de la República del Salvador, San Salvador, 3 Nov. 1863, copy in Coll. 20, Central America Political Ephemera, LALTU.

65. AGCA, B, leg. 2443, exps. 53347 and 53362.

66. Carrera to Aycinena, San Salvador, 11 Nov. 1863, Quetzaltepeque, 15 Nov. 1863, and Cerro Redondo, 27 Nov. 1863, AGCA, B, leg. 2442, exp. 53229, and leg. 2443, exps. 53238 and 53269; *Relación de las fiestas con que se celebró en los dias 29 y 30 de noviembre, 1 y 2 de diciembre, al regreso a la capital de Excmo. Señor Presidente y de las fuerzas expedicionarias* (1864); AGCA, B78.25, leg. 729, exp. 17041.

67. *Relación de la fiesta*, 7.

68. Carrera, *Mensaje . . . día 10 de diciembre de 1863*, 1–3.

69. *Gaceta de Guatemala*, 31 Dec. 1863, 30 Jan., 7 and 13 Mar. 1864.

70. Ibid., 21 Jan.–7 Mar. 1864.

71. Rafael Carrera to Chepita Silva, Escuintla, 17 and 23 Jan., 1864, GCUK.

72. See, for example, Carrera to General Tomás Martínez, Guatemala, 7 Sept. 1864, AGCA, B, leg. 2482, exp. 54914.

73. "La civilización atacada en el último retiro por el salvajismo," *La Estrella de Panamá*, 28 Jan. 1864; Mariano Castro, "El Jeneral Carrera," *Gaceta de Guatemala*, 28 Feb. 1864. The next issue of the *Gaceta*, 7 Mar. 1863, offered a correction on the point of Carrera collecting only a small part of the war expenses. It now claimed that Carrera had demanded nothing, but that President Dueñas had insisted that the Salvadoran government make some contribution to the expenses of the Guatemalan army. Although Carrera had not requested it, he accepted "this small subsidy from the Salvadoran provisional government." *La Estrella de Panamá* also published Castro's defense of Carrera, on 2 Feb. 1864, along with a note from Lorenzo Montúfar denying authorship of the anti-Carrera article. See also the letter ridiculing Barrios from "M.C.," "¡¡Barrios ofreciendo su espada!!" in *La Estrella de Panamá*, 16 Feb. 1864.

74. *Gaceta de Guatemala*, 1 Feb. and 4 Mar. 1865.

75. Ibid., 4 July 1865; *Recopilación de las leyes emitadas por el gobierno democrático de la República de Guatemala, desde el 3 de junio de 1871, hasta el 30 de junio de 1881* (1881), 1:6.

76. López Vallecillos, *Barrios*, 2:479–98.

77. *Gaceta de Guatemala*, 7 June 1860, and 22 June 1861.

78. See especially the *Gaceta de Guatemala*, 4 Sept. 1864.

79. Those rumors were reported widely, not only in Central America, but also in the United States. *Gaceta de Guatemala*, 24 Apr., 14 July, and 1 Oct. 1864.

80. *Gaceta de Guatemala*, 9–16 Aug. 1864. It was also published separately in pamphlet form, E. Masseras, *El programa del imperio* (1864).

81. *Gaceta de Guatemala*, 14 Oct. 1864.

16. The Transition to Liberalism

1. Marroquín Rojas, *Morazán y Carrera*, 8.

2. Lazardi, "Carrera," 73–75.

3. Author's interview with Dr. Horacio Figueroa Marroquín, Guatemala City, 9 Nov. 1986.

4. *Gaceta de Guatemala*, 21 Mar.–20 Apr. 1865; Manuel Coronado Aguilar, *Apuntes histórico-guatemalenses*, 2d ed. (1975), 379–83.

5. *Relación de las exéquias del Excmo. Sr. Presidente Capitán Gral. D. Rafael Carrera, celebrada en la S. I. Catedral de Guatemala el día 17 de abril de 1865* (1865),

8–40. Miguel Angel García reprinted a large number of the obituaries, eulogies, and other publications relating to Carrera's death in "Carrera," 11:16–46.

6. Wayne M. Clegern, "Transition from Conservatism to Liberalism in Guatemala, 1865–1871," in William S. Coker, ed., *Hispanic-American Essays in Honor of Max Leon Moorhead* (1979), 98–110, argues for the Cerna administration being a transitional period between conservative and liberal dictatorships. He is persuasive in his contention that there was considerable economic liberalism under Cerna, but fear of political liberalism. Clegern is presently completing a book-length manuscript on this period, "Origins of Liberal Dictatorship in Central America: Guatemala, 1865–1873."

7. *Gaceta de Guatemala*, 20 Apr. 1865.

8. Juan Matheu to Pedro de Aycinena, Guatemala, 2 May 1865, *Gaceta de Guatemala*, 8 May 1865.

9. "Acta de la sesión de la Asamblea General el Día 3 de Mayo de 1865," *hojas sueltas* collection, Hemeroteca of the AGCA.

10. *Gaceta de Guatemala*, 8 and 17 May 1865.

11. Cerna's report on agricultural production in Chiquimula in the *Gaceta de Guatemala*, 23 May 1860; AGCA, B, leg. 28587, AMG, Comunicaciones, Chiquimula.

12. *Programa de la recepción del Sr. Presidente electo* (Guatemala, 19 May 1865), and *Vicente Cerna, Mariscal de Campo, Presidente de la República de Guatemala, a sus conciudadanos* (Guatemala, 24 May 1865) in Coll. 20, Central America Political Ephemera, LALTU; *Gaceta de Guatemala*, 29 May 1865.

13. Aycinena to José Milla, Guatemala, 27 May 1865; Echeverría to Milla, Guatemala, 27 May 1865; and Cerezo to Milla, Guatemala, 27 May 1867, *Gaceta de Guatemala*, 4 June 1865.

14. *Gaceta de Guatemala*, 4 July 1865.

15. AGCA, B, AMG, leg. 28604, 28605, and 28606, contain a great deal of evidence of this effort.

16. "Mensaje dirijido por el Excmo. Sr. Presidente de la República de Guatemala, Mariscal de Campo D. Vicente Cerna, á la Cámara de Representantes; en la apertura de sus terceras sesiones del tercer período constitucional, el día 25 de Noviembre de 1865," *Gaceta de Guatemala*, 29 Nov. 1865.

17. *Gaceta de Guatemala*, 19 Dec. 1865.

18. "Mensage dirijido por Excmo. Sr. Presidente de la República de Guatemala, Mariscal de Campo D. Vicente Cerna, a la Cámara de Representantes; en la apertura de sus cuartas sesiones del tercer período constitucional," Guatemala, 24 Nov. 1866, *Gaceta de Guatemala*, 5 Dec. 1866.

19. José Torón España, "Oposición del Representante García Granados al gobierno del Mariscal Don Vicente Cerna," *Historia y Antropología: Ensayos en honor de J. Daniel Contreras R.*, edited by Jorge Luján Muñoz (1982), 171–86.

20. Rodríguez, *Central America*, 98; Jesús J. Amurrio González, *El positivismo en Guatemala* (1970.) Recently, Charles A. Hale, *The Transformation of Liberalism in*

Late Nineteenth-Century Mexico (1989), has detailed the process of positivist modification of Mexican liberalism after 1850. It would appear that much the same sort of transformation occurred in Guatemala.

21. *Gaceta de Guatemala*, 3 Jan. 1866.

22. Ibid., 23 June 1866.

23. "Reglamento de la Cámara de Representantes," *Gaceta de Guatemala*, 3–10 July 1868.

24. *Gaceta de Guatemala*, 16 May 1862.

25. AGCA, B, leg. 28615; *Gaceta de Guatemala*, 21 Mar. 1868.

26. *Gaceta de Guatemala*, 29 Dec. 1868.

27. AGCA, B, AMG, leg. 28609.

28. Julio Medina to Corregidor, Izabal, 4 Sept. 1868; and Corregidor de Izabal to Juan Zerón, Izabal, 5 Sept. 1868, AGCA, B, leg. 28614, AMG, 1868; C. J. M. R. Gullick, *Exiled from St. Vincent: The Development of Black Carib Culture in Central America up to 1945* (1976); and William V. Davidson, "Black Carib (Garifuna) Habitats in Central America," in *Frontier Adaptations in Lower Central America*, edited by Mary W. Helms and Franklin O. Loveland (1976), 85–94.

29. AGCA, B, AMG, leg. 28627.

30. Salazar, *Tiempo viejo*, 147; Bancroft, *Central America*, 3:415–16; *Algunas reflexiones*, 3–5.

31. AGCA, leg. 28610, exp. 333, AMG, Marcelino Valladares, Tiburcio Barrientos, and Francisco Marroquín, vecinos de San Juan de los Cabreras, Jurisdicción de Sansare, Dpto. de Chiquimula, al Presidente de la República, 13 Apr. 1867.

32. Bancroft, *Central America*, 3:414–15.

33. *Gaceta de Guatemala*, 7 Dec. 1867 and 27 Nov. 1868.

34. Ibid., 29 Dec. 1868.

35. A detailed "Reglamento y Ceremonial para la elección y posesión del Presidente de la República" was also decreed on 8 Jan. 1869, in accordance with the Acta Constitutiva of 1851. *Gaceta de Guatemala*, 16 Jan. 1869.

36. Clegern, "Transition," 98–99. On this process in Mexico, see Hale, *Transformation*, 3–9, 89–90.

37. *Gaceta de Guatemala*, 22 Jan. 1869.

38. Julio C. Castellanos Cambranes, *Café y campesinos en Guatemala, 1853–1897* (1985), 81–135.

39. *Gaceta de Guatemala*, 22 Jan. 1869.

40. Ibid., 3 Apr. 1869; Bancroft, *Central America*, 3:414–16; Castellanos Cambranes, *Café y campesinos* 162–65; Enrique del Cid Fernández, *Cruz y Barrios: Incendio y saqueo de la Villa de Huehuetenango* (1966).

41. *Algunas reflexiones*, 6–7.

42. *Gaceta de Guatemala*, 12 May 1869.

43. Ibid., 19 Nov. 1870.

44. Miller, *La iglesia*, 49–52.

45. Cerna, *Mensaje* . . . *25 de noviembre de 1869*, 1–2.

46. Others voting for the motion were A. Arroyo, Estrada, Escamilla, M. Larrave, and Samayoa. *Gaceta de Guatemala*, 29 Dec. 1869.

47. The Council of State was solidly conservative: Pedro Aycinena, Juan Matheu, Manuel Echeverría, Raymundo Arroyo, José Antonio Azmitia, Manuel F. González, Luis Molina, and Gregorio Urruela. Juan Matheu to Vicente Cerna, Guatemala, 2 Dec. 1869, *Gaceta de Guatemala*, 8 Dec. 1869.

48. González Centeno, *Serapio Cruz*, 65–72; García, "Carrera" 11:47.

49. Clegern, "Transition," 101–3; García, "Carrera," 11:183.

50. In addition, however, Escamilla began to attend the sessions on the twentieth, and Estrada showed up in early May. *Gaceta de Guatemala*, 21 Apr. 1870.

51. Cerna, *Mensage* . . . *4 de abril de 1870*.

52. Those elected by the departments and the corporations are listed in the *Gaceta de Guatemala*, 18 Sept. 1870.

53. *Gaceta de Guatemala*, 7 Dec. 1870.

54. Cerna, *Mensage* . . . *25 de noviembre de 1870*.

55. AGCA, leg. 28623, AMG.

56. Zeceña, *La revolución*, 50–53.

57. Meneray, "Kingdom," 176–82; Cayetano Alcázar Molina, *Los virreinatos en el siglo XVIII* (1945), 206–7.

58. Dunn, *Guatimala*, 232; Wortman, *Government and Society*, 140–53, 286–87; Mariano de Montealegre, Baltasar de Echevarría, y Gregorio Castro al Sr. Director Gral., Real Factoría de Tabaco de Costarrica, San José, 1 Dec. 1814, and accompanying documents, AGCA, A, leg. 2298, exp. 34043; Informe de las reformas hechas en el edificio que ocupa la factoría de San Vicente, 1819, AGCA, A, leg. 2301, exp. 34108; Victor Hugo Acuña Ortega, *Historia económica del tabaco, época colonial* (1974); Cardoso and Pérez Brignoli, *Centro América*, 122–24; and José Luis Vega Carballo, "El nacimiento de un régimen de burguesía dependiente: El caso de Costa Rica," in Congreso Centroamericano de Historia Demográfica, Económica y Social, I, Santa Barbara, Costa Rica, 1973, *Ensayos de historia centroamericana* (1974), 97–101.

59. Rodríguez, *Cádiz Experiment*, 43, 142; Wortman, *Government and Society*, 237–38; see also the report of José Velasco, Director General of Tobacco Revenue, of 4 Nov. 1824, reflecting the difficulties of the tobacco administration following independence, in AGCA, B, leg. 96, exp. 2637.

60. *El Tiempo*, 15 Oct. 1840.

61. *Gaceta Oficial*, 9 Aug. and 28 Sept. 1842.

62. See, for example, the reports for 1846–48, when it netted only a few hundred dollars per year, in *Gaceta de Guatemala*, 20 July 1847 and 28 June 1848.

63. See the report of the minister of finance on this subject in AGCA, B, leg. 3653, exp. 8619.

64. *Gaceta de Guatemala*, 19 May 1849.

65. Ibid., 28 Feb. 1850.

66. Ibid., 19 Jan. 1855, 20 July 1855, 24 Sept. 1858, 14 Oct. 1858, 15 Nov. 1861.

67. Pineda de Mont, *Recopilación*, 1:5.

68. Rodríguez, *Cádiz Experiment*, 103, 155, 227; Valentín Solórzano Fernández, *Historia de la evolución económica de Guatemala* (1947), 183–84.

69. AGCA, B, leg. 1391, exp. 32124.

70. *El Tiempo*, 11 Dec. 1839.

71. José Luis Reyes M., *Catálogo razonado de las leyes de Guatemala* (1945), 38–39; AGCA, B, AMG, 1857, leg. 18574.

72. *Gaceta Oficial*, 28 Nov. 1843.

73. Ibid., 23 May 1845.

74. "Orden Núm. 9," *Gaceta de Guatemala*, 31 Jan. 1849.

75. *Gaceta de Guatemala*, 29 Aug. 1851.

76. Ibid., 19 Mar. 1852.

77. "Bases q. propone la junta de hacienda para el remate de los estancos de chicha de la República en el año económico de 1852 a 1853," *Gaceta de Guatemala*, 5 Mar. 1852.

78. *Gaceta de Guatemala*, 1 July 1853, 7 Sept. 1855; *Acuerdo abriendo los remates de estancos de aguardientes* (Guatemala: Palacio Nacional, 20 June 1853) and Rafael Carrera, *Decreto Núm. 95* (Guatemala, 21 Nov. 1853), Coll. 20, Central America Political Ephemera, LALTU.

79. AGCA, B, AMG, 1857, leg. 2857.

80. AGCA, B, AMG, 1858, leg. 28576.

81. Decree of 4 Sept. 1856, *Gaceta de Guatemala*, 7 Sept. 1856.

82. *Gaceta de Guatemala*, 9 Oct. 1856.

83. *Gaceta de Guatemala*, 16 Jan. 1858.

84. *Gaceta de Guatemala*, 8 Aug. 1866. The "Estatutos de la Compañía de Aguardientes de Guatemala" appeared in the *Gaceta* on 9 Oct. 1866.

85. Decreto no. 3, Quetzaltenango, 11 June 1871, *Recopilación de las leyes . . . 1881*, 1:6.

86. Seventy-three Jesuits, most of them foreign, sailed from San José on 10 Sept. 1871. The government of García Granados also expelled the archbishop and bishops because of their adhesion to the previous government. Paul Burgess, *Justo Rufino Barrios: A Biography* (1926), 90; Victor Miguel Díaz, *Barrios ante la posteridad* (1935), 110–13; Bancroft, *Central America*, 3:426.

87. *Recopilación de las leyes . . . 1881*, 1:3–4.

88. *Gaceta de Guatemala*, 8 June 1871.

89. Bancroft, *Central America*, 3:420–24; Clegern, "Transition," p 104.

90. For a collection of documents reflecting liberal thought in the Reforma of 1871, see J. M. García Laguardia, comp., *El pensamiento liberal de Guatemala* (1977).

91. Rodríguez, *Central America*, 93–94.

17. Infrastructure Development in Conservative Guatemala

1. Ruggiero Romano. "American Feudalism," *Hispanic American Historical Review* 64 (1984):124–34.

2. Martínez Peláez, *La patria del criollo*, 618–27.

3. For a useful overview of export agriculture in Guatemala, see Julio C. Pinto Soria, "La agricultura de exportación en Guatemala: Un acercamiento histórico," *Tikalia* 4, no. 1 (1988):1–15.

4. Woodward, *Class Privilege*. The *Real cédula de erección* (Madrid, 1793), is reproduced in the Spanish version of Woodward, *Privilegio de clase y desarrollo económico: Guatemala 1793–1871* (1981), 231–52; see also R. S. Smith, "Origins of the Consulado," and his "The Institution of the Consulado in New Spain," *Hispanic American Historical Review* 24 (1944):37–76.

5. Pineda de Mont, *Recopilación*, 1:749–50; *El Tiempo*, 24 Aug. 1839; AGCA, B12.7, exp. 4941, leg. 214, fol. 198; Woodward, *Privilegio de clase*, 257–59.

6. Decreto legislativo no. 58, Ley Electoral, 25 de octubre de 1851. Art. 7 y 8, *Gaceta de Guatemala*, 31 Oct. 1851; "Acta Constitutiva de la República de Guatemala," 19 Oct. 1851, Art. 10, *Gaceta de Guatemala*, 25 Oct. 1851.

7. AGCA, B12.7, leg. 213, exp. 4868; *El Tiempo*, 5 Oct. 1840. Lists of the membership were published in the annual reports of the Economic Society. See, for example, Enrique Palacios, *Memoria leída en la junta general que celebró la Sociedad Económica de Amigos del País, el 26 de diciembre de 1861* (1861), 21–23. On the history of this institution in Guatemala see Shafer, *Economic Societies* 199–364 *passim;* Manuel Rubio Sánchez, *Historia de la Sociedad Económica de Amigos del País* (1981); José Luis Reyes M., *Apuntes para una monografía de la Sociedad Económica de Amigos del País* (1964); and Elisa Luque Alcaide, *La Sociedad Económica de Amigos del País de Guatemala* (1962). For the order reestablishing this institution in 1829, see Pineda de Mont, *Recopilación*, 1:798–99.

8. AGCA, B, leg. 1390, exp. 322099; *Gaceta Oficial*, 6 Dec. 1845.

9. AGCA, B, leg. 1390, exp. 32099; *El Tiempo*, 20 Jan. 1841. The school opened on 15 March 1841. *Gaceta Oficial*, 20 Mar. 1841. Regulations for this school were published in the *Gaceta Oficial*, 1 Dec. 1842.

10. These began in January 1843 under the direction of Cleto Peralta. *Gaceta Oficial*, 13 Jan. 1843; AGCA, B, leg. 1390, exp. 32099; *Gaceta de Guatemala*, 22 Nov. 1850.

11. The instructor of the shorthand classes, Manuel Pineda, was declared to be the only man in the state who knew shorthand. He began his lessons at the Economic Society in Sept. 1844 from 11:00 A.M. to noon daily. *Gaceta Oficial*, 22 Aug. and 27 Sept. 1844.

12. Woodward, *Class Privilege*, 47–54; Shafer, *Economic Societies* 361.

13. *Gaceta de Guatemala*, 1 and 8 Feb., 10 May, and 29 Nov. 1850.

14. *El Noticioso de Guatemala*, 11 Sept. 1862.

15. *Gaceta de Guatemala*, 30 Jan. 1862, 29 Sept. 1863, and 20 Jan. 1866.

16. *Gaceta de Guatemala*, 16 Apr. 1869; 12 July 1870; *La Semana*, 18 May 1869.

17. Shafer, *Economic Societies*, 127, 262; AGCA, B, leg. 1390, exp. 32104.

18. *Gaceta Oficial*, 6 Nov. 1846; *Gaceta de Guatemala*, 13 Feb. and 16 Apr. 1852, 24 Feb. and 31 Mar. 1854, 9 Mar. 1855, 4 Jan. 1856, 21 Nov. 1860, and 15 and 22 Jan. 1861; Batres Jáuregui, *América Central*, 3:240; Palacios, *Memoria leída*, 9–10, 15–17; *La Sociedad Económica de Guatemala*, January 1866–May 1870.

19. On the Ministerio de Fomento, see David J. McCreery, *Development and the State in Reforma Guatemala* (1983).

20. Woodward, *Class Privilege*, 56–59, 133–34, including a table on 58–59 showing amounts spent annually for roads and ports. The annual incomes of the Consulado for the period 1839–71 varied considerably from year to year, but after 1850 usually fell within a range of $35,000 to $55,000.

21. Juan Bautista de Irisarri headed a Consulado commission that carried out extensive reconnaissance of Pacific Coast sites in the 1790s. Although the Consulado approved his project in principal, it took no concrete steps to develop such a port, perhaps fearing it might enable Salvadoran indigo producers to bypass the Guatemalan merchants. Irisarri's death in 1805 left the Pacific Coast ports without an effective advocate. Woodward, *Class Privilege*, 60–67.

22. Stephens, *Incidents*, 1:34–35, provides an especially descriptive account of Izabal at this point.

23. Woodward, *Class Privilege*, 67–69; Francisco M. Beteta to Secretario de Estado y del Despacho de Hacienda, Guatemala, 7 July 1826, AGCA, B, leg. 3483, exp. 79641, fol. 535.

24. Stephens, *Incidents*, 1:287–88.

25. *El Tiempo*, 19 Oct. 1839.

26. *El Tiempo*, 11 Feb. and 28 June 1840; *Gaceta Oficial*, 4 Nov. 1842. Legislative decree no. 64 of 25 Nov. 1839 gave the Consulado authorization to develop the ports of both coasts, and this act served as the basic law for port improvements throughout the conservative years.

27. Woodward, *Class Privilege*, 71–72.

28. Legislative decree of 14 Dec. 1839, *El Tiempo*, 20 Nov. 1839.

29. J. Mariano Vidaurre and Manuel F. Pavón to Secretario del Despacho de Gobernación y Justicia, Guatemala, 25 Oct. 1839, *El Tiempo*, 3 Nov. 1839; M. Cerezo to los Secretarios de la Asamblea Constituyente, Guatemala, 24 Mar. 1843, *Gaceta Oficial*, 1 Apr. 1843.

30. *Gaceta de Guatemala*, 16 Apr. 1847.

31. *La Semana*, 22 Jan.–19 Feb. 1865.

32. *La Semana*, 29 Apr. 1868; *Gaceta de Guatemala*, 1 May 1868.

33. Woodward, *Class Privilege*, 74–75.

34. *Gaceta de Guatemala*, 18 Jan. 1857.

35. Woodward, *Class Privilege*, 74–78.

36. Wayne Anderson, "The Development of Export Transportation in Liberal Guatemala, 1871–1920" (1985); Woodward, *Class Privilege*, 79–80.

37. AGCA, A, leg. 183, exp. 3750; leg. 2190, exp. 15739, fol. 136; leg. 2193, exp. 15746, fol. 97; leg. 2798, exp. 24573; leg. 6930, exp. 57158.

38. AGCA, B, leg. 3483, exp. 79641, fol. 219.

39. Pineda de Mont, *Recopilación*, 1:774; Griffith, *Santo Tomás*, 21.

40. *El Tiempo*, 17 June 1840; 20 Jan. 1841; Prior of the Consulado to the Secretary General of the Supremo Gobierno del Estado de Guatemala, 20 Apr. 1841, AGCA, B, leg. 3612, exp. 84383.

41. Consulado de Comercio, *Memoria leída por el secretario del Consulado de Comercio . . .* (1845), 4.

42. Woodward, *Class Privilege*, 92. Decreto no. 16, Ministerio de Gobernación, 10 May 1847, AGCA, AMG, 1847.

43. *Gaceta de Guatemala*, 14 July 1855.

44. Consulado de Comercio, *Memoria leída por el secretario del Consulado de Comercio . . .* (1856), 5; *Gaceta de Guatemala*, 9 Apr. and 28 May 1856.

45. *Gaceta de Guatemala*, 25 Feb. 1853.

46. Rafael Carrera, *Mensaje dirigido por el Excmo. señor Presidente de la República . . . el día 10 de diciembre de 1863* (1863), 6; *Gaceta de Guatemala*, 18 Apr. and 16 June 1863; 31 Mar. 1864; *La Semana*, 22 Jan. 1865. This company was organized in 1862, with William Remsen as president and Henry R. Morgan as secretary. Its board of directors included Pierre Albino Marié, Henry Charles Bishop, W. R. Traves, and John Slosson. Its chief engineer, who negotiated the Guatemalan contract, was a Frenchman named de Brame. *Gaceta de Guatemala*, 15 Jan. and 16 June 1863. After the Motagua project proved to be unfeasible, the company later turned to activities in Belize, but it eventually folded. Clegern, *Colonial Dead End*, 31.

47. *Gaceta de Guatemala*, 9 and 27 Oct. 1867; Pineda de Mont, *Recopilación*, 1:792–97; Pedro Pérez Valenzuela, *Santo Tomás de Castilla; Apuntes para la historia de las colonizaciones en la costa atlántica* (1956), 228–34.

48. *Gaceta de Guatemala*, 4 Oct. 1860; Consulado de Comercio, *Informe y estados que dió cuenta á la junta de gobierno del Consulado de Comercio . . .* (1861), 18–22; *Memoria sobre los trabajos en que se han ocupado el Consulado de Comercio . . .* (1862), 12–14.

49. *Gaceta Oficial*, 24 Dec. 1842 and 10 Mar. 1843.

50. *Gaceta de Guatemala*, 12 and 19 July, 19 Sept., 20 and 27 Dec. 1850, 11 July and 28 Nov. 1851.

51. Consulado de Comercio, *Memoria leída por el secretario del Consulado. . . 1856*, 5–7.; *Gaceta de Guatemala*, 14 Feb. 1856 and 15 Dec. 1858.

52. The *Memorias* of the Consulado of 1861, 1862, and 1865, and the reports of the Consulado engineer, published regularly in the *Gaceta de Guatemala* after 1866, reveal the Consulado's strong priority for this road over all others; see also *La Semana*, 6 Aug. 1866.

53. *Gaceta de Guatemala*, 13 Feb. 1852.

54. Ibid., 26 Sept. 1851; 19 Dec. 1851.

55. *Gaceta de Guatemala*, 26 Mar. 1852; 25 June and 2 July 1852; and 6 May and

25 Aug. 1860; 26 Apr. and 22 Sept. 1861; 7 May 1864; 22 June 1865; Consulado de Comercio, *Memoria . . . 19 de mayo de 1853*, 6; and *Memoria . . . 8 de mayo de 1861 a igual fecha de 1862*, 11; *La Semana*, 25 Sept. 1865; *La Sociedad Económica*, 15 and 31 Dec. 1870; Report of the Corregidor of Sololá, 11 Sept. 1859, on the building of a bridge at Rusmalchiqui, in AGCA, B, AMG, 1858, leg. 28577; and 1866, legs. 28604, 28606, and 28607.

56. Consulado de Comercio. *Memoria leída por el secretario del Consulado de Comercio . . .* (1844), para. 32; and *Memoria . . . de 19 de mayo de 1845*, 5; *Gaceta Oficial*, 13 Feb. 1844.

57. *Gaceta de Guatemala*, 5 Dec. 1851; 23 Jan. 1852; 11 June 1852; 6 Mar. 1866; 23 Nov. 1866; *La Semana*, 27 Aug. 1865.

58. *La Semana*, 27 Aug. 1865; *Gaceta de Guatemala*, 26 Jan. 1868.

59. *El Costarricense* (San José), 10 Apr. 1847; AGCA, B, leg. 214, exp. 4941, fol. 581; *El Tiempo*, 5 Dec. 1839; Crowe, *Gospel*, 138–39. Watson, Thomson and Company of Glasgow had been actively advertising their iron bridges in Central America. They provided prefabricated suspension bridges, twelve *varas* wide in lengths ranging from six varas at $550 to fifty varas at $2,900.

60. Woodward, *Class Privilege*, 98–99.

61. *Gaceta Oficial*, 26 Nov. 1841.

62. Decreto Ejecutivo no. 65, 24 Dec. 1851, *Gaceta de Guatemala*, 2 Jan. 1852, approved by the Cámara de Representantes, 10 Dec. 1852, *Gaceta de Guatemala*, 22 Apr. 1853.

63. *Gaceta de Guatemala*, 1 Mar. 1857; 15 May and 10 July 1866; 21 June 1870; *El Noticioso de Guatemala*, 2 Nov. 1861; Félix Belly, *A travers l'Amérique centrale, le Nicaragua et la canal interocéanique* (1867), 1:131; *La Sociedad Económica de Guatemala*, 15 and 31 Dec. 1870.

64. *Gaceta de Guatemala*, 7 Feb. 1866. Cobos's "Informe sobre la carretera proyectada entre Tactic y el Puerto de Telemán" is published in its entirety in the *Gaceta*, 18 Feb. 1866.

65. AGCA, B, AMG, 1866, leg. 28604.

66. *La Semana*, 26 Jan. and 29 Aug. 1869; AGCA, B, leg. 28605, AMG, 1866

67. *Gaceta de Guatemala*, 8 July 1858.

68. Ibid., 4 Feb. 1868.

69. *La Semana*, 29 May 1869.

70. *Gaceta de Guatemala*, 26 Apr. and 28 June 1870.

71. *Gaceta de Guatemala*, 19 Dec. 1866, 27 Dec. 1867; AGCA, B, leg. 3664, exp. 86687. A Paris-based company, the Sociedad Internacional de Telegrafía Eléctrica, had proposed an ambitious plan to link Central America with the world by telegraph as early as 1857. Guatemala, unlike Costa Rica, which had entered into negotiations with the French company, did not pursue any telegraph project until after the death of Carrera. *Gaceta de Guatemala*, 14 Jan. 1858.

72. Belly, *A travers*, 1:128. See Woodward, *Class Privilege*, for further discussion of the Consulado's involvement in public works construction.

73. AGCA, B, leg. 213, exp. 4884.

74. Naylor, "British Commercial Relations," 112, 118; *Gaceta de Guatemala*, 13 Aug. 1849.

75. *Gaceta de Guatemala*, 6 Sept. 1850.

76. Ibid., 7 Sept. 1855.

77. Albion, "British Shipping," 363.

78. *Gaceta de Guatemala*, 3 May and 20 Dec. 1850.

79. Ibid., 30 May and 8 Oct. [*sic* Nov.] 1851.

80. Ibid., 16 Sept., 18 Nov., and 23 Dec. 1853, and 13 Jan. and 17 Feb. 1854.

81. Ibid., 21 Mar. 1856.

82. *Gaceta de Guatemala*, 12 and 14 Feb. 1856; the contract was revised in 1858 to provide for a $12,000 annual subsidy if the company would add a second ship and increase service to twice per month (ibid., 8 Apr. 1858), but apparently the second ship was not put into service, for in 1868 the contract was renewed for five more years at the $8,000 annual subsidy (ibid., 18 Apr. 1868).

83. *Gaceta de Guatemala*, 15 Jan. 1857.

84. Ibid., 14 July 1864.

85. Ibid., 31 Mar. 1858; AGCA, B, AMG, 1858, leg. 28576.

86. AGCA, B, AMG, 1865, leg. 28601; *Gaceta de Guatemala*, 19 Aug. 1865.

87. AGCA, B, AMG, leg. 28626.

88. AGCA, B, AMG, leg. 28620 and leg. 28623; Vicente Cerna, *Mensage dirigido por el Excelentísimo Señor Presidente de la República de Guatemala, Mariscal de Campo don Vicente Cerna, a la Cámara de Representantes, en la continuación de las últimas sesiones del tercer período constitucional, el día de 4 de abril de 1870* (1870), 4.

89. "Acuerdo sobre ordenanza y reforma de correos," *Gaceta de Guatemala*, 11 June 1866.

90. Naylor, "British Commercial Relations," 115.

91. Marston Bates's statement that "the National idea, both in Europe and Latin America, got solidified into units whose size was determined by the systems of communication and transportation that were available around 1800" seems to be especially true for Central America. *Where Winter Never Comes, A Study of Man and Nature in the Tropics* (1952), 254.

18. Production for Consumption and Export

1. AGCA, B, leg. 3605, exp. 83479.

2. José Antonio de Larrave, Corregidor de Guatemala, Ordinance, 28 Dec. 1840, *hojas sueltas* collection, Hemeroteca of the AGCA.

3. AGCA, B, leg. 3600, exp. 82802.

4. *El Procurador de los Pueblos*, 26 Sept. 1840.

5. *El Tiempo*, 26 Nov. 1840.

6. Juan Matheu to Ministro de Hacienda y Guerra, Guatemala, 25 Feb. 1845,

AGCA, B, leg. 3612, exp. 84444. For discussion of opposition to free trade in the early 1840s, see the *Gaceta Oficial*, 18 and 30 Aug. 1842.

7. *Gaceta de Guatemala*, 17 May 1844.

8. *Gaceta Oficial*, 27 June 1844.

9. AGCA, B, leg. 28552, exp. 1194.

10. *Gaceta de Guatemala*, 19 and 24 Feb. 1844.

11. See, for example, "Teoría de M. Rossi," *Gaceta Oficial*, 12 Apr. 1845.

12. José M. de Castilla, Director, and M. Dardón, Secretario, to Supremo Gefe del Estado, Guatemala, 4 Aug. 1845, *Gaceta Oficial*, 10 Sept. 1845, AGCA, B, leg. 3611, exp. 84342.

13. Rafael Carrera, *Decreto Núm. 96* (Guatemala, 28 Nov. 1853); and *Gaceta de Guatemala*, 31 Aug. 1855.

14. *Gaceta de Guatemala*, 9–20 May 1858.

15. *Gaceta de Guatemala*, 19 March 1852.

16. Acuerdo del Ministerio de Gobernación, 16 Apr. 1852, *Gaceta de Guatemala*, 23 Apr. 1852.

17. Gregorio Rosales, *Instrucción para teñir y dar colores a las lanas, para el uso de los tintoreros de los departamentos de los altos. . .* (1852).

18. An arroba was about twenty-five pounds. Manuel Fuentes Franco, "Informe del Corregidor de San Marcos sobre existencia de ganado menor y lana que se obtiene anualmente en aquel departamento," 20 Oct. 1854, *Gaceta de Guatemala*, 17 Nov. 1854.

19. AGCA, B, leg. 28590, Ministro de Gobernación, Comunicaciones, 1859.

20. Ibid,, 21 Mar. 1850.

21. Naylor, "British Commercial Relations," 174.

22. Dunlop, *Travels*, 79–86, 317, 334–35.

23. L. E. Elliott, *Central America: New Paths in Ancient Lands* (1925), 129.

24. Griffith, *Empires*, and "Attitudes."

25. Smith, "Financing," 508, citing AGCA, B, leg. 131, exp. 3123.

26. Griffith, *Empires*, 29.

27. Naylor, "British Commercial Relations," 183; Merle A. Renikka, *A History of the Orchid* (1972), 169–72, and "The Late Mr. G. Ure Skinner," *Gardeners' Chronicle*, no. 8 (1867). There are sixty-four letters (1836–57) from Skinner to W. J. Hooker written from Central America scattered through several bound volumes of the "Hooker Letters, Miscellaneous Correspondence, 1828–1928," in the Library of the Royal Botanical Gardens, Kew, Richmond, Surrey, England. Many of these letters include detailed descriptions of Skinner's travels in Central America and observations of the flora and fauna.

28. Naylor, "British Commercial Relations," 82–83, 90–96, 154, 159–61; Frederick Chatfield to P. N. Arriaga, Guatemala, 5 May 1851, *Gaceta de Guatemala*, 9 May 1851, in which Chatfield sends a table showing how British tariffs have dropped on Guatemalan produce during the period 1801–49 as their volume has increased.

29. Thompson, *Narrative*, 419; Dunn, *Guatimala*, 15, 216–18; Griffith, *Santo Tomás*, 8–9; Naylor, "British Commercial Relations," 154; Solórzano Fernández, *Historia*, 244–45; Browning, *El Salvador*, 145.

30. Ministerio de Hacienda de Indias to Secretario de Marina *et al.*, Madrid, 16 Feb. 1829, and Prior y Cónsules del Consulado de la Habana to Secretario de Estado y del Despacho de Hacienda de Indias, Havana, 29 Jan. 1828, Archivo General de Indias Sevilla (hereinafter cited as AGI), Sección 10, Ultramar, leg. 324; Montgomery, *Journey to Guatemala*, 36; Young, *Narrative*, 138–39, 162–68.

31. Naylor, "British Role," 367.

32. Report compiled by José Ramón Velasco, *Semanario de Guatemala*, 21 May 1836.

33. *Semanario de Guatemala*, 9 July 1836.

34. *El Editor: Periódico de los Tribunales*, 1 June 1837.

35. *El Tiempo*, 19 Oct. 1839.

36. Griffith, *Empires*, 208–10.

37. *Gaceta Oficial*, 26 Nov. 1841.

38. *El Tiempo*, 28 Dec. 1840.

39. Report of Joaquín de Arce in *El Tiempo*, 24 Oct. 1840. The Acajutla exports of Guatemalan produce included cochineal, sarsaparilla, balsam, and hides.

40. Decreto no. 34, 24 Dec. 1841, and Decreto no. 152, 12 May 1842, AGCA, B, leg. 213, exp. 4911; Decreto no. 48, 28 Oct. 1842, in Coll. 20, Central America Political Ephemera, LALTU.

41. *Gaceta Oficial*, 7 July 1843.

42. Ibid., 27 June and 11 July 1845.

43. Executive Decree of 22 Nov. 1851, AGCA, B, leg. 3606, exp. 83791.

44. Executive Decree no. 65, 24 Dec. 1851, *Gaceta de Guatemala*, 2 Jan. 1852, 22 Apr. 1853.

45. Schoonover, "Metropole Rivalry," 24–25, 36–37; Thomas Schoonover, "Germany in Central America, 1820s to 1929: An Overview," *Jahrbuch für Geschichte von Staat, Wirtschaft und Gesellschaft Lateinamerikas* 25 (1988):33–43; and Thomas and Ebba Schoonover, "Statistics for an Understanding of Foreign Intrusions into Central America from the 1820s to 1930," *Anuario de Estudios Centroamericanos* 15, no. 1 (1989): 93–118 and 16, no. 1 (1990): 135–56.

46. *Gaceta de Guatemala*, 4 Aug. 1854.

47. Ibid., 25 Nov. 1856.

48. Browning, *El Salvador*, 141.

49. *La Semana*, 13–22 Aug. 1866; Shirley Lucas McAfee, "A Study of Agricultural Labor in Guatemala, 1821–1871" (1955), 55–58; AGCA, B, leg. 28615; *Gaceta de Guatemala*, 1 May 1868.

50. *Gaceta de Guatemala*, 13 Oct. 1869 and 24 May 1870.

51. One of the best descriptions of cochineal production in Guatemala is found in Dunlop, *Travels*, 62, 122–36. Dunlop managed a cochineal plantation near Amatitlán in 1845. Woodward, *Class Privilege*, 33–41; John Baily, *Central America*

(1850), 164; Chinchilla Aguilar, *Historia*, 80; Orden no. 12 del Congreso Constituyente del Estado de Guatemala, 21 Sept. 1824, AGCA, B, leg. 2298, exp. 29367; Orden no. 44 del Congreso Constituyente del Estado de Guatemala, 7 Oct. 1824, and "El Gefe Interino de Guatemala a los pueblos que lo forman," 8 Oct. 1824, AGCA, B, leg. 192, exp. 4158, fols. 46–49; and Circular from Guatemalan government to its jefes políticos, 8 Oct. 1824, AGCA, B, leg. 1188, exp. 28798.

52. Dunlop, *Travels*, 95.

53. Naylor, "British Role," 371.

54. Solórzano Fernández, *Historia*, 259–60.

55. *Gaceta Oficial*, 19 July 1846. A chart in the *Gaceta* showing this information provides considerable additional data on the specific costs of packaging and shipping the cochineal.

56. The letter and an accompanying chart appeared in the *Gaceta Oficial*, 7 Aug. 1846, and gives additional detail on expenses in producing cochineal. Based on the official figures in Table 12, it would appear that the government overestimated the value of the crop in 1846.

57. In 1850 the remainder of British cochineal came from Mexico (16.1 percent), the Canary Islands (7 percent), and elsewhere (1.3 percent). *Gaceta de Guatemala*, 5 Dec. 1851.

58. Rafael Meldola, Arthur C. Green, and John C. Cain, eds., *Jubilee of the Discovery of Mauve and of the Foundation of the Coal Tar Colour Industry by Sir W. H. Perkin* (1906), 66; Herbert Heaton, *Economic History of Europe*, rev. ed. (1948), 511–12.

59. *Gaceta de Guatemala*, 21 Sept. and 14 Oct. 1860.

60. "Agricultura: Cochinilla," *Gaceta de Guatemala*, 2 July and 12 Aug. 1860.

61. See, for example, the broadside published on 1 Sept. 1860, *Ultimas noticias relativas a la grana y el nuevo tinte con que se había pretendido sustituirla*, in *hojas sueltas* collection, Hemeroteca of the AGCA; and various notices from the government in the *Gaceta de Guatemala*, especially in September and October, 1860.

62. *Gaceta de Guatemala*, 17 Oct. 1860, 23 Mar. 1861, and 8 Apr. 1865; Consulado de Comercio, *Memoria sobre los trabajos en que se ha ocupado el Consulado de Comercio . . .* (1862), 3–5; Salazar, *Tiempo viejo*, 9–10.

63. Belly, *A travers*, (1867), 1:144–45.

64. Carolyn Hall, *El café y el desarrollo histórico-geográfico de Costa Rica* (1976); Lanuza Matamoros, *Estructuras*, 164–80.

65. Auto acordado, Guatemala, 10 May 1805, AGCA, A, leg. 2317, fol. 96.

66. AGCA, B, leg. 3606, exp. 83745, fol. 21v.

67. Consulado de Comercio, *Memoria leída por el secretario del Consulado de Comercio del estado de Guatemala al abrirse la sesión de 19 de mayo de 1845* (1845), 4–7; Sociedad Economica, *Memoria de la junta general de la Sociedad Económica del estado de Guatemala, celebrado el 14 de setiembre de 1845* (1845), 9–10.

68. Woodward, *Class Privilege*, 50–51. The *Gaceta de Guatemala*, 1850–60, contains many articles reflecting the Consulado's and Economic Society's efforts in this respect. See also Manuel Aguilar, *Memoria sobre el cultivo del café, arreglada la práctica*

que se observa en Costa Rica, escrita por el Ldo. Manuel Aguilar, y dada imprimir por el Consulado de Comercio de Guatemala (1845).

69. *Gaceta de Guatemala*, 4 Mar. 1853, 13 May 1853, 24 Sept. 1859, 29 Mar. 1862, and 18 Oct. 1862.

70. Pineda de Mont, *Recopilación*, 2:618; *Gaceta de Guatemala*, 16 Jan. 1858.

71. *Gaceta de Guatemala*, 4 June 1859.

72. Ibid., 16 Nov. 1859 and 14 June 1860. Julio Rosignon, in the *Gaceta*, noted the advantages for coffee cultivation in the Verapaz, including the possibility of exporting it via the Río Polochic.

73. *El Noticioso de Guatemala*, 17 Feb. 1862.

74. *Gaceta de Guatemala*, 13 Apr. 1862; *El Noticioso de Guatemala*, 28 Dec. 1861.

75. Aycinena to Ministro de Gobernación, Guatemala, 17 Apr. 1866., AGCA, B, leg. 28604.

76. See the report of Enrique Palacios to the Economic Society on coffee cultivation in Escuintla in *El Noticioso de Guatemala*, 18 Jan. 1862; and the informe of the Corregidor of Escuintla, Miguel Urrutia, in the *Gaceta de Guatemala*, 8 Sept. 1861.

77. "Cultivo de café," *Gaceta de Guatemala*, 27 July 1862.

78. Solórzano Fernández, *Historia*, 265–66; Schwemmer, "Belgium Colonization Company," 416; and Guillermo Náñez Falcón, "Paul Erwin Dieseldorff, German Entrepreneur in the Alta Verapaz of Guatemala, 1889–1937" (1970); Castellanos Cambranes, *Café y Campesinos*, 103–6.

79. *Mensage dirigido por el Exmo. Señor Presidente de la República de Guatemala, Capitán General Don Rafael Carrera, a la Cámara de Representantes; en la apertura de sus sestas sesiones del segundo período constitucional, el día 25 de noviembre de 1861* (1862), 5–6; *Mensaje dirijido por el Excmo. Señor Presidente de la República de Guatemala, Capitán Gral. Don Rafael Carrera, a la Cámara de Representantes; en la apertura de sus sétimas sesiones del segundo período constitucional, el día 25 de noviembre de 1862* (1862), 4.

80. Informes from the Corregidor of San Marcos, Marcos Zelaya, to the Ministro de Gobernación, 16 Feb. and 18 Mar. 1865, AGCA, B, leg. 28602.

81. Dunn, *Guatimala*, 215; Ralph Lee Woodward, Jr., "Guatemalan Cotton and the American Civil War," *Inter-American Economic Affairs* 18 (Winter 1984):87–94.

82. Frank L. Owsley, *King Cotton Diplomacy: Foreign Relations of the Confederate States of America*, 2d ed. (1959), 3.

83. The British Consul in Guatemala, Charles L. Wyke, described the seed as being from the "best cotton of New Orleans." *Gaceta de Guatemala*, 22 July 1858.

84. *Gaceta de Guatemala*, 19 and 26 Apr., 1 May 1860.

85. Ibid., 18 June 1862, 21 Sept. 1864.

86. AGCA, B, leg. 1390, exp. 32099; leg. 3606, exp. 83745; leg. 3611, exp. 84320.

87. The Consulado began to give strong support to cotton cultivation in 1859. Luis Batres to Ministro del Interior, Guatemala, 22 Jan. 1859, AGCA, B, leg. 28590, Comunicaciones, Ministro de Gobernación, 1862; *Gaceta de Guatemala*,

25 Nov. 1863, 7 Mar. 1864, 16 June 1864, 3 Dec. 1864; *El Noticioso de Guatemala*, 2 and 11 Dec. 1861, 17 Feb. and 2 May 1862; Solórzano Fernández, *Historia*, 272.

88. *Gaceta de Guatemala*, 29 Mar. 1862, 13 May 1853.

89. Ibid., 18 June 1862.

90. Ibid., 24 Dec. 1864.

91. *Gaceta de Guatemala*, 11 Dec., 1864; Solórzano Fernández, *Historia*, 272. For a discussion of the twentieth-century revival and some disastrous effects of the careless use of pesticides to grow cotton in Central America see Robert G. Williams, *Export Agriculture and the Crisis in Central America* (1986).

92. Woodward, *Class Privilege*, 49.

93. AGCA, B, leg. 1392, exp. 32226; *Gaceta de Guatemala*, 26 Apr. 1850.

94. *Gaceta Oficial*, 6 Dec. 1845.

95. *Gaceta de Guatemala*, 20 May 1853.

96. Ibid., 29 Sept. 1859, 13 Oct. 1869.

97. Aycinena published an instructional pamphlet in 1839: *Breve instrucción sobre el cultivo de las moreras, para la crianza de gusano de seda con algunos cálculos del producto de este ramo de industria, tomadas de los autores que han escrito últimamente sobre la materia.*

98. *Gaceta de Guatemala*, 24 and 30 Nov. 1862; Manuel Rubio Sánchez, *Historia del cultivo de la morera de China y de la industria del gusano de seda en Guatemala* (1984).

99. *Gaceta de Guatemala*, 4 June 1864.

100. Based on reports in the *Gaceta Oficial* and *Gaceta de Guatemala*, 1843–1866, the number of cattle slaughtered in Guatemala City for the years available were as follows:

1834–35	5,718
1840 (Jan.–July)	2,676
1845	4,974
1846	4,788
1847 (Dec.)	610
1849	5,581
1850	5,785
1851	5,809
1860	7,347
1861	7,877
1862	7,161
1865	6,156

Weights or quantity of meat yielded from these cattle are rarely given in the records. The report for December 1847, however, indicated that the 610 cattle slaughtered in that month yielded 9,218 arrobas of meat (average 377.79 pounds) and 313 arrobas, 6 lbs. of lard (average 12.84 pounds). "Demostración del número de reses beneficiadas en el rastro de esta ciudad en el mes de diciembre próximo pasado, y carne que han producido," Guatemala, 8 Jan. 1848, *Gaceta de Guatemala*,

28 Jan. 1848. Actual consumption may have been higher, for it is unlikely that all beef consumed was included in these statistics.

101. The number of weeks in each year for which data is available is as follows: 1853, 29; 1854, 29; 1855, 2; 1856, 5; 1857, 4; 1858, 36; 1859, 12; 1860, 25; 1861, 10; 1862, 20; 1863, 5; 1864, 0; 1865, 0; 1866, 3.

102. Rafael Carrera, *Mensaje . . . a la Cámara de Representantes . . . 25 de noviembre de 1854*, 6; see also *Gaceta de Guatemala*, 24 March, 14 June, 20 Oct., and 24 Nov. 1854.

103. Ralph Lee Woodward, Jr., "Population and Development in Guatemala, 1840–1870," *Annals of the Southeastern Council on Latin American Studies* 14 (1983): 10–11. Among such disasters during the Carrera period were the following:

1837–38	Cholera epidemic
1837–39	War of the Mountain
1838–40	Civil war between State of Guatemala and Central American federation.
1840	Drought
1841	Hurricane on the Pacific coast
1842–44	Drought
1845	Eruption of Volcán Pacaya
1847–52	Resumption of War of the Mountain
1848–49	Civil war between liberals and conservatives
1851–52	War with Honduras and El Salvador
1854	Locust plague
1855–57	War in Nicaragua with thousands of Guatemalan casualties
1856	Excessive rainfall
1857–58	Cholera epidemic
1860	Drought
1861	Excessive rainfall
1862	Bad harvests and excessive rainfall
1863	War with El Salvador
1865	Cholera epidemic
1866	Hurricane on Pacific Coast, especially damaging to Escuintla
1867	Tidal wave on Caribbean Coast
1868–69	Drought
1868–71	Liberal revolution.

Robert Claxton, "Historia de la meteorología y sequía en Guatemala, 1563 a 1925," to be published in the *Revista del Pensamiento Centroamericano*, is especially revealing of natural disasters affecting Guatemalan history.

104. The *Gaceta de Guatemala*, 1847–71, contains a great deal of evidence of this sort of government action.

105. *Gaceta de Guatemala*, 2 and 9 June, 20 Oct., and 24 Nov. 1854

19. Currency and Government Finance

1. *Gaceta de Guatemala*, 26 Feb. 1856.

2. Bancroft, *Central America*, 3:664–65, gives the following trade balances for Guatemala in the third quarter of the nineteenth century—1851–57: $7,672,682 imports, $9,613,099 exports; 1860–64: $6,268,227 imports, $7,386,541 exports; 1871–75: $12,304,289 imports, $12,418,083 exports; 1876–80: $15,054, 152 imports, $22,552,867 exports.

3. Solís, *Casa de Moneda*; Kurt Prober, *Historia numismática de Guatemala*, 2d ed. (1973).

4. Thompson, *Narrative*, 520.

5. 1 June 1836. *Gaceta de Guatemala*, 24 May 1850.

6. Naylor, *Influencia británica*, 68–73; Solís, *Casa de Moneda*, 3A:711–27.

7. The government requested this report, which was prepared by a committee composed of Julián González, José Nájera, Juan Matheu, Felipe Prado, and Juan Uriarte. *El Tiempo*, 28 June 1840. See also the editorial on this subject in *El Tiempo*, 13 July 1840.

8. Executive decrees of 30 June and 2 July 1840 prohibited payment of public debts, and, effectively, their use as legal tender, with silver coins minted in Cuzco bearing the Seal of the Sun, those of Bolivia with the bust of Bolívar, and those of Peru with the effigy of Liberty. The decrees suggested that there were many counterfeits of these coins and many of them contained less than the correct amount of silver. *El Tiempo*, 6 and 8 July 1840. Subsequent legislative decrees of 15 July and 22 Sept. 1840 approved this prohibition, but emphasized that it did not include silver pesos that were legitimately coined in the South American republics. *El Tiempo*, 30 Sept. 1840; *Procurador de los Pueblos*, 19 Sept. 1840.

9. Juan José Aycinena to Marcial Zebadúa, Guatemala, 28 July 1842, *Gaceta Oficial*, 3 Aug. 1842; and *Gaceta Oficial*, 5 Jan. 1843.

10. *Gaceta Oficial*, 26 Apr. 1845. For the Consulado's response to the proposal, see ibid., 26 July 1845.

11. *Gaceta de Guatemala*, 1 Aug. and 19 Dec. 1851.

12. Solís, *Casa de Moneda*, 3A:731–33.

13. *Gaceta de Guatemala*, 6 May 1853.

14. The legislature passed this law in January 1857, and it was signed by President Carrera on 6 April 1857. AGCA, B, AMG, leg. 28576; *Gaceta de Guatemala*, 8 Mar. 1857 and 6 July 1859.

15. Voting for the bill were Juan Andreu, Zebadúa, Echeverría, Pedro Aycinena, Cerezo, Zavala, Palomo, Valenzuela, Montúfar, Espinosa, Santa Cruz, Juan Fermín Aycinena, Galdames, Arroyo, Ruiz, José Luna, Rodríguez, Horjales, Solís, Aparicio, Saravía, Matheu, and Pavón. Opposed were Machado, Nicolás Larrave, Manuel González, García Parra, Miguel González, Andrés Andreu, Juan Estrada, Arcadio Estrada, Pacheco, García Granados, David Luna, Manuel Larrave, Esca-

milla, and Dardón. For photographs of these coins, see Solís, *Casa de Moneda*, 3A:plates at conclusion of the volume.

16. *Gaceta de Guatemala*, 11 May 1855; and 27 Nov., 29 and 31 Dec. 1858.

17. Ibid., 24 Sept. 1858 and 6 Jan. 1859.

18. Ibid., 6 Mar. 1856; Carrera, *Mensage . . . 1858*, 3; Moorhead, "Rafael Carrera," 138.

19. Carrera, *Mensage . . . 1858*, 5; *Gaceta de Guatemala*, 13 Jan., 10 Feb., and 10 Sept. 1859; and 13 May 1860.

20. *Gaceta de Guatemala*, 27 Jan. 1860.

21. Circular from José Nájera, Minister of Finance, announcing the new coin, 28 Mar. 1860, *hojas sueltas* collection, Hemeroteca of the AGCA.

22. *Gaceta de Guatemala*, 26 Sept. 1860.

23. Ibid., 15 Jan. 1863.

24. Ibid., 26 Feb. 1870.

25. Enrique Palacios, *La cuestión monetaria en Guatemala* (1870), 16–19; *Gaceta de Guatemala*, 19 June 1869.

26. Palacios, *La cuestión*, 3.

27. Ibid, 9–31; *Gaceta de Guatemala*, 13 Oct. 1870.

28. *Gaceta de Guatemala*, 21 Sept. 1864. See also the letter by the Baron du Teil, 13 Nov. 1864, praising the new Banco de Guatemala in the *Gaceta*, 29 Nov. 1864.

29. The founders of the bank included Thomas Jump, G. J. Hockmeyer, Vicente Zebadúa, José and Juan Urruela, Miguel García Granados, the du Teil brothers, Eugenio Laprade, and José María Samayoa. *Proyecto de concesión para establecer en la República de Guatemala un banco nacional* (1866); Vicente Cerna, *Mensaje dirijido por el Excmo. señor Presidente de la República de Guatemala, Mariscal de Campo don Vicente Cerna, á la Cámara de Representantes; en la apertura de sus cuartas sesiones del tercer período constitucional, el día 25 de noviembre de 1866* (1866); Pineda de Mont, *Recopilación*, 1:765–70; *Gaceta de Guatemala*, 23 Aug. 1867.

30. *Gaceta de Guatemala*, 1 Sept. 1866.

31. Executive Decree of Gefe del Estado de Guatemala, 17 Nov. 1827 (Guatemala, 1827), 1–2.

32. Chester Lloyd Jones, *Costa Rica and Civilization in the Caribbean* (1935), 99; Smith, "Financing," 486–88. A copy of the contract with Barclay and Herring Company from the Aycinena family archive was provided the author by Mr. Richmond Brown.

33. *Semanario de Guatemala*, 28 July 1836, citing *El Vijia del Istmo*, no. 12.

34. Smith, "Financing." Costa Rica received nothing from this loan, yet it had to repay more than $100,000. González Viquez, *Capítulos*, 24. According to Jones, *Costa Rica*, 100, Costa Rica paid its share of £26,755 with two thousand *tercios* of tobacco, which were sent to Nicaragua and sold for indigo. This earned only £16,210 when sold in London. Although this amount was considerably short of the total, the British creditors reportedly decided to accept it in full payment rather than carry the risky investment any longer. This left Costa Rica free of foreign

debt, and it continued to remain free of major foreign debt for another thirty years.

35. Ezequiel Martínez Estrada, *Diferencias y semejanzas entre los países de la América Latina* (1962), 261; Karnes, *Failure of Union*, 112–13; *Gaceta Oficial*, 3 Aug. 1842; Rodríguez, *Palmerstonian*, 245–52.

36. *Gaceta de Guatemala*, 5 Aug. 1858.

37. Ibid., 31 Mar. 1848 and 4 July 1851.

38. Ibid., 10 May 1850 and 22 Feb. 1857.

39. Ibid., 9 Aug. 1850.

40. For the entire history of the country's foreign debt through 1935, see *Sixty-second Annual Report of the Council* (London: Corporation of Foreign Bondholders, 1936), cited in Moorhead, "Rafael Carrera," 1942. The agreement, negotiated between the representative of the bondholders, Lawrence, and the Guatemalan government, was published in the *Gaceta de Guatemala*, 31 May 1856. John Samuel, of Issacs & Samuel, subsequently became the Guatemalan consul general in London.

41. AGCA, B, leg. 214, exp. 4941, fol. 130–66 lists the merchants and planters and the amounts they each contributed to this *donativo*.

42. *El Tiempo*, 11 Aug. and 9 Nov. 1839.

43. *Boletín Oficial*, 10 June 1838.

44. *Noticioso Guatemalteco*, 17 Mar. 1838.

45. There is a discussion of this question in the assembly on 3 June 1839 in *Actas de la Asamblea Constituyente y Acuerdos Oficiales del Gobierno*, no. 2 (Guatemala, 27 Aug. 1839), 10.

46. *El Tiempo*, 14 Nov. 1839; L. Montúfar, *Reseña*, 3:381.

47. Salazar, *Historia de veintiún años*, 14.

48. Martínez Peláez, *La patria del criollo*, 489–90, 748.

49. Subsequently, in October 1841, the assembly agreed that the members of the Consejo de Gobierno, which succeeded the old Consejo de Representantes, might receive from the treasury up to eighty pesos monthly while they served on the Council, providing they had no other income during the period. In the event that they had an income smaller than eighty pesos per month, the treasury would pay them the difference between their income and the eighty pesos. It also provided that the official from the assembly's secretariat who served as secretary to the council would receive an additional $100 per year. Guatemala, Asamblea Constituyente. *Colección de las ordenes de observancia* (1842), 29–30.

50. *El Tiempo*, 7 Jan. 1840. An "Estado que manifiesta los gastos de la administración de Estado de Guatemala, según las reformas hechas por la Asamblea Constituyente," ibid., 19 Dec. 1839, revealed the following civilian salaries for fiscal 1839:

ASSEMBLY during recess:	
Archivist	$ 600
Porter	45
EXECUTIVE BRANCH	
President of the state	2,500

Secretary of interior government	1,400
Secretary of the Treasury	1,400
First officer	600
Second officer	480
2 Scribes at $360 each	720
Archivist	300
Porter	180
2 Servants at $96 each	192

INTERIOR GOVERNMENT (*Gobernación*)

Corregidor for each of 7 departments at $1,200 and one in Amatitlán at $1,000	9,400
Secretary for each of the 8 at $300	2,400
4 police lieutenants in the capital at $360 each	1,440

TREASURY

Chief accountant	1,200
First officer	360
Scribe	300

Administration of the treasury

Treasurer	1,500
Accountant	1,200
Inspector	1,100
Sales tax inspector	500
Scribe	300
Porter	200
Servant	96

Tobacco Office

Agent	1,200
Auditor	1,000
Scribe	300
Porter/guard	200

Administration of customs

Administrator in Izabal	1,300
Accountant in Izabal	1,200
Scribe in Izabal	600
Administrator in Iztapa	1,000
Administrator in Antigua	1,000
Administrators in Escuintla, Chimaltenango, Chiquimula, Verapaz, Petén, and other Subaltern collectors get 6 percent of what they collect.	

Security

Chief guard in the capital	500
11 sentries and 2 guards at $360 each	4,680
2 guards in Izabal at $300 each	600

2 guards in Iztapa at $300 each	600
4 guards in Antigua at $300 each	1,200
1 guard in Chimaltenango	300
2 guards in Escuintla at $300 each	600
1 guard in Chiquimula	300
1 guard in Verapaz	300
Mint	
Superintendent of the mint	600
Inspector	400
Assayer	150
2 engravers at $600 and $400 each	1,000
JUDICIAL BRANCH	
Regent (Chief Justice)	1,600
4 magistrates at $1,500 each	6,000
Attorney general	1,500
Court scribe	500
Public defender	300
Solicitor for public defender	200
2 scribes at $300	600
First officer	400
Archivist/collector	300
Porter	200
Servant	120
Justice Section	
Judge of original jurisdiction in each of the 7 departments at $1,000 each	7,000
2 scribes in the capital at $200 each	400
2 commissars at $120 each	240

51. AGCA, B92.2, leg. 1392, exps. 32210 and 33212; and leg. 3612, exp. 84420. For a discussion of academic salaries in this period see Chapter 21.

52. The corregidor of Sololá, for example, in an estimate of costs for building a bridge included the following labor costs: one mason at six reales ($0.75) per day; two helpers at three reales ($0.375) per day; four carpenters at four reales ($0.50) per day. AGCA, B, AMG, leg. 28577, Comunicaciones año 1858.

53. The full text of the *Montepío Civil y Militar* appears in the *Gaceta de Guatemala*, 13 May 1858.

54. AGCA, B12.7, leg. 214, exp. 4941, fol. 607.

55. Mariano Rivera Paz, *Informe* (14 July 1840); *El Tiempo*, 26 Aug. 1840.

56. *El Tiempo*, 23 May 1840 and 7 Jan. 1841.

57. *El Tiempo*, 26 Aug. 1840.

58. Rodríguez, *Palmerstonian*, 149–50.

59. *Noticioso Guatemalteco*, 17 March 1838.

60. *Informe presentada la Asamblea Constituyente del Estado, en la sesión de 7 de octubre*

proponiendo un nuevo plan de contribuciones (Guatemala, 1839), AGCA, *El Libro Verde*, vol. no. 4148, item 462, 2–7, 12–16.

61. *El Tiempo*, 14 Dec. 1839.

62. *Gaceta Oficial*, 28 Sept. 1842.

63. Dunlop, *Travels*, 186.

64. *Gaceta de Guatemala*, 12 and 19 Dec. 1851, 12 Nov. 1852; "Estado de la deuda flotante de la República de Guatemala en noviembre de 1852 y en fin de octubre de 1835," *Gaceta de Guatemala*, 24 Feb. 1854; Rafael Carrera, *Informe dirijido por el Exmo. Sr. Presidente de la República de Guatemala, Capitán Jeneral don Rafael Carrera, á la Cámara de Representantes, en la apertura de sus segundas sesiones, el día 25 de noviembre de 1853* (1853), 8.

65. See the bitter denunciation of such taxes by an anonymous Nicaraguan, "Contribuciones i empréstitos," *Rejistro Oficial* (León), 7 Feb. 1846.

66. *Gaceta de Guatemala*, 18 Apr. and 31 Dec. 1864.

67. *Gaceta de Guatemala*, 1854–1871.

68. *Gaceta de Guatemala*, 6 Dec. 1857.

69. García Granados, *Memorias*, 2:55.

70. This law, signed by Rivera Paz on 22 Oct. 1840, repealed a law of 18 Aug. 1835 that had allowed higher rates. *El Tiempo*, 26 Nov. 1840. Discussion of the debate over this law in the assembly is found in several numbers of *El Tiempo* in September and October 1840.

71. *Gaceta de Guatemala*, 27 Apr. 1862. French banks consistently offered lower rates to investors than other European banks, but fluctuations did occur, as is indicated in the following table, showing interest rates offered by European banks as published in the *Gaceta de Guatemala*, 11 Feb. 1865 and 11 Sept. 1866:

	January 1865	*August 1866*
London	6 percent	10 percent
Paris	4.5 percent	4.5 percent
Vienna	6 percent	5 percent
Berlin	7 percent	6 percent
Amsterdam	6 percent	6 percent
Brussels	6 percent	6 percent
Madrid	9 percent	9 percent

European rates in the period from 1850 to 1870 fluctuated between 5 percent and 9 percent generally, and declined after that to as low as 3 percent by the end of the century. Jean Bouvier, *Initiation au vocabulaire et aux mécanismes économiques contemporains (XIX–XX siècles)* (1969), 298.

72. Ciro F. S. Cardoso, "Historia económica del café en Centroamérica (siglo XIX): Estudio comparativo," *Estudios Sociales Centroamericanos* 4, no. 10 (1975):34; Lanuza, *Estructuras*, 76.

73. The mines were named San Jorge, San Rafael, San Antonio, San José Guadalupe, and Santa Catarina, all in Alotepeque. AGCA, B, leg. 3629, exps. 84863 and 84864.

74. Index to the Archivo de la Sociedad Económica, AGCA, B, leg. 1390, exp. 32099; and *Gaceta de Guatemala*, 19 June 1847.

75. *Gaceta de Guatemala*, 2 June 1848.

76. *Gaceta de Guatemala*, 1 Aug. and 19 Sept. 1851.

77. AGCA, B, leg. 28557, exp. 1377; leg. 28556, exp. 1323.

78. *Gaceta de Guatemala*, 23 Mar. 1855.

79. *Gaceta de Guatemala*, 11 Sept. 1856.

80. The agreement signed with the government on 9 Aug. appears in the *Gaceta de Guatemala*, 19 Aug. 1865.

81. *Gaceta de Guatemala*, 17 Oct. 1857.

82. Gustavo Enrique Palma Murga, *Algunas relaciones entre la iglesia y los grupos particulares durante el período de 1860 a 1870: Su incidencia en el movimiento liberal de 1871* (1977), 86, citing AGCA, leg. 28563, unnumbered exp.

83. *Gaceta de Guatemala*, 31 Mar. and 15 Apr. 1858.

84. *Gaceta de Guatemala*, 10 July 1858.

85. AGCA, B, AMG, Comunicaciones, 1862, leg. 28590; *Gaceta de Guatemala*, 22 July 1862.

86. See Edelman's advertisement in the *Gaceta de Guatemala*, 13 Dec. 1864.

87. AGCA, B, AMG, leg. 28620.

88. Palma Murga, *Relaciones*, 141–88, 225–30.

20. Conservative Social Policy

1. For a detailed description of this effort, see John Tate Lanning, *The Eighteenth-Century Enlightenment in the University of San Carlos de Guatemala* (1956), 244–59.

2. Rubén Reina, *The Law of the Saints: A Pokomam Pueblo and Its Community Culture* (1966), 14.

3. *El Tiempo*, 24 Jan. and 5 Dec. 1840, 7 Jan. 1841.

4. *Gaceta de Guatemala*, 21 Sept. 1855, 26 Apr. 1856, 22 Jan., 18 Apr., and 25 July 1861; 1 Feb., 13 Apr., 16 May, 14 and 18 June, and 17 Sept. 1862; and 8 Jan. 1863.

5. Williford, "Las Luces," 37; Woodward, "Social Revolution," 53–54.

6. *Gaceta de Guatemala*, 21 and 28 June 1850; 26 Sept. 1851; AGCA, B, AMG, leg. 28576, Año 1858.

7. *Gaceta de Guatemala*, 13 Feb. 1844, and 25 Oct. and 15 Dec. 1858; AGCA, B, AMG, legs. 28575 and 28576, Año 1858.

8. *Gaceta Oficial*, 6 Dec. 1845.

9. *Estado del Hospital General de San Juan de Dios de Guatemala* (1814).

10. Dunlop, *Travels*, 84–85.

11. *Gaceta de Guatemala*, 15 Feb. 1850.

12. Ibid., 17 Feb. 1854; 14 Jan. and 10 Oct. 1858; 18 Apr. 1859, and 7 Oct. 1868.

13. W. George Lovell and Christopher H. Lutz, "Core and Periphery in Colonial Guatemala," Smith, ed., *Guatemalan Indians*, 30–52.

14. Madigan, "Santiago Atitlán," 148.

15. Dunlop, *Travels*, 130–38; Moorhead, "Rafael Carrera," 146–47.

16. Martínez Peláez, *La patria del criollo*, 412.

17. *Gaceta de Guatemala*, 10 Oct. 1851.

18. *Gaceta de Guatemala*, 14 Nov. 1851; Skinner-Klée, *Legislación*, 31–33.

19. Castellanos Combranes, *Café y campesinos*.

20. *Gaceta de Guatemala*, 21 Aug. 1847.

21. Ibid., 12 Mar. 1852.

22. Ibid., 2 Apr., 18 May, 4 and 11 June, 1852.

23. Pineda de Mont, *Recopilación*, 1:512–13.

24. Burgess, *Barrios*, 163.

25. See, for example, *Gaceta de Guatemala*, 27 Mar. and 19 Apr. 1850.

26. AGCA, AMG, Sololá, Año 1857, B, leg. 28574.

27. Queja presentada por las indígenas de San Felipe, Suchitepéquez, 8 Apr. 1862, AGCA, B, leg. 28587, AMG. Suchitepéquez, Año 1862. This long petition from the Indians of San Felipe is interesting for its variety of complaints against the Ladinos of the area. The principal dispute centered over the construction of a new church, for which the Indians had obtained the wood at considerable labor and sacrifice. They had also collected among themselves nine hundred pesos, representing one peso apiece. These community funds had been looted, and the Indians were complaining directly to the government in Guatemala. The investigation revealed a somewhat different side of the story from the Ladinos, but the community funds were eventually restored. At the same time, the government was careful not to discourage the extension of coffee cultivation.

28. Castellanos Cambranes, *Café y campesinos*, 89.

29. *Gaceta de Guatemala*, 8 Nov. 1862; Fiscal Beteta to Ministro de Gobernación, Guatemala, 19 Feb. 1866; AGCA, AMG, leg. 28607.

30. Castellanos Cambranes, *Café y campesinos*, 90, citing Juez Preventivo al Corregidor de Suchitepéquez, 10 Sept. 1865, AGCA, AMG, leg. 28600.

31. Castellanos Cambranes, *Café y campesinos*, 90–165.

32. AGCA, AMG, leg. 28624, exp. 3. The author is grateful for copies of these documents provided by Julio Castellanos Cambranes (hereinafter cited as Castellanos collection).

33. See, for example, the 1864 litigation over lands in Sololá in AGCA, AMG, leg. 28607 (Castellanos collection).

34. *Gaceta de Guatemala*, 17 Nov. and 29 Dec. 1858; AGCA, B78.24, leg. 718, exp. 16257; leg. 720, exp. 16411.

35. Records in the AMG for the years 1866–71 reflect a notable increase in such complaints.

36. Juan E. Valdés, Corregidor del Verapaz, to Ministro de Gobernación, Salamá, 28 Apr. 1866, AGCA, B, leg. 28604.

37. Castellanos Cambranes, *Café y campesinos*, 81–119.

38. The series continued on 7 Feb. and concluded on 24 Feb. 1867.

39. AGCA, AMG, legs. 28606 & 28607 (Castellanos collection).

40. Vecinos de San Cristóbal Cajcoj al Presidente de la República, enclosed with Corregidor Juan E. Valdés to Ministro de Gobernación, 14 Sept. 1866, AGCA, AMG, leg. 28604 (Castellanos collection).

41. Valdez to Ministro de Gobernación, ibid.

42. For a description of this problem in late twentieth-century Central America, see Williams, *Export Agriculture*.

43. Informe de la Administración de la Municipalidad de Ciudad Vieja al Corregidor, 31 Dec. 1866, AGCA, AMG, leg. 28604 (Castellanos collection).

44. AGCA, AMG, leg. 28612 (Castellanos collection).

45. AGCA, AMG, Leg. 28610 (Castellanos collection).

46. See, for example, the regulations issued by the corregidor of Sololá on 16 Nov. 1868 and the reservations pointed out regarding them by the Fiscal to the Ministro de Gobernación on 24 Feb. 1869. AGCA, AMG, leg. 28621 (Castellanos collection).

47. 26 Dec. 1870, AGCA, AMG, leg. 28624 (Castellanos collection). These regulations read, in part, as follows:

Considerando: Que en este Departamento van haciéndose de día mas graves las dificultades que se experimentan entre los dueños de fincas, ya sea por los abusos que cometen los mismos interesados, o ya porque los mozos que solicitan trabajo se han acostumbrado a burlarse de sus compromisos, recibiendo dinero sin ningún temor con 2 o 3 personas a cuenta de sus jornales; teniendo presente que en años anteriores se han reglamentado disposiciones con el objeto de evitar estos abusos y que nada han favorecido . . . he tenido a bien ordenar los siguientes:

Art. 1—Ningún dueño de finca o administrador de ella, podrá en lo sucesivo acomodar mozos para el trabajo sin que le presenten su cuenta o saldo del patrón de quien últimamente sirvieron, o constancia de la autoridad de su pueblo de no tener adeudado en ninguna finca; el que contraviniere estas disposiciones, sufrirá la multa de 10 pesos por cada mozo que hubiere acomodado, aplicable a los fondos municipales.

Art. 2—Será obligación de los encargados de recoger o habilitar gente para el trabajo, presentarse al Gobernador o Alcalde del pueblo donde se soliciten para que estas autoridades tomen el nombre de los mozos y el lugar a donde van a trabajar, con el fin de saber su paradero, a cuyo objeto se llevará un libro donde sienten las partidas expuestas, debiendo así mismo pagar los interesados un real por cada mozo de los que se saquen, cuya asignación la tomarán dichas autoridades.

Art. 3—Sin embargo de las disposiciones anteriores continuasen los mozos huyéndose de las fincas con la mira de defraudar el dinero que han recibido, los dueños de las fincas, o administradores de ellas se dirijirán a las autoridades de los pueblos de donde fueron sacados, con el objeto de que sean perseguidos, y habidos que sean deberán ser remitidos por las mismas autoridades a la finca en que cometieron la fuga, para que devenguen lo que tienen recibido.

Del cumplimiento de estas disposiciones, quedan responsables las Municipalidades y Gobernadores de todos los pueblos del Departamento.

48. Woodward, "Population and Development," 12–13.

21. Education and Culture

1. *Gaceta de Guatemala*, 15 Nov. 1850.

2. AGCA, A, leg. 2991, exp. 28497.

3. Rubén Reina described this process in Chinautla, in his *Law of the Saints*, 14–15; Rodríguez, *Cádiz Experiment*, 25.

4. Rodríguez, *Cádiz Experiment*, 209.

5. *Gaceta de Guatemala*, 10 Dec. 1847, 12 June 1865.

6. Williford, "Educational Reforms," 462–63.

7. "Mensaje del Gefe del Estado de Guatemala, Doctor Mariano Gálvez, al abrir sus sesiones ordinarias la Asamblea, Lejislativa de 1837," *El Editor: Periódico de los Tribunales*, 4 Mar. 1837; Williford, "Las luces," 35–38; Holleran, *Church and State*, 120.

8. Morazán to the Federal Congress, San Salvador, 21 May 1836, in Apartado, "Morazán," 371.

9. *El Tiempo*, 6 Sept. 1839.

10. *Procurador de los Pueblos*, 26 Sept. 1840.

11. Crowe, *Gospel*, 288–90.

12. Dunlop, *Travels*, 86, 335.

13. *Manifiesto documentado que la Municipalidad de Guatemala da al público relativo a sus procedimientos en virtud de la orden suprema que mandó cesar al Sr. Federico Crowe la escuela que de hecho tiene abierta* (Guatemala, 1847), item no. 124 in *El Libro Verde*, AGCA, 1–2, 5.

14. *Gacetá Oficial*, 24 Mar. 1843.

15. M. F. Pavón to Dr. Francisco García Peláez, Guatemala, 3 Oct. 1844, *Gacetá Oficial*, 12 Oct. 1844.

16. *Gacetá Oficial*, 31 May 1846.

17. Ibid., 6 June 1846.

18. *Gaceta de Guatemala*, 10 Dec. 1847.

19. Ibid., 2 Aug. 1850.

20. *Gaceta de Guatemala*, 30 Apr. 1856; Zeceña to Presidente de la Cámara de Representantes, 13 Jan. 1855, ibid., 16 Jan. 1855.

21. A breakdown of these statistics by department follows:

Departments	No. of Schools	No. of Pupils	Annual Expenditures	Average per Pupil
Guatemala	22	765	$4,528	$5.92
Sacatepéquez	18	538	2,544	4.73
Amatitlán	9	392	1,212	3.09
Escuintla	11	290	1,764	6.08
Santa Rosa	19	373	912	2.45
Jutiapa	22	539	1,362	2.53
Chiquimula	23	978	2,580	2.64
Izabal	2	39	660	16.92
Verapaz	11	263	936	3.56
Quetzaltenango	7	514	1,820.25	3.54
Chimaltenango	12	359	1,608	4.48
Sololá	13	212	1,164	5.49
Totonicapán	9	319	928.50	2.91
Suchitepéquez	9	266	1,098	4.13
San Marcos	8	250	648	2.59
Huehuetenango	11	189	687	3.63
Totals	206	6,286	$24,451.75	$3.89

Gaceta de Guatemala, 24 Sept. 1852.

22. Ibid., 18 Sept. 1852.

23. Ibid., 24 Sept. 1852.

24. Consulado de Comercio, *Memoria . . . 19 de mayo de 1854*, 8.

25. Consulado de Comercio, *Memoria . . . 6 de junio de 1862*, 15–16.

26. *Gaceta de Guatemala*, 18 Aug. 1854.

27. Acuerdo, Ministerio de Gobernación, 5 May 1854, *Gaceta de Guatemala*, 12 May 1854.

28. *Gaceta de Guatemala*, 14 and 28 May 1856. Sr. Sevilla offered evening classes, from 7 to 9 p.m. at a charge of $6 per month, and daytime lessons in the homes of his clients at $8 per month.

29. *Gaceta de Guatemala*, 10 Sept. 1858.

30. Ibid., 10 Jan. 1858.

31. AGCA, AMG, 1858, leg. 28576.

32. *Gaceta de Guatemala*, 28 Sept. 1867 and 27 Nov. 1868.

33. Ibid., 26 Apr. 1856.

34. Ibid., 13 Mar. 1864.

35. Ibid., 2 Nov. 1861. The table follows, with mathematical errors corrected:

| | Public Schools | | | | Private Schools | | | |
| | Boys | | Girls | | Boys | | Girls | |
Departments	Schls.	Pupils	Schls.	Pupils	Schls.	Pupils	Schls.	Pupils
Guatemala	20	760	7	190	5	112	18	286
Chiquimula	20	593	1	28	0	0	0	0
San Marcos	17	415	4	235	2	0	2	0
Sololá	16	364	3	146	0	0	0	0
Verapaz	11	302	4	116	0	0	3	33
Sacatepéquez	10	344	2	174	3	30	3	66
Chimaltenango	10	343	4	213	0	0	0	0
Quetzaltenango	8	360	2	123	2	54	0	0
Santa Rosa	8	250	2	33	0	0	0	0
Totonicapan	7	207	3	95	0	0	0	0
Suchitepéquez	7	217	2	148	0	0	1	13
Jutiapa	7	257	0	0	8	139	0	0
Amatitlán	6	203	3	136	2	54	1	15
Huehuetenango	6	151	1	41	0	0	0	0
Escuintla	5	125	1	64	0	0	0	0
Petén	1	103	1	73	4	24	2	26
Izabal	1	29	0	0	0	0	0	0
Totals	160	5,023	40	1,815	26	413	30	439

Summary

Public and private schools of both sexes, including those of music and liceos	280
Expenses of all these establishments	$30,524
Number of pupils in these schools	8,125

Note: In addition to those indicated, there are another seven private institutions of learning, known by the name of Liceos, most of which are in this capital. They have 235 tuition-paying pupils, and two of these institutions also receive a total of 648 pesos annually from municipal funds.

There are also in several departments some private music schools, and seventeen public ones with 200 students, and funded with 2,256 pesos annually from municipal funds.

36. "Comunidad," *Gaceta de Guatemala*, 12 June 1865.

37. "Informe del Corregimiento de Guatemala," *Gaceta de Guatemala*, 30 Apr. 1866.

38. *Gaceta de Guatemala*, 15 Feb. 1869.

39. Ibid., 9 May 1866.

40. Ibid., 19 Apr. 1866.

41. "Informe del Corregidor de San Marcos," *Gaceta de Guatemala*, 15 Mar. 1866.

42. *Gaceta de Guatemala*, 23 Mar. 1866.

43. "Estado que demuestra el número de escuelas de primeras letras que huyo

en los pueblos de este Depto. en el año pxmo. pdo. de 656," *Gaceta de Guatemala*, 25 Feb. 1866.

44. *Gaceta de Guatemala*, 23 Mar., 19 Apr., and 9 May 1866.

45. Ibid., 26 July 1866.

46. John Tate Lanning, *The University in the Kingdom of Guatemala* (1955).

47. Lanning, *Eighteenth-Century Enlightenment*.

48. Crowe, *Gospel*, 282.

49. Tobar Cruz, *Los montañeses* (1959), 43–44; Williford, "Educational Reforms," 473; Holleran, *Church and State*, 120–21; Marure, *Efemérides*, 72–73. The academy was originally called Academia de Estudios, but later changed to Academia de Ciencias.

50. *El Tiempo*, 12 March 1840. The university reform act of 16 Sept. 1855 increased the range of faculty salaries to $200–$500 annually. *Gaceta de Guatemala*, 28 Sept. 1855.

51. Decreto no. 110 of the Asamblea Constituyente, 7 Nov. 1840, *hojas sueltas* collection, LALTU; Marure, *Efemérides*, 126; *El Tiempo*, 19 Sept. 1840.

52. Marure, *Efemérides*, 73; *El Tiempo*, 5 Dec. 1840.

53. Chandler, *Aycinena*, contains reprints of many of Aycinena's writings during the period as well as a bibliography of his works, 269–74. See especially Aycinena's "La educación de la juventud, 1845," ibid., 257–68. Quirino Flores served as vice rector under Aycinena. A complete list of the faculty in the restored university, as of December 1842, may be found in the *Gaceta Oficial*, 10 Dec. 1842.

54. *Gaceta Oficial*, 21 Oct. 1845.

55. Ibid., 21 Oct. 1845.

56. A report of the rector of 6 Sept. 1846, in the *Gaceta Oficial*, 6 Nov. 1846, detailed the university's continuing debt from 1840–46.

57. *Gaceta Oficial*, 29 Sept. 1843. After its first year of operation, 1840–41, the university had granted thirty-eight bachelor's degrees. *Gaceta Oficial*, 10 Sept. 1841.

58. *Gaceta de Guatemala*, 29 Sept. 1847, 2 Nov. 1849, and 15 Nov. 1850.

59. *Gaceta Oficial*, 9 Aug. 1845.

60. Ibid., 27 Feb. 1846.

61. *Gaceta de Guatemala*, 19 June 1847. In its opening session, on 13 June 1847, presentations were made by Manuel Beteta, Manuel Zerón, and Vicente Dardón, all of whom were of liberal persuasion.

62. *Gaceta de Guatemala*, 10 Nov. 1848.

63. *Gaceta de Guatemala*, 7 June 1850. Carrera gave another $1,000 the following year for the same purpose. Ibid., 13 Aug. 1851.

64. *Gaceta de Guatemala*, 1 Nov. 1850.

65. Ibid., 2 Apr. 1852.

66. Statistics on each year are given annually in the *Gaceta de Guatemala*.

67. Both were grandsons of the first marques de Aycinena, Juan Fermín. *Gaceta de Guatemala*, 12 Oct. 1855, 26 Apr. 1859.

68. Chandler, *Aycinena*, 9; *Gaceta de Guatemala*, 21 Nov. 1865.

69. Miller, *La iglesia*, 41; Pineda de Mont, *Recopilación*, 3:203–11; *Gaceta de Guatemala*, 28 Sept. 1855; 5 Oct. 1855.

70. *Gaceta de Guatemala*, 21 Feb. 1856.

71. Ibid., 21 July 1856.

72. Carroll E. Mace, *New Information About Dance Dramas of Rabinal and the "Rabinal-Achí"* (1967) and *Two Spanish-Quiché Dance Dramas of Rabinal* (1970); Barbara Bode, "The Dance of the Conquest of Guatemala" (1958).

73. See the description of the 1862 Carnival in the *Gaceta de Guatemala*, 8 Feb. [*sic* March] 1862.

74. This sort of "corrida de toros" is still carried on in connection with annual fiestas or ferias in some Guatemalan towns, as, for example, in San Antonio Aguascalientes during the annual Corpus Christi fiesta.

75. Robert H. Claxton, "Miguel Rivera Maestre, Guatemalan Scientist-Engineer," *Technology and Culture* 14 (July 1973):384–403.

76. Williford, "Las Luces," 38–40. On the Fedriani episode, see also Espinoza Altamirano, *El libro*, 43, and L. Montúfar, *Reseña*, 2:79–81.

77. *El Tiempo*, 21 Dec. 1839.

78. *Gaceta Oficial*, 14 July 1843; "Reglamento de la Sociedad Filarmónica de Guatemala bajo los auspicios de la Sociedad Económica," 1859, AGCA, AMG, B, leg. 28577; *Gaceta de Guatemala*, 30 Jan. 1864.

79. *Gaceta Oficial*, 24 July 1846.

80. *Gaceta de Guatemala*, 3 Nov. 1847.

81. Ibid., 13 Aug. 1852; AGCA, AMG, B, leg. 28576.

82. Balance de la c[ontra]ta del teatro, Juan Matheu al S. Ministro de Gobernación, 6 Nov. 1858, AGCA, AMG, B, leg. 28576.

83. *Gaceta de Guatemala*, 14 Aug. 1858, 23 May 1859.

84. Ibid., 15 and 29 Sept., 22 Oct., and 5 Nov. 1859.

85. Ibid., 11 Nov. 1859.

86. Juan Matheu and Miguel Ruiz, "Comunicación de la Comisión encargada del Teatro," 20 Sept. 1859, *Gaceta de Guatemala*, 29 Sept. 1859.

87. *Gaceta de Guatemala*, 1 Mar. 1860.

88. Reviews and announcements of performances are in the *Gaceta de Guatemala* for these years.

89. Batres Jáuregui, *América Central*, 3:240.

90. Dunlop, *Travels*, 336–37.

91. *El Tiempo*, 11 Oct. 1839 and 12 Sept. 1840; *Gaceta de Guatemala*, 3 Aug. 1849 and 24 Dec. 1864.

92. Salazar, *Tiempo viejo*, 97–100.

93. *Gaceta de Guatemala*, 20 Apr. 1855.

94. Ibid., 23 Feb. 1858.

95. Ibid., 9 July 1852.

22. Conclusions

1. Vela, *Barrundia*, 1:232.

2. In addition to his writings in the contemporary Guatemalan newspapers, many of Milla's books reflected a romantic defense of the Carrera government, notably *Cuadros de costumbres*, 5th ed., 4 vols. (1958); *Historia de un Pepe*, 8th ed. (1964); *Libro sin nombre*, 5th ed. (1964); and *Memorias de un abogado* (1956).

3. García, "Carrera," 11:46–83. Sarmiento's views were originally set down in 1845 in a series of Chilean newspaper articles attacking the caudillos Facundo Quiroga and Juan Manuel de Rosas that subsequently became Sarmiento's best-known work, *Life in the Argentine Republic in the Days of the Tyrants; or Civilization and Barbarism*, translated by Mrs. Horace Mann (1868). More recently, however, Sarmiento had been a major political figure in Argentine provincial and national government, including among his activities a term as president from 1868 to 1874. He had remained active in public affairs after that date until his death in 1888, the same year that the Guzmán-Gámez dialogue had taken place in Nicaragua.

4. Moorhead, "Rafael Carrera," 82.

5. This theme is developed more fully in the author's "Changes in the Nineteenth-Century Guatemalan State and its Indian Policies," in Smith, ed., *Guatemalan Indians*, 52–71. On the role of the peasants as independent actors in nineteenth-century Guatemala, see also Solórzano F., "Rafael Carrera," 5–35.

6. E. Bradford Burns has pursued this theme at some length in his *Poverty of Progress: Latin America in the Nineteenth Century* (1980).

7. See especially Schoonover's "Germany in Central America," and "Metropole Rivalry," and Schoonover and Schoonover, "Statistics."

8. Colin M. Maclachlan, *Spain's Empire in the New World: The Role of Ideas in Institutional and Social Change* (1988), 135.

Bibliography

Primary Sources

Archives and Libraries

AGCA. See Archivo General de Centro América.

AGI. See Archivo General de Indias.

AMG. Archivo del Ministerio de Gobernación. In Archivo General de Centro América, Guatemala.

ANCR. See Archivo Nacional de Costa Rica.

Archivo General de Centro América, Guatemala. Government records, 1760–1871.

Archivo General de Indias, Sevilla. Audiencia de Guatemala and Sección Ultramar.

Archivo Nacional de Costa Rica, San José. Government records, 1824–71.

Benson Latin American Collection, University of Texas, Austin. Arturo Taracena Collection of nineteenth-century publications.

BLAC. See Benson Latin American Collection.

Casa de Cultura. Quetzaltenango. Arturo Taracena Collection of nineteenth-century manuscripts and publications.

FO. See Great Britain. Public Record Office.

GCUK. See Spencer Library, University of Kansas.

Great Britain. Public Record Office. Microfilm records of Foreign Office and Colonial Office, nineteenth century, in LALTU.

LALTU. See Latin American Library, Tulane University.

Latin American Library, Tulane University, New Orleans, Louisiana. Contemporary publications and manuscripts, 1804–75.

NAB. See National Archives of Belize.

National Archives of Belize, Belmopan. Government records, nineteenth century.

PRO. See Great Britain. Public Record Office.

Spencer Library, University of Kansas, Lawrence. William J. Griffith Collection. Letters of Rafael Carrera, 1846–64.

Newspapers

El Album Republicano. Guatemala, 1848.

El Amigo de Guatemala. Guatemala, 1838.

El Amigo de la Patria. Guatemala, 1820–22. In *Edición preconmemorativa del sesquicentenario de la independencia de Centro América*. 5 vols. Guatemala: Editorial José de Pineda Ibarra, 1969.

Archivo Americano y Espírituo de la Prensa del Mundo. Buenos Aires, 1845.

El Atleta. San Salvador, 1839.

El Bien Común. San Salvador, 1838.

Boletín de Noticias del Ejército. Guatemala, 1848.

Boletín Oficial. Guatemala, 1831–38, 1871–72.

El Ciudadano. Quezaltenango, 1836.

El Costarricense. San José, Costa Rica, 1847.

El Editor Constitucional. Guatemala, 1820–21. In *Edición preconmemorativa del sesquicentenario de la independencia de Centro América*. 5 vols. Guatemala: Editorial José de Pineda Ibarra, 1969.

El Editor: Periódico de los Tribunales. Guatemala, 1837.

La Estrella de Panamá. 1864.

La Gaceta. Guatemala, 1833.

Gaceta de Guatemala. Guatemala, 1847–71.

Gaceta del Gobierno de Los Altos. Quezaltenango, 1839.

Gaceta del Gobierno Supremo del Estado del Salvador en la República de Centro-América. San Salvador, 1848.

Gaceta Estraordinaria del Gobierno. Guatemala, 1827.

Gaceta Oficial. Guatemala, 1841–47.

Gaceta Oficial de Honduras. Comayagua, 1859.

Gazeta de Guatemala. Guatemala, 1800–1803, 1809–10.

Gazeta del Gobierno. Guatemala, 1828.

Gazeta Federal. Guatemala, 1832.

Illustrated London News. 1853.

Mentor Costarricense. San José, Costa Rica, 1845.

El Museo Guatemalteco. Guatemala, 1856–57.

El Nicaragüense. Granada, Nicaragua, 1856.

Niles Register. Washington, D.C., 1841.

El Noticioso de Guatemala. Guatemala, 1861–62.

Noticioso Guatemalteco. Guatemala, 1838.

La Nueva Era. Guatemala, 1837–38.

El Observador. Guatemala, 1838.

Observer. New York, 1864.

La Oposición. Guatemala, 1837–38.

El Popular. Quezaltenango, 1839.

Procurador de los Pueblos. Guatemala, 1840.

El Progreso. Guatemala, 1875.

Registro Oficial. San Fernando [Masaya], Nicaragua, 1845; León, Nicaragua, 1846.

La Semana. Guatemala, 1865–66.

Semanario de Guatemala. Guatemala, 1836.

Semi-Diario de los Libres. Guatemala, 1837–38.

El Siglo de Lafayette. Guatemala, 1831.

La Sociedad Económica de Guatemala. 1866–70.

Sucesos del Dia. Guatemala, 1849.

El Tiempo. Guatemala, 1839–41.

La Verdad. Guatemala, 1837.

Published Documents, Government Publications, Memorias, Informes, and Other Contemporary Publications

Acta de la Junta General de autoridades, funcionarios públicos, prelados eclesiásticos, gefes militares y diputaciones de las corporaciones, en que se aclamó presidente perpétuo de la República de Guatemala, al Exmo. Señor Capitán General Don Rafael Carrera. Guatemala, 1854.

Actas de la Asamblea Constituyente y Acuerdos Oficiales del Gobierno. Guatemala, 1839.

Aguilar, E. *El Presidente del Estado del Salvador para conocimiento de todos los centro-americanos publica los documentos que comprueban la complicidad que el Sr. Obispo Viteri ha tenido en las facciones que vinieron armadas de Honduras para trastornar el orden de este estado el 1 de noviembre último.* San Salvador: Imprenta del Estado, 1846.

Aguilar, M. *Memoria sobre el cultivo del café, arreglada la práctica que se observa en Costa Rica, escrita por el Ldo. Manuel Aguilar, y dada imprimir por el Consulado de Comercio de Guatemala.* Guatemala: Imprenta de la Paz, 1845.

Algunas reflexiones sobre la última sedición, artículos publicados en los números 37, 38, y 39 de La Semana. Guatemala: Imprenta de la Paz, 1870.

Arce, Manuel José. *Memoria.* Edited by Modesto Barrios. San Salvador: Ministerio de Cultura, 1959.

Astaburuaga y Cienfuegos, Francisco Solano. *República de Centro América, o idea de su historia i de su estado actual.* Santiago de Chile: Imprenta del Ferrocarril, 1857.

Aycinena, Juan José. *Breve instrucción sobre el cultivo de las moreras, para la crianza de gusano de seda con algunos cálculos del producto de este ramo de industria, tomadas de los autores que han escrito últimamente sobre la materia.* Guatemala: Imprenta de A. España, 1839.

———. *Exposición que hace al público el Presbo. Dr. Juan José de Aycinena sobre el asunto de la llamada de los padres de la Compañía de Jesús por la intervención que en ella tuvo como Ministro de relaciones, justicia y negocios eclesiásticos del Estado de Guatemala en el año de 1843.* Guatemala, 7 June 1845.

———. *Reclamación y protesta del Supremo Gobierno del Estado de Guatemala, sobre la ocupación de Soconusco, por tropas de la República mexicana, con los documentos en que se fundan.* Guatemala: Imprenta de la Paz, 1843.

Baily, John. *Central America*. London: T. Saunders, 1850.

Belly, Félix. *A travers l'Amérique centrale, le Nicaragua et le canal interocéanique*. 2 vols. Paris: Librairie de la Suisse Romande, 1867.

Bolaños-Geyer, Alejandro, ed. and trans. *Diario de John Hill Wheeler, Ministro de los Estados Unidos en Nicaragua, 1854–1857*. Managua: Banco de América, 1974.

————. *Documentos diplomáticos de William Carey Jones, agente especial de los Estados Unidos ante Costa Rica y Nicaragua, 1857–1858*. Managua: Banco de América, 1974.

————. *La guerra de Nicaragua según* Frank Leslie's Illustrated Newspaper *y* Harper's Weekly. Managua: Banco de América, 1976.

————. *El testamento de Scott, declaración del Capitán Joseph N. Scott, como testigo de la defensa en juicio entablado por el depositario de la compañía accesoria del tránsito contra Cornelius Vanderbilt, en 1861, en Nueva York*. Managua: Banco de América, 1975.

Bonaparte. See N. L. B.

Bumgartner, Louis, ed. "Demonstraciones públicas de lealtad que ha hecho el comercio de la ciudad de Guatemala." *Anales de la Sociedad de Geografía e Historia de Guatemala* 38, no. 1/4 (1965): 68–78.

Burdon, John, ed. *Archives of British Honduras*. 3 vols. London: Sifton, Praed, 1931–35.

Carrera, Rafael. Annual messages (*Informes, Mensages*, and *Mensajes*) to the legislature. Guatemala: Imprenta de la Paz, 1852–64.

————. *El fiel observante de los derechos de los pueblos que componen Centro-América, AL PUBLICO*. Guatemala: Imprenta del Exército, 28 November 1842.

————. *Informe que dirijió el presidente de la República de Guatemala al Cuerpo Representativo, en su instalacion el dia 15 de Agosto de 1848*. Guatemala: Imprenta de la Paz, 1848.

————. *Manifiesto del Exmo. Señor Presidente del Estado de Guatemala, en que se exponen los fundamentos del Decreto expedido en 21 de Marzo del presente año, erigiendo dicho Estado en república independiente*. Guatemala: Imprenta de la Paz, 1847.

————. *Memorias del General Carrera, 1837 a 1840*. Edited by Ignacio Solís. Guatemala: Sánchez y de Guise, 1906. 2d ed. Edited by Francisco Polo Sifontes. Colección Historia, Serie Historia Republicana, Publicación Especial no. 12. Guatemala: Instituto de Antropología e Historia de Guatemala, 1979.

————. *Pronunciamiento del General Rafael Carrera y del ejército de la Constitucion del Estado de Guatemala*. Mataquescuintla, 24 March 1839.

Cerna, Vicente. Annual *Mensajes* to the legislature. Guatemala: Imprenta de la Paz, 1865–70.

Cobos, Salvador. *Informes dirigidos al Consulado de Comercio*. Guatemala: Imprenta de la Paz, 1869.

Colección de algunos de los interesantes documentos que se encontraron en los equipajes tomados en la accion de los días 18 y 19 de marzo. Se publican de orden del gobierno para conocimiento del público de los Estados aliados. Guatemala: Imprenta del Gobierno, [1840].

Constitución política del Estado de Guatemala, decretada por el Congreso Constituyente en 16 de septiembre de 1845. Guatemala: Imprenta del Gobierno, 1845.

Consulado de Comercio. Annual *Informes* and *Memorias*. Guatemala: Consulado de Comercio, 1804, 1843–65.

————. *Instrucción para el cultivo y beneficio de cáñamo, arreglado á lo que se practica en otros paises, y con las modificaciones que se han creido convenientes á nuestra clima*. Guatemala: Consulado de Comercio, 1848.

————. *Instrucción para plantar los nopales, cultivar y beneficiar la grana cochinilla fina*. Guatemala: Real Consulado, 1820.

Convención provisional de los Estados de Centro-América, formada a concecuencia de la disolución del Gobierno Federal y en virtud de los convenios y tratados que se publican reuinidos y por su orden, para mejor conocimiento del público. Guatemala: Imprenta de la Academia de Estudios, 1839.

Cortés y Larraz, Pedro. *Descripción geográfica-moral de la Diócesis de Guatemala hecha por su arzobispo*. 2 vols. Guatemala: Sociedad de Geografía e Historia de Guatemala, 1958.

Crowe, Frederick. *The Gospel in Central America; Containing a Map of the Country, Physical and Geographical, Historical and Political, Moral and Religious: A History of the Baptist Mission in British Honduras and of the Introduction of the Bible into the Spanish American Republic of Guatemala*. London: Charles Gilpin, 1850.

Dávila, Fernando Antonio. *Discurso pronunciado en el acto de la instalacion de la Asamblea Constituyente del Estado, por su primér Presidente el Sr. Presbítero Fernando Antonio Dávila*. Guatemala: Imprenta del Gobierno, 1839.

Dunlop, Robert. *Travels in Central America; Being a Journal of Nearly Three Years' Residence in the Country; Together with a Sketch of the History of the Republic, and an Account of its Climate, Productions, Commerce, etc*. London: Longman, Brown, Green & Longman, 1847.

Dunn, Henry. *Guatimala* [sic], *or, The Republic of Central America, in 1827–8*. London: J. Nisbet, 1829.

Ferrera, Francisco. *Memoria presentado a la Cámara Lejislativa por el Ministro de Guerra que suscribe*. Comayagua, Honduras, 26 January 1846.

Fuentes y Guzmán, Francisco Antonio de. *Recordación Florida*. 3 vols. Guatemala: Sociedad de Geografía e Historia de Guatemala, 1933.

Gallardo, Ricardo. *Las constituciones de la República Federal de Centro-América*. 2 vols. Madrid: Instituto de Estudios Políticos, 1958.

Gálvez, Mariano. *Documentos sobre arreglar un plan de administración antes de encargarse el Ministerio de Relaciones el Ministro nombrado Ldo. Marcial Zebadúa*. Guatemala: Imprenta Nueva, 1833.

García Granados, Miguel. *Memorias del General don Miguel García Granados*. 2 vols. Guatemala: El Progreso, Tipografía Nacional, 1877–93.

García Laguardia, J. M., comp. *El pensamiento liberal de Guatemala: (Antología)*. San José, Costa Rica: EDUCA, 1977.

García Peláez, Francisco de Paula. *Discurso pronunciado el 15 de septiembre de 1856 XXV aniversario de la independencia de Guatemala.* Guatemala, 1856.

Gavarrete, Francisco. *Catecismo de geografía de Guatemala para el uso de las escuelas de primeras letras de la República.* Guatemala: Imprenta de la Paz, 1860.

―――. *Geografía de la república de Guatemala.* 2d ed. Guatemala: Imprenta de la Paz, 1868.

―――. *Geografía de la república de Guatemala.* 3d ed. Guatemala: Emilio Goubaud, 1874.

González, M. *Memoria sobre el estado actual del comercio de Guatemala: Obstáculos que impiden su progreso y medios de removerlos, que por acuerdo del Consulado Nacional extendió su secretario interino.* Guatemala: Consulado de Comercio, 1823.

Griffith, William J., ed. "The Personal Archive of Francisco Morazán." *Philological and Documentary Studies* 2, no. 6 (Middle American Research Institute publication no. 12): 197–286. New Orleans: Tulane University, 1977.

Guatemala. Asamblea Constituyente. *Colección de las ordenes de observancia general emitadas por la Asamblea Constituyente del Estado de Guatemala en los años 1839, 1840, 1841 y 1842.* Guatemala: Imprenta de la Paz, 1842.

―――. *Decreto ejecutivo del Gefe del Estado de Guatemala.* Guatemala: Ministro General del Gobierno del Estado de Guatemala, Departamento de Hacienda, 17 November 1827.

―――. *Dictamen de la comision de negocios eclesiásticos de la Asamblea Constituyente, sobre el reestablecimiento de las Ordenes Regulares.* Guatemala: Imprenta del Gobierno, 1839.

Guatemala y El Salvador. Guatemala: N.p., n.d [December 1862].

Guía de forasteros de Guatemala para el año 1853. Guatemala: n.p., [1853?].

Informes de las secretarias del gobierno en los ramos de gobernación, hacienda, guerra, y relaciones exteriores; a la asamblea constituyente de la república en agosto de 1851. Guatemala: Imprenta de la Paz, 1851.

El Libro Verde. 3 vols. This is a bound collection of Central American (mostly Guatemalan) nineteenth-century pamphlets and handbills in the AGCA. A microfilm copy is in the LALTU.

Manning, William Ray, ed. *Diplomatic Correspondence of the United States Concerning Independence of Latin American Nations.* 3 vols. New York: Oxford University Press, 1925.

―――. *Diplomatic Correspondence of the United States, Inter-American Affairs, 1831–1860.* Vol. 3, Central America, 1831–1850. Washington, D.C.: Carnegie Endowment for International Peace, 1933.

Marure, Alejandro. *Bosquejo histórico de las revoluciones de Centroamérica, desde 1811 hasta 1834.* 2d ed. 2 vols. Biblioteca Guatemalteca de Cultura Popular, nos. 36 and 37. Guatemala: Ministerio de Educación Pública, 1960. (1st ed., Guatemala: El Progreso, 1877–78).

―――. *Efemérides de los hechos notables acaecidos en la República de Centro-América desde el año 1821 hasta el de 1842.* 2d ed. Guatemala: Tipografía Nacional, 1895.

—————. *Memoria sobre la insurrección de Santa Rosa y Mataquescuintla en Centro América, comparada con la que estalló en Francia, en el año de 1790, en los departamentos de la Vendée*. Guatemala: Imprenta del Gobierno, 1838.

—————. *Observaciones sobre la intervencion que ha tenido el ex-Presidente de Centro-América, General Francisco Morazán, en los negocios políticos de Guatemala, durante las convulsiones que ha sufrido este Estado, de mediados de 837 á principios de 839*. Guatemala: Imprenta de la Acad. de Estudios, 1839.

Masseras, E. *El programa del imperio*. Guatemala: Imprenta de la Paz, 1864.

Mayorga, Juan de Dios. *Manifiesto sobre el decreto de nuevo convocatoria que expidió el Supremo Gobierno en 5 del corriente*. Guatemala, 25 Nov. 1827 (LALTU).

—————. *Observaciones sobre la conducta política del Dr. C. Mariano Gálvez con respecto a los horribles males que con ella ha causado a Centro-América*. Guatemala: Imprenta Nueva, 1831.

Mendieta, Salvador. *La enfermedad de Centro América*. 3 vols. Barcelona: Tipografía Maucci, 1934.

Menéndez, Isidro, comp. *Recopilación de las leyes del Salvador en Centro América*. 2d ed. 2 vols. San Salvador: República de El Salvador, 1956.

México. *Exposición sobre el derecho que tiene la Provincia de Chiapa para pronunciar libremente su voluntad, y el que tiene Goatemala para ser independiente*. México: Imprenta de Tomás Lorrain, 1823.

—————. *Incorporación de Chiapas a México: Discursos*. México: Tip. de la Oficina Impresora de Estampillas, 1922.

Milla y Vidaurre, José. *Cuadros de costumbres*. 5th ed. 4 vols. Guatemala: Ministerio de Educación Pública, 1958.

—————. *Historia de un Pepe*. 8th ed. Guatemala: Ed. José de Pineda Ibarra, 1964.

—————. *Libro sin nombre*. 5th ed. Guatemala: Ministerio de Educación Pública, 1964.

—————. *Memorias de un abogado*. Guatemala: Ministerio de Educación Pública, 1956.

Molina Mata, Marcelo. *Mensaje del Gobierno Provisional a la Asamblea Constituyente de Los Altos al abrir sus sesiones en la Ciudad de Totonicapam 26 de diciembre de 1838*. N.p.: Imprenta del Estado de Los Altos, 1838.

Montgomery, George Washington. *Narrative of a Journey to Guatemala in Central America, in 1838*. New York: Wiley & Putnam, 1839.

Montúfar Coronado, Manuel. *Memorias para la historia de la revolución de Centro América*. Jalapa, México: Blanco y Aburto, 1832.

Montúfar y Rivera Maestre, Lorenzo. *Reseña histórica de Centro-América*. Guatemala: Tipografía "El Progreso" & Tipografía "La Unión," 1878–88.

Morazán, Francisco. *Manifiesto al pueblo centro-americano*. David: Nueva Granada, 16 July 1841.

Morelet, Arthur. *Travels in Central America*. New York: Leypoldt, Holt & Williams, 1871.

N. L. B. [Napoleon Louis Bonaparte]. *Canal de Nicaragua, or a Project to Connect the*

Atlantic and Pacific Oceans by Means of a Canal. London: Mills & Son, 1846.

Noticia biográfica del Señor Don Luis Batres, Consejero de Estado y Vice-Presidente de la Cámara de Representantes. Guatemala: Imprenta de la Paz, 1862.

Palacios, Enrique. *La cuestión monetaria en Guatemala*. Guatemala: Imprenta de la Paz, 1870.

————. *Memoria leída en la junta general que celebró la Sociedad Económica de Amigos del País, el 26 de diciembre de 1861*. Guatemala: Sociedad Económica, 1861.

Paredes, Mariano. *Informe dirijido por el Presidente de la República al cuerpo representativo, en la apertura de las sesiones el dia 16 de agosto de 1851*. Guatemala: Imprenta de la Paz, 1851.

Pavón, M. F. *Informe sobre los diferentes ramos de la administración pública, presentado al Exmo. Señor Presidente, por El L. M. F. Pavón, al dejar la secretaria del despacho*. Guatemala: Imprenta de la Paz, 1844.

Pineda de Mont, Manuel, comp. *Recopilación de las leyes de Guatemala*. 3 vols. Guatemala: Imprenta de la Paz, 1869–72.

Proyecto de concesión para establecer en la República de Guatemala un banco nacional. Guatemala, 12 Dec. 1866.

Proyecto de la Confederación Centro-Americano entre los Estados del Salvador, Honduras y Nicaragua acordado en la Ciudad de Chinandega a 27 de Julio de 1842. San Salvador: Imprenta del Estado, 1842.

Recopilación de las leyes emitidas por el gobierno democrático de la República de Guatemala, desde el 3 de junio de 1871, hasta el 30 de junio de 1881. 2 vols. Guatemala: Tipografía de "El Progreso," 1881.

Relación de la fiesta que el Colegio Seminario dió al Excmo. Sr. Presidente de Guatemala Don. Rafael Carrera, y a su ejército espedicionario, el 9 de marzo de 1864. Guatemala: Imprenta de la Paz, 1864.

Relación de las exéquias del Excmo. Sr. Presidente Capitán Gral. D. Rafael Carrera, celebrada en la S. I. Catedral de Guatemala el dia 17 de abril de 1865. Guatemala: Imprenta de la Paz, 1865.

Relación de las fiestas con que se celebró en los dias 29 y 30 de noviembre, 1 y 2 de diciembre, al regreso a la capital de Excmo. Señor Presidente y de las fuerzas expedicionarias. Guatemala: Imprenta de la Paz, 1864.

Richardson, James D., comp. *A Compilation of the Messages and Papers of the Presidents, 1789–1902*. 10 vols. Washington, D.C.: U.S. Congress, 1900–1903.

Rivera Paz, Mariano. *Informe dado a la Asamblea Constituyente por el Presidente del Estado de Guatemala, sobre los sucesos ocurridos desde que la misma Asamblea suspendió sus sesiones, y sobre el estado en que se halla la Administración Pública*. Guatemala: Imprenta de la Paz, 14 July 1840.

————. *Informe del Presidente del Estado de Guatemala a la Asamblea Constituyente sobre los sucesos ocurridos desde que esta suspendió sus sesiones: Sobre el estado de la administración pública, y medidas dictadas para su mejoramiento. Leydo en las sesiones de los dias 23 y 24 de noviembre de 1842*. Guatemala: Imprenta de la Paz, 1842.

————. *Memoria que presentó a la Asamblea Constituyente en su primera sesión el Con-*

sejero Gefe de Estado de Guatemala, por medio del Secretario del Despacho de Relaciones. Guatemala: Imprenta del Gobierno del Estado, 31 May 1839.

Rodríguez Cerna, José, comp. *Colección de Tratados de Guatemala*. 3 vols. Guatemala: Secretaría de Relaciones Exteriores, 1939–44.

Romero, José Luis, and Luis Alberto Romero. *Pensamiento conservador (1815–1898)*. Caracas: Biblioteca Ayacucho, 1978.

Rosales, Gregorio. *Instrucción para teñir y dar colores a las lanas, para el uso de los tintoreros de los departamentos de los altos: Formada por el Presb. D. Gregorio Rosales, Cura de S. Lucas y miembro de la Sociedad Económica de Amigos del País, y por disposición del Exmo. Sr. Capitán General D. Rafael Carrera, Presidente de la República*. Guatemala: Imprenta de la Paz, 1852.

Salazar, Ramón. *Tiempo viejo: Recuerdos de mi juventud*. 2d ed. Guatemala: Editorial del Ministerio de Educación Pública, 1957.

Sarmiento, Domingo Faustino. *Life in the Argentine Republic in the Days of the Tyrants; or Civilization and Barbarism*. Translated by Mrs. Horace Mann. New York: Hurd and Houghton, 1868.

Smith, Robert S., ed. " 'Statutes of the Guatemalan Indigo Growers' Society' by M. de Gálvez," *Hispanic American Historical Review* 30 (1950): 336–45.

Sociedad Económica. *Memoria de la junta general de la Sociedad Económica del estado de Guatemala, celebrado el 14 de setiembre de 1845*. Guatemala: Sociedad Económica, 1845.

Solís, Ignacio. *Memorias de la Casa de Moneda de Guatemala y del desarrollo económico del país*. 3 tomes in 4 vols. Edited by Julio Castellanos Cambranes. Guatemala: Ministerio de Finanzas, 1978–79.

Squier, Ephraim G. *Notes on Central America*. New York: Harper Brothers, 1855.

———. *Travels in Central America, Particularly in Nicaragua*. 2 vols. New York: D. Appleton, 1853.

Stephens, John Lloyd. *Incidents of Travel in Central America, Chiapas and Yucatan*. 2 vols. New York: Harper, 1841.

Thompson, George A. *Narrative of an Official Visit to Guatemala from Mexico*. London: John Murray, 1829.

United States, Department of State. *Papers Relating to the Foreign Relations of the United States, 1862*. Washington, D.C.: Government Printing Office, 1863.

Unos Españoles. *Documentos relativos a la cuestión sobre los españoles, que ha pasado al conocimiento de la Asamblea Constituyente el Sr. Ministro de Relaciones*. Guatemala: Imprenta Nueva de la Luna, 24 April 1849.

Valle, José del. *Instrucción sobre la plaga de langosta; medios de exterminarla, o de disminuir sus efectos: Y de precaber la escasez de comestibles*. Nueva Guatemala, 1804.

Valle, Rafael Heliodoro, ed. *La anexión de Centroamérica a México (documentos y escritos de 1821–1828)*. 6 vols. México: Secretaría de Relaciones Exteriores, 1924–49.

———. *Cartas de Bentham a José del Valle*. México: Editorial Cultura, 1942.

Valois, Alfred de. *Mexique, Havane et Guatemala—Notes de voyage*. Paris: Collection Hetzel, E. Dentu, 1861.

Vega Bolaños, Andrés. *Gobernantes de Nicaragua: Notas y documentos.* Managua: Editorial Rodríguez, 1944.

Young, Thomas. *Narrative of a Residence on the Mosquito Shore, During the Years 1839, 1840 & 1841, with an Account of Truxillo and the Adjacent Islands of Bonacca and Roatan.* London: Smith, Elder, 1842.

Zeceña, Basilio. *Oración pronunciada en la Santa Iglesia Catedral en el aniversario de la independencia; por el Sr. Presb. D. Basilio Zeceña, Doctor en Sagrada Teología, Cura de San Juan Sacatepéquez.* Guatemala: Imprenta de la Paz, 1851.

Secondary Sources

Acuña Ortega, Victor Hugo. "Historia económica del tabaco, época colonial." San José: Tésis de grado, Universidad de Costa Rica, 1974.

Albion, R. G. "British Shipping and Latin America, 1806–1914." *Journal of Economic History* 11 (Fall 1951): 361–74.

Alcázar Molina, Cayetano. *Los virreinatos en el siglo XVIII.* Barcelona: Salvat Editores, 1945.

Amurrio González, Jesús J. *El positivismo en Guatemala.* Guatemala: Universidad de San Carlos, 1970.

Anderson, Wayne. "The Development of Export Transportation in Liberal Guatemala, 1871–1920." Ph.D. diss., Tulane University, 1985.

Aparicio y Aparicio, Edgar Juan, Marqués de Vistabella. "La familia de Arzú." *Revista de la Academia Guatemalteca de Estudios Genealógicos, Heráldicos e Históricos* 3–4 (1969–70): 69–113.

Apartado, Manuel del. "Vida de Morazán." Unpublished manuscript, San Salvador, July 1959, in Latin American Library, Tulane University.

Archer, Christon I. *The Army in Bourbon Mexico, 1760–1810.* Albuquerque: University of New Mexico Press, 1977.

Arcila Farías, Eduardo. "Evolución de la economía en Venezuela." In *Venezuela independiente, 1810–1960.* Caracas: Fundación Eugenio Mendoza, 1962.

Armytage, Frances. *The Free Port System in the British West Indies: A Study in Commercial Policy.* London: Longmans, Green, for the Royal Empire Society, 1953.

Arriola, Jorge Luis. "García Peláez, uno de los precursores del liberalismo económico en Guatemala." *Anales de la Sociedad de Geografía e Historia de Guatemala* 40 (January-June 1967): 29–36.

Balmori, Diana, Stuart F. Voss, and Miles Wortman. *Notable Family Networks in Latin America.* Chicago: University of Chicago Press, 1984.

Bancroft, Hubert H. *History of Central America.* 3 vols. San Francisco: History Company, 1886–87.

Barbier, Jacques, and Allan Kuethe, eds. *The North American Role in the Spanish Imperial Economy, 1760–1819.* Manchester: Manchester University Press, 1984.

Barrera Túnchez, José A. "Aspectos generales de la situación demográfica de Guatemala." In *Seminario sobre el crecimiento de la población y desarrollo*. Guatemala: Dirección General de Estadística, 1968.

Bates, Marston. *Where Winter Never Comes, A Study of Man and Nature in the Tropics*. New York: Scribner's, 1952.

Batres Jáuregui, Antonio. *La América Central ante la historia*. 3 vols. Guatemala: Marroquín Hermanos, Sánchez y de Guise, and Tipografía Nacional, 1915–49.

————. *El Doctor Mariano Gálvez y su época*. 2d ed. Guatemala: Ministerio de Educación Pública, 1957.

Beltranena Sinibaldi, Luis. *Fundación de la República de Guatemala*. Guatemala: Tipografía Nacional, 1971.

Bode, Barbara O. "The Dance of the Conquest in Guatemala." Master's thesis, Tulane University, 1958.

Bolaños-Geyer, Alejandro. *Con Walker en Nicaragua*. Masaya, Nicaragua: By the author, 1977.

————. *El filibustero Clinton Rollins*. Masaya, Nicaragua: By the author, 1976.

————. *William Walker, The Gray-Eyed Man of Destiny. Book One: The Crescent City*. St. Louis, Mo.: By the author, 1988.

Bouvier, Jean. *Initiation au vocabulaire et aux mécanismes économiques contemporains (XIX-XX siècles)*. Paris: Société d'Edition d'Enseignement Supérieur, 1969.

Brown, Richmond. "Friends and Relations: Charles Lennox Wyke and the Central American Diplomacy of Great Britain, 1852–1860." Master's thesis, Tulane University, 1986.

Browning, David. *El Salvador, Landscape and Society*. Oxford: Clarendon Press, 1971.

Bumgartner, Louis. *José del Valle of Central America*. Durham, N.C.: Duke University Press, 1963.

Burgess, Paul. *Justo Rufino Barrios: A Biography*. Philadelphia: Dorrance, 1926.

Burns, E. Bradford. *The Poverty of Progress: Latin America in the Nineteenth Century*. Berkeley: University of California Press, 1980.

Cabat, Geoffrey A. "The Consolidation of 1804 in Guatemala." *The Americas* 28 (1971): 20–38.

Calderón Quijano, José Antonio. *Belice 1663?–1821: Historia de los establecimientos británicos del Río Valis hasta la independencia de Hispanoamérica*. Seville: Escuela de Estudios Hispano-Americanos, 1944.

Cardoso, Ciro F. S. "Historia económica del café en Centroamérica (siglo XIX): Estudio comparativo." *Estudios Sociales Centroamericanos* 4, no. 10 (1975): 9–55.

Cardoso, Ciro F. S., and Héctor Pérez Brignoli. *Centro América y la economía occidental (1520–1930)*. San José: Editorial de la Universidad de Costa Rica, 1977.

Carr, Albert Z. *The World and William Walker*. New York: Harper & Row, 1963.

Carrera, Mario Alberto. *Breve biografía de Pepe Milla. Microbiografías de autores guatemaltecos*, no. 4. Guatemala: Piedra Santa, n.d.

Castellanos Cambranes, Julio. *Café y campesinos en Guatemala, 1853–1897*. Guatemala: Editorial Universitaria de Guatemala, 1985.

Chamberlain, Robert S. *Francisco Morazán, Champion of Central American Federation*. Coral Gables, Fla.: University of Miami Press, 1950.

Chandler, D. S. "Jacobo de Villaurrutia and the Audiencia of Guatemala." *The Americas* 32 (1976): 402–17.

Chandler, David L. *Juan José de Aycinena, idealista conservador de la Guatemala del siglo XIX*. Guatemala: Centro de Investigaciones Regionales de Mesoamérica, 1988.

Chinchilla Aguilar, Ernesto. *Historia y tradiciones de la ciudad Amatitlán*. Guatemala: Ministerio de Educación Pública, 1961.

Cid Fernández, Enrique del. *Cruz y Barrios: Incendio y saqueo a la Villa de Huehuetenango*. Guatemala: Editorial del Ejército, 1966.

————. *Origen, trama y desarrollo del movimiento que proclamó vitalicia la presidencia del General Rafael Carrera*. Guatemala: Editorial del Ejército, 1966.

Claxton, Robert H. "Historia de la meteorología y sequía en Guatemala, 1563 a 1925." *Revista del Pensamiento Centroamericano*. Managua, forthcoming.

————. "Miguel Rivera Maestre: Guatemalan Scientist-Engineer." *Technology and Culture* 14 (July 1973): 384–403.

Clegern, Wayne M. *British Honduras, Colonial Dead End, 1859–1900*. Baton Rouge: Louisiana State University Press, 1967.

————. "Guatemalan Defense of the British Honduras Boundary of 1859." *Hispanic American Historical Review* 40 (1960): 570–81.

————. *Origins of Liberal Dictatorship in Central America: Guatemala, 1865–1873*. Boulder: University of Colorado Press, 1994.

————. "Transition from Conservatism to Liberalism in Guatemala, 1865–1871." In *Hispanic-American Essays in Honor of Max Leon Moorhead*, 98–110. Edited by William S. Coker. Pensacola, Fla.: Perdido Bay Press, 1979.

Cobos Batres, Manuel. *Carrera*. Guatemala: By the author, n.d. [1935].

Coronado Aguilar, Manuel. *Apuntes históricos-guatemalenses*. 2d ed. Guatemala: Editorial José Pineda Ibarra, 1975.

————. "El General Rafael Carrera ante la historia." *Anales de la Sociedad de Geografía e Historia de Guatemala* 38 (1965): 217–59.

Cox de Collins, Anita. "San Marcos Huista: Unas notas." *Guatemala Indígena* 5 (1970): 129–95.

Creedman, Theodore S. *Historical Dictionary of Costa Rica*. Metuchen, N.J.: Scarecrow, 1977.

Davidson, William V. "Black Carib (Garifuna) Habitats in Central America." In *Frontier Adaptations in Lower Central America*, 85–94. Edited by Mary W. Helms and Franklin O. Loveland. Philadelphia: Institute for the Study of Human Issues, 1976.

Díaz, Víctor Miguel. *Barrios ante la posteridad*. Guatemala: Tipografía Nacional, 1935.

Domínguez Sosa, Julio Alberto. *Ensayo histórico sobre los tribus nonualcos y su caudillo Anastasio Aquino.* San Salvador: Ministerio de Educación, 1964.

Donoso, Ricardo. *Antonio José de Irisarri, escritor y diplomático, 1786–1868.* 2d ed. Santiago de Chile: Facultad de Filosofía y Educación, 1966.

Dougherty, John E. "Mexico and Guatemala, 1856–1872: A Case Study in Extra-Legal Relations." Ph.D. diss., University of California, Los Angeles, 1969.

Durand, J. D. "World Population Estimates, 1700–2000." *Proceedings of the World Population Conference, Belgrade, 30 August-10 September 1965.* New York: Department of Economic and Social Affairs, United Nations, 1967.

Durón, Rómulo E. *Album morazánico: Homenaje del gobierno que preside el doctor y general don Tiburcio Carías Andino al general don Francisco Morazán, con motivo del primer centenario de su fallecimiento.* 2 vols. Tegucigalpa: Talleres Tipográficos Nacionales, 1942.

Eisen, Arlene. "The Indians in Colonial Spanish America." In *Spanish Bureaucratic-Patrimonialism in America*, 101–23. Edited by Magali Sarfatti. Berkeley: Institute of International Studies, University of California, 1966.

Elliott, L. E. *Central America: New Paths in Ancient Lands.* New York: Dodd, Mead & Co., 1925.

Escobar, Jorge Alberto. "El añil en la economía de El Salvador." *Economía Salvadoreña* 11 (1962): 23–36.

Escobar Medrano, Edgar. *Mariano Rivera Paz y su época.* Guatemala: Universidad de San Carlos de Guatemala, 1982.

Espinoza Altamirano, Horacio. *El libro del ciudadano.* Guatemala: Tipografía Nacional, 1930.

Facio, Rodrigo. *Trayectoria y crisis de la federación centroamericana.* San José, Costa Rica: Imprenta Nacional, 1949.

Fernández Hall, Francisco. "Historiadores de Guatemala posteriores a la independencia nacional: El Doctor don Francisco de Paula García Peláez." *Anales de la Sociedad de Geografía e Historia* 15, no. 3 (March 1939): 261–78.

Fiehrer, Thomas M. "The Barón de Carondelet as an Agent of Bourbon Reform: A Study of Spanish Colonial Administration in the Years of the French Revolution." Ph.D. diss., Tulane University, 1977.

Figuero Marroquín, Horacio. Personal interview with the author, Guatemala City, 9 November 1986.

Flemion, Philip F. *Historical Dictionary of El Salvador.* Metuchen, N.J.: Scarecrow Press, 1972.

———. "Manuel José Arce and the Formation of the Federal Republic of Central America." Ph.D. diss., University of Florida, 1969.

Flores, Romeo R. "Las representaciones de 1805." *Historia Mexicana* 17 (January-March 1968): 469–73.

Floyd, Troy S. *The Anglo-Spanish Struggle for Mosquitia.* Albuquerque: University of New Mexico Press, 1967.

———. "The Guatemalan Merchants, the Government, and the *Provincianos,*

1750–1800." *Hispanic American Historical Review* 41 (1961): 90–110.

Folkman, David. *The Nicaragua Route.* Salt Lake City: University of Utah Press, 1972.

Fry, Michael F. "Política agraria y reacción campesina en Guatemala: La región de La Montaña, 1821–1838." *Mesoamérica* 15 (June 1988): 25–46.

Gall, Francis. "En el centenario del fallecimiento de García Peláez: Palabra del presidente de la Sociedad de Geografía e Historia de Guatemala al declarar abierto el acto académico del 25 de enero de 1967." *Anales de la Sociedad de Geografía e Historia* 40, no. 1/2 (January-June 1967): 19–29.

Gálvez G., María Albertina. *Emblemas nacionales.* Guatemala: Ministerio de Educación Pública, 1958.

García, Miguel Angel. "Carrera." *Diccionario histórico-enciclopédico de la República de El Salvador* 10: 408–592; 11: 1–184. San Salvador: Imprenta Nacional, 1948.

——— . *Gral. Don Manuel José Arce. (Diccionario histórico enciclopédico de la República de El Salvador).* 3 vols. San Salvador: Imprenta Nacional, 1945.

García, Miguel Angel, ed. *San Salvador desde la conquista hasta el año de 1899 (Diccionario histórico enciclopédico de la República de El Salvador).* 3 vols. San Salvador: Imprenta Nacional, 1952–58.

García Laguardia. Jorge Mario. *Orígenes de la democracia constitucional en Centroamérica.* San José, Costa Rica: EDUCA, 1971.

García Peláez, Francisco de Paula. *Memorias para la historia del antiguo reyno de Guatemala.* 3 vols. Guatemala: L. Luna, 1851–52.

Gerhard, Peter. *The Southeast Frontier of New Spain.* Princeton: Princeton University Press, 1979.

González, Jorge. "Una historia de Los Altos: Origen, desarrollo y extinción de un movimiento autonomista regional." Master's thesis, Tulane University, 1989.

González Centeno, Rodolfo. *El Mariscal de Campo Don Serapio Cruz, sus notables campañas militares.* Guatemala: Editorial del Ejército, 1982.

González Viquez, Cleto. *Capítulos de un libro sobre historia financiera de Costa Rica.* San José: Editorial Costa Rica, 1977.

Griffith, William J. "Attitudes Toward Foreign Colonization: The Evolution of Nineteenth-Century Guatemalan Immigration Policy." In *Applied Enlightenment: 19th Century Liberalism* (Middle American Research Institute publication no. 23), 71–110. Edited by Margaret A. L. Harrison and Robert Wauchope. New Orleans: Tulane University, 1972.

——— . *Empires in the Wilderness: Foreign Colonization and Development in Guatemala, 1834–1844.* Chapel Hill: University of North Carolina Press, 1965.

——— . "The Historiography of Central America since 1830." *Hispanic American Historical Review* 40 (1960): 548–69.

——— . "Juan Galindo, Central American Chauvinist." *Hispanic American Historical Review* 40 (1960): 25–52.

——— . *Santo Tomás, anhelado emporio del comercio en el Atlántico.* Guatemala: Sociedad de Geografía e Historia, 1959.

Gullick, C. J. M. R. *Exiled from St. Vincent: The Development of Black Carib Culture in Central America up to 1945*. Malta: Progress Press, 1976.

Guzmán Böckler, Carlos, and Jean-Loup Herbert. *Guatemala: Una interpretación histórico-social*. México: Siglo XXI, 1970.

Haeussler Yela, Carlos C. *Diccionario General de Guatemala*. 3 vols. Guatemala: By the author, 1983.

Hale, Charles A. *The Transformation of Liberalism in Late Nineteenth-Century Mexico*. Princeton: Princeton University Press, 1989.

Hall, Carolyn. *El café y el desarrollo histórico-geográfico de Costa Rica*. San José: Editorial Costa Rica, 1976.

Halperin-Donghi, Tulio. *The Aftermath of Revolution in Latin America*. Translated by Josephine de Bunsen. New York: Harper, 1973.

Hamnett, Bryan R. *Politics and Trade in Southern Mexico, 1750–1821*. Cambridge: Cambridge University Press, 1971.

Heaton, Herbert. *Economic History of Europe*. Rev. ed. New York: Harper & Brothers, 1948.

Hernández de León, Federico. *El libro de efemérides: Capítulos de la historia de la América Central*. 7 vols. Guatemala: Tip. Sánchez de Guise and Tipografía Nacional, 1925–66.

Herrarte, Alberto. *La unión de Centroamérica (tragedia y esperanza), ensayo político-social sobre la realidad de Centro América*. 2d ed. Guatemala: Ministerio de Educación Pública, 1963.

Holleran, Mary P. *Church and State In Guatemala*. Studies in History, Economics and Public Law, no. 549. New York: Columbia University Press, 1949.

Humphreys, Robin A. *The Diplomatic History of British Honduras, 1638–1901*. London: Oxford University Press, 1961.

Ingersoll, Hazel M. B. "The War of the Mountain: A Study of Reactionary Peasant Insurgency in Guatemala, 1837–1873." Ph.D. diss., George Washington University, 1972.

Jérez, Víctor. "General Don Carlos Salazar." In *San Salvador y sus hombres*, 2d ed., 98. Edited by Academia Salvadoreña de la Historia. San Salvador: Ministerio de Educación, 1967.

Jones, Chester Lloyd. *Costa Rica and Civilization in the Caribbean*. Madison: University of Wisconsin Press, 1935.

———. *Guatemala, Past and Present*. Minneapolis: University of Minnesota Press, 1940.

Karnes, Thomas L. *The Failure of Union, Central America, 1824–1960*. Chapel Hill: University of North Carolina Press, 1961.

Kayser, Elmer L. *The Grand Social Enterprise: A Study of Jeremy Bentham in his Relationship to Liberal Materialism*. London: P. S. King Son, 1932.

Kenyon, Gordon. "Mexican Influence in Central America, 1821–1823." *Hispanic American Historical Review* 41 (1961): 175–205.

Kern, Robert, ed. *The Caciques: Oligarchical Politics and the System of Caciquismo in the Luso-Hispanic World*. Albuquerque: University of New Mexico Press, 1973.

Kuethe, Allan J. *Military Reform and Society in New Granada, 1773–1808*. Gainesville: University Presses of Florida, 1978.

Lambert, Jacques. *Latin America: Social Structures and Political Institutions*. Berkeley: University of California Press, 1969.

Langenberg, Inge. *Urbanisation und Bevölkerungsstruktur der Stadt Guatemala in der ausgehenden Kolonialzeit: Eine sozialhistorische Analyse der Stadtverlegung und ihrer Auswirkungen auf die demographische, berufliche, un soziale Gliederung der Bevölkerung (1773–1824)*. Koln, Wien: Bohlau, 1981.

―――. "Urbanización y cambio social: El traslado de la ciudad de Guatemala y sus consecuencias para la población y sociedad urbana al fin de la época colonial, 1773–1824." *Anuario de Estudios Americanos* 36 (1979): 351–74.

Lanning, John Tate. *The Eighteenth-Century Enlightenment in the University of San Carlos de Guatemala*. Ithaca, N.Y.: Cornell University Press, 1956.

―――. *The University in the Kingdom of Guatemala*. Ithaca, N.Y.: Cornell University Press, 1955.

Lanuza Matamoras, Alberto. *Estructuras socioeconómicas, poder y estado en Nicaragua, de 1821 a 1875*. Serie Tésis de Grado no. 2. San José, Costa Rica: Programa Centroamericano de Ciencias Sociales, 1976.

Lavrin, Asunción. "The Execution of the Law of *Consolidación* in New Spain: Economic Aims and Results." *Hispanic American Historical Review* 53 (1973): 27–49.

Lazardi, S. A. "El Excelentísimo Señor Gral. Don Rafael Carrera." *El Progreso Nacional* 2 (7 May 1895): 73–75.

Leysbeth, Nicolas. *Historique de la colonisation belge a Santo-Tomas Guatemala*. Bruxelles: Nouvelle Société D'Editions, 1938.

López Vallecillos, Italo. *Gerardo Barrios y su tiempo*. 2 vols. San Salvador: Ministerio de Educación, 1967.

Lovell, W. George. *Conquest and Survival in Colonial Guatemala: A Historical Geography of the Cuchumatán Highlands, 1500–1821*. Kingston and Montreal: McGill-Queen's University Press, 1985.

Luján Muñoz, Jorge, ed. *Economía de Guatemala, 1750–1940: Antología de lecturas y materiales*. 2 vols. Guatemala: Facultad de Humanidades, Universidad de San Carlos de Guatemala, 1980.

Luque Alcaide, Elisa. *La Sociedad Económica de Amigos del País de Guatemala*. Sevilla: Escuela de Estudios Hispanoamericanos, 1962.

Lutz, Christopher H. *Historia sociodemográfica de Santiago de Guatemala, 1541–1773*. Antigua, Guatemala, and South Woodstock, Vt.: Centro de Investigaciones Regionales de Mesoamérica, 1982.

Mace, Carroll E. *New Information About Dance Dramas of Rabinal and the "Rabinal-Achí."* New Orleans: Xavier University, 1967.

―――. *Two Spanish-Quiché Dance Dramas of Rabinal*. New Orleans: Tulane University, Studies in Romance Languages and Literature, 1970.

MacLachlan, Colin M. *Spain's Empire in the New World: The Role of Ideas in Institutional and Social Change*. Berkeley: University of California Press, 1988.

MacLeod, Murdo J. *Spanish Central America, A Socioeconomic History, 1520–1720*. Berkeley: University of California Press, 1973.

Madigan, Douglas G. "Santiago Atitlán: A Socioeconomic and Demographic History." Ph.D. diss., University of Pittsburgh, 1976.

Marroquín Rojas, Clemente. *Francisco Morazán y Rafael Carrera*. Guatemala: Marroquín Hnos., 1965.

——— . *Historia de Guatemala*. Guatemala: Tipografía Nacional, 1971.

Martínez Estrada, Ezequiel. *Diferencias y semejanzas entre los países de la América Latina*. México: Universidad Nacional Autónoma de México, Escuela de Ciencias Políticas y Sociales, 1962.

Martínez López, E. *Biografía del General Francisco Morazán*. 4th ed. San Pedro Sula: Editora Nacional, Ministerio de Educación Pública, 1966.

Martínez Peláez, Severo. *La patria del criollo*. Guatemala: Editorial Universitaria, 1970.

——— . "Los motines de indios en el período colonial guatemalteca." In Congreso Centroamericano de Historia Demográfica, Económica y Social, I, Santa Barbara, Costa Rica, 1973, *Ensayos de historia centroamericana*. Colección Seminario y Documento 17 (San José, Costa Rica: Centro de Estudios Democráticos de América Latina, 1974), 27–47.

May, Robert E. *The Southern Dream of a Caribbean Empire, 1854–1861*. Baton Rouge: Louisiana State University Press, 1973.

McAfee, Shirley Lucas. "A Study of Agricultural Labor in Guatemala, 1821–1871." Master's thesis, Tulane University, 1955.

McAlister, Lyle N. *The "Fuero Militar" in New Spain, 1764–1800*. Gainesville: University of Florida Press, 1957.

——— . "The Military." In *Continuity and Change in Latin America*, 136–60. Edited by John J. Johnson. Stanford: Stanford University Press, 1964.

McCreery, David J. "Debt Servitude in Rural Guatemala, 1876–1936." *Hispanic American Historical Review* 63 (1983): 748–50.

——— . *Development and the State in Reforma Guatemala*. Athens: Ohio University Press, 1983.

Mejía, Medardo. *Historia de Honduras*. Vol. 4. Tegucigalpa: Universidad Nacional Autónoma de Honduras, 1988.

——— . *Trinidad Cabañas, soldado de la República Federal*. Tegucigalpa: Instituto Morazánico, 1971.

Mejía Nieto, Arturo. *Morazán, presidente de la desaparecida república centroamericana*. Buenos Aires: Nova, 1947.

Meldola, Rafael, Arthur C. Green, and John C. Cain, eds. *Jubilee of the Discovery of Mauve and of the Foundation of the Coal Tar Colour Industry by Sir W. H. Perkin*. London: Perkin Memorial Committee, 1906.

Meléndez Chaverri, Carlos. *La ilustración en el antiguo Reino de Guatemala*. San José, Costa Rica: EDUCA, 1970.

Meneray, Wilbur E. "The Kingdom of Guatemala During the Reign of Charles III, 1759–1788." Ph.D. diss., University of North Carolina, 1975.

Miceli, Keith. "Rafael Carrera: Defender and Promoter of Peasant Interests in Guatemala, 1837–1848." *The Americas* 31 (1974): 72–95.

Miller, Hubert J. *La iglesia y el estado en tiempo de Justo Rufino Barrios*. Guatemala: Editorial Universitaria, 1976.

Mobil, José A. *100 personajes históricos de Guatemala*. Guatemala: Serviprensa Centroamericana, 1979.

Moorhead, Max Leon. "Rafael Carrera of Guatemala: His Life and Times." Ph.D. diss., University of California, Berkeley, 1942.

Morales, María Eugenia. *Movimiento de los Lucíos: Un acercamiento histórico sociológico*. Guatemala: Universidad de San Carlos de Guatemala, Escuela de Historia, 1983.

Morales Baños, Antonio. *Morazán y Carrera o Liberales y Conservadores, 1821–1841*. Guatemala: Editoria del Ejército, 1985.

Morse, Richard M. "Toward a Theory of Spanish American Government." *Journal of the History of Ideas* 15 (1954): 71–93.

Mosk, Sanford. "The Coffee Economy of Guatemala, 1850–1918: Development and Signs of Instability." *Inter-American Economic Affairs* 9, no. 3 (1955): 6–20.

"La muerte del suegro del General Rafael Carrera." *Revista del Departamento de Historia y Hemeroteca Nacional* (San Salvador) 2, no. 3 (1939): 27–29.

Munro, Dana. *The Five Republics of Central America*. New York: Oxford University Press, 1918.

Náñez Falcón, Guillermo. "Paul Erwin Dieseldorff, German Entrepreneur in the Alta Verapaz of Guatemala, 1889–1937." Ph.D. diss., Tulane University, 1970.

Naylor, Robert A. "British Commercial Relations with Central America, 1821–1851." Ph.D. diss., Tulane University, 1958.

———. "The British Role in Central America Prior to the Clayton-Bulwer Treaty of 1850." *Hispanic American Historical Review* 40 (1960): 361–82.

———. "Guatemala: Indian Attitudes Toward Land Tenure." *Journal of Inter-American Studies* 9 (1967): 619–39.

———. *Influencia británica en el comercio centroamericano durante las primeras décadas de la independencia (1821–1851)*. Antigua, Guatemala: Centro de Investigaciones Regionales de Mesoamérica, 1988.

———. *Penny Ante Imperialism: The Mosquito Shore and the Bay of Honduras, 1600–1914*. Cranbury, N.J.: Fairleigh Dickinson University Press, 1988.

Ordóñez Jonama, Ramiro. "Familias fundadoras en el Valle de la Ermita." *Revista de la Academia Guatemalteca de Estudios Genealógicas, Heráldicas e Históricos* 2 (1968): 167–237.

———. "La familia Varón de Berrieza." *Revista de la Academia Guatemalteca de Estudios Genealógicas, Heráldicas e Históricos* 9 (1987): 523–826.

Ortega Aranciba, Francisco. *Cuarenta años (1838–1878) de historia de Nicaragua.* 3d ed. Managua: Banco de América, Fondo de Promoción Cultural, 1974.

Owsley, Frank L. *King Cotton Diplomacy: Foreign Relations of the Confederate States of America.* 2d ed. Chicago: University of Chicago Press, 1959.

Palma Murga, Gustavo Enrique. *Algunas relaciones entre la iglesia y los grupos particulares durante el período de 1860 a 1870. Su incidencia en el movimiento liberal de 1871.* Guatemala: Escuela de Historia, Universidad de San Carlos, 1977.

Palomares, Ricardo. "Jeremy Bentham in Spanish America." Ph.D. diss., University of North Carolina, 1978.

Parker, Franklin D. *The Central American Republics.* London: Oxford University Press, 1964.

———. *José Cecilio del Valle and the Establishment of the Central American Federation.* Tegucigalpa: Universidad de Honduras, 1954.

Pastor, Rodolfo. *Historia de Centroamérica.* México: El Colegio de México, 1988.

Payne, Walter A. *A Central American Historian, José Milla (1822–1882).* Gainesville: University of Florida Press, 1957.

Peláez Almengor, Oscar Guillermo. "Alejandro Marure, la historia y el proyecto político." Tesis de licenciado en Historia, Universidad de San Carlos de Guatemala, 1989.

Pérez Valenzuela, Pedro. *La Nueva Guatemala de la Asunción; terremoto de Santa Marta; fundación en el llano de la Virgen.* Guatemala: Tipografía Nacional, 1934.

———. *Santo Tomás de Castilla; Apuntes para la historia de las colonizaciones en la costa atlántica.* Guatemala: Tipografía Nacional, 1956.

Pinto Soria, Julio C. "La agricultura de exportación en Guatemala: Un acercamiento histórico." *Tikalia, La Revista de la Facultad de Agronomía* 4, no. 1 (1988): 1–15.

———. *Guatemala en la década de la independencia.* Guatemala: Editorial Universitaria, 1978.

———. *Raíces históricas del estado en Centroamérica.* 2d ed. Guatemala: Editorial Universitaria, 1983.

Pompejano, Daniele. *Centro America: La crisi dell'ancien régime (Guatemala 1840–1870).* Messina, Italy: By the author, 1990.

Prober, Kurt. *Historia numismática de Guatemala.* 2d ed. translated by Jorge Luis Arriola. Guatemala: Banco de Guatemala, 1973.

Radell, David, and James Parsons. "Realejo: A Forgotten Colonial Port and Shipbuilding Center in Nicaragua." *Hispanic American Historical Review* 51 (1971): 295–312.

Reed, Nelson. *The Caste War of Yucatán.* Stanford: Stanford University Press, 1964.

Reid, John T. *Modern Spain and Liberalism: A Study in Literary Contrasts.* Stanford: Stanford University Press, 1937.

Reina, Rubén. *The Law of the Saints: A Pokomam Pueblo and its Community Culture.* New York: Bobbs-Merrill, 1966.

Reina Valenzuela, José. *José Trinidad Cabañas: Estudio biográfico*. Tegucigalpa: El Ejército de las Fuerzas Armadas de Honduras, 1984.

Renikka, Merle A. *A History of the Orchid*. Coral Gables, Fla.: University of Miami Press, 1972.

Reyes M., José Luis. *Apuntes para una monografía de la Sociedad Económica de Amigos del País*. Guatemala: Centro Editorial José de Pineda Ibarra, 1964.

————. *Catálogo razonado de las leyes de Guatemala (contiene adiciones al de don Alejandro Marure, que lo dejó hasta 1850; al del licenciado Andrés Fuentes Franco, hasta 1856 y su continuación hasta 1871)*. Guatemala: Tipografía Nacional, 1945.

Roca, Antonio de la, and Efraín Arriola Porres. *Los que fueron . . . (de viris illustribus) 1777–1951 (Biografías mínimas de varones ilustres)*, no. 4. Quezaltenango: Editorial Unión, 1955.

Rodríguez, José N. *Estudios de historia militar de Centro-América*. Guatemala: Tipografía Nacional, 1930.

Rodríguez, Mario. *The Cádiz Experiment in Central America*. Berkeley: University of California Press, 1978.

————. *Central America*. Englewood Cliffs, N.J.: Prentice- Hall, 1965.

————. "The Livingston Codes in the Guatemalan Crisis of 1837–1838." In *Applied Enlightenment: 19th Century Liberalism* (Middle American Research Institute publication no. 23), 1–32. Edited by Margaret A. L. Harrison and Robert Wauchope. New Orleans: Tulane University, 1972.

————. *A Palmerstonian Diplomat in Central America, Frederick Chatfield, Esq.* Tucson: University of Arizona Press, 1964.

Rodríguez Beteta, Virgilio. *La política inglesa en Centroamérica durante el siglo XIX*. Guatemala: Editorial "José de Pineda Ibarra," Ministerio de Educación Pública, 1963.

Romano, Ruggiero. "American Feudalism." *Hispanic American Historical Review* 64 (1984): 121–34.

Rosengarten, Frederick, Jr. *Freebooters Must Die! The Life and Death of William Walker, the Most Notorious Filibuster of the Nineteenth Century*. Wayne, Pa.: Haverford House, 1976.

Rosenthal, Mario. *Guatemala, the Story of an Emerging Latin-American Democracy*. New York: Twayne, 1962.

Rubio Sánchez, Manuel. "Breve historia del desarrollo de café en Guatemala." *Anales de la Sociedad de Geografía e Historia de Guatemala* 27 (1953–54): 169–238.

————. *Historia de el Realejo*. Managua: Fondo de Promoción Cultural, Banco de América, 1975.

————. "Historia de la grana cochinilla en Guatemala." Manuscript in LALTU, 1982.

————. *Historia del añil o xiquilite en Centro América*. 2 vols. San Salvador: Ministerio de Educación Pública, 1976.

————. *Historia de la Sociedad Económica de Amigos del País*. Guatemala: Editorial Académica Centroamericana, 1981.

————. *Historia del cultivo de la morera de China y de la industria del gusano de seda en Guatemala*. Guatemala: Academia de Geografía e Historia de Guatemala, 1984.

————. *Historia del Fuerte de San Rafael de Matamoros*. Guatemala: Editorial José de Pineda Ibarra, 1982.

————. *El Mariscal de Campo José Clara Lorenzana*. Guatemala: Editorial del Ejército, 1987.

————. *Los Mariscales de Campo: I—Francisco Cáscara*. Guatemala: Editorial del Ejército, 1984.

————. "El real consulado de comercio." *Antropología e Historia de Guatemala* 19 (July-December 1967): 59–73.

Salazar, Ramón A. *Historia de veintiún años: la independencia de Guatemala*. Guatemala: Tipografía Nacional, 1928.

————. *Manuel José Arce (hombres de la independencia)*. Guatemala: Ministerio de Educación Pública, 1952.

————. *Mariano de Aycinena*. Guatemala: Ministerio de Educación, 1952.

————. *Tiempo viejo, recuerdos de mi juventud*. 2d ed. Guatemala: Ministerio de Educación Pública, 1957.

Samayoa Guevara, Héctor Humberto. *Los gremios de artesanos en la ciudad de Guatemala (1524–1821)*. Guatemala: Editorial Universitaria, 1962.

Sanabria Martínez, Victor. *Anselmo Llorente y Lafuente, primer obispo de Costa Rica: Apuntamientos históricos*. 2d ed. San José: Editorial Costa Rica, 1972.

Sánchez Albornoz, Nicolás. *La población de América Latina desde los tiempos precolombinos al año 2,000*. Madrid: Alianza Editorial, 1973.

Schmit, Patricia Brady. "Guatemalan Political Parties: Development of Interest Groups, 1820–1822." Ph.D. diss., Tulane University, 1977.

Schoonover, Thomas. "Germany in Central America, 1820s to 1929: An Overview." *Jahrbuch für Geschichte von Staat, Wirtschaft und Gesellschaft Lateinamerikas* 25 (1988): 33–59.

————. "Metropole Rivalry in Central America, 1820s-1929: An Overview." In *Central America: Historical Perspectives on the Contemporary Crises*, 21–46. Edited by Ralph Lee Woodward, Jr. Westport, Conn.: Greenwood, 1988.

————. "Misconstrued Mission: Expansionism and Black Colonization in Mexico and Central America During the Civil War." *Pacific Historical Review* 49 (1980): 607–20.

Schoonover, Thomas, and Ebba Schoonover. "Statistics for an Understanding of Foreign Intrusions into Central America from the 1820s to 1930." *Anuario de Estudios Centroamericanos* 15, no. 1 (1989): 93–118; 16, no. 1 (1990): 135–56.

Schwemmer, Ora-Westley. "The Belgian Colonization Company, 1840–1858." Ph.D. diss., Tulane University, 1966.

Scroggs, William O. *Financiers and Fillibusters: The Story of William Walker and his Associates*. New York: Macmillan, 1916.

Shafer, Robert J. *The Economic Societies in the Spanish World, 1763–1821*. Syracuse: Syracuse University Press, 1958.

Sherman, William L. *Forced Native Labor in Sixteenth-Century Central America*. Lincoln: University of Nebraska Press, 1979.

Skinner-Klée, Jorge. *Legislación indigenista de Guatemala*. México: Instituto Indigenista Interamericana, 1954.

Smith, Carol A., ed. *Guatemalan Indians and the State, 1540 to 1988*. Austin: University of Texas Press, 1990.

Smith, Robert S. "Financing the Central American Federation, 1821–1838." *Hispanic American Historical Review* 43 (1963): 483–510.

———. "Indigo Production and Trade in Colonial Guatemala." *Hispanic American Historical Review* 39 (1959): 181–211.

———. "The Institution of the Consulado in New Spain." *Hispanic American Historical Review* 24 (1944): 37–76.

———. "Origins of the Consulado de Guatemala." *Hispanic American Historical Review* 26 (1946): 150–61.

Snow, Lewis. "The Páez Years: Venezuelan Economic Legislation, 1830–1846." Ph.D. diss., University of North Carolina, 1970.

Solano, Francisco de. "Tierra, comercio y sociedad: Un análisis de la estructura social agraria centroamericana durante el siglo XVIII." *Revista de Indias* 31 (July-December 1971): 311–65.

Solórzano F., Juan Carlos. "Rafael Carrera, ¿reacción conservadora o revolución campesina? Guatemala 1837–1873." *Anuario de Estudios Centroamericanos* 13, no. 2 (1987): 5–35.

Solórzano Fernández, Valentín. "García Peláez: Cátedra prima de economía política en el Reino de Guatemala, 1814." *Anales de la Sociedad de Geografía e Historia de Guatemala* 40, no. 1/2 (January-June 1967): 19–29.

———. *Historia de la evolución económica de Guatemala*. México: Universidad Nacional Autónoma de México, 1947.

Soto V., Marco A. *Guerra Nacional de Centroamérica*. Guatemala: Ministerio de Educación Pública, 1957.

Stansifer, Charles L. "E. George Squier: Yanqui versatil en Centro América." *Revista Conservadora del Pensamiento Centroamericano* 15, no. 73 (October 1966): 13–20.

———. *Ephraim George Squier: Diversos aspectos de su carrera en Centroamérica*. Managua: Libro del Mes, *Revista Conservadora del Pensamiento Centroamericano* 20, no. 98 (November 1968): following page 32, 1–64.

Strobeck, Susan. "The Political Activities of Some Members of the Aristocratic Families of Guatemala, 1821–1839." Master's thesis, Tulane University, 1958.

Sturtevant, David R. *Popular Uprisings in the Philippines, 1840–1940*. Ithaca, N.Y.: Cornell University Press, 1976.

Szaszdi, Adam. *Nicolás Raoul y la república federal de Centroamérica*. Madrid: Universidad de Madrid, Seminario de Estudios Americanistas, 1958.

Taracena Flores, Arturo. "Biografías sintéticas de guatemaltecos distinguidos." *Re-*

vista de la Academia Guatemalteca de Estudios Genealógicos, Heráldicos e Históricos 3–4 (1970): 375–87.

Tjarks, Germán. *El Consulado de Buenos Aires y sus proyecciones en la historia del Río de la Plata.* 2 vols. Buenos Aires: Universidad de Buenos Aires, Facultad de Filosofía y Letras, 1962.

Tobar Cruz, Pedro. *Los montañeses.* 2d ed. Guatemala: Ministerio de Educación Pública, 1959.

———. *Los montañeses, facción de los Lucíos.* Guatemala: Editorial Universitaria, Universidad de San Carlos, 1971.

Torón España, José. "Oposición del Representante García Granados al gobierno del Mariscal Don Vicente Cerna." In *Historia y Antropología: Ensayos en honor de J. Daniel Contreras R.*, 171–86. Edited by Jorge Luján Muñoz. Guatemala: Facultad de Humanidades, Universidad de San Carlos, 1982.

Townsend Ezcurra, Andrés. *Las provincias unidas de Centroamérica: Fundación de la República.* San José: Editorial Costa Rica, 1973.

Toynbee, Arnold, and Eaisaku Ikeda. *The Toynbee-Ikeda Dialogue: Man Himself Must Choose.* Tokyo: Kodansha International, 1976.

Vega Carballo, José Luis. "El nacimiento de un régimen de burguesía dependiente: El caso de Costa Rica." In Congreso Centroamericano de Historia Demográfica, Económica y Social, I, Santa Barbara, Costa Rica, 1973, *Ensayos de historia centroamericana*, 93–118. San José, Costa Rica: Centro de Estudios Democráticos de América Latina, 1974.

Vela, David. *Barrundia ante el espejo de su tiempo.* 2 vols. Guatemala: Editorial Universitaria, 1956–57.

Vicens Vives, Jaime. *Approaches to the History of Spain.* Berkeley: University of California Press, 1967.

Villacorta Calderón, J. Antonio. *Historia de la capitanía general de Guatemala.* Guatemala: Tipografía Nacional, 1942.

Villalobos R., Sergio. "Problemas del comercio colonial." In *Temas de historia económica hispanoamericana.* Vol. 1, *Nova Americana*, 57–62. Paris: Ecole Pratique des Hautes Etudes and Universidad de Chile, Centro de Investigaciones de Historia Americana, 1965.

Walker, William. *The War in Nicaragua.* Mobile, Ala.: S. H. Goetzel & Co., 1860.

Wall, James T. *Manifest Destiny Denied: America's First Intervention in Nicaragua.* Washington, D.C.: University Press of America, 1981.

Weaver, Joanne. "Liberal Historian or Conservative Thinker? Alejandro Marure and Guatemalan History, 1821–1851." Master's thesis, Tulane University, 1975.

Webre, Stephen A. "The Social and Economic Bases of Cabildo Membership in Seventeenth-Century Santiago de Guatemala." Ph.D. diss., Tulane University, 1980.

Williams, Robert G. *Export Agriculture and the Crisis in Central America.* Chapel Hill: University of North Carolina Press, 1986.

Williford, Miriam. "The Educational Reforms of Dr. Mariano Gálvez." *Journal of Inter-American Studies* 10 (1968): 461–73.

————. *Jeremy Bentham on Spanish America: An Account of his Letters and Proposals to the New World.* Baton Rouge: Louisiana State University Press, 1980.

————. "Las Luces y La Civilización: The Social Reforms of Mariano Gálvez." In *Applied Enlightenment: 19th Century Liberalism* (Middle American Research Institute publication no. 23), 33–41. Edited by Margaret A. L. Harrison and Robert Wauchope. New Orleans: Tulane University, 1972.

Wolf, Eric B., and Edward C. Hansen. "Caudillo Politics: A Structural Analysis." *Comparative Studies in Society and History* 9, no. 2 (1967): 168–79.

Woods, Jamie. "Expansionism as Diplomacy: The Career of Solon Borland in Central America 1853–1854." *The Americas* 40 (1984): 399–417.

Woodward, Ralph Lee, Jr. *Central America, a Nation Divided.* 2d ed. New York: Oxford University Press, 1985.

————. "Central America from Independence to c. 1870." In *The Cambridge History of Latin America*, vol. 3, 471–506, 874–79. Edited by Leslie Bethell. Cambridge: Cambridge University Press, 1985.

————. *Class Privilege and Economic Development: The Consulado de Comercio of Guatemala, 1793–1871.* Chapel Hill: University of North Carolina Press, 1966.

————. "Crecimiento de población en Centro América durante la primera mitad del siglo de la independencia nacional: investigación reciente y estimados hasta la fecha." *Mesoamérica, Revista del Centro de Investigaciones Regionales de Mesoamérica* 1, no. 1 (1980): 219–29.

————. "Economic and Social Origins of the Guatemalan Political Parties (1773–1823)." *Hispanic American Historical Review* 45 (1965): 544–66.

————. "Economic Development and Dependency in Nineteenth-Century Guatemala." In *Political Economy of the World-System Annuals*, vol. 9, 59–78. Series edited by Immanuel Wallerstein. Vol. 9, *Crisis in the Caribbean Basin*, edited by Richard Tardanico. Newbury Park, Calif.: Sage, 1987.

————. "Guatemalan Cotton and the American Civil War." *Inter-American Economic Affairs* 18 (Winter 1984): 87–94.

————. "The Historiography of Modern Central America Since 1960." *Hispanic American Historical Review* 67 (1987): 461–96.

————. "Liberalism, Conservatism, and the Response of the Peasants of La Montaña to the Government of Guatemala, 1821–1850." *Plantation Society in the Americas* 1 (1979): 109–29.

————. "La política centroamericana de Rafael Carrera, 1840–1865." *Anuario de Estudios Centroamericanos* (Costa Rica) 9 (1983): 55–68.

————. "Population and Development in Guatemala, 1840–1870." *Annals of the Southeastern Council on Latin American Studies* 14 (1983): 5–18.

————. *Privilegio de clase y desarrollo económico: Guatemala 1793–1871.* San José, Costa Rica: EDUCA, 1981.

————. "Social Revolution in Guatemala: The Carrera Revolt." In *Applied*

Enlightenment: 19th Century Liberalism (Middle American Research Institute publication no. 23), 45–70. Edited by Margaret A. L. Harrison and Robert Wauchope. New Orleans: Tulane University, 1972.

Wortman, Miles L. "Bourbon Reforms in Central America, 1750–1786." *The Americas* 32 (October 1975): 222–38.

——. *Government and Society in Central America, 1680–1840.* New York: Columbia University Press, 1982.

——. "Government Revenue and Economic Trends in Central America, 1787–1819." *Hispanic American Historical Review* 55 (1975): 251–86.

Wright, Peter C. *The Role and Effects of Literacy in a Guatemalan Ladino Peasant Community.* Tampa: University of South Florida, 1965.

Zamora Castellanos, P. "El castillo de Carrera." *Revista militar* (Guatemala) 3, no. 2 (1 December 1923): 57–59.

——. *Vida militar de Centro América.* Guatemala: Tipografía Nacional, 1924.

Zea Carrascosa, Manuel Octavio. *Semblanzas: Ministros de la Guerra y de la Defensa Nacional de Guatemala, síntesis biográfica de los hombres que rigieron los destinos de la Institución Armada desde el año de 1823 hasta nuestros días.* Guatemala: Ministerio de la Defensa Nacional, 1971.

Zeceña, Mariano. *La revolución de 1871 y sus caudillos: Estudios políticos.* 3d ed. (Biblioteca Guatemalteca de Cultura Popular, vol. 17). Guatemala: Ministerio de Educación Pública, 1957.

Index

Printed in the United States
206440BV00003B/9/P